■ **Illustrations** have been selected to reinforce main points. They include numerous maps, artwork and photographs, figures, and tables. Frequently a map or a picture is more effective than words alone in explaining or emphasizing a particular development.

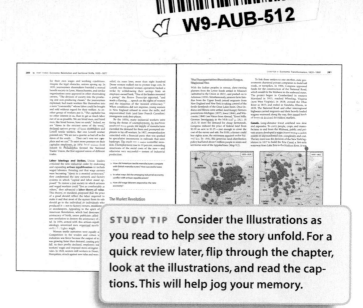

■ **Boxed features** are a central element of each chapter. They present primary sources as a way to experience the immediacy of the past through the words and perspectives of those who lived it. The features — Comparing American Voices, Reading American Pictures, and Voices from Abroad — emphasize important developments in the narrative.

Review at the end of the chapter

■ **A summary** concludes each chapter and highlights the main chapter themes.

■ **Connections** immediately following the summary link the chapter's main themes back to the part introduction and provide a bridge to the next chapter.

■ **Chapter review questions** ask you to relate the themes presented in the different sections of the chapter. They model the types of broad questions your instructor might ask on an exam.

■ **Timelines** help you keep the chronology of events straight.

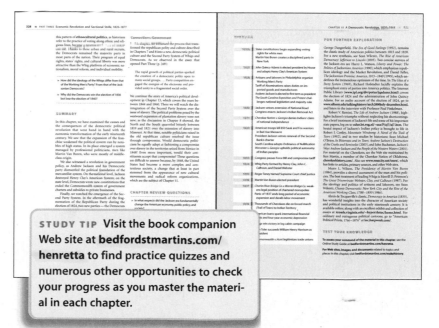

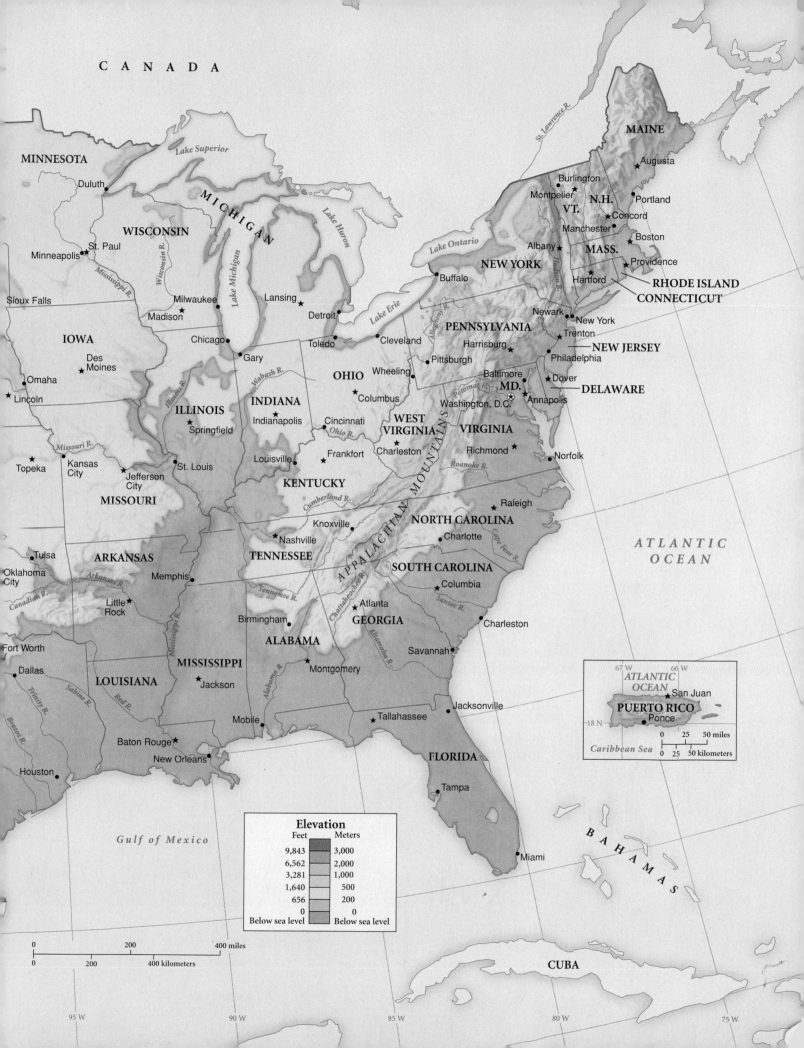

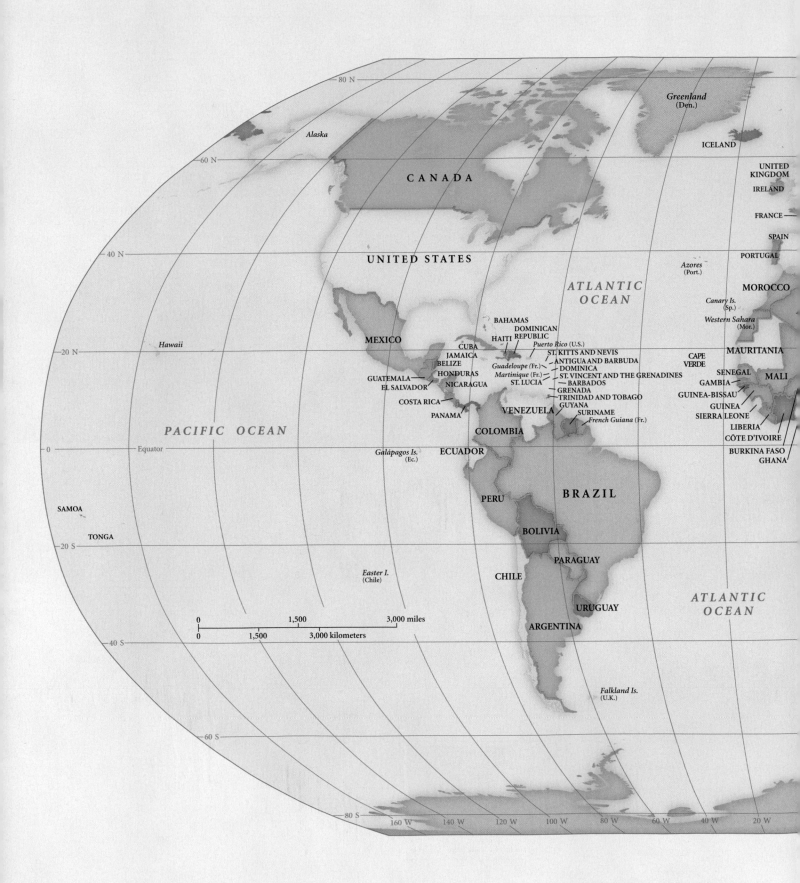

Greenland
(Den.)

ICELAND

Alaska

CANADA

UNITED
KINGDOM

IRELAND

FRANCE

SPAIN

PORTUGAL

UNITED STATES

ATLANTIC
OCEAN

Azores
(Port.)

MOROCCO

Canary Is.
(Sp.)

Western Sahara
(Mor.)

Hawaii

MEXICO

BAHAMAS
DOMINICAN
REPUBLIC
HAITI   Puerto Rico (U.S.)
CUBA   ST. KITTS AND NEVIS
JAMAICA   ANTIGUA AND BARBUDA
BELIZE   Guadeloupe (Fr.)   DOMINICA
GUATEMALA   HONDURAS   Martinique (Fr.) ST. VINCENT AND THE GRENADINES
EL SALVADOR   NICARAGUA   ST. LUCIA   BARBADOS
                              GRENADA
COSTA RICA   TRINIDAD AND TOBAGO
                              GUYANA
PANAMA   VENEZUELA   SURINAME
                          French Guiana (Fr.)
COLOMBIA

MAURITANIA

CAPE
VERDE

SENEGAL   MALI

GAMBIA
GUINEA-BISSAU
GUINEA
SIERRA LEONE
LIBERIA
CÔTE D'IVOIRE
BURKINA FASO
GHANA

PACIFIC OCEAN

Equator

Galápagos Is.
(Ec.)

ECUADOR

PERU

BRAZIL

SAMOA

TONGA

BOLIVIA

Easter I.
(Chile)

PARAGUAY

CHILE

URUGUAY

ATLANTIC
OCEAN

ARGENTINA

Falkland Is.
(U.K.)

0   1,500   3,000 miles
0   1,500   3,000 kilometers

80 N
60 N
40 N
20 N
0
20 S
40 S
60 S
80 S

160 W   140 W   120 W   100 W   80 W   60 W   40 W   20 W

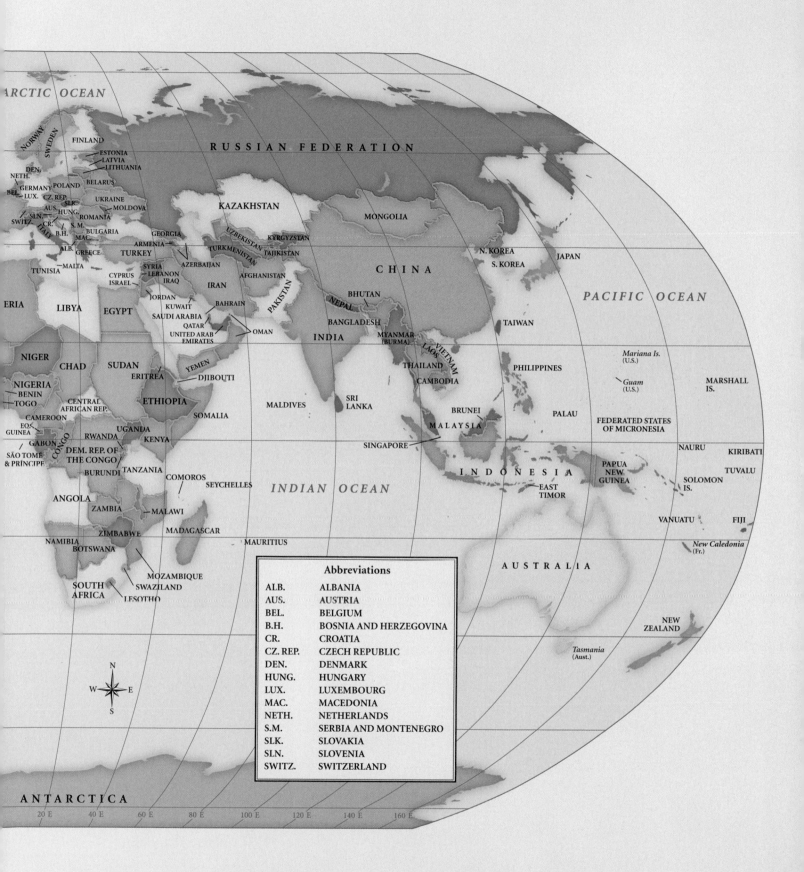

ARCTIC OCEAN

NORWAY
SWEDEN
FINLAND

RUSSIAN FEDERATION

DEN.
NETH.
BEL.
GERMANY POLAND
LUX. CZ. REP.
AUS. SLK.
SLN. HUNG.
SWITZ. CR. S.M.
ITALY B.H.
ALB.
MAC.
MALTA
TUNISIA

ESTONIA
LATVIA
LITHUANIA
BELARUS
UKRAINE
MOLDOVA
ROMANIA
BULGARIA
GEORGIA
GREECE
TURKEY

KAZAKHSTAN

MONGOLIA

UZBEKISTAN
ARMENIA
TURKMENISTAN
KYRGYZSTAN
TAJIKISTAN

N. KOREA
JAPAN
S. KOREA

PACIFIC OCEAN

CYPRUS
ISRAEL
SYRIA
LEBANON
IRAQ
AZERBAIJAN
AFGHANISTAN

CHINA

ERIA
LIBYA
EGYPT
JORDAN
KUWAIT
SAUDI ARABIA
BAHRAIN
QATAR
UNITED ARAB
EMIRATES
OMAN

IRAN
PAKISTAN

NEPAL
BHUTAN

BANGLADESH
INDIA

MYANMAR
(BURMA)
LAOS
VIETNAM

TAIWAN

Mariana Is.
(U.S.)

NIGER
CHAD
SUDAN
YEMEN
ERITREA
DJIBOUTI

THAILAND
CAMBODIA

PHILIPPINES

Guam
(U.S.)

MARSHALL
IS.

NIGERIA
BENIN
TOGO
CENTRAL
AFRICAN REP.
ETHIOPIA
SOMALIA

MALDIVES

SRI
LANKA

EQ.
GUINEA
CAMEROON
UGANDA
KENYA
GABON
RWANDA
CONGO
SÃO TOMÉ
& PRÍNCIPE
DEM. REP. OF
THE CONGO
BURUNDI
TANZANIA
COMOROS
SEYCHELLES

BRUNEI
MALAYSIA
SINGAPORE

PALAU

FEDERATED STATES
OF MICRONESIA

NAURU
KIRIBATI

INDONESIA
PAPUA
NEW
GUINEA

TUVALU
SOLOMON
IS.

ANGOLA
ZAMBIA
MALAWI
MADAGASCAR

INDIAN OCEAN

EAST
TIMOR

VANUATU
FIJI

NAMIBIA
ZIMBABWE
BOTSWANA
MOZAMBIQUE
SWAZILAND
SOUTH
AFRICA
LESOTHO

MAURITIUS

New Caledonia
(Fr.)

AUSTRALIA

N
W E
S

Abbreviations	
ALB.	ALBANIA
AUS.	AUSTRIA
BEL.	BELGIUM
B.H.	BOSNIA AND HERZEGOVINA
CR.	CROATIA
CZ. REP.	CZECH REPUBLIC
DEN.	DENMARK
HUNG.	HUNGARY
LUX.	LUXEMBOURG
MAC.	MACEDONIA
NETH.	NETHERLANDS
S.M.	SERBIA AND MONTENEGRO
SLK.	SLOVAKIA
SLN.	SLOVENIA
SWITZ.	SWITZERLAND

NEW
ZEALAND

Tasmania
(Aust.)

ANTARCTICA

20 E   40 E   60 E   80 E   100 E   120 E   140 E   160 E

America's History

Volume One: To 1877

America's History

Volume One: To 1877

Sixth Edition

James A. Henretta
University of Maryland

David Brody
University of California, Davis

Lynn Dumenil
Occidental College

Bedford / St. Martin's
Boston • New York

For Bedford/St.Martin's

Executive Editor for History: Mary Dougherty
Director of Development for History: Jane Knetzger
Senior Developmental Editor: William J. Lombardo
Senior Production Editor: Bridget Leahy
Senior Production Supervisor: Joe Ford
Executive Marketing Manager: Jenna Bookin Barry
Editorial Assistants: Holly Dye and Amy Leathe
Production Assistants: Amy Derjue and Lidia MacDonald-Carr
Copyeditors: Barbara Bell and Lisa Wehrle
Text Design: Catherine Hawkes, Cat and Mouse Design
Indexer: EdIndex
Photo Research: Pembroke Herbert and Sandi Rygiel/Picture Research Consultants & Archives
Cover Design: Donna Lee Dennison
Cover Art: Penn's Treaty with the Indians, 1771–1772. Benjamin West. Oil on canvas. 75 x 107 in, 191.8 x 273.7 cm.
  Gift of Mrs. Sarah Harrison (The Joseph Harrison Jr. Collection). Pennsylvania Academy of the Fine Arts;
  Map of the Province of Pensilvania. © www.mapsofpa.com / Harold Cramer.
Cartography: Mapping Specialists Limited
Composition: TechBooks
Printing and Binding: R.R. Donnelley & Sons Company

President: Joan E. Feinberg
Editorial Director: Denise B. Wydra
Director of Marketing: Karen Melton Soeltz
Director of Editing, Design, and Production: Marcia Cohen
Managing Editor: Elizabeth M. Schaaf

Library of Congress Control Number: 2006940141

Manufactured in the United States of America.

1 0 9 8 7
f e d c b a

For information, write: Bedford/St. Martin's, 75 Arlington Street, Boston, MA 02116
(617-399-4000)

ISBN-10: 0–312–44350–1   ISBN-13: 978–0–312–44350–4   (combined edition)
ISBN-10: 0–312–45285–3   ISBN-13: 978–0–312–45285–8   (Vol. 1)
ISBN-10: 0–312–45286–1   ISBN-13: 978–0–312–45286–5   (Vol. 2)
ISBN-10: 0–312–46548–3   ISBN-13: 978–0–312–46548–3   (high school edition)

Acknowledgments

Acknowledgments and copyrights can be found at the back of the book on pages C-1–C-2, which constitute an extension of the copyright page.

ONE OF THE GIFTS OF textbook writing is the second and third chances it affords. Where else, after all, does the historian have the opportunity to revisit work and strive, on a regular basis, to make it better? Relishing the opportunity, we have, with each edition, sharpened the narrative, refined arguments, restructured chapters, and incorporated fresh scholarship. In this, the sixth edition, we pick up that task again, only this time with a more ambitious goal. We want to bring *America's History* into the twenty-first century. *America's History* was conceived nearly thirty years ago and built into it were assumptions — both intellectual and pedagogical — that, for this edition, we have reconsidered. On the intellectual side, this has led us to a thorough rethinking and recasting of our post-1945 chapters. On the pedagogical side, it has led us to a back-to-basics approach, utilizing an array of learning tools that we are confident will engage and instruct today's students. On both counts, *America's History* will strike instructors as quite new. But we have not departed from the core idea with which we began — to write a comprehensive text that has explanatory power and yet is immediately accessible to every student who enrolls in the survey course.

From the very inception of *America's History*, we set out to write a *democratic* history, one that would convey the experiences of ordinary people even as it recorded the accomplishments of the great and powerful. We focus not only on the marvelous diversity of peoples who became American but also on the institutions — political, economic, cultural, and social — that forged a common national identity. And we present these historical trajectories in an integrated way, using each perspective to make better sense of the others. In our discussion of government and politics, diplomacy and war, we show how they affected — and were affected by — ethnic groups and economic conditions, intellectual beliefs and social changes, and the religious and moral values of the times. Just as important, we place the American experience in a global context. We trace aspects of American society to their origins in European and African cultures, consider the American Industrial Revolution within the framework of the world economy, and plot the foreign relations of the United States as part of an ever-shifting international system of imperial expansion, financial exchange, and diplomatic alliances. In emphasizing the global context, we want to remind students that America never existed alone in the world; that other nations experienced developments comparable to our own; and that, knowing this, we can better understand, through comparative discussions at opportune moments, what was distinctive and particular to the American experience.

In these eventful times, college students — even those who don't think much about America's past or today's news — have to wonder about 9/11 or the Iraq war or the furor over illegal immigration: How did that happen? This question is at the heart of historical inquiry. And in asking it, the student is thinking historically. In *America's History* we aspire to satisfy that student's curiosity. We try to ask the right questions — the big ones and the not-so-big — and then write history that illuminates the answers. We are writing narrative history, but harnessed to historical argument, not simply a retelling of "this happened, then that happened."

Structure

One way of overcoming the student's sense that history is just one-damn-thing-after-another is to show her that American history is constituted of distinct periods or eras that give it shape and meaning. Accordingly, we devised early on a six-part structure, corresponding to what we understood to be the major phases of American development. Part Six, carrying the story from 1945 to the present, stood somewhat apart because it was, by definition, unfinished. In earlier editions, that made sense, but as we move into the twenty-first century, it becomes increasingly clear that we have entered a new phase of American history, and that the era that began in 1945 has ended. So now we have a fully realized Part Six, which we call the Age of Cold War Liberalism, 1945–1980, and a new Part Seven, with the breaking point at 1980 signaling the advent of a conservative America in an emerging post–Cold War world. Students who know only this new age will find in Part Six a coherent narrative history of the times of their parents and grandparents. In Part Seven, they will find an account of an era truly their own, carried to the present with a full chapter on the post-2000 years.

Given the importance of the part structure in the text's scheme, we have taken pains to provide students with the aids to comprehension they need to benefit fully from this organization. Each part begins with a two-page overview. First, a **thematic timeline** highlights the key developments in politics, the economy, society, culture, and foreign affairs; then these themes are fleshed out in a corresponding **part essay**. Each part essay focuses on the crucial engines of historical change—in some eras primarily economic, in others political or diplomatic—that created new conditions of life and transformed social relations. The part organization, encapsulated in the thematic timelines and opening essays, helps students understand the major themes and periods of American history, to see how bits and pieces of historical data acquire significance as part of a larger pattern of development.

The individual chapters are similarly constructed with student comprehension in mind. A **chapter outline** gives readers an overview of the text discussion, followed by a **thematic introduction** that orients them to the central issues and ideas of the chapter. Then, at the end of the chapter, we remind students of important events in a **chapter timeline** and reiterate the themes in an **analytic summary**. The summaries have been thoroughly revised, with the aim of underlining as concretely as possible the main points of the chapter. In addition, we have added a new feature, **Connections**, that enables students to take a longer view, to see how the chapter relates to prior and forthcoming chapters. We are also more attentive to the need of students for effective study aids. Within each chapter, we now append focus questions to each section, and at the chapter's end, a set of study questions. And where students are likely to stumble, we provide a **glossary** that defines the **key concepts** bold faced in the text where first mentioned.

Features: Back to Basics

In keeping with our back-to-basics approach, *America's History* has rebuilt its features program around primary sources, providing students with an opportunity to experience the past through the words and perspectives of those who lived it and, equally important, to encounter historical evidence and learn how to extract meaning from it. The cornerstone of this program is the two-page **Comparing American Voices** feature that appears in every chapter. Each contains several primary sources— excerpts from letters, diaries, autobiographies, and public testimony—offering varying, often conflicting, views on a single event or theme discussed in the chapter. An introduction establishes the historical context, generally with reference to the chapter, and headnotes identify and explain the provenance of the individual documents. These are followed by a series of questions—under the heading Analyzing the Evidence—that focus the student's attention on revealing aspects of the documents and show her how historians—herself included—can draw meaning from contemporary evidence. Instructors will find in Comparing American Voices a major resource for inducting beginning students into the processes of historical analysis. Carried over from the previous edition is **Voices from Abroad,** featuring first-person testimony by foreign visitors and observers, but now also equipped with questions like those in Comparing American Voices, and with a similar pedagogical intent.

America's History has always been noted for its rich offering of maps, figures, and pictures that help students visualize the past. Over 120 **full-color maps** encourage a geographic perspective, many of them with annotations that call out key points. All the maps are cross-referenced in the narrative text, as are the tables and figures. Nearly 40 percent of the **art** and **photographs** are new to this edition, selected to reflect changes in the text and to underscore chapter themes. Most appear in full color, with unusually **substantive captions** that actively engage students with the image and encourage them to analyze visuals as primary documents. To advance further this pedagogical aim, we have developed a new feature that we call **Reading American Pictures**, a full page in each chapter devoted to the visual study of one or more carefully selected contemporary paintings, cartoons, or photographs. These are introduced by a discussion of the context in which they were produced and followed by questions designed to prompt students to treat them as another form of historical evidence. We anticipate that the exercise will provoke lively classroom discussion. In our pedagogical program focusing on primary sources, Reading American Pictures is offered as the visual counterpart to Comparing American Voices and Voices from Abroad.

Textual Changes

Of all the reasons for a new edition, of course, the most compelling is to improve the text itself. Good narrative history is primarily a product of good sentences and good paragraphs. So our labors have been mostly in the trenches, so to speak, in a line-by-line striving for the vividness and human presence that are hallmarks of narrative history. We are also partisans of economical writing, by necessity if we are to incorporate what's new in the field and in contemporary affairs while holding *America's History* to a manageable length. This is a challenge we welcome, believing as we do that brevity is the best antidote to imprecise language and murky argument. Of the more substantive changes, a notable one arose from the refocusing of our features program on primary sources. Whereas previous editions contained boxed essays on American lives, we have now integrated those stories of ordinary and notable Americans into the narrative, much expanding and enlivening its people-centered approach.

Within chapters we have been especially attentive to chronology, which sometimes involved a significant reordering of material. In Part Two (1776–1820), chapters 6 and 7 now provide a continuous political narrative from the Declaration of Independence to the Era of Good Feelings. In Part Three (1820–1877), feedback from instructors persuaded us to consolidate our treatment of the pre–Civil War South into a single, integrated chapter. In Part Four (1877–1914), our chapter on Gilded Age politics has been reorganized to improve chronology and placed after the chapter on the city so as to provide students with a seamless transition to the Progressive era. In Part Five (1914–1945), the three chapters on the 1920s, the Great Depression, and the New Deal have been melded into two crisper, more integrated chapters. All of the chapters in Part Six (1945–1980) and the new Part Seven (1980–2006) have been thoroughly reworked as part of our rethinking of the post-1945 era. In the companion Chapters 26 and 27, we now offer a thematic treatment of the 1950s, while Chapters 28 and 29 provide a coherent narrative account of liberalism's triumph under Kennedy and Johnson and its dramatic decline after 1968. Part Seven represents a much expanded coverage of the post-1980 years, with new chapters devoted to social and economic developments and America since 2000. Altogether, these organizational changes represent the biggest shake-up of *America's History* since its inception.

The revising process also affords us a welcome opportunity to incorporate fresh scholarship. In Part One, we have added new material on life in Africa, the slave trade, the emergence of an African American ethnicity, and on such non-English ethnic colonial groups as the Scots Irish and the Germans. In Chapter 11, we have a completely new section on urban popular culture (masculinity, sexuality, minstrel shows, and racism) drawing on recent advances in cultural history, inventive scholarship that also informs Chapter 18 (on the late-nineteenth-century city) and several twentieth-century chapters, including in Chapter 27 our treatment of consumer culture in the 1950s. Chapter 16 contains fresh information about the impact of farming on the ecosystem of the Great Plains. In Chapter 20, the opening section has been recast to incorporate recent insights into the middle-class impulse behind progressivism, and a new section treats the industrial strife that reoriented progressivism toward the problem of the nation's labor relations. Of the many revisions in the post-1945 chapters, perhaps the most notable derive from the opening of Soviet archives, which allows us at last to see the Cold War from both sides of the Iron Curtain, and also to amend our assessment of the impact of communism on American life. In addition, Part Six contains fresh material on the civil rights movement, on the Vietnam War, and on the revival of American conservatism. Even richer are the additions to Part Seven, "Entering a New Era: Conservatism, Globalization, Terrorism, 1980–2006," especially in the treatment of social movements and the information technology revolution in Chapter 31, and a completely new post-2000 Chapter 32, which, unlike all the preceding chapters, relies not on secondary sources, but primarily on a reading of the contemporary press and the public record.

Supplements

For Students

Documents to Accompany** America's History, **Sixth Edition. Edited by Melvin Yazawa, University of New Mexico (Volume 1), and Kevin Fernlund, University of Missouri, St. Louis (Volume 2), this primary source reader is designed to accompany *America's History*, Sixth Edition, and offers a chorus of voices from the past to enrich the study of U.S. history. Both celebrated figures and ordinary people, from Frederick Douglass to mill workers, demonstrate the diversity of America's history while putting a human face on historical experience. A wealth of speeches, petitions, advertisements, and posters paint a vivid picture of the social and political life of the time, providing depth and breadth to the textbook discussion. Brief introductions set each document in context, while questions for analysis help link the individual source to larger historical themes.

NEW *E-Documents to Accompany* America's History, *Sixth Edition*. The most robust gathering of primary sources to accompany any U.S. history survey text is now available online. *E-Documents to Accompany* America's History, *Sixth Edition* is perfect for adding an electronic dimension to your class or integrating with your existing online course.

Online Study Guide at bedfordstmartins.com/ henretta. The popular Online Study Guide for *America's History* is a free and uniquely personalized learning tool to help students master themes and information presented in the textbook and improve their historical skills. Assessment quizzes let students evaluate their comprehension and provide them with customized plans for further study through a variety of activities. Instructors can monitor students' progress through the online Quiz Gradebook or receive e-mail updates.

Maps in Context: A Workbook for American History. Written by historical cartography expert Gerald A. Danzer (University of Illinois, Chicago), this skill-building workbook helps students comprehend essential connections between geographic literacy and historical understanding. Organized to correspond to the typical U.S. history survey course, *Maps in Context* presents a wealth of map-centered projects and convenient pop quizzes that give students hands-on experience working with maps. Available free when packaged with the text.

NEW *The Bedford Glossary for U.S. History.* This handy supplement for the survey course gives students clear, concise definitions of the political, economic, social, and cultural terms used by historians and contemporary media alike. The terms are historically contextualized to aid comprehension. Available free when packaged with the text.

NEW *History Matters: A Student Guide to U.S. History Online.* This new resource, written by Alan Gevinson, Kelly Schrum, and Roy Rosenzweig (all of George Mason University), provides an illus-trated and annotated guide to 250 of the most useful Web sites for student research in U.S. history as well as advice on evaluating and using Internet sources. This essential guide is based on the acclaimed "History Matters" Web site developed by the American Social History Project and the Center for History and New Media. Available free when packaged with the text.

Bedford Series in History and Culture. Over 100 titles in this highly praised series combine first-rate scholarship, historical narrative, and important primary documents for undergraduate courses. Each book is brief, inexpensive, and focused on a specific topic or period. Package discounts are available.

Historians at Work Series. Brief enough for a single assignment yet meaty enough to provoke thoughtful discussion, each volume in this series examines a single historical question by combining unabridged selections by distinguished historians, each with a different perspective on the issue, with helpful learning aids. Package discounts are available.

Trade Books. Titles published by sister companies Farrar, Straus and Giroux; Henry Holt and Company; Hill and Wang; Picador; and St. Martin's Press are available at deep discounts when packaged with Bedford/St. Martin's textbooks. For more information, visit bedfordstmartins.com/tradeup.

Critical Thinking Modules at bedfordstmartins.com/ historymodules. This Web site offers over two dozen online modules for interpreting maps, audio, visual, and textual sources, centered on events covered in the U.S. history survey. An online guide correlates modules to textbook chapters.

Research and Documentation Online at **bedfordstmartins.com/resdoc.** This Web site provides clear advice on how to integrate primary and secondary sources into research papers, how to cite sources correctly, and how to format in MLA, APA, *Chicago,* or CBE style.

The St. Martin's Tutorial on Avoiding Plagiarism at **bedfordstmartins.com/plagiarismtutorial.** This online tutorial reviews the consequences of plagiarism and explains what sources to acknowledge, how to keep good notes, how to organize research, and how to integrate sources appropriately. This tutorial includes exercises to help students practice integrating sources and recognize acceptable summaries.

Bedford Research Room at bedfordstmartins.com/researchroom. The Research Room, drawn from Mike Palmquist's *The Bedford Researcher,* offers a wealth of resources—including interactive tutorials, research activities, student writing samples, and links to hundreds of other places online—to support students in courses across the disciplines. The site also offers instructors a library of helpful instructional tools.

For Instructors

Instructor's Resource Manual. Written by Jason Newman (Cosumnes River College, Los Rios Community College District), the *Instructor's Resource Manual for AMERICA'S HISTORY,* Sixth Edition, provides both first-time and experienced instructors with valuable teaching tools—annotated chapter outlines, lecture strategies, in-class activities, discussion questions, suggested writing assignments, and related readings and media—to structure and customize their American history course. The manual also offers a convenient, chapter-by-chapter guide to the wealth of supplementary materials available to instructors teaching *America's History.*

Computerized Test Bank. A fully updated Test Bank CD-ROM offers over 80 exercises for each chapter, allowing instructors to pick and choose from a collection of multiple-choice, fill-in, map, and short and long essay questions. To aid instructors in tailoring their tests to suit their classes, every question includes a textbook page number so instructors can direct students to a particular page for correct answers. Also, the software allows instructors to edit both questions and answers to further customize their texts. Correct answers and model responses are included.

Transparencies. This set of over 160 full-color acetate transparencies of all maps and selected images in the text helps instructors present lectures and teach students important map-reading skills.

Book Companion Site at bedfordstmartins.com/henretta. The companion Web site gathers all the electronic resources for *America's History,* including the Online Study Guide and related Quiz Gradebook, at a single Web address, providing convenient links to lecture, assignment, and research materials such as PowerPoint chapter outlines and the digital libraries at Make History.

NEW Make History at bedfordstmartins.com/makehistory. Comprising the content of our five acclaimed online libraries—Map Central, the U.S. History Image Library, DocLinks, HistoryLinks, and PlaceLinks—Make History provides one-stop access to relevant digital content including maps, images, documents, and Web links. Students and instructors alike can search this free, easy-to-use database by keyword, topic, date, or specific chapter of *America's History* and can download any content they find. Instructors using *America's History* can also create entire collections of content and store them online for later use or post their collections to the Web to share with students.

Instructor's Resource CD-ROM. This disc provides instructors with ready-made and customizable PowerPoint multimedia presentations built around chapter outlines, maps, figures, and selected images from the textbook. The disc also includes all maps and selected images from the textbook in jpeg format, the *Instructor's Resource Manual* in pdf format, and a quick-start guide to the Online Study Guide.

Course Management Content. E-content is available for *America's History* in Blackboard, WebCT, and other platforms. This e-content includes nearly all of the offerings from the book's Online Study Center as well as the book's test bank.

Videos and Multimedia. A wide assortment of videos and multimedia CD-ROMs on various topics in American history is available to qualified adopters.

NEW *The AP U.S. History Teaching Toolkit for* America's History, *Sixth Edition.* Written by AP experts Jonathan Chu (University of Massachusetts, Boston) and Ellen W. Parisi (Williamsville East High School and D'Youville College), this entirely new AP resource is the first comprehensive history resource for AP teachers. The *AP U.S. History Teaching ToolKit* provides materials to teach the basics of and preparation for the AP U.S. history examination, including entire DBQs. The *ToolKit* also includes a wealth of materials that address the course's main challenges, especially coverage, pacing, and methods for conveying the critical knowledge and skills that AP students need.

NEW *AP U.S. History Testbank for* America's History, *Sixth Edition.* Written by Ellen W. Parisi (Williamsville East High School and D'Youville College) specifically for AP teachers and students, the *AP U.S. History Test Bank* is designed to help students recall their textbook reading and prepare for the format and difficulty level of the AP exam. Each chapter of *America's History,* Sixth Edition, has a twenty-question multiple-choice quiz and five AP-style questions that mimic the exam questions. Each major part of *America's History* has a corresponding test containing fifty AP-style questions, which can be used for both student self-testing and in-class practice exams. All multiple-choice questions include five distracters.

Acknowledgments

We are very grateful to the following scholars and teachers who reported on their experiences with the fifth edition or reviewed chapters of the sixth edition. Their comments often challenged us to rethink or justify our interpretations and always provided a check on accuracy down to the smallest detail.

Elizabeth Alexander, *Texas Wesleyan University*
Marjorie Berman, *Red Rocks Community College*
Rebecca Boone, *Lamar University*
Michael L. Cox, *Barton County Community College*
Glen Gendzel, *Indiana University-Perdue*
Jessica Gerard, *Ozarks Technical Community College*
Martin Halpern, *Henderson State University*
Yvonne Johnson, *Central Missouri State University*
Sanford B. Kanter, *San Jacinto College South*
Anthony Kaye, *Penn State University*
William J. Lipkin, *Union County College*
Daniel Littlefield, *University of South Carolina*
James Meriwether, *California State University, Bakersfield*
William Moore, *University of Wyoming*
Allison Parker, *SUNY Brockport*
Phillip Payne, *St. Bonaventure University*
Louis W. Potts, *University of Missouri, Kansas City*
Yasmin Rahman, *University of Colorado at Boulder*
Kim Richardson, *Community College at Jacksonville*
Howard Rock, *Florida International University*
Donald W. Rogers, *Central Connecticut State University*
Jason Scott Smith, *University of New Mexico*
David Steigerwald, *The Ohio State University, Marion*
David G. Thompson, *Illinois Central College*
Christine S. White, *San Jacinto College South*

We also extend our thanks and gratitude to our high school colleagues and college instructors associated with the College Board who commented on *America's History* and reviewed the new AP supplements tailored specifically for our textbook.

Tom Alleman, *Carbon High School*
Margaret Bramlett, *St. Paul's Episcopal School*
Cameron Flint, *Cloverleaf High School*
Tim Greene, *Jersey Shore Senior High School*
Jonathan Lurie, *Rutgers University*
Jackie McHargue, *Duncanville High School*
Christine Madsen, *Flintridge Prep School*
Louisa Moffitt, *Marist School*
Joseph J. O'Neill, *Mount Saint Charles Academy*
La Juana J. Reban Coleman, *NMHU Center at Rio Rancho*
Rex Sanders, *A & M Consolidated High School*
Mary van Weezel, *Lakeland Regional High School*
Joe Villano, *Marist College (retired)*

As the authors of *America's History,* we know better than anyone else how much this book is the work of other hands and minds. We are grateful to Mary Dougherty and Jane Knetzger, who oversaw the project, and William Lombardo, who used his extensive knowledge and critical skills as a well-trained historian to edit our text and suggest a multitude of improvements. As usual, Joan E. Feinberg has been generous in providing the resources we needed to produce the sixth edition. Bridget Leahy did more than we had a right to expect in producing an outstanding volume. Karen Melton Soeltz and Jenna Bookin Barry in the marketing department have been instrumental in helping this book reach the classroom. We also thank the rest of our editorial and production team for their dedicated efforts: Amy Leathe, Holly Dye, Amy Derjue, and Lidia MacDonald-Carr; Pembroke Herbert and Sandi Rygiel at Picture Research Consultants and Archives; and Sandy Schechter. Finally, we want to express our appreciation for the invaluable assistance of Patricia Deveneau and Jason Newman, whose work contributed in many ways to the intellectual vitality of this new edition of *America's History.*

James A. Henretta
David Brody
Lynn Dumenil

CONTENTS

PART TWO

The New Republic, 1763–1820

**6 Making War and
Republican Governments,
1776–1789** *169*

**7 Politics and Society
in the New Republic,
1787–1820** *203*

MAPS

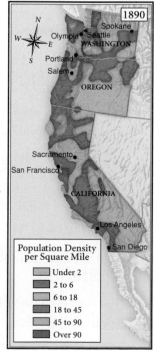

FIGURES AND TABLES

SPECIAL FEATURES

ABOUT THE AUTHORS

JAMES A. HENRETTA is Priscilla Alden Burke Professor of American History at the University of Maryland, College Park. He received his undergraduate education at Swarthmore College and his Ph.D. from Harvard University. He has taught at the University of Sussex, England; Princeton University; UCLA; Boston University; as a Fulbright lecturer in Australia at the University of New England; and at Oxford University as the Harmsworth Professor of American History. His publications include *The Evolution of American Society, 1700–1815: An Interdisciplinary Analysis;* "*Salutary Neglect*": *Colonial Administration under the Duke of Newcastle; Evolution and Revolution: American Society, 1600–1820; The Origins of American Capitalism;* and an edited volume, *Republicanism and Liberalism in America and the German States, 1750–1850.* His most recent publication is a long article, "Charles Evans Hughes and the Strange Death of Liberal America," (*Law and History Review,* 2006), derived from his ongoing research on The Liberal State in New York, 1820–1975.

DAVID BRODY is Professor Emeritus of History at the University of California, Davis. He received his B.A., M.A., and Ph.D. from Harvard University. He has taught at the University of Warwick in England, at Moscow State University in the former Soviet Union, and at Sydney University in Australia. He is the author of *Steelworkers in America; Workers in Industrial America: Essays on the 20th Century Struggle;* and *In Labor's Cause: Main Themes on the History of the American Worker.* His most recent book is *Labor Embattled: History, Power, Rights* (2005). He has been awarded fellowships from the Social Science Research Council, the Guggenheim Foundation, and the National Endowment for the Humanities. He is past president (1991–1992) of the Pacific Coast branch of the American Historical Association.

LYNN DUMENIL is Robert Glass Cleland Professor of American History at Occidental College in Los Angeles. She is a graduate of the University of Southern California and received her Ph.D. from the University of California, Berkeley. She has written *The Modern Temper: American Culture and Society in the 1920s* and *Freemasonry and American Culture: 1880–1930.* Her articles and reviews have appeared in the *Journal of American History;* the *Journal of American Ethnic History: Reviews in American History;* and the *American Historical Review.* She has been a historical consultant to several documentary film projects and is on the Pelzer Prize Committee of the Organization of American Historians. Her current work, for which she received a National Endowment for the Humanities Fellowship, is on World War I, citizenship, and the state. In 2001–2002 she was the Bicentennial Fulbright Chair in American Studies at the University of Helsinki.

America's History

Volume One: To 1877

ECONOMY	SOCIETY	GOVERNMENT	RELIGION	CULTURE
From staple crops to internal growth	Ethnic, racial, and class divisions	From monarchy to republic	From hierarchy to pluralism	The creation of American identity
1450 ▸ Native American subsistence economy ▸ Europeans fish off North American coast	▸ Sporadic warfare among Indian peoples ▸ Spanish conquest of Mexico (1519–1521)	▸ Rise of monarchical nation-states in Europe	▸ Protestant Reformation begins (1517)	▸ Diverse Native American cultures in eastern woodlands
1600 ▸ First staple export crops: furs and tobacco	▸ English-Indian wars ▸ African servitude begins in Virginia (1619)	▸ James I claims divine right to rule England ▸ Virginia House of Burgesses (1619)	▸ English Puritans and Catholics migrate to America to escape persecution	▸ Puritans implant Calvinism, education, and freehold ideal
1640 ▸ New England trades with sugar islands ▸ First mercantilist regulation: Navigation Act (1651)	▸ White indentured servitude in Chesapeake ▸ Indians retreat inland ▸ Virginia laws deprive Africans of rights (1671)	▸ Puritan Revolution in England ▸ Stuart restoration (1660) ▸ Bacon's Rebellion in Virginia (1675)	▸ Puritans in Massachusetts Bay quash "heresy" ▸ Religious liberty in Rhode Island	▸ Aristocratic aspirations in Chesapeake region
1680 ▸ Tobacco trade stagnates ▸ Rice cultivation begins in South Carolina	▸ Indian slavery in the Carolinas ▸ Ethnic rebellion in New York (1689)	▸ Dominion of New England (1686–1689) ▸ Glorious Revolution in England (1688–1689)	▸ Rise of tolerance	▸ Emergence of African American language and culture
1720 ▸ Mature yeoman farm economy in north ▸ Cultivation of rice expands ▸ Imports from Britain increase	▸ Scots-Irish and German migration ▸ Growing inequality in rural and urban areas	▸ Rise of the colonial representative assemblies ▸ Era of salutary neglect in colonial administration	▸ German and Scots-Irish Pietists in Middle Atlantic region ▸ Great Awakening	▸ Expansion of colleges, newspapers, and magazines ▸ Franklin and the American Enlightenment
1760 ▸ End of British military aid sparks postwar recession	▸ Uprisings by tenants and backcountry farmers ▸ Artisan protests in seaport cities	▸ Britain victorious over French in "Great War for Empire" (1757–1763) ▸ British ministry tightens control of American colonies	▸ Evangelical Baptists in Virginia	▸ First signs of an American identity

Historians know that societies are made over time, not born in a moment. They are the creation of decades, even centuries, of human endeavor and experience. Historians also know that the first Americans were hunters and gatherers who migrated to the Western Hemisphere from Asia. Over hundreds of generations, these migrants—the Native Americans—came to live in a wide variety of environments and cultures. In much of North America, they developed kinship-based societies that relied on farming and hunting. But in the lower Mississippi River Valley, Native Americans fashioned a hierarchical social order similar to that of the great civilizations of the Aztecs, Mayas, and Incas of Mesoamerica.

In Part One, we describe how Europeans, with their steel weapons, attractive trade goods, and most importantly their diseases, shredded the fabric of most Native American cultures. Throughout the Western Hemisphere, men and women of European origin— the Spanish in Mesoamerica and South America, the French in Canada, the English along the Atlantic coast— gradually achieved domination over the native peoples.

Our story focuses on the Europeans who settled in the English mainland colonies. They came hoping to transplant their traditional societies, cultures, and religious beliefs in the soil of the New World. But things did not work out exactly as they planned. In learning to live in the new land, English, Germans, and Scots-Irish created societies in British North America that differed from those of their homelands in their economies, social character, political systems, religions, and cultures. Here, in brief, is the story of that transformation as we explain it in Part One.

ECONOMY   Many European settlements succeeded as economic ventures. Traditional Europe was made up of poor, overcrowded, and unequal societies that periodically suffered devastating famines.

But with few people and a bountiful natural environment, the settlers in North America created a bustling economy. Indeed, in the northern mainland colonies, communities of independent farm families in rural areas and merchants and artisans in America's growing port towns and cities prospered in what British and German migrants called "the best poor man's country."

SOCIETY   At the same time, many European settlements became places of oppressive captivity for Africans, with profound consequences for America's social development. To replace the dwindling supply of white indentured servants from Europe, planters in the Chesapeake region imported enslaved African workers to grow tobacco. Wealthy British and French planters in the West Indies, aided by African traders and political leaders, bought hundreds of thousands of slaves from many African regions and forced them to labor on sugar plantations. Slowly and with great effort, the slaves and their descendants created a variety of African American cultures within the European-dominated societies in which they lived.

GOVERNMENT   Simultaneously, the white settlers in the English mainland colonies devised an increasingly free and competitive political system. The first migrants transplanted authoritarian institutions to America and, until 1689, English authorities intervened frequently in their economic and political affairs. Thereafter, local governments and representative assemblies became more important and created a tradition of self-rule that would spark demands for political independence from Britain in the years following the conclusion of the Great War for Empire in 1763.

RELIGION   The American experience profoundly changed religious institutions and values. Many migrants left Europe because of conflicts among rival Christian churches and persecution by government officials; they hoped to practice their religion in America without interference. Religion flourished in the English colonies, especially after the evangelical revivals of the 1740s, but the churches became less dogmatic. Many Americans rejected the harshest tenets of Calvinism (a strict Protestant faith); others embraced the rationalism of the European Enlightenment. As a result, American Protestant Christianity became increasingly tolerant, democratic, and optimistic.

CULTURE   The new American society witnessed new forms of family and community life. The first English settlers lived in patriarchal families ruled by dominant fathers and in communities controlled by men of high status. However, by 1750, many American fathers no longer strictly managed their children's lives and, because of widespread property ownership, many men and some women enjoyed personal independence. This new American society was increasingly pluralistic, composed of migrants from many European ethnic groups—English, Scots, Scots Irish, Dutch, and Germans—as well as West African slaves and Native American peoples. Distinct regional cultures developed in New England, the Middle Atlantic colonies, the Chesapeake, and the Carolinas. Consequently, an overarching American identity based on the English language, English legal and political institutions, and shared experiences emerged very slowly.

Thus, the story of the English colonial experience is both depressing and uplifting. On the one hand, Europeans and their diseases destroyed many Native American peoples and European slaveowners held an increasing number of African Americans in bondage. On the other hand, white migrants enjoyed unprecedented opportunities for economic security, political freedom, and spiritual fulfillment.

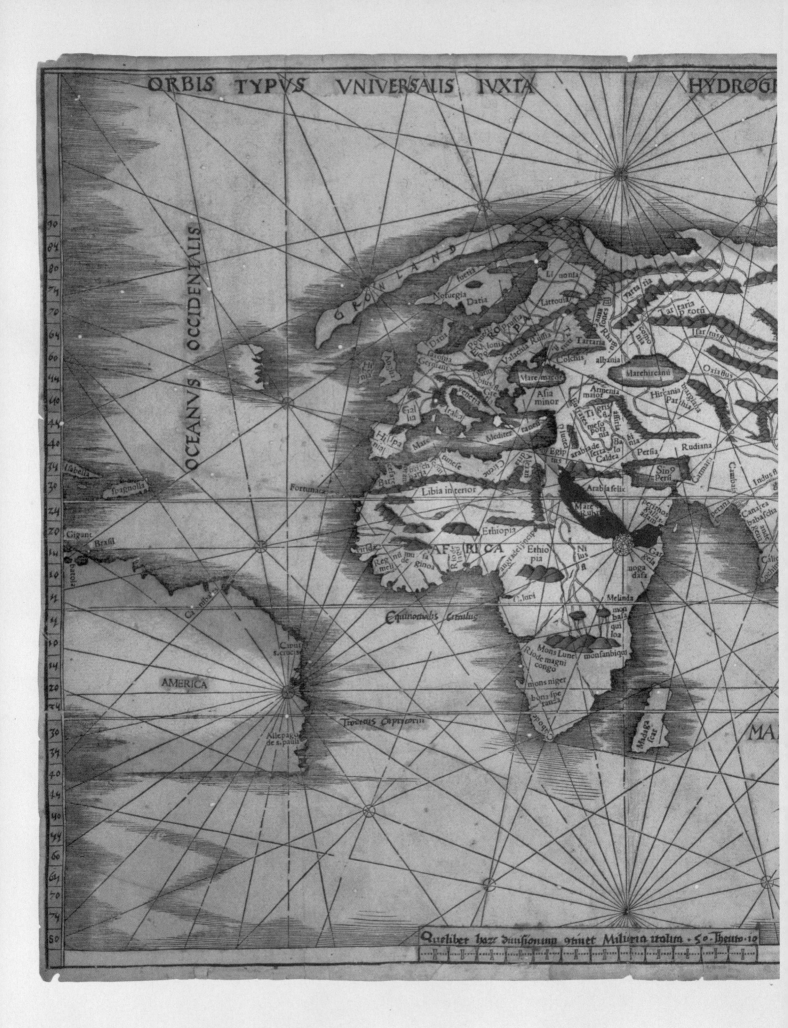

1 Worlds Collide: Europe, Africa, and America

1450–1620

"BEFORE THE FRENCH CAME AMONG us," an elder of the Natchez people of Mississippi explained, "we were men . . . and we walked with boldness every road, but now we walk like slaves, which we shall soon be, since the French already treat us . . . as they do their black slaves." Before the 1490s, the Natchez and the other native peoples of the Western Hemisphere knew nothing about the light-skinned inhabitants of Europe and the dark-complexioned peoples of Africa. But Portuguese merchants seeking gold, ivory, and slaves had been trading along the west coast of Africa for fifty years. When Christopher Columbus, a European searching for a sea route to Asia, encountered the peoples of the Western Hemisphere in 1492, the destinies of four continents quickly became intertwined. On his second voyage, Columbus carried a cargo of enslaved Africans, initiating the centuries-long trade that would produce a multitude of triracial societies in the Americas.

As the Natchez elder knew well, the resulting mixture of peoples was based on exploitation, not equality. But by the time he urged his people to resist, the French intruders were too numerous and strong. With the help of Indian allies, they killed hundreds of Natchez rebels and sold the survivors into slavery on the sugar plantations of the West Indies. And the fate of the Natchez was not unique. In the three centuries following

◀ **Orbis Typus Universalis**

This map of the world, drawn by German cartographer Martin Waldseemüller in 1507, was one of the first to use *America* as the name of the New World. Only the northwestern area of present-day Brazil and a few (mislocated) Caribbean islands appear on Waldseemüller's map. Europeans had yet to comprehend the size and shape of the Western Hemisphere.
John Carter Brown Library, Brown University.

Columbus's voyage, many Native American peoples came under the domination of the Spanish, Portuguese, French, English, and Dutch who colonized the Western Hemisphere and used African slaves to work their agricultural plantations.

How did this happen? How did Europeans become leaders in world trade and extend their influence across the Atlantic? What made Native Americans vulnerable to conquest by European adventurers? And what led to the transatlantic trade in African slaves? In the answers to these questions lie the origins of the United States and the dominance of people of European descent in the modern world.

Native American Societies

Inca Cup

This painted wooden drinking cup (*q'iru*) shows how the Incas, who ruled a great sixteenth-century empire in present-day Peru (see Map 1.5), made use of history and tradition. Around A.D. 1000, the Tiwanaku people ruled an empire in the highlands of Peru; one of the central motifs of their culture was a sacred staircase symbolizing heavens, earth, and the underworld. By placing that Tiwanaku motif on the central band of this cup and combining its symbol with their own — the man with the staff, shield, and headdress — the Incas grounded their claim of royal authority in the prestige of the Tiwanaku. Courtesy, National Museum of the American Indian, Smithsonian Institution.

When the Europeans arrived, most Native Americans — about 40 million — lived in Mesoamerica (present-day Mexico and Guatemala) and along the western coast of South America (present-day Peru); another 7 million resided in lands to the north, in what is now the United States and Canada. Some Native peoples lived in simple hunter-gatherer or agricultural communities governed by kin ties, but most lived in societies ruled by warrior-kings and priests. In Mesoamerica and Peru, Indian peoples created civilizations whose art, religion, society, and economy were as complex as those of Europe and the Mediterranean.

The First Americans

According to the elders of the Navajo people, history began when their ancestors emerged from under the earth; for the Iroquois, the story of their Five Nations began when people fell from the sky. But most twenty-first-century anthropologists and historians believe that the first inhabitants of the Western Hemisphere were migrants from Asia. Some came by water; most probably came by land. Strong archaeological and genetic evidence suggests that in the last Ice Age, which began about twenty thousand years ago, small bands of tribal hunters followed herds of game across a 100-mile-wide land bridge between Siberia and Alaska. An

oral history of the Tuscarora Indians, who settled in present-day North Carolina, tells of a famine in the Old World and a journey over ice toward where "the sun rises," a trek that brought their ancestors to a lush forest with abundant food and game.

Most anthropologists would argue that the main migratory stream from Asia lasted from about fifteen thousand to nine thousand years ago, after which the glaciers melted and the rising ocean waters submerged the land bridge and created the Bering Strait (Map 1.1). Around eight thousand years ago, a second movement of peoples, now traveling by water across the narrow strait, brought the ancestors of the Navajos and the Apaches to North America. A third migration around five thousand years ago introduced the forebears of the Aleut and Inuit peoples, the "Eskimos." Subsequently, the peoples of the Western Hemisphere were largely cut off from the rest of the world for three hundred generations.

For many centuries, the first Americans lived as hunter-gatherers, subsisting on the abundant wildlife and vegetation. Gradually, as the larger species of animals — mammoths, giant beaver, and horses — died out because of overhunting and climatic change, hunters became adept at killing more-elusive game — rabbits, deer, and elk. By about 3000 B.C., some Native American peoples in the region near present-day Mexico had begun to farm. They planted beans, squash, and maize (corn), as well as tomatoes, potatoes, and manioc (cassava) — crops that would eventually enrich the food supply of the entire world. In fact, the Indians gradually bred maize into an extremely nutritious plant that had a higher yield per acre than did wheat, barley, or rye, the staple cereals of Europe. They also learned to plant beans and squash together with corn, a mix of crops that provided a nourishing diet and kept the soil fertile. The resulting agricultural surplus made urban society possible, laying the economic foundation for populous and wealthy societies in Mexico, Peru, and the Mississippi River Valley (Map 1.2).

The Mayas and the Aztecs

The flowering of civilization in Mesoamerica began around 700 B.C. among the Olmec people, who lived along the Gulf of Mexico. Subsequently, the Mayas of the Yucatán Peninsula of Mexico and the neighboring rain forests of Guatemala built large urban centers that relied on elaborate systems of water storage and irrigation. By A.D. 300, more than 20,000 people were living in the Mayan city of Tikal [*tee-kall*]. Most were farmers, whose labor had built the city's huge stone temples. An elite class claiming

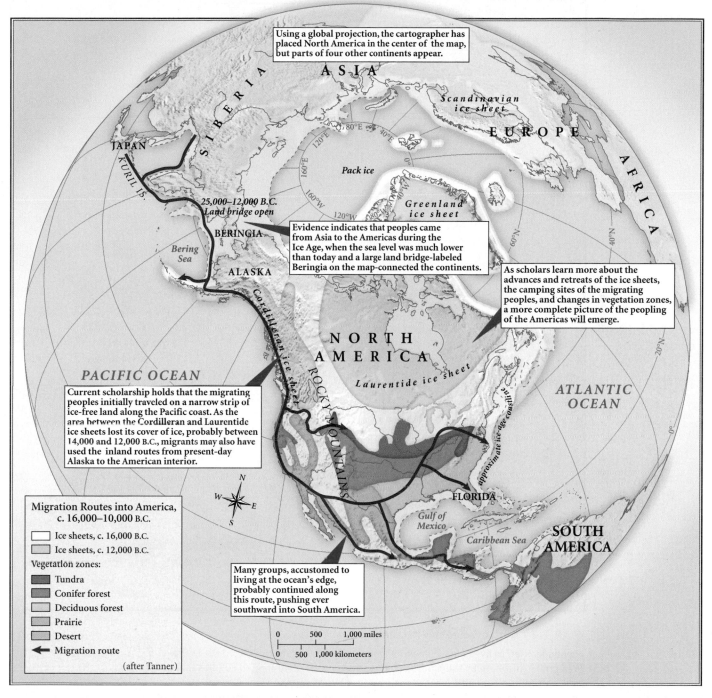

Using a global projection, the cartographer has placed North America in the center of the map, but parts of four other continents appear.

Evidence indicates that peoples came from Asia to the Americas during the Ice Age, when the sea level was much lower than today and a large land bridge-labeled Beringia on the map-connected the continents.

As scholars learn more about the advances and retreats of the ice sheets, the camping sites of the migrating peoples, and changes in vegetation zones, a more complete picture of the peopling of the Americas will emerge.

Current scholarship holds that the migrating peoples initially traveled on a narrow strip of ice-free land along the Pacific coast. As the area between the Cordilleran and Laurentide ice sheets lost its cover of ice, probably between 14,000 and 12,000 B.C., migrants may also have used the inland routes from present-day Alaska to the American interior.

Many groups, accustomed to living at the ocean's edge, probably continued along this route, pushing ever southward into South America.

ASIA

SIBERIA

JAPAN

KURIL IS.

25,000–12,000 B.C.
Land bridge open

BERINGIA

Bering Sea

ALASKA

PACIFIC OCEAN

Cordilleran ice sheet

ROCKY MOUNTAINS

NORTH AMERICA

Laurentide ice sheet

Scandinavian ice sheet

EUROPE

AFRICA

Pack ice

Greenland ice sheet

ATLANTIC OCEAN

approximate ice-age coastline

FLORIDA

Gulf of Mexico

Caribbean Sea

SOUTH AMERICA

Migration Routes into America, c. 16,000–10,000 B.C.

Ice sheets, c. 16,000 B.C.
Ice sheets, c. 12,000 B.C.

Vegetation zones:
Tundra
Conifer forest
Deciduous forest
Prairie
Desert
← Migration route

(after Tanner)

N
W   E
S

0   500   1,000 miles
0   500   1,000 kilometers

MAP 1.1 The Ice Age and the Settling of the Americas

Some sixteen thousand years ago, a sheet of ice covered much of Europe and North America. Making use of a broad bridge of land connecting Siberia and Alaska, hunting peoples from Asia migrated to North America in search of woolly mammoths and other large game animals, and ice-free habitats. By 10,000 B.C., the descendants of these migrant peoples had moved south to present-day Florida and central Mexico. In time, they would settle as far south as the tip of South America and as far east as the Atlantic coast of North America.

MAP 1.2 Native American Peoples, 1492

Having learned to live in many environments, Native Americans populated the entire Western Hemisphere by the time Columbus arrived there. They created cultures that ranged from centralized agriculture-based societies (the Mayas and the Aztecs), to societies that combined farming and hunting (the Iroquois and Algonquins), to seminomadic tribes of hunter-gatherers (the Micmacs and Ottowas). Their diversity — of tradition, language, and tribal identity — in large part prevented Native Americans from uniting to resist the European invaders.

descent from the gods ruled Mayan society and lived in splendor on goods and taxes extracted from peasant families. Drawing on the religious and artistic traditions of the Olmecs, Mayan artisans decorated temples and palaces with depictions of jaguars, warrior-gods, and complex religious ritu-

als. Mayan astronomers created a calendar that recorded historical events and accurately predicted eclipses of the sun and the moon. And Mayan scholars developed hieroglyphic writing to record royal lineages and wars and other noteworthy events. These skills in calculation and writing enhanced the authority of the class of warriors and priests that ruled Mayan society, and they provided the people with a sense of history and identity. By facilitating the movement of goods and ideas, they also increased the prosperity of Mayan society and the complexity of its culture.

Beginning around 800, Mayan civilization went into decline. Evidence suggests that a two-century-long drought led to an economic crisis and prompted overtaxed peasants to desert the temple cities and retreat to the countryside. By 900, many religious centers had been abandoned. The few Mayan city-states that remained intact would vigorously resist the Spanish invaders in the 1520s.

A second major Mesoamerican civilization developed in the highlands of Mexico around the city of Teotihuacán [tee-o-ti-hue-kon], with its magnificent Pyramid of the Sun. At its zenith, about A.D. 500, Teotihuacán had more than one hundred temples, some four thousand apartment buildings, and a population of at least 100,000. By 800, the city was failing, the likely victim of both long-term drought and the recurrent invasions of seminomadic warrior peoples. Eventually one of these invading peoples, the Aztecs, established an even more extensive empire.

The Aztecs entered the great central valley of Mexico from the north and settled on an island in Lake Texcoco. There, in 1325, they began to build a new city, Tenochtitlán [ten-och-tit-lan], Mexico City today. The Aztecs learned the ways of the resident peoples, mastered their complex irrigation systems and written language, and established an elaborate culture with a hierarchical social order. Priests and warrior-nobles ruled over twenty **clans** of free Aztec commoners who farmed communal land. The nobles also used huge numbers of non-Aztec slaves and serfs to labor on their private estates.

An aggressive people, the Aztecs soon subjugated most of central Mexico. Their rulers demanded both economic and human tribute from scores of subject peoples, sacrificing untold thousands of men and women to ensure fertile fields and the daily return of the sun.

Aztec merchants forged trading routes that crisscrossed the empire, and imported furs, gold, textiles, food, and obsidian from as far north as the Rio Grande and as far south as present-day Panama. By 1500, Tenochtitlán had grown into a metropolis, with magnificent palaces and temples and more than 200,000 inhabitants — making it far larger than most European cities. Aztec artisans worked in stone, pottery, cloth, leather, and especially obsidian, a hard volcanic glass used to make sharp-edged weapons and tools. The splendor of the city and its elaborate crafts dazzled both subject peoples and

Spanish soldiers. "These great towns and pyramids and buildings arising from the water, all made of stone, seemed like an enchanted vision," marveled one Spaniard. The Aztecs' strong institutions, military power, and wealth posed a formidable challenge to any adversary, at home or from afar.

The Indians of the North

The societies north of the Rio Grande generally were less complex and less coercive than those to the south. They lacked occupational diversity, social hierarchy, and strong state institutions. Most northern peoples lived in self-governing tribes made up of clans, groups of related families that traced their lineage to a real or legendary common ancestor. Clan elders and local chiefs set war policy, conducted ceremonies, and resolved personal feuds. They also made social policy — banning marriage between members of the same clan, for example, to prevent inbreeding — and disciplined those who violated that policy and other customs. But elders and chiefs usually did not form a distinct ruling class; instead, they ruled with limited powers through a kinship system of government that was local and worked by consent.

The culture of these lineage-based societies did not encourage the accumulation of material goods. Individual ownership of land was virtually unknown: As a French missionary among the Iroquois noted, they "possess hardly anything except in common." The elders would urge members to share food and other scarce goods, encouraging an ethic of reciprocity rather than one of accumulation. "You are covetous, and neither generous nor kind," the Micmac Indians of Nova Scotia would tell acquisitive French fur traders in the late 1600s. "As for us, if we have a morsel of bread, we share it with our neighbor."

The Hopewell Culture. Over the centuries, some Indian peoples did become materialistic, engaging in trade or conquest (see Reading American Pictures, "Maize for Blankets: Indian Trading Networks on the Great Plains," p. 10). By A.D. 100, the vigorous Hopewell people of present-day Ohio had increased their food supply by domesticating plants, organized themselves in large villages, and set up a trading network that stretched from present-day Louisiana to Wisconsin. They imported obsidian from the Yellowstone region of the Rocky Mountains, copper from the Great Lakes, and pottery and marine shells from the Gulf of Mexico. The Hopewells built large burial mounds and surrounded them with extensive circular, rectangular,

Maize for Blankets: Indian Trading Networks on the Great Plains

Tom Lovell, *Trade Among Indian Peoples.* Courtesy of Abell-Hanger Foundation and of the Permian Basin Petroleum Museum, Library and Hall of Fame of Midland, Texas, where the painting is on permanent display.

In most Native American societies, there were no merchants, store-keepers, or traders. Yet, as the text explains, many Indian peoples exchanged goods with their neighbors and often acquired wares produced in distant lands. Those "wares" included captives taken in battle, who were put to work as slaves or integrated into the society through marriage or adoption. This 1973 painting offers a historical reconstruction of the commerce in goods at the fortified Towa pueblo of Cicúye (in what is Pecos, New Mexico, today), which stands on a high mountain pass between the Rio Grande Valley and the Great Plains (and looms in the background to the left). The Towa people are trading with Apaches.

ANALYZING THE EVIDENCE

➤ Why did the location of the Pecos pueblo make it a major trading post? One clue comes from a Spanish explorer who visited Pecos in 1541 with Francisco Vásquez de Coronado's expedition (see Chapter 2). He reported that Indians from the Great Plains exchanged "*cueros de Cíbola* [bison hides] and deer skins" for the "maize and blankets" produced by the Pueblo peoples. Do you see any other pueblo products in this painting?

➤ What do the clothing, material goods, and lodgings of the two peoples — the Towas and the Apaches — tell us about their respective ways of life?

➤ How have the Apaches transported their goods to Pecos? Based on what you have read in the text, can you explain why no horses are shown in the painting, which is set in A.D. 1500?

➤ Look closely at what the men and women are doing. What does the painting tell you about gender roles in Native American societies?

The Great Serpent Mound

Scholars long believed that the serpent was the work of Adena peoples (500 B.C.–A.D. 200) because of its proximity to an Adena burial site. Recent research places the mound at a much later date (A.D. 950–1200) and, because of the serpent imagery, ties it to the culture of Mississippian peoples. The head of the serpent is aligned with the sunset of the summer solstice, an event of great religious significance to a sun worshipping culture. © Bettmann/Corbis

or octagonal earthworks that in some cases still survive. Skilled Hopewell artisans fashioned striking ornaments to bury with the dead: copper beaten into intricate designs, mica cut into the shape of serpents or human hands, and stone pipes carved to represent frogs, hawks, bears, and other spiritually powerful beings. For unknown reasons, the elaborate trading network of the Hopewells gradually collapsed around 400.

The Southwestern Peoples and Environmental Decline. A second complex culture developed among the Pueblo peoples of the Southwest — the Hohokams, Mogollons, and Anasazis. By A.D. 600, Hohokam [*ho-ho-kam*] people in the high country along the border of present-day Arizona and New Mexico were using irrigation to grow two crops a year, fashioning fine pottery in red-on-buff designs, and worshiping their gods on Mesoamerican-like platform mounds; by 1000, they were living in elaborate multiroom stone structures called **pueblos**. To the east, in the Mimbres Valley of present-day New Mexico, the

Mogollon [*mo-gee-yon*] people developed a distinctive black-on-white pottery. And by A.D. 900, to the north, the Anasazi (or Ancestral Pueblo) people had become master architects. They built residential-ceremonial villages in steep cliffs, a pueblo in Chaco Canyon that housed one thousand people, and 400 miles of straight roads. But the culture of the Pueblo peoples gradually collapsed after 1150, as soil exhaustion and extended droughts disrupted maize production and prompted the abandonment of Chaco Canyon and other communities. The descendants of these peoples — including the Acomas, Zunis, and Hopis — later built strong but smaller village societies better suited to the dry and unpredictable climate of the American Southwest.

Mississippian Culture. The last large-scale culture to emerge north of the Rio Grande was the Mississippian. By about A.D. 800, the farming technology of Mesoamerica had reached the Mississippi River Valley, perhaps carried by Mayan refugees from the war-torn Yucatán Peninsula. By planting new strains of maize and beans, the Mississippian peoples produced an agricultural surplus that allowed them to live in small, fortified temple cities, where they developed a robust culture. By 1150, the largest city, Cahokia [*ka-ho-kee-ah*], near present-day St. Louis, boasted a population of 15,000 to 20,000 and more than one hundred temple mounds, one of them as large as the great Egyptian pyramids. Here, too, as in Mesoamerica, the tribute paid by peasant farmers supported a privileged class of nobles and priests who waged war against neighboring chiefdoms, patronized artisans, and claimed descent from the sun god.

By 1350, the Mississippian civilization was in rapid decline. The large population had overburdened the environment, depleting nearby forests and herds of deer. The Indians also fell victim to tuberculosis and other deadly urban diseases. Still, Mississippian institutions and practices endured for centuries.

When Spanish conquistador Hernán de Soto invaded the region in the 1540s, he found the Apalachee [*ap-a-la-chee*] and Timucua [*tee-moo-kwa*] Indians living in permanent settlements under the command of powerful chiefs. "If you desire to see me, come where I am," a chief told de Soto, "neither for you, nor for any man, will I set back one foot." A century and a half later, French traders and priests found the Natchez people living in a society rigidly divided among hereditary chiefs, two groups of nobles and honored people, and a bottom class of peasants. "Their chiefs possess all authority," a Frenchman noted. "They distribute their favors and presents at will." Undoubtedly influenced by Mesoamerican rituals, the Natchez marked the death of a chief by sacrificing his wives and burying their remains in a ceremonial mound (see Voices from Abroad, "Father Le Petite: The Customs of the Natchez, 1730," p. 13).

Iroquois Women at Work, 1724

As this European engraving suggests, Iroquois women were responsible for growing food crops. Several of the women at the top are hoeing the soil into small hillocks, while others are planting corn and beans. The lower section shows other women tapping sugar maples and boiling the sweet sap to make maple syrup. The woman at the left is probably grinding corn into flour. Later she would add water to make flat patties for baking. Newberry Library, Chicago.

Father Le Petite

The Customs of the Natchez, 1730

The beliefs and institutions of the Mississippians (A.D. 1000–1450) survived for centuries among the native peoples of the Southeast, and helped them resist the attacks of Spanish conquistador Hernán de Soto in the 1540s. Mississippian customs lasted longest among the Natchez people, who lived in present-day Mississippi. A fine description of their society appears in a letter written around 1730 by Father Le Petite, one of the hundreds of Jesuit priests who lived among the Indians in the French colonies of Louisiana and Canada. Here, Father Le Petite accurately describes several Indian customs to his religious superiors in France. However, he misunderstands the reasons why the chief is succeeded by his sister's son rather than his own son. In a matrilineal society, lines of descent and inheritance pass through women, not men.

My Reverend Father, The peace of Our Lord.

This Nation of Savages inhabits one of the most beautiful and fertile countries in the World, and is the only one on this continent which appears to have any regular worship. Their Religion in certain points is very similar to that of the ancient Romans. They have a Temple filled with Idols, which are different figures of men and of animals, and for which they have the most profound veneration. Their Temple in shape resembles an earthen oven, a hundred feet in circumference. They enter it by a little door about four feet high, and not more than three in breadth. Above on the outside are three figures of eagles made of wood, and painted red, yellow, and white. Before the door is a kind of shed with folding-doors, where the Guardian of the Temple is lodged; all around it runs a circle of palisades [pointed wooden stakes], on which are seen exposed the skulls of all the heads which their Warriors had brought back from the battles in which they had been engaged with the enemies of their Nation. . . .

The Sun is the principal object of veneration to these people; as they cannot conceive of anything which can be above this heavenly body, nothing else appears to them more worthy of their homage. It is for the same reason that the great Chief of this Nation, who knows nothing on the earth more dignified than himself, takes the title of brother of the Sun, and the credulity of the people maintains him in the despotic authority which he claims. To enable them better to converse together, they raise a mound of artificial soil, on which they build his cabin, which is of the same construction as the Temple. When a great Chief dies, his many wives are killed and are buried with him and personal goods in a great ceremonial mound.

The old men prescribe the Laws for the rest of the people, and one of their principles is . . . the immortality of the soul, and when they leave this world they go, they say, to live in another, there to be recompensed or punished.

In former times the Nation of the *Natchez* was very large. It counted sixty Villages and eight hundred Suns or Princes; now it is reduced to six little Villages and eleven Suns. [Its] Government is hereditary; it is not, however, the son of the reigning Chief who succeeds his father, but the son of his sister, or the first Princess of the blood. This policy is founded on the knowledge they have of the licentiousness of their women. They are not sure, they say, that the children of the chief's wife may be of the blood Royal, whereas the son of the sister of the great Chief must be, at least on the side of the mother.

SOURCE: Reuben Gold Thwaites, ed., *The Jesuit Relations and Allied Documents* (Cleveland: Murrow Brothers, 1900), 68: 121–135.

ANALYZING THE EVIDENCE

➤ Which of Le Petite's remarks suggest a link between the Natchez and the Aztecs of Mesoamerica? How might this link have been established?

➤ Given what you have learned about the Native American population decline, how would you explain that sixty Natchez villages had been reduced to six?

The Eastern Woodland Peoples. The cultures of the native peoples of eastern North America were diverse. Like the Natchez, the Creeks, Choctaws, and Chickasaws who lived in present-day Alabama and Mississippi had once been organized in powerful chiefdoms. However, the devastating epidemics of European diseases introduced by de Soto's expedition in the 1540s killed a majority of their populations and destroyed their traditional institutions. The survivors of the various chiefdoms intermarried and settled in smaller and less powerful agricultural communities.

In these Muskogean-speaking societies—and among the Algonquian-speaking peoples who lived farther north and to the east, in present-day Virginia—farming became the work of women. While the men hunted and fished, the women used flint hoes to raise corn, squash, and beans. Because of the importance of farming, a **matrilineal** system developed among many eastern Indian peoples, including the Five Nations of the Iroquois, who lived in present-day New York State. Women cultivated the fields around semipermanent settlements and passed the use rights to the fields to their daughters. In these matrilineal societies, the father stood outside the main lines of descent and authority; the principal responsibility for child raising fell on the mother and her brothers, who often lived with their sisters rather than with their wives. Among these farming peoples, religious rituals centered on the agricultural cycle. The Iroquois, for example, celebrated green corn and strawberry festivals. Although the eastern Indian peoples of 1500 ate a balanced diet of meat and vegetables, they enjoyed few material comforts and their populations grew slowly.

When Europeans intruded into their lives, most eastern woodland Indians lived in relatively small kinship-based societies. The strong city-states that had once flourished in the Southwest and in the Mississippi River Valley had vanished. Consequently, there were no great Indian empires or religious centers here—as there were in Mesoamerica—that could sustain a campaign of military and spiritual resistance to European invaders. "When you command, all the French obey and go to war," the Chippewa chief Chigabe [*chig-ah-bee*] remarked to a French general, but "I shall not be heeded and obeyed by my nation." Because household and lineage were the basis of his society, Chigabe explained, "I cannot answer except for myself and for those immediately allied to me."

➤ What were the major similarities and differences between the civilizations of Mesoamerica and the Mississippian culture to the north?

➤ How did the climate affect the rise and decline of various Native peoples?

➤ How were eastern woodland Indian societies organized and governed?

Europe Encounters Africa and the Americas, 1450 – 1550

In 1400, few observers would have predicted that Europeans would dominate the trade of Africa and become overlords of the Western Hemisphere. One thousand years after the fall of the great Roman empire, Europe remained a mosaic of small and relatively weak kingdoms. Moreover, around 1350, a vicious epidemic from the subcontinent of India—the Black Death—had killed one-third of Europe's population. Peoples in other regions had stronger economies and governments and seemed more likely to seize control of world commerce. In 1417, for example, a large Chinese fleet had traveled thousands of miles to trade along the eastern coast of Africa; and Muslim merchants controlled all of Europe's trade with Asia.

European Agricultural Society

In 1450, there were just a few large cities in Western Europe: Only Paris, London, and Naples had as many as 100,000 residents. Most Europeans were **peasants** who lived in small agricultural communities. Peasant families usually owned or leased a small dwelling in the village center and had the right to farm the surrounding fields. The fields were open—not divided by fences or hedges—which made cooperative farming a necessity. The community decided which crops to grow, and every family followed its dictates. Because output was limited and there were few good roads, most trade was local. Neighboring families exchanged surplus grain and meat and bartered their farm products for the services of local millers, weavers, and blacksmiths. Most peasants yearned to be **yeomen**, to own enough land to support their families in comfort, but relatively few achieved that goal.

The Seasonal Cycle and the Peasants' Lot. For European peasants, as for Native Americans, the rhythm of life followed the seasons. The agricultural year began in late March, when the ground thawed and dried and the villagers began the exhausting work of spring plowing and then planting

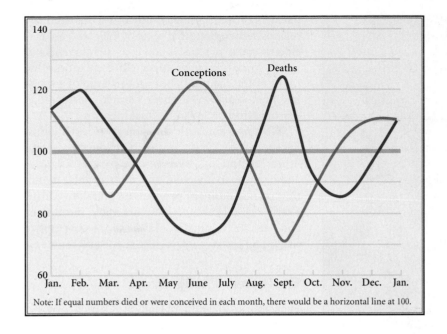

FIGURE 1.1 The Rhythm of Rural Life

The annual cycle of nature profoundly affected the life of European peasants for many centuries. Each year the death rate soared in February (from viruses) and September (from fly-borne dysentery). Early summer was the healthiest season, the time of the fewest deaths and the most conceptions (as measured by births nine months later).

Note: If equal numbers died or were conceived in each month, there would be a horizontal line at 100.

wheat, rye, and oats. During these busy months, men sheared the thick winter wool of their sheep, which the women washed and spun into yarn. In June, peasants cut the first crop of hay and stored it as winter fodder for their livestock. During the summer, life was more relaxed, and families had the time to repair their houses and barns. Fall brought the strenuous harvest, followed by solemn feasts of thanksgiving and riotous bouts of merry-making. As winter approached, peasants slaughtered excess livestock and salted or smoked the meat. During the cold months, they threshed grain and wove textiles, visited friends and relatives, and celebrated the winter solstice or the birth of Christ. Just before the farming cycle began again in the spring, they held carnivals, celebrating with drink and dance the end of the long winter night. Even births and deaths followed the seasons: More successful conceptions took place in early summer than any other time of the year. And many rural people died in January and February, victims of viral diseases and then again in August and September, casualties of epidemics of fly-borne dysentery (Figure 1.1).

For most peasants, survival meant constant labor, breaking the soil with primitive wooden plows or harvesting hay and grain with small hand sickles. In the absence of high-quality seeds, chemical fertilizers, and pesticides, output was pitifully small—less than one-tenth of present-day yields. The margin of existence was also small, and that corroded family relationships. Malnourished mothers fed their babies sparingly, calling them "greedy and gluttonous," and many newborn girls were "helped to die" so that their older brothers would have enough to eat. Disease killed about half of all peasant children before the age of twenty-one. Indeed, when the Black Death ravaged Europe, it took the lives of millions. Even in less dangerous times, assault, murder, and rape were woven into the fabric of daily life, and hunger was a constant companion. "I have seen the latest epoch of misery," a French doctor reported as famine and plague struck. "The inhabitants . . . lie down in a meadow to eat grass, and share the food of wild beasts."

Often destitute, usually exploited by landlords and nobles, many peasants simply accepted their condition. Others hoped for a better life for themselves and their children. It was the peasants of Spain, Germany, and Britain who would supply the majority of white migrants to the Western Hemisphere.

Hierarchy and Authority

In traditional societies—Mesoamerican or European—authority came from above. In Europe, kings and princes owned vast tracts of land, forcibly conscripted men for military service, and lived in splendor off the labor of the peasantry. Yet monarchs were far from supreme: Local nobles also owned large estates and controlled hundreds of peasant families. Collectively, these nobles challenged royal authority with both their military power and their legislative institutions, such as the French *parlements* and the English House of Lords.

Artisan Family

Work was slow and output was limited in the preindustrial world, and survival required the efforts of all family members. Here a fifteenth-century French woodworker planes a panel of wood while his wife twists flax fibers into linen yarn for the family's clothes and their young son cleans up wood shavings from the workshop floor. Giraudon/Art Resource, New York.

Just as kings and nobles ruled society, so men governed families. Rich or poor, the man was the head of the house, his power justified by the teachings of the Christian church. As one English clergyman put it, "The woman is a weak creature not embued with like strength and constancy of mind"; consequently, law and custom "subjected her to the power of man." Once she married, an Englishwoman assumed her husband's surname and had to submit, under threat of legally sanctioned physical "correction," to his orders. Moreover, she surrendered to her husband the legal right to all her property. Her sole protection: When he died, she received a **dower**, usually the use during her lifetime of one-third of the family's land and goods.

Men also controlled the lives of their children, who usually were required to work for their father into their middle or late twenties. Then landowning peasants would give land to their sons and dowries to their daughters and choose marriage partners of appropriate wealth and status. In many regions, fathers bestowed most of their land on their eldest son, a practice known as **primogeniture**, which forced many younger children to join the ranks of the roaming poor. In this kind of society, few men—and even fewer women—had much personal freedom or individual identity.

Hierarchy and authority prevailed in traditional European society both because of the power of established institutions—family, church, and village—and because, in a violent and unpredictable world, they offered ordinary people a measure of security. Carried by migrants to America, these institutions and need for security would shape the character of family and society well into the eighteenth century.

The Power of Religion

For centuries, the Roman Catholic Church served as the great unifying institution in Western Europe. The pope in Rome stood at the head of a vast religious hierarchy of cardinals, bishops, and priests. Catholic books and theologians preserved Latin, the great language of classical scholarship, and Christian dogma provided a common understanding of God, the world, and human history. Equally important, the Church provided a bulwark of authority and discipline. Every village had a church, and the holy shrines that dotted the byways of Europe were reminders of the Church's power and teachings.

Christian doctrine penetrated deeply into the everyday lives of peasants. Originally, most Europeans were **pagans**. Like the Indians of North America, they were animists: They believed that unpredictable spiritual forces governed the natural world and that those spirits had to be paid ritual honor. As Christianity spread, priests taught the peasants that spiritual power came from outside nature, from God, a supernatural being, who had sent his divine son, Jesus Christ, into the world to save humanity from its sins. The Church also devised a religious calendar that transformed pagan agricultural festivals into Christian holy days. Thus the winter solstice, which for pagans marked the return of the sun, became the feast of Christmas, to mark the birth of Christ. To avert famine and plague, Christianized peasants no longer made ritual offerings to nature; instead, they offered prayers to Christ and the saints.

The Church also taught that Satan, a lesser and evil supernatural being, was constantly challenging God by tempting people to sin. If a devout Christian fell mysteriously ill, the cause might be an evil spell cast by a witch in league with Satan. If prophets spread **heresies**,—doctrines that were inconsistent with the teachings of the Church—they

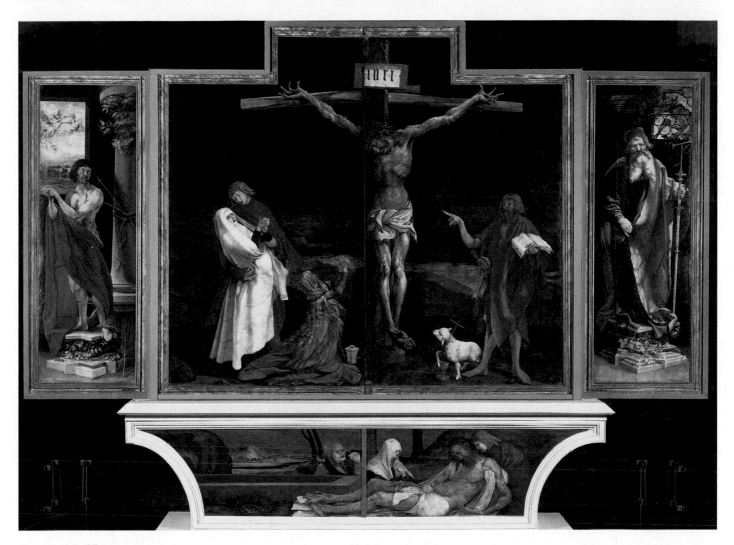

Christ's Crucifixion

The German painter Grünewald rendered this graphic portrayal of Christ's death on the cross and subsequent burial. It was meant to remind believers not only of Christ's sacrifice but also of the ever-present prospect of their own death. The panel to the left depicts the martyr Saint Sebastian, killed by dozens of arrows; the panel to the right probably portrays the abbot of the monastery in Isenheim, Germany, that commissioned the altarpiece. Musée Unterlinden, Colmar, Colmar-Giraudon/Art Resource.

were surely the tools of Satan. Suppressing false doctrines became an obligation of Christian rulers. So did combating Islam, a religion that like Christianity proclaimed a single god (monotheism). Following the death in A.D. 632 of the prophet Muhammad, the founder of Islam, the newly converted Arab peoples of the Mediterranean used force and persuasion to spread the Muslim faith into sub-Saharan Africa, India, and Indonesia, and deep into Spain and the Balkan regions of Europe. Between 1096 and 1291, Christian armies undertook a series of Crusades to halt this advance and win back the holy lands where Christ had lived.

The crusaders had some military successes against the Muslims, but their most profound impact was on European society. Religious warfare intensified Europe's Christian identity and prompted the persecution of Jews and their expulsion from many European countries. The Crusades also broadened the intellectual and economic horizons of the privileged classes of Western Europe, who absorbed the scholarship of the Arab world and set out to capture the Arab-dominated trade routes that stretched from Constantinople to Beijing and from the Mediterranean to the East Indian seas (Maps 1.3 and 1.4).

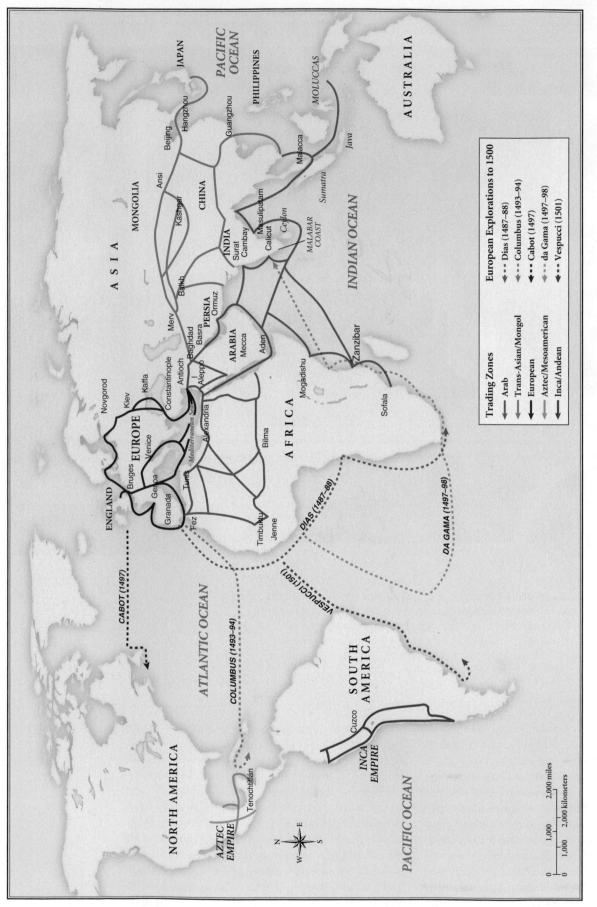

MAP 1.3 The Eurasian Trade System and European Maritime Ventures, c. 1500

For centuries, the Mediterranean Sea was the meeting point for the commerce of Europe, North Africa, and Asia — via the Silk Road from China and the Spice Trade from India. During the 1490s, Portuguese, Spanish, and Dutch monarchs and merchants subsidized maritime explorers who discovered new trade routes and challenged the commercial primacy of the Muslim-dominated Mediterranean.

Astronomers at Istanbul (Constantinople), 1581

Arab and Turkish scholars transmitted ancient texts and learning to Europeans during the Middle Ages and provided much of the geographical and astronomical knowledge European explorers used during the sixteenth century, the great Age of Discovery. University Library, Istanbul, Turkey & Bridgeman Art Library.

The Renaissance Changes Europe, 1300–1500

Stimulated by exposure to Arab society, first Italy and then the countries of northern Europe recovered from the Black Death and experienced a rebirth of cultural life and economic energy. Arabs had access to the silks and spices of the East and had acquired magnetic compasses, water-powered mills, and mechanical clocks, mostly from the Chinese. Moreover, Arab scholars carried on the legacy of Byzantine civilization, which had preserved the great achievements of the Greeks and Romans in medicine, philosophy, mathematics, astronomy, and geography. The Crusades exposed Europeans to Byzantine and Arab learning and reacquainted them with the achievements of classical antiquity.

Innovations in Economics, Art, and Politics. The Renaissance had the most profound impact on the upper classes. Merchants from the Italian city-states of Venice, Genoa, Florence, and Pisa dispatched ships to Alexandria, Beirut, and other eastern Mediterranean ports, where they purchased goods from China, India, Persia, and Arabia, and sold them throughout Europe. The enormous profits from this commerce created powerful merchants, bankers, and textile manufacturers who conducted trade, lent vast sums of money, and spurred technological innovation in silk and wool production. These Italian moneyed elites ruled their city-states as **republics**, with no prince or king. They celebrated **civic humanism**, an **ideology** that praised public virtue and service to the state and in time profoundly influenced European and American conceptions of government.

Perhaps no other age in European history has produced such a flowering of artistic genius. Michelangelo, Andrea Palladio, and Filippo Brunelleschi designed and built great architectural masterpieces, while Leonardo da Vinci, Jacopo Bellini, and Raphael produced magnificent religious paintings, setting styles and standards that have endured into the modern era.

This creative energy inspired Renaissance rulers. In *The Prince* (1513), Niccolò Machiavelli offered unsentimental advice on how monarchs could increase their political power. The kings of Western Europe followed his advice, creating royal law courts and bureaucracies to reduce the power of the landed classes and forging alliances with merchants and urban artisans. Monarchs allowed merchants to trade throughout their realms, granted privileges to the artisan organizations called **guilds**, and safeguarded commercial transactions in royal law courts, thereby encouraging domestic manufacturing and foreign trade. In return, kings and princes extracted taxes from towns and loans from merchants to support their armies and officials. This mutually enriching alliance of monarchs and merchants propelled Europe into its first age of overseas expansion.

Prince Henry and Maritime Expansion. Under the direction of Prince Henry (1394–1460), Portugal led a surge of maritime commercial expansion. Prince Henry was the third son of King João I of Portugal and his English wife, Philippa of Lancaster. In 1415, as a young soldier of the Crusading Order of Christ, he instigated a successful attack on the Muslim port of Ceuta in northern Morocco, where he learned of Arab merchants' rich trade in gold and slaves across the Sahara Desert. In his search for a maritime route to the sources of this trade in West Africa, Henry patronized Renaissance thinkers and drew on the work of Arab and Italian geographers. In 1420, he founded a center for oceanic navigation and astronomical observation at Sagres, in the south of Portugal. There he oversaw the making of more precise maps and

Prince Henry of Portugal

As the third son of the king, Henry stood little chance of succeeding to the throne. So he devoted his energies to Christian crusades against the Moors and to maritime explorations. In the 1430s, his mariners finally rounded Cape Bojador and began to trade with the peoples of sub-Saharan Africa. The Granger Collection, New York.

pushed forward the development of the caravel, a three-masted ship with two regular sails and one lateen (triangular) sail for maneuverability. Most important, Henry urged his captains to find a way around Cape Bojador in North Africa, a region of fierce winds and treacherous currents, and to explore the feared "Sea of Darkness" to the south. Eventually Henry's mariners sailed far into the Atlantic, where they discovered and colonized the Madeira and Azore Islands; and from there they explored the sub-Saharan African coast. By 1435, Portuguese sea captains had reached the coast of Sierra Leone, where they exchanged salt, wine, and fish for African ivory and gold. By the 1440s, they were trading in humans as well, the first Europeans to engage in the long-established and extensive African trade in slaves. By the time he died, Henry had succeeded in his mission of enhancing Portugal's wealth through maritime commerce with West Africa.

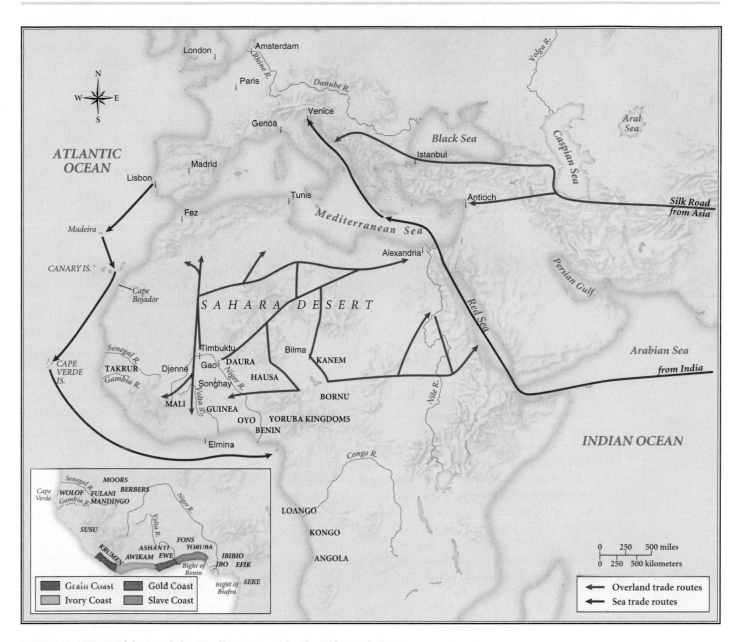

MAP 1.4   West Africa and the Mediterranean in the Fifteenth Century

Trade routes across the Sahara Desert had long connected West Africa with the Mediterranean. Gold, ivory, and slaves moved north and east; fine textiles, spices, and the Muslim faith traveled south. Beginning in the 1430s, the Portuguese opened up maritime trade with the coastal regions of West Africa, which were home to many peoples and dozens of large and small states. Within a decade, they would take part in the slave trade there.

West African Society and Slavery

Vast and diverse, West Africa stretches along the coast from present-day Senegal to Angola. In the 1400s, tropical rain forest covered much of the coast, but a series of great rivers—the Senegal, Gambia, Volta, Niger, and Congo—provided relatively easy access to the woodlands and savannas of the interior, where most people lived. There were few coastal cities because there was little seaborne trade (Map 1.4).

West African Life. Most West Africans lived in extended families in small villages and farmed modest plots. Normally, the men cleared the land and the women planted and harvested the crops. On the plains, farmers grew millet and cotton, and

Fulani Village in West Africa

Around 1550, the Fulani people conquered the lands to the south of the Senegal River. To protect themselves from subject peoples and neighboring tribes, the Fulanis constructed fortified villages like the one shown here. The Fulanis were originally nomadic herders and, as the enclosed pasture shows, continued to keep livestock. Notice the cylindrical houses of mud brick with their thatched roofs. Frederic Shoberl, ed., *The World in Miniature: Africa*, 4 vols. (London: Ackermann, 1821).

set their livestock out to graze; the forest peoples planted yams and harvested oil-rich palm nuts. Forest dwellers exchanged palm oil and kola nuts, a highly valued stimulant, for the textiles and leather goods produced by savanna dwellers. Similarly, merchants collected valuable salt, which was produced along the coast and mined in great deposits in the Sahara, and traded it for iron, gold, and manufactures along the Niger and other rivers.

West Africans lived in diverse ethnic groups and spoke four basic languages, each with many dialects. Among West Atlantic–speakers, the Fulani and Wolof peoples were most numerous. Mande-speakers in the upper Niger region included the Malinke and Bambara peoples; the Yorubas and the Ibos of southern Nigeria spoke varieties of the Kwa language. Finally, the Mossis and other Voltaic-speakers inhabited the area along the upper Volta River. Most of these peoples lived in societies that were similar to those of the Mayas and Aztecs—socially stratified states ruled by kings and princes. Some lived in city-states that produced high-quality metal, leather, textiles, and pottery. Other West Africans dwelled in stateless societies organized by household and lineage, much like those of the eastern woodland Indians.

Spiritual beliefs varied greatly. West Africans who lived immediately south of the Sahara—the Fulanis in Senegal, Mande-speakers in Mali, and the Hausas in northern Nigeria—learned about Islam from Arab merchants and missionaries. Although some worshiped only the Muslim god, Allah, most recognized a number of other gods and the spirits they believed lived in the earth, in animals, and in plants. Many Africans also believed their kings had divine attributes and that they were able to contact the spirit world. They also treated their ancestors with great respect, partly because they believed that

the dead resided in a nearby spiritual realm and could intercede in their lives. Most West African peoples had secret societies, such as the Poro for men and the Sande for women, that united people from different lineages and clans. These societies educated their members in sexual practices, conducted adult initiation ceremonies, and used public humiliation to enforce codes of conduct and morality.

The European Impact. Early European traders had a positive impact on West Africa by introducing new plants and animals. Portuguese merchants brought coconuts from East Africa, oranges and lemons from the Mediterranean, pigs from Western Europe, and, after 1492, maize, manioc, and tomatoes from the Americas. Portuguese merchants also expanded existing African trade networks. From small, fortified trading posts on the coast, they shipped metal products, manufactures, and slaves along the coast and to inland regions, and took gold, ivory, and pepper in return. For much of the inland trade, the Portuguese relied on Africans: Portuguese ships could travel just 150 miles up the slow-flowing Gambia and lesser distances on the other rivers. Yellow fever, malaria, and dysentery quickly struck down Europeans who spent time in the interior of West Africa, often killing as many as half of them each year.

As they traded with Africans, Portuguese adventurers continued their quest for an ocean route to Asia. In 1488, Bartholomeu Dias rounded the Cape of Good Hope, the southern tip of Africa; ten years later, Vasco da Gama reached India. Although the Arab, Indian, and Jewish merchants who controlled the trade along India's Malabar Coast tried to exclude him, da Gama acquired a highly profitable cargo of cinnamon and pepper, spices used to flavor and preserve meat. To capture the trade in spices and Indian textiles, da Gama returned to India in 1502 with twenty-one fighting vessels, which outmaneuvered and outgunned the Arab fleets. Soon the Portuguese government set up fortified trading posts for its merchants at key points around the Indian Ocean, in Indonesia, and along the coast of Asia to China and Japan. In a transition that laid the foundation for the momentous growth of European wealth and power, the Portuguese used the route around Africa to replace Arabs as the leaders in world commerce.

African Slavery. Portuguese traders joined African states and Arab merchants in the slave trade. Bonded labor — slavery, serfdom, indentured servitude — was the norm in most premodern societies, and in Africa it took the form of slavery. Some people were held in bondage as security for debts; others were sold into servitude by their kin, often in exchange for food in times of famine; many others were captured in wars. Most slaves worked as agricultural laborers or served in slave armies. And most were treated as property. Sometimes their descendants were allowed to became members of society, usually with a low class or caste status; but others endured hereditary bondage. Sonni Ali, the ruler from 1464 to 1492 of the powerful upper-Niger Islamic kingdom of Songhay, personally owned twelve "tribes" of hereditary agricultural slaves, many of them seized in raids against stateless peoples.

A significant number of West Africans became **trade slaves**, sold as agricultural workers by one kingdom to another, or carried overland in caravans by Arab traders to the Mediterranean region. When the great Tunisian traveler Ibn Battua returned to North Africa from the Kingdom of Mali around 1350, he trekked across the Sahara with a caravan of six hundred female slaves, who were destined for domestic service or concubinage in North Africa, Egypt, and the Ottoman Empire. Some decades later, the first Portuguese in Senegambia found that the Wolof king, who stood at the head of a horse-mounted warrior aristocracy, "supports himself by raids which result in many slaves. . . . He employs these slaves in cultivating the land allotted to him; but he also sells many to the [Arab] merchants in return for horses and other goods."

To exploit this trade, Portuguese merchants established forts at small port cities — first at Elmina in 1482 and later at Gorée, Mpinda, and Loango — where they bought gold and slaves from African princes and warlords. Initially, they carried a few thousand African slaves each year to work on sugar plantations in the Cape Verde Islands, the Azores, and the Madeira Islands; they also sold slaves in Lisbon, which soon had a black population of 9,000. After 1550, the maritime slave trade expanded enormously as Europeans set up sugar plantations in the newly discovered lands of Brazil and the West Indies.

Europeans Explore America

Explorers financed by the Spanish monarchs, King Ferdinand of Aragon and Queen Isabel of Castile, discovered the Western Hemisphere for Europeans. As Renaissance rulers, Ferdinand and Isabel saw national unity and foreign commerce as the keys to power and prosperity. Married in an arranged match to combine their Christian kingdoms, the young rulers (r. 1474–1516) completed the centuries-long *reconquista.* In 1492, their armies captured Granada, the last Islamic state in Western Europe. Using Catholicism to build a sense of "Spanishness," they launched the brutal Inquisition against suspected Christian heretics and expelled or forcibly converted thousands of Jews and Muslims.

Simultaneously, Ferdinand and Isabel sought trade and empire, and enlisted the services of Christopher Columbus, a mariner from Genoa. Misinterpreting the findings of Italian geographers, Columbus believed that the Atlantic Ocean, long feared by Arab merchants as a 10,000-mile-wide "green sea of darkness," was a much narrower channel of water separating Europe from Asia. Although dubious about Columbus's theory, Ferdinand and Isabel arranged financial backing from Spanish merchants and charged Columbus with finding a western route to Asia and carrying Christianity to its peoples.

Columbus set sail in three small ships in August 1492. Six weeks later, after a perilous voyage of 3,000 miles, he disembarked on an island in the present-day Bahamas. Believing he had reached Asia — "the Indies," in fifteenth-century parlance — Columbus called the native inhabitants Indians and the islands the West Indies. Surprised by the rude living conditions of the native people, Columbus expected them to "easily be made Christians." With ceremony and solemnity, he bestowed the names of the Spanish royal family and Catholic holy days on the islands, thereby intending to claim them for Spain and for Christendom. Columbus then explored the neighboring Caribbean islands and demanded tribute from the local Taino [*tie-no*], Arawak [*r-a-wak*], and Carib peoples. Buoyed by the natives' stories of rivers of gold lying "to the west," Columbus left forty men on the island of Hispaniola (present-day Haiti and the Dominican Republic) and returned triumphantly to Spain.

Although Columbus brought back no gold, the Spanish monarchs supported three more voyages over the next twelve years. During those expeditions, Columbus began the colonization of the

West Indies, transporting more than a thousand Spanish settlers — all men — and hundreds of domestic animals. He also began the transatlantic trade in slaves, carrying Indians to bondage in Europe and Africans to work as artisans and farmers in the new Spanish settlements. Because Columbus failed to find either golden treasures or great kingdoms, his death in 1506 went virtually unnoticed.

A German geographer soon labeled the "new" continents "America" in honor of a Genoese explorer, Amerigo Vespucci (see the Waldseemüller map, p. 4). Vespucci, who had explored the region around 1500, denied that it was Asia and called it a *nuevo mundo*, a "new world." For its part, the Spanish crown continued to call the continents *Las Indias* ("the Indies") and wanted to make them a new Spanish world.

The Spanish Conquest

Spanish adventurers ruled the peoples of the Indies with an iron hand. After subduing the Arawaks and Tainos on Hispaniola, the Spanish probed the mainland for gold and slaves. In 1513, Juan Ponce de León explored the coast of Florida and gave the peninsula its name. That same year, Vasco Núñez de Balboa crossed the Isthmus of Darien (Panama) and became the first European to see the Pacific Ocean. Rumors of rich Indian kingdoms in the interior encouraged other Spaniards, including hardened veterans of the *reconquista,* to launch an invasion. They also had the support of the Spanish monarchs, who offered successful conquistadors (conquerors) titles, and vast estates and Indian laborers to farm them.

Cortés, Malinche, and the Fall of the Aztecs.
Hernán Cortés (1485–1547) conquered an empire and destroyed a civilization. Cortés came from a family of minor gentry in Spain and, seeking military adventure and material gain, sailed to Santo Domingo in 1506. Ambitious and charismatic, he distinguished himself in battle, putting down a revolt and serving in the conquest of Cuba. These exploits, and marriage to a well-connected Spanish woman, won Cortés an extensive Cuban estate and a series of administrative appointments.

Eager to increase his fortune, Cortés jumped at the chance in 1519 to lead an expedition to the mainland. He landed with six hundred men near the Mayan settlement of Potonchan, which he quickly overpowered. Then Cortés got lucky. The defeated Mayas presented him with twenty slave women to serve as servants and concubines, among them Malinali, a young woman of noble birth. Not only was she "of pleasing appearance and sharp-witted and outward-going" — the words of a Spanish soldier; she also spoke Nahuatl, the Aztecs' lan-

Malinche and Cortés

In this Aztec pictograph (c. 1540), Cortés is shown with Malinche (Mariana in Spanish), his Nahuatl-speaking interpreter, advisor, and mistress. Signifying her dual identity as an Indian and a European, Malinche wears native clothes but holds a rosary. Bibliothèque Nationale de France, Paris.

guage. Cortés took her as his mistress and interpreter, and soon she became his guide. When the Spanish leader learned from Malinali the extent of the Aztec empire, his goal became power rather than plunder. He would depose its king, Moctezuma [*mok-tah-zoo-mah*], and take over his realm.

Of Malinali's motives for helping Cortés there is no record. Like his Spanish followers, she may have been dazzled by his powerful personality. Or, more likely, she may have calculated that Cortés was her best hope for escaping slavery and reclaiming her noble status. Whatever her reasons, Malinali's loyalty to her new master was complete. As the Spanish marched on the Aztec capital of Tenochtitlán in 1519, she risked her life by warning Cortés of a surprise attack in the city of Cholula and served as his translator as he negotiated his way into the Aztec capital. "Without her," concluded Bernal Díaz del Castillo, the Spanish chronicler of the conquest, we would "have been unable to surmount many difficulties."

Awed by the military prowess of the Spanish invaders, Moctezuma received Cortés with great ceremony, only to become his captive. When the emperor's supporters tried to expel the invaders, they faced superior European military technology. The sight of the Spaniards in full metal armor, with guns that shook the heavens and inflicted devastating wounds, made a deep impression on the Aztecs, who knew how to purify gold but not how to produce iron tools or weapons. Moreover, the Aztecs had no wheeled carts or cavalry, and their warriors, fighting on foot with flint- or obsidian-tipped spears and arrows, were no match for mounted Spanish conquistadors wielding steel swords and aided by vicious attack dogs. Although heavily outnumbered and suffering great losses, Cortés and his men were able to fight their way out of the Aztec capital.

The Aztec emperor could easily have crushed the Spanish invaders if he had ruled a united empire. But many Indian peoples hated the Aztecs, and Cortés deftly exploited their anger. With the help of Malinali, now known by the honorific Nahuatl name Malinche, he formed military alliances with the subject peoples whose wealth had been appropriated by Aztec nobles and whose people had been sacrificed to the Aztec sun god. The Aztec empire collapsed, the victim not of superior military technology but of a vast internal rebellion instigated by the wily Cortés (see Comparing American Voices, "The Spanish Conquest of Mexico," pp. 26–27).

The Impact of Disease. The Spanish also had a silent ally—disease. Separated from the Eurasian land mass for thousands of years, the inhabitants of the Americas had no immunities to common European diseases. A massive smallpox epidemic lasting seventy days ravaged Tenochtitlán following the Spanish exodus, "striking everywhere in the city," according to an Aztec source, and killing Moctezuma's brother and thousands more. "They could not move, they could not stir. . . . Covered, mantled with pustules, very many people died of them." Subsequent outbreaks of smallpox, influenza, and measles killed hundreds of thousands of Indians and sapped the morale of the survivors. Exploiting this demographic weakness, Cortés quickly extended Spanish rule over the Aztec empire. His lieutenants then moved against the Mayan city-states in the Yucatán Peninsula, eventually conquering them as well.

In 1524, Francisco Pizarro led a Spanish military expedition toward Peru, home of the rich and powerful Inca empire, which stretched 2,000 miles along the Pacific coast of South America. To govern this far-flung empire, the Inca rulers had laid 24,000 miles of roads and built dozens of administrative centers, carefully constructed of finely crafted stone. A semidivine Inca king ruled the empire with the help of a hierarchical bureaucracy staffed by noblemen, many of them the king's relatives. By the time Pizarro and his small force of 168 men and 67 horses finally reached Peru in 1632, half of the Inca population had died from European diseases spread by Indian traders. Weakened militarily and fighting over succession to the throne, the Inca nobility was easy prey for Pizarro's army. In the mere space of

sixteen years, Spain had become the master of the wealthiest and most populous regions of the Western Hemisphere (Map 1.5).

The Ecological Legacy of the Conquest. The Spanish invasion changed life forever in the Americas. Disease and warfare wiped out virtually all of the Indians of Hispaniola—at least 300,000 people. In Peru, the population plummeted from 9 million in 1530 to fewer than 500,000 a century later. Mesoamerica suffered the greatest losses: In 1500, it boasted a population of 30 million; by 1650, its Native American population had fallen to just 3 million—one of the great demographic disasters in world history.

Once the conquistadors had triumphed, the Spanish monarchs quickly created an elaborate bureaucratic empire. From its headquarters in Madrid, the Council of the Indies issued laws and decrees to viceroys and other Spanish officials in America. Still, the conquistadors and their descendants remained powerful because they held *encomiendas,* royal grants that gave them legal control of the labor of the native population. They ruthlessly exploited the surviving Native Americans, forcing them to raise crops and cattle both for local consumption and for export to Europe. The Spaniards also permanently altered the natural environment by introducing grains and grasses that supplanted the native flora. Horses, once native to the Western Hemisphere but long extinct, spread quickly and widely across the Americas, and dramatically changed the way of life of many Indian peoples, especially on the Great Plains of North America.

The Spanish conquest had a significant ecological impact on Europe and Africa as well. In a process historians call the **Columbian Exchange,** the food products of the Western Hemisphere—especially maize, potatoes, manioc, sweet potatoes, and tomatoes—were transferred to the peoples of other continents, significantly increasing agricultural yields and population growth worldwide. A less welcome gift was the virulent strain of syphilis Columbus's crew members took back to Europe with them. Similarly, the livestock and crops—and weeds and human diseases—of Africa and Eurasia became part of life in the Americas. Nor was that all. The gold and silver that had formerly honored Aztec gods now gilded the Catholic churches of Europe and flowed into the countinghouses of Spain, making that nation the richest and most powerful in Europe.

By 1550, the once magnificent civilizations of Mexico and Peru lay in ruins. "Of all these wonders"—the great city of Tenochtitlán, the bountiful irrigated fields, the rich orchards, the

The Spanish Conquest of Mexico

How could a Spanish force of six hundred men take control of an empire of 20 million people? That the Spaniards had horses, guns, and steel swords certainly gave them a military advantage. Still, a concerted attack by the armies of the Aztecs and their allies would have overwhelmed the invaders as they initially approached the Mexican capital. Why did the Aztecs wait months to attack Cortés and his men?

These documents, which describe Cortés's initial entry into Tenochtitlán, come from the memoir of a participant and an oral history. Consider them first as *sources:* How trustworthy are they? In what ways might they be biased? Then think about their *content:* Where do the accounts agree? What key events do they identify?

FRIAR BERNARDINO DE SAHAGÚN
Aztec Elders Describe the Behavior of Moctezuma

During the 1550s, Friar Bernardino de Sahagún published The Florentine Codex: General History of New Spain. *According to Sahagún, the authors of the codex were Aztec elders who lived through the conquest. They told their stories to Sahagún in a repetitive style, according to the conventions of Aztec oral histories, and he translated them into Spanish.*

Moctezuma enjoyed no sleep, no food, no one spoke to him. Whatsoever he did, it was as if he were in torment. Ofttimes it was as if he sighed, became weak, felt weak. . . . Wherefore he said, "What will now befall us? Who indeed stands [in charge]? Alas, until now, I. In great torment is my heart; as if it were washed in chili water it indeed burns." And when he had so heard what the messengers reported, he was terrified, he was astounded. . . . Especially did it cause him to faint away when he heard how the gun, at [the Spaniards'] command, discharged: how it resounded as if it thundered when it went off. It indeed bereft one of strength; it shut off one's ears. And when it discharged, something like a round pebble came forth from within. Fire went showering forth; sparks went blazing forth. And its smoke smelled very foul; it had a fetid odor which verily wounded the head. And when [the shot] struck a mountain, it was as if it were destroyed, dissolved . . . as if someone blew it away.

All iron was their war array. In iron they clothed themselves. With iron they covered their heads. Iron were their swords. Iron were their crossbows. Iron were their shields. Iron were their lances. And those which bore them upon their backs, their deer [horses], were as tall as roof terraces.

And their bodies were everywhere covered; only their faces appeared. They were very white; they had chalky faces; they had yellow hair, though the hair of some was black. . . . And when Moctezuma so heard, he was much terrified. It was as if he fainted away. His heart saddened; his heart failed him. . . . [But] he made himself resolute; he put forth great effort; he quieted, he controlled his heart; he submitted himself entirely to whatsoever he was to see, at which he was to marvel. . . . [Moctezuma then greets Cortés, as described above.]

And when [the Spaniards] were well settled, they thereupon inquired of Moctezuma as to all the city's treasure . . . the devices, the shields. Much did they importune him; with great zeal they sought gold. . . . Thereupon were brought forth all the brilliant things; the shields, the golden discs, the devils' necklaces, the golden nose crescents, the golden leg bands, the golden arm bands, the golden forehead bands.

SOURCE: Friar Bernardino de Sahagún, *Florentine Codex: General History of New Spain,* trans. Arthur J. O. Anderson and Charles E. Dibble (Santa Fe and Salt Lake City: School of American Research and University of Utah Press, 1975), 12: 17–20, 26.

BERNAL DÍAZ DEL CASTILLO
Cortés and Moctezuma Meet

Bernal Díaz was an unlikely chronicler of great events. Born poor, he went to America as a common soldier in 1514 and served under conquistadors in Panama and Cuba. In 1519, he joined Cortés's expedition, fought in many battles, and, as a reward, received an estate in present-day Guatemala. In his old age, Díaz wrote The True History of the Conquest of New Spain, *a compelling memoir written from a soldier's perspective. In fresh and straightforward prose, he depicts the conquest as a divinely blessed event that saved the non-Aztec peoples of Mexico from a barbarous regime.*

The Great Moctezuma had sent these great Caciques in advance to receive us, and when they came before Cortés they bade us welcome in their language, and as a sign of peace, they touched their hands against the ground. . . .

When we arrived near to Mexico, . . . the Great Moctezuma got down from his litter, and those great Caciques supported him with their arms beneath a marvelously rich canopy of green coloured feathers with much gold and silver embroidery . . . which was wonderful to look at. The Great Moctezuma was richly attired according to his usage, and he was shod with sandals, the soles were of gold and the upper part adorned with precious stones. . . .

Many other Lords walked before the Great Moctezuma, sweeping the ground where he would tread and spreading cloths on it, so that he should not tread on the earth. Not one of these chieftains dared even to think of looking him in the face, but kept their eyes lowered with great reverence. . . .

When Cortés was told that the Great Moctezuma was approaching, and he saw him coming, he dismounted from his horse, and when he was near Moctezuma, they simultaneously paid great reverence to one another. Moctezuma bade him welcome and our Cortes replied through Doña Marina [Malinche, Cortés's Indian mistress and interpreter] wishing him very good health. . . . And then Cortes brought out a necklace which he had ready at hand, made of glass stones, . . . which have within them many patterns of diverse colours, these were strung on a cord of gold and with musk so that it should have a sweet scent, and he placed it round the neck of the Great Moctezuma. . . .

Then Cortés through the mouth of Doña Marina told him that now his heart rejoiced having seen such a great Prince, and that he took it as a great honour that he had come in person to meet him. . . .

Thus space was made for us to enter the streets of Mexico, without being so much crowded. But who could now count the multitude of men and women and boys who were in the streets and in canoes on the canals, who had come out to see us. It was indeed wonderful. . . . Coming to think it over it seems to be a great mercy that our Lord Jesus Christ was pleased to give us grace and courage to dare to enter into such a city; and for the many times He has saved me from danger of death . . . I give Him sincere thanks. . . .

They took us to lodge in some large houses, where there were apartments for all of us, for they had belonged to the father of the Great Moctezuma, who was named Axayaca. . . .

Cortés thanked Moctezuma through our interpreters, and Moctezuma replied, "Malinche, you and your brethren are in your own house, rest awhile," and then he went to his palaces, which were not far away, and we divided our lodgings by companies, and placed the artillery pointing in a convenient direction, and the order which we had to keep was clearly explained to us, and that we were to be much on the alert, both the cavalry and all of us soldiers. A sumptuous dinner was provided for us according to their use and custom, and we ate it at once. So this was our lucky and daring entry into the great city of Tenochtitlan Mexico on the 8th day of November the year of our Saviour Jesus Christ, 1519.

SOURCE: Bernal Díaz del Castillo, *The True History of the Conquest of New Spain,* trans. A. P. Maudslay (1632; London: Routledge, 1928), 272–275.

ANALYZING THE EVIDENCE

➤ Díaz's account is a memoir written long after the event. What effect does that have on the structure and tone of his writing? How is the Aztec description, as translated by Sahagún, different in those respects?

➤ Why does Moctezuma pay "great reverence" to Cortés? Why does Cortés return the honor? What is the strategy of each leader?

➤ How does Díaz explain the Spaniards' easy entry into Tenochtitlán? What explanation do the Aztec elders suggest? Why do you think they are different?

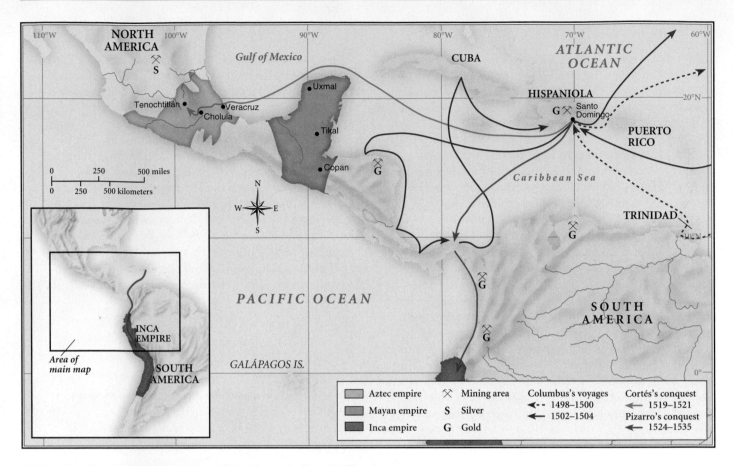

MAP 1.5   The Spanish Conquest of the Great Indian Civilizations

The Spanish first invaded and settled the islands of the Caribbean. Rumors of a golden civilization led to Cortés's invasion of the Aztec empire in 1519. By 1535, other Spanish conquistadors had conquered the Mayan temple cities and the Inca empire in Peru, completing one of the great conquests in world history.

overflowing markets — "all is overthrown and lost, nothing left standing," recalled Bernal Díaz, who had been a young soldier in Cortés's army. Moreover, the surviving Indian peoples lost a vital part of their cultural identity when Spanish priests suppressed their worship of traditional gods and converted them to Catholicism. As early as 1531, an Indian convert reported a vision of a dark-skinned Virgin Mary, later known as the Virgin of Guadalupe, a Christian version of the "corn mother" who traditionally protected the maize crop.

A new society took shape on the lands emptied by disease and exploitation. Between 1500 and 1650, no fewer than 350,000 Spaniards migrated to Mesoamerica and western South America. More than 75 percent of the Spanish settlers were men, and many of them took Indian women as wives or mistresses. Consequently, a substantial mixed-race population, called **mestizos**, quickly appeared, along with an elaborate race-based **caste system**. Around 1800, near the end of the colonial era,

Spanish America stretched from the tip of South America to the northern border of present-day California. It contained about 17 million people: a dominant caste of 3.2 million Spaniards; 5.5 million people of mixed Indian and European race and cultural heritage; 1.0 million African slaves; and 7.5 million Indians, who lived mostly on marginal lands. For the original Native American peoples, the consequences of the European invasion that began in 1492 were tragic and irreversible.

➤ Compare and contrast the main characteristics of traditional European society and West African society. How were they each similar to and different from Native American societies?

➤ Why and how did Portugal and Spain pursue overseas commerce and conquest?

➤ What was the impact of the Columbian Exchange on the Americas, Europe, and Africa?

The Protestant Reformation and the Rise of England

Even as Catholic fervor prompted the forced conversion of the Indians in America and the Muslims and Jews in Spain, Christianity ceased to be a unifying force in European society. During the early sixteenth century, new religious doctrines preached by Martin Luther and other reformers divided Europe between Catholic and Protestant states and plunged the continent into a century-long series of religious wars. During these conflicts, France replaced Spain as the most powerful European state, and Holland and England emerged as Protestant nations determined to colonize the Western Hemisphere.

The Protestant Movement

Over the centuries, the Catholic Church had become a large and wealthy institution. Renaissance popes and cardinals used the Church's wealth to patronize the arts, and some clerics used their power for personal gain. Pope Leo X (r. 1513–1521) received half a million ducats (about $20 million in 2006 dollars) a year from the sale of religious offices. Corruption at the top encouraged ordinary priests and monks to seek economic or sexual favors. One English reformer denounced the clergy as a "gang of scoundrels" who should be "rid of their vices or stripped of their authority," but he was ignored. Other critics of the Church, such as Jan Hus of Bohemia, were executed as heretics.

In 1517, Martin Luther, a German monk and professor at the university in Wittenberg, took up the cause of reform. His *Ninety-five Theses* condemned many Catholic practices, including **indulgences**, certificates that allegedly pardoned sinners from punishment in the afterlife. Outraged by Luther's charges, the pope dismissed him from the Church, and the Holy Roman Emperor, King Charles I of Spain (r. 1516–1556), threatened Luther with punishment. However, the princes of northern Germany, who were resisting the emperor's authority for political reasons, protected Luther from arrest, thus allowing the Protestant movement to survive.

Luther took issue with Roman Catholic doctrine in three major respects. First, he rejected the belief that Christians could secure salvation through good deeds or the purchase of indulgences; instead, Luther argued that people could be saved only by grace, which came as a free gift from God. Second, the German reformer downplayed the role of the clergy and the pope as mediators between God and the people, and proclaimed a much more democratic outlook. "Our baptism consecrates us all without exception and makes us all priests." Third, Luther said that believers must look to the Bible—not to Church officials or doctrine—as the ultimate authority in matters of faith. And so that every literate German could read the Bible, for centuries only available in Latin, he translated it into German.

Peasants as well as princes heeded Luther's attack on authority and, to his dismay, mounted social protests of their own. In 1524, many German peasants rebelled against their manorial lords. Fearing social revolution, Luther urged obedience to established political institutions and condemned the teachings of the Anabaptists (who rejected the baptism of infants) and other new groups of religious dissidents. Assured of Luther's social conservatism, most princes in northern Germany embraced his teachings and broke from Rome, thereby gaining the power to appoint bishops and control the Church's property within their domains. To restore Catholic doctrine and his political authority, the Holy Roman Emperor dispatched armies to Germany, setting off a generation of warfare. Eventually, the Peace of Augsburg (1555) divided Germany into Lutheran states in the north and Catholic principalities in the south.

John Calvin, a French theologian in Geneva, Switzerland, established the most rigorous Protestant regime. Even more than Luther, Calvin stressed human weakness and God's omnipotence. His *Institutes of the Christian Religion* (1536) depicted God as an awesome and absolute sovereign who governed the "wills of men so as to move precisely to that end directed by him." Calvin preached the doctrine of **predestination**, the idea that God chooses certain people for salvation before they are born and condemns the rest to eternal damnation. In Geneva, he set up a model Christian community, eliminating bishops and placing spiritual power in the hands of ministers chosen by the congregation. Ministers and pious laymen ruled the city, prohibiting frivolity and luxury and imposing religious discipline. "We know," wrote Calvin, "that man is of so perverse and crooked a nature, that everyone would scratch out his neighbor's eyes if there were no bridle to hold them in." Calvin's authoritarian doctrine won converts all over Europe; it became the theology of the Huguenots in France, the Reformed churches in Belgium and Holland, and the Presbyterians and Puritans in Scotland and England (Map 1.6).

In England, King Henry VIII (r. 1509–1547) initially opposed Protestantism. However, in 1534, when the pope refused to annul his marriage to the Spanish princess Catherine of Aragon, Henry broke

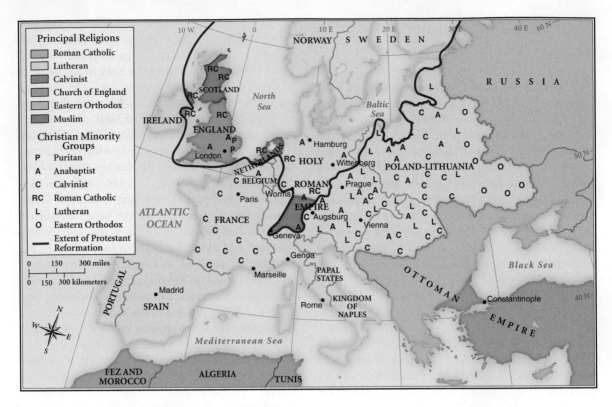

MAP 1.6   Religious Diversity in Europe, 1600

By 1600, Europe was permanently divided among rival churches. Catholicism remained dominant in the south; but Lutheran princes and monarchs ruled northern Europe, and Calvinism had strongholds in Switzerland, Holland, and Scotland. By persecuting radical religious sects, legally established churches — both Protestant and Catholic — encouraged the migration of sect members to America.

with Rome and placed himself at the head of a national church, the Church of England, which promptly granted the king an annulment. Henry made few changes in Catholic doctrine, organization, and ritual, but he did allow the spread of Protestant beliefs and teachings. Faced with popular pressure for greater reform, Henry's daughter and successor, Queen Elizabeth I (r. 1558–1603), approved a Protestant confession of faith that incorporated both the Lutheran doctrine of salvation by grace and the Calvinist belief in predestination. To satisfy traditionalists, Elizabeth retained the Catholic ritual of Holy Communion — now conducted in English rather than Latin — as well as the hierarchy of bishops and archbishops.

Elizabeth's compromises angered radical Protestants, who condemned the power of bishops as "anti-Christian and devilish and contrary to the Scriptures." These reformers were inspired by the presbyterian system pioneered in Calvin's Geneva and developed by John Knox for the Church of Scotland. In Scotland, congregations elected lay elders (presbyters) who helped ministers and participated in the synods (councils) that decided Church doctrine. By 1600, at least five hundred ministers in the Church of England wanted to eliminate bishops and install a presbyterian form of church government.

Other radical English Protestants called themselves "unspotted lambs of the Lord" or Puritans. These extraordinarily devout Calvinists wanted to "purify" the Church of England of all Catholic teachings and magical or idolatrous practices. Puritans refused to burn incense or to appeal to dead saints for their intervention; a carefully argued sermon was the focus of their service. Puritans placed special emphasis on the "conversion experience," the felt infusion of God's grace, and the "calling," the duty to serve God in one's ordinary life and work. To ensure that all men and women had direct access to God's commands in the Bible, they encouraged literacy and Bible-study. Finally, most Puritans wanted authority over spiritual and financial matters to rest primarily with local congregations. Eventually, thousands of English Puritans would migrate to

A Dutch Merchant Family

This painting of Pierre de Moucheron and his family by Dutch artist Cornelius de Zeeuw captures both the prosperity and the severe Calvinist ethos of sixteenth-century Holland. It also depicts the character of the traditional patriarchal family, in which status reflected a rigid hierarchy of gender and age. Rijksmuseum, Amsterdam.

North America and establish churches there based on these radical Protestant doctrines.

The Dutch and English Challenge Spain

Luther's challenge to Catholicism in 1517 came just two years before Cortés began his conquest of the Aztec empire, and the two events became linked. Gold and silver from Mexico and later Peru made Spain the wealthiest nation in Europe and King Philip II (r. 1556–1598) its most powerful ruler. In addition to Spanish America, Philip presided over wealthy city-states in Italy, the commercial and manufacturing provinces of the Spanish Netherlands (present-day Holland and Belgium), and, after 1580, Portugal and all its possessions in America, Africa, and the East Indies. "If the Romans were able to rule the world simply by ruling the Mediterranean," a Spanish priest boasted, "what of the man who rules the Atlantic and Pacific oceans, since they surround the world?"

Philip's Wars and Spain's Decline. Philip, an ardent Catholic, tried to root out Islam in North Africa and Protestantism in the Netherlands and in England. He failed in both efforts. A massive Spanish fleet defeated a Turkish armada at Lepanto in the eastern Mediterranean in 1571, freeing 15,000 Christian galley slaves, but Muslims continued to rule nearby Morocco and Algiers. To the north, the Spanish-controlled Netherlands had grown wealthy from trade with the vast Portuguese empire and from weaving wool and linen. These provinces had also become hotbeds of Calvinism. To protect their Calvinist faith and political liberties, the Dutch and Flemish revolted against Spain in 1566. In 1581, after fifteen years of war and with the help of other Protestant states, the seven northern provinces declared their independence, becoming the Dutch Republic (or Holland).

Elizabeth I of England helped the Dutch cause by dispatching six thousand troops to Holland. She also supported military expeditions to extend direct English rule over Gaelic-speaking Catholic regions of Ireland. Calling the Irish "wild savages," English troops brutally massacred thousands, prefiguring the treatment of Indians in America. In 1588, to meet Elizabeth's challenge, Philip sent the Spanish Armada—130 ships and thirty thousand men—against England. Philip intended to restore Catholicism to England and Ireland and then wipe out Calvinism in Holland. But he failed utterly when English ships and a fierce storm destroyed the Spanish fleet.

Shrugging off this defeat, Philip continued to spend his American gold on religious wars. This ill-advised policy diverted resources from industrial investment in Spain and weakened its economy. Oppressed by high taxes on agriculture and fearful

Elizabeth I (r. 1558–1603)
Dressed in richly decorated clothes that symbolize her power, Queen Elizabeth I relishes the destruction of the Spanish Armada (pictured in the background) and proclaims her nation's imperial ambitions. The queen's hand rests on a globe, asserting England's claims in the Western Hemisphere. Woburn Abbey Collection, by permission of the Marquess of Tavistock and the Trustees of the Bedford Estates.

of military service, more than 200,000 residents of Castile, the richest region of Spain, migrated to America. By the time of Philip's death in 1598, Spain was in serious decline.

As mighty Spain faltered, tiny Holland prospered—the economic miracle of the seventeenth century. Amsterdam emerged as the financial capital of northern Europe, and the Dutch Republic replaced Portugal as the dominant trader in Indonesia and West Africa. Dutch merchants also looked across the Atlantic: They created the West India Company, which invested in sugar plantations in Brazil and established the fur-trading colony of New Netherland along the Hudson River in North America.

Elizabeth's Mercantile Policies. England also emerged as a European power in the sixteenth century, its economy stimulated by an increase in population, from 3 million in 1500 to 5 million in 1630. Equally important, its royal government supported the expansion of commerce and manufacturing. English merchants had long supplied European weavers with high-quality wool; by around 1500, they had created their own textile industry. That industry relied on **outwork**: Merchants bought wool from the owners of great estates and then hired landless peasants to spin and weave the wool into cloth. The government helped textile entrepreneurs by setting low rates for wages, and it helped merchants by awarding monopoly privileges in foreign markets. Queen Elizabeth granted monopolies to the Levant Company (Turkey) in 1581, the Guinea Company (Africa) in 1588, and the East India Company (India) in 1600.

This system of state-assisted manufacturing and trade became known as **mercantilism**. By encouraging domestic manufacturing, Elizabeth hoped to reduce imports and increase exports, giving England a favorable balance of trade. The queen and her advisors wanted gold and silver to flow into the country in payment for English goods, stimulating further economic expansion and enriching the merchant community. Increased trade also meant greater revenues from import duties, which swelled the royal treasury and enhanced the power of the national government. By 1600, Elizabeth's mercantile policies had laid the foundations for overseas colonization. Now the English, as well as the Dutch, had the merchant fleets and wealth needed to challenge Spain's domination of the Western Hemisphere, and strong social and economic reasons for doing so.

The Social Causes of English Colonization

England sent more than merchant fleets and manufactures to America. The rapid growth of the English population also provided a large body of settlers, many fleeing economic hardship. The massive expenditure of American gold and silver by Philip II had doubled the money supply of Europe and sparked a major economic upheaval known today as the **Price Revolution** (Figure 1.2).

The landed nobility in England was the first casualty of the Price Revolution. Aristocrats customarily rented out their estates on long leases for fixed rents, which gave them a secure income and plenty

Figure 1.2   Inflation and Living Standards in Europe, 1400–1700

As American gold and silver poured into Europe after 1520 and was minted into money, people used it to bid up the price of grain. Grain remained in short supply because Europe's population almost doubled between 1500 and 1700, from 68 million to 120 million. The increased supply of money in combination with the increased demand for goods led to the Price Revolution.

As the graph shows, from 1500 through 1630, grain prices rose more quickly than wages. Thus real wages — what wages actually purchase — fell from a high point in about 1430 to a low point in about 1650. As real wages rose after 1650, people lived better.

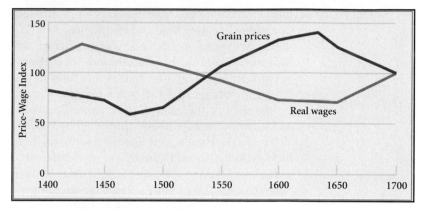

The base period for the graph is 1700: That is, the price and wage levels in 1700 have the index value of 100. In 1630, the index for grain was about 140, which means that grain cost about 40 percent more relative to wages than it would cost in 1700.

of leisure. As one English nobleman put it, "We eat and drink and rise up to play and this is to live like a gentleman." Then inflation struck. In less than two generations, the price of goods more than tripled while the nobility's income from rents barely increased. As the income of the aristocracy fell, that of the **gentry** and the yeomen rose. The gentry, who were nonnoble landholders with substantial estates, kept pace with inflation by renting land on short leases at higher rates. Yeomen, described by a European traveler as "middle people of a condition between gentlemen and peasants," owned small farms that they worked with family help. As wheat prices tripled, yeomen used the profits to build larger houses and provide their children with land.

As always, economics influenced politics. As nobles lost wealth, the influence of their branch of Parliament, the House of Lords, weakened. At the same time, members of the rising gentry entered the House of Commons, the political voice of the propertied classes. Supported by the yeomen, the gentry demanded new rights and powers for the Commons, among them control of taxation. Thus the Price Revolution encouraged the rise of representative institutions in which rich commoners and small property owners had a voice. This development had profound consequences for English — and American — political history.

The Price Revolution likewise transformed the lives of peasants, who made up three-fourths of the English population (Figure 1.3). The economic stimulus of Spanish gold spurred the expansion of the textile industry. To increase the supply of wool, profit-minded landlords and wool merchants persuaded Parliament to pass **enclosure acts,** laws that allowed owners to fence in the open fields that surrounded many peasant villages and put sheep to graze on them. Those peasant families who were

dispossessed of their lands lived on the brink of poverty, spinning and weaving wool or working as wage laborers on farms. Wealthy men had "taken farms into their hands," an observer noted in 1600, "whereby the peasantry of England is decayed and become servants to gentlemen."

In 1600, Europe experienced the first of a series of remarkably long and cold winters, a phenomenon that lasted a century and was known as the Little Ice Age. The resulting crop failures brought soaring grain prices and social discontent. "Thieves and rogues do swarm the highways," warned one

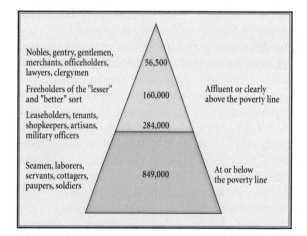

Figure 1.3   The Structure of English Society, 1688

This famous chart, the work of Gregory King (1648–1712), an early statistician, shows the results of centuries of aristocratic rule. A small privileged elite perches atop the thin pyramid, and a mass of poor working people forms its base. Most English families (some 849,000 according to King) lived at or below the poverty line and, according to King, were "Decreasing the Wealth of the Kingdom." In fact, the labor of the poor produced much of the wealth owned by the 500,500 families in the higher reaches of society.

justice of the peace, "and bastards be multiplied in parishes." Seeking food and security, tens of thousands of young men and women signed an **indenture**, a contract in which the individual agreed to work without wages for four or five years in exchange for passage to America and room and board for the term of the contract. Dispossessed peasants and weavers, their livelihood threatened by a recession in the cloth trade, were likewise ready to try their luck across the ocean. Thousands of yeomen families were also on the move, looking for affordable land on which to settle their children. This large-scale migration of English yeomen families and impoverished laborers would lead to a new collision with Indian peoples, this time in North America.

> ➤ How did Protestant religious doctrine differ from that of Roman Catholicism?

> ➤ Why did Spain lose its position as the dominant European power?

> ➤ What factors prompted the large-scale migration of English men and women to America?

SUMMARY

In this chapter we have seen that the first human inhabitants of the Western Hemisphere were hunter-gatherers from Asia. Their descendants would form many cultures and speak many languages. In Mesoamerica, the Mayan and Aztec peoples developed populous agricultural societies that operated within highly sophisticated religious and political systems; so, too, did the Incas along the western coast of South America. The Hopewell, Pueblo, and Mississippian peoples of North America also created complex societies and elaborate cultures; but in 1500, most Indians to the north of the Rio Grande lived in small self-governing communities of foragers, hunters, and farmers.

We have also traced the maritime expansion of Europe. Trade initially brought Europeans to the Americas. The Spanish crown, eager to share in Portugal's mercantile success, financed expeditions to uncover new trade routes to Asia. When Christopher Columbus revealed a "new world" to Europeans in 1492, Spanish adventurers undertook to conquer it. By 1535, conquistadors had destroyed the wealthy civilizations of Mesoamerica and Peru and introduced diseases that would kill millions of Native Americans. And through the exchange of crops, animals, and plants, they fundamentally altered the ecology of much of the world.

Population growth, religious warfare, and American gold and silver transformed European society in the sixteenth century. As the costs of religious warfare sapped Spain's strength, the rise of strong and purposeful governments in Holland, France, and England, along with a class of increasingly powerful merchants, enhanced the economies of those countries and whetted their appetite for overseas expansion.

Connections: Society

In the essay opening Part One (p. 3), we noted that

> Europeans, with their steel weapons and their diseases, shredded the fabric of most Native American cultures.

In this chapter, you've read the first part of that story—the Spanish invasion of Mesoamerica and South America. In Chapter 2, we compare the interaction of Native Americans with various European peoples: the Spanish in New Mexico and Florida; the French in Louisiana; and the Dutch and English in the Northeast. The chapter concludes with an analysis of Native Americans in New England as of 1700. Later chapters explain how and why Native Americans continued to shape the history of the eastern seaboard, even as their numbers and strength underwent a sharp decline. Part One concludes with the Great War for Empire (1754–1763). That war was known in the British colonies as the French and Indian War, and rightly so: It was fought by Native Americans to defend their lands from Anglo-American settlers.

The coming of those settlers to the Chesapeake region and New England between 1600 and 1675, and their initial wars with the Native peoples, will be a major theme of Chapter 2.

CHAPTER REVIEW QUESTIONS

> ➤ How do you explain the different ways in which the Indian peoples of Mesoamerica and North America developed?

> ➤ What made Native American peoples vulnerable to conquest by European adventurers?

> ➤ What led to the transatlantic trade in African slaves?

> ➤ What was mercantilism? How did this doctrine shape the policies of European monarchs to promote domestic manufacturing and foreign trade?

> ➤ How did Europeans become leaders in world trade and extend their influence across the Atlantic?

TIMELINE

13,000–3000 B.C.	Asian migrants reach North America
3000 B.C.	Farming begins in Mesoamerica
A.D. 100–400	Flourishing of Hopewell culture
300	Rise of Mayan civilization
500	Zenith of Teotihuacán civilization
600	Pueblo cultures emerge
632–1100	Arab people adopt Islam and spread its influence
800–1350	Development of Mississippian culture
1096–1291	Crusades link Europe with Arab learning
1300–1450	Italian Renaissance
1325	Aztecs establish capital at Tenochtitlán
1440s	Portugal enters trade in African slaves
1492	Christopher Columbus makes first voyage to America
1513	Juan Ponce de León explores Florida
1517	Martin Luther sparks Protestant Reformation
1519–1521	Hernán Cortés conquers Aztec empire
1520–1650	Price Revolution
1532–1535	Francisco Pizarro vanquishes Incas
1534	Henry VIII establishes Church of England
1536	John Calvin publishes *Institutes of the Christian Religion*
1550–1630	English crown endorses mercantilism
	Parliament passes enclosure acts
1556–1598	Reign of Philip II, King of Spain
1558–1603	Reign of Elizabeth I, Queen of England
1560s	Puritan movement begins in England
1588	English and storms defeat Spanish Armada

FOR FURTHER EXPLORATION

Kenneth Pomeranz, *The Great Divergence: Europe, China, and the Making of the Modern World Economy* (2000), examines the settlement of America from the perspective of world history. Brian M. Fagan, *The Great Journey: The People of Ancient America* (1987), and Alvin M. Josephy Jr., ed., *America in 1492: The World of the Indian Peoples Before the Arrival of Columbus* (1991), offer a panorama of early Indian societies, and are more reliable than Charles C. Mann, 1491: *New Revelations of the Americas Before Columbus* (2005). For the European background of colonization, begin with George Huppert, *After the Black Death* (2nd ed., 1998), a highly readable study of Western Europe's recovery from the devastating epidemic of the mid-fourteenth century. William D. Phillips, with Carla Rahn Phillips, discusses European expansion in *The Worlds of Christopher Columbus* (1992), an engaging biography that describes the enormous consequences of Columbus's voyages. Two interesting Public Broadcasting Service (PBS) videos examine the ancient civilizations of Mesoamerica: *Odyssey: Maya Lords of the Jungle* (1 hour) and *Odyssey: The Incas* (1 hour). For additional information, log on to "1492: An Ongoing Voyage" (**www.loc.gov/exhibits/1492/intro.html**), which surveys the native cultures of the Western Hemisphere and offers full-color images of artifacts and art. Material on an early Indian civilization in the Southwest is available at "Sipapu: The Anasazi Emergence into the Cyber World" (**sipapu.gsu.edu/**).

Peter Laslett, *The World We Have Lost* (3rd ed., 1984), paints a vivid portrait of society in seventeenth-century England; important recent studies include Andrew McRae, *God Speed the Plough* (2002), and Ethan Shagan, *Popular Politics and the English Reformation* (2003). "Martin Luther" (**www.luther.de/e/index. html**) offers biographies of the leading figures of the Protestant Reformation and striking images of the era. Giles Milton, *Nathaniel's Nutmeg: Or, the True and Incredible Adventures of the Spice Trader Who Changed the Course of History* (1999), tells the rousing tale of international seagoing competition among European powers for control of the spice trade and, subsequently, the New World. Also see the BBC's interactive Web site on the history of navigation (**www.bbc.co.uk/history/discovery/exploration/navigation_animation.shtml**), which made that competition possible.

TEST YOUR KNOWLEDGE

To assess your command of the material in this chapter, see the Online Study Guide at **bedfordstmartins.com/henretta**.

For Web sites, images, and documents related to topics and places in this chapter, visit **bedfordstmartins.com/makehistory**.

T B

2

The Invasion and Settlement of North America

1550–1700

ESTABLISHING COLONIES IN NORTH AMERICA was not for the faint of heart. First came a long voyage over stormy, dangerous waters, a trip that took many lives. Of three hundred migrants to New France in 1663, for example, seventy died en route. Those who survived, although weakened by spoiled food and shipboard diseases, immediately had to build shelter and plant crops. Many also faced hostile Indian peoples. "We neither fear them or trust them," declared Puritan settler Francis Higginson; instead, he went on, they relied on "our musketeers." Still, despite great risks and uncertain rewards, English, French, and Spanish migrants by the tens of thousands crossed the Atlantic during the seventeenth century. They were either driven by poverty and religious persecution at home or drawn by the promise of land, gold, or — according to one pious migrant — promoting "the Christian religion to such People as yet live in Darkness."

For Native Americans, the European invasion was a catastrophe. Whether they came as settlers, missionaries, or fur traders, the white-skinned people brought new diseases and religions that threatened the Indians' lives, lands, and cultures. "Our fathers had plenty of deer and skins, . . . and our coves were full of fish and fowl," Narragansett chief Miantonomi reminded the Montauk people in 1642, "but these English having gotten our land . . . their cows and horses eat the grass, and their

◄ **A European View of Virginia**

Many Europeans received their first impressions of America from the engravings of Theodore de Bry (1528–1598), who published an illustrated edition of Thomas Hariot's *A briefe and true report of the new found land of Virginia* in 1590. De Bry based his famous engravings on the paintings of John White, who had accompanied the English expedition to Roanoke. Whereas White pictured the Indians in realistic and casual poses, de Bry rendered them as sculpturelike figures with muscular bodies and European faces. William L. Clements Library, University of Michigan.

hogs spoil our clam banks, and we shall all be starved." Miantonomi called for united resistance: "We [are] all Indians [and must] say brother to one another, . . . otherwise we shall all be gone shortly." The Narragansett leader's unsuccessful plea foretold the course of North American history: The European invaders would advance, and the Indian peoples would be dispossessed.

The Rival Imperial Models of Spain, France, and Holland

In Mesoamerica, the Spanish seized the Indians' lands, converted them to Catholicism, and made them dig for gold and farm large estates. In the more sparsely populated eastern regions of North America, French and Dutch merchants created fur-trading colonies, and the native peoples retained their lands and political autonomy (Table 2.1). Whatever the Europeans' mission, all across the continent Indian peoples diminished in numbers and soon rebelled.

New Spain: Colonization and Conversion

In their ceaseless quest for gold, Spanish explorers penetrated deeply into the southern and western areas of what would become the United States. In the 1540s, Francisco Vásquez de Coronado searched in vain for the fabled seven golden cities of Cíbola; what he discovered instead were the southern reaches of the Grand Canyon, the Pueblo peoples of the Southwest, and the grasslands of present-day Kansas. Simultaneously, Hernán de Soto and a force of six hundred cut a bloody swath across the Southeast, doing battle with the Apalachees (in what is northern Florida today) and the Coosas (in northern Alabama) but finding no gold (Map 2.1).

By the 1560s, Spanish officials gave up the search for Indian gold and focused on the defense of their empire. Roving English "sea dogs" were plundering Spanish treasure ships and Caribbean seaports, and French Protestants were settling in Florida despite Spain's claim to the land there. Following King Philip II's order to cast out the trespassing Frenchmen "by the best means," Spanish troops massacred three hundred members of the "evil Lutheran sect" near the mouth of the St. John River. To safeguard the route of the treasure fleet, in 1565 Spain established a fort at St. Augustine, making it the first permanent European settlement in the future United States. Raids by the Calusas and Timuacuas wiped out a dozen other Spanish military outposts in Florida, and Algonquins destroyed Jesuit religious missions along the east coast, one as far north as the Chesapeake Bay.

TABLE 2.1 **European Colonies in North America before 1660**

Colony	Date	First Settlement	Type	Religion	Chief Export/ Economic Activity
New Spain	1520	Mexico City	Royal	Catholic	Gold, silver, grain, hides
New France	1608	Quebec	Royal	Catholic	Furs
New Netherland	1613	Fort Orange (Albany)	Corporate	Dutch Reformed	Furs
New Sweden	1628	Fort Christina	Corporate	Lutheran	Furs, farming
English Colonies					
Virginia	1607	Jamestown	Corporate (merchant)	Anglican	Tobacco
Plymouth	1620	Plymouth	Corporate (religious)	Separatist Puritan	Mixed farming, livestock
Massachusetts Bay	1629	Boston	Corporate	Puritan	Mixed farming, livestock
Maryland	1634	St. Mary's	Proprietary (religious)	Catholic	Tobacco, grain
Connecticut	1635	Hartford	Corporate (religious)	Puritan	Mixed farming, livestock
Rhode Island	1636	Providence	Corporate (religious)	Separatist Puritan	Mixed farming, livestock

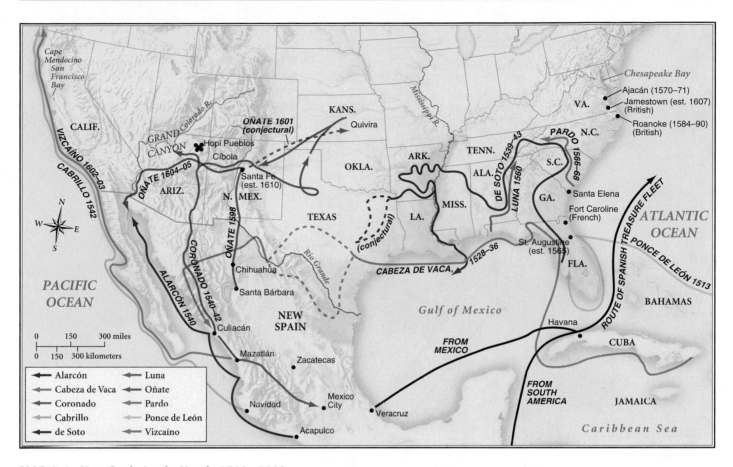

MAP 2.1 New Spain Looks North, 1513–1610

The search for gold drew Spanish explorers first to Florida and then deep into the present-day United States. When the wide-ranging expeditions of Hernán de Soto and Francisco Vásquez de Coronado failed to find gold or flourishing Indian civilizations, authorities in New Spain limited settlements in the northern territories to St. Augustine in Florida (to protect the treasure fleet) and Santa Fe in the upper Rio Grande Valley.

Franciscan Missions. These military setbacks prompted the Spanish crown to adopt a new policy toward the Indian peoples, one of Christianization. The Comprehensive Orders for New Discoveries, issued in 1573, placed responsibility for pacification of new lands primarily in the hands of missionaries, not conquistadors. Over the next century, dozens of Franciscan friars set up missions among the Apalachees in Florida and the Pueblo peoples in the lands they named Nuevo México. Although the friars often learned Indian languages, they systematically attacked the natives' culture. And their methods were anything but peaceful. Protected by Spanish soldiers, missionaries whipped Indians who continued to practice **polygamy,** smashed their religious idols, and severely punished those who worshiped traditional gods. On one occasion, forty-seven "sorcerers" in Nuevo México were whipped and sold into slavery.

For the Franciscans, religious conversion, cultural assimilation, and forced labor went hand in hand. They encouraged the Indians to talk, cook, dress, and walk like Spaniards. They ignored Spanish laws that protected the native peoples, and allowed privileged Spanish landowners (*encomenderos*) in New Mexico to extract goods and forced labor from the native population. The missions also depended on Indian workers to grow crops and carry them to market, often on their backs.

Popé and the Pueblo Revolt of 1680. Native Americans initially tolerated the Franciscans because they feared military reprisals and hoped to learn the friars' spiritual secrets. But when Christian prayers failed to protect their communities from European diseases, droughts, and raids by nomadic Apaches and Pawnees, many Pueblo people returned to their ancestral religions. Thus, the people of Hawikuh refused to become "wet-heads" (as the Indians called baptized Christians) "because with the water of baptism they would have to die."

In 1598, the tense relations between Indians and Spaniards in New Mexico exploded into open

La V.ᵐᵉ Mᵃ. Maria de Iesus de Agreda. Predicando á los Chichimecos del Nuebo-mexico. Antꞵ de Coꞵro fᵗ.

Conversion in New Mexico

Franciscan friars, helped by nuns of various religious orders, introduced Catholicism to the Indian peoples north of the Rio Grande. This 1631 engraving shows one nun, María de Jesús de Agreda, preaching to nomadic peoples (the Chichimecos) in New Mexico. The friars would also flaunt their rich vestments, gold crosses, and silver chalices to persuade Native Americans to worship the Christian god. Nettie Lee Benson Latin American Collection, University of Texas at Austin.

warfare. An expedition of five hundred Spanish soldiers and settlers led by Juan de Oñate seized corn and clothing from the Pueblo peoples and murdered or raped those who resisted. When Indians of the Acoma pueblo retaliated by killing eleven soldiers, the Spanish troops destroyed the pueblo and murdered five hundred men and three hundred women and children. Faced with bitterly hostile native peoples, most of the settlers left New Mexico. In 1610, the Spanish returned, founded the town of Santa Fe, and reestablished the system of missions and forced labor. Over the next two generations, European diseases, forced tribute, and raids by nomadic plains Indians reduced the population of Pueblo peoples from 60,000 to just 17,000.

As a prolonged drought threatened the survivors with extinction, the Indian shaman Popé called for the Pueblo peoples to expel the Spaniards and "return to the laws of their ancients." He "who

shall kill a Spaniard will get an Indian women for a wife," Popé promised, and be "free from the labor . . . performed for the religious and the Spaniards." In 1680, in a carefully coordinated rebellion, Popé and his followers from two dozen pueblos killed more than four hundred Spaniards and forced the remaining fifteen hundred colonists (and five hundred Pueblo and Apache slaves) to flee 300 miles to El Paso. Repudiating Christianity, the Pueblo peoples desecrated churches and tortured and killed twenty-one missionaries. They burned "the seeds which the Spaniards sowed," planted "only maize and beans, which were the crops of their ancestors," and rebuilt the sacred kivas, the round stone structures in which they had long worshiped. Like those who would later lead Native American resistance, Popé marched forward while looking backward, hoping to restore the traditional religion and way of life.

It was not to be. A decade later, Spain reasserted control over most of the Pueblo peoples. The oppressed Natives rebelled again in 1696, only to be subdued. Exhausted by a generation of warfare, they agreed to a compromise that allowed them to practice their own religion and ended forced labor. In return, they accepted a dependent position in New Mexico and helped the Spanish defend their settlements and farms there against attacks by nomadic Apaches and Comanches.

Spain had maintained its northern empire, but it failed to convert and assimilate the Indian peoples. Some Natives had married Spaniards and their offspring formed a bicultural mestizo population. However, most Pueblo Indians continued to practice the old ways. As a Franciscan friar admitted, "They are still drawn more by their idolatry and infidelity than by the Christian doctrine."

The situation in Florida was equally disappointing to Spanish officials. Raids by the English in Carolina in the early 1700s destroyed most of the Spanish missions there, and killed or enslaved most Catholic converts. These setbacks persuaded Spanish officials to delay the settlement of the distant northern province of California until the 1760s. For the time being, Santa Fe and St. Augustine stood as vulnerable defensive northern outposts of Spain's American empire.

New France: Furs, Souls, and Warfare

Far to the northeast, the French were likewise trying to convert the native peoples to Catholicism. In the 1530s, Jacques Cartier had claimed the lands bordered by the Gulf of St. Lawrence for France. By the 1580s, hundreds of ships from many nations were arriving annually off the coast of Newfoundland to catch fish, whales, and seals. However, the first permanent settlement came only in 1608, when Samuel de Champlain founded Quebec. The small French fur-trading post was struggling in 1627, when Cardinal Richelieu, chief minister of King Louis XIII (r. 1610–1643), transferred control of the region to the Company of One Hundred Associates. The company agreed to send out four thousand settlers but fell well short of that target. Then, in 1662, King Louis XIV (r. 1643–1714) turned New France into a royal colony and began subsidizing the migration of indentured servants there. Those who signed indentures would serve a term of thirty-six months, be paid a yearly salary, and eventually receive a leasehold farm — terms far more generous than those for indentured servants in the English colonies.

Still, despite brutal famines in France, few Frenchmen and -women migrated to New France.

This reluctance puzzled a contemporary observer, who asked: "Is it possible that peasants are so afraid of losing sight of the village steeple, that they would rather languish in their misery and poverty?" In fact, various state policies and laws discouraged migration. In his fervor to expand France's boundaries, Louis XIV drafted tens of thousands of potential migrants into military service. The Catholic monarch also barred Huguenots (French Calvinist Protestants) from migrating to New France. Moreover, the French legal system gave peasants strong rights to their village lands, which they were loathe to give up. Finally, most French people thought of New France (also called Canada, from the Huron-Iroquois word for village) as a cold and forbidding place, "a country at the end of the world." Of the 27,000 men and women who migrated to New France before 1760, almost two-thirds eventually returned to France. In 1698, the European population of the colony was only 15,200; by contrast, there were 100,000 residents in English settlements at that time.

Lacking settlers, New France became a vast enterprise for acquiring furs, which were in great demand in Europe to make felt hats and fur garments. To secure plush beaver pelts from the Huron Indians, who controlled trade north of the Great Lakes, Champlain provided them with blankets and iron utensils. He also gave them guns to fight the expansionist-minded Five Nations of the Iroquois of New York (see Voices from Abroad, "Samuel de Champlain: Going to War with the Hurons," p. 42). Searching for new sources of furs to the west, explorer Jacques Marquette reached the Mississippi River in present-day Wisconsin in 1673 and traveled as far south as Arkansas. Then, in 1681, Robert de La Salle traveled down the majestic river to the Gulf of Mexico, trading as he went. As a French priest noted with disgust, La Salle and his associates hoped "to buy all the Furs and Skins of the remotest Savages, who, as they thought, did not know their Value; and so enrich themselves in one single voyage." To honor Louis XIV, La Salle named the region Louisiana; it would include the thriving port of New Orleans on the Gulf of Mexico, which was established in 1718.

The Rise of the Iroquois. Despite their small numbers, the French had a disastrous impact. By unwittingly introducing European diseases, they triggered epidemics that killed from 25 percent to 90 percent of many Indian peoples. Moreover, by bartering guns for furs, the French sparked a series of deadly wars. The Five Iroquois Nations were the prime aggressors. From their strategic geographical location in central New York, the Iroquois could obtain guns and goods from Dutch merchants at

Samuel de Champlain

Going to War with the Hurons

Although Samuel de Champlain is best known as the founder of Quebec, he was primarily a soldier and an adventurer. After fighting in the French religious wars, Champlain joined the Company of New France and set out to create a French empire in North America. In 1603, he traveled down the St. Lawrence River as far as Quebec. He then lived for several years in the company's failed settlement in Maine before returning to Quebec in 1608. To ensure French access to the western fur trade, Champlain joined the Hurons in a raid against the Iroquois in 1609, which he later described in a book of his American adventures.

Pursuing our route, I met some two or three hundred savages, who were encamped in huts near a little island called St. Eloi. . . . We made a reconnaissance, and found that they were tribes of savages called Ochasteguins [Hurons] and Algonquins, on their way to Quebec to assist us in exploring the territory of the Iroquois, with whom they are in deadly hostility. . . . [We joined with them and] went to the mouth of the River of the Iroquois [the Richelieu River, where it joins the St. Lawrence River], where we stayed two days, refreshing ourselves with good venison, birds, and fish, which the savages gave us.

In all their encampments, they have their Pilotois, or Ostemoy, a class of persons who play the part of soothsayers, in whom these people have faith. One of these builds a cabin, surrounds it with small pieces of wood and covers it with his robe: after it is built, he places himself inside, so as not to be seen at all, when he seizes and shakes one of the posts of his cabin, muttering some words between his teeth, by which he says he invokes the devil, who appears to him in the form of a stone, and tells them whether they will meet their enemies and kill many of them. . . . They frequently told me that the shaking of the cabin, which I saw, proceeded from the devil, who made it move, and not the man inside, although I could see the contrary. . . . They told me also that I should see fire come out from the top, which I did not see at all.

Now, as we began to approach within two or three days' journey of the abode of our enemies, we advanced only at night. . . . By day, they withdraw into the interior of the woods, where they rest, without straying off, neither making any noise, even for the sake of cooking, so as not to be noticed in case their enemies should by accident pass by. They make no fire, except in smoking, which amounts to almost nothing. They eat baked Indian meal, which they soak in water, when it becomes a kind of porridge. . . .

In order to ascertain what was to be the result of their undertaking, they often asked me if I had had a dream, and seen their enemies, to which I replied in the negative. . . . [Then one night] while sleeping, I dreamed that I saw our enemies, the Iroquois, drowning near a mountain, within sight. When I expressed a wish to help them, our allies, the savages, told me we must let them all die. . . . This, upon being related [to our allies], gave them so much confidence that they did not doubt any longer that good was to happen to them. . . .

[After our victory over the Iroquois,] they took one of the prisoners, to whom they made a harangue, enumerating the cruelties which he and his men had already practiced toward them without any mercy, and that, in like manner, he ought to make up his mind to receive as much. They commanded him to sing, if he had courage, which he did; but it was a very sad song.

Meanwhile, our men kindled a fire; and, when it was well burning, they brand, and burned this poor creature gradually, so as to make him suffer greater torment. Sometimes they stopped, and threw water on his back. Then they tore out his nails, and applied fire to the extremities of his fingers and private member. Afterwards, they flayed the top of his head, and had a kind of gum poured all hot upon it.

SOURCE: Samuel de Champlain, *Voyages of Samuel de Champlain, 1604–1618*, ed. W. L. Grant (New York: Charles Scribner's Sons, 1907), 79–86.

ANALYZING THE EVIDENCE

- ➤ How do you account for the differences between the Hurons' and Champlain's perceptions of the soothsayer's hut? What does it suggest about their respective views of the world?

- ➤ Having read this passage, what would you say was the role of dreams in Huron culture?

- ➤ At the beginning of this passage, Champlain refers to the Indians as savages. Would the torture he describes help to explain that characterization? How do you think a modern anthropologist would explain the Indians' custom of torturing war captives?

Albany and quickly attack other Indian peoples by water. Iroquois warriors moved to the east along the Mohawk River as far as New England, and south along the Delaware and Susquehanna Rivers as far as the Carolinas. They traveled north via Lake Champlain and the Richelieu River to Quebec. And they journeyed west via the Great Lakes and the Allegheny-Ohio river system to exploit the rich fur-bearing lands of the upper Mississippi River Valley.

The rise of the Iroquois was breathtakingly rapid, just as their subsequent decline was tragically sobering. In 1600, the Iroquois numbered about 30,000 and lived in large towns of 500 to 2,000 inhabitants. Over the next two decades, they organized themselves in a confederation of Five Nations: Senecas, Cayugas, Onondagas, Oneidas, and Mohawks. Partly in response to a virulent smallpox epidemic in 1633, which cut their number by a third, the Iroquois waged a devastating series of wars against the Hurons (1649), Neutrals (1651), Eries (1657), and Susquehannocks — all Iroquoian-speaking peoples. They razed the villages and killed most of the men, cooking and eating their flesh to gain access to their spiritual powers. They took thousands of women and children as captives, adopting them into Iroquois lineages and clans in formal ceremonies. These rituals transferred to the captives the names of the Iroquois dead, along with their social roles and duties. The Hurons simply ceased to exist as a distinct people and culture. Those who survived the Iroquois raids migrated westward and joined other remnant peoples to form a new tribe, the Wyandots.

These triumphs gave the Iroquois control of the fur trade with the French in Quebec and the Dutch in New Amsterdam. Equally important, they changed the character of Iroquois society. By 1657, adopted prisoners made up as much as half of the population of many Iroquois communities. Cultural diversity within the confederacy increased further when the Five Nations made peace with the French and allowed Jesuit missionaries to live among them. As the Jesuits won converts, Iroquois villages split into bitter religious factions. Many Christian Indians moved to French-sponsored mission towns, and tradition-minded Iroquois took control of the Five Nations.

During the 1670s, those traditionalists repudiated their ties with the French and formed an alliance, called the Covenant Chain, with English officials in New York. Seeking furs to sell to merchants in Albany, they embarked on a new series of western "beaver wars." Iroquois warriors pushed a dozen Algonquian-speaking peoples allied with the French — Ottawas, Foxes, Sauks, Kickapoos, Miamis, and Illinois — out of their traditional lands north of the Ohio River and into a multitribal region west of Lake Michigan (in present-day Wisconsin). The Iroquois' victory came at a high cost: more than 2,200 warriors dead. To end the bloodshed, in 1701 the Iroquois made treaties with the French as well as the English, a diplomatic maneuver that brought peace for two generations.

The Jesuit Missions. The French priests who sought converts, first among the Hurons and then among their Iroquois conquerors, were members of the Society of Jesus (or Jesuits), a Catholic religious order founded to combat the Protestant Reformation. Between 1625 and 1763, hundreds of French Jesuits lived among the Indian peoples of the Great Lakes region. These priests — to a greater extent than the Spanish Franciscan monks — came to understand and respect the Indians' values. One Jesuit noted the Huron belief that "our souls have desires which are inborn and concealed, yet are made known by means of dreams." For their part, many Indian peoples initially welcomed the French "Black Robes" as powerful spiritual beings with magical secrets, among them the ability to forge iron. But when prayers to the Christian god did not protect them from disease or attack, they grew skeptical. A Peoria chief charged that a priest's "fables are good only in his own country; we have our own [religious beliefs], which do not make us die as his do." In the face of epidemics and droughts, some Indian peoples vented their anger on French missionaries and fur traders. "If you cannot make rain, they speak of nothing less than making away with you," lamented one Jesuit.

Whatever the limits of their spiritual powers, the French Jesuits did not exploit the labor of the Indian peoples. Moreover, they tried to keep brandy, which wreaked havoc among the natives, from becoming a bargaining chip in the French fur trade. Finally, the Jesuits won converts by adapting Christian beliefs to the Indians' needs. In the 1690s, for example, they introduced the cult of the Virgin Mary to the young women of the Illinois people. Its emphasis on chastity reinforced the Algonquian belief that unmarried women were "masters of their own body."

Still, despite the Jesuits' efforts, the French fur-trading system brought cultural devastation to the Indian peoples of the Great Lakes region. Epidemics killed tens of thousands, and Iroquois warriors murdered thousands more. Nor did the Iroquois escape unscathed. In 1666 and again in the 1690s, French armies invaded their land, burned villages and cornfields, and killed many warriors. "Everywhere there was peril and everywhere mourning," recalled an oral Iroquois legend.

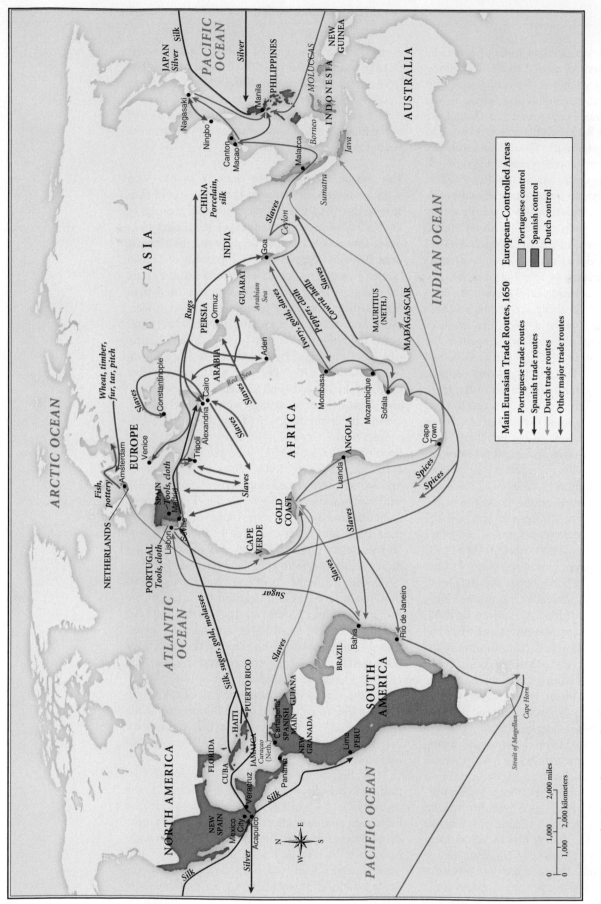

MAP 2.2 The Eurasian Trade System and European Spheres of Influence, 1650

Between 1550 and 1650, Spanish, Portuguese, and Dutch merchants took control of the maritime trade routes between Europe and India, Indonesia, and China. They also created the South Atlantic system (see Chapter 3), which carried slaves, sugar, and manufactured goods between Europe, Africa, and the valuable plantation settlements in Brazil and the Caribbean Islands. (To trace long-term changes in trade and empires, see Map 1.3 on p. 18 and Map 5.1 on p. 139.)

New Netherland: Commerce and Conquest

By 1600, Holland had emerged as the financial and commercial hub of northern Europe. Exploiting the country's strategic location—at the mouth of the great Rhine River and near the Baltic sea—enterprising Dutch merchants controlled the trade in western and northern Europe. In addition, Dutch entrepreneurs dominated the European banking, insurance, and textile industries; and its merchants owned more tons of shipping and employed more sailors than did the combined fleets of England, France, and Spain. Indeed, the Dutch managed much of the world's commerce. During their struggle for independence from Spain (and its Portuguese dependency), the Dutch seized Portuguese forts in Africa, Brazil, and Indonesia, which gave them control of the Atlantic trade in slaves and the Indian Ocean commerce in East Indies spices and Chinese silks (Map 2.2).

In 1609, Dutch merchants, long active in the Baltic and Russian fur trade, dispatched an Eng-lishman, Henry Hudson, to locate a new source of supply in North America. After Hudson explored the river that bears his name, the merchants set up a fur-trading post at Fort Orange (Albany). In 1621, the Dutch government chartered the West India Company and gave it a monopoly over the American fur trade and the West African slave trade. Three years later, the company founded the town of New Amsterdam on Manhattan Island, and made it the capital of New Netherland.

The new colony did not thrive. The population of the Dutch Republic was small—just 1.5 million people, compared to 5 million in Britain and 20 million in France—and relatively prosperous. Consequently, few Dutch settlers moved to the fur-trading posts, which made them vulnerable to rival European nations. To encourage migration, the West India Company granted huge estates along the Hudson River to wealthy Dutchmen with the proviso that each proprietor settle fifty tenants on the land within four years or lose his grant. By 1646, only one proprietor, Kiliaen Van

New Amsterdam, c. 1640

As the wooden palisade suggests, New Amsterdam was a fort-like trading post at the edge of a vast land populated by alien Indian peoples. It was also a pale miniature version of Amsterdam, a city with many canals. The first settlers built houses in the Dutch style, with their gable ends facing the street (notice the two middle houses), and excavated a canal across lower Manhattan Island (New York City's Canal Street today). Library of Congress.

Rensselaer, had succeeded. In 1664, New Netherland had just 5,000 residents, and fewer than half of them were Dutch.

Although the colony failed to attract settlers, it flourished as a fur-trading enterprise. In 1633, Dutch traders at Fort Orange exported thirty thousand beaver and otter pelts. Their success reflected their practice of offering high-quality goods at relatively low prices and the policy of peace they adopted toward the powerful Iroquois. Dutch settlers near New Amsterdam were more aggressive. They seized prime farming land from their Algonquian-speaking neighbors and took over the Indians' trading network, in which corn and wampum from Long Island were exchanged for furs from Maine. The Algonquins responded with force. In the 1640s, in a bloody two-year war, more than two hundred Dutch residents and one thousand Indians died, many of them women, children, and elderly men. During the fighting, the Dutch formed an alliance with the Mohawks, a longtime foe of the Algonquins. Thereafter, the Mohawks controlled Indian access to Albany, and the Mohawk dialect became the language of business in the small fur-trading outpost.

After the crippling Indian war of the 1640s, the West India Company largely ignored New Netherland, focusing instead on the profitable trade in African slaves to sugar plantations in Brazil. In New Amsterdam, Dutch officials ruled shortsightedly. Governor Peter Stuyvesant rejected the demands of English Puritan settlers on Long Island for a representative system of government and alienated the colony's increasingly diverse population of Dutch, English, and Swedish migrants. It is not surprising, then, that the residents of New Amsterdam offered little resistance to English invaders in 1664.

Initially, the Duke of York, the overlord of the new English colony of New York, ruled with a mild hand: He allowed the Dutch residents to retain their property, legal system, and religious institutions. That changed after a Dutch assault in 1673, which momentarily recaptured the colony. In retaliation, the duke's governor, Edmund Andros, shut down the Dutch courts, imposed English law, and demanded an oath of allegiance. Dutch residents avoided the English courts, settling disputes by arbitration, and resisted cultural assimilation by speaking Dutch, marrying among themselves, and worshipping at the Dutch Reformed Church. Once dominant over the Algonquins, the Dutch had themselves become a subject people. As a group of Anglicans noted in 1699, New York "seemed rather like a conquered Foreign Province held by the terror of a Garrison, than an English colony."

> ➤ How were Spanish, French, and Dutch colonial strategies similar? How did they differ? In what ways were the similarities and differences reflected in the nations' settlements in the New World?

> ➤ Why did the Five Nations of the Iroquois unite? What were the goals of the confederation? How successful were the Iroquois in achieving those goals?

The English Arrive: The Chesapeake Experience

Unlike their European rivals, the English founded populous colonies in North America. Settlers in the Chesapeake Bay region used force to take possession of Indian lands. They created a society based on tobacco that brought wealth to certain prominent families who ruthlessly pursued their dreams of wealth by exploiting the labor of English indentured servants and African slaves.

Settling the Tobacco Colonies

The first English settlements in North America were organized by minor nobles in the 1580s and by merchants and religious dissidents after 1600. Although the English monarch and ministry approved these ventures, they neither directed nor controlled them. This meant that English colonies, unlike the state-supervised Spanish and French settlements, enjoyed considerable autonomy.

In part because they lacked the direct support of the English government, the ventures of the 1580s were abject failures. Sir Humphrey Gilbert's settlement in Newfoundland collapsed for lack of financing, and Sir Ferdinando Gorges's colony along the coast of Maine floundered because of the harsh climate. Sir Walter Raleigh's three expeditions to North Carolina likewise ended in disaster when the colony on Roanoke Island vanished without a trace. (Roanoke is still known today as the "lost colony.")

Following these failures, merchants took charge of English expansion and, like the French and Dutch, initially focused on trade with the native population. In 1606, King James I (r. 1603–1625) granted to the Virginia Company of London all the

Carolina Indians Fishing, 1585

The artist John White was one of the English settlers in Sir Walter Releigh's ill-fated colony on Roanoke Island, and his watercolors provide a rich visual record of Native American life. Here the Indians who resided near present-day Albermarle Sound in North Carolina are harvesting a protein-rich diet of fish from its shallow waters. Trustees of the British Museum.

lands stretching from present-day North Carolina to southern New York. To honor the memory of Elizabeth I, the never-married "Virgin Queen," the company's directors named the region Virginia and promised to "propagate the [true] Christian religion" among the "infidels and Savages" (Map 2.3).

The Jamestown Settlement. Commerce was the Virginia Company's primary goal. The first expedition, in 1607, was limited to male traders — no women, farmers, or ministers — who were the employees or "servants" of the company. The company directed them to procure their own food and to ship gold, exotic crops, and Indian merchandise to England. Some of the traders were young gentlemen with personal ties to the company's shareholders: a bunch of "unruly Sparks, packed off by their

Friends to escape worse Destinies at home." Others were cynical men bent on turning a quick profit: All they wanted, one of them said, was to "dig gold, refine gold, load gold."

But there was no gold, and the traders were ill equipped to deal with the new environment. Arriving in Virginia after an exhausting four-month voyage, they settled in May on a swampy, unhealthy peninsula, which they named Jamestown in honor of the king. Because they lacked access to fresh water and refused to plant crops, they quickly died off; only 38 of the 120 traders were alive nine months later. Death rates remained high. By 1611, the Virginia Company had dispatched 1,200 settlers to Jamestown, but fewer than half had survived. "Our men were destroyed with cruell diseases, as Swellings, Fluxes, Burning Fevers, and by warres,"

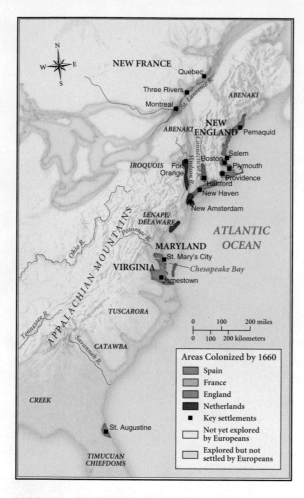

MAP 2.3 Eastern North America, 1650

By 1650, four European nations had permanent settlements along the eastern coast of North America, but only England had substantial numbers of settlers, some 25,000 in New England and another 15,000 in the Chesapeake region. The Europeans also had a presence in the interior, as colonial authorities established diplomatic relations with neighboring Indian peoples and as French and Dutch fur traders carried European goods—and diseases—to distant tribes.

reported one of the settlement's leaders, "but for the most part they died of meere famine."

At first the local Indians were suspicious of the settlers, perhaps because they remembered the violent end to a mission established in the 1570s by Spanish Jesuit missionaries. However, Powhatan, chief of the Algonquian-speaking peoples of the region, treated the English traders as potential allies and a source of valuable goods. A "grave majestical man," according to explorer John Smith, Powhatan allowed his followers—some fourteen thousand people in all—to exchange their corn for English cloth and iron hatchets. To integrate the newcomers peacefully into his chiefdom, Powhatan arranged a

marriage between his daughter Pocahontas and John Rolfe, an English colonist. His tactic failed in part because Rolfe had imported tobacco seed from the West Indies and cultivated the crop, which fetched a high price in England. Eager to become rich by planting tobacco, thousands of English settlers embarked for Virginia. Now Powhatan accused the English of coming "not to trade but to invade my people and possess my country."

To foster the flow of migrants, the Virginia Company instituted new policies. In 1617, it allowed individual settlers to own land, granting one hundred acres to every freeman and allowing those who imported servants to claim an additional fifty acres for every one. The company also issued a "greate Charter" that created a system of representative government. The House of Burgesses, which first convened in 1619, could make laws and levy taxes, although the governor and the company council in England could veto its acts. By 1622, land ownership, self-government, and a judicial system based on "the lawes of the realme of England" had attracted some 4,500 new recruits. Virginia was on the verge of becoming a settler colony.

Opechancanough and the Indian Revolt of 1622.
The influx of land-hungry English migrants sparked all-out revolt by the Indian peoples. The uprising was led by a mysterious chief named Opechancanough, who was Powhatan's brother and successor. Some evidence suggests that Opechancanough was taken to Spain as a young man and converted to Catholicism, and that when he returned to Virginia as part of a Jesuit mission, he killed the missionaries. It is certain that thirty years later, in 1609, Opechancanough personally confronted the English invaders, capturing Captain John Smith but sparing his life. Subsequently, the Indian chief "stood aloof" from the English settlers and "would not be drawn to any Treaty." In particular, he resisted proposals to take Indian children from their parents so that they might be "brought upp in Christianytie." When Opechancanough became the main chief in 1621, he assumed a new name, Massatamohtnock, and a new mission: "Before the end of two moons," he told the chief of the Potomacks, "there should not be an Englishman in all their Countries."

Massatamohtnock almost succeeded. In 1622, he coordinated a surprise attack by twelve Indian tribes that killed 347 English settlers, nearly a third of the white population. The English fought back by seizing the Indians' fields and food and, after a decade of intermittent fighting, finally secured the safety of the colony. The victorious settlers sold captured warriors into slavery, "destroy[ing] them who sought to

John Smith and Chief Opechancanough

The powerful Indian chief Opechancanough towers over English explorer John Smith. This engraving depicts the confrontation between the two men in 1609 over English access to Indian supplies of food; the scenes in the background depict the major uprising led by Opechancanough — now called Massatamohtnock — in 1622. Library of Congress.

C. Smith taketh the King of Pamavnkee prisoner 1608

destroy us," and took control of "their cultivated places . . . possessing the fruits of others' labour."

Shocked by the Indian uprising, James I revoked the charter of the Virginia Company and, in 1624, made Virginia a royal colony. Now the king and his ministers appointed the governor and a small advisory council. James retained the House of Burgesses but stipulated that his Privy Council, a committee of leading ministers, must ratify all legislation. The king also decreed the legal establishment of the Church of England, which meant that all property owners had to pay taxes to support its clergy. These institutions — a royal governor, an elected assembly, and an established Anglican church — became the model for royal colonies throughout English America.

Lord Baltimore Settles Catholics in Maryland.
A second tobacco-growing colony developed in neighboring Maryland, but with a different set of insti-

tutions. King Charles I (r. 1625–1649), James's successor, was secretly sympathetic toward Catholicism and had a number of Catholic friends. In 1632, he granted the lands bordering the vast Chesapeake Bay to Cecilius Calvert, a Catholic aristocrat who carried the title Lord Baltimore. As the proprietor of Maryland (named for Queen Henrietta Maria, the king's wife), Baltimore could sell, lease, or give the land away as he pleased. He also had the authority to appoint public officials and to found churches and appoint ministers.

Lord Baltimore wanted Maryland to become a refuge for Catholics, who were subject to persecution in England. In 1634, twenty gentlemen, mostly Catholics, and two hundred artisans and laborers, mostly Protestants, established St. Mary's City, which overlooked the mouth of the Potomac River. To minimize religious confrontations, the proprietor instructed the governor (his brother, Leonard Calvert) to allow "no scandall nor offence to be given to any of the Protestants" and to "cause

All Acts of Romane Catholicque Religion to be done as privately as may be."

Maryland's population grew quickly because the Calverts imported scores of artisans and offered ample grants of land to wealthy migrants. But political conflict constantly threatened the colony's stability. When Governor Calvert violated the charter by governing without the "Advice, Assent, and Approbation" of the freemen, they elected a representative assembly. The assembly insisted on the right to initiate legislation, which Lord Baltimore grudgingly granted. Anti-Catholic agitation by Protestant settlers also endangered Maryland's religious mission. To protect his coreligionists, who remained a minority, Lord Baltimore persuaded the assembly to enact the Toleration Act (1649), which granted all Christians the right to follow their own religious beliefs and hold church services.

Tobacco and Disease.

In Maryland, as in Virginia, tobacco quickly became the basis of the economy. Indians had long used tobacco as a medicine and a stimulant, and the English came to crave the nicotine it contained. By the 1620s, they were smoking, chewing, and snorting tobacco with abandon. James I initially condemned tobacco as a "vile Weed" whose "black stinking fumes" were "baleful to the nose, harmful to the brain, and dangerous to the lungs." But the king's attitude changed as taxes on imported tobacco bolstered the royal treasury.

European demand for tobacco set off a forty-year economic boom in the Chesapeake region. "All our riches for the present do consist in tobacco," a planter remarked in 1630. Exports rose from about 3 million pounds in 1640 to 10 million pounds in 1660. Newly arrived planters moved up the river valleys, establishing large plantations a good distance from one another but easily reached by water.

Despite the economic boom, life in the Chesapeake colonies was harsh. The scarcity of towns deprived settlers of community (Map 2.4). Families were equally scarce because there were few women settlers, and marriages often ended with the death of a young spouse. Pregnant women were especially vulnerable to malaria, which was spread by the mosquitoes that flourished in the warm climate (Table 2.2). Many mothers died after bearing a first or second child, so that orphaned children (along with unmarried young men) formed a large segment of the society. Sixty percent of the children born in Middlesex County, Virginia, before 1680, lost one or both of their parents by the time they were thirteen. Although 15,000 English migrants arrived in Virginia between 1622 and 1640, the population during that period rose only from 2,000 to 8,000.

The Tobacco Economy

Most farmers in Virginia — poor and rich — raised tobacco. Wealthy planters used indentured servants and slaves, like those pictured here, to grow and process the crop. The workers cured the tobacco stalks by hanging them for several months in a well-ventilated shed; then they stripped the leaves and packed them tightly into large plantation-made barrels, or hogsheads, for shipment to Europe. Library of Congress.

Masters, Servants, and Slaves

Despite the difficulty of life in the Chesapeake region, the prospect of owning land lured migrants there. By 1700, more than 100,000 Englishmen and -women had come to Virginia and Maryland, most as indentured servants. English shipping registers reveal their backgrounds. Three-quarters of the 5,000 indentured servants who embarked from the port of Bristol were young men, many of them displaced by the enclosure of their village lands (see Chapter 1). They came to Bristol searching for work; and, once there, they were persuaded by merchants and sea captains to sign labor contracts. The indentures bound the men — and a much smaller number of women — to work for a master in the Chesapeake

MAP 2.4 River Plantations in Virginia, c. 1640

The first migrants settled in widely dispersed plantations — and different disease environments — along the James River. The growth of the tobacco economy promoted this pattern: Wealthy planter-merchants would trade with English ship captains from their riverfront plantations. Consequently, few substantial towns or trading centers developed in the Chesapeake region.

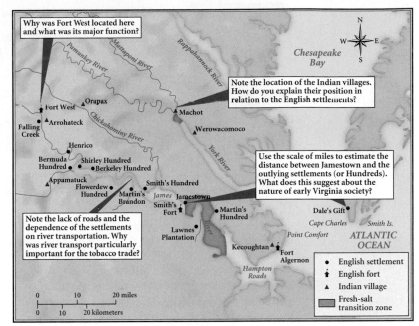

Why was Fort West located here and what was its major function?

Note the location of the Indian villages. How do you explain their position in relation to the English settlements?

Use the scale of miles to estimate the distance between Jamestown and the outlying settlements (or Hundreds). What does this suggest about the nature of early Virginia society?

Note the lack of roads and the dependence of the settlements on river transportation. Why was river transport particularly important for the tobacco trade?

- • English settlement
- ⊧ English fort
- ▲ Indian village
- Fresh-salt transition zone

colonies for four or five years, after which they would be free to marry and work for themselves.

Indentured Life. For merchants, servants were valuable cargo: Their contracts fetched high prices from Chesapeake planters. For the plantation owners, they were an incredible bargain. During the tobacco boom, a male servant could produce five times his purchase price in a single year. To ensure maximum production, most masters ruled their servants strictly, beating them for bad behavior and withholding permission to marry. If servants ran away or became pregnant, masters went to court to increase the term of their service. Female servants were especially vulnerable to abuse. As a Virginia law of 1692 stated, "dissolute masters have gotten their maids with child; and yet claim the benefit of their service." Planters got rid of uncooperative servants by selling their contracts to new masters. As one Englishman remarked in disgust, in Virginia "servants were sold up and down like horses."

Most indentured servants did not escape from poverty. Half the men died before completing the term of their contract, and another quarter

TABLE 2.2	Environment, Disease, and Death in Virginia, 1618–1624		
Zones of James River Estuary	Colony Population in Zone (percent)	Annual Mortality in Zone (percent)	Proportion of All Deaths in Colony (percent)
Freshwater	28.5	16.7	6.9
Freshwater/saltwater	49.3	27.1	64.6
Saltwater	22.2	23.3	18.4

Early Virginia was a deadly place. Historians estimate that at least 28 percent of the population died each year, most of typhoid fever and dysentery (the "bloody flux"). Only a constant stream of migrants allowed the population of the colony to grow at all. Most settlers lived along the James River estuary, but their location along the river determined their chance of survival. The most dangerous environment was the zone with a mix of freshwater and salt water. The influx of salt water during the dry summer months trapped human and animal waste from upriver and contaminated the water and its fish, oysters, and crabs. The year-round saltwater zone was the next most deadly, both because of fecal contamination and because of salt poisoning from drinking brackish well water.

SOURCE: Adapted from Carville V. Earle, "Environment, Disease, and Mortality in Early Virginia," in *The Chesapeake in the Seventeenth Century,* ed. Thad W. Tate and David L. Ammerman (New York: W. W. Norton, 1979), table 3.

TABLE 2.3	Indentured Servants in the Chesapeake Labor Force, 1640–1700				
Decade Ending	White Population	White Population in Labor Force (percent)	White Labor Force	White Servant Population	White Servants in Labor Force (percent)
1640	8,000	75	6,000	1,790	30
1660	24,000	66	15,800	4,300	27
1680	55,600	58	32,300	5,500	17
1700	85,200	46	38,900	3,800	10

The population of the Chesapeake increased more than tenfold between 1640 and 1700, and its character changed significantly. As more women migrated to Virginia and bore children, the percentage of the population in the labor force fell dramatically, from 75 percent to 46 percent. So did the region's reliance on indentured servants: In 1640, white servants made up about 30 percent of the labor force; by 1700, they accounted for just 10 percent.

SOURCE: Adapted from Christopher Tomlins, "Reconsidering Indentured Servitude" (unpublished paper, 2001), table 3.

although freed remained poor. Only a quarter acquired the property and respectability they had been looking for (Table 2.3). Female servants generally fared better. Men in the Chesapeake had grown "very sensible of the Misfortune of Wanting Wives," so many female servants married well-established men. By migrating to the Chesapeake, these few — and very fortunate — men and women escaped a life of landless poverty in England.

African Laborers. Fate was equally mixed for the first African workers in the Chesapeake colonies. In 1619, John Rolfe noted that "a Dutch man of warre . . . sold us twenty Negars." But for a generation, the number of Africans in the region remained small. About 400 Africans lived in the Chesapeake colonies in 1649, just 2 percent of the population; by 1670, only 5 percent of the population was black. Although many Africans served their English masters for life, they were not legally enslaved. English **common law** did not acknowledge **chattel slavery,** the ownership of a human being as property. Moreover, some of these African workers came from the Kingdom of Kongo, where Portuguese missionaries had converted the king to Christianity, and they had some knowledge of European ways. By calculation, hard work, or conversion to Christianity, many of these first African laborers found a way to escape their bondage. Some ambitious African freemen in the Chesapeake region even purchased slaves, bought the labor contracts of white servants, or married Englishwomen.

This mobility for Africans came to an end in the 1660s with the collapse of the tobacco boom. Tobacco had once sold for 24 pence a pound; now it fetched just a tenth of that. The "low price of Tobacco requires it should bee made as cheap as possible," declared Virginia planter Nicholas Spencer, and "blacks can make it cheaper than whites." As the English-born elite imported fewer English servants

and more African slaves, Chesapeake legislatures grew more conscious of race and enacted laws undercutting the status of blacks. By 1671, the Virginia House of Burgesses had forbidden Africans to own guns or join the militia. It also had barred them — "tho baptized and enjoying their own Freedom" — from buying the labor contracts of white servants and from winning their freedom by converting to Christianity. Being black was now a mark of inferior legal status, and slavery was becoming a permanent and hereditary condition. As an English clergyman observed, "These two words, Negro and Slave had by custom grown Homogeneous and convertible."

The Seeds of Social Revolt

As the tobacco boom went bust in the 1660s, long-standing social conflicts flared into political turmoil. The drop in tobacco prices stemmed primarily from an imbalance in the market: A rapid increase in production was outstripping limited demand. But it also reflected Parliament's decision in 1651 to pass the Act of Trade and Navigation and to add new provisions in 1660 and 1663. The Navigation Acts allowed only English or colonial-owned ships to enter American ports, thereby excluding Dutch merchants, who paid the highest prices for tobacco, sold the best goods, and provided the cheapest shipping services. They also required the colonists to ship tobacco and other "enumerated articles" (including sugar) only to England, where monarchs continually raised import duties, stifling the profitability of the market. By the 1670s, tobacco planters were getting just a penny a pound for their crop.

Despite low prices, tobacco exports from the region doubled between 1670 and 1700. The reason was simple: As the Chesapeake region's population increased, so did the number of planters. Lacking another cash crop, they planted tobacco, which provided yeomen families with just enough to scrape by. Worse off were newly freed indentured servants, who could not earn enough to buy tools and seed or to pay the fees required to claim their fifty-acre head rights. Many ex-servants had to sell their labor again, either by signing new indentures or becoming wage workers or tenant farmers.

Increasingly, an elite of planter-merchants dominated the Chesapeake colonies. Like the English gentry, they prospered from the ownership of large estates that they leased to the growing population of former servants. Many well-to-do planters also became commercial middlemen and moneylenders. They set up retail stores and charged commissions for shipping the tobacco produced by yeomen farmers to merchants in England. This elite accumulated nearly half the land in Virginia by securing grants from royal governors. In Maryland, well-connected Catholic planters were equally powerful; by 1720, one of those planters, Charles Carroll, owned 47,000 acres of land, which he farmed with the labor of scores of tenants, indentured servants, and slaves.

Bacon's Rebellion

As these aggressive planter-entrepreneurs confronted a multitude of young, landless laborers, political and social conflict rocked Virginia during the 1670s. This violent struggle left a contradictory legacy: a decrease in class conflict among whites and greater reliance on black slaves, which greatly intensified hostility between Europeans and Africans.

The Corrupt Regime of Governor William Berkeley. William Berkeley first served as governor of Virginia between 1642 and 1652, and played a key role in suppressing a second major Indian uprising in 1644. Appointed governor again in 1660, Berkeley bestowed large land grants on members of his council. The councilors promptly exempted their lands from taxation and appointed their friends as local justices of the peace and county judges. To suppress dissent in the House of Burgesses, Berkeley bought off legislators with land grants and lucrative appointments as sheriffs, tax collectors, and estate appraisers. Unrest increased when the corrupt Burgesses changed the voting system to exclude landless freemen, who by now constituted half the adult white men in the colony. Property-holding yeomen retained the vote; but frustrated by falling tobacco prices, rising taxes, and political corruption, they were no longer willing to support Berkeley and the landed gentry.

An Indian conflict lit the flame of social rebellion. When the English intruded into Virginia in 1607 there were 30,000 Native Americans living there; by 1675, the number of Indians had dwindled to a mere 3,500. By comparison, the number of Europeans had multiplied to 38,000 and the number of Africans to about 2,500. Most Indians lived on treaty-guaranteed territory along the frontier, land that was now coveted by impoverished white **freeholders** and aspiring tenants. They demanded that the natives be expelled or exterminated. Opposition came from wealthy planters along the seacoast, who wanted a ready supply of tenant farmers and wage laborers, and from Berkeley and the planter-merchants, who traded with the Native Americans for furs.

Fighting broke out late in 1675, when a band of Virginia militiamen murdered thirty Indians. Defying Berkeley's orders, a larger force of one thousand militiamen then surrounded a fortified Susquehannock village and killed five chiefs who had come out to negotiate. The Susquehannocks, recent migrants from present-day northern Pennsylvania, retaliated by raiding outlying plantations and killing three hundred whites. To avoid an Indian war, Berkeley proposed a defensive military strategy—a series of frontier forts to deter Indian intrusions. The settlers dismissed this scheme as useless. They also questioned Berkeley's motivation, insisting his plan was simply a plot by planters and merchants to impose high taxes and take "all our tobacco into their own hands."

Nathaniel Bacon, Rebel Leader. Nathaniel Bacon emerged as the leader of the rebels. A young English migrant, Bacon had settled on a frontier estate and his English connections had secured him an appointment to the governor's council. Because of his considerable wealth and commanding personal presence, Bacon also commanded the respect of his neighbors. When Berkeley refused to grant Bacon a military commission to lead an attack on nearby Indians, the headstrong planter marched a force of frontiersmen against the Indians anyway and slaughtered some of the peaceful Doeg people. Condemning the frontiersmen as "rebels and mutineers," Berkeley expelled Bacon from the council and had him arrested. But Bacon's men quickly won his release and forced the governor to hold legislative elections. The newly elected House of Burgesses enacted far-reaching political reforms that curbed the powers of the governor and the council and restored voting rights to landless freemen.

These much-needed reforms came too late. Bacon remained bitter toward Berkeley, and the poor farmers and indentured servants that he now led resented years of exploitation by wealthy planters and arrogant justices of the peace. As one yeoman rebel complained, "A poor man who has only his labour to maintain himself and his family pays as much [in taxes] as a man who has 20,000 acres." Backed by four hundred armed men, Bacon issued a "Manifesto and Declaration of the People" that

Nathaniel Bacon

Condemned as a rebel and a traitor in his own time, Nathaniel Bacon emerged in the late nineteenth century as an American hero, a harbinger of the Patriots of 1776. This stained-glass window probably was designed by famed jeweler and glassmaker Tiffany & Co. of New York. It was installed in a Virginia church, endowing Bacon with semisacred status. The Association for the Preservation of Virginia Antiquities.

demanded the death or removal of all Indians and an end to the rule of wealthy "parasites." "All the power and sway is got into the hands of the rich," Bacon proclaimed, as his army burned Jamestown to the ground and plundered the plantations of Berkeley's allies. When Bacon died suddenly of dysentery in October 1676, the governor took his revenge, dispersing the rebel army, seizing the estates of well-to-do rebels, and hanging twenty-three men.

Bacon's Rebellion was a pivotal event in the history of Virginia and the Chesapeake. Thereafter, landed planters retained their dominance by curbing corruption and appointing ambitious yeomen to public office. They appeased the lower social orders by cutting taxes and supporting white expansion onto Indian lands. Most important, the uprising confirmed the planters' growing reliance on African

slaves. To forestall another rebellion by poor whites, Chesapeake planters turned away from indentured servants; in 1705, the Burgesses explicitly legalized chattel slavery, and planters began importing thousands of African laborers. Those fateful decisions committed subsequent generations of Americans to a social system based on racial exploitation.

➤ What were the special characteristics of the population of Virginia in the seventeenth century and what accounted for them?

➤ What were the various systems of forced labor that took hold in the Chesapeake colonies?

➤ Compare the Indian uprising in Virginia in 1622 with Bacon's Rebellion in 1675. What were the consequences of each for Virginia's economic and social development?

Puritan New England

As the scramble for wealth escalated in the Chesapeake, 500 miles to the north Puritan settlers created colonies with a strong moral dimension. Between 1620 and 1640, thousands of Puritans fled to America in what was both a worldly quest for land and a spiritual quest to preserve the "pure" Christian faith. By distributing land broadly, the Puritans set out to build a society of independent farm families. And by establishing a "holy commonwealth" in America, they hoped to reform the Church of England. Although sharp conflicts over religious dogma ultimately led to the founding of a number of different colonies, all New England Puritans defined their mission in spiritual terms. Indeed, their "errand into the wilderness" gave a moral dimension to American history that survives today.

The Puritan Migration

New England differed from other European colonies in America. Unruly male adventurers founded New Spain and Jamestown, and male traders dominated life in New France and New Netherland. By contrast, the leaders of the Plymouth and Massachusetts Bay colonies were pious Protestants, and the settlers there included women and children as well as men (Map 2.5).

The Pilgrims. The Pilgrims who settled in Plymouth were religious separatists, Puritans who had left the Church of England. When King James I threatened to drive Puritans "out of the land, or else do worse," the Pilgrims left England and lived among Dutch Calvinists in Holland. Subsequently,

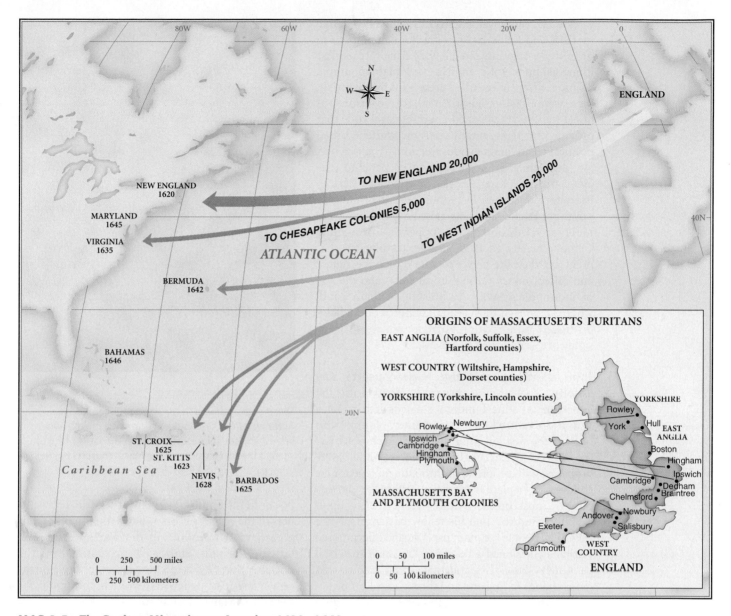

MAP 2.5   The Puritan Migration to America, 1620–1640

Forty-five thousand Puritans left England between 1620 and 1640, but they created religious societies only in the New England colonies of Plymouth, Massachusetts Bay, and Connecticut. Within New England, migrants from the three major centers of English Puritanism — Yorkshire, East Anglia, and the West Country — commonly settled among those from their own region. They named American communities after their English towns of origin and practiced their traditional regional customs. Thus settlers from Rowley in Yorkshire transplanted their system of open-field agriculture to Rowley in Massachusetts Bay.

thirty-five of these exiles resolved to migrate to America to maintain their English identity. Led by William Bradford and joined by sixty-seven migrants from England, they sailed to America in 1620 aboard the *Mayflower* and settled near Cape Cod in southeastern Massachusetts. Lacking a royal charter, they created their own covenant of government, the Mayflower Compact, to "combine ourselves together into a civil body politick." The Compact, the first American constitution, used the

Puritans' self-governing religious congregation as the model for its political structure.

The first winter in Plymouth tested the Pilgrims. Like the early settlers in Virginia, the Pilgrims faced hunger and disease: Of the 102 migrants who arrived in November, only half survived until spring. But then Plymouth became a healthy and thriving community. The cold climate inhibited the spread of mosquito-borne diseases, and the Pilgrims' religious discipline established a strong work ethic. Moreover, because a smallpox epidemic in 1618 had killed most of the local Wampanoag people, the migrants faced few external threats. The Pilgrims built solid houses and planted ample crops, and their number grew rapidly. By 1640, there were 3,000 settlers in Plymouth. To ensure political stability, they issued a written legal code that provided for representative self-government, broad political rights, and religious freedom of conscience.

Meanwhile, England plunged deeper into religious turmoil. King Charles I repudiated certain Protestant doctrines, including the role of grace in salvation. English Puritans, now powerful in Parliament, accused the king of "popery"—of holding Catholic beliefs. In 1629, Charles dissolved Parliament, claimed the power to rule by "divine right," and raised money through royal edicts and the sale of monopolies. When Archbishop William Laud, whom Charles chose to head the Church of England, dismissed hundreds of Puritan ministers, thousands of Puritans fled to America.

John Winthrop and the Massachusetts Bay Colony. That exodus began in 1630 with the departure of nine hundred Puritans led by John Winthrop, a well-educated country squire who became the first governor of the Massachusetts Bay colony. Calling England morally corrupt and "overburdened with people," Winthrop sought land for his children and a place in Christian history for his people. "We must consider that we shall be as a City upon a Hill," Winthrop told his fellow passengers. "The eyes of all people are upon us." Like the Pilgrims, the Puritans envisioned a reformed Christian society, a genuinely "New" England that would inspire religious change in England and throughout Europe.

Winthrop and his associates established the government of the Massachusetts Bay Colony in the town of Boston. They transformed their **joint-stock corporation**, the General Court of shareholders, into a representative political system with a governor, council, and assembly. To ensure rule by the godly, the Puritans limited the right to vote and hold office to men who were church members. Ignoring the policy of religious tolerance in Plymouth Colony, they established Puritanism as the state-supported religion, barred other faiths from conducting services, and used the Bible as a legal guide. "Where there is no Law," the colony's government declared, magistrates should rule "as near the law of God as they can." Over the next decade, about ten thousand Puritans migrated to the colony, along with ten thousand others fleeing hard times in England.

In establishing churches, New England Puritans tried to recreate the simplicity of the first Christians. They eliminated bishops and placed

Governor John Winthrop

This portrait, painted in the style of Flemish artist Anthony Van Dyke, captures Winthrop's gravity and intensity. His religious orthodoxy and belief in elite rule shaped the early history of the Massachusetts Bay Colony. Courtesy American Antiquarian Society, Worcester.

power in the hands of the laity, the ordinary members of the congregation—hence their name, Congregationalists. Following the teachings of John Calvin, Puritans embraced predestination, the doctrine that God had chosen (before their birth) only a few "elect" men and women, the Saints, for salvation. Many church members lived in great anxiety, uncertain that God had selected them.

Puritans dealt with this uncertainty in three ways. Some congregations stressed the conversion experience, the intense spiritual sensation of being born again upon receiving God's grace. Other Puritans focused on preparation, the confidence in salvation that came from years of spiritual guidance from their ministers. Still others believed that God considered the Puritans his chosen people, the new Israelites, who would be saved if they obeyed his laws (see Reading American Pictures, "Skeletons and Angels: Exploring Colonial New England Cemeteries," p. 58).

Roger Williams and Rhode Island. To maintain God's favor, the Puritan magistrates of Massachusetts Bay purged their society of religious dissidents. One target was Roger Williams, the minister of the Puritan church in Salem, a coastal town north of Boston. Williams endorsed the Pilgrim's separation of church and state in Plymouth, condemning the legal establishment of Congregationalism in Massachusetts Bay. He taught that political magistrates had authority over only the "bodies, goods, and outward estates of men," not their spiritual lives. Moreover, the Salem minister questioned the Puritans' seizure of Indian lands. The magistrates banished him from the colony in 1636.

Williams and his followers settled about fifty miles south of Boston, founding the town of Providence on land purchased from the Narragansett Indians. Other religious dissidents settled nearby at Portsmouth and Newport. In 1644, the settlers obtained a corporate charter from Parliament for a new colony—Rhode Island—with full authority "to rule themselves." In Rhode Island as in Plymouth, there was no legally established church: Every congregation was independent, and individuals could worship God as they pleased.

Anne Hutchinson. Puritan magistrates in Massachusetts Bay also felt their authority threatened by Anne Hutchinson, the wife of a merchant and a mother of seven who worked as a midwife. Hutchinson held weekly prayer meetings for women in her house and accused various Boston clergymen of placing too much emphasis on good behavior. Recalling Martin Luther's rejection of indulgences, Hutchinson denied that salvation could be earned through good deeds. She insisted that there was no "covenant of works," that God bestowed salvation through the "covenant of grace." Moreover, Hutchinson declared that God "revealed" divine truth directly to the individual believer, a doctrine the Puritan magistrates denounced as heretical.

The magistrates also resented Hutchinson because of her sex. Like other Christians, Puritans believed that both men and women could be saved, but gender equality stopped there. They believed that women were inferior to men in earthly affairs, and so instructed married women: "Thy desires shall bee subject to thy husband, and he shall rule over thee." They likewise denied women significant roles within the church. According to John Robinson, a Pilgrim minister, women "are debarred by their sex from ordinary prophesying, and from any other dealing in the church wherein they take authority over the man." Puritan women could not be ministers or lay preachers, and they had no vote in the congregation.

In 1637, the magistrates put Hutchinson on trial for teaching that inward grace freed an individual from the rules of the church. Hutchinson defended her views with great skill; even Winthrop admitted that she was "a woman of fierce and haughty courage." But the judges scolded her for not attending to "her household affairs, and such things as belong to women" and found her guilty of holding heretical views. Banished, she followed Roger Williams into exile in Rhode Island.

These coercive policies in Winthrop's colony, along with the desire for better farm land, prompted some Puritans to migrate to the Connecticut River Valley. In 1636, pastor Thomas Hooker and his congregation established the town of Hartford, and other Puritans settled along the river at Wethersfield and Windsor. In 1662, they secured a charter from King Charles II (r. 1660–1685) for a self-governing colony. Like Massachusetts Bay, the Connecticut plan of government provided for a legally established church and an elected governor and assembly; however, it granted voting rights to most propertyowning men, not just church members as in the original Puritan colony.

The English Puritan Revolution. As Puritan migrants established colonies in America, England fell into a religious war. When Archbishop Laud imposed a Church of England prayer book on Presbyterian Scotland in 1642, a Scottish army invaded England. Thousands of English Puritans (and hundreds of American Puritans) joined the invaders, demanding reform of the established church and greater authority for Parliament. After several years of civil war, the parliamentary forces led by Oliver Cromwell were victorious. In 1649, Parliament executed King Charles I, proclaimed a republican commonwealth, and banished bishops and elaborate rituals from the Church of England.

The Puritan triumph was short-lived. Popular support for the Commonwealth ebbed, especially after 1653, when Cromwell took dictatorial control. After his death in 1658, moderate Protestants and a resurgent aristocracy restored the monarchy and the hierarchy of bishops. For many Puritans, Charles II's accession in 1660 represented the victory of the Antichrist, the false prophet described in the final book of the New Testament.

For the Puritans in America, the restoration of the monarchy began a new phase of their "errand into the wilderness." They had come to New England to preserve the "pure" Christian church, expecting to return to Europe in triumph. When the failure of the English Revolution dashed that sacred mission, Puritan ministers exhorted their congregations to create a holy society in America.

Puritanism and Witchcraft

Like Native Americans, Puritans believed that the physical world was full of supernatural forces. Devout Christians saw signs of God's (or Satan's) power in blazing stars, birth defects, and other unusual events. Noting that the houses of many ministers "had been

Skeletons and Angels: Exploring Colonial New England Cemeteries

Susanna Jayne, died 1776, Marblehead, Massachusetts. Peabody Essex Museum, Salem, Massachusetts.

Elder Robert Murray, died December 13, 1790, Old Hill Burial Ground, Newburyport, Massachusetts. From the collection of photographs *New England Gravestones*, vol. 1772–1778, copyright Jenn Marcelais.

Before 1800, New England was a much healthier place than Europe. As the text explains, most Puritan infants who survived past one year — especially before 1730 — lived into their sixties. Yet when historians ventured into American cemeteries, they found that Puritan gravestones often depicted death in terrifying terms. Surprisingly, after 1730, as epidemics ravaged growing colonial cities and densely populated farming towns, and death rates rose, the images on gravestones became less frightening. How do we reconcile the statistical and visual evidence?

ANALYZING THE EVIDENCE

➤ Look at Susanna Jayne's gravestone. Why do you think the Puritans used such terrifying images? Do those images carry a religious message? What clues can you find on the stone about Puritan culture?

➤ How does Elder Murray's gravestone reflect the changing image of death in the eighteenth century? How would you relate this shift in imagery to changes in Puritan religious beliefs?

➤ The angel curved on the 1790 gravestone bears Elder Murray's face. It was not uncommon to reproduce an image of the person who had died on his or her grave-

stone. Why do you think a family would choose to use a personal image on a gravestone? Could you argue that the need to personalize a gravestone reflects the rise of American individualism? Why or why not?

➤ There are thousands of antique gravestone in New England cemeteries, the work of scores of carvers, and you can find photographs of many of them on the Web. One good resource is **www.gravematter. com**. What patterns do you see in the images? How would a historian prove that a hypothesis — for example, the use of personal images on gravestones increased with the rise of individualism — is sound?

smitten with Lightning," Cotton Mather, a prominent Puritan theologian, wondered "what the meaning of God should be in it."

This belief in "spirits" stemmed in part from Christian teachings—the Catholic belief in miracles, for example, and the Protestant faith in grace. It also reflected a pagan influence. When Samuel Sewall, a well-educated Puritan merchant and judge, moved into a new house, he fended off evil spirits by driving a metal pin into the floor. Thousands of ordinary Puritan farmers followed the pagan astrological charts—they were printed in almanacs—to determine the best times to plant crops, marry, and make other important decisions.

Zealous ministers attacked these beliefs and practices as "superstition" and condemned the "cunning" individuals who claimed special powers as healers or prophets. Indeed, many Christians believed these conjurers were Satan's "wizards" or "witches." The people of Andover, one of the Massachusetts Bay settlements, "were much addicted to sorcery," claimed one observer, and "there were forty men in it that could raise the Devil as well as any astrologer." Between 1647 and 1662, civil authorities in New England hanged fourteen people for witchcraft, mostly older women accused of being "double-tongued" or of having "an unruly spirit."

The most dramatic episode of witch-hunting occurred in Salem in 1692. It began when several young girls experienced strange seizures and then accused various neighbors of bewitching them. When judges at the trials allowed the use of "spectral" evidence—visions seen only by the girls—the accusations spun out of control. Eventually, Massachusetts Bay authorities arrested and tried 175 people for the crime of witchcraft and executed nineteen of them. The causes of this mass hysteria were complex and are still debated. Some historians point to group rivalries: Many of the accusers were the daughters or servants of poor farmers in a rural area of Salem, whereas many of the alleged witches were wealthier church members or their friends. Because eighteen of those put to death were women, other historians claim the trials and executions were part of the broader Puritan effort to subordinate women. Still other scholars focus on political instability in Massachusetts Bay in the early 1690s (see Chapter 3) and fears raised by recent Indian attacks in nearby Maine, in which the parents of some of the young accusers had been killed.

Whatever the cause, the Salem witch-hunts marked a turning point. Many settlers were horrified by the executions, a response that discouraged additional legal prosecutions. Another reason for the demise of witchcraft accusations in New England was the influence of the European Enlightenment,

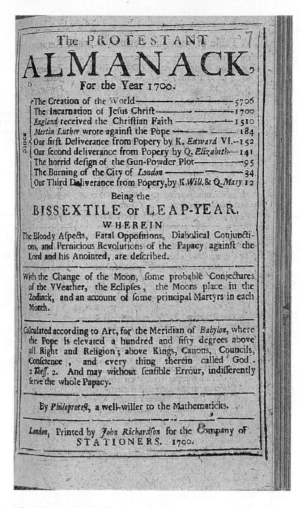

The Protestant Almanack, 1700

The conflict between Protestants and Catholics took many forms. To reinforce the religious identity of English Protestants, the Company of Stationers published a yearly almanac that charted not only the passage of the seasons but also the "Pernicious Revolutions of the Papacy against the Lord and his Anointed." By permission of the Syndics of Cambridge University Library.

a major intellectual movement that began around 1675 and promoted a rational, scientific view of the world. Increasingly, educated people explained accidents and sudden deaths by reference to the "laws of nature." In contrast to Cotton Mather (1663–1728), who believed that lightning might be a supernatural sign, Benjamin Franklin and other well-read men of the next generation would conceive of lightning as a natural phenomenon.

A Yeoman Society, 1630–1700

In building their communities, New England Puritans consciously rejected the feudal practices of traditional European society. They had "escaped out of the pollutions of the world," declared the

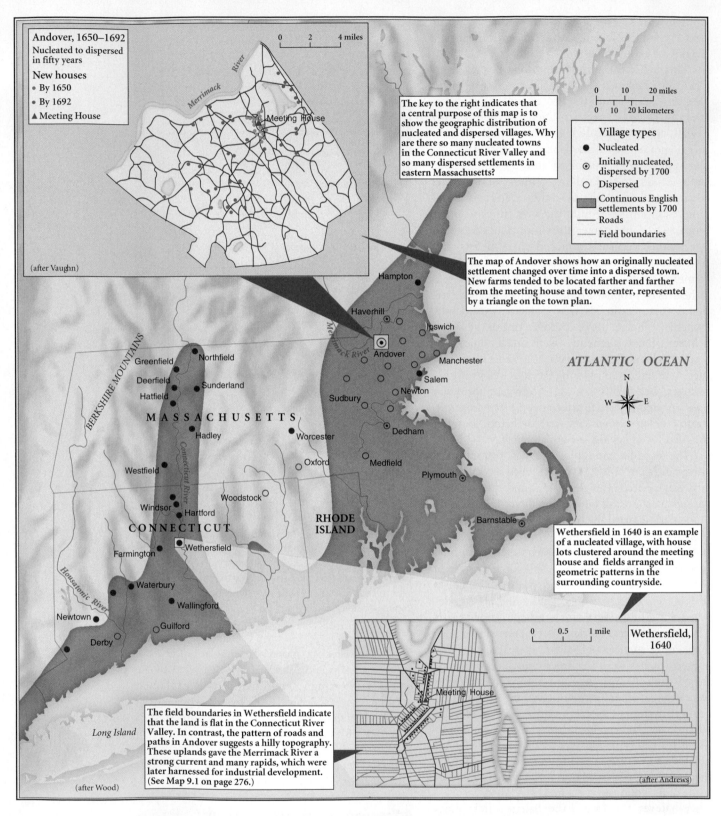

Andover, 1650–1692
Nucleated to dispersed in fifty years
New houses
• By 1650
• By 1692
▲ Meeting House

(after Vaughn)

The key to the right indicates that a central purpose of this map is to show the geographic distribution of nucleated and dispersed villages. Why are there so many nucleated towns in the Connecticut River Valley and so many dispersed settlements in eastern Massachusetts?

Village types
• Nucleated
◉ Initially nucleated, dispersed by 1700
○ Dispersed
▨ Continuous English settlements by 1700
— Roads
— Field boundaries

The map of Andover shows how an originally nucleated settlement changed over time into a dispersed town. New farms tended to be located farther and farther from the meeting house and town center, represented by a triangle on the town plan.

ATLANTIC OCEAN

Wethersfield in 1640 is an example of a nucleated village, with house lots clustered around the meeting house and fields arranged in geometric patterns in the surrounding countryside.

The field boundaries in Wethersfield indicate that the land is flat in the Connecticut River Valley. In contrast, the pattern of roads and paths in Andover suggests a hilly topography. These uplands gave the Merrimack River a strong current and many rapids, which were later harnessed for industrial development. (See Map 9.1 on page 276.)

Wethersfield, 1640

(after Andrews)

(after Wood)

MAP 2.6 Settlement Patterns in New England Towns, 1630–1700

Initially, most Puritan towns were compact: Regardless of the local topography — hills or plains — families lived close to one another in the village center and traveled daily to work in the surrounding fields. This pattern is clearly apparent in the 1640 map of Wethersfield, which is situated on the broad plains of the Connecticut River Valley. The first settlers in Andover, Massachusetts, also chose to live in the village center. However, the rugged topography of eastern Massachusetts encouraged the townspeople to disperse; and by 1692, many Andover residents were living on their own farms.

An Affluent Puritan Woman

This well-known painting (c. 1671) of Elizabeth Freake and her daughter, Mary, is perhaps the finest portrait we have of a seventeenth-century American. The skill of the artist, probably a visiting English portraitist, and the finery of Mrs. Freake's dress and bonnet suggest the growing cosmopolitanism and prosperity of Boston's merchant community. Worcester Art Museum.

settlers of Watertown in Massachusetts Bay, and vowed "to sit down . . . close together." They refused to live as tenants of wealthy aristocrats or submit to oppressive taxation by a distant government. Instead, the General Courts of Massachusetts Bay and Connecticut bestowed the title to each township on a group of settlers, or **proprietors**, who then distributed the land among the male heads of families.

Widespread ownership of land did not mean equality of wealth or status. "G.od had Ordained different degrees and orders of men," proclaimed Boston merchant John Saffin, "some to be Masters and Commanders, others to be Subjects, and to be commanded." Town proprietors normally awarded the largest plots to men of high social status, who often became selectmen and justices of the peace. However, all families received some land, and most adult men had a vote in the **town meeting**, the main institution of local government (Map 2.6).

In this society of independent households and self-governing communities, ordinary farmers had much more political power than Chesapeake yeomen and European peasants did. Although Nathaniel Fish was one of the poorest men in the town of Barnstable — he owned just a two-room cottage, eight acres of land, an ox, and a cow — he was a voting member of the town meeting. Each year, Fish and other Barnstable farmers levied taxes, enacted ordinances governing fencing and road building, regulated the use of common fields for grazing livestock, and chose the selectmen who managed town affairs. Moreover, they selected the town's representatives to the General Court, which gradually displaced the governor as the center of political authority. For Fish and thousands of other ordinary settlers, New England had proved to be the promised land, a new world of opportunity.

➤ What problems did the Puritans have with the Church of England? What beliefs made the Puritans different?

➤ The Puritans of Massachusetts Bay had fled an established church and religious persecution in England. Why, then, did they promptly establish their own church and persecute dissenters?

➤ Describe the political structure that developed in the New England colonies. What was the relationship between local government and the Puritan churches?

The Eastern Indians' New World

Native Americans along the Atlantic coast of North America also lived in a new world, but for them it was a bleak and dangerous place. Europeans had invaded their lands, introduced deadly diseases, and erected hundreds of permanent settlements. Some Indian peoples, among them the Pequots in New England and the Susquehannocks in Virginia, resisted the invaders by force. Others, most prominently the Iroquois, used European guns and manufactures to dominate other tribes. Still other native peoples retreated into the mountains or moved west to preserve their traditional cultures.

Puritans and Pequots

As the Puritans embarked for New England, they pondered the morality of intruding on Native American lands. "By what right or warrant can we enter into the land of the Savages?" they asked themselves. Responding to such concerns, John Winthrop detected God's hand in these events and pointed to a recent smallpox epidemic that devastated the local Indian peoples. "If God were not pleased with our inheriting these parts," he asked, "why doth he still make roome for us by diminishing them as we increase?" Citing the Book of Genesis, the magistrates of Massachusetts Bay declared that the Indians had not "subdued" their land and therefore had no "just right" to it.

Believing they were God's chosen people, the Puritans often treated Native Americans with a brutality equal to that of the Spanish conquistadors and Nathaniel Bacon's frontiersmen. When Pequot warriors attacked English farmers who had intruded onto their lands in the Connecticut River Valley in 1636, a Puritan militia attacked a Pequot village and massacred some five hundred men, women, and children. "God laughed at the Enemies of his People," one soldier boasted, "filling the Place with Dead Bodies."

Like most Europeans, English Puritans saw the Indians as "savages" and culturally inferior peoples. But the Puritans were not *racists* as the term is understood today. They did not believe that Native Americans were genetically inferior to them; in fact, they believed they were white people with sun-darkened skin. "Sin," not race, accounted for the Indians' degeneracy. "Probably the devil" delivered these "miserable savages" to America, Cotton Mather suggested, "in hopes that the gospel of the Lord Jesus Christ would never come here to destroy or disturb his absolute empire over them."

This interpretation of the Indians' history inspired another Puritan minister, John Eliot, to convert them to Christianity. Eliot translated the Bible into Algonquian and undertook numerous missions to Indian villages in the Massachusetts Bay Colony. Because the Puritans demanded that Indians understand the complexities of Protestant theology, only a few Native Americans became full members of Puritan congregations. The Puritans created **praying towns** that were similar to the Franciscan missions in New Mexico. By 1670, more than 1,000 Indians lived in fourteen special towns like Natick (Massachusetts) and Maanexit (Connecticut). Even the coastal Indians who remained in their ancestral villages had lost much of their independence and traditional culture.

Metacom's Rebellion

By the 1670s, there were three times as many whites as Indians in New England. The English population now totaled some 55,000, while the number of Native peoples had plummeted — from an estimated 120,000 in 1570 to 70,000 in 1620, to barely 16,000. To Metacom, leader of the Wampanoags, the future looked grim. When his people copied English ways by raising hogs and selling pork in Boston, Puritan officials accused them of selling at "an under rate" and placed restrictions on their trade. When they killed wandering livestock that damaged their cornfields, authorities denounced them for violating English property rights.

Metacom (King Philip), Chief of the Wampanoags
The Indian uprising of 1675–1676 left an indelible mark on the history of New England. This painting from the 1850s, done on semitransparent cloth and lit from behind for effect, was used by traveling performers to tell the story of King Philip's War. Notice that Metacom is not pictured as a savage but is depicted with dignity. No longer in danger of Indian attack, nineteenth-century whites in New England could adopt a romanticized version of their region's often brutal history. Shelburne Museum.

Like Opechancanough in Virginia and Popé in New Mexico, Metacom concluded that only military resistance could save Indian lands and culture. So in 1675, the Wampanoags' leader, whom the English called King Philip, forged a military alliance with the Narragansetts and Nipmucks and began attacking white settlements throughout New England. Almost every day, settler William Harris fearfully reported, he heard new reports of the Indians' "burneing houses, takeing cattell, killing men & women & Children: & carrying others captive." Bitter fighting continued into 1676, ending only when the Indian warriors ran short of guns and powder and when the Massachusetts Bay government hired Mohegan and Mohawk warriors, who ambushed and killed Metacom (see Comparing American Voices, "The Causes of the War of 1675–1676," pp. 64–65).

The rebellion was a deadly affair. The Indians went to war, a party of Narragansetts told Roger

Williams, because the English "had forced them to it." The fighting was long and hard. Indians destroyed 20 percent of the English towns in Massachusetts and Rhode Island and killed 1,000 settlers, nearly 5 percent of the adult population. The very future of the Puritan experiment hung in the balance. Had "the Indeans not been divided," remarked one settler, "they might have forced us [to evacuate] to Som Islands: & there to have planted a little Corne, & fished for our liveings." But the Natives' own losses—from famine and disease, death in battle, and sale into slavery—were much larger: About 4,500 Indians died, a quarter of an already-diminished population. Many of the surviving Wampanoag, Narragansett, and Nipmuck peoples migrated farther into the New England backcountry, where they intermarried with Algonquin tribes allied to the French. Over the next century, these displaced Indian peoples would take their revenge, joining with French Catholics to attack their Puritan enemies.

The Human and Environmental Impact of the Fur Trade

As English towns slowly filled the river valleys along the Atlantic coast, the Indians who lived in the great forested areas beyond the Appalachian Mountains remained independent. Yet the distant Indian peoples—the Iroquois, Ottawas, Crees, Illinois, and many more—also felt the European presence through the fur trade. As they bargained for woolen blankets, iron cooking ware, knives, and guns, Indians learned to avoid the French at Montreal, who demanded two beaver skins for a woolen blanket. Instead, they dealt with the Dutch and English merchants at Albany, who asked for only one pelt and who could be played off against one another. "They are marvailous subtle in their bargains to save a penny," an English trader complained. "They will beate all markets and try all places . . . to save six pence." Still, because the Indians had no way of knowing the value of their pelts in Europe, they rarely secured the highest possible price.

Nor could they control the impact of European traders and settlers on their societies. All Indian peoples were diminished in number and vitality as they encountered European diseases, European guns, and European rum. "Strong spirits . . . Causes our men to get very sick," a Catawba leader in Carolina protested, "and many of our people has Lately Died by the Effects of that Strong Drink." Most Native societies also lost their economic independence. As they exchanged furs for European-made iron utensils and woolen blankets, Indians neglected their traditional artisan skills, making fewer flint hoes, clay pots, and skin garments. A Cherokee chief complained in the 1750s, "Every necessity of life we must have from the white

Ætatis suæ 21. Aᵒ. 1616.

An English View of Pocahontas

By depicting the Indian princess Pocahontas as a well-dressed European woman, the artist casts her as a symbol of peaceful assimilation to English culture. In actuality, marriages between white men (often fur traders) and Indian women usually resulted in bilingual families that absorbed elements from both cultures. National Portrait Gallery, Smithsonian Institution/Art Resource, New York.

people." Religious autonomy vanished as well. When French missionaries won converts among the Hurons, Iroquois, and Illinois, they divided Indian communities into hostile religious factions.

Likewise, constant warfare for furs altered the dynamics of tribal politics by shifting power from cautious elders to headstrong young warriors. The sachems (chiefs), a group of young Seneca warriors said scornfully, "were a parcell of Old People who say much but who Mean or Act very little." The position and status of Indian women changed in especially complex ways. Traditionally, eastern woodland women had asserted authority as the chief providers of food and handcrafted goods. As a French Jesuit noted of the Iroquois, "The women are always the first to deliberate . . . on private or community matters. They hold their councils apart and . . . advise the chiefs . . . , so that the latter may deliberate on them in their turn." The disruption of farming by warfare and the influx of European goods undermined the economic basis of women's power. Paradoxically, though, among the Iroquois and other victorious tribes, the influence of women may have increased because they assumed responsibility for the cultural assimilation of hundreds of captives.

The Causes of the War of 1675–1676

The causes of—and responsibility for—every American war have been much debated, and the war of 1675–1676 between Puritans and Native Americans is no exception. The English settlers called it King Philip's War, as if the Wampanoag chief instigated it. Is that the case? What were the underlying causes of the uprising? When did it actually begin? We have no firsthand Indian accounts of its origins, but three English accounts tell the story from different perspectives. Given the differences among these accounts and their fragmentary character, how can historians reconstruct what "really happened"? Moreover, from whose point of view, the Indians' or the Europeans', should the story be told?

JOHN EASTON
A Relacion of the Indyan Warre

John Easton was the deputy governor of Rhode Island and a Quaker. Like many other Quakers, he was a pacifist and did what he could to prevent the war. He wrote this "Relacion" shortly after the conflict ended.

In [January 1675], an Indian was found dead; and by a coroner inquest of Plymouth colony judged murdered. . . . The dead Indian was called Sassamon, and a Christian that could read and write. . . .

The report came that the three Indians had confessed and accused Philip [of employing them to do so, and that consequently] . . . the English would hang Philip. So the Indians were afraid, and reported that the English had . . . by threats [led] Philip [to believe] that they might kill him to have his land. . . . So Philip kept his men in arms.

Plymouth governor [Josias Winslow] required him to disband his men, and informed him his jealousy was false. Philip answered he would do no harm, and thanked the governor for his information. The three Indians were hung [on June 8, 1675]. . . . And it was reported [that] Sassamon, before his death, had informed [the English] of the Indian plot, and that if the Indians knew it they would kill him, and that the heathen might destroy the English for their wickedness as God had permitted the heathen to destroy the Israelites of old.

So the English were afraid and Philip was afraid and both increased in arms; but for forty years' time reports and jealousies of war had been very frequent, that we did not think that now a war was breaking forth. But about a week before it did we had cause to think it would; then to endeavor to prevent it, we sent a man to Philip. . . .

He called his council and agreed to come to us; [Philip] came himself, unarmed, and about forty of his men, armed.

Then five of us went over. Three were magistrates. We sat very friendly together [June 14–18]. We told him our business was to endeavor that they might not . . . do wrong. They said that that was well; they had done no wrong; the English had wronged them. We said we knew the English said that the Indians wronged them, and the Indians said the English wronged them, but our desire was the quarrel might rightly be decided in the best way, and not as dogs decide their quarrels.

The Indians owned that fighting was the worst way; then they propounded how right might take place; we said by arbitration. They said all English agreed against them; and so by arbitration they had had much wrong, many square miles of land so taken from them, for the English would have English arbitrators. . . .

Another grievance: the English cattle and horses still increased that when [the Indians] removed thirty miles from where English had anything to do, they could not keep their corn from being spoiled [by the English livestock]. . . .

So we departed without any discourtesies; and suddenly [circa June 25] had [a] letter from [the] Plymouth governor, [that] they intended in arms to [subjugate] Philip . . . and in a week's time after we had been with the Indians the war thus begun.

SOURCE: John Easton, "A Relacion of the Indyan Warre, by Mr. Easton, of Roade Isld., 1675," in *Narratives of the Indian Wars, 1675–1699,* ed. Charles H. Lincoln (New York: Charles Scribner's Sons, 1913), 7–17.

EDWARD RANDOLPH
Short Narrative of My Proceedings

Edward Randolph was an English customs official who denounced the independent policies of the Puritan colonies and tried to subject them to English control. His "Short Narrative,"

Various are the reports and conjectures of the causes of the present Indian warre. Some impute it to an impudent zeal in the magistrates of Boston to Christianize those heathen before they were civilized and enjoining them the strict observation of their laws, which, to a people so rude and licentious, hath proved even intolerable. . . . While the magistrates, for their profit, put the laws severely in execution against the Indians, the people, on the other side, for lucre and gain, entice and provoke the Indians to the breach thereof, especially to drunkenness, to which those people are so generally addicted that they will strip themselves to their skin to have their fill of rum and brandy. . . .

Some believe there have been vagrant and jesuitical [French] priests, who have made it their business, for some years past, to go from Sachem to Sachem, to exasperate the Indians against the English and to bring them into a confederacy, and that they were promised supplies from France and other parts to extirpate the English nation out of the continent of America. . . .

Others impute the cause to some injuries offered to the Sachem Philip; for he being possessed of a tract of land called Mount Hope . . . some English had a mind to dispossess him thereof, who never wanting one pretence or other to attain their end, complained of injuries done by Philip and his Indians to their stock and cattle, whereupon Philip was often summoned before the magistrate, sometimes imprisoned, and never released but upon parting with a considerable part of his land.

But the government of the Massachusetts . . . do declare [the following acts] are the great evils for which God hath given the heathen commission to rise against them. . . . For men wearing long hair and periwigs made of women's hair; for women . . . cutting, curling and laying out the hair. . . . For profaneness in the people not frequenting their [church] meetings.

SOURCE: Albert B. Hart, ed., *American History Told by Contemporaries* (New York: Macmillan, 1897), 1: 458–460.

BENJAMIN CHURCH
Entertaining Passages

Captain Benjamin Church fought in the war and helped end it by capturing King Philip's wife and son and leading the expedition that killed the Indian leader. Forty years later, in 1716, Church's son Thomas wrote an account of the war based on his father's notes and recollections.

While Mr. Church was diligently settling his new farm . . . Behold! The rumor of a war between the English and the natives gave a check to his projects. . . . Philip, according to his promise to his people, permitted them to march out of the neck [of the Mount Hope peninsula, where they lived]. . . . They plundered the nearest houses that the inhabitants had deserted [on the rumor of a war], but as yet offered no violence to the people, at least none were killed. . . . However, the alarm was given by their numbers, and hostile equipage, and by the prey they made of what they could find in the forsaken houses.

An express came the same day to the governor [circa June 25], who immediately gave orders to the captains of the towns to march the greatest part of their companies [of militia], and to rendezvous at Taunton. . . .

The enemy, who began their hostilities with plundering and destroying cattle, did not long content themselves with that game. They thirsted for English blood, and they soon broached it; killing two men in the way not far from Mr. Miles's garrison. And soon after, eight more at Mattapoisett, upon whose bodies they exercised more than brutish barbarities. . . .

These provocations drew out the resentments of some of Capt. Prentice's troop, who desired they might have liberty to go out and seek the enemy in their own quarters [circa June 26].

SOURCE: Benjamin Church, *Entertaining Passages Relating to Philip's War Which Began in the Year, 1675*, ed. Thomas Church (Boston: B. Green, 1716).

ANALYZING THE EVIDENCE

➤ Where do the documents agree and disagree about the causes of the war? Given what you know from the discussion in the text, how might the war have been prevented?

➤ In specific terms, what did the magistrates of Massachusetts Bay believe to be the prime cause of the war? Could historians verify or disprove their explanation? How? What additional sources of evidence might be useful?

➤ Make an argument for when the war began. Which documents provide the most compelling evidence? Why?

There is no doubt that the sheer extent of the fur industry—the slaughter of hundreds of thousands of beaver, deer, otter, and other animals—profoundly altered the environment. As early as the 1630s, a French Jesuit worried that the Montagnais people, who lived north of the St. Lawrence, were killing so many beaver that they would "exterminate the species in this Region, as has happened among the Hurons." As the animal populations died off, streams ran faster (there were fewer beaver dams) and the underbrush grew denser (there were fewer deer to trim the vegetation). The native environment, as well as its animals and peoples, were now part of a new American world.

➤ Compare the causes of the uprisings led by Popé in New Mexico and Metacom in New England. Which was more successful? Why?

➤ What were the major social and environmental developments that made America a new world for both Europeans and Indians?

SUMMARY

We have seen that Spain created a permanent settlement in North America in 1565; a half-century later, France, the Dutch Republic, and England did the same. These invasions of Native American lands had much in common. All spread devastating European diseases. All reduced the Indians to subject peoples. All sparked wars or revolts. And, except for the Dutch, all involved efforts to convert the Native peoples to Christianity. There were important differences as well. The French and the Dutch established fur-trading colonies; the Spanish and the English came in large numbers and formed settler colonies—although the Spanish intermarried with the Indians while the English did not.

There were also significant similarities and differences between the English settlements in the Chesapeake region, in which bound laborers raised tobacco for export to Europe, and those in New England, where pious Puritans lived in farming towns and fishing communities. Although the social structure of the Chesapeake colonies was less equal than that of the New England settlements, both regions boasted representative political institutions. Both regions also experienced Indian revolts and wars in the first decades of settlement (in Virginia in 1622 and in New England in 1636) and again in 1675–1676. Indeed, the simultaneous eruption of the Indian conflict that ignited Bacon's Rebellion and Metacom's War is evidence that the histories of the two regions of English settlement were beginning to converge.

Connections: Religion

In the part opener (p. 3), we state:

> The American experience profoundly changed religious institutions and values. Many migrants left Europe because of conflicts among rival Christian churches; in America, they hoped to practice their religion without interference.

In Chapter 2, we began our analysis of religion in English America by discussing the migration of Anglicans to Virginia, Catholics to Maryland, and Puritans to New England. We saw how the conditions of American life, especially religious diversity and weak state institutions, thwarted attempts by religious traditionalists to create strong established churches in the Chesapeake colonies and to enforce spiritual conformity in New England. We will revisit issues of religious uniformity and tolerance in Chapter 3, with a discussion of the Quaker settlement of Pennsylvania and West New Jersey in the 1680s, and in Chapter 4, with an analysis of the migration to British North America between 1720 and 1760 of tens of thousands of Scots-Irish Presbyterians, German Lutherans, and other European Protestants.

The forced migration of hundreds of thousands of Africans, one of the central themes of Chapter 3, will add complexity to our story of religion in colonial America. Some African slaves were Muslims; many more relied for spiritual substance and moral guidance on African gods and the powers they saw in nature. As we will see in Chapter 4, the Great Awakening, a far-reaching religious revival during the 1740s and 1750s, brought only a few Africans into the Christian fold; instead, it increased religious diversity among peoples of European ancestry. As the timeline for Part One (p. 2) suggests, religious liberty, pluralism, and tolerance are key themes of the American religious experience.

CHAPTER REVIEW QUESTIONS

➤ Outline the goals of the directors of the Virginia Company and the leaders of the Massachusetts Bay Company. Where did they succeed? In what ways did they fall short?

➤ Explain why there were no major witchcraft scares in the Chesapeake colonies and no uprising like Bacon's Rebellion in New England. Consider the possible social, economic, and religious causes of both phenomena.

TIMELINE

1539–1543	Coronado and de Soto lead gold-seeking expeditions
1565	Spain establishes a fort at St. Augustine
1598	Acomas rebel in New Mexico
1603–1625	Reign of James I, king of England
1607	English traders settle Jamestown (Virginia)
1608	Samuel de Champlain founds Quebec
1613	Dutch set up fur-trading post on Manhattan Island
1619	First Africans arrive in the Chesapeake region
	House of Burgesses convenes in Virginia
1620	Pilgrims found Plymouth Colony
1620–1660	Chesapeake colonies experience tobacco boom
1621	Dutch West India Company granted charter
1622	Opechancanough's uprising
1624	Virginia becomes a royal colony
1625–1649	Reign of Charles I, king of England
1630	Puritans found Massachusetts Bay Colony
1634	Maryland is settled
1636	Puritan-Pequot War
1636	Roger Williams founds Providence
1637	Anne Hutchinson banished from Massachusetts Bay
1640s	Iroquois initiate wars over fur trade
1642–1659	Puritan Revolution in England
1651	First Navigation Act
1660	Restoration of English monarchy
	Tobacco prices fall and remain low
1664	English conquer New Netherland
1675	Bacon's Rebellion
1675–1676	Metacom's uprising
1680	Popé's rebellion in New Mexico
1692	Salem witchcraft trials
1705	Virginia enacts law defining slavery

FOR FURTHER EXPLORATION

For a comprehensive and insightful narrative of the Spanish exploration and settlement of the lands to the north of the Rio Grande, consult David Weber, *The Spanish Frontier in North America* (1992). Bernard Bailyn, *The Peopling of British North America: An Introduction* (1986), presents a brief, vivid history of English migration and settlement. In *American Slavery, American Freedom* (1975), Edmund Morgan offers a compelling portrait of white servitude and black slavery in early Virginia. John Demos, *The Unredeemed Captive: A Family Story from Early America* (1994), relates the gripping tale of Eunice Williams, the daughter of a Puritan minister who was captured by and lived her life among the Mohawks. Two other fine studies of Native American life are James Merrell, *The Indians' New World: Catawbas and Their Neighbors from European Contact Through the Era of Removal* (1989), and Colin Calloway, *New Worlds for All: Indians, Europeans, and the Remaking of Early America* (1997). Arthur Quinn, *A New World: An Epic of Colonial America from the Founding of Jamestown to the Fall of Quebec* (1994), is a lively narrative filled with portraits of important political figures, macabre events, and high hopes that end disastrously. A recent biography is Francis J. Bremer, *John Winthrop: America's Forgotten Founding Father* (2003).

Two fine Web sites explore the history of the Pilgrims at Plymouth: "Caleb Johnson's Mayflower History" (**www.mayflowerhistory.com/**) and "The Plymouth Colony Archive Project" (**etext.lib.virginia.edu/users/deetz/**). For insight into life in colonial New England in 1628, see the excellent PBS series *Colonial House* (in eight parts) and the accompanying Web site (**www.pbs.org/wnet/colonialhouse/about.html**). Extensive materials on the witchcraft trials can be viewed at "Salem Witchcraft Trials" (**etext.lib.virginia.edu/salem/witchcraft/**). "Colonial Williamsburg" (**www.colonialwilliamsburg.org/history/**) offers an extensive collection of documents, illustrations, and secondary texts about colonial life, as well as information about the archaeological excavations at Williamsburg. "Historic Jamestowne" (**www.historicjamestowne.org/index.php**) offers documentation on recent archaeological finds and gives visitors the opportunity to participate in a virtual dig.

APBS video, *Surviving Columbus* (2 hours), traces the experiences of the Pueblo Indians over 450 years. "First Nations Histories" (**www.tolatsga.org/Compacts.html**) presents histories of many North American Indian peoples and information on their politics, language, culture, and demography.

TEST YOUR KNOWLEDGE

To assess your command of the material in this chapter, see the Online Study Guide at **bedfordstmartins.com/henretta**.

For Web sites, images, and documents related to topics and places in this chapter, visit **bedfordstmartins.com/makehistory**.

3

The British Empire in America
1660–1750

W HEN CHARLES II CAME TO THE throne in 1660, England was a second-class trading country, its merchants picking up the crumbs left by the much more efficient Dutch. "What we want is more of the trade the Dutch now have," declared the Duke of Albemarle, a trusted minister of the king and a proprietor of Carolina. To get it, the English government passed a series of Navigation Acts, which excluded Dutch ships from its colonies, and went to war to enforce the new legislation. By the 1720s, the recently unified kingdom of Great Britain (comprising England and Scotland) had taken control of commerce in the Atlantic. Trade in West Indian sugar and African slaves "is our chief support," Secretary of State Lord Carteret told the House of Lords in 1739. As ardent imperialist Malachy Postlethwayt explained, the British empire "was a magnificent superstructure of American commerce and naval power on an African foundation."

To protect the empire's valuable West Indian sugar colonies from European rivals — the Dutch in New Netherland, the Spanish in Mesoamerica and Florida, and especially the Catholic French in Quebec and the West Indies — British ministers repeatedly went to war and with considerable success. Boasted one English pamphleteer, "We are, of any nation, the best situated for trade, . . . capable of giving

◄ **Power and Race in the Chesapeake**

In this 1670 painting by Gerard Soest, Lord Baltimore holds a map of his proprietary colony, Maryland. The colony will soon belong to his grandson Cecil Calvert, who is pointing to his magnificent inheritance. The presence of a young African servant foretells the importance of slave labor in the post-1700 economy of the Chesapeake colonies.
Enoch Pratt Free Library of Baltimore.

maritime laws to the world." So when Edward Randolph, an imperial official in New England, reported in the early 1670s that "there is no notice taken [here] of the act of navigation," the home government set out to impose its political will on the American settlements.

Although that coercion was only partially successful, the mainland colonies became increasingly important to the prosperity of the British empire. "We have within ourselves and in our colonies in America an inexhaustible fund to supply ourselves" with a vast array of goods, another English pamphleteer proudly announced. The cost of creating this increasingly prosperous transatlantic commercial system was borne primarily by hundreds of thousands of enslaved Africans, who endured brutal, often deadly conditions on the plantations of the West Indies.

The Politics of Empire, 1660–1713

Before 1660, England governed its New England and Chesapeake colonies haphazardly. Taking advantage of that laxness and the English civil war, local oligarchies of Puritan magistrates and tobacco planter-merchants ran their societies as they wanted. After the monarchy was restored in 1660, royal bureaucrats tried to impose order on the unruly settlements and, with the help of Indian allies, went to war against rival European powers to further their imperial ambitions.

The Great Aristocratic Land Grab

When Charles II (r. 1660–1685) ascended the English throne, he quickly established a string of new settlements — the Restoration Colonies, as historians call them (Table 3.1). In 1663, Charles, a generous man who was always in debt, rewarded eight noblemen with the gift of Carolina, an area long claimed by Spain and populated by thousands of Indians. The following year, he bestowed an equally huge grant on his brother James, the Duke of York. James took possession of New Jersey and the just-conquered Dutch colony of New Netherland, which he renamed New York. Then James conveyed the ownership of New Jersey to two of the Carolina proprietors.

In one of the great land grabs in history, a handful of English nobles had taken title to vast provinces. Like Lord Baltimore's Maryland, their new colonies were proprietorships: The aristocrats owned all the land and could rule as they wished as long as their laws conformed broadly to those of England. Most proprietors envisioned a traditional European society presided over by the gentry and the Church of England. The Fundamental Constitutions of Carolina (1669), for example, prescribed a **manorial system**, a society in which a mass of serfs would be governed by a small number of powerful nobles.

The Carolinas. The manorial system proved to be a fantasy. The first settlers in North Carolina were primarily poor families and runaway servants from

TABLE 3.1	English Colonies Established in North America, 1660–1750				
Colony	Date	Type	Religion	Status in 1775	Chief Export/ Economic Activity
Carolina	1663	Proprietary	Church of England	Royal	
North	1691				Farming, naval stores
South	1691				Rice, indigo
New Jersey	1664	Proprietary	Church of England	Royal	Wheat
New York	1664	Proprietary	Church of England	Royal	Wheat
Pennsylvania	1681	Proprietary	Quaker	Proprietary	Wheat
Georgia	1732	Trustees	Church of England	Royal	Rice
New Hampshire (separated from Massachusetts)	1741	Royal	Congregationalist	Royal	Mixed farming, lumber, naval stores
Nova Scotia	1749	Royal	Church of England	Royal	Fishing, mixed farming, naval stores

Virginia, and equality-minded English Quakers, a radical Protestant sect also known as the Society of Friends. They "think there is no difference between a Gentleman and a labourer," complained one Anglican clergyman. Refusing to work on large manors, the settlers raised corn, hogs, and tobacco on modest family farms. And in 1677, inspired by Bacon's Rebellion in Virginia, the residents of Albemarle County staged their own uprising. Angered by taxes on tobacco exports and other levies imposed to support the Anglican church, they rebelled again in 1708. By deposing a series of governors, the "stubborn and disobedient" residents — the description was a wealthy Anglican landowner's — forced the proprietors to abandon their dreams of a feudal society.

In what would become South Carolina, the colonists also refused to accept the Fundamental Constitutions. Many of the white settlers there were migrants from the overcrowded sugar-producing island of Barbados, and they had their own vision of a hierarchical society. They used slaves — both Africans and Native Americans — to raise cattle and food crops for export to the West Indies. Carolina merchants also opened a lucrative trade with neighboring Indian peoples by exchanging English manufactures for deerskins. The Carolinians' reliance on slave labor encouraged their Indian trading partners to take captives from other Native American peoples and exchange them for alcohol and guns. By 1708, white Carolinians were working their coastal plantations with 1,400 Indian and 2,900 African slaves, and brutal Indian warfare continued in the backcountry. South Carolina would remain a violent frontier settlement until the 1720s.

William Penn and the Quakers. In dramatic contrast to the Carolinians, settlers in Pennsylvania

William Penn's Treaty with the Indians, 1683

In 1771, Benjamin West executed this famous picture of William Penn's meeting with the Lenni-Lanapes (or Delawares), who called themselves "the Common People." A Quaker, Penn refused to seize Indian lands by force; instead he negotiated purchases from the Indians. Penn was favorably impressed by the Lenni-Lanapes: "For their persons they are generally tall, straight, well built, and of singular proportion," he wrote in 1683. "They tread strong and clever, and mostly walk with a lofty chin." Pennsylvania Academy of the Fine Arts, Philadelphia.

pursued a pacifistic policy toward Native Americans and quickly became prosperous. In 1681, Charles II bestowed Pennsylvania (which included present-day Delaware) on William Penn in payment for a large debt owed to Penn's father. The younger Penn was born to wealth, owned substantial estates in Ireland and England, and lived in lavish style — with a country mansion, fine clothes, and eight servants. Seemingly destined for courtly pursuits, Penn instead joined the Society of Friends, a religious sect that condemned war and extravagance. Penn designed Pennsylvania as a refuge for his fellow Quakers, who were persecuted in England because they refused to serve in the military or pay taxes to support the Church of England. Penn himself spent more than two years in jail for preaching his beliefs.

Like the Puritans, the Quakers wanted to restore Christianity to its early simplicity and spirituality. But they rejected the Puritans' pessimistic religious doctrine of Calvinism, which restricted salvation to a small elect. Instead, they followed the teachings of two English visionaries, George Fox and Margaret Fell, who argued that God had imbued all men and women with an "inner light" of grace or understanding.

Penn's Frame of Government (1681) applied the Quakers' radical beliefs to the political structure of his colony. It ensured religious freedom by prohibiting a legally established church, and it promoted political equality by allowing all property-owning men to vote and hold office. These enlightened provisions prompted thousands of Quakers, mostly yeoman farm families from northwestern England, to come to Pennsylvania. Initially, they settled along the Delaware River near the city of Philadelphia, which Penn himself laid out in an grid with wide main streets and many parks. To attract European Protestants, Penn published pamphlets in Dutch and German that promised cheap land and freedom from religious persecution. In 1683, migrants from the German region of Saxony founded Germantown (just outside Philadelphia), and thousands of other Germans soon followed. Ethnic diversity, pacifism, and freedom of conscience made Pennsylvania the most open and democratic of the Restoration Colonies.

From Mercantilism to Imperial Dominion

As Charles II gave away his American lands, his ministers were devising policies to keep colonial trade in English hands. Since the 1560s, the English crown had used government subsidies and charters to stimulate English manufacturing and foreign trade. Now the English government extended these mercantilist policies to the American settlements through a series of Navigation Acts (Table 3.2).

Mercantilism: Theory and Practice. According to mercantilist theory, the colonies would produce agricultural goods and raw materials, which Eng-

---

TABLE 3.2 Navigation Acts, 1651–1751

	Date	Purpose	Result
Act of 1651	1651	Cut Dutch trade	Mostly ignored
Act of 1660	1660	Ban foreign shipping; enumerated goods only to England	Partially obeyed
Act of 1663	1663	European imports only through England	Partially obeyed
Staple Act	1673	Ensure enumerated goods go only to England	Mostly obeyed
Act of 1696	1696	Prevent frauds; Create Vice-Admiralty Courts	Mostly obeyed
Woolen Act	1699	Prevent export or intercolonial sale of textiles	Partially obeyed
Hat Act	1732	Prevent export or intercolonial sale of hats	Partially obeyed
Molasses Act	1733	Cut American imports of molasses from French West Indies	Extensively violated
Iron Act	1750	Prevent manufacture of finished iron products	Extensively violated
Currency Act 1751	1751	End use of paper currency as legal tender in New England	Mostly obeyed

lish merchants would carry to England. Certain goods and materials then would be traded immediately in the European market; others would be manufactured into finished products and then exported to Europe (see Chapter 1). The Navigation Act of 1651 excluded Dutch merchants from the English colonies and required that goods imported into England or its American settlements be carried on ships owned by English or colonial merchants. New parliamentary acts in 1660 and 1663 strengthened the ban on foreign traders and stipulated that the colonists had to ship their sugar and tobacco only to England. To provide even more business for English merchants, the acts required that European exports to America pass through England. To pay the customs officials who enforced the mercantilist laws, the Revenue Act of 1673 imposed a "plantation duty" on American exports of sugar and tobacco.

The English government backed its mercantilist policy with the force of arms. In three commercial wars between 1652 and 1674, the English navy drove the Dutch from New Netherland; and by attacking Dutch forts and ships along the Gold Coast of Africa, the English encroached on Holland's dominance of the Atlantic slave trade. Meanwhile, English merchants expanded their fleets, which grew from 150,000 tons of shipping in 1640 to 340,000 tons in 1690, and seized control of commerce in the North Atlantic.

Many colonists refused to comply with the mercantilist laws, continuing to welcome Dutch merchants and to import sugar and molasses from the French West Indies. The Massachusetts Bay assembly boldly declared: "The laws of England are bounded within the [four] seas and do not reach America." Outraged by this insolence, an English official in the colony called for troops to "reduce Massachusetts to obedience." Instead, the Lords of Trade—the administrative body charged with colonial affairs—opted for a punitive legal strategy. In 1679, it denied the claim of Massachusetts Bay to New Hampshire and eventually established a completely separate colony there with a royal governor. Then, in 1684, the Lords of Trade persuaded the English Court of Chancery to annul the charter of Massachusetts Bay on the grounds that the Puritan government had violated the Navigation Acts and virtually outlawed the Church of England.

The Absolutism of James II. The Puritans' troubles had only begun. The accession to the throne of James II (r. 1685–1688) prompted more imperial regulations. The new king was an aggres-

The Target of the Glorious Revolution: James II

In Godfrey Kneller's portrait of James II (r. 1685–1688), the king's stance and facial expression suggest his forceful, arrogant personality. James's arbitrary measures and Catholic sympathies prompted rebellions in England and America, and cost him the throne. National Portrait Gallery, London.

sive and inflexible ruler. During the reign of Oliver Cromwell, James had grown up in exile in France, and he admired its authoritarian king, Louis XIV. Believing that monarchs had a "divine-right" to rule, James instructed the Lords of Trade to subject the American colonies to strict royal control. In 1686, the Lords revoked the corporate charters of Connecticut and Rhode Island and merged them with the Massachusetts Bay and Plymouth colonies to form a new royal province, the Dominion of New England. As governor of the Dominion, James II appointed Sir Edmund Andros, a former governor of New York. Two years later, James II added New York and New Jersey to the Dominion, creating a vast colony that stretched from Maine to the Delaware River (Map 3.1).

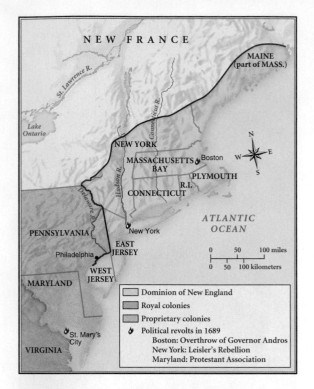

MAP 3.1 The Dominion of New England, 1686–1689

In the Dominion, James II created a vast royal colony that stretched nearly 500 miles along the Atlantic coast. During the Glorious Revolution in England, politicians and ministers in Boston and New York City led revolts that ousted Dominion officials and repudiated their authority. King William and Queen Mary replaced the Dominion with governments that balanced the power held by imperial authorities and local political institutions.

The king's administrative innovations in the Dominion went far beyond mercantilism, which primarily regulated trade. The Dominion extended to America the oppressive model of colonial rule the English government had imposed on Catholic Ireland. When England had retaken control of New York from the Dutch in 1674, James II refused to allow an elective assembly and ruled by decree. Now he imposed absolutist rule on the entire Dominion by ordering Governor Andros to abolish the existing legislative assemblies. In Massachusetts, Andros immediately banned town meetings, angering villagers who prized local self-rule. He also advocated public worship in the Church of England, offending Puritan Congregationalists. Even worse from the colonists' perspective, the governor challenged all land titles granted under the original Massachusetts Bay charter. Andros offered to provide new deeds, but only if the colonists would agree to pay an annual fee.

The Glorious Revolution in England and America

Fortunately for the colonists, James II angered English political leaders as much as Andros alienated the American settlers. The king revoked the charters of many English towns, rejected the advice of Parliament, and aroused popular opposition by openly practicing Roman Catholicism. Then, in 1688, James's Spanish Catholic wife gave birth to a son, raising the prospect of a Catholic heir to the throne. To forestall that outcome, Protestant bishops and parliamentary leaders in the Whig Party led a quick and bloodless coup known as the Glorious Revolution. Buoyed by strong popular sentiment and the support of military leaders, they forced James into exile and in 1689 enthroned Mary, his Protestant daughter by his first wife, and her Dutch Protestant husband, William of Orange. The Whigs did not advocate democracy: They wanted political power, especially the power to levy taxes, in the hands of the gentry, merchants, and other substantial property owners. By forcing King William and Queen Mary to accept the Declaration of Rights in 1689, Whig politicians created a constitutional monarchy that enhanced the powers of the House of Commons at the expense of the crown.

To justify their coup, the members of Parliament relied on political philosopher John Locke. In his *Two Treatises on Government* (1690), Locke rejected the divine-right theory of monarchical rule advocated by James II; instead, he argued that the legitimacy of government rests on the consent of the governed, and that individuals have inalienable natural rights to life, liberty, and property. Locke's celebration of individual rights and representative government had a lasting influence in America, where many political leaders wanted to expand the powers of the colonial assemblies.

Uprisings in Massachusetts and Maryland. More immediately, the Glorious Revolution sparked rebellions by Protestant colonists in Massachusetts, Maryland, and New York. When the news of the coup reached Boston in April 1689, Puritan leaders, supported by two thousand militiamen, seized Governor Andros, accused him of Catholic sympathies, and shipped him back to England. Heeding American complaints of authoritarian rule, the new monarchs broke up the Dominion of New England. However, they refused to restore the old Puritan-dominated government of Massachusetts Bay; instead, in 1692, they created a new royal colony (which included Plymouth and Maine). The new colony's charter empowered the king to appoint the governor and customs officials; it also gave the vote to all male property owners, not just Puritan church members; and it eliminated Puritan restrictions on the Church of England.

The uprising in Maryland had economic as well as religious causes. Since 1660, falling tobacco prices had hurt smallholders, tenant farmers, and former indentured servants. These economically vulnerable people were overwhelmingly Protestants, and they resented the rising taxes and the high fees imposed by wealthy proprietary officials, who were primarily Catholics. When Parliament ousted James II, a Protestant association mustered seven hundred men and forcibly removed the Catholic governor. The Lords of Trade supported this Protestant initiative: It suspended Lord Baltimore's proprietorship, imposed royal government, and made the Church of England the legal religion in the colony. This arrangement lasted until 1715, when Benedict Calvert, the fourth Lord Baltimore, converted to the Anglican faith, and the king restored the proprietorship to the Calvert family.

Jacob Leisler's Rebellion. In New York, Jacob Leisler led the rebellion against the Dominion of New England. Leisler was a German soldier who had worked for the Dutch West India Company, become a merchant, and married into a prominent Dutch family in New York. He was also a militant Calvinist, rigid and hot tempered. When New England settlers on Long Island, angered by James's prohibition of representative institutions, learned of the king's ouster, they repudiated the Dominion. The rebels quickly won the support of Dutch Protestant artisans in New York City, who welcomed

A Prosperous Dutch Farmstead

Dutch farmers in the Hudson River Valley prospered because of their easy access to market and their exploitation of black slaves, which they owned in much greater numbers than did their English neighbors. To record his good fortune, Martin Van Bergen of Leeds, New York, had this mural painted over his mantelpiece. New York State Historical Association, Cooperstown.

the succession of Queen Mary and her Dutch husband. Led by Leisler, the Dutch militia ousted Lieutenant Governor Nicholson, an Andros appointee and an alleged Catholic sympathizer.

Initially, all classes and ethnic groups rallied behind Leisler, who headed the new government. However, Leisler's denunciations of political rivals as "popish dogs" and "Roages, Rascalls, and Devills" soon alienated many English-speaking New Yorkers. When Leisler imprisoned forty of his political opponents, imposed new taxes, and championed the artisans' cause, the prominent Dutch merchants who had traditionally controlled the city's government condemned his rule. In 1691, the merchants found an ally in Colonel Henry Sloughter, the new English governor, who had Leisler indicted for treason. Convicted by an English jury, Leisler was hanged and then decapitated, an act of ethnic vengeance that offended Dutch residents and corrupted New York politics for a generation.

The Glorious Revolution of 1688–1689 led to a new political era in both England and America. In England, William and Mary ruled as constitutional monarchs and promoted an empire based on commerce. Equally important, because the new monarchs wanted colonial support for a war against Catholic France, they accepted the overthrow of the authoritarian Dominion of New England and allowed the restoration of self-government in Massachusetts and New York. Parliament created the Board of Trade in 1696 to supervise the American settlements, but it had limited success. Settlers and proprietors resisted the board's attempt to install royal governments in every colony, as did many English political leaders, who feared an increase in monarchical power. The result was another period of lax administration. The home government cut the high duties on West Indian sugar instituted by James II and imposed only a few laws and taxes on the mainland settlements. It allowed local merchants and landowners to run the American colonies and encouraged enterprising English merchants and financiers to develop them as sources of trade.

Imperial Wars and Native Peoples

In a world of nations competing for commerce, the growth of wealth in Britain depended on both mercantile skills and military power. Between 1689 and 1815, Britain fought a series of increasingly intense wars with France (Table 3.3). To win a dominant position in Western Europe and the Caribbean, government leaders in Britain created a powerful central state that spent three-quarters of its revenue on military and naval expenses. As the wars spread to the North American mainland, they involved growing numbers of colonists and Native American warriors, now armed with European guns. Indeed, many Indian peoples understood European goals and diplomacy well enough to turn the fighting to their own advantage.

Mayhem in Florida and the Carolinas. The first significant battles in North America occurred during the War of the Spanish Succession (1702–1713), which pitted Britain against France and Spain. To secure their foothold in the Carolinas, English settlers attacked Spanish Florida. The Carolinians armed the Creeks, whose fifteen thousand members

TABLE 3.3	English Wars, 1650–1750		
War	**Date**	**Purpose**	**Result**
Anglo-Dutch	1652–1654	Commercial markets	Stalemate
Anglo-Dutch	1664	Markets-Conquest	England takes New Amsterdam
Anglo-Dutch	1673	Commercial markets	England makes maritime gains
King William's	1689–1697	Maintain European balance of power	Stalemate in North America
Queen Anne's	1702–1713	Maintain European balance of power	British get Hudson Bay and Nova Scotia
Jenkins's Ear	1739–1741	Expand markets in Spanish America	English merchants expand influence
King George's	1740–1748	Maintain European balance of power	Capture and return of Louisbourg

farmed the fertile lands along the present-day border of Georgia and Alabama. A joint English-Creek expedition burned the Spanish town of St. Augustine but failed to capture the nearby fort. Fearing that future Carolinian-backed Indian raids would endanger Florida and pose a threat to Havana in nearby Cuba, the Spanish reinforced St. Augustine and unsuccessfully attacked Charleston (South Carolina).

The Creeks had their own agenda: They wanted to be the dominant tribe in the region. That meant defeating their longtime enemies, the pro-French Choctaws to the west and the Spanish-allied Apalachees to the south. Beginning in 1704, a force of Creek and Yamasee warriors destroyed the remaining Franciscan missions in northern Florida, attacked the Spanish settlement at Pensacola, and captured 1,000 Apalachees, whom they sold to South Carolinian slave traders for sale in the West Indies. Simultaneously, a Carolina-supplied Creek expedition attacked the Iroquois-speaking Tuscarora people of North Carolina, killing hundreds, executing 160 male captives, and sending 400 women and children into slavery. The surviving Tuscaroras migrated to the north and joined the Iroquois in New York (now the Six Iroquois Nations). The Carolinians, having used Indian guns against the Spaniards and their native allies, now died by them. When English traders demanded the payment of trade debts in 1715, the Creeks and Yamasees revolted. They killed 400 colonists before being overwhelmed by the Carolinians and their new allies, the Cherokees.

Native Americans also figured significantly in the warfare between French Catholics in Canada and English Protestants in New England. With French aid, Catholic Mohawk and Abenaki warriors took revenge on their Puritan enemies. They destroyed English settlements in Maine, and in 1704 attacked the western Massachusetts town of Deerfield, where they killed 48 residents and carried 112 into captivity. In response, New England militia attacked French settlements and, in 1710, joined with British naval forces to seize Port Royal in French Acadia (Nova Scotia). However, a major British-New England expedition against the French stronghold at Quebec failed miserably.

The Iroquois' Policy of Peace. The New York frontier remained quiet. French and English merchants did not want to disrupt the lucrative fur trade, and the Iroquois, tired of war, had adopted a policy of "aggressive neutrality." In 1701, the Iroquois concluded a peace treaty with France and its Indian allies. Simultaneously, they renewed the Covenant Chain, a series of military alliances with the English government in New York and various Indian peoples (see Chapter 2). For the next half-century, the Iroquois exploited their strategic location between the English and the French colonies by trading with both but refusing to fight for either one. The Delaware leader Teedyuscung urged an alliance with the Iroquois by showing his people a pictorial message: "You see a Square in the Middle, meaning the Lands of the Indians; and at one End, the Figure of a Man, indicating the English; and at the other End, another, meaning the French. Let us join together to defend our land against both."

Despite the military stalemate in the colonies, Britain won major territorial and commercial concessions through its victories in Europe. In the Treaty of Utrecht (1713), Britain obtained Newfoundland, Acadia, and the Hudson Bay region of northern Canada from France, as well as access through Albany to the western Indian trade. From Spain, Britain acquired the strategic fortress of Gibraltar at the entrance to the Mediterranean and a thirty-year contract to supply slaves to Spanish America. These gains solidified Britain's commercial supremacy, preserved the Protestant monarchy instituted in 1689, and brought peace to eastern North America for a generation (Map 3.2).

➤ What was the role of the colonies in the British mercantilist system?

➤ Explain the causes and the results of the Glorious Revolutions in England and America.

➤ How did Native Americans attempt to turn European rivalries to their advantage? How successful were they?

The Imperial Slave Economy

Britain's increasing interest in American affairs reflected the growth of a new agricultural and commercial order — the South Atlantic System — which produced sugar, tobacco, rice, and other subtropical products for a growing international market. At the center of this economy stood plantation societies ruled by powerful European planter-merchants and worked by hundreds of thousands of enslaved Africans. Indeed, by 1650, Africans

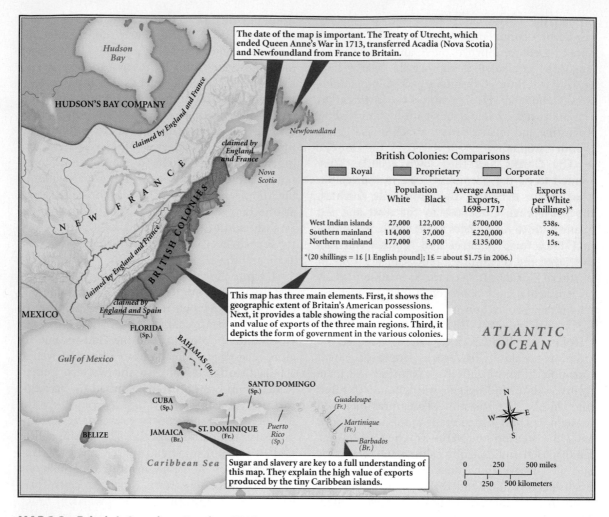

The date of the map is important. The Treaty of Utrecht, which ended Queen Anne's War in 1713, transferred Acadia (Nova Scotia) and Newfoundland from France to Britain.

British Colonies: Comparisons

Royal   Proprietary   Corporate

	Population White	Black	Average Annual Exports, 1698–1717	Exports per White (shillings)*
West Indian islands	27,000	122,000	£700,000	538s.
Southern mainland	114,000	37,000	£220,000	39s.
Northern mainland	177,000	3,000	£135,000	15s.

*(20 shillings = 1£ [1 English pound]; 1£ = about $1.75 in 2006.)

This map has three main elements. First, it shows the geographic extent of Britain's American possessions. Next, it provides a table showing the racial composition and value of exports of the three main regions. Third, it depicts the form of government in the various colonies.

Sugar and slavery are key to a full understanding of this map. They explain the high value of exports produced by the tiny Caribbean islands.

MAP 3.2   Britain's American Empire, 1713

Many of Britain's possessions in the West Indies were tiny islands, mere dots on the Caribbean Sea. However, in 1713, these small pieces of land were by far the most valuable parts of the empire. Their sugar crops brought wealth to English merchants, commerce to the northern colonies, and a brutal life and early death to hundreds of thousands of African workers.

formed the majority of transatlantic migrants to the Western Hemisphere (Table 3.4).

The South Atlantic System

The South Atlantic System had its center in Brazil and the West Indies, and sugar was its primary product. Before 1500, people in most lands had few sweeteners—mostly honey and fruit juices. Then Portuguese planters developed sugar plantations in the Atlantic islands off the African coast and, after 1550, in Brazil. As the cultivation of sugarcane spread, first Europeans and then other peoples developed a craving for the potent new sweetener. By 1900, sugar would account for an astonishing 20 percent of the calories consumed by the world's people.

European merchants, investors, and planters ran the South Atlantic System. Following mercantilist principles, they provided the organizational skill, ships, and money needed to grow and process sugarcane, carry the partially refined sugar to Europe, and supply the plantations with tools and equipment. To provide labor for the sugar plantations, the merchants imported slaves from Africa. Between 1520 and 1650, Portuguese traders transported 95 percent of the 820,000 Africans carried across the Atlantic—about 4,000 slaves a year before 1600 and 10,000 annually thereafter. Over the next half century, the Dutch dominated the Atlantic slave trade; between 1700 and 1800, the British became the prime carriers, transporting about half of the 6.1 million Africans

TABLE 3.4	African Slaves Imported to the Americas, 1520–1810

Destination	Number of Africans Arriving
South America	
Brazil	3,650,000
Dutch America	500,000
West Indies	
British	1,660,000
French	1,660,000
Central America (Spanish)	1,500,000
North America (British)	500,000
Europe	175,000
Total	**9,645,000**

tenants or overseers for wealthy planters, hundreds of English farmers looked elsewhere for cheap land. Many migrated to the new mainland colony of Carolina; many others to the large island of Jamaica, which England had seized from Spain in 1655. English sugar merchants and landowners invested heavily in Jamaica, which by 1750 would become the wealthiest British colony. That year, Jamaica had seven hundred large sugar plantations worked by more than 105,000 slaves.

Sugar was a rich man's crop because it could be produced most efficiently on large plantations. Scores of workers planted and cut the sugarcane, which was then processed by expensive equipment — crushing mills, boiling houses, distilling equipment — into raw sugar, molasses, and rum. Affluent planter-merchants controlled the sugar industry and drew annual profits of more than 10 percent on their investment. As Scottish economist Adam Smith noted in his famous treatise *The Wealth of Nations* (1776), sugar was the most profitable crop in Europe and America.

sent to the Americas. To secure this vast number of workers, European merchants relied on African-run slave-catching systems. These systems extended far into the interior and funneled captives to the slave ports of Elmina on the Gold Coast, Whydah in the Bight (bay) of Benin, Bonny and Calabar in the Bight of Biafra, and, farther south, the ports of Loango, Cabinda, and Luanda (see Map 3.3).

The West Indies Turn to Sugar. The cultivation of sugar — and, after 1750, coffee — drove the slave trade. In the 1620s, the English colonized a number of small West Indian islands: St. Christopher, Nevis, Montserrat, and especially Barbados, which had an extensive amount of arable land. Until the 1650s, the colonists were primarily English, smallholders along with a few planters and their indentured servants, who exported tobacco and livestock hides. Actually, there were more English residents in the West Indies (some 44,000) than in the Chesapeake (12,000) and New England (23,000) colonies combined.

It was sugar that dramatically transformed these islands into slave-based plantation societies. Eager for a source of raw sugar for refineries in Amsterdam, Dutch merchants provided ambitious English planters with money to buy land, with sugar-processing equipment, and with slaves. By 1680, enslaved Africans made up a majority of the population of Barbados, and the majority of them were owned by the 175 planters who now dominated the island's economy. Unwilling to work as

The Impact of Sugar on Europe. In fact, the South Atlantic System brought wealth to the entire British — and European — economy. Most of the owners of British West Indian plantations were absentee landlords: They lived in England, where they spent their profits and formed a powerful "sugar lobby." Moreover, the Navigation Acts required that sugar from the British islands be sold to British consumers or exported by British merchants to foreign markets. By 1750, British reshipments of American sugar and tobacco to Europe accounted for half of all the nation's exports. Substantial profits also flowed into Britain from the slave trade. The Royal African Company and other English traders sold slaves in the West Indies for three to five times what they paid for them in Africa. In addition, the value of the guns, iron, rum, cloth, and other European products exchanged for slaves amounted only to about one-tenth (in the 1680s) to one-third (by the 1780s) of the value of the goods those slaves subsequently produced in America.

These massive profits drove the expansion of the slave trade. At the height of the trade, in the 1790s, Britain was exporting 300,000 guns annually to Africa, to exchange for captives and equip slave raiders, and a British ship carrying 300 to 350 slaves left an African port every other day. The trade to Africa and America stimulated British shipbuilding and manufacturing. English shipyards built hundreds of vessels, and thousands of English and Scottish men and women worked in trade-related industries: building port facilities and warehouses,

A Sugar Mill in the French West Indies, 1655

Making sugar required hard labor and considerable expertise. Field slaves did the hard work, cutting the sugarcane and carrying or carting it to the oxen- (or wind-) powered mill, where it was pressed to yield the juice. Then skilled slave artisans took over. They carefully heated the juice and, at the proper moment, added ingredients that granulated the sugar and separated it from the molasses, which was later distilled into rum. The Granger Collection, New York.

refining sugar and tobacco, distilling rum from molasses (a by-product of sugar), and manufacturing textiles and iron products for the growing markets in Africa and America. Moreover, commercial expansion provided Britain with a supply of experienced sailors and helped the Royal Navy become the most powerful fleet in Europe.

Africa, Africans, and the Slave Trade

The South Atlantic system increased prosperity in Europe, but it did so at enormous economic, political, and human cost to West and West-Central Africa. Between 1550 and 1870, the Atlantic slave trade uprooted almost 11 million Africans, draining the lands south of the Sahara Desert of people and wealth. Equally important, the slave trade changed the nature of West African society. By directing commerce away from the savannas and diminishing cultural contact with the Islamic world across the Sahara, the Atlantic slave trade diminished the vitality of many interior states and peoples. Simultaneously, it prompted the growth of militaristic centralized states in the coastal areas, and the use of imported European goods throughout the continent (Map 3.3).

Slavery in Africa. Warfare and slaving had been an integral part of African life for centuries, in part because of conflicts among numerous states and ethnic groups. As the demand for sugar increased the demand for slaves (and the price Europeans would pay for them), slaving wars increased dramatically in scale. Indeed, they became a favorite

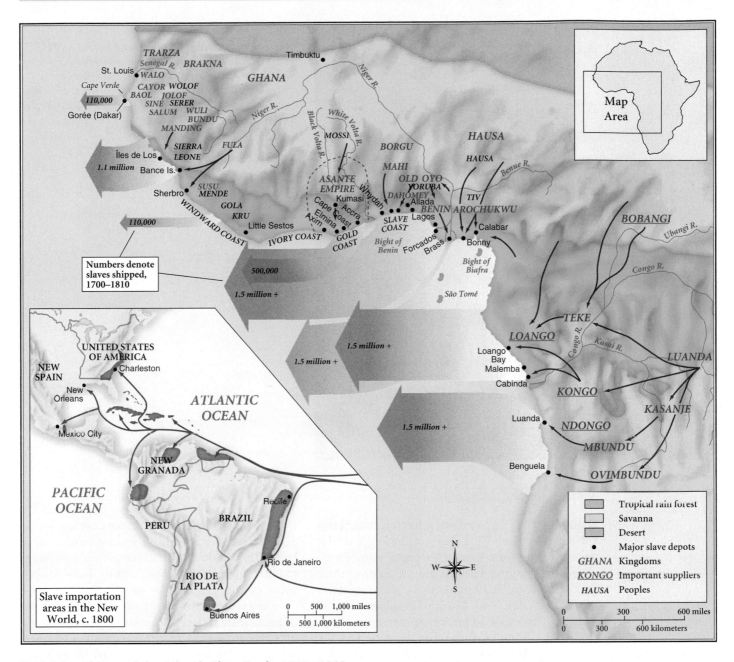

MAP 3.3 Africa and the Atlantic Slave Trade, 1700–1810

The tropical rain forest of West Africa was home to scores of peoples and dozens of kingdoms. Some kingdoms became aggressive slavers. Dahomey's army, for example, seized tens of thousands of captives in wars with neighboring peoples and sold them to European traders. About 15 percent of the captives died during the grueling Middle Passage, the transatlantic voyage between Africa and the Americas. Most of the survivors labored on sugar plantations in Brazil and the British and French West Indies (see Table 3.4).

tactic of ambitious kings and plundering warlords. "Whenever the King of Barsally wants Goods or Brandy," an observer noted, "the King goes and ransacks some of his enemies' towns, seizing the people and selling them." Supplying the Atlantic trade became a way of life in Dahomey, where the royal house made the sale of slaves a state monopoly and used European guns to establish a military despotism. Dahomey's army, which included a contingent of five thousand women, systematically raided the interior for captives; between 1680 and 1730, these raids accounted for many of the twenty

A View of the Middle Passage
This 1846 watercolor shows the cargo hold of a slave ship on a voyage to Brazil, which imported large numbers of Africans until the 1860s. Painted by a ship's officer, the picture minimizes the brutality of the Middle Passage — none of the slaves are in chains — and captures the Africans' humanity and dignity. Bridgeman Art Library.

thousand slaves exported annually from Allada and Whydah. In the 1720s, the Asante kings in the forests of the Gold Coast also began using European firearms and slave trading to expand their political dominion. Conquering neighboring states along the coast and Muslim kingdoms in the savanna, they created a prosperous empire of 3 million to 5 million people. Yet participation in the European slave trade remained a choice for Africans, not a necessity. For over a century, the powerful kingdom of Benin, famous for its cast bronzes and carved ivory, kept its many male slaves for labor at home and, for a time, prohibited the export of all slaves, male and female.

The trade in humans produced untold misery. Hundreds of thousands of young Africans died, and millions more were condemned to the brutal life of slaves in the Americas. In many African societies, class divisions hardened as people of noble birth enslaved and sold those of lesser status. Gender relations shifted as well. Men constituted two-thirds of the slaves sent across the Atlantic because European planters paid more for "men and stout men boys," and because African slave traders sold

women captives in local or Saharan slave markets as agricultural workers, house servants, and concubines. The resulting imbalance between the sexes changed the nature of marriage in many African societies, encouraging men to take several wives.

The expansion of the Atlantic trade went hand in hand with an intensification of the commerce in slaves in Africa. At the height of his power, Sultan Mawlay Ismail of Morocco (r. 1672–1727) owned 150,000 black slaves, obtained by trade in Timbuktu and by force in Senegal. In Africa, as in the Americas, slavery was eroding the dignity of human life.

From Captive to Worker. Those Africans sold into the South Atlantic system had the bleakest fate. Torn from their villages, they were marched in chains to Elmina and other coastal ports. From there they made the perilous **Middle Passage** to the New World in hideously overcrowded ships. The captives had little to eat and drink, and some would die from dehydration. The feces, urine, and vomit prompted dangerous outbreaks of dysentery, which took more lives. "I was so overcome by the heat, stench, and foul air that I nearly fainted," reported a European doctor who ventured below deck. Some slaves jumped overboard, choosing to drown rather than endure more suffering (see Voices from Abroad, "Olaudah Equiano: The Brutal 'Middle Passage,'" p. 84). Believing that "they would be made into oil and eaten," many Africans staged violent revolts. Slaves attacked their captors on no fewer than two thousand voyages, roughly one of every ten Atlantic passages. Nearly 100,000 slaves died in these uprisings, and more than a million others—about 15 percent of those transported—died of sickness on the monthlong journey. Most died of dysentery or scurvy; others died of measles, yellow fever, and smallpox, which survivors often carried to American port cities and plantations.

For those who lived through the Middle Passage, things only got worse. Life on the sugar plantations of northwestern Brazil and the West Indies was a lesson in systematic violence and relentless exploitation. The slaves worked ten hours a day under the hot semitropical sun; slept in flimsy huts; and lived on a starchy diet of corn, yams, and dried fish. And they were subject to brutal discipline: "The fear of punishment is the principle [we use] . . . to keep them in awe and order," one planter declared. With sugar prices high and the cost of slaves low, many planters simply worked their slaves to death and then bought more. Between 1708 and 1735, British planters imported about 85,000 Africans into Barbados, but the island's black population increased by only 4,000 (from 42,000 to 46,000) during that period. The constant influx of new slaves kept the black population thoroughly "African" in its languages, religions, and culture. "Here," wrote a Jamaican observer, "each different nation of Africa meet and dance after the manner of their own country . . . [and] retain most of their native customs."

Slavery in the Chesapeake and South Carolina

Following Bacon's Rebellion, planters in Virginia and Maryland took advantage of the increased British trade in African slaves (see Chapter 2). In a "tobacco revolution," they created a new plantation regime based on African slavery rather than English indentured servitude. By 1720, Africans made up nearly 20 percent of the Chesapeake population, and slavery had become a central feature of the society, not just one of several forms of unfree labor. Equally important, slavery was now defined in racial terms. Virginia passed a law in 1692 that

Olaudah Equiano

This 1780 portrait by an unknown artist in England shows the freed slave and author Olaudah Equiano. Equiano was among the first individuals of African descent to develop a consciousness of African identity that transcended traditional ethnic and national boundaries. Royal Albert Memorial Museum, Exeter, England.

prohibited sexual intercourse between English and Africans; and a 1705 statute defined virtually all resident Africans as slaves: "All servants imported or brought into this country by sea or land who were not Christians in their native country shall be accounted and be slaves."

Conditions for slaves in Virginia and Maryland were much less severe than they were in the West Indies, and slaves lived relatively long lives. Sugar required strenuous labor during the planting and harvesting seasons, whereas tobacco cultivation required steady but undemanding labor. Slaves planted the young tobacco seedlings in the spring, hoed and weeded the crop during the summer, and in the fall picked and hung the leaves to cure over the winter. Moreover, diseases did not spread easily among slaves in the Chesapeake colonies, where plantation quarters were smaller and less crowded than those in the West Indies. In addition, because tobacco profits were low, planters could not always afford to buy new slaves and so treated those they had less harshly than West Indian planters did.

Olaudah Equiano

The Brutal "Middle Passage"

Olaudah Equiano, known also as Gustavus Vassa, claimed to have been born in Igboland (in present-day southern Nigeria). But two scholars, one African and one Euro-American, writing independently, have recently argued that Equiano was not born in Africa. One of them has discovered strong evidence that he was born into slavery in South Carolina and suggests that he drew on conversations with African-born slaves to create a fictitious history of an idyllic childhood in West Africa, his kidnapping and enslavement at the age of eleven, and a traumatic passage across the Atlantic. It now appears that Equiano worked as a plantation slave as a young boy and was then was purchased by an English sea captain. Equiano bought his freedom in 1766, settled in London, became an antislavery activist, and, in 1789, published the memoir containing these selections.

My father, besides many slaves, had a numerous family of which seven lived to grow up, including myself and a sister who was the only daughter. . . . I was trained up from my earliest years in the art of war, my daily exercise was shooting and throwing javelins, and my mother adorned me with emblems after the manner of our greatest warriors. One day, when all our people were gone out to their works as usual and only I and my dear sister were left to mind the house, two men and a woman got over our walls, and in a moment seized us both, and without giving us time to cry out or make resistance they stopped our mouths and ran off with us into the nearest wood. . . .

At length, after many days' travelling, during which I had often changed masters, I got into the hands of a chieftain in a very pleasant country. This man had two wives and some children, and they all used me extremely well and did all they could to comfort me, particularly the first wife, who was something like my mother. Although I was a great many days' journey from my father's house, yet these people spoke exactly the same language with us. This first master of mine, as I may call him, was a [blacksmith], and my principal employment was working his bellows.

I was again sold and carried through a number of places till . . . at the end of six or seven months after I had been kidnapped I arrived at the sea coast.

The first object which saluted my eyes when I arrived on the coast was the sea, and a slave ship which was then riding at anchor and waiting for its cargo. I now saw myself deprived of all chance of returning to my native country . . . ; and I even wished for my former slavery in preference to my present situation, which was filled with horrors of every kind. . . . I was soon put down under the decks, and there I received such a salutation in my nostrils as I had never experienced in my life; so that with the loathsomeness of the stench and crying together, I became so sick and low that I was not able to eat, nor had I the least desire to taste any thing. I now wished for the last friend, death, to relieve me; but soon, to my grief, two of the white men offered me eatables, and on my refusing to eat, one of them held me fast by the hands and laid me across I think the windlass, and tied my feet while the other flogged me severely. I had never experienced anything of this kind before, and although, not being used to the water, I naturally feared that element the first time I saw it, yet nevertheless could I have got over the nettings, I would have jumped over the side, but I could not. . . . One day, when we had a smooth sea and moderate wind, two of my wearied countrymen who were chained together (I was near them at the time), preferring death to such a life of misery, somehow made it through the nettings and jumped into the sea.

At last we came in sight of the island of Barbados; the white people got some old slaves from the land to pacify us. They told us we were not to be eaten but to work, and were soon to go on land where we should see many of our country people. This report eased us much; and sure enough soon after we were landed there came to us Africans of all languages.

SOURCE: *The Interesting Narrative of the Life of Olaudah Equiano, or Gustavus Vassa, the African, Written by Himself* (London, 1789), 15, 22–23, 28–29.

ANALYZING THE EVIDENCE

➤ In what ways is Equiano's description of slavery in Africa consistent with the analysis in the text?

➤ What evidence does Equiano offer in his description of the Middle Passage that explains the average slave mortality rate of about 15 percent during the Atlantic crossing?

➤ Assuming that the scholars are correct, that Equiano was not born in Africa, why do you think he wrote this fictious narrative of his childhood instead of describing the facts of his own life in slavery?

In fact, some tobacco planters consciously increased their workforce by buying female slaves and encouraging them to have children. In 1720, women made up one-third of Africans in Maryland, and the black population had begun to increase naturally. One absentee owner instructed his plantation agent "to be kind and indulgent to the breeding wenches, and not to force them when with child upon any service or hardship that will be injurious to them." Moreover, he added, "the children are to be well looked after." By midcentury, slaves made up almost a third of the Chesapeake population, and more than three-quarters of them were American born.

Slaves in South Carolina labored under much more oppressive conditions. The colony grew slowly until 1700, when Africans from rice-growing societies, who knew how to plant and process the nutritious grain, turned it into a profitable export. To expand production, white planters imported thousands of slaves and changed the face of the colony (Figure 3.1). By 1705, there were more Africans in South Carolina than there were whites, and slaves made up 80 percent of the population in rice-growing areas.

Those areas were inland swamps, and the work was dangerous and exhausting. Slaves planted, weeded, and harvested the rice in ankle-deep mud. Pools of putrid water bred mosquitoes, which

transmitted disease among the workers, taking hundreds of African lives. Other slaves, forced to move tons of dirt to build irrigation works, died from exhaustion. "The labour required [for growing rice] is only fit for slaves," a Scottish traveler remarked, "and I think the hardest work I have seen them engaged in." In South Carolina, as in the West Indies and Brazil, there were many deaths and few births, and the importation of new slaves constantly "re-Africanized" the black population.

The Emergence of an African American Community

Slaves came from many different states and peoples in West Africa and the West-Central African regions of Kongo and Angola (Table 3.5). Plantation owners in South Carolina preferred laborers from the Gold Coast and Gambia, who had a reputation as hardworking farmers. But as African sources of slaves shifted southward after 1730, more than 30 percent of the colony's workforce came from Kongo and Angola. Some white planters welcomed ethnic diversity as a deterrent to slave revolts. "The safety of the Plantations," declared a widely read English pamphlet, "depends upon having Negroes from all parts of Guiny, who do not understand each other's languages and Customs and cannot agree to Rebel." However, planters often had to take the workers offered by slave traders, whatever their region of origin. Of the slaves imported into the Upper James River region of Virginia after 1730, 41 percent embarked from ports in the Bight of Biafra (present-day Nigeria), where Kwa dialects were spoken. Another 25 percent came from West-Central Africa and were probably Kikongo- and Kimbundu-speakers. The rest hailed from the Windward and Gold coasts, Senegambia, and Sierra Leone, and spoke Mande and other regional languages.

Initially, the slaves did not think of themselves as Africans or blacks but as members of a specific family, clan, or people — Wolof, Hausa, Ibo, Yoruba, Teke, Ngola — and they associated with those who shared their language and customs. In the Upper James River region, where Ibo men and women arrived in equal numbers, they probably married other Ibos and so retained their African culture. Discoveries of spoons with incised handles, like those used by Ibo diviners, point to the persistence of traditional ways.

Over time, the slaves made friendships and married across ethnic lines, thereby transcending the cultural groups of their homeland. In the West Indies and the Carolina lowlands, the largely

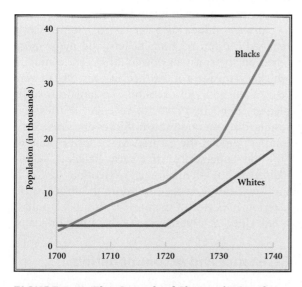

FIGURE 3.1 The Growth of Slavery in South Carolina, 1700–1740

To grow more rice, white planters in South Carolina imported thousands of enslaved Africans. By 1705, South Carolina had a black majority, which allowed the development among slaves of a strong Afro-centric language and culture.

TABLE 3.5	African Slaves Imported into North America by Region of Departure and Ethnicity, 1700–1775		
Region of Departure	**Ethnicity**	**Number**	**Percentage**
Senegambia	Mandinka, Fulbe, Serer, Jola, Wolof, Bambara	47,300	17
Sierra Leone	Vai, Mende, Kpelle, Kru	33,400	12
Gold Coast	Ashanti, Fanit	19,500	7
Bight of Benin, Bight of Biafra	Ibo, Ibibio	47,300	17
West-Central Africa	Kongo, Tio, Matamba	44,600	16
Southeast Africa	Unknown	2,800	1
Other or unknown		83,500	30
Total		**278,400**	**100**

The numbers are estimated from known voyages involving 195,000 Africans. The ethnic origins of the slaves are tentative because peoples from different regions often left from the same port and because the regions of departure of 83,500 slaves (30 percent) are not known.

SOURCE: Aaron S. Fogleman, "From Slaves, Convicts, and Servants to Free Passengers: The Transformation of Immigration in the Era of the American Revolution," *Journal of American History* 85 (June 1998), table A.4.

African-born population created new languages. One was the Gullah dialect, which combined English and African words in an African grammatical structure. "They have a language peculiar to themselves," a missionary reported, "a wild confused medley of Negro and corrupt English, which makes them very unintelligible except to those who have conversed with them for many years." In the Chesapeake region, where there were more American-born slaves, most people of African descent gradually gave up their native tongues. In the 1760s, a European visitor to Virginia reported with surprise that "all the blacks spoke very good English."

A common language—Gullah or English or French (in Louisiana and the French West Indies)—was key to the development of an African American community. A nearly equal number of men and women, which encouraged marriage, stable families, and continuity between generations, was another. In South Carolina, the high death rate among slaves undermined ties of family and kinship; but after 1725, Chesapeake-area blacks created strong nuclear families and extended kin relationships. For example, all but 30 of the 128 slaves on one of Charles Carroll's estates in Maryland were members of two extended families. These African Americans gradually developed a culture of their own, passing on family names, traditions, and knowledge to the next generation. As one observer suggested, blacks had created their own cultural world, "a Nation within a Nation."

As the slaves forged a new identity, they carried on certain African practices but let others go. Many Africans arrived in the colonies with ritualistic scars that white planters called "country markings"; this sign of ethnic identity fell into disuse on the culturally diverse plantations. But the slaves' African heritage took many other tangible forms: in their hairstyles; in the traditional motifs they used in wood carvings and pottery; in the large wooden mortars and pestles with which they hulled rice; and in the design of their houses, in which rooms often were arranged from front to back in a distinctive "I" pattern, not side by side as was common in English dwellings.

African values also persisted. Some slaves retained Muslim religious beliefs, and many more relied on the spiritual powers of obeah, conjurers who knew the ways of the African gods. Obeah were "consulted upon all occasions," a Jamaican sugar planter noted in 1774, "to revenge injuries and insults, discover and punish thieves and adulterers; [and] to predict the future." Many slaves clung to "the old Superstition of a false Religion," complained an English missionary in Georgia (see Reading American Pictures, "Jumping the Broomstick: Viewing an African Ceremony in South Carolina," p. 88). Until the 1790s, few slaves became Christians.

Resistance and Accommodation

There were drastic limits on African American creativity. Most slaves were denied education. They accumulated few material goods and had little opportunity to weave cloth or decorate pottery with traditional African designs. A well-traveled European who visited a slave hut in Virginia in the late eighteenth century found it "more miserable than

Hulling Rice in West Africa and Georgia

An eighteenth-century engraving depicts West African women using huge wooden mortars and pestles to strip the tough outer hull from rice kernels. A century and a half later, African American women in Georgia used the same tools to prepare rice for their families.

Library of Congress/Georgia Department of Archives and History, Atlanta.

the most miserable of the cottages of our peasants. The husband and wife sleep on a mean pallet, the children on the ground; a very bad fireplace, some utensils for cooking. . . . They work all week, not having a single day for themselves except for holidays."

Slaves who resisted did so at their peril. Planters resorted to the lash to punish slaves who refused to work; and some would amputate slaves' fingers, toes, or ears. Declaring the chronic runaway Ballazore an "incorrigeble rogue," a Virginia planter ordered all his toes cut off: "Nothing less than dismembering will reclaim him." Thomas Jefferson, who witnessed this cruelty on his father's Virginia plantation, noted that each generation of whites was "nursed, educated, and daily exercised in tyranny": The relationship "between master and slave is a perpetual exercise of the most unremitting despotism on the one part, and degrading submission on the other." A fellow Virginian, planter George Mason, agreed: "Every Master is born a petty tyrant."

The extent of white violence depended on the size and density of the slave population. As Virginia planter William Byrd II complained in 1736, "Numbers make them insolent." In the rural areas of the northern colonies, where there were few

slaves, physical violence was sporadic. But assertive black slaves on the sugar and rice plantations in the West Indies and South Carolina were routinely whipped. Because Africans outnumbered Europeans eight to one in these plantation areas, planters prohibited slaves from leaving the plantation without special passes. They also forced their poor white neighbors to patrol the countryside at night, a duty that (authorities regularly reported) was "almost totally neglected."

Slaves dealt with their plight in several ways. Some newly arrived Africans fled to the frontier, where they established traditional villages or married into Indian tribes. Blacks who were fluent in English fled to towns, where they tried to pass as free men and women. Most African Americans remained enslaved and bargained continually with their masters over the terms of their bondage. Some blacks bartered extra work for better food and clothes; others seized a small privilege and dared the master to revoke it. That is how Sundays gradually became a day of rest—and a right rather than a privilege. When bargaining failed, slaves would protest silently, working slowly or stealing. Others, provoked beyond endurance, killed their owners or overseers: In the

Jumping the Broomstick: Viewing an African Ceremony

African Culture in South Carolina, c. 1800. Abby Aldrich Rockefeller Folk Art Center, Colonial Williamsburg.

African slaves carried their customs to British North America, where they created a new culture that combined the traditions of many African and European peoples. How can we better understand this cultural synthesis? Slaves left few written records; but we do have visual evidence, like this painting of a dance — possibly at a wedding ceremony — by an unknown artist.

ANALYZING THE EVIDENCE

➤ The painting is set on a rice plantation in the low country of South Carolina. What clues can you see in the image that confirm the location?

➤ Does the evidence in the picture suggest that these people are recent arrivals from Africa? What artifacts in the picture might be African in origin? What have you learned from the text about the conditions on rice plantations that would contribute to a steady stream of African-born workers on those plantations?

➤ Many African peoples mingled with one another on large plantations. Do you see any evidence in

the painting that suggests tribal differences? What suggests that the two dancers in the center — perhaps a bride and groom — come from different African peoples?

➤ Around 1860, a Virginia slave recounted the story of her parents' marriage: "Ant Lucky read sumpin from de Bible, an' den she put de broomstick down an' dey locked dey arms together an' jumped over it. Den dey was married." In the scene depicted in this painting, the man in the red breeches is holding a long stick. If this is a wedding, is there any evidence of Christianity in the ceremony? Look carefully at the men's and women's clothes. Do they reveal signs of European cultural influence?

1760s, in Amherst County, Virginia, a slave killed four whites; in Elizabeth City County, eight slaves strangled their master in bed. A few blacks even plotted rebellion, despite white superiority in guns and, in most regions, in numbers as well.

Predictably, South Carolina witnessed the largest slave uprising, the Stono Rebellion of 1739. The governor of the Spanish colony of Florida instigated the revolt by promising freedom to fugitive slaves. By February 1739, at least sixty-nine slaves had escaped to St. Augustine, and rumors circulated "that a Conspiracy was formed by Negroes in Carolina to rise and make their way out of the province." When war between England and Spain broke out in September (see p. 95), seventy-five Africans rose in revolt and killed a number of whites near the Stono River. According to one account, some of the rebels were Portuguese-speaking Catholics from the Kingdom of Kongo attracted by the prospect of life in a Catholic colony. Displaying their skills as soldiers — decades of brutal slave raiding in Kongo had militarized the society there — the rebels marched toward Florida "with Colours displayed and two Drums beating." White militia killed many of the Stono rebels, preventing a general uprising; and frightened whites imported fewer new slaves and tightened discipline on the plantations.

William Byrd and the Rise of the Southern Gentry

As the southern colonies became full-fledged slave societies, life changed not only for blacks but also for whites. Consider the career of William Byrd II (1674–1744). Byrd's father was a London goldsmith who became a successful planter-merchant in Virginia. Like many first-generation planters, the elder Byrd hoped to return to England and marry his children into landed-gentry families. To smooth his son's entry into gentry society, Byrd sent him to be educated in England when the boy was just seven. But his status-conscious classmates at the Felsted School shunned the child, calling him a "colonial." This was the young Byrd's first taste of the gradations of rank that permeated English society.

Other rejections followed. Lacking aristocratic connections, Byrd was denied a post with the Board of Trade, was passed over three times for the royal governorship of Virginia, and — the most crushing psychological blow — failed utterly in his almost desperate efforts to marry a rich Englishwoman. His Virginia estate of 43,000 acres and 200 African slaves failed to impress the father of his intended bride. In 1726, at age 52, Byrd finally gave up his father's dream and moved back to Virginia, a "lonely . . . silent country" where he sometimes felt he was "being buried alive." Accepting his lesser destiny as a member of the colony's gentry, Byrd built an elegant brick mansion on the family's estate at Westover, sat in "the best pew in the church," and won the king's appointment to the governor's council.

William Byrd II's experience mirrored that of many planter-merchants, trapped in Virginia and South Carolina by the curse of their inferior colonial status. They used their economic muscle to control white yeomen families and tenant farmers,

"Virginian Luxuries"

This painting by an unknown artist (c. 1810) depicts the physical and sexual exploitation inherent in a slave society. On the right, an owner chastises a male slave by beating him with a cane; on the left, ignoring the cultural and legal rules prohibiting sexual intercourse between whites and blacks, a white master prepares to bed his black mistress. Abby Aldrich Rockefeller Folk Art Collection, Colonial Williamsburg Foundation.

and resorted to brute strength to exploit enslaved blacks, the American equivalent of the oppressed peasants and serfs of Europe. The planters used Africans to grow food as well as tobacco; build houses, wagons, and tobacco casks; and make shoes and clothes. By making their plantations self-sufficient, the Chesapeake elite survived the depressed tobacco market between 1670 and 1720. Small-scale planters who needed to buy cloth and other goods fared less well and fell into debt.

To prevent another uprising like Bacon's Rebellion, the Chesapeake gentry addressed the concerns of middling and poor whites (see Chapter 2). They began by gradually lowering taxes on smallholders: In Virginia, the annual poll tax fell from forty-five pounds of tobacco in 1675 to just five pounds in 1750. In addition, the gentry encouraged smallholders to improve their economic lot by investing in slaves. By 1770, 60 percent of the English families in the Chesapeake colonies owned at least one slave. There was change, too, on the political front, as planters allowed poor yeomen and some tenants to vote. The strategy of the leading families—the Carters, Lees, Randolphs, and Robinsons—was to curry favor with these voters by bribing them with rum, money, and the promise of minor offices in county governments. In return, they expected the yeomen and tenants to elect them to office and defer to them. This horse trading solidified the social position of the planter elite, which used its control of the House of Burgesses to limit the power of the royal governor. Hundreds of yeomen farmers benefited as well, tasting political power and garnering substantial fees and salaries as deputy sheriffs, road surveyors, estate appraisers, and grand jurymen.

Even as wealthy Chesapeake gentlemen were allying themselves with smallholders, they were consciously setting themselves apart from their less affluent neighbors. As late as the 1720s some leading planters were boisterous, aggressive men who enjoyed the amusements of common folk—from hunting, hard drinking, and gambling on horse races to demonstrating their manly prowess by seducing female servants and slaves. As time passed, they began, like William Byrd II to model themselves on the English aristocracy. Consciously cultivating **gentility**—a refined but elaborate lifestyle—wealthy planters replaced their modest wooden houses with mansions of brick and mortar. Robert "King" Carter, for example, built a house that was seventy-five feet long, forty-four feet wide, and forty feet high; and then he filled it with fine furniture and rugs. The planters acknowledged the source of their acquired gentility, sending their sons to London to be educated as lawyers and gentlemen. But, unlike Byrd's father, they intended them to return to America, marry local heiresses, and assume their fathers' roles, managing plantations, socializing with fellow gentry, and running the political system.

Wealthy Chesapeake and South Carolina women also emulated the English elite. They read English newspapers and fashionable magazines, wore the finest English clothes, and dined in the English fashion, with an elaborate afternoon tea. To improve their daughters' marriage prospects, they hired English tutors to teach young women etiquette. Once married, gentry women deferred to their husbands, reared pious children, and maintained elaborate social networks, in time creating a new ideal—the southern gentlewoman. Using the profits generated by enslaved Africans in the South Atlantic system of commerce, wealthy planters formed an increasingly well educated, refined, and stable ruling class.

The Northern Maritime Economy

The South Atlantic system had broad geographical reach. As early as the 1640s, New England farmers supplied the sugar islands with bread, lumber, fish, and meat. As a West Indian explained, planters in the islands "had rather buy foode at very deare rates than produce it by labour, soe infinite is the profitt of sugar works." By 1700, the economies of the West Indies and New England were closely interwoven. Soon farmers and merchants in New York, New Jersey, and Pennsylvania were also shipping wheat, corn, and bread to the Caribbean sugar islands. By the 1750s, about two-thirds of New England's exports and half of those from the Middle Colonies were going to places like Jamaica and Barbados.

In fact, the South Atlantic system linked the entire British empire. In return for the sugar they sent to England, West Indian planters received credit—in the form of **bills of exchange**—from London merchants. The planters used the bills to buy slaves from Africa and to pay North American farmers and merchants for their provisions and shipping services. The American farmers and merchants then exchanged the bills for British manufactures, primarily textiles and iron goods.

The West Indian trade created the first American merchant fortunes and the first urban industries (Map 3.4). Merchants in Boston, Newport, Providence, Philadelphia, and New York invested their profits in new ships and in factories that refined raw sugar into finished loaves. They also distilled West Indian molasses into rum—more than half a million gallons in Boston alone by the 1740s.

Preserving Fish, Eighteenth-Century Style

Without refrigeration, how can fish be kept from spoiling? Salt and sun were the answers. As fish were caught, sailors quickly gutted and cleaned them. Once on shore, they cut the fish into fillets (or "flakes"), added a liberal dose of salt, and placed them on wooden racks to dry in the sun. Properly preserved and packed, the fish remained edible for months, and merchant ships carried them to consumers in the West Indies and Europe.
© Bettmann/Corbis.

Merchants in Salem, Marblehead, and other small New England ports built a major fishing industry by selling salted mackerel and cod to the sugar islands and to southern Europe. Baltimore merchants transformed their town into a major port by developing a bustling export business in wheat, while traders in Charleston shipped deerskins, indigo, and rice to European markets.

As transatlantic commerce expanded — from five hundred voyages annually in the 1680s to fifteen hundred annually in the 1730s — American port cities grew in size and complexity. Seeking jobs and excitement, British and German migrants and young people from the countryside (servant girls, male laborers, and apprentice artisans) flocked to urban areas. By 1750, the populations of Newport and Charleston were nearly 10,000; Boston had 15,000 residents; and New York had almost 18,000. The largest port was Philadelphia, whose population by 1776 had reached 30,000, the size of a large provincial city in Europe. Smaller coastal towns emerged as centers of the lumber and shipbuilding industries. Seventy sawmills dotted the Piscataqua River in New Hampshire, providing low-cost wood for homes, warehouses, and especially shipbuilding. Taking advantage of the Navigation Acts, which allowed colonists to build and own trading vessels, hundreds of shipwrights turned out ocean-going vessels, while other artisans made ropes, sails, and metal fittings for the new fleet. By the 1770s, colonial-built ships made up one-third of the British merchant fleet.

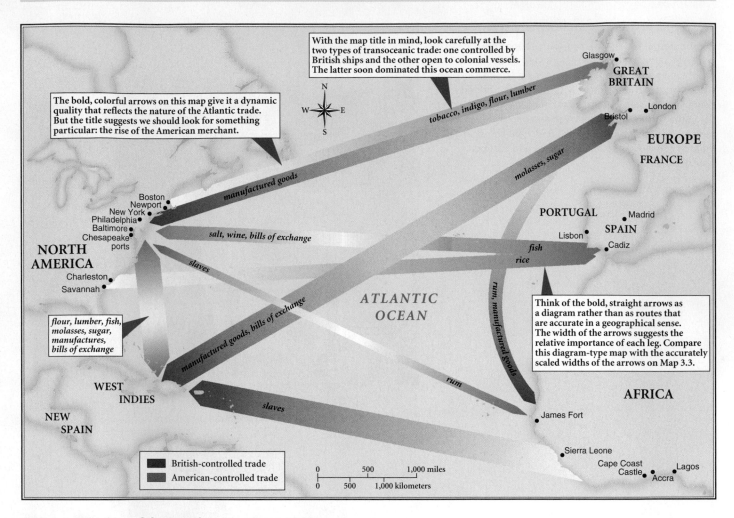

With the map title in mind, look carefully at the two types of transoceanic trade: one controlled by British ships and the other open to colonial vessels. The latter soon dominated this ocean commerce.

The bold, colorful arrows on this map give it a dynamic quality that reflects the nature of the Atlantic trade. But the title suggests we should look for something particular: the rise of the American merchant.

Think of the bold, straight arrows as a diagram rather than as routes that are accurate in a geographical sense. The width of the arrows suggests the relative importance of each leg. Compare this diagram-type map with the accurately scaled widths of the arrows on Map 3.3.

flour, lumber, fish, molasses, sugar, manufactures, bills of exchange

British-controlled trade
American-controlled trade

MAP 3.4   The Rise of the American Merchant, 1750

Throughout the colonial era, British merchant houses dominated the transatlantic trade in manufactures, sugar, tobacco, and slaves. However, by 1750, American-born merchants in Boston, New York, and Philadelphia had seized control of the commerce between the mainland and the West Indies. In addition, Newport traders played a small role in the slave trade from Africa, and Boston and Charleston merchants grew rich carrying fish and rice to southern Europe.

The South Atlantic System extended far into the interior. A fleet of small vessels sailed back and forth on the Hudson and Delaware rivers, delivering cargoes of European manufactures and picking up barrels of flour and wheat to carry to New York and Philadelphia for export to the West Indies and Europe. By the 1750s, hundreds of professional teamsters in Maryland were transporting 370,000 bushels of wheat and corn and 16,000 barrels of flour to urban markets each year — more than ten thousand wagon trips. To service this traffic, entrepreneurs and artisans set up taverns, horse stables, and barrel-making shops in towns along the wagon roads. Lancaster, a prosperous wheat-producing town in Pennsylvania, for example, boasted more than two hundred German and English artisans and a dozen merchants.

Prosperous merchants dominated seaport cities. In 1750, about forty merchants controlled over 50 percent of Philadelphia's trade; they had taxable assets averaging £10,000, a huge sum at the time. Like the Chesapeake gentry, these urban merchants modeled themselves after the British upper classes, importing design books from England and building Georgian-style mansions to display their wealth. Their wives created a genteel culture by decorating their houses with fine furniture and entertaining guests at elegant dinners.

Artisan and shopkeeper families, the middle ranks of seaport society, made up nearly half the population. Innkeepers, butchers, seamstresses, shoemakers, weavers, bakers, carpenters, masons, and dozens of other skilled workers formed mutual self-help societies and toiled to gain a competency — an income sufficient to maintain their families in modest comfort and dignity. Wives and husbands often worked as a team, teaching the "mysteries of the craft" to their children. Some artisans aspired to wealth and status, an entrepreneurial ethic that prompted them to hire apprentices and expand production. However, most were not well-to-do, and many were quite poor. During his working life, a tailor was lucky to accumulate £30 worth of property, far less than the £2,000 owned at death by an ordinary merchant or the £300 listed in the **probate inventory** of a successful blacksmith.

Laboring men and women formed the lowest ranks of urban society. Merchants needed hundreds of dockworkers to unload manufactured goods and molasses from inbound ships and reload them with barrels of wheat, fish, and rice. Often they filled these demanding jobs with black slaves, who constituted 10 percent of the workforce in Philadelphia and New York City; otherwise, they hired unskilled wageworkers. Poor white and black women — single, married, or widowed — eked out a living by washing clothes, spinning wool, or working as servants or prostitutes. To make ends meet, most laboring families sent their children out to work at an early age. Indispensable to the economy, yet virtually propertyless, urban laborers rented rooms in crowded tenements in back alleys. In good times, their jobs bought security for their families or as much cheap New England rum as they could drink.

Periods of stagnant commerce threatened the financial security of merchants and artisans. For laborers, seamen, and seamstresses, whose household budgets left no margin for sickness or unemployment, depressed trade meant hunger or dependence on charity from the Overseers of the Poor, and — for the most desperate — petty thievery or prostitution. The sugar- and slave-based South Atlantic system brought economic uncertainty as well as jobs and opportunities to farmers and workers in the northern colonies.

➤ Describe the major elements of the South Atlantic system. How did the system work? How did it shape the development of the various colonies?

➤ What role did Africans play in the expansion of the Atlantic slave trade? What role did Europeans play?

➤ In what colonies were enslaved Africans most successful in creating African American communities? Where were they least successful? How do you explain the differences?

The New Politics of Empire, 1713–1750

The South Atlantic system changed the politics of empire. British ministers, pleased with the commercial success of staple crops, ruled the colonies with a gentle hand. The colonists took advantage of that leniency to strengthen their political institutions and, eventually, would challenge the rules of the mercantilist system.

The Rise of Colonial Assemblies

After the Glorious Revolution of 1688–1689, representative assemblies in America followed the example of the English Whigs, limiting the powers of crown officials. In Massachusetts during the 1720s, the assembly repeatedly ignored the king's instructions to provide the royal governor with a permanent salary. Legislatures in North Carolina, New Jersey, and Pennsylvania likewise refused for several years to pay their governors a salary. Using this and other tactics, the colonial legislatures gradually took control of taxation and local appointments, which angered imperial bureaucrats and absentee proprietors. "The people in power in America," complained William Penn during a struggle with the Pennsylvania assembly, "think nothing taller than themselves but the Trees."

Leading the increasingly powerful assemblies were members of the colonial elite. Although most property-owning white men had the right to vote, only men of wealth and status stood for election. In New Jersey in 1750, 90 percent of assemblymen came from political families (Figure 3.2). In Virginia in the 1750s, seven members of the influential Lee family sat in the House of Burgesses and, along with other powerful families, dominated its major committees. In New England, affluent descendants of the original Puritans intermarried and formed a core of political leaders. "Go into every village in New England," John Adams wrote in 1765, "and you will find that the office of justice of the peace, and even the place of representative, have generally descended from generation to generation, in three or four families at most."

However, neither elitist assemblies nor wealthy property owners could impose unpopular edicts on

Percentage of New Jersey assemblymen with fathers or other relatives who had been assemblymen

FIGURE 3.2 Family Connections and Political Power, New Jersey, 1700–1776

By the 1750s, nearly every member of the New Jersey assembly came from a family with a history of political leadership, clear testimony to the emergence of an experienced governing elite in the mainland colonies.

the people. Purposeful crowd actions were a fact of colonial life. It was the uprising of ordinary citizens that overthrew the Dominion of New England in 1689. In New York, mobs closed houses of prostitution; in Salem (Massachusetts), they ran people with infectious diseases out of town. In Boston in 1710, angry crowds prevented merchants from exporting scarce grain; and in New Jersey in the 1730s and 1740s, mobs of farmers battled with proprietors who were forcing tenants off disputed lands. When officials in Boston restricted the sale of farm produce to a single public market, a crowd destroyed the building and its members defied the authorities to arrest them. "If you touch One you shall touch All," an anonymous letter warned the sheriff, "and we will show you a Hundred Men where you can show one." These expressions of popular power, combined with the growing authority of the assemblies, created a new political system. By the 1750s, colonial legislatures were broadly responsive to popular pressure and increasingly unresponsive to British control.

Salutary Neglect

British colonial policy during the reigns of George I (r. 1714–1727) and George II (r. 1727–1760) allowed the rise of American self-government. Royal bureaucrats, flush with growing tax receipts, relaxed their supervision of internal colonial affairs and focused instead on defense and trade. In 1775, British political philosopher Edmund Burke would praise this strategy as **salutary neglect**.

Salutary neglect was a by-product of the political system developed by Sir Robert Walpole, the Whig leader in the House of Commons from 1720 to 1742. By providing supporters with appointments and pensions, Walpole won parliamentary approval for his policies. However, his use of patronage weakened the imperial system by filling the Board of Trade with political hacks. When Governor Gabriel Johnson arrived in North Carolina in the 1730s, he vowed to curb the powers of the assembly and "make a mighty change in the face of affairs." Receiving little support from the Board of Trade, Johnson renounced reform and decided "to do nothing which can be reasonably blamed, and leave the rest to time, and a new set of inhabitants."

Sir Robert Walpole, the King's Minister

All eyes are on Sir Robert Walpole (left) as he offers advice to the Speaker of the House of Commons. A brilliant politician, the treasury secretary used patronage to command a majority in the Commons and won the confidence of George I and George II, the German-speaking monarchs from the duchy of Hanover. Walpole's personal motto, "Let sleeping dogs lie," helps explain his colonial policy of salutary neglect.

© National Trust Photographic Library/John Hammond.

Walpole's tactics also weakened the empire by undermining the integrity of the political system. **Radical Whigs** protested that Walpole had betrayed the Glorious Revolution by using patronage and bribery to create the strong Court (or Kingly) Party. The Country Party—its members were landed gentlemen—likewise warned that Walpole's policies of high taxes and a bloated royal bureaucracy threatened British liberties. Heeding these arguments, colonial legislators complained that royal governors abused their patronage powers. To preserve American liberty, the colonists strengthened the powers of the representative assemblies, unintentionally laying the foundation for the American independence movement (see Comparing American Voices, "The Rise of Representative Assemblies," pp. 96–97).

Protecting the Mercantile System

Apart from patronage, Walpole's American policy had as its primary goal the protection of British commercial interests. Initially, Walpole pursued a cautious foreign policy to allow Britain to recover from a generation of war (1689–1713) against Louis XIV of France. But in 1732, he provided a parliamentary subsidy for the new colony of Georgia, which was intended by its reform-minded trustees as a refuge for Britain's poor. Envisioning a society of independent family farmers, the trustees limited most land grants to five hundred acres and initially outlawed slavery.

Walpole had little interest in social reform; he wanted Georgia subsidized to protect the valuable rice-growing colony of South Carolina. Britain's expansion into Georgia, a region long claimed by Spain, outraged Spanish officials, who were already angry because British merchants were illegally selling slaves and manufactured goods in Spain's American colonies. In fact, to counter Britain's commercial expansion, Spanish naval forces had stepped up their seizure of illegal traders—and sexually mutilated an English sea captain, Robert Jenkins.

Yielding to Parliamentary pressure, Walpole declared war on Spain in 1739. The War of Jenkins's Ear (1739–1741) was a largely unsuccessful attack on Spain's empire in North America. In 1740, British regulars failed to capture St. Augustine because South Carolina whites—still shaken by the Stono Rebellion—refused to commit militia units to the expedition. A year later, a major British and American assault on the prosperous Spanish seaport of Cartagena (in present-day Colombia) failed. Instead of enriching themselves with Spanish

booty, hundreds of troops from the mainland colonies died in the attack, mostly from tropical diseases.

The War of Jenkins's Ear quickly became part of a general European conflict, the War of the Austrian Succession (1740–1748). Massive French armies battled British-subsidized German forces in Europe, and French naval forces roamed the West Indies, vainly trying to conquer a British sugar island. There was little fighting in North America until 1745, when three thousand New England militiamen, supported by a British naval squadron, captured Louisbourg, a French fortress at the entrance to the St. Lawrence River. To the dismay of New England Puritans, who feared invasion from Catholic Quebec, the Treaty of Aix-la-Chapelle (1748) returned Louisbourg to France. The treaty ensured British control over Georgia and reaffirmed its military superiority over Spain; more important, it made clear to colonial leaders that England would act in its own interests, not theirs.

The American Economic Challenge

The Walpole ministry had similar intentions about American economic activities. According to the Navigation Acts, the colonies were to produce staple crops and to consume British manufactured goods. To enforce the British monopoly on manufacturing, Parliament passed a series of additional Navigation Acts prohibiting Americans from selling colonial-made textiles (Woolen Act, 1699), hats (Hat Act, 1732), and iron products such as plows, axes, and skillets (Iron Act, 1750). As exports of tobacco, rice, and wheat grew by 400 percent between 1700 and 1750, colonists on the American mainland purchased more British textiles and iron goods.

However, the Navigation Acts had a major loophole: They allowed Americans to own ships and transport goods. Colonial merchants exploited those provisions to control 95 percent of the commerce between the mainland and the West Indies, and 75 percent of the transatlantic trade in manufactures. Quite unintentionally, the mercantilist system had created a dynamic community of colonial merchants, from which many of the early advocates for American independence would come.

Moreover, by the 1720s, the British sugar islands could not absorb all the flour, fish, and meat produced by mainland settlers. So, ignoring Britain's intense rivalry with France, colonial merchants sold their produce in the French West Indies. These supplies helped French planters produce

The Rise of Representative Assemblies

During the first six decades of the eighteenth century, the representative assemblies in British North America gradually expanded their authority and power. This development reflected greater popular respect for the assemblies, and, in turn, meant increased resistance to imperial policies. The shift in power from imperial authorities to colonial legislatures was piecemeal, the result of a series of small, seemingly inconsequential struggles. As you read this correspondence sent by two royal governors to officials back in England, look closely at the character of the disputes and think about how they were resolved.

ALEXANDER SPOTSWOOD
Confronting the House of Burgesses

As a reward for his military service in the wars against Louis XIV of France, Alexander Spotswood was made governor of Virginia in 1710. An often imperious and contentious man, Spotswood, though an effective governor, was a controversial one. He told the House of Burgesses to its face that the voters had mistakenly chosen "a set of representatives whom heaven has not generally endowed with the ordinary qualifications requisite to legislators." As the following selections show, Spotswood set out to reform the voting system that, in his judgment, produced such mediocre representatives. His efforts to oust popular members of the gentry from the House of Burgesses made him few friends; and in 1722, his enemies in Virginia used their influence in London to have him removed from office.

To ye Council of Trade, Virginia, October 15, 1712
MY LORDS:
. . . The Indians continue their Incursions in North Carolina, and the Death of Colo. Hyde, their Gov'r, which happened the beginning of last Month, increases the misery of that province, so much weakened already by their own divisions, that no measures projected by those in the Governm't for curbing the Heathen can be prosecuted.

This Unhappy State of her Maj't's Subjects in my Neighbourhood is ye more Affecting to me because I have very little hopes of being enabled to relieve them by our Assembly, which I have called to meet next Week; for the Mob of this Country, having tried their Strength in the late Election and finding themselves able to carry whom they please, have generally chosen representatives of their own Class, who as their principal Recommendation have declared their resolution to raise no Tax on the people, let the occasion be what it will. This is owing to a defect in the Constitution, which allows to every one, tho' but just out of the Condition of a Servant, and that can but purchase half an acre of Land, an equal Vote with the Man of the best Estate in the Country.

The Militia of this Colony is perfectly useless without Arms or ammunition, and by an unaccountable infatuation, no arguments I have used can prevail on these people to make their Militia more Serviceable, or to fall into any other measures for the Defence of their Country. . . .

December the 17th 1714
The Governor this day laying before the Council a letter from the Right Honorable the Lords Commissioners for Trade dated the 23d of April 1713 directing him to advise with the Council & to recommend to the Generall Assembly to pass a law for qualifying the Electors & the persons Elected Burgesses to serve in the Generall Assembly of this Colony in a more just & equal manner than the Laws now in force do direct. . . . The Council declare that they cannot advise the Governor to move for any alteration in the present method of Electing of Burgesses, some being of opinion that this is not a proper time, & others that the present manner of electing of Burgesses & the qualifications of the elected is sufficiently provided for by the Laws now in force. . . .

To Mr. Secretary James Stanhope, July 15, 1715
I cannot forbear regretting yt I must always have to do with ye Representatives of ye Vulgar People, and mostly with such members as are of their Stamp and Understanding, for so long as half an Acre of Land, (which is of small value in this Country,) qualifys a man to be an Elector, the meaner sort of People will ever carry ye Elections, and the humour generally runs to choose such men as are their most familiar Companions, who very eagerly seek to be Burgesses merely for the lucre of the Salary, and who, for fear of not being

chosen again, dare in Assembly do nothing that may be disrelished out of the House by ye Common People. Hence it often happens yt what appears prudent and feasible to his Maj's Governors and Council here will not pass with the House of Burgesses, upon whom they must depend for the means of putting their designs in Execution. . . .

To the Lords Commissioners of Trade, May 23, 1716
. . . The behaviour of this Gentleman [Philip Ludwell Jr., the colony's auditor] in constantly opposing whatever I have offered for ye due collecting the Quitt rents and regulating the Acc'ts; his stirring up ye humours of the people before the last election of Burgesses; tampering with the most mutinous of that house, and betraying to them the measures resolved on in Council for his Maj't's Service, would have made me likewise suspend him from ye Council, but I find by the late Instructions I have received from his Maj'tie that Power is taken from ye Govern'r and transferred upon the majority of that Board, and while there are no less than seven of his Relations there, it is impossible to get a Majority to consent to the Suspension of him. . . .

GEORGE CLINTON
A Plea for Help

George Clinton served as governor of New York from 1744 to 1752. Like many governors appointed during the era of salutary neglect, Clinton owed his appointment to his social status and political connections. As the second son of the seventh Earl of Lincoln, he would not inherit the family's estate or his father's position in the House of Lords; to provide an income for Clinton, his family traded its votes in Parliament for patronage appointments to various naval and political positions. Once installed as governor of New York, Clinton found himself dependent on the assembly for the payment of his salary and the salaries of all the members of his government. Here, he explains his problems to the Board of Trade; by the end of Clinton's governorship, the Board was advocating increased imperial control over colonial life and politics.

My Lords,
I have in my former letters inform'd Your Lordships what Incroachments the Assemblys of this province have from time to time made on His Majesty's Prerogative & Authority in this Province in drawing an absolute dependence of all the Officers upon them for their Saleries & Reward of their services, & by their taking in effect the Nomination to all Officers . . . .

1stly, That the Assembly refuse to admit of any amendment to any money bill, in any part of the Bill; so that the Bill must pass as it comes from the Assembly, or all the Supplies granted for the support of Government, & the most urgent services must be lost.

2ndly, It appears that they take the Payment of the [military forces], passing of Muster Rolls into their own hands by naming the Commissaries for those purposes in the Act.

3rdly, They by granting the Saleries to the Officers personally by name & not to the Officer for the time being, intimate that if any person be appointed to any Office his Salary must depend upon their approbation of the Appointment. . . .

I must now refer it to Your Lordships' consideration whether it be not high time to put a stop to these usurpations of the Assembly on His Majesty's Authority in this Province and for that purpose may it not be proper that His Majesty signify his Disallowance of the Act at least for the payment of Saleries.

SOURCES: R. A. Brock, ed., *The Official Letters of Alexander Spotswood* (Richmond: Virginia Historical Society, 1885), 2: 1–2, 124, 154–155; H. R. MacIwaine, ed., *Executive Journals of the Council of Colonial Virginia* (Richmond: Virginia State Library, 1928), 3: 392; and E. B. O'Callaghan, ed., *Documents Relative to the Colonial History of the State of New York* (Albany, 1860), 2: 211.

ANALYZING THE EVIDENCE

➤ What policies did Spotswood want to pursue? Why couldn't he persuade the House of Burgesses to implement them? According to Spotswood, what was wrong with Virginia's political system? How did he propose to reform it?

➤ Unlike the House of Burgesses, whose members were elected by qualified voters, the members of the governor's council in Virginia were appointed by the crown, usually on the recommendation of the governor. What was the council's response to Spotswood's plan to reform the political system? Based on the Ludwell incident, where did the political sympathies of the council lie?

➤ What were Clinton's complaints about the actions of the New York assembly? Did those actions represent a more or less serious threat to imperial power than the activities of the Virginia Burgesses? Based on the material here, which governor was a stronger representative of the crown's interests?

Bristol Docks and Quay

Bristol, in southwest England, served as a hub for the trade with Africa, the West Indies, and the American mainland. This detail from an eighteenth-century painting of the bustling seaport shows horses drawing large hogsheads of West Indian sugar to local factories and workers readying smaller barrels of rum and other goods for export to Africa.

City of Bristol Museum and Art Gallery.

low-cost sugar and outsell Britain in the European sugar market. When American rum distillers began to buy cheap molasses from the French islands, the West Indian "sugar lobby" persuaded Parliament to enact the Molasses Act of 1733. The act allowed the mainland colonies to export fish and farm products to the French islands but — to give a price advantage to British sugar planters — placed a high tariff on French molasses. American merchants and legislators protested that the Molasses Act would cut farm exports, cripple the distilling industry, and, by slashing colonial income, reduce the colonists' purchases of British goods. When Parliament ignored their petitions, American merchants smuggled in French molasses by bribing customs officials. Luckily for the Americans, sugar prices rose sharply in the late 1730s and enriched planters in the British West Indies, so the act was not rigorously enforced.

The lack of adequate currency in the colonies prompted another conflict with British officials.

New England Sea Captains in Surinam

Flouting the Navigation Acts, New England traders developed a flourishing trade with plantation owners and merchant houses in the Dutch colony of Surinam on the east coast of South America (between Venezuela and Brazil). The traders carried fish and other footstuffs to the Dutch settlement and returned with cargoes of Surinamese molasses and Asian goods cotton cloth, ceramics, and tea provided by Dutch merchants. This tavern scene, painted by Boston artist John Greenwood in the 1750s, pokes fun at the hard-drinking New England sea captains. The Saint Louis Art Museum.

To pay for manufactured goods, American merchants sent to Britain the bills of exchange and the gold and silver coins they earned in the West Indian trade. These payments drained the colonial economy of money, which made it difficult for Americans to borrow funds or to buy and sell goods among themselves. To remedy the problem, ten colonial assemblies established **land banks** that lent paper money to farmers, who used their land as collateral for the loans. Farmers used the currency to buy tools or livestock or to pay their creditors, thereby stimulating trade. However, some assemblies, like the legislature in Rhode Island, issued large amounts of paper money (which consequently fell in value) and required merchants to accept it as legal tender. English merchants and other creditors rightly complained that they were being forced to accept worthless money. So in 1751, Parliament passed the Currency Act, which barred the New England colonies from establishing new land banks and prohibited the use of paper money to pay private debts.

These conflicts over trade and paper money angered a new generation of political leaders in England. In 1749, Charles Townshend of the Board of Trade charged that the American assemblies had assumed many of the "ancient and established prerogatives wisely preserved in the Crown"; he vowed to replace salutary neglect with more-rigorous imperial control.

The wheel of empire had come full circle. In the 1650s, England had set out to build a centrally managed colonial empire and, over the course of a century, achieved the economic part of that goal. Mercantilist legislation, commercial warfare against European rivals, and the forced labor of a million African slaves brought prosperity to Britain. However, internal unrest (the Glorious Revolution) and a policy of salutary neglect had weakened Britain's authority over its American colonies. Recognizing the threat self-government posed to the empire, British officials in the late 1740s vowed to reassert their authority in America, an initiative that would have disastrous results.

➤ How did the ideas and policies of the Whigs in England affect British and colonial political systems between 1700 and 1760?

➤ What was the British policy of salutary neglect? Why did the British follow this policy? What consequences did it have for the British colonies in North America?

SUMMARY

In this chapter we have examined two long-term processes of change, one in politics and one in society and economy. The political story began in the 1660s and 1670s, with Britain's attempt to centralize control over its American possessions. Parliament passed the Acts of Trade and Navigation to give Britain a monopoly over colonial products and trade. Then, King James II abolished representative institutions in the northern colonies and created the authoritarian Dominion of New England. The Glorious Revolution of 1688–1689 partially reversed these policies by restoring American self-government and by allowing colonists, during the subsequent era of salutary neglect, to avoid rigid compliance with mercantilist policies.

The core of the social and economic story centers on the development of the South Atlantic system of production and trade. It involved an enormous expansion of African slave raiding, the Atlantic slave trade, and the cultivation of sugar, rice, and tobacco in America. This complex story also includes the creation of exploited African American labor forces in the West Indies and the southern mainland, and of prosperous communities of European American farmers, merchants, and artisans in the northern mainland colonies. How would the stories develop? In 1750, slavery and the South Atlantic system seemed firmly in place; however, the days of salutary neglect appeared to be numbered.

Connections: Economy and Government

In the part opener (p. 3), we noted,

> many European settlements became places of oppressive captivity for Africans, with pro-

found consequences for America's social development. . . . planters in the Chesapeake region imported enslaved African workers. Wealthy British and French planters in the West Indies, . . . bought hundreds of thousands of slaves from many African regions and forced them to labor on sugar, tobacco, and rice plantations.

As we can see in retrospect, the enormous expansion of the South Atlantic system of slavery and staple-crop production effected a dramatic change in the British colonies. In 1675, the three major English settlements—in the Chesapeake, New England, and Barbados—were small in numbers and reeling from Indian attacks, social revolts, and overpopulation. By 1750, all this had changed. British settlements in North America and the Caribbean had more than 2 million residents; produced vast amounts of sugar, rice, and tobacco; and were no longer in danger of being wiped off the map by Indian attacks. The South Atlantic system had brought wealth and opportunity to the white inhabitants not only of the sugar islands, the Chesapeake, and the Carolinas but also to the merchants and farm families of the New England and Middle Atlantic colonies.

If expansion solved some problems, it created others. As we have seen in Chapter 3, imperial officials imposed mercantilist laws regulating the increasingly valuable colonies and repeatedly went to war to safeguard them. This story of expanding imperial authority and warfare continues in Chapter 4, in the description of Britain's "Great War for Empire," a vast military conflict intended to expand British commercial power throughout the world and to establish Britain as the dominant nation in Europe.

CHAPTER REVIEW QUESTIONS

➤ Describe the dramatic expansion of the British empire in North America in the late seventeenth and early eighteenth centuries. What role did the South Atlantic System play?

➤ In what ways did politics in the British empire change in the decades following the Glorious Revolution? How do you explain those changes?

TIMELINE

1651	First Navigation Act
1660–1685	Reign of King Charles II
1663	Charles II grants Carolina proprietorship
1664	English capture New Netherland; rename it New York
1681	William Penn founds Pennsylvania
1685–1688	Reign of King James II
1686–1689	Dominion of New England
1688–1689	Glorious Revolution in England
1689	William and Mary ascend the throne in England
	Revolts in Massachusetts, Maryland, and New York
1689–1713	England, France, and Spain at war
1696	Parliament creates Board of Trade
1705	Virginia enacts slavery legislation
1714–1750	Britain follows policy of salutary neglect, allowing American assemblies to gain power
1720–1742	Sir Robert Walpole leads Parliament
1720–1750	African American community forms
	Rice exports from South Carolina soar
	Planter aristocracy emerges
	Seaport cities expand
1732	Parliament charters Georgia, challenging Spain
	Hat Act
1733	Molasses Act
1739	Stono Rebellion in South Carolina
1739–1748	War with Spain in the Caribbean and France in Canada
1750	Iron Act restricts colonial iron manufactures
1751	Currency Act prohibits land banks and use of paper money as legal tender

FOR FURTHER EXPLORATION

The best concise overview of America's place in England's empire is Michael Kammen, *Empire and Interest: The American Colonies and the Politics of Mercantilism* (1970). Linda Colley, *Britons: Forging the Nation, 1707–1837* (1992), explores the impact of empire on Britain. A clearly written study of multicultural tensions in early New York is Joyce Goodfriend, *Before the Melting Pot: Society and Culture in Colonial New York City, 1664–1730* (1992). Two fine portrayals of imperial military and political affairs in the eighteenth century are Fred Anderson, *A People's Army: Massachusetts Soldiers and Society in the Seven Years' War* (1984), a compelling picture of army life, and Richard Bushman, *King and People in Provincial Massachusetts* (1985), a nicely crafted story of the decline of British authority in New England.

Betty Wood, *Origins of American Slavery* (1998), and David Eltis, *The Rise of African Slavery in the Americas* (2000), offer fine surveys of this important topic. For compelling discussions of the diversity and evolving character of African bondage, see Ira Berlin, *Many Thousands Gone: The First Two Centuries of Slavery in North America* (1999), and Philip D. Morgan, *Slave Counterpoint: Black Culture in the Eighteenth-Century Chesapeake and Low Country* (1998). Olaudah Equiano, *The Interesting Narrative of the Life of Olaudah Equiano* (1789, 1995), provides a powerful account of slavery and the emergence of an African sense of identity. On Africa, consult Paul Bohannan and Philip Curtin, *Africa and the Africans* (3rd ed., 1988).

The PBS video *Africans in America, Part 1: Terrible Transformation, 1450–1750* (1.5 hours) covers the African American experience in the colonial period; the Web site (**www.pbs.org/wgbh/aia/part1/title.html**) contains a wide variety of pictures, historical documents, and scholarly commentary. The writings of enslaved and free African Americans are available at "Digital History" (**www.digitalhistory.uh.edu/black_voices/black_voices.cfm**). Jerome S. Handler and Michael L. Tuite Jr. present a comprehensive "Visual Record" of "The Atlantic Slave Trade and Slave Life in the Americas" (**hitchcock.itc.virginia.edu/Slavery/**). Also see the Library of Congress exhibit "African-American Odyssey" (**lcweb2.loc.gov/ammem/aaohtml/**), which provides digital access to court records, pamphlets, and slave narratives covering the period from 1740 to the present.

TEST YOUR KNOWLEDGE

To assess your command of the material in this chapter, see the Online Study Guide at **bedfordstmartins.com/henretta**.

For Web sites, images, and documents related to topics and places in this chapter, visit **bedfordstmartins.com/makehistory**.

4

Growth and Crisis in Colonial Society

1720–1765

I N 1736, ALEXANDER MACALLISTER LEFT the Highlands of Scotland for the backcountry of North Carolina, where his wife and three sisters soon joined him. Over the years, MacAllister prospered as a landowner and mill proprietor and had only praise for his new home. Carolina was "the best poor man's country I have heard in this age," he wrote to his brother Hector, urging him to "advise all poor people . . . to take courage and come." In North Carolina, there were no landlords to keep "the face of the poor . . . to the grinding stone," and so many Highlanders were arriving that "it will soon be a new Scotland." Here, on the far margins of the British empire, MacAllister wrote, people could "breathe the air of liberty, and not want the necessarys of life." Tens of thousands of European migrants — primarily Highland Scots, Scots-Irish, and Germans — heeded that advice, and they swelled the population of Britain's North American settlements from 400,000 in 1720 to almost 2 million by 1765.

The rapid increase in the number of white settlers — and enslaved Africans — transformed the character of life in every region of British America. Long-settled towns in New England became densely settled and then overcrowded; antagonistic ethnic and religious communities jostled uneasily with one another in the Middle Atlantic colonies; and the influx of the MacAllisters and thousands of other Celtic and German migrants altered the social and political landscape in the backcountry of

◄ **George Whitefield, Evangelist**

No painting could capture Whitefield's magical appeal, although this image conveys his open demeanor and religious intensity. When Whitefield spoke to a crowd near Philadelphia, an observer noted, his words were "sharper than a two-edged sword. . . . Some of the people were pale as death; others were wringing their hands . . . and most lifting their eyes to heaven and crying to God for mercy." *George Whitefield Preaching*, by John Collet (c. 1725–80). © Private Collection/The Bridgeman Art Library.

the South. Moreover, in every colony, two European cultural movements — the Enlightenment and Pietism — changed the tone of intellectual and spiritual life. Finally, and perhaps most important, as the migrants and the landless children of long-settled families moved inland, they sparked wars with the Native peoples and with France and Spain, the other European powers vying for empire in North America. A generation of dynamic growth produced a decade of deadly warfare that would set the stage for a new era in American history.

Freehold Society in New England

In the 1630s, the Puritans left a country where a handful of nobles and gentry owned 75 percent of the arable land and relied on servants, leaseholding tenants, and wageworkers to farm it. In New England, the Puritans set out to create a yeoman society, consisting primarily of freeholders, or landowning farm families. They succeeded all too well. By 1750, the region's rapidly growing yeoman population had settled on most of the best farmland, threatening the future of the freehold ideal.

Farm Families: Women and the Rural Household Economy

The Puritans' commitment to independence did not extend to women. Puritan ideology placed the husband at the head of the household and accorded him almost complete control over his dependents. As Reverend Benjamin Wadsworth of Boston advised women in *The Well-Ordered Family* (1712), being richer, more intelligent, or of higher social status than their husbands mattered little: "Since he is thy Husband, God has made him the head and set him above thee." Therefore, Wadsworth concluded, it was a wife's duty "to love and reverence" her husband.

Their subordinate role was made clear to women throughout their lives. Small girls watched their mothers defer to their fathers. As young women, they saw the courts prosecute many women and very few men for the crime of fornication (having sexual intercourse outside of marriage). And they learned that their marriage portions would be inferior in kind and size to those of their brothers: Instead of land, which was highly prized, daughters usually received livestock or household goods. Ebenezer Chittendon of Guilford (Connecticut), for example, left all his land to his sons, decreeing that "Each Daughter [shall] have half so much as Each Son, one half in money and the other half in Cattle." Because English law had eliminated

many customary restrictions on the disposition of wealth, fathers generally were free to divide their property as they pleased.

In rural New England — in fact, throughout the colonies — women assumed the role of dutiful helpmeets (helpmates) to their husbands. Farmwives tended the garden that provided the family with fresh vegetables and herbs. They spun thread and yarn from flax or wool, and wove it into cloth for shirts and gowns. They knitted sweaters and stockings, made candles and soap, churned milk into butter and pressed curds into cheese, fermented malt for beer, preserved meats, and mastered dozens of other household tasks. And the most "notable," the most accomplished practitioners of these domestic arts, won praise from the community because their labor and skills were crucial to the rural household economy.

Bearing and rearing children were equally important tasks. Most women in New England married in their early twenties and by their early forties had given birth to six or seven children, usually delivered with the help of a neighbor or a midwife. Large families sapped the physical and emotional strength of most mothers for twenty or more of their most active years. One Massachusetts woman confessed that she had little time for religious activities because "the care of my Babes takes up so large a portion of my time and attention." Yet, more women than men became full members of Puritan congregations: "In a Church of between *Three* and *Four* Hundred *Communicants*," the eminent minister Cotton Mather noted, "there are but few more than *One* Hundred *Men*; all the Rest are Women." According to revivalist Jonathan Edwards, many women became full members both because they feared the dangers of childbirth and because that status meant that "their children may be baptized."

As the size of farms shrank in long-settled communities, many couples chose to have fewer children. After 1750, women in Andover, a typical farm village in Massachusetts, bore an average of only four children and had time and energy to pursue other tasks. Farm women now made extra yarn, cloth, or cheese to exchange with neighbors or sell to shopkeepers, which raised their families' standard of living. Or, like Susan Huntington of Boston, the wife of a prosperous merchant, they spent more time in "the care & culture of children, and the perusal of necessary books, including the scriptures."

Still, women's lives remained tightly bound by a web of legal and cultural restrictions. Ministers praised women's piety but excluded them from an equal role in the church. When Hannah Heaton, a farmwife in Connecticut, grew dissatisfied with her

Reflections on Mortality, 1775

This powerful image reveals both the artistic skills of colonial women working in the traditional mediums of quilting, embroidering, and weaving and the continuing concern of Puritan culture with the inevitability of death. Has the child of Prudence Punderson, a Rhode Island woman, already died and is soon to be placed in the coffin to the left? Or is Punderson picturing the progression of the child's life — from cradle, to marriage (note the image on the wall to the far right), to motherhood, and finally to death and burial? Connecticut Historical Society.

Congregationalist minister, thinking him unconverted and a "blind guide," she sought out Quaker and Baptist churches that welcomed questioning women and allowed them to become spiritual leaders. However, by the 1760s, many evangelical congregations were advocating traditional gender roles. "The government of Church and State must be . . . family government" controlled by its "king," declared the Danbury (Connecticut) Baptist Association. Willingly or not, most New England women abided by the custom that, as essayist Timothy Dwight put it, they should be "employed only in and about the house and in the proper business of the sex." This would not be the last time that men and women would clash over their proper social roles.

Farm Property: Inheritance

By contrast, European men who migrated to the colonies escaped many traditional constraints, including the curse of landlessness. "The hope of having land of their own & becoming independent of Landlords is what chiefly induces people into America," an official noted in the 1730s. For men who had been peasants and dependent on powerful lords in Europe, owning property gave them a new social identity.

Actually, property ownership and family authority were closely related. Most migrating Europeans wanted large farms that would provide sustenance for themselves and ample land for their children. Parents with small farms could not provide their offspring with land, so they placed them

as indentured servants in more-prosperous households. When the indentures ended at age eighteen or twenty-one, their propertyless sons faced a decades-long climb up the agricultural ladder, from laborer to tenant and finally to freeholder.

Sons and daughters in well-to-do farm families were luckier: They received a marriage portion when they reached the age of twenty-three to twenty-five. The marriage portion — land, livestock, or farm equipment — repaid children for their past labor and allowed parents to choose their children's partners, which they did not hesitate to do. Parents' security during old age depended on a wise choice of son- or daughter-in-law. Although children could refuse an unacceptable match, they did not have the luxury of simply falling in love with whomever they pleased.

Marriage under eighteenth-century English common law was not a contract between equals. A bride relinquished to her husband the legal ownership of her land and her personal property. After his death, she received a dower right — the right to use, but not sell, a third of the family's property. The widow's death or remarriage canceled this use right, and her portion was divided among the children. The widow's property rights were subordinate to those of the family line, which stretched across the generations.

It was a father's duty to provide inheritances for his children, and men who failed to do so lost status in the community. Some fathers willed the family farm to a single son, providing their other children with money, apprenticeship contracts, or uncleared frontier tracts, or requiring the inheriting son to do so. Other yeomen moved their families to the frontier, where life initially was hard, but land for their children was cheap and abundant. "The Squire's House stands on the Bank of the Susquehannah," traveler Philip Fithian reported from the Pennsylvania backcountry in the early 1760s. "He tells me that he will be able to settle all his sons and his fair Daughter Betsy on the Fat of the Earth."

These farmers' historic accomplishment was the creation of whole communities of independent property owners. A French visitor noted the sense of personal dignity in this rural world, which contrasted sharply with European peasant life. Throughout the northern colonies, he found "men and women whose features are not marked by poverty, by lifelong deprivation of the necessities of life, or by a feeling that they are insignificant subjects and subservient members of society."

The Crisis of Freehold Society

How long would this happy circumstance last? Because of high rates of natural increase, New England's population doubled with each generation. The Puritan colonies had about 100,000 people in 1700, nearly 200,000 in 1725, and almost 400,000 in 1750. In long-settled areas, many farms had been divided and then subdivided; now they were so small—fifty acres or less—that many parents could not provide their children with an adequate inheritance. In the 1740s, Reverend Samuel Chandler of Andover was "much distressed for land for his children," seven of whom were male. A decade later, in nearby Concord, about 60 percent of the farmers owned less land than their fathers had.

Because parents had less to give their sons and daughters, they had less control over their children's lives. The system of arranged marriages broke down as young people engaged in premarital sex and used the urgency of pregnancy to win their fathers' permission to marry. Throughout New England, the number of premarital conceptions rose dramatically, from about 10 percent of first-born children in the 1710s to more than 30 percent in the 1740s. Given another chance, young people "would do the same again," an Anglican minister observed, "because otherwise they could not obtain their parents' consent to marry."

New England families met the threat to the free-holder ideal through a variety of strategies. Some parents chose to have smaller families by using various methods of birth control—abstention, coitus interruptus, or primitive condoms. Other families petitioned the provincial government for frontier land grants and hacked new farms out of the forests

of central Massachusetts, western Connecticut, and, eventually, New Hampshire and Vermont. Still others used their small plots more productively, replacing the traditional English crops of wheat and barley with high-yielding potatoes and Indian corn. Corn was an especially wise choice: It offered a hearty food for people, and its leaves furnished feed for cattle and pigs, which in turn provided farm families with milk and meat. Gradually, New England changed from a grain to a livestock economy, becoming the major supplier of salted and pickled meat to the plantations of the West Indies.

Finally, New England farmers survived on their smaller plots by developing the full potential of what one historian has called the "household mode of production." In this system, families exchanged labor and goods with one another. Women and children worked in groups to spin yarn, sew quilts, and shuck corn. Men lent one another tools, draft animals, and grazing land. Farmers plowed fields owned by artisans and shopkeepers, who repaid them with shoes, furniture, or store credit. In part because money was in short supply, no currency changed hands. Instead, farmers, artisans, and shopkeepers recorded their debits and credits in personal account books and every few years "balanced" the books by transferring small amounts of cash to one another. This system of community exchange allowed households—and the region's economy—to maximize their output and so preserve the freehold ideal.

➤ In what ways were the lives of women and men in New England similar? Different?

➤ By midcentury, the traditional strategies New England's farming families had relied on to provide marriage portions for children and security in old age for parents had become problematic. Why? How did farming households respond?

The Middle Atlantic: Toward a New Society, 1720–1765

The Middle Atlantic colonies—New York, New Jersey, and Pennsylvania—became home to peoples of differing origins, languages, and religions. Scots-Irish Presbyterians, English and Welsh Quakers, German Lutherans and Moravians, Dutch Reformed Protestants, and others formed ethnic and religious communities that coexisted uneasily with one another.

Economic Growth and Social Inequality

Ample fertile land and a longer growing season than New England attracted migrants to the Middle Atlantic colonies, and grain exports to Europe and the West Indies financed their rapid settlement. Between 1720 and 1770, growing demand doubled the price of wheat. By increasing their exports of wheat, corn, flour, and bread, Middle Atlantic farmers brought prosperity to the region, which, in turn, attracted more settlers. The population of the area surged from 120,000 in 1720 to 450,000 in 1765 (Figure 4.1).

Tenancy in New York. Despite the demand for land, many migrants refused to settle in New York's fertile Hudson River Valley. There, the Van Rensselaers and other Dutch landlords presided over manors created by the Dutch West India Company; and wealthy British families, such as the Clarkes and the Livingstons, dominated vast tracts granted by English governors (Map 4.1). Like the Chesapeake planters, the New York landlords aspired to live as European gentry, but few migrants wanted to labor as poor, dependent peasants. To attract tenants, the manorial lords had to grant them long leases and the right to sell their improvements—

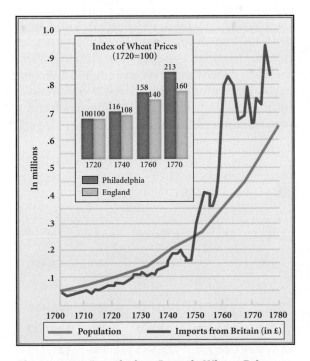

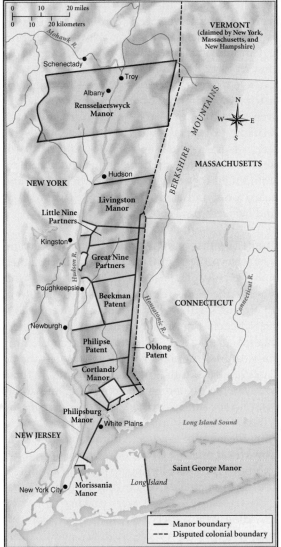

MAP 4.1 The Hudson River Manors

Dutch and English manorial lords owned much of the fertile eastern shore of the Hudson River, where they leased farms, on perpetual contracts, to German tenants and refused to sell land to freehold-seeking migrants from overcrowded New England. This powerful landed elite produced Patriot leaders, such as Gouverneur Morris and Robert Livingston, and prominent American families, such as the Roosevelts.

Figure 4.1 Population Growth, Wheat Prices, and British Imports in the Middle Colonies

Wheat prices doubled in Philadelphia between 1720 and 1770 as demand in the West Indies and Europe swelled. Exports of grain and flour paid for English manufactures, which the colonists imported in large quantities after 1750.

their houses and barns, for example—to the next tenant. The number of tenant families on the vast Van Rensselaer estate rose slowly at first, from 82 to 345 between 1714 and 1752, but then jumped to 700 by 1765.

Most tenant families hoped that with hard work and luck, they could sell enough wheat to buy their own farmsteads. But preindustrial technology limited their output, especially during the crucial harvest season. As the wheat ripened, it had to be harvested quickly, before it sprouted and became useless. A worker with a hand sickle could reap only half an acre of wheat, rye, or oats a day, limiting the number of acres a family could harvest. The cradle scythe, a tool introduced during the 1750s, doubled or tripled the amount of grain a worker could cut. Even so, during the harvest season, a family with two adult workers could reap only about twelve acres of grain—perhaps 150 to 180 bushels of wheat. After family needs were met, the remaining grain might be worth £15, enough to buy salt and sugar, tools, and cloth, but little else. The road to land ownership was not an easy one.

Quaker Pennsylvania. In rural Pennsylvania and New Jersey, at least initially, wealth was distributed more evenly. The first Quakers arrived with roughly the same resources and lived simply in small houses with one or two rooms, a sleeping loft, a few benches or stools, some wooden trenchers (platters), and a few wooden noggins (cups). Only the wealthiest families ate off pewter or ceramic plates imported from England or Holland. In time, however, the expanding trade in wheat and an influx of poor settlers led to social divisions. By the 1760s, affluent eastern Pennsylvania farmers were using the labor of slaves and immigrant workers to grow wheat on large farms. At the same time, other ambitious men were buying up land and dividing it into small tenancies, which they let out on profitable leases. Still others were making money by providing new settlers with farming equipment, sugar and rum from the West Indies, and financial services. These large-scale farmers, rural landlords, speculators, storekeepers, and gristmill operators formed a distinct class of agricultural capitalists. They displayed their wealth by building large stone houses and furnishing them with expensive mahogany tables and four-poster beds, and laying their tables with elegant linen and handsomely decorated Dutch dinnerware.

At the other end of the social scale, one-half of the white population of the Middle Atlantic colonies owned no land and little personal property. Some propertyless men were the sons of farmers and would eventually inherit at least part of the family estate. But many were Scots-Irish "inmates"—single men or families, explained a tax assessor, "such as live in small cottages and have no taxable property, except a cow." In the predominantly German settlement of Lancaster, Pennsylvania, a merchant noted an "abundance of Poor people" who "maintain their Families with great difficulty by day Labour." Although these Scots-Irish and German migrants hoped to become tenants and eventually landowners, sharply rising land prices prevented many of them from realizing their dreams.

Merchants and artisans took advantage of the ample supply of labor to organize an outwork system. They bought wool or flax from farmers and paid propertyless workers and land-poor farm families to spin it into yarn or weave it into cloth. In the 1760s, an English traveler reported that hundreds of Pennsylvanians had turned "to manufacture, and live upon a small farm, as in many parts of England." Indeed, many communities had become as crowded and as socially divided as communities in rural England, and many smallholders feared a return to the lowly status of the European peasant.

TABLE 4.1	Estimated European Migration to the British Mainland Colonies, 1700–1780

Period	Germany	Northern Ireland	Southern Ireland	Scotland	England	Wales	Other	Total
1700–1719	4,000	2,000	2,500	700	1,700	1,200	300	**12,400**
1720–1739	17,900	6,900	10,400	2,800	7,100	4,700	1,000	**50,800**
1740–1759	52,700	25,400	18,200	6,800	16,300	10,700	2,300	**132,400**
1760–1779	23,700	36,200	13,400	25,000	19,000	12,400	2,300	**132,000**
Total	**98,300**	**70,500**	**44,500**	**35,300**	**44,100**	**29,000**	**5,900**	**327,600**

After 1720, European migration to British America increased dramatically, peaking between 1740 and 1780, when more than 264,000 settlers arrived in the mainland colonies. Immigration from Germany was at its highest in the mid-1750s, while that from Ireland, Scotland, England, and Wales continued to increase during the 1760s and early 1770s. Most migrants, including those from Southern Ireland, were Protestants.

SOURCE: Adapted from Aaron Fogelman, "Migrations to the Thirteen British North American Colonies, 1700–1775: New Estimates," *Journal of Interdisciplinary History* 22 (1992).

Cultural Diversity

The middle colonies were not a melting pot: European migrants held tightly to their traditions, creating a patchwork of ethnically and religiously diverse communities (Table 4.1). In 1748, a traveler counted no fewer than twelve religious denominations in Philadelphia, including Anglicans, Baptists, Quakers, Swedish and German Lutherans, Mennonites, Scots-Irish Presbyterians, and Roman Catholics.

Migrants preserved their cultural identity by marrying within their own ethnic group and maintaining the customs of their native land (see Comparing American Voices, "Ethnic Customs and Conflict," pp. 110–111). A major exception were the Huguenots, Calvinists who were expelled from Catholic France in the 1680s and moved to Holland, England, and the British colonies. Those Huguenots who settled in American port cities — Boston, New York, and Charleston — soon lost their French identity by intermarrying with other Protestants. More typical were the Welsh Quakers. Seventy percent of the children of the original Welsh migrants to Chester County, Pennsylvania, married other Welsh Quakers, as did 60 percent of the third generation.

In Pennsylvania and western New Jersey, Quakers were the dominant social group, at first because of their numbers and later because of their wealth and social cohesion. Because Quakers were pacifists, Pennsylvania officials dealt with Native Americans by negotiating treaties and buying land rather than seizing it. However, in 1737, Governor

A Quaker Meeting for Worship

Quakers dressed plainly and met in unadorned buildings, sitting in silence until inspired by an "inner light." Women spoke with near-equality to men, a tradition that prepared Quaker women to take a leading part in the nineteenth-century women's rights movement. In this English work, titled *Quaker Meeting*, an elder (his hat on a peg above his head) conveys his thoughts to the congregation. Museum of Fine Arts, Boston.

Ethnic Customs and Conflict

As we note in the text, people from many European regions migrated to British North America during the eighteenth century, bringing with them their languages, religions, and customs. What happened next? Did the migrants continue their old ways in the new land? Or did the new environment change them? Did they remain distinct groups? Or did they gradually create a composite Euro-American race and culture? The two accounts here, the first a contemporary essay and the second a memoir, offer insights on these cultural issues.

J. HECTOR ST. JOHN DE CREVÈCOEUR
"What, Then, Is the American, This New Man?"

A Frenchman by birth, Crevècoeur (1735–1813) came to America during the French and Indian War, married a merchant's daughter, and settled in Orange County, New York, where he lived as a "gentleman farmer." In 1782, he published Letters from an American Farmer, *a justly famous book of essays that explored the character of his new land and its people.*

The next wish of this traveler will be to know whence came all these people. They are a mixture of English, Scotch, Irish, French, Dutch, Germans, and Swedes. From this promiscuous breed, that race now called Americans have arisen. The eastern provinces [New England] must indeed be excepted as being the unmixed descendants of Englishmen. I have heard many wish that they had been more intermixed also; I for my part, I am no wisher and think it much better as it has happened. I respect them for what they have done; for the accuracy and wisdom with which they have settled their territory; for the decency of their manners; for their early love of letters; their ancient college [Harvard], . . . for their industry. . . . There never was a people, situated as they are, who with so ungrateful a soil have done more in so short a time. . . .

In this great American asylum, the poor of Europe have by some means met together, . . . and here they are become men: in Europe they were as so many useless plants, wanting vegetative mould and refreshing showers; they withered, and were mowed down by want, hunger, and war; but now, by the power of transplantation, like all other plants they have taken root and flourished! Formerly they were not numbered in any civil lists of their country, except in those of the poor; here they rank as citizens. . . .

What, then, is the American, this new man? He is either an European or the descendant of an European; hence that strange mixture of blood, which you will find in no other country. I could point out to you a family whose grandfather was an Englishman, whose wife was Dutch, whose son married a French woman, and whose present four sons have now four wives of different nations. *He* is an American, who, leaving behind him all his ancient prejudices and manners, receives new ones from the new mode of life he has embraced, the new government he obeys, and the new rank he holds. . . . From involuntary idleness, servile dependence, penury, and useless labour, he has passed to toils of a very different nature, rewarded by ample subsistence. This is an American.

How much wiser, in general, the honest Germans than almost all other Europeans; . . . and [by] the most persevering industry, they commonly succeed. . . . The Scotch and the Irish [are different]. . . . The effects of their new situation do not strike them so forcibly, nor has it so lasting an effect. Whence the difference arises I know not, but out of twelve families of emigrants of each country, generally seven Scotch will succeed, nine German, and four Irish. The Scotch are frugal and laborious, but their wives cannot work so hard as German women, who on the contrary vie with their husbands, and often share with them the most severe toils of the field, which they understand better. . . . The Irish do not . . . prosper so well; they love to drink and to quarrel; they are litigious and soon take to the gun, which is the ruin of everything; they seem beside to labour under a greater degree of ignorance in husbandry than the others; . . . perhaps it is that their industry had less scope and was less exercised at home. . . . [In Ireland,] their potatoes, which are easily raised, are perhaps an inducement to laziness: their wages are too low and their whisky too cheap.

SOURCE: J. Hector St. John de Crevècoeur, *Letters from an American Farmer,* ed. Albert E. Stone (New York: Penguin, 1981) 68–71, 85.

JOSEPH PLUMB MARTIN

A Narrative of a Revolutionary Soldier

Born in western Massachusetts, Joseph Plumb Martin (1760–1850) enlisted in the army in 1776 and served through the War of Independence. He then settled in Maine, where he worked as a town official and laborer, barely providing for his family. In 1830, he published his Narrative, *which was based on his wartime diary.*

I, with some of my comrades who were in the battle of the White plains in the year 76, one day took a ramble on the ground. . . . We saw a number of the graves of those who fell in that battle; some of the bodies had been so slightly buried that the dogs or hogs, or both, had dug them out of the ground. . . . Here were Hessian sculls as thick as a bomb shell—poor fellows! They were left unburied in a foreign land, . . . they should have kept at home. . . . But, the reader will say, they were forced to come and be killed here; forced by their rulers who have absolute power of life and death over their subjects. Well then, reader, bless a kind Providence that has made such a distinction between your condition and theirs. And be careful too that you do not allow yourself ever to be brought to such an abject, servile and debased condition. . . .

There were three regiments of Light Infantry, composed of men from the whole main army,—it was a motly group,— Yankees, Irishmen, Buckskins and what not. The regiment that I belonged to, was made up of about one half New-Englanders and the remainder were chiefly Pennsylvanians, two setts of people as opposite in manners and customs as Light and darkness, consequently there was not much cordialty subsisting between us; for, to tell the sober truth, I had in those days, as [soon] have been incorporated with a tribe of western Indians, as with any of the southern troops; especially of those which consisted mostly (as the Pennsylvanians did) of foreigners. But I was among them and in the same regiment too, . . . and had to do duty with them; to make a bad matter worse, I was often, when on duty, the only Yankee that happened to be on the same tour for several days together. "The bloody Yankee," or "the d—d Yankee," was the mildest epithets that they would bestow upon me at such times. It often made me think of home, or at *least* of my regiment of fellow-Yankees. . . .

After . . . being constantly interrogated by the passing officers, who we were, and how we came to be behind our troops, I concluded, that as most or all the troops had passed us, to stay where I then was, and wait the coming up of the baggage of our troops, thinking that the guard or drivers might have directions where to find them. . . . While we were waiting we had an opportunity to see the baggage of the army pass. When that of the middle States passed us,

it was truly amusing to see the number and habiliments of those attending it; of all specimens of human beings, this group capped the whole; a caravan of wild beasts could bear no comparison with it. There was "Tag, Rag and Bobtail;" "some in rags and some in jags," but none "in velvet gowns." Some with two eyes, some with one, and some, I believe, with none at all. They "beggared all description; their dialect, too, was as confused as their bodily appearance was odd and disgusting; there was the Irish and Scotch brogue, murdered English, that insipid Dutch and some lingos which would puzzle a philosopher to tell whether they belonged to this world or some "undiscovered country."

SOURCE: Joseph Plumb Martin, *A Narrative of a Revolutionary Soldier*, with an introduction by Thomas Fleming (New York: Signet, (2001), 116–117, 170.

ANALYZING THE EVIDENCE

➤ Crevècoeur is known for suggesting that their environment forged a common character in the American people. Is this what he actually says? Consider his comments about the people of New England and about the relative success of Germans, Scots, and Irish.

➤ What do Martin's remarks suggest about the political consciousness of New Englanders? About the extent of geographical and ethnic consciousness in early America?

➤ How are the accounts of ethnicity by Crevècoeur and Martin consistent with one another? In what ways do they conflict? How would you explain the similarities and differences?

Thomas Penn used dubious tactics to oust the Lenni-Lanape (or Delaware) Indians (see the painting on p. 71) from a vast area of land, creating bitterness that would lead to war in the 1750s. By this time, Quakers had begun to extend their religious values of equality and justice to African Americans. Many Quaker meetings (congregations) condemned the institution of slavery, and some expelled members who continued to keep slaves.

German Migration. The Quaker vision of a "peaceable kingdom" attracted 100,000 German migrants who were fleeing their homelands because of war and military conscription, religious persecution, and high taxes. First to arrive, in 1683, were the Mennonites, a group of religious dissenters drawn by the promise of religious freedom. In the 1720s, overcrowding and religious upheaval in southwestern Germany and German-speaking cantons in Switzerland brought a larger wave of migrants. "Wages were far better" in Pennsylvania, Heinrich

Schneebeli reported to his friends in Zurich, and "one also enjoyed there a free unhindered exercise of religion." A third wave of Germans and Swiss—nearly 40,000 strong—landed in Philadelphia between 1749 and 1756. Some of these newcomers were redemptioners, indentured servants who migrated as a family; but many more were propertied farmers and artisans in search of ample land for their children (see Voices from Abroad, "Gottlieb Mittelberger: The Perils of Migration," p. 113).

Germans soon dominated many districts of eastern Pennsylvania, and thousands more moved down the Shenandoah Valley into the western parts of Maryland, Virginia, and the Carolinas (Map 4.2). The migrants carefully guarded their language and cultural heritage. A minister in North Carolina admonished young people "not to contract any marriages with the English or Irish," explaining "we owe it to our native country to do our part that German blood and the German language be preserved in America." Well beyond 1800, these settlers spoke

MAP 4.2 Ethnic and Racial Diversity in the British Colonies, 1775

In 1700, most colonists in British North America were of English origin; by 1775, settlers of English descent constituted only about 50 percent of the total population. African Americans now accounted for one-third of the residents of the South, while thousands of German and Scots-Irish migrants contributed to ethnic and religious diversity in the middle colonies and southern backcountry (see Table 4.1).

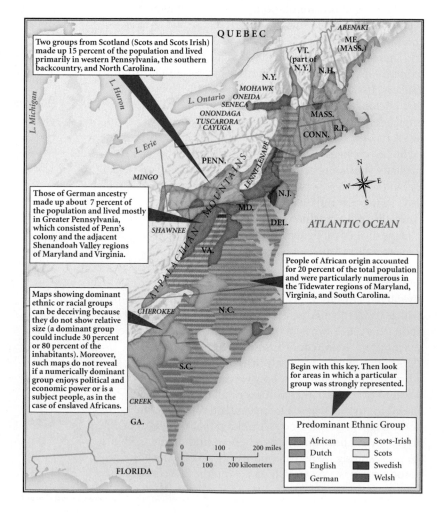

Gottlieb Mittelberger

The Perils of Migration

Gottlieb Mittelberger was a Lutheran minister who migrated to Pennsylvania with thousands of other Germans in the 1740s. Dismayed by the lack of piety among the colonists and the lack of state support for religious authority, he returned to his homeland after a few years. In Journey to America, a book published in Germany in 1750, Mittelberger examined America with a critical eye, warning his readers of the difficulties of migration, the dangers of indentured servitude, and the hazards of life in a competitive society.

[The journey from Germany to Pennsylvania via Holland and England] lasts from the beginning of May to the end of October, fully half a year, amid such hardships as no one is able to describe adequately with their misery. Both in Rotterdam and in Amsterdam the people are packed densely, like herrings so to say, in the large sea-vessels. One person receives a place of scarcely 2 feet width and 6 feet length in the bedstead, while many a ship carries four to six hundred souls. . . .

During the journey the ship is full of pitiful signs of distress — smells, fumes, horrors, vomiting, various kinds of sea sickness, fever, dysentery, headaches, heat, constipation, boils, scurvy, cancer, mouth-rot, and similar afflictions, all of them caused by the age and the highly-salted state of the food, especially of the meat, as well as by the very bad and filthy water, which brings about the miserable destruction and death of many. . . .

Children between the ages of one and seven seldom survive the sea voyage; and parents must often watch their offspring suffer miserably, die, and be thrown into the ocean, from want, hunger, thirst, and the like. I myself, alas, saw such a pitiful fate overtake thirty-two children on board our vessel, all of whom were finally thrown into the sea. Their parents grieve all the more, since their children do not find repose in the earth, but are devoured by the predatory fish of the ocean. . . .

When the ships finally arrive in Philadelphia after the long voyage only those are let off who can pay their sea freight or can give good security. The others, who lack the money to pay, have to remain on board until they are purchased and until their purchasers can thus pry them loose from the ship. In this whole process the sick are the worst off, for the healthy are naturally preferred and purchased first; and so the sick and wretched must often remain on board in front of the city for 2 or 3 weeks, and frequently die.

The sale of human beings in the market on board the ship is carried on thus: Every day Englishmen, Dutchmen and High-German people select among the healthy persons such as they deem suitable for their business, and bargain with them how long they will serve for their passage-money, which most of them are still in debt for. When they have come to an agreement, it happens that adult persons bind themselves in writing to serve 3, 4, 5 or 6 years for the amount due by them, according to their age and strength. But very young people, from 10 to 15 years, must serve till they are 21 years old.

Many parents must sell and trade away their children like so many head of cattle; for if their children take the debt upon themselves, the parents can leave the ship free and unrestrained. . . . It often happens that whole families, husband, wife, and children, are separated by being sold to different purchasers, especially when they have not paid any part of their passage money. . . .

When a serf has an opportunity to marry in this country, he or she must pay for each year which he or she would have yet to serve, 5 to 6 pounds. Thus let him who wants to earn his piece of bread honestly and in a Christian manner and who can only do this by manual labor in his native country stay there rather than come to America.

SOURCE: Gottlieb Mittelberger, *Journey to Pennsylvania,* ed. and trans. Oscar Handlin and John Clive (Cambridge, Mass.: Harvard University Press, 1960), 11–21.

ANALYZING THE EVIDENCE

➤ Most historians accept Mittelberger's account as generally accurate. How, then, do you explain the extent of German migration to the British colonies in North America?

➤ Why do you think most German migrants took passage to Philadelphia and not another colonial seaport?

➤ Compare Mittelberger's account of his Atlantic crossing with that of Olaudah Equiano (see Chapter 3, p. 84). How are they similar? How are they different?

German Farm in Western Maryland

Beginning in the 1730s, wheat became a major export crop in Maryland and Virginia. This engraving probably depicts a German farm: The harvesters are using oxen, not horses, and women are working in the field alongside the men. Using "a new method of reaping" that is possibly of German origin, the harvesters cut only the grain-bearing tip of the plants, leaving the wheat stalks in the fields to be eaten by livestock. Library of Congress.

German, read German-language newspapers, conducted church services in German, and preserved German farming practices, which sent women into the fields to plow and reap. Most German migrants were Protestants and lived easily as subjects of Britain's German-born and German-speaking monarchs, George I and George II. They engaged in local politics primarily to protect their churches and cultural practices, insisting, for example, that married women should have the right to hold property and write wills, as they did in Germany.

The Scots-Irish Influx. Migrants from Ireland accounted for the largest group of incoming Europeans, about 115,000 in number. Although some were Irish and Catholic, most were Scots and Presbyterians, the descendants of the Calvinist Protestants sent to Ireland by the English government during the seventeenth century to solidify its rule. Once in Ireland, the Scots faced hostility from both Irish Catholics and English officials and landlords. The Irish Test Act of 1704 restricted voting and office holding to Anglicans. English mercantilist regulations placed heavy import duties on the linens made by Scots-Irish weavers, and Scots-Irish farmers paid heavy taxes. "Read this letter, Rev. Baptist Boyd," a migrant to New York wrote back to his minister, "and tell all the poor folk of ye place that God has opened a door for their deliverance . . .

all that a man works for is his own; there are no revenue hounds to take it from us here."

Lured by reports like this one, thousands of Scots-Irish sailed for the colonies. The first migrants landed in Boston in the 1710s and settled primarily in New Hampshire. By 1720, though, most were sailing to Philadelphia, attracted by the religious tolerance there. In search of cheap land, they moved inland to central Pennsylvania and the fertile Shenandoah Valley, which stretched from Maryland to North Carolina. Governor William Gooch of Virginia welcomed their presence, which helped to secure "the Country against the Indians"; but an Anglican planter worried that the Scots-Irish "swarm like the Goths and Vandals of old, & will over-spread our continent soon." Like the Germans, the Scots-Irish retained their culture, living in ethnic communities and holding firm to the Presbyterian Church.

Religious Identity and Political Conflict

In Western Europe, the leaders of church and state condemned religious diversity. "To tolerate all [religions] without controul is the way to have none at all," an Anglican clergyman declared. Both English and German ministers carried these sentiments to Pennsylvania. "The preachers do not have the power to punish anyone, or to force anyone to go to church," complained Gottlieb Mittelberger, an influential minister. As a result, "Sunday is very badly kept. Many people plough, reap, thresh, hew or split wood and the like." He concluded: "Liberty in Pennsylvania does more harm than good to many people, both in soul and body."

Mittleberger was mistaken. Although ministers in Pennsylvania could not invoke government authority to uphold religious values, the result was not social anarchy. Instead, religious sects enforced moral behavior through communal self-discipline. Quaker families attended a weekly worship meeting and a monthly discipline meeting. Every three months, a committee from the monthly meeting reminded each mother and father to provide their children with proper religious instruction. Parents took the committee's words to heart. "If thou refuse to be obedient to God's teachings," Walter Faucit of Chester County admonished his son, "thou will be a fool and a vagabond." The committee also supervised adult behavior: A Chester County meeting, for example, disciplined one of its members "to reclaim him from drinking to excess and keeping vain company." Significantly, Quaker meetings granted permission to marry only to couples with land and livestock sufficient to support a family. As a result, the children of well-to-do Friends usually married within the sect, while poor Quakers remained unmarried, wed later in life, or married without permission—in which case they were often barred from Quaker meetings. These marriage rules helped build a self-contained and prosperous Quaker community.

In the 1740s, Quaker dominance in Pennsylvania came under attack. As German and Scots-Irish migration increased, Quakers became a minority, just 30 percent of the population. Simultaneously, Scots-Irish settlers in central Pennsylvania challenged the pacifism of the Quaker-dominated assembly by demanding an aggressive Indian policy. To maintain their influence, Quaker politicians looked for allies among the German migrants, many of whom embraced the Quakers' policies of pacifism and no compulsory militia service. In return, German leaders demanded fair representation of their communities in the provincial assembly and legislation that respected their inheritance customs. These ethnic-based conflicts over Indian policy and representation threw politics in Pennsylvania into turmoil. One European visitor noted that the attempts of Scots-Irish Presbyterians, German Baptists, and German Lutherans to form "a general confederacy" against the Quakers were likely to fail because of "a mutual jealousy, for religious zeal is secretly burning" (Map 4.3).

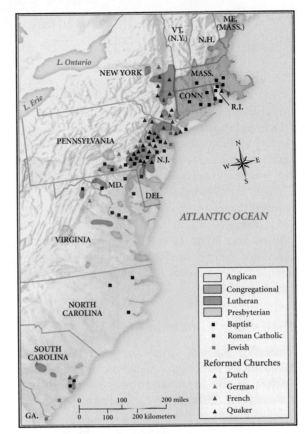

MAP 4.3 Religious Diversity in 1750

By 1750, religious diversity was on the rise, not only in the multiethnic middle colonies, but in all of British North America. Baptists had increased their numbers in New England, long the stronghold of Congregationalists, and would soon become important in Virginia. Already there were good-sized pockets of Presbyterians, Lutherans, and German Reformed in the South, where Anglicanism was the established religion.

By the 1750s, ethnic and religious passions flared in the Middle Atlantic colonies. In Pennsylvania, Benjamin Franklin disparaged the "boorish" character and "swarthy complexion" of German migrants; while in New York, a Dutchman declared that he "Valued English Law no more than a Turd." The region's experiment in cultural and religious diversity prefigured the bitter ethnic and social conflicts that would characterize much of American society in the centuries to come.

➤ What issues divided the various ethnic and religious groups of the middle colonies?

➤ How did Quakers maintain their economic and political primacy as Europeans from other cultures and traditions flooded into Pennsylvania during the eighteenth century?

The Enlightenment and the Great Awakening, 1720–1765

Two great European cultural movements reached America between the 1720s and the 1760s: the Enlightenment and Pietism. The Enlightenment, which emphasized the power of human reason to understand and shape the world, appealed especially to urban artisans and to well-educated men and women from merchant or planter families. Pietism, an evangelical Christian movement that stressed the individual's personal relationship with God, attracted many more adherents, primarily farmers and urban laborers. The two movements promoted independent thinking in different ways; together, they transformed American intellectual and cultural life.

The Enlightenment in America

Many early settlers in America turned to folk wisdom to explain the workings of the natural world. Swedish settlers in the lower counties of Pennsylvania (present-day Delaware), for example, attributed magical powers to the great white mullein, a common wildflower, and treated fevers by tying the plant's leaves around their feet and arms. Others relied on religion. Most Christians believed the earth stood at the center of the universe and that God (and Satan, by witchcraft and other means) intervened directly and continuously in human affairs. When a measles epidemic struck Boston in the 1710s, the Puritan minister Cotton Mather thought that only God could end it.

The European Enlightenment. Colonists held to their beliefs despite the scientific revolution of the sixteenth and seventeenth centuries, which challenged both folk and traditional Christian worldviews. In the 1530s, the astronomer Copernicus observed that the earth traveled around the sun, not vice versa. That discovery suggested that humans occupied a more modest place in the universe than Christian theology assumed. Eventually, Sir Isaac Newton, in his *Principia Mathematica* (1687), used the sciences of mathematics and physics to explain the movement of the planets around the sun. Newton's laws of motion and gravity described how the universe could operate by means of natural forces. This explanation, which did not require the constant intervention of a supernatural being, undermined the traditional Christian understanding of the cosmos.

In the century between the publication of *Principia Mathematica* and the outbreak of the French Revolution in 1789, the philosophers of the European Enlightenment used empirical research and scientific reasoning to study all aspects of life, including social institutions and human behavior. Enlightenment thinkers advanced four fundamental principles: the lawlike order of the natural world, the power of human reason, the "natural rights" of individuals (including the right to self-government), and the progressive improvement of society.

English philosopher John Locke was a major contributor to the Enlightenment. In his *Essay Concerning Human Understanding* (1690), Locke focused on the impact of environment and experience on human behavior. He argued that the character of individuals and societies was not fixed, that it could be changed through education, rational thought, and purposeful action. Locke's *Two Treatises on Government* (1690) advanced the revolutionary theory that political authority was not given by God to monarchs, as James II and other kings had insisted (see Chapter 3). Instead, it derived from social compacts that people made to preserve their "natural rights" to life, liberty, and property. In Locke's view, a people should have the right to change government policies—or even the form of government—through the decision of a majority.

Locke's ideas and those of other Enlightenment thinkers came to America by way of books, travelers, and educated migrants. Some clergymen responded to these ideas by devising a rational form of Christianity. Rejecting the supernatural and the early Puritans' arbitrary and vengeful God, Congregationalist minister Andrew Eliot maintained that "there is nothing in Christianity that is contrary to reason." Reverend John Wise of Ipswich, Massachusetts, used Locke's political principles to defend the Puritans' practice of vesting power in ordinary church members. Just as the social compact formed the basis of political society, Wise argued, so the religious covenant among the lay members of the congregation made them—not the bishops of the Church of England or even ministers like himself—the proper interpreters of religious truth. The Enlightenment influenced Cotton Mather as well. When a smallpox epidemic threatened Boston in the 1720s, this time Mather turned to a scientific rather than a religious remedy, joining with physician Nicholas Boyleston to publicize the new technique of inoculation.

Benjamin Franklin and the American Enlightenment. Benjamin Franklin was the exemplar of the American Enlightenment. Born in Boston

Benjamin Franklin's Influence

Benjamin Franklin's work as a scientist and inventor captivated subsequent generations of Americans. This painted panel (c. 1830) from a fire engine of the Franklin Volunteer Fire Company of Philadelphia depicts Franklin's experiment in 1752 in which he demonstrated the presence of electricity in lightning. Cigna Museum and Art Collection, Philadelphia/Photo by Joseph Painter.

in 1706 to a devout Calvinist family and, as a youth, apprenticed to his half-brother, a printer, Franklin was a self-taught man. While working as a printer and journalist in Philadelphia, he formed "a club of mutual improvement" that met weekly to discuss "Morals, Politics, or Natural Philosophy." These discussions and Enlightenment literature, rather than the Bible, shaped Franklin's mind. As Franklin explained in his *Autobiography* (1771), "From the different books I read, I began to doubt of Revelation [God-revealed truth] itself."

Like many urban artisans, wealthy Virginia planters, and affluent seaport merchants, Franklin became a **deist**. Influenced by Enlightenment science, deists believed that God had created the world but allowed it to operate through the laws of nature. The deists' god was a divine "watchmaker" who did not intervene directly in history or in people's lives. Rejecting the authority of the Bible, deists relied on people's "natural reason," their innate moral sense, to define right and wrong. A one-time slave owner, Franklin came to question the moral legitimacy of racial bondage and repudiated it as he began to contest the colonists' political bondage to the British.

Franklin popularized the practical outlook of the Enlightenment in *Poor Richard's Almanack* (1732–1757), an annual publication read by thousands. In 1743, he helped found the American Philosophical Society, an institution devoted to "the promotion of useful knowledge." Taking this message to heart, Franklin invented bifocal lenses for eyeglasses, the Franklin stove, and the lightning rod. His book on electricity, published in England in 1751, won praise as the greatest contribution to science since Newton's discoveries. Inspired by Franklin, ambitious printers in America's seaport cities published newspapers and gentlemen's magazines, the first significant nonreligious publications to appear in the colonies. The European Enlightenment, then, added a secular dimension to colonial intellectual life, preparing the way for the great American contributions to republican political theory by a new generation of intellectuals led by John Adams, James Madison, and Thomas Jefferson.

American Pietism and the Great Awakening

As many educated Americans turned to deism, thousands of colonists embraced Pietism, a Christian movement that emphasized "pious" behavior (hence the name) and had its origins in Germany around 1700. In its belief that individuals could form a mystical union with God and in its emotional services, Pietism appealed to the heart rather than the mind (see Reading American Pictures, "Almanacs and Meetinghouses: Exploring Popular Culture," p. 119). In the 1720s, German migrants carried Pietism to America, quickly sparking a religious **revival.** In Pennsylvania and New Jersey, Dutch minister Theodore Jacob Frelinghuysen moved from church to church, preaching rousing emotional sermons to German settlers. In private prayer meetings, he encouraged church members to spread the message of spiritual urgency. A decade later, William Tennent and his son Gilbert copied Frelinghuysen's approach and led revivals among Scots-Irish Presbyterians throughout the Middle Atlantic region.

Jonathan Edwards: Preacher and Philosopher.
Simultaneously, an American-born Pietist movement appeared in Puritan New England. The original Puritan settlers were intensely pious Christians, but over the decades their spiritual zeal had faded. In the 1730s, Jonathan Edwards restored that zeal to Congregational churches in the Connecticut River Valley. Edwards was born in 1703, the fifth child and only son among the eleven children of Timothy and Esther Stoddard Edwards. His father was a poorly paid rural minister, but his mother was the daughter of Solomon Stoddard, a famous preacher who taught that God was compassionate and that Sainthood was not limited to a select few.

As a young man, Edwards rejected Stoddard's thinking. Taking inspiration from the harsh theology of John Calvin, he preached that men and women were helpless, that they were completely dependent on God. In his most famous sermon, "Sinners in the Hands of an Angry God" (1741), Edwards declared: "There is Hell's wide gaping mouth open; and you have nothing to stand upon, nor any thing to take hold of: there is nothing between you and Hell but the air; 'tis only the power and mere pleasure of God that holds you up." According to one observer, the response was electric: "There was a great moaning and crying through the whole house, What shall I do to be saved — oh, I am going to Hell."

Surprisingly, Edwards's writings contributed to Enlightenment thought. The New England minister accepted Locke's argument in the *Essay Concerning Human Understanding* (1690), that ideas are the product of experience as conveyed by the senses; however, Edwards went on to claim that people's ideas depended on their passions. Edwards used his theory of knowledge to justify his preaching,

Almanacs and Meetinghouses: Exploring Popular Culture

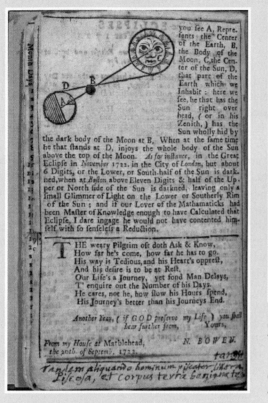

(above) **Mauck Meeting House, Mill Creek, Virginia.** H. Wickliffe Rose Papers, Yale University Library.

(left) **Explaining the Great Eclipse of 1722.** American Antiquarian Society, Worcester, Massachusetts.

From the writings of educated people and learned ministers, we know that the Enlightenment and Pietism changed the way they looked at the world. But what was the impact of these movements on ordinary people who had less education and lived predominantly as farmers or common folk? From almanacs, which enjoyed a wide readership, and churches, which were designed, built, and used by congregants, we can find clues to the impact of these transatlantic cultural and religious movements on colonial Americans.

ANALYZING THE EVIDENCE

➤ Almanacs provided information about a wide variety of subjects. Consider the page from Nathaniel Bowen's *Almanac.* How does Bowen explain why London was "wholly hid" by the "Great Eclipfe" in November 1722, while Boston was only partially darkened?

➤ Is Bowen's explanation based on a scientific or a religious view of the solar system? Would people who read and understood Bowen's account begin to see the world as Enlightenment thinkers did, to accept that it was governed by predictable "laws of nature"?

➤ What does the photograph of the interior of Mauck Meeting House tell us about the experience of Pietism in eighteenth-century Virginia? What is missing that you would expect to find in a church?

Who do you think sat on the raised bench? How would this relatively small and intimate space encourage communal worship? What can you conclude about Pietistic religious culture from this image?

➤ A building is concrete evidence of history: You can see it and touch it and experience it to learn more about the people who built and used it. Can you think of other types of concrete evidence that might provide insight into how ordinary people lived their lives in the eighteenth century? What do these sources reveal that print sources cannot? Think about your life and the meaning you attach to everyday objects.

Jonathan Edwards, c. 1750

In this portrait by Joseph Badger, Edwards looks directly at the viewer, as he looked directly at his congregation in Northampton, Massachusetts, and urged them to be "born again and made new creatures." At the time, Edwards was in his mid-forties and at the height of his powers as a scholar — but not as a pastor. When Edwards restricted full church membership to those who were Saints — the Calvinist "elect"—his congregation voted 200 to 20 to dismiss the great preacher and philosopher. Impoverished, Edwards moved to the frontier town of Stockbridge, where he ministered, without great success, to the Housatonic Indians. Yale University Art Gallery, Bequest of Eugene Philips Edwards.

arguing that vivid words would "fright persons away from Hell" and promote conversions. News of Edwards's success stimulated religious fervor up and down the Connecticut River Valley.

George Whitefield and the Great Awakening.
George Whitefield transformed the local revivals inspired by Edwards and the Tennants into a Great Awakening that spanned the British colonies in North America. Whitefield had his own awakening after reading German Pietist tracts, and he became a follower of John Wesley, the founder of English Methodism. In 1739, Whitefield carried Wesley's fervent message to America. Over the next two years, he attracted huge crowds of "enthusiasts" as he preached at settlements from Georgia to Massachusetts (see the painting on p. 102). "Religion is become the Subject of most Conversations," the *Pennsylvania Gazette* reported. "No books are in Request but those of Piety and Devotion." The usu-

ally skeptical Benjamin Franklin was so impressed by Whitefield's preaching that when the revivalist asked for contributions, Franklin emptied the coins in his pockets "wholly into the collector's dish, gold and all." By the time Whitefield reached Boston, Reverend Benjamin Colman reported, the people were "ready to receive him as an angel of God."

Whitefield owed his appeal to skillful publicity and to his compelling presence. "He looked almost angelical; a young, slim, slender youth . . . cloathed with authority from the Great God," wrote a Connecticut farmer. Like most evangelical preachers, Whitefield did not read his sermons (which he sold in large numbers) but spoke from memory. He gestured eloquently, raised his voice for dramatic effect, and even assumed a female persona — a woman in labor struggling to deliver the word of God. When the young preacher told his spellbound listeners that they had all sinned and must seek salvation, hundreds of men and women suddenly felt a "new light" within them. As "the power of god come down," Hannah Heaton recalled, "my knees smote together . . . it seemed to me I was a sinking down into hell . . . but then I resigned my distress and was perfectly easy quiet and calm . . . it seemed as if I had a new soul & body both." Strengthened and self-confident, these "New Lights" were eager to spread Whitefield's message throughout their communities.

Religious Upheaval in the North

Like all cultural explosions, the Great Awakening was controversial. Conservative ministers — "Old Lights" — condemned the "cryings out, faintings and convulsions" that had become a part of revivalist meetings. Charles Chauncy, a minister in Boston, also attacked the New Lights' practice of allowing women to speak in public: It was, he stated, "a plain breach of that commandment of the LORD, where it is said, Let your WOMEN keep silence in the churches." In Connecticut, Old Lights persuaded the legislature to prohibit evangelists from speaking to established congregations without the ministers' permission. When Whitefield returned to Connecticut in 1744, he found many pulpits closed to him. But the New Lights refused to be silenced. Dozens of farmers, women, and artisans roamed the countryside, condemning the Old Lights as "unconverted" sinners and willingly accepting imprisonment: "I shall bring glory to God in my bonds," a dissident preacher wrote from jail.

As the Awakening proceeded, it undermined the allegiance to legally established churches and their tax-supported ministers. In New England, New Lights left the Congregational Church and founded

Figure 4.2   Church Growth by Denomination, 1700–1780

Some churches — such as the Dutch Reformed, Anglican, and Congregational — grew at a steady pace, primarily from the natural increase of their members. After 1740, the fastest-growing denominations were immigrant churches — German Reformed, Lutheran, and Presbyterian — and those, like the Baptists, with an evangelical message.

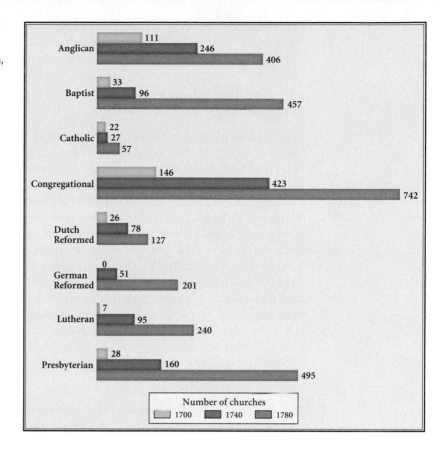

125 "separatist" churches that supported their ministers through voluntary contributions (Figure 4.2). Other religious dissidents joined Baptist congregations, which also condemned government support of churches. "God never allowed any civil state upon earth to impose religious taxes," declared Baptist preacher Isaac Backus. In New York and New Jersey, the Dutch Reformed Church split in two because New Lights refused to accept the doctrines and practices handed down by conservative church authorities in Holland.

In a sense, the Awakening challenged the authority of all ministers, an authority that rested in large part on respect for their education and knowledge of the Bible. In an influential pamphlet, *The Dangers of an Unconverted Ministry* (1740), Gilbert Tennent asserted that ministers' authority should come not from theological training but from the conversion experience. Reaffirming Martin Luther's belief in the priesthood of all Christians, Tennent suggested that anyone who had experienced the redeeming grace of God could speak with ministerial authority. Isaac Backus also celebrated a spiritual democracy, noting that "the common people now claim as good a right to judge and act in matters of religion as civil rulers or the learned clergy." When challenged by her minister, Sarah Harrah Osborne, a New Light "exhorter" in Rhode Island, refused "to shut up my mouth and doors and creep into obscurity."

In many rural villages, revivalism reinforced the communal values of farm families by questioning the moneygrubbing practices of merchants and land speculators. Jonathan Edwards spoke for many rural colonists when he charged that a miserly spirit was more suitable "for wolves and other beasts of prey, than for human beings." Said Gilbert Tennent: "In any truly Christian society mutual love is the Band and Cement."

As religious enthusiasm spread, churches founded new colleges to educate their young men and train ministers. New Light Presbyterians established the College of New Jersey (Princeton) in 1746, and New York Anglicans founded King's College (Columbia) in 1754. Baptists set up the College of Rhode Island (Brown) in 1764; and the Dutch Reformed Church subsidized Queen's College (Rutgers) in New Jersey two years later. The intellectual legacy of the Awakening, however, was not education for the privileged few but a new sense of authority among the many. A European visitor to Philadelphia remarked in surprise, "The poorest day-laborer . . . holds it his right to advance his opinion, in religious as well as political matters, with as much freedom as the gentleman."

Social and Religious Conflict in the South

In the southern colonies, where the Church of England was legally established, religious enthusiasm triggered sharp social conflict. Anglican ministers were few in number and generally ignored the spiritual needs of African Americans (about 40 percent of the population), and landless whites (another 20 percent) attended church irregularly. Middling white freeholders (35 percent of the residents) formed the core of most Anglican congregations. Prominent planters and their families (just 5 percent) held the real power in the church, and they used their control of parish finances to discipline their ministers. One clergyman complained that dismissal awaited any minister who "had the courage to preach against any Vices taken into favor by the leading Men of his Parish."

The Presbyterian Revival. In the southern colonies, the Great Awakening challenged the dominance of both the Church of England and the planter elite. In 1743, bricklayer Samuel Morris, inspired by reading George Whitefield's sermons led a group of Virginia Anglicans out of the church. Seeking a more vital religious experience, Morris and his followers invited New Light Presbyterian ministers to lead their prayer meetings. Soon Presbyterian revivals spread not only to the Scots-Irish in the backcountry but also to English residents in the Tidewater region, where they threatened the social authority of the Virginia gentry. Traditionally, planters and their well-dressed families arrived at Anglican services in elaborate carriages drawn by well-bred horses, and the men flaunted their power by marching in a body to their front-pew seats. Those ritual reminders of the gentry's social superiority would be meaningless if all the freeholders were attending Presbyterian churches. Moreover, religious pluralism threatened the tax-supported status of the Anglican Church.

To halt the spread of New Light ideas, Virginia's governor William Gooch denounced them as "false teachings," and Anglican justices of the peace closed down Presbyterian meetinghouses. This harassment kept most white yeomen families and poor tenants in the Church of England; so did the fact that most Presbyterian ministers were well-educated men who refused to preach in

the "enthusiastic" style that appealed to ordinary folk.

The Baptist Insurgency. New Light Baptist ministers had no problem reaching out to ordinary folk, and they won large numbers of converts in Virginia during the 1760s. The Baptists were radical Protestants whose central ritual was adult (rather than infant) baptism. Once men and women had experienced the infusion of grace — had been "born again" — they were baptized in an emotional public ceremony, often involving complete immersion in water. The vigorous preaching and democratic message of the Baptist preachers drew thousands of yeomen and tenant farm families into their congregations.

Even slaves were welcome at Baptist revivals. During the 1740s, George Whitefield had urged Carolina slave owners to bring blacks into the Christian fold, but white hostility and the commitment of Africans to their ancestral religions kept the number of converts low. The first significant conversion of slaves to Christianity came in Virginia in the 1760s, as second- and third-generation African Americans responded to the Baptists' message that all people were equal in God's eyes. Sensing a threat to the system of racial slavery, the House of Burgesses imposed heavy fines on Baptists who preached to slaves without their owners' permission.

The Baptists posed a direct threat to the traditional authority of the gentry. Their preachers repudiated the social hierarchy, urging followers to call one another "brother" and "sister"; and they condemned the customary pleasures of Chesapeake planters. As planter Landon Carter complained, the Baptists were "destroying pleasure in the Country; for they encourage ardent Prayer; strong & constant faith, & an intire Banishment of *Gaming*, *Dancing*, & Sabbath-Day Diversions." Stung by such criticisms, the gentry responded with violence. Hearing Baptist Dutton Lane condemn "the vileness and danger" of drunkenness and whoring, planter John Giles took the charge personally: "I know who you mean! and by God I'll demolish you." In Caroline County, an Anglican posse attacked a prayer meeting led by Brother John Waller. A Baptist described the attack: "[He] was violently jerked off the stage; they caught him by the back part of his neck, beat his head against the ground, and a gentleman gave him twenty lashes with his horsewhip."

Despite these attacks, Baptist congregations continued to multiply. By 1775, about 15 percent of Virginia's whites and hundreds of black slaves had joined Baptist churches. To signify their state of grace, some Baptist men "cut off their hair, like Cromwell's round-headed chaplains." Many others refused to attend "a horse race or other unnecessary, unprofitable, sinful assemblies." Still others forged a new evangelical masculinity — "crying, weeping, lifting up the eyes, groaning" when touched by the Holy Spirit, but defending themselves with vigor. "Not able to bear the insults" of a heckler, a group of Baptists "took [him] by the neck and heels and threw him out of doors," setting off a bloody brawl.

The Baptist revival in the Chesapeake may have changed the form of worship, but it did not change the social order to a significant extent. Rejecting the requests of evangelical women, Baptist men kept church authority in the hands of "free born male members"; and Anglican slaveholders retained their power over the political system. Still, the Baptist insurgency infused the lives of poor tenant families with spiritual meaning and empowered yeomen to defend their economic interests. Moreover, as Baptist ministers spread Christianity among slaves, the cultural gulf between blacks and whites shrank, undermining one justification for slavery and giving blacks a new religious identity. Within a generation, African Americans would develop distinctive versions of Protestant Christianity.

➤ What was the significance of the Enlightenment in America?

➤ In what ways did the Enlightenment and the Great Awakening prompt Americans to challenge traditional sources of authority?

➤ How did the Baptist insurgency in Virginia challenge conventional assumptions about race, gender, and class in the colony?

The Midcentury Challenge: War, Trade, and Social Conflict, 1750–1765

Between 1750 and 1765, a series of events transformed colonial life. First, Britain embarked on a war against the French in America, which became a worldwide conflict — the Great War for Empire. Second, a surge in trade boosted colonial consumption but placed some Americans deeply in debt to British creditors. Third, a great westward migration of colonists sparked new conflicts with Indian

peoples, armed disputes between settlers and speculators, and backcountry rebellions against eastern-controlled governments.

The French and Indian War Becomes a War for Empire

By 1754, both France and Britain had laid claim to much of the land west of the Appalachians (Map 4.4). Still, only a few Europeans had moved into that vast area. One factor in limiting access from the British colonies was topography: There were few natural routes running east and west. More important, the Iroquois and other Indian peoples controlled the great valleys of the Ohio and Mississippi rivers, and they firmly opposed — through diplomacy and violent raids — extensive white settlement.

The End of the Play-off System. For decades, the Native peoples had used their control of the fur trade to bargain for guns and subsidies from French and British officials. By the 1740s, however, the Iroquois' strategy of playing off the French against the British was breaking down. The Europeans resented the rising cost of "gifts" of arms and money; equally important, alliances between the Indians and the British crumbled as Anglo-American demands for land escalated. In the late 1740s, the Mohawks rebuffed attempts by Sir William Johnson, an Indian agent and land speculator, to settle Scottish migrants west of Albany. The Iroquois also responded angrily when Governor Robert Dinwiddie of Virginia, along with Virginia land speculators and London merchants, formed the Ohio Company in 1749. The company's royal grant of 200,000 acres lay in the upper Ohio River Valley, an area the Iroquois controlled through alliances with the Delaware and Shawnee peoples. "We don't know what you Christians, English and French intend," the outraged Iroquois complained, "we are so hemmed in by both, that we have hardly a hunting place left."

To repair the British relationship with the Iroquois, the Board of Trade called a meeting at Albany in June 1754. At the Albany Congress, delegates from many of Britain's mainland colonies denied any designs on Iroquois lands; and they asked the Indians for their help against New France. Although still small in numbers, the French colony had a broad reach. In the 1750s, the 15,000 French farm families who lived along the St. Lawrence River provided food and supplies not only to the fur-trading settlements of Montreal and Quebec but also to the hundreds of fur traders, missionaries, and soldiers who lived among the

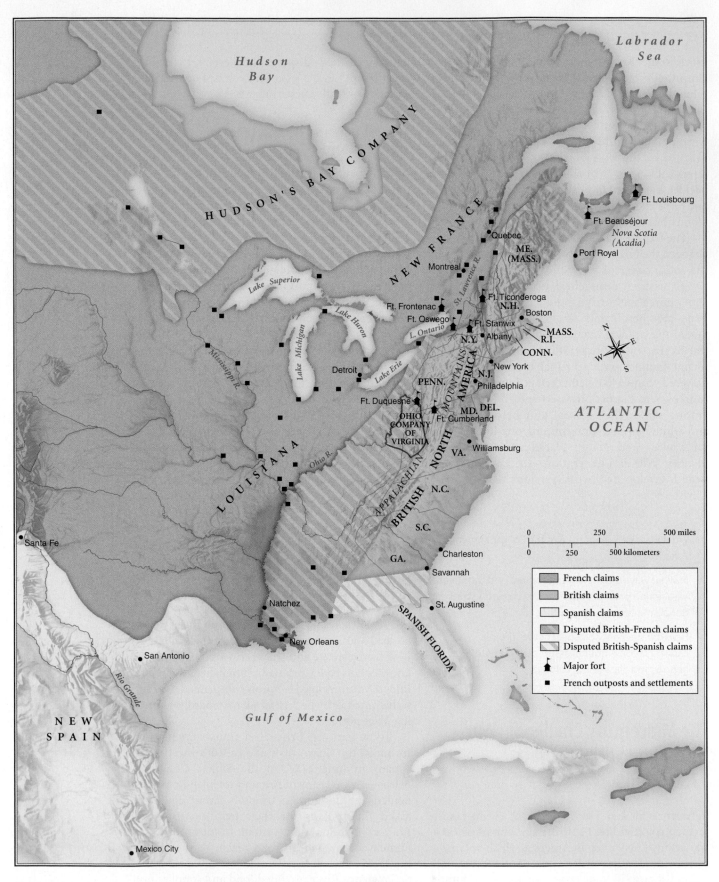

MAP 4.4 European Spheres of Influence in North America, 1754

France and Spain laid claim to vast areas of North America and relied on their Indian allies to combat the numerical superiority of British settlers. For their part, Native Americans played off one European power against another. As a British official observed: "To preserve the Ballance between us and the French is the great ruling Principle of Modern Indian Politics." By expelling the French from North America, the Great War for Empire disrupted this balance and left the Indian peoples on their own to resist encroaching Anglo-American settlers.

western Indian peoples. To counter the French, Benjamin Franklin proposed a Plan of Union to the delegates at Albany. Franklin's plan included a continental assembly that would manage trade, Indian policy, and defense in the West, and so increase British influence there. But neither Franklin's plan nor a proposal by the Board of Trade for a political "union between ye Royal, Proprietary, & Charter Governments" was in the cards. British ministers worried that a union would spark demands for American independence, and colonial leaders feared that a consolidated government would undermine the authority of the assemblies.

Meanwhile, the Ohio Company's land grant alarmed French authorities. For decades, they had given their Indian allies guns and other gifts to stop British settlers from pouring into the Ohio River Valley. Now they built a series of military forts, including Fort Duquesne at the point where the Monongahela and Allegheny rivers join to form the Ohio River (present-day Pittsburgh). Confrontation came when Dinwiddie dispatched a military expedition led by Colonel George Washington, a young Virginia planter and Ohio Company stockholder. In July 1754, French troops seized Washington and his men and sent them back to Virginia, prompting American and British expansionists to demand war. Henry Pelham, the British prime minister, urged calm: "There is such a load of debt, and such heavy taxes already laid upon the people, that nothing but an absolute necessity can justifie our engaging in a new War."

Expansionism Triumphant. Pelham could not control the march of events. In Parliament, William Pitt, a rising British statesman, and Lord Halifax, the new head of the Board of Trade, were strong advocates for colonial expansion. They persuaded Pelham to dispatch military forces to America to join with colonial militias in attacking French forts. In June 1755, British and New England troops captured Fort Beauséjour in Nova Scotia (Acadia). Subsequently, troops from Puritan Massachusetts seized nearly 10,000 Acadians and deported them to France, the West Indies, and Louisiana (where they became known as Cajuns). English and Scottish Protestants took over the farms the French Catholics left behind.

These Anglo-American successes were quickly offset by a stunning defeat. In July 1755, 2,000 British regulars and Virginia militiamen advancing on Fort Duquesne without benefit of Indian scouts marched into a deadly ambush. A much smaller force of French soldiers and Delaware and Shawnee warriors rained fire on the British force, taking the life of the British commander, General Edward Braddock, and killing or wounding half of his troops. "We have been beaten, most shamefully beaten, by a handfull of Men," Washington complained bitterly as he led the militiamen back to Virginia.

The Great War for Empire

By 1756, the conflict in America had spread to Europe, where it was known as the Seven Years' War and arrayed France, Spain, and Austria against Britain and Prussia. When Britain mounted major offensives in India and West Africa as well as in North America, the conflict became a Great War for Empire. Since 1700, Britain had reaped unprecedented profits from its overseas trading empire; it was determined to crush France, the main obstacle to further expansion.

William Pitt emerged as the architect of the British war effort. Pitt was the grandson of the East Indies merchant "Diamond" Pitt, a committed expansionist and an arrogant man. "I know that I can save this country and that I alone can," he declared. In fact, Pitt was a master of strategy, both commercial and military, and planned to cripple France by seizing its colonies. In designing the critical campaign against New France, Pitt exploited a demographic advantage: On the North American mainland, King George II's 2 million subjects outnumbered the French by 14 to 1. To mobilize the colonists, Pitt paid half the cost of their troops and supplied them with arms and equipment, an expenditure of nearly £1 million a year. He also committed a fleet of British ships and 30,000 British regulars to the American conflict.

The Conquest of Canada. Beginning in 1758, the powerful Anglo-American forces moved from one triumph to the next. They forced the French to abandon Fort Duquesne (which they renamed Fort Pitt) and then captured Fort Louisbourg, a French stronghold at the mouth of the St. Lawrence. In 1759, a force led by General James Wolfe sailed down the St. Lawrence and took Quebec, the heart of France's American empire. The Royal Navy prevented French reinforcements from crossing the Atlantic; and in 1760, British forces captured Montreal, completing the conquest of Canada (Map 4.5).

Elsewhere the British also went from success to success. Fulfilling Pitt's dream, the East India Company ousted French traders from India; and British forces seized French Senegal in West Africa and the sugar islands Martinique and Guadeloupe in the French West Indies. From Spain, the British won

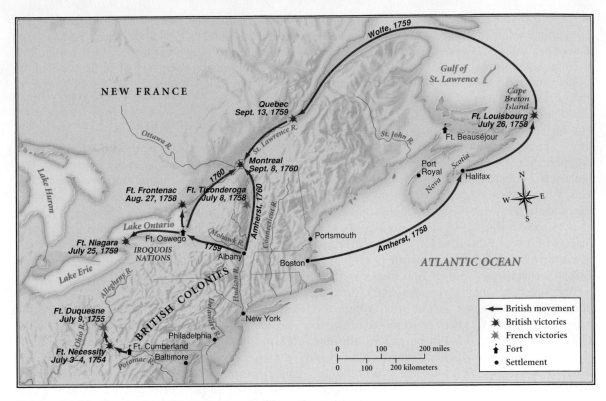

MAP 4.5 The Anglo-American Conquest of New France

After full-scale war with France broke out in 1756, it took almost three years for the British ministry to equip colonial forces and dispatch an army to America. Then British and colonial troops attacked the heartland of New France, capturing Quebec in 1759 and Montreal in 1760. The conquest both united and divided the allies. Colonists celebrated the great victory — "The Illuminations and Fireworks exceeded any that had been exhibited before," reported the *South Carolina Gazette*. However, British officers held the colonial soldiers in disdain. Said one: "[They are] the dirtiest, most contemptible, cowardly dogs you can conceive."

Cuba and the Philippine Islands. The Treaty of Paris of 1763 confirmed Britain's triumph. It granted the British sovereignty over half the continent of North America, including French Canada, all French territory east of the Mississippi River, and Spanish Florida. The French empire in North America was reduced to a handful of sugar islands in the West Indies and two rocky islands off the coast of Newfoundland.

Pontiac's Rebellion. Britain's territorial acquisitions alarmed Indian peoples from New York to Michigan, who rightly feared an influx of Anglo-American settlers. Hoping that the French would return as a counterweight to British power, the Ottawa chief Pontiac declared, "I am French, and I want to die French." Neolin, a Delaware prophet, went further; he taught that the suffering of the Indian peoples stemmed from their dependence on Europeans' goods, guns, and rum, and called for their expulsion: "If you suffer the English among you, you are dead men. Sickness, smallpox, and their poison [rum] will destroy you entirely." In 1763, inspired by Neolin's vision and his growing anti-British sentiments, Pontiac led a group of loosely confederated tribes (stretching geographically from the New York Senecas to the Minnesota Chippewas) in a major uprising known as Pontiac's Rebellion. The Indian force seized nearly every British garrison west of Fort Niagara, besieged the fort at Detroit, and killed or captured more than 2,000 settlers. But the Indian alliance gradually weakened, and British military expeditions defeated the Delawares near Fort Pitt and broke the siege of Detroit. In the peace settlement, Pontiac and his allies accepted the British as their new political "fathers." In return, the British issued the Proclamation of 1763, which expressly prohibited

Pipe of Peace

In 1760, the Ottawa chief Pontiac welcomed British troops to his territory. Here he is shown offering a pipe of peace to their commander, Major Robert Rogers. Three years later, as British troops built forts in Indian lands and Anglo-American settlers moved west, Pontiac led a coordinated Indian uprising against the new European intruders. Library of Congress.

white settlements west of the Appalachians. It was an edict the colonists would ignore.

British Industrial Growth and the Consumer Revolution

Britain owed its military and diplomatic success to its unprecedented economic resources. Since 1700, when it had wrested control of many oceanic trade routes from the Dutch, Britain had been the dominant commercial power in the Atlantic and Indian oceans. By 1750, it had also become the first country to use new manufacturing technology and work discipline to expand output. This combination of commerce and industry would soon make Britain the most powerful nation in the world.

Mechanical power was a key ingredient of Britain's Industrial Revolution. British artisans designed and built water mills and steam engines that efficiently powered a wide array of machines: lathes for shaping wood, jennies and looms for spinning and weaving textiles, and hammers for forging iron. The new power-driven machinery produced woolen and linen textiles, iron tools, furniture, and chinaware in greater quantities than traditional manufacturing methods—and at lower cost. Moreover, the entrepreneurs who ran the new workshops drove their employees hard, forcing them to keep pace with the machines and to work long hours. To market the abundant products produced in the factories, English and Scottish merchants extended a full year's credit to colonial

shopkeepers instead of the traditional six months'. Americans soon were purchasing 30 percent of all British exports.

To pay for British manufactured goods, the colonists increased their exports of tobacco, rice, indigo, and wheat. In Virginia, farmers moved into the Piedmont, a region of plains and rolling hills just inland from the Tidewater counties. Using credit advanced by Scottish tobacco merchants, planters bought land, slaves, and equipment. The merchants took their payment in tobacco and exported it to expanding markets in France and central Europe. In South Carolina, rice planters increased their wealth and luxurious lifestyles by using British government subsidies to develop indigo plantations. By the 1760s, they were exporting large quantities of the deep blue dye to English textile factories; at the same time, they were selling 65 million pounds of rice a year to Holland and southern Europe. Simultaneously, New York, Pennsylvania, Maryland, and Virginia became the breadbasket of the Atlantic world, supplying Europe's exploding population with wheat at ever-increasing prices. In Philadelphia, export prices for wheat jumped almost 50 percent between 1740 and 1765.

Americans used their profits from trade to buy English manufactures in a "consumer revolution" that raised their standard of living (Figure 4.3). However, this first American spending binge, like most subsequent splurges, landed many consumers in debt. Even during the booming wartime economy

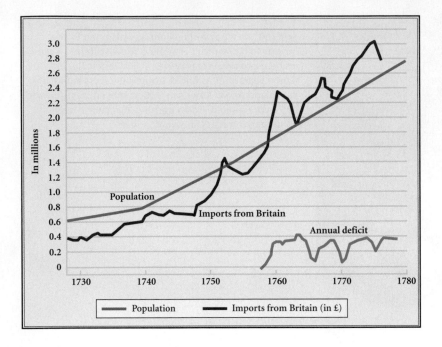

Figure 4.3 Mainland Population, British Imports, and the American Trade Deficit

Around 1750, British imports were growing at a faster rate than the American population, indicating that the colonists were consuming more per capita. But Americans went into debt to pay for these goods, running an annual trade deficit with their British suppliers that by 1772 meant a cumulative debt of £2 million.

of the 1750s, exports paid for only 80 percent of imported British goods. The remaining 20 percent—the Americans' trade deficit—was financed by Britain through the extension of credit and through Pitt's military expenditures. When the military subsidies ended in 1763, the colonies found themselves in an economic recession. Colonial merchants looked anxiously at their overstocked warehouses and feared bankruptcy. "I think we have a gloomy prospect before us," a Philadelphia trader noted in 1765, "as there are of late some Persons failed, who were in no way suspected." The increase in transatlantic trade had raised living standards; but it also had made Americans more dependent on overseas credit and markets.

The Struggle for Land in the East

In good times and bad, the colonial population continued to grow, intensifying the demand for arable land. The families who founded the town of Kent, Connecticut, in 1738 were descended from the original settlers of the colony. Like earlier generations, they had moved inland to establish new farms, but they had now reached the colony's western boundary. To provide for the next generation, many Kent families joined the Susquehanna Company. Started in 1749, the company undertook to settle lands in the Wyoming Valley and other areas along the upper Susquehanna River (in what is today the northeastern corner of Pennsylvania). As Connecticut settlers took up farm-

steads there, the company urged the Connecticut legislature to claim the region based on Connecticut's "sea-to-sea" royal charter of 1662. However, Charles II had also granted the Wyoming Valley region to William Penn, and the Penn family had sold farms there to Pennsylvania residents. By the late 1750s, settlers from Connecticut and Pennsylvania were at war, burning down their rivals' houses and barns.

Simultaneously, three distinct but related land disputes broke out in the Hudson River Valley (Map 4.6). Dutch tenant farmers, Wappinger Indians, and migrants from Massachusetts asserted ownership rights to lands long claimed by the Van Rensselaer, Livingston, and other manorial families. When the manorial lords turned to the legal system to uphold their claims, Dutch and English farmers in Westchester, Dutchess, and Albany counties rioted to close the courts. At the request of New York's royal governor, General Thomas Gage and two British regiments joined with local sheriffs and manorial bailiffs to put down the mob. They suppressed the tenant farmers, intimidated the Wappingers, and evicted the Massachusetts squatters.

Other land disputes erupted in New Jersey and the southern colonies, where resident landlords and English aristocrats successfully asserted legal claims based on long-dormant seventeenth-century charters. One court decision upheld the right of Lord Granville, an heir of an original Carolina proprietor, to collect an annual tax on

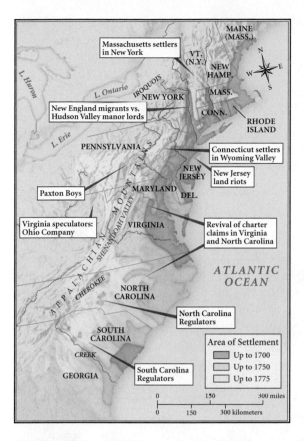

MAP 4.6 Westward Expansion and Land Conflicts, 1750–1775

Between 1750 and 1775, the mainland population more than doubled — from 1.2 million to 2.5 million — triggering both migration westward and legal battles over land, which had become increasingly valuable. Violence broke out in eastern areas, where tenant farmers and smallholders contested landlords' titles, and in the backcountry, where migrating settlers fought with Indians, rival claimants, and the officials of eastern-dominated governments.

land in North Carolina; another decision awarded ownership of the entire northern neck of Virginia (along the Potomac River) to Lord Fairfax.

This revival of proprietary claims by manorial lords and English nobles reflected the rising price of land on the Atlantic coastal plain. It also reflected the maturity of the colonial courts, which now had enough authority to uphold property rights. And both developments underscored the increasing resemblance between rural societies in Europe and America. Long-settled tenants and yeomen, fearing they would soon be reduced to the status of European peasants, joined with new migrants from Europe to look for cheap land near the Appalachian Mountains.

Western Uprisings and Regulator Movements

As would-be landowners moved westward, they sparked new disputes over Indian policy, political representation, and debts. During the war with France, Delaware and Shawnee warriors had extracted revenge for Thomas Penn's land swindle of 1737 by attacking frontier farms throughout central and western Pennsylvania, destroying property and killing and capturing hundreds of residents. Scots-Irish settlers demanded military action to expel all Indians, but Quaker leaders refused. In 1763, the Scots-Irish Paxton Boys took matters into their own hands and massacred twenty members of the peaceful Conestoga tribe. When Governor John Penn tried to bring the murderers to justice, about 250 armed Scots-Irish advanced on Philadelphia. Benjamin Franklin intercepted the angry mob at Lancaster and arranged a truce, narrowly averting a pitched battle with the militia. Prosecution of the Paxton Boys failed for lack of witnesses, and the Scots-Irish dropped their demands that the Indians be expelled; but the episode left a legacy of racial hatred and political resentment.

The South Carolina Regulators. Violence also broke out in the backcountry of South Carolina, where land-hungry Scottish and Anglo-American settlers clashed repeatedly with Cherokees during the war with France. When the war ended in 1763, a group of landowning vigilantes, the Regulators, tried to suppress outlaw bands of whites that were stealing cattle and other property. The Regulators also had political goals: They demanded that the eastern-controlled government provide the western districts with more courts and greater representation in the assembly, and distribute the tax burden fairly across the colony. Fearing slave revolts, the lowland rice planters who ran the South Carolina assembly chose to compromise with the Regulators rather than fight them. In 1767, the assembly created local courts in the western counties and reduced the fees for legal documents; but it refused to reapportion seats or to lower taxes in the backcountry. Like the Paxton Boys in Pennsylvania, the South Carolina Regulators attracted attention to western needs but ultimately failed to wrest power from the eastern elite.

Civil Strife in North Carolina. In 1766, a more radical Regulator movement arose in the backcountry of North Carolina. The economic recession

A Hudson River Manor

Philipse Manor encompassed 90,000 acres, and included mills and warehouses as well as a grand house. In this unattributed painting, the artist has dressed the women in the foreground in classical costumes, thereby linking the Philipses to the noble families of the Roman republic. To preserve their aristocratic lifestyle and the quasi-feudal leasehold system of agriculture, the Philipses joined with other Hudson River manorial lords to suppress tenant uprisings in the 1760s. Historic Hudson Valley, Tarrytown, New York.

of the early 1760s caused a sharp fall in tobacco prices, and many farmers could not pay their debts. When creditors sued for what they were owed, judges directed sheriffs to seize the debtors' property and sell it to pay debts and court costs. Backcountry farmers—including many German and Scots-Irish migrants—denounced the merchants' lawsuits, both because they generated high fees for lawyers and court officials and because they violated the rural custom of community exchange, which allowed loans to remain unpaid for years.

To save their farms from grasping creditors and tax-hungry officials, North Carolina's debtors defied the government's authority. Disciplined mobs of farmers intimidated judges, closed courts, and freed their comrades from jail. Significantly, the Regulators proposed a coherent set of reforms. They demanded legislation to lower legal fees and allow payment of taxes in the "produce of the country" rather than in cash. They also insisted on greater representation in the assembly and a fair tax system, proposing that each person be taxed "in proportion to the profits arising from his estate." To no avail. In May 1771, Royal Governor William Tryon decided to suppress the Regulators. Mobilizing British troops and the eastern militia, Tryon defeated a large Regulator

Governor Tryon and the Regulators Meet at Hillsborough, 1768

Orange County, North Carolina, was home to the Sandy Creek Association, a group of Quakers led by Herman Husband, a powerful advocate of social justice. Early in 1768 its members joined with other Piedmont farmers to create the Regulator movement. When the legislature ignored their petitions protesting corruption by government officials, the Regulators refused to pay taxes and shut down the courts. In September 1768, Royal Governor William Tryon and the low country militia confronted a group of Regulators near Hillsborough. As this engraving suggests, the possibility of violence was high and only narrowly averted. Three years later, Tryon and the Regulators engaged in a pitched battle near the Alamance River, twenty miles west of Hillsborough.

Picture Research Consultants and Archives.

force at the Alamance River. When the fighting ended, thirty men lay dead, and Tryon summarily executed seven insurgent leaders. Not since Bacon's Rebellion in Virginia in 1675 (see Chapter 2) had a domestic political conflict caused so much bloodshed.

In 1771, as in 1675, colonial conflicts became entwined with imperial politics. In Connecticut, Reverend Ezra Stiles defended the North Carolina Regulators. "What shall an injured & oppressed people do," he asked, when faced with "Oppression and tyranny?" His remarks reflected growing resistance to measures the British began introducing in 1765 to enhance their control of the colonies. As they had in 1686, when James II imposed the Dominion of New England, the American colonies still depended on Britain for their trade and mili-

tary defense. However, by the 1760s, the mainland settlements had developed an increasingly complex society with the potential to exist independently. British policies would determine the direction the maturing colonies would take.

➤ What were the major consequences of the Great War for Empire on the imperial balance of power, British-colonial relations, Indian peoples, and Anglo-American settlers?

➤ What impact did the Industrial Revolution in England have on the American colonies?

➤ What were the causes of unrest in the American backcountry in the mid-eighteenth century?

SUMMARY

In this chapter we explored the dramatic social and cultural changes between 1720 and 1765 in the British mainland colonies. Looking at the colonies as a whole, we noted an astonishing increase in population — from 400,000 to almost 2 million — the result of natural growth, immigration, and the forced transport of large numbers of slaves from Africa. At the same time, American settlers were introduced to and became well acquainted with two major cultural movements: the Enlightenment and Pietism. They also had access to a steady supply of new consumer goods churned out by English factories.

On the regional level, we noted that the colonists confronted three major challenges. First, by 1750, overpopulation had become a problem in many older settlements in New England, where farms could no longer be subdivided by inheritance and still support a family. To preserve the yeoman ideal of independent farming, some families migrated to new regions while others developed an "exchange" economy to maximize their resources. Second, in the middle colonies, where fertile land was more plentiful, English Quaker, German, and Scots-Irish residents struggled to maintain their religious and cultural identities while avoiding bruising ethnic conflicts. Finally, the pressures of westward migration disrupted life throughout the backcountry — the frontier regions from New England to the Carolinas. In 1754, Anglo-American expansion into the Ohio River Valley led to conflicts with Indian peoples, civil and political unrest among white settlers, and, ultimately, the Great War for Empire.

By 1765, Britain stood triumphant in Europe and America. But social and cultural developments in the colonies in combination with new British policies would soon revolutionize the character of life there.

Connections: Culture

In the part opener (p. 3), we provided a broad outline of cultural changes in America between 1600 and 1765:

> The new American society witnessed the appearance of new forms of family and community life. . . . [It was also] increasingly pluralistic, made up of migrants from many European ethnic groups — English, Scots, Scots-Irish, Dutch, and Germans — as well as West African slaves and Native Americans. Distinct regional cultures developed in New England, the Middle Atlantic colonies, the Chesapeake, and the Carolinas.

Now that we have tracked the trajectory of Britain's North American colonies, we can see a crucial turning point around 1700. Until that time, most settlers came from England, bringing with them traditional English social and political structures: Fathers ruled families, and authoritarian leaders dominated politics. Then came a massive wave of migrants — enslaved Africans, Germans, Scots-Irish, and Scots. By 1765, these migrants and their descendants constituted a majority of the population. As the people in British North America became more diverse, life there became less repressive and more open to innovation.

A second phase of cultural change began around 1740. An increasingly complex economy encouraged farmers to join the market economy; a responsive system of government prompted more men to seek office; a decline in parental power allowed young women greater choice in their marriage partners; and an outburst of religious enthusiasm shook established churches and advanced religious liberty. Taken together, these developments provided the colonists in British North America (as we put it in concluding the Part Opener) "unprecedented opportunities for economic security, political freedom, and spiritual fulfillment."

CHAPTER REVIEW QUESTIONS

➤ How did the three mainland regions in British North America — New England, the middle colonies, and, as discussed in Chapter 3, the South — become more like one another between 1720 and 1750? In what ways did they become increasingly different? From these comparisons, what conclusions can you draw about the character of American society in the mid-eighteenth century?

➤ Compare and contrast the ethnic complexity of the middle colonies with the racial (and, in the backcountry, the ethnic) diversity of the southern colonies. What conflicts did this diversity cause?

TIMELINE

1710s–1730s	Enlightenment ideas spread from Europe to America
	Germans and Scots-Irish settle in the Middle Atlantic colonies
	Theodore Jacob Frelinghuysen preaches Pietism to German migrants
1730s	William and Gilbert Tennent lead Presbyterian revivals among Scots-Irish
	Jonathan Edwards preaches in New England
1739	George Whitefield sparks the Great Awakening
1740s–1760s	Conflict between Old Lights and New Lights
	Shortage of farmland in New England threatens freehold ideal
	Growing ethnic and religious pluralism in Middle Atlantic colonies
	Religious denominations establish colleges
1743	Benjamin Franklin founds American Philosophical Society
	Samuel Morris starts Presbyterian revivals in Virginia
1749	Virginia speculators create Ohio Company, and Connecticut farmers form Susquehanna Company
1750s	Industrial Revolution in England
	Consumer revolution increases American imports and debt
1754	French and Indian War begins
	Iroquois and colonists meet at Albany Congress; Franklin's Plan of Union
1756	Britain begins Great War for Empire
1759–1760	Britain completes conquest of Canada
1760s	Land conflict along New York and New England
	Baptist revivals win converts in Virginia
1763	Pontiac's Rebellion leads to Proclamation of 1763
	Treaty of Paris ends Great War for Empire
	Scots-Irish Paxton Boys massacre Indians in Pennsylvania
1771	Royal governor puts down Regulator revolt in North Carolina

FOR FURTHER EXPLORATION

The social history of eighteenth-century America comes to life in the stories of individuals. In *Good Wives: Image and Reality in the Lives of Women in Northern New England, 1650–1750* (1982), Laurel Thatcher Ulrich paints a vivid picture of women's experiences. For further insight into the day-to-day lives of women, see the PBS video *A Midwife's Tale*, which tells the story of Martha Ballard; for additional materials on Ballard, see **www.pbs.org/amex/midwife** and **www.DoHistory.org**. Benjamin Franklin's *Autobiography* (1771; available in many editions) demonstrates Franklin's Enlightenment sensibilities, describes his pursuit of wealth and influence, and provides an entertaining look at the bustling city of Philadelphia. Also see the Library of Congress exhibit and Web page, "Benjamin Franklin . . . in His Own Words" (**www.loc.gov/exhibits/treasures/franklin-home.html**). For more on Franklin's life and times, see "The Electric Franklin" (**www.ushistory.org/franklin/index.htm**).

A less-successful quest for self-betterment is the subject of another autobiography, *The Infortunate: The Voyage and Adventures of William Moraley, an Indentured Servant* (1992), edited by Susan E. Klepp and Billy G. Smith. Harry S. Stout's *The Divine Dramatist: George Whitefield and the Rise of Modern Evangelicalism* (1991) shows how the charismatic preacher's flair for theatrics and self-promotion enabled him to preach effectively. "Jonathan Edwards On-Line" (**www.JonathanEdwards.com/**) presents the writings of the great philosopher and preacher; but note that the site uses Edwards's arguments to advance one side of a present-day theological debate.

On day-to-day economic life, see "Colonial Currency and Colonial Coin" (**www.coins.nd.edu/ColCurrency/index.html**), which contains detailed essays as well as pictures of colonial money. For a rich collection of documents and visual materials on the lives of migrant German sectarians, see "Bethlehem Digital History Project" (**bdhp.moravian.edu/**).

For an examination of the relationships between settlers and Indians, see Jane T. Merritt, *At the Crossroads: Indians and Empires on a Mid-Atlantic Frontier, 1700–1763* (2003), and three regional studies: Matthew C. Ward, *Breaking the Backcountry: The Seven Years' War in Virginia and Pennsylvania, 1754–1765* (2003); John Oliphant, *Peace and War on the Anglo-Cherokee Frontier, 1756–63* (2001); and Gregory Evans Dowd, *War Under Heaven: Pontiac, the Indian Nations, and the British Empire* (2002). Also see "The War That Made America," a PBS series about the French and Indian War, and the accompanying Web site (**www.thewarthatmadeamerica.com/**).

TEST YOUR KNOWLEDGE

To assess your command of the material in this chapter, see the Online Study Guide at **bedfordstmartins.com/henretta**.

For Web sites, images, and documents related to topics and places in this chapter, visit **bedfordstmartins.com/makehistory**.

PART TWO

The New Republic
1763–1820

	GOVERNMENT	DIPLOMACY	ECONOMY	SOCIETY	CULTURE
	Creating republican institutions	European entanglements	Expanding commerce and manufacturing	Defining liberty and equality	Pluralism and national identity
1763	▸ Stamp Act Congress (1765) ▸ Committees of correspondence ▸ First Continental Congress (1774)	▸ Treaty of Paris (1763) gives Britain control of Canada and Florida	▸ Merchants defy Sugar and Stamp Acts ▸ Boycotts spur domestic manufacturing	▸ Artisans seek influence ▸ Quebec Act (1774) allows Catholicism	▸ Patriots call for American unity ▸ Concept of popular sovereignty takes hold
1775	▸ Second Continental Congress (1775) ▸ States devise and implement constitutions	▸ Independence declared (1776) ▸ Treaty of Alliance with France (1778)	▸ Manufacturing expands during war ▸ Severe inflation threatens economy	▸ Judith Sargent Murray writes On the Equality of the Sexes (1779) ▸ Emancipation begins in the North	▸ Thomas Paine's Common Sense (1776) calls for a republic
1780	▸ Articles of Confederation ratified (1781) ▸ Legislatures assert supremacy in states ▸ Philadelphia convention drafts U.S. Constitution (1787)	▸ Treaty of Paris (1783) ▸ Britain restricts U.S. trade with West Indies ▸ U.S. government signs treaties with Indian peoples	▸ Bank of North America founded (1781) ▸ Commercial recession (1783–1789) ▸ Land speculation continues in West	▸ Virginia enacts religious freedom legislation (1786) ▸ Politicians and ministers endorse republican motherhood	▸ Noah Webster defines American English ▸ State cessions and land ordinances create national domain in West ▸ German settlers keep own language
1790	▸ Conflict over Alexander Hamilton's economic policies ▸ First national parties: Federalists and Republicans	▸ Wars between France and Britain ▸ Jay's Treaty and Pinkney's Treaty (1795) ▸ Undeclared war with France (1798)	▸ First Bank of the United States (1792–1811) ▸ States charter business corporations ▸ Outwork system grows	▸ Bill of Rights ratified (1791) ▸ Creation of French Republic (1793) sparks ideological debate ▸ Sedition Act limits freedom of press (1798)	▸ Indians form Western Confederacy (1790) ▸ Second Great Awakening (1790–1860) ▸ Divisions emerge between South and North
1800	▸ Jefferson's "Revolution of 1800" reduces activism of national government ▸ Chief Justice Marshall asserts judicial powers	▸ Napoleonic Wars (1802–1815) ▸ Louisiana Purchase (1803) ▸ Embargo Act (1807)	▸ Cotton farming expands ▸ Farm productivity improves ▸ Embargo encourages U.S. manufacturing	▸ New Jersey denies suffrage to propertied women (1807) ▸ Atlantic slave trade legally ends (1808)	▸ Tenskwatawa and Tecumseh revive Western Confederacy
1810	▸ Triumph of Republican Party and end of Federalist Party ▸ State constitutions democratized	▸ War of 1812 (1812–1815) ▸ Monroe Doctrine (1823)	▸ Second Bank of the United States chartered (1816–1836) ▸ Supreme Court rules for business ▸ Emergence of a national economy	▸ Suffrage for white men expands ▸ American Colonization Society (1817) ▸ Missouri Compromise (1819–1821)	▸ War of 1812 tests national unity ▸ Religious benevolence produces social reform

"The American war is over," Philadelphia Patriot Benjamin Rush declared in 1787, "but this is far from being the case with the American Revolution. On the contrary, nothing but the first act of the great drama is closed. It remains yet to establish and perfect our new forms of government." As we will suggest in Part Two, the job was even greater than Rush imagined. The republican revolution that began with the Patriot resistance movement of 1765 and took shape with the Declaration of Independence in 1776 reached far beyond politics. It challenged almost all the values and institutions of the colonial social order and forced Americans to consider fundamental changes in their economic, religious, and cultural practices. Here, in summary, are the main themes of our discussion of America's new political and social order.

GOVERNMENT Once Americans had repudiated their allegiance to Britain and the monarchy, they faced the task of creating a new system of government. In 1776, no one knew how the states should go about setting up republican institutions. Nor did Patriot leaders know if there should be a permanent central authority along the lines of the Continental Congresses that led the resistance movement and the war. It would take time and experience to find out. It would take even longer to assimilate a new institution — the political party — into the workings of government. However, by 1820, years of difficult political compromise and constitutional revision had resulted in republican national and state governments that commanded the allegiance of their citizens.

DIPLOMACY To create and preserve their new republic, Americans of European descent had to fight two wars against Great Britain, an undeclared war against France, and many battles with Indian peoples. The wars against Britain divided the country into bitter factions — Patriots against Loyalists in the War of Independence, and prowar Republicans against antiwar Federalists in the War of 1812 — and expended much blood and treasure. The extension of American sovereignty and settlements into the trans-Appalachian west was a cultural disaster for many Indian peoples, who were brutally driven from their lands by white farmers. Despite these external and internal wars, by 1820, the United States had emerged as a strong independent state. Freed from a half-century of entanglement in the wars and diplomacy of Europe, its people began to exploit the riches of the continent.

ECONOMY By the 1760s, the expansion of markets and commerce had established the foundations for a vigorous national economy. Beginning in the 1780s, northern merchants financed a banking system and organized a rural outwork system. Simultaneously, state governments used charters and special privileges to help businesses and to improve roads, bridges, and waterways. African American slaves remained vital to the southern economy as planters began to export a new staple crop — cotton — to markets in the North and Europe. Many yeomen farm families migrated westward to grow grain; while those in the East turned to the production of raw materials — leather and wool, for example — for burgeoning manufacturing enterprises, and augmented their income with sales of shoes, textiles, tinware, and other handicrafts. By 1820, the young American republic was on the verge of achieving economic as well as political independence.

SOCIETY As Americans undertook to create a republican society, they divided along lines of gender, race, religion, and class. In particular, they disagreed over fundamental issues like legal equality for women, the status of slavery, the meaning of free speech and religious liberty, and the extent of public responsibility for social inequality. As we shall see, political leaders managed to resolve some of these disputes. Legislatures abolished slavery in the North, broadened religious liberty by allowing freedom of conscience, and, except in New England, ended the system of established churches. However, Americans continued to argue over social equality, in part because their republican creed placed authority in the family and in society into the hands of men of property. This arrangement denied power not only to slaves but also to free blacks, women, and poor white men.

CULTURE The diversity of peoples and regions that characterized the British colonies in North America complicated efforts after the Revolution to define a distinct American culture and identity. Native Americans still lived in their own clans and nations; and black Americans, one-fifth of the enumerated population, were developing a new, African American culture. Although white Americans were bound by vigorous regional cultures and their ancestral heritage — English, Scottish, Scots-Irish, German, or Dutch — in time, their political institutions began to unite them, as did their increasing participation in the market economy and in Evangelical Protestant churches. By 1820, to be an American meant, for many members of the dominant white population, to be a republican, a Protestant, and an enterprising individual in a capitalist-run market system.

5 Toward Independence: Years of Decision

1763–1776

A S THE GREAT WAR FOR empire ended in 1763, Seth Metcalf joined other American colonists in celebrating the triumph of British arms. A Massachusetts soldier during the conflict, Metcalf thanked "the Great Goodness of God" for the "General Peace" that was so "percularly Advantageous to the English Nation." Just two years later, Metcalf was less certain of God's favor. "God is angry with us of this land," the pious Calvinist wrote in his journal, "and is now Smiting [us] with his Rod Especially by the hands of our Rulers."

The rapid disintegration of the bonds uniting Britain and America—an event that Metcalf could explain only in terms of Divine Providence—mystified many Americans. How had it happened, the president of King's College in New York asked in 1775, that such a "happily situated" people were ready to "hazard their Fortunes, their Lives, and their Souls, in a Rebellion"? Unlike other colonial peoples of the time, white Americans lived in a prosperous society with a strong tradition of self-government. They had little to gain and much to lose by rebelling.

Or so it seemed in 1763, before the British government began to reform the imperial system. "This year Came an act from England Called the Stamp Act . . . which is thought will be very oppressive to the Inhabitants of North America," Metcalf reflected, "But Mobbs keep it back."

◀ **British Troops Occupy Concord, 1775**

In April 1775, hundreds of British troops stationed in Boston marched to Lexington and Concord, Massachusetts, in search of Patriot arms and munitions. The raid led to a violent and deadly confrontation with the Patriot militia, an outcome prefigured by the unknown artist's depiction of a graveyard in the foreground of this painting. Courtesy, Concord Museum.

The British reforms quickly prompted violent resistance and a downward spiral of ideological debate and political conflict that ended in a war for American independence. Was this outcome inevitable? Could careful statecraft and political compromise have saved the empire? The likely answer is yes. But neither statecraft nor compromise was in evidence; instead, the inflexibility of British ministers and the passionate determination of Patriot leaders would destroy the British empire in North America.

Imperial Reform, 1763–1765

The Great War for Empire left a mixed legacy. Britain had driven the French out of Canada and the lands to the west of the Appalachian Mountains, and the Spanish out of Florida; and it now dominated all of eastern North America (Map 5.1). But the cost of the war had been high. To cope with the nation's enormous debt, the British ministry imposed new taxes on the American possessions. More fundamentally, the war spurred Parliament to redefine the character of the empire: Salutary Neglect, with its emphasis on trade and colonial self-government, gave way to imperial authority and the direct rule of Parliament.

The Legacy of War

The war changed the relationship between Britain and its North American colonies. During the fighting, British generals and American leaders disagreed sharply on military strategy. Moreover, the presence of 25,000 British troops revealed sharp cultural differences. The arrogance of British officers and their demands for deference shocked many Americans: British soldiers "are but little better than slaves to their officers," declared a Massachusetts militiaman. The hostility was mutual. British general James Wolfe complained that colonial troops were drawn from the dregs of society and that "there was no depending on them in action."

Disputes over Trade and Troops. The war also exposed the weakness of the royal governors. In theory, the governors had extensive political powers, including command of the provincial militia; in reality, they had to share power with the colonial assemblies, which outraged British officials. In Massachusetts, complained the Board of Trade, "almost every act of executive and legislative power is ordered and directed by votes and resolves of the General Court." To strengthen imperial authority, Parliament passed the Revenue Act of 1762. The act tightened up the collection of trade duties, which colonial merchants had evaded for decades by bribing customs officials. The ministry also instructed the Royal Navy to seize American vessels carrying supplies from the mainland to the French West Indies. It was absurd, declared an outraged British politician, that French armies that were attempting "to Destroy one English province . . . are actually supported by Bread raised in another."

Britain's victory over France provoked a fundamental shift in military policy: the peacetime deployment of an army of ten thousand men in North America. Underlying that decision were several factors. King George III (r. 1760–1820) wanted military commands for his friends. The king's ministers feared a possible rebellion by the 60,000 French residents of Canada, Britain's new province to the north. The Native Americans were also a concern: Pontiac's Rebellion had nearly overwhelmed Britain's frontier forts; only a substantial military force could restrain the Indian peoples and deter land-hungry whites from settling west of the Appalachian Mountains in defiance of the Proclamation of 1763 (see Chapter 4). Finally, British politicians worried about the colonists' loyalty now that the French no longer controlled Canada. "The main purpose of Stationing a large Body of Troops in America," declared treasury official William Knox, "is to secure the Dependence of the Colonys on Great Britain." By deploying an army in America, the British ministry signaled its willingness to use military force to subdue conquered Frenchmen, unruly Indians, or rebellious colonists.

The National Debt. Troops cost money, which was in short supply because Britain's national debt had soared from £75 million in 1756 to £133 million in 1763. Indeed, the interest on the war debt was consuming 60 percent of the national budget, forcing cutbacks in other government expenditures. To restore fiscal stability, the prime minister, Lord Bute, needed to raise taxes. He began in England. The Treasury Department opposed increasing the land tax, which was already high and was paid primarily by the gentry and aristocracy, who had great influence in Parliament. So instead, Bute taxed those with little or no political power—the poor and middling classes—imposing higher import duties on tobacco and sugar, which raised their cost to consumers. The ministry also increased excise

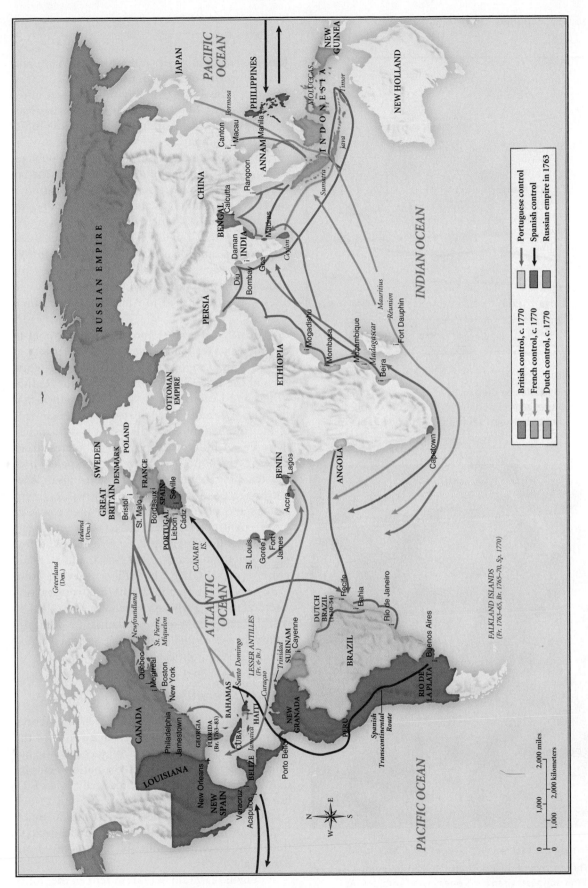

MAP 5.1 Eurasian Trade and European Colonies, c. 1770

By 1770, the Western European nations that had long dominated maritime trade had created vast colonial empires. Spain controlled the western halves of North and South America, Portugal owned Brazil, and Holland ruled Indonesia. Britain, a newer imperial power, boasted settler societies in North America, rich sugar islands in the West Indies, slave ports in West Africa, and a growing presence on the Indian subcontinent. Only France had failed to acquire and hold on to a significant colonial empire. (To trace changes in empire and trade routes, see Map 1.3 on p. 18 and Map 2.2 on p. 44.)

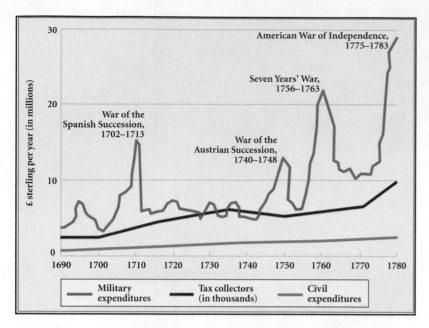

FIGURE 5.1 The Growing Power of the British State, 1690–1780

As Britain built a great navy and subsidized the armies of its European allies, the government's military expenditures soared, as did the number of tax collectors. The tax bureaucracy doubled in size between 1700 and 1735, and doubled again between 1750 and 1780.

George Grenville, Architect of the Stamp Act

This portrait of the British prime minister, painted in 1763, suggests Grenville's energy and ambition. As events were to show, he was determined to reform the imperial system and to ensure that the colonists shared the cost of the empire. The Earl of Halifax, Garrowby, Yorkshire.

levies — essentially sales taxes — on salt, beer, and distilled spirits, once again passing on the costs of the war to the king's ordinary subjects. Left unresolved was the question of taxing the American colonists, who, like Britain's poor, had little influence in Parliament.

To ensure adherence to its new fiscal policies, the British government doubled the size of the tax bureaucracy (Figure 5.1). Customs agents patrolled the coasts of southern Britain, arrested smugglers, and seized tons of French wines and Flemish textiles. Convicted smugglers faced heavy penalties, including death or forced "transportation" to America. Despite protests by the colonial assemblies, nearly fifty thousand English criminals had already been banished to America as indentured servants.

The price of empire abroad had turned out to be higher taxes and government intrusion at home. This development confirmed the worst fears of the British opposition parties, the Radical Whigs and Country Party. They complained that the huge war debt placed the treasury at the mercy of the "monied interest," the banks and financiers who reaped millions of pounds in interest from government bonds. Moreover, the expansion of the tax bureaucracy had created thousands of patronage positions filled with "worthless pensioners and placemen." To reverse the growth of government power — and the consequent threats to personal liberty and property rights — reformers in Britain demanded that Parliament be made more representative. The Radical Whig John Wilkes called for an end to **rotten boroughs**, tiny electoral districts whose voters were controlled by wealthy aristocrats and merchants. In domestic affairs as in colonial policy, the war had transformed British political life.

George Grenville: Imperial Reformer

A member of Parliament since 1741, George Grenville was widely conceded to be "one of the ablest men in Great Britain." When Grenville became prime minister in 1763, the nation's empire in America had expanded dramatically (Map 5.2); but the war had left Britain in debt, and British taxpayers were paying nearly five times as much in taxes as free Americans were. Grenville decided that new revenue would have to come from America.

Grenville carefully set out to reform the imperial system and began with a two-part plan. One part consisted of the Currency Act of 1764, which extended the ban on paper money as legal tender

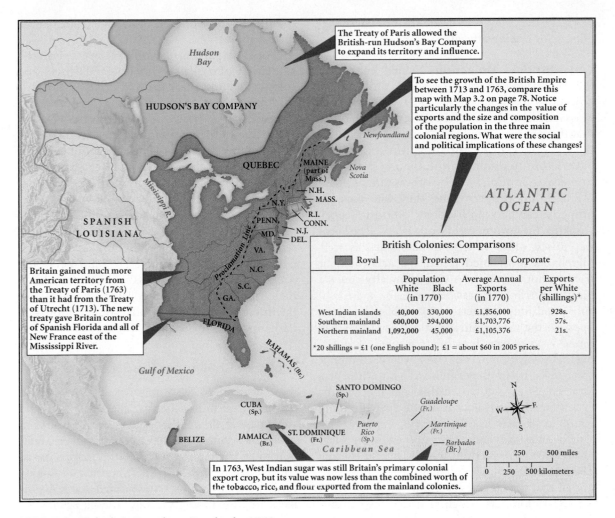

The Treaty of Paris allowed the British-run Hudson's Bay Company to expand its territory and influence.

To see the growth of the British Empire between 1713 and 1763, compare this map with Map 3.2 on page 78. Notice particularly the changes in the value of exports and the size and composition of the population in the three main colonial regions. What were the social and political implications of these changes?

Britain gained much more American territory from the Treaty of Paris (1763) than it had from the Treaty of Utrecht (1713). The new treaty gave Britain control of Spanish Florida and all of New France east of the Mississippi River.

British Colonies: Comparisons

Royal   Proprietary   Corporate

	Population White (in 1770)	Black	Average Annual Exports (in 1770)	Exports per White (shillings)*
West Indian islands	40,000	330,000	£1,856,000	928s.
Southern mainland	600,000	394,000	£1,703,776	57s.
Northern mainland	1,092,000	45,000	£1,105,376	21s.

*20 shillings = £1 (one English pound); £1 = about $60 in 2005 prices.

In 1763, West Indian sugar was still Britain's primary colonial export crop, but its value was now less than the combined worth of the tobacco, rice, and flour exported from the mainland colonies.

MAP 5.2   Britain's American Empire in 1763

The Treaty of Paris gave Britain control of the eastern half of North America and a dominant position in the West Indies. To protect the empire's new territories, British ministers dispatched troops to Florida and Quebec; they also sent troops to uphold the terms of the Proclamation of 1763, which prohibited Anglo-American settlement west of the Appalachian Mountains.

from New England to all the American colonies. Now American shopkeepers, planters, and farmers would have to pay their debts to British merchants in gold or silver coin, which was always in short supply.

The Sugar Act and Colonial Rights. Grenville also won parliamentary approval of the Sugar Act of 1764 to replace the widely ignored Molasses Act of 1733 (see Chapter 3). The prime minister and his subordinates who wrote the law understood the pattern of colonial trade: They knew that mainland settlers had to sell at least some of their wheat, fish, and lumber in the French sugar islands to accumulate funds to buy British manu-

factures. Grenville consequently resisted demands from British sugar planters, who wanted to retain a duty of 6 pence per gallon on French molasses, and instead settled on a duty of 3 pence per gallon.

This carefully crafted policy garnered little support in America. New England merchants — among them John Hancock of Boston — had made their fortunes smuggling French molasses, and they knew their profits would be reduced if the new regulations were enforced. These merchants and New England distillers, who relied on cheap French molasses to make rum, feared a rise in the price of molasses. They claimed publicly that the Sugar Act would wipe out trade with the French islands;

privately, they vowed to evade the duty by smuggling or by bribing officials.

Constitutional Objections. More important, the merchants' political allies raised constitutional objections to the Sugar Act. The Speaker of the Massachusetts House of Representatives argued that the new legislation was "contrary to a fundamental Principall of our Constitution: That all Taxes ought to originate with the people." "They who are taxed at pleasure by others cannot possibly have any property, and they who have no property, can have no freedom," warned Stephen Hopkins, the governor of Rhode Island. The Sugar Act raised other constitutional issues as well. Merchants prosecuted under the act would be tried without a jury by a **vice-admiralty court**, a maritime tribunal presided over by a British-appointed judge. American assemblies had long opposed the vice-admiralty courts, and they had found ways to have merchants accused of violating the Navigation Acts be tried by local common-law courts, where they often were acquitted by a jury. The Sugar Act closed this legal loophole by extending the jurisdiction of the vice-admiralty courts to all customs offenses.

The new taxes and trials imposed by the Sugar Act revived old American fears of British control. The influential Virginia planter Richard Bland admitted that the colonies had long been subject to the Navigation Acts, which restricted their manufactures and commerce. But, he protested, the American settlers "were not sent out to be the Slaves but to be the Equals of those that remained behind." John Adams, a young Massachusetts lawyer who was defending John Hancock on a charge of smuggling, phrased his concern in terms of the vice-admiralty courts: Those courts, he said, "degrade every American . . . below the rank of an Englishman."

While the logic of American arguments appeared compelling, some of the facts were wrong. The Navigation Acts certainly favored British merchants and manufacturers. However, trying accused smugglers in vice-admiralty courts was not discriminatory; similar rules had long been in force in Britain. The real issue was the growing administrative power of the British state. Having lived for decades under a policy of salutary neglect, a policy that allowed them to ignore certain provisions of the Navigation Acts, Americans understood the potential impact of the new policies: As a committee of the Massachusetts House of Representatives put it, they would "deprive the colonies of some of their most essential Rights as British subjects."

For their part, British officials insisted on the supremacy of parliamentary laws and denied that colonists should enjoy the traditional legal rights of Englishmen. When the royal governor of Massachusetts, Francis Bernard, heard that the Massachusetts House had objected to the Sugar Act, claiming there should be no taxation without representation, he asserted that Americans did not have that constitutional right: "The rule that a British subject shall not be bound by laws or liable to taxes, but what he has consented to by his representatives must be confined to the inhabitants of Great Britain only." In the eyes of George Grenville and other imperial reformers, the Americans were second-class subjects of the king, their rights limited by the Navigation Acts and the interests of the British state as determined by Parliament.

An Open Challenge: The Stamp Act

Another new tax, the Stamp Act of 1765, sparked the first great imperial crisis. The new levy would cover part of the cost of keeping British troops in America—some £200,000 a year (about $50 million today). The tax would require stamps on all court documents, land titles, contracts, playing cards, newspapers, and other printed items. A similar stamp tax in England was yielding £290,000 a year; Grenville hoped the American levy would raise £60,000. The prime minister knew that some Americans would object to the tax on constitutional grounds, and so raised the issue explicitly in the House of Commons: Did any member doubt "the power and sovereignty of Parliament over every part of the British dominions, for the purpose of raising or collecting any tax?" No one rose to object.

Confident of Parliament's support, Grenville threatened to impose a stamp tax unless the colonists paid for their own defense. The London merchants who served as agents for the colonial legislatures immediately protested that Americans did not have a continent-wide body that could impose taxes. Representatives from the various colonies had met together officially only once, at the Albany Congress of 1754, and not a single assembly had accepted that body's proposals for a colonial union (see Chapter 4). Benjamin Franklin, who was in Britain as the agent of the Pennsylvania assembly, proposed another solution to Grenville's challenge: American representation in Parliament.

"If you chuse to tax us," he suggested, "give us Members in your Legislature, and let us be one People."

With the exception of William Pitt, British politicians rejected Franklin's idea as too radical. They maintained that the colonists already had **virtual representation** in Parliament, that they were represented by members who were transatlantic merchants and West Indian sugar planters. Colonial leaders were equally skeptical of Franklin's plan. Americans were "situate at a great Distance from their Mother Country," the Connecticut assembly declared, and therefore "cannot participate in the general Legislature of the Nation."

When Grenville moved forward with the Stamp Act, his goal was not only to raise revenue but also to assert a constitutional principle: "the Right of Parliament to lay an internal Tax upon the Colonies." The House of Commons ignored American petitions opposing the act and passed the new legislation by an overwhelming vote of 205 to 49. At the request of General Thomas Gage, the British military commander in America, Parliament also passed the Quartering Act, which required colonial governments to provide barracks and food for British troops stationed within their borders. Finally, Parliament approved Grenville's proposal that violations of the Stamp Act be tried in vice-admiralty courts.

The design for reform was complete. Using the doctrine of parliamentary supremacy, Grenville had begun to fashion a centralized imperial system in America. He intended that system to function much like the system in Ireland: British officials would run the colonies with little regard for the local assemblies. Grenville's plan would provoke a constitutional confrontation not only on the specific issues of taxation, jury trials, and military quartering, but also on the general question of representative self-government.

➤ How did the Great War for Empire change the relationship between England and its American colonies?

➤ What were the goals of British imperial reformers?

➤ Why did the colonists object to the new taxes in 1764 and again in 1765? What arguments did they use?

➤ Why did these conflicts over specific policies turn into a constitutional crisis?

The Dynamics of Rebellion, 1765–1770

In the name of reform, Grenville had thrown down the gauntlet to the Americans. The colonists had often resisted unpopular laws and arbitrary governors, but they had faced an all-out attack on their institutions only once — in 1686, when James II had unilaterally imposed the Dominion of New England. The danger now was even greater: The new reforms were backed by both the king and Parliament. But the Patriots, as the defenders of American rights came to be called, met the challenge posed by Grenville and then by Charles Townshend. They organized protests, encouraged riots, and articulated a compelling ideology of resistance.

Politicians Protest, and the Crowd Rebels

In May 1765, Patrick Henry, a young headstrong member of the Virginia House of Burgesses, condemned Grenville's new legislation and attacked

The Intensity of Patrick Henry

This portrait, painted in 1795, when Henry was in his sixties, captures the Patriot's seriousness and intensity. As an orator, Henry drew on Evangelical Protestantism to create a new mode of political oratory. "His figures of speech . . . were often borrowed from the Scriptures," a contemporary noted, and the content of his speeches mirrored "the earnestness depicted in his own features." Mead Art Museum, Amherst College.

The BOSTONIAN'S Paying the EXCISE-MAN, or TARRING & FEATHERING.

London Printed for Rob.ˢ Sayer & J.Bennett, Map & Printseller. Nᵒ53, Fleet Street, as the Act directs 31 Octᵗ 1774.

George III for supporting it. By comparing the king to Charles I, whose tyranny had led to religious and political conflict in the 1640s, Henry seemed to be calling for a new republican revolution. Although the assembly members were shaken by Henry's remarks, which bordered on treason, they condemned the Stamp Act as "a manifest Tendency to Destroy American freedom." In Massachusetts, James Otis, another republican-minded firebrand, persuaded the House of Representatives to call an all-colony congress "to implore Relief" from the act.

The Stamp Act Congress. Nine colonial assemblies sent delegates to the Stamp Act Congress, which met in New York City in October 1765. The congress issued a set of resolutions protesting the loss of American "rights and liberties," especially the right to trial by jury. The Stamp Act Resolves also challenged the constitutionality of the Stamp and Sugar acts by declaring that only the colonists' elected representatives could tax them. Still, the delegates were moderate men who wanted compromise, not confrontation. They assured Parliament that Americans "glory in being subjects of the best of Kings" and humbly petitioned for repeal of the Stamp Act. Other influential Americans, however, were advocating resistance, and they began to organize a boycott of British goods.

Popular opposition to the Stamp Act took more violent forms. When the act went into effect on

November 1, 1765, disciplined mobs demanded the resignation of stamp-tax collectors, most of whom had been born in the colonies. In Boston, the **Sons of Liberty** beheaded and burned an effigy of collector Andrew Oliver and then destroyed Oliver's new brick warehouse. Two weeks later, Bostonians attacked the house of Lieutenant Governor Thomas Hutchinson, long known as a defender of social privilege and imperial authority, breaking his furniture, looting his wine cellar, and setting fire to his library.

The men who inspired the mobs were wealthy merchants, like John Hancock, and Patriot lawyers, like John Adams; leading the crowds were middling artisans and minor merchants. "Spent the evening with the Sons of Liberty," Adams wrote in his diary, "John Smith, the brazier [metalworker], Thomas Crafts, the painter, Edes, the printer, Stephen Cleverly, the brazier; Chase, the distiller; [and] Joseph Field, Master of a vessel." Many of these men knew one another through their work; others were drinking buddies at the taverns that became centers of Patriot agitation.

In New York City, nearly three thousand shopkeepers, artisans, laborers, and seamen marched through the streets breaking streetlamps and windows and crying "Liberty!" And resistance to the Stamp Act spread far beyond the port cities. In nearly every colony, crowds of angry people — the "rabble," their detractors called them — intimidated royal officials. Near Wethersfield, Connecticut, five hundred farmers seized a tax collector, Jared Ingersoll, and forced him to resign his office in "the Cause of the People."

The Motives of the Crowd. Crowd protests were common in both Britain and America. Every November 5, Protestant mobs on both sides of the Atlantic burned effigies of the pope to celebrate the failure in 1605 of a Catholic plot, led by Guy Fawkes, to blow up the Houses of Parliament. Colonial mobs regularly destroyed brothels and rioted against the impressment (forced service) of merchant seamen by the Royal Navy. Governments tolerated the mobs because they usually did little damage and because, short of calling out the militia, they had no means of stopping them.

If rioting was traditional, its political goals were new. In New York City, for example, the leaders of the Sons of Liberty were two minor merchants, Isaac Sears and Alexander McDougall. Both Radical Whigs, Sears and McDougall were afraid that imperial reform would undermine political liberty. Other members of the mob had other agendas. Many artisans and their journeymen joined the protests because imports of low-priced British shoes and other manufactures threatened their livelihood. Some rioters also feared the financial burden of new taxes. Unlike "the Common people of England," a well-traveled colonist observed, "the people of America . . . never would submitt to be taxed that a few may be loaded with palaces and Pensions . . . while they themselves cannot support themselves and their needy offspring with Bread."

Religion motivated other protesters. Roused by the Great Awakening, evangelical Protestants resented the arrogance of British military officers and the corruption of royal bureaucrats. In New England, where many people lived into their sixties, and memories lived even longer, rioters looked back to the antimonarchy sentiments of their great-grandparents. A letter to a Boston newspaper signed "Oliver Cromwell," the name of the English republican revolutionary, promised to save "all the Free-born Sons of America." Finally, the mobs included apprentices, day laborers, and unemployed sailors — young men looking for excitement, who, when fortified by drink, were eager to resort to violence.

Throughout the colonies, popular resistance nullified the Stamp Act. Fearing a massive assault on Fort George on Guy Fawkes Day, New York lieutenant governor Cadwallader Colden called on General Gage to use his small military force to protect the stamps. Gage refused. "Fire from the Fort might disperse the Mob, but it would not quell them," he told Colden, and the result would be "an Insurrection, the Commencement of Civil War." Frightened collectors gave up their stamps, and angry Americans forced officials to accept legal documents without them. Popular insurrection gave a democratic cast to the emerging American Patriot movement. "Nothing is wanting but your own Resolution," declared a New York rioter, "for great is the Authority and Power of the People."

Because communication across the Atlantic was slow, the British response to the Stamp Act Congress and the Sons of Liberty mobs would not be known until the spring of 1766. However, royal officials in America already knew that they had lost the popular support that had sustained the empire for three generations. Lamented a customs collector in Philadelphia: "What can a Governor do without the assistance of the Governed?"

The Ideological Roots of Resistance

The American resistance movement emerged first in the seaports because British policies directly affected their residents. The Sugar Act raised the cost of molasses to urban distillers; the Stamp Act taxed the newspapers sold by printers and the contracts and other legal documents prepared by lawyers for merchants; and the flood of British manufactures threatened the livelihood of seaport artisans. The first protests, then, focused on economic grievances. According to one pamphleteer, Americans were being compelled to give the British "our money, as oft and in what quantity they please to demand it." Other writers alleged that the British had violated specific "liberties and privileges" embodied in colonial charters.

Initially, the resistance movement had no acknowledged leaders, no organization, and no clear goals. In time, however, lawyers took the lead, in part because merchants hired them to protect their goods from seizure by customs officials. Lawyers had another professional interest as well: As practitioners of English common law, they understood the importance to their clients of trial by jury and so opposed the extension of judge-run vice-admiralty courts. Composing pamphlets of remarkable political sophistication, Patriot lawyers gave the resistance movement its rationale, its political agenda, and its leaders.

Patriot writers drew on three intellectual traditions. The first was English common law, the centuries-old body of legal rules and procedures that protected the lives and property of the monarch's subjects. In the famous *Writs of Assistance* case of 1761, Boston lawyer James Otis invoked English legal precedents to dispute the legitimacy of a general search warrant that allowed customs officials to conduct wide-ranging inspections. And in demanding a jury trial for John Hancock, John Adams appealed to the jury-trial provision in the "29th Chap. of Magna Charta," an ancient document (1215) that "has for many Centuries been esteemed by Englishmen, as one of the . . . firmest Bulwarks of their Liberties." Other lawyers protested when the ministry declared that colonial judges served "at the pleasure" of the royal governors, claiming that would undermine the independence of the judiciary.

A second major intellectual resource was rationalist thought of the Enlightenment. Virginia planter Thomas Jefferson invoked David Hume and Francis Hutcheson, Enlightenment philosophers who applied reason in their critiques of traditional political practices and in their proposals to correct social ills. Jefferson and other Patriot writers also drew on John Locke, who argued that all individuals possessed certain "natural rights"—among them life, liberty, and property—and that governments must protect those rights (see Chapter 4). And they turned to French philosopher Montesquieu, who argued that a separation of powers among government departments prevented arbitrary rule.

The republican and Whig strands of the English political tradition provided a third ideological source for American Patriots. Puritan New England had long venerated the Commonwealth era, the brief period between 1649 and 1660 when England was a republic (see Chapter 2). After the Glorious Revolution of 1688–1689, the colonists praised the ban on royally imposed taxes and the other constitutional restrictions placed on the monarchy by English Whigs. And, Bostonian Samuel Adams and other Patriot leaders applauded Britain's Radical Whigs for denouncing political corruption among royal officials. Joseph Warren, a physician and a Patriot, reported that many Bostonians believed the Stamp Act was part of a plot "to force the colonies into rebellion," after which the ministry would use "military power to reduce them to servitude."

These diverse intellectual traditions and arguments—publicized in newspapers and pamphlets—helped to turn a series of impromptu riots and tax protests into a coherent Patriot-led political movement. The Patriots organized a highly successful boycott of British manufactures to force a repeal of the new imperial measures.

Sam Adams, Boston Agitator

This painting by John Singleton Copley (c. 1772) shows the radical Patriot pointing to the Massachusetts Charter of 1692, suggesting that Adams's determination to protect "charter rights" explained his opposition to British policies. However, Adams also was influenced by the natural-rights tradition. Deposited by the City of Boston. Courtesy Museum of Fine Arts, Boston.

TABLE 5.1	Ministerial Instability in Britain, 1760–1782	
Leading Minister	**Dates of Ministry**	**American Policy**
Lord Bute	1760–1763	Mildly reformist
George Grenville	1763–1765	Ardently reformist
Lord Rockingham	1765–1766	Accommodationist
William Pitt/Charles Townshend	1766–1770	Ardently reformist
Lord North	1770–1782	Coercive

Parliament Compromises, 1766

When news of the Stamp Act riots and the boycott reached Britain, Parliament was already in turmoil. Disputes over domestic policy had led George III to dismiss Grenville as the prime minister (Table 5.1). It was left to his successor, Lord Rockingham, to address the growing resistance in the colonies. The members of Parliament were divided. Grenville's followers demanded that imperial reform continue, if necessary at the point of a gun. The issue for them was the constitutional supremacy of Parliament: They were determined to maintain its status as one of the few powerful representative bodies in eighteenth-century Europe. "The British legislature," declared Chief Justice Sir James Mansfield, "has authority to bind every part and every subject, whether such subjects have a right to vote or not."

Three other factions were advocating for repeal of the Stamp Act. The Old Whigs, now led by Lord Rockingham, had long maintained that America was more important for its "flourishing and increasing trade" than for its tax revenues. A second group, representing the interests of British merchants and manufacturers, pointed out that the American trade boycott was cutting deeply into British exports. A committee of "London Merchants trading to America" joined with traders in the ports of Liverpool, Bristol, and Glasgow to petition Parliament for repeal. "The Avenues of Trade are all shut up," complained a Bristol merchant. "We have no Remittances and are at our Witts End for want of Money to fulfill our Engagements with our Tradesmen." Finally, former prime minister William Pitt and his allies in Parliament argued that the Stamp Act was a mistake and demanded it "be repealed absolutely, totally, and immediately." Pitt tried to draw a subtle distinction between taxation and legislation: Parliament lacked the authority to tax the colonies, he said, but its power over America was "sovereign and supreme, in every circumstance of government and legislation whatsoever." As Pitt's ambiguous formula suggested, the Stamp Act raised the difficult constitutional question of the extent of Parliament's sovereign powers.

Rockingham was a young and inexperienced minister facing complex issues. In the end, he decided on compromise. To mollify the colonists and help British merchants, he repealed the Stamp Act and reduced the duty imposed by the Sugar Act on French molasses to a penny a gallon. Then he pacified imperial reformers and hardliners with the Declaratory Act of 1766, which explicitly reaffirmed Parliament's "full power and authority to make laws and statutes . . . to bind the colonies and people of America . . . in all cases whatsoever." By ending the Stamp Act crisis swiftly, Rockingham hoped it would be forgotten just as quickly.

Charles Townshend Steps In

Often the course of history is changed by a small event—an illness, a personal grudge, a chance remark. So it was in 1767, when Rockingham's ministry collapsed over domestic issues and George III named William Pitt to head a new government. Pitt was chronically ill with gout, a painful disease of the joints, and often missed parliamentary debates, leaving the chancellor of the exchequer, Charles Townshend, in command. Pitt was sympathetic toward America; Townshend was not. As a member of the Board of Trade in the 1750s, Townshend had strongly supported restrictions on the colonial assemblies, and he was an outspoken advocate for the Stamp Act. So in 1767, when Grenville, now a member of Parliament, demanded that the colonists pay for the British troops in America, Townshend made an unplanned and fateful decision. Convinced of the necessity of imperial reform and eager to reduce the English land tax, he promised to find a new source of revenue in America.

The Townshend Act. The new tax legislation, the Townshend Act of 1767, had both fiscal and political goals. The statute imposed duties on colonial imports of paper, paint, glass, and tea, and would raise about £40,000 a year. To pacify Grenville, Townshend allocated some of this revenue for American military expenses. However, most of the money would fund a colonial civil list — paying the salaries of royal governors, judges, and other imperial officials. By freeing royal officials from financial dependence on the American assemblies, the ministry made it easier for them to enforce parliamentary laws and the king's instructions. And to strengthen imperial power further, Townshend devised the Revenue Act of 1767. This legislation created a board of customs commissioners in Boston and vice-admiralty courts in Halifax, Boston, Philadelphia, and Charleston. By using Parliament-imposed taxes to finance imperial administration, Townshend intended to undermine the autonomy and authority of American political institutions.

The Restraining Act. The full implications of Townshend's policies became clear in New York, where the assembly refused to comply with the Quartering Act of 1765. Fearing an unlimited drain on its treasury, the New York legislature first denied General Gage's requests for barracks and supplies for his troops and then offered limited assistance. In response, Townshend demanded full compliance, and Parliament threatened to impose a special duty on New York's imports and exports. The Earl of Shelburne, the new secretary of state, went even further: He proposed the appointment of a military governor with the authority to seize funds from New York's treasury and "to act with Force or Gentleness as circumstances might make necessary." Townshend decided on a less provocative but equally coercive measure, the Restraining Act of 1767, which suspended the New York assembly. Faced with the loss of self-government, New Yorkers reluctantly appropriated the funds to quarter the troops.

The Restraining Act raised the stakes for the colonists. Previously, the British Privy Council had invalidated a small proportion — about 5 percent — of colonial laws, like those establishing land banks. Townshend's Restraining Act went much further, declaring that American representative assemblies were completely dependent on the will of Parliament.

America Debates and Resists Again

The Townshend duties revived the constitutional debate over taxation. During the Stamp Act crisis, some Americans, including Benjamin Franklin, made a distinction between external and internal taxes. They suggested that external duties on trade, which Britain had long imposed through the Navigation Acts, were acceptable to Americans, but that direct, or internal, taxes, which had not previously been levied in the colonies, were not. Townshend thought this distinction was "perfect nonsense," but he indulged the Americans and laid duties only on trade.

The Second Boycott. Even so, most colonial leaders refused to accept the legitimacy of Townshend's measures. They agreed with lawyer John Dickinson, author of *Letters from a Farmer in Pennsylvania* (1768), that the real issue was not whether a tax was external or internal but the intention of the legislation. Because the Townshend duties were designed to raise revenue, they were taxes imposed without consent. In February 1768, the Massachusetts House of Representatives sent a letter condemning the Townshend Act to the other assemblies, and Boston and New York merchants began a new boycott of British goods. Public support for nonimportation quickly emerged in the smaller port cities of Salem, Newport, and Baltimore. Throughout Puritan New England, ministers and public officials discouraged the purchase of "foreign superfluities" and promoted the domestic manufacture of cloth and other necessities.

The Daughters of Liberty. American women, ordinarily excluded from public affairs, became crucial to the nonimportation movement through their production of **homespuns**. During the Stamp Act boycott in 1765, the wives and daughters of Patriot leaders had increased their output of yarn and cloth. Resistance to the Townshend duties mobilized many more women, including pious farmwives who spun yarn at the homes of their ministers. Some gatherings were openly patriotic. At one in Berwick, Maine, "true Daughters of Liberty" celebrated American products by "drinking rye coffee and dining on bear venison." Other women's groups combined support for the boycott with charitable work, spinning flax and wool to donate to the needy. Just as Patriot men followed tradition by joining crowd actions, so women's protests reflected their customary attention to the well-being of the community.

Newspapers celebrated the Daughters of Liberty. One Massachusetts town proudly claimed an annual output of thirty thousand yards of cloth; East Hartford, Connecticut, reported seventeen thousand yards. Although this surge in domestic production did not compensate for the loss of

British imports, which had averaged about 10 million yards of cloth each year, it brought thousands of women into the public arena.

Actually, the boycott mobilized many Americans to take political action. In the seaport cities, the Sons of Liberty published the names of merchants who imported British goods; they also broke the merchants' store windows and harassed their employees. By March 1769, tactics like these had convinced merchants and sailors in Philadelphia to join the nonimportation movement. Two months later, the members of the Virginia House of Burgesses vowed not to buy duted articles, luxury goods, or slaves imported by British merchants. "The whole continent from New England to Georgia seems firmly fixed," the *Massachusetts Gazette* proudly announced. "Like a strong, well-constructed arch, the more weight there is laid upon it, the firmer it stands; and thus with America, the more we are loaded, the more we are united." Reflecting colonial self-confidence, Benjamin Franklin called for a return to the pre-1763 mercantilist system and proposed a "plan of conciliation" that was really a demand for British capitulation: "Repeal the laws, renounce the right, recall the troops, refund the money, and return to the old method of requisition."

Britain Responds. American resistance only increased British determination. When the Massachusetts House's letter opposing the Townshend duties reached London, Lord Hillsborough, the secretary of state for American affairs, branded it "unjustifiable opposition to the constitutional authority of Parliament." To strengthen the "Hand of Government" in Massachusetts and help the customs commissioners there, Hillsborough dispatched General Thomas Gage and four thousand British troops to Boston. Gage accused Massachusetts leaders of "Treasonable and desperate Resolves" and advised the ministry to "Quash this Spirit at a Blow." Parliament threatened to appoint a special commission to hear evidence of treason, and Hillsborough proposed to isolate Massachusetts from the other colonies and then use the army to bring the rebellious New Englanders to their knees (Map 5.3). In 1765, American resistance to taxation had provoked a parliamentary debate; in 1768, it produced a plan for military coercion.

Lord North Compromises, 1770

At this critical moment, the British ministry's resolve faltered. A series of harsh winters and dry summers cut grain output and raised food prices in Great Britain. In Scotland and northern England, thousands of tenants deserted their farms and boarded ships bound for America; and food riots spread across the English countryside. There were riots, too, in Ireland over the growing military budget there.

Adding to the ministry's difficulties was Radical Whig John Wilkes. Supported by associations of merchants, tradesmen, and artisans, Wilkes stepped up his attacks on government corruption and won election to Parliament. Overjoyed, American Patriots drank toasts to Wilkes and bought thousands of teapots and mugs emblazoned with his picture. When Wilkes was imprisoned for libel against parliament, an angry crowd protested his arrest. Troops killed seven protesters in the highly publicized

John Wilkes, British Radical

Wilkes won fame on both sides of the Atlantic as the author of *North Briton, Number 45* (depicted on the left), which called for major reforms in the British political system. At a dinner in Boston, Radical Whigs raised their wineglasses to Wilkes, toasting him forty-five times! But Wilkes had many enemies in Britain, including the artist who created this image. Wilkes is depicted as a cunning demagogue, brandishing the cap of Liberty to curry favor with the mob. Miriam and Ira D. Wallach Division of Art, Prints and Photographs, The New York Public Library. Astor, Lenox and Tilden Foundations.

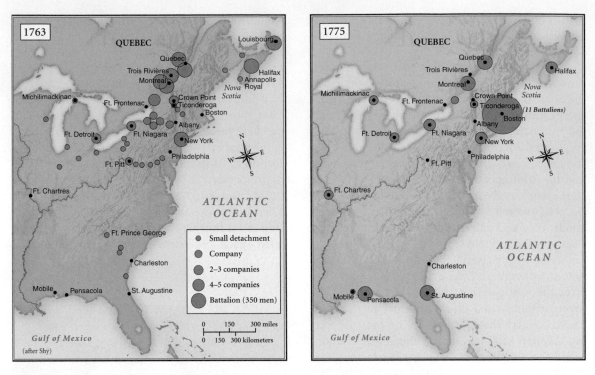

MAP 5.3   British Troop Deployments, 1763 and 1775

As the imperial crisis deepened, British military priorities changed. In 1763, most British battalions were stationed in Canada to deter Indian uprisings and French Canadian revolts. After the Stamp Act riots of 1765, the British established large garrisons in New York and Philadelphia. By 1775, eleven battalions of British regulars occupied Boston, the center of the Patriot movement.

Massacre of Saint George's Field, sparking more disturbances.

Nonimportation Succeeds. The American trade boycott also had a major impact on the British economy. The colonies usually had an annual trade deficit of £500,000; but in 1768, they imported less from Britain, cutting the deficit to £230,000. By 1769, the boycott of British goods, coupled with the colonies' staple exports and shipping services to overseas markets, had yielded a balance-of-payments surplus of £816,000. To revive their flagging sales to America, British merchants and manufacturers petitioned Parliament for repeal of the Townshend duties. British government revenues, which were heavily dependent on excise taxes and duties on imported goods, also had suffered from the boycott. By late 1769, some ministers felt that the Townshend duties were a mistake, and the king no longer supported Hillsborough's plan to use military force against Massachusetts.

Early in 1770, Lord North became prime minister. A witty man and a skillful politician, North set out to save the empire by designing a new compromise. Arguing that it was foolish to tax British exports to America (thereby raising their price and decreasing consumption), North persuaded Parliament to repeal most of the Townshend duties. However, he retained the tax on tea as a symbol of Parliament's supremacy. Gratified by North's initiative, colonial merchants called off the boycott (Figure 5.2).

Even an outbreak of violence did not rupture the compromise. During the boycott, New York artisans and workers had taunted British troops, mostly with words but occasionally with stones and their fists. In retaliation, the soldiers tore down a Liberty Pole (a Patriot flagpole), setting off a week of street fighting. In Boston, friction between residents and British soldiers over constitutional principles and everyday issues, like competition for part-time jobs, triggered a violent conflict. In March 1770, a group of soldiers fired into a crowd of rowdy demonstrators, killing five men, including one of the leaders, Crispus Attucks, an escaped slave who was working as a seaman. Convinced of a ministerial conspiracy against liberty, Radical Whigs labeled the

FIGURE 5.2 Trade as a Political Weapon, 1763–1776

Political upheaval did not affect the mainland colonies' exports to Britain, which rose slightly over the period, but imports fluctuated greatly. The American boycott of 1768–1769 led to a sharp fall in imports of British manufactures; but those imports soared after the Townshend duties were repealed.

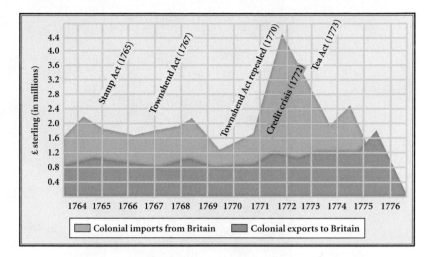

incident a "massacre" and filled the popular press with accusations that the British had planned the killings.

Sovereignty Debated. Although most Americans ignored the Radical Whigs' charges and remained loyal to the empire, five years of conflict over taxes and constitutional principles had taken their toll. In 1765, American leaders had accepted Parliament's authority; the Stamp Act Resolves had opposed only certain "unconstitutional" legislation. By 1770, the most outspoken Patriots — Benjamin Franklin in Pennsylvania, Patrick Henry in Virginia, and Samuel Adams in Massachusetts — had repudiated parliamentary supremacy and claimed equality for the American assemblies within the empire. Perhaps thinking of various European "composite monarchies," in which kings ruled far-distant provinces acquired by inheritance or conquest, Franklin suggested that the colonies were now "distinct and separate states" with "the same Head, or Sovereign, the King."

Franklin's suggestion outraged Thomas Hutchinson, the American-born royal governor of Massachusetts, whose house had been destroyed by a Stamp Act mob. A strong supporter of imperial rule, Hutchinson emphatically rejected the idea of "two independent legislatures in one and the same state"; in his mind, the British empire was a whole, its sovereignty indivisible. "I know of no line," he told the Massachusetts assembly, "that can be drawn between the supreme authority of Parliament and the total independence of the colonies."

There the matter rested. The British had twice imposed taxes on the colonies, and American Patri-

ots had twice forced a retreat. If Parliament insisted on exercising Britain's claim to sovereign power a third time, some Americans were prepared to resist by force. Nor did they flinch when reminded that George III condemned their agitation. As the Massachusetts House told Hutchinson, "There is more reason to dread the consequences of absolute uncontrolled supreme power, whether of a nation or a monarch, than those of total independence." Fearful of civil war, Lord North's ministry hesitated to force the issue.

➤ What were the core constitutional principles over which the colonists and the ministers in Parliament disagreed?

➤ If Grenville's and Townshend's initiatives had been successful, how would the character of the British imperial system have changed?

➤ Weigh the importance of economic and ideological motives in creating and sustaining the colonial resistance movement. Which was more important? Why?

The Road to Independence, 1771–1776

The repeal of the Townshend duties in 1770 seemed to restore harmony to the British empire; but below the surface lay strong passions and mutual distrust. In 1773, those emotions erupted, destroying any hope of compromise. Within two years, the Americans and the British

Patriot Propaganda

Silversmith Paul Revere issued this engraving of the confrontation between British redcoats and snowball-throwing Bostonians. To whip up opposition to the military occupation of their town, Revere and other Patriots called the incident "The Boston Massacre." The shooting confirmed their Radical Whig belief that "standing armies" were instruments of tyranny. Library of Congress.

clashed in armed conflict, and Patriot legislators were forming provisional governments and building military forces, the two essentials for independence.

A Compromise Ignored

Once aroused, political passions are not easily quieted. In Boston, radical Patriots continued to warn Americans of the dangers of imperial domination. In November 1772, Samuel Adams persuaded the Boston town meeting to establish a committee of correspondence to urge Patriots "to state the Rights of the Colonists of this Province." Soon, eighty Massachusetts towns had similar committees. Then smugglers in Rhode Island burned the *Gaspée,* a customs vessel, and the British government set up a royal commission to investigate the incident. The commission's broad powers, particularly its authority to send Americans to Britain for trial, prompted the Virginia House of Burgesses to set up its own committee of correspondence "to communicate with the other colonies" about the situation in Rhode Island. By mid-1773, similar committees

The Boston Tea Party

Led by radical Patriots disguised as Mohawk Indians, Bostonians dump taxed tea owned by the East India Company into the harbor. The rioters made clear their "pure" political motives by punishing those who sought personal gain: A Son of Liberty who stole some of the tea was "stripped of his booty and his clothes together, and sent home naked." Library of Congress.

had appeared in Connecticut, New Hampshire, and South Carolina.

The Tea Act. These committees sprang into action when, at Lord North's behest, Parliament enacted the Tea Act in May 1773. The act provided financial relief for the British East India Company, which was deeply in debt because of military expeditions to extend Britain's influence in India. The Tea Act gave the company a government loan and canceled the import duty on its tea. But the act offended many Americans. Since 1768, when the Townshend Act had placed a duty of 3 pence a pound on tea, most colonists had bought tea smuggled in by Dutch traders. By relieving the East India Company of import duties, the Tea Act made its tea cheaper than that sold by Dutch merchants. So the act encouraged Americans to drink East India tea — and pay the Townshend duty.

Radical Patriots accused the ministry of bribing Americans to give up their principled opposition to British taxation. As an anonymous woman wrote in the *Massachusetts Spy,* "The use of [British] tea is considered not as a private but as a public evil . . . a handle to introduce a variety of . . . oppressions

amongst us." American merchants joined the protest because the East India Company planned to distribute its tea directly to shopkeepers, thereby excluding them from the profits of the trade. "The fear of an Introduction of a Monopoly in this Country," British general Frederick Haldimand reported from New York, "has induced the mercantile part of the Inhabitants to be very industrious in opposing this Step and added Strength to a Spirit of Independence already too prevalent."

The committees of correspondence organized resistance to the Tea Act. Committee members held public bonfires at which they persuaded their fellow townspeople — sometimes gently, sometimes not — to consign British tea to the flames. The Sons of Liberty patrolled the wharves and prevented East India Company ships from landing new supplies. In response, Royal Governor Hutchinson of Massachusetts hatched a scheme to land the tea and collect the tax. When a shipment of tea arrived in Boston Harbor on the *Dartmouth,* Hutchinson immediately passed the ship through customs so that it could enter the harbor. If the Sons of Liberty blocked the tea from coming ashore, Hutchinson intended to order British troops to unload the tea and supervise its sale by auction. But the Patriots foiled the governor's plan: After nightfall on December 16, 1773, a group of artisans and laborers disguised as Indians boarded the *Dartmouth*, broke open 342 chests of tea (valued at about £10,000, or roughly $800,000 today), and threw them into the harbor. "This destruction of the Tea is so bold and it must have so important Consequences," John Adams wrote in his diary, "that I cannot but consider it as an Epoch in History."

The Coercive Acts. The British Privy Council was outraged, as was the king. "Concessions have made matters worse," George III declared. "The time has come for compulsion." Early in 1774, Parliament decisively rejected a proposal to repeal the duty on American tea; instead, it enacted four Coercive Acts to force Massachusetts to pay for the tea and to submit to imperial authority. The Port Bill closed Boston Harbor; the Government Act annulled the Massachusetts charter and prohibited most local town meetings; the Quartering Act—a new one—required the colony to build barracks for British troops; and the Justice Act allowed trials for capital crimes to be transferred to other colonies or to Britain (see Reading American Pictures, "How Did the British View the Crisis in the Colonies?," p. 155).

Patriot leaders throughout the mainland branded the measures "intolerable" and rallied support for Massachusetts. In far-off Georgia, a Patriot warned the "Freemen of the Province" that "every privilege you at present claim as a birthright, may be wrested from you by the same authority that blockades the town of Boston." "The cause of Boston," George Washington declared in Virginia, "now is and ever will be considered as the cause of America." The committees of correspondence had created a firm sense of unity among Patriots.

In 1774, Parliament also passed the Quebec Act, recognizing Roman Catholicism in Quebec. This humane concession to Quebec's predominantly Catholic population reignited religious passions in New England, where Protestants associated Catholicism with arbitrary royal government and popish superstition. Because the act extended the boundaries of Quebec into the Ohio River Valley, it also angered influential land speculators and politicians in Virginia and other colonies (Map 5.4). Although the ministry did not intend the Quebec Act to be a coercive measure, many colonial leaders saw it as proof of Parliament's intention to intervene in American domestic affairs.

The Continental Congress Responds

In response to the Coercive Acts, Patriot leaders invited all colonial assemblies to send delegates to a new continent-wide body, the Continental Congress. Twelve did. The recently acquired mainland colonies—Florida, Quebec, Nova Scotia, and Newfoundland—refused to attend, as did Georgia, where the royal governor controlled the legislature. And the assemblies of Barbados, Jamaica, and the other British sugar islands, fearful of revolts by their predominately African populations, reaffirmed their allegiance to the crown.

The delegates who met in Philadelphia in September 1774 had specific concerns. Southern representatives, fearing a British plot "to overturn the constitution and introduce a system of arbitrary government," advocated a new economic boycott. Independence-minded representatives from New England demanded political union and defensive military preparations. However, many delegates from the Middle Atlantic colonies favored a political compromise.

Led by Joseph Galloway of Pennsylvania, these men of "loyal principles" proposed a compromise that was much like the plan Franklin had proposed in Albany two decades earlier: Each colony would retain its assembly, which would legislate on local matters, and a new continent-wide body would handle general American affairs. The king would appoint a president-general, who would preside over a legislative council selected by the colonial assemblies. Although Galloway's plan gave the council veto power over parliamentary legislation that affected America, the delegates refused to endorse it. With British troops occupying Boston, most thought it was too conciliatory (see Comparing American Voices, "The Debate over Representation and Sovereignty," pp. 158–159).

Instead, a majority of the delegates passed a Declaration of Rights and Grievances, which demanded the repeal of the Coercive Acts. They also repudiated the Declaratory Act of 1766, which had proclaimed Parliament's supremacy over the colonies, and stipulated that British control be limited to matters of trade. Finally, the Congress approved a program of economic retaliation. It ordered a new non-importation pact that would take effect in December 1774. If Parliament did not repeal the Intolerable Acts by September 1775, the Congress vowed to cut off virtually all colonial exports to Britain, Ireland, and the British West Indies. Ten years of constitutional conflict had culminated in the threat of all-out commercial warfare.

Even at this late date, a few British leaders hoped for compromise. In January 1775, William Pitt, now sitting in the House of Lords as the Earl of Chatham, asked Parliament to renounce its power to tax the

How Did the British View the Crisis in the Colonies?

"An Attempt to Land a Bishop in America," 1768. Library of Congress.

"The Bostonians in Distress," 1774. Library of Congress.

Britain's colonial policy between 1763 and 1775 created controversy in Britain as well as in America. Grenville's ministry enacted the Stamp Act in 1765; the next year, Rockingham's government repealed it. The conflict over policy split Tory hard-liners, who believed the Patriots should be coerced into paying taxes and quartering troops, from Old Whigs, who preferred compromise. Their debates roiled the Halls of Parliament and spilled onto the pages of London's newspapers, where they took the form of controversial essays and political cartoons, like the two here. People of the time immediately understood the meaning—and the political bias—of these cartoons; more than two centuries later, we have to work a bit harder to understand what they are "saying."

ANALYZING THE EVIDENCE

➤ "An Attempt to Land a Bishop in America" addressed the dispute over a proposal to dispatch a bishop of the Church of England to America to supervise the clergy there. What is the cartoonist's position on the proposal?

➤ Look carefully at the signs and banners in "An Attempt to Land a Bishop in America." They celebrate John Locke, the advocate of self-government, and call for "Liberty and Freedom of Conscience." To interpret the words in the balloon, "No Lords Spiritual or Temporal in New England," think back to the Puritans and what they thought of bishops (see Chapter 2). What other aspects of the cartoon point to the artist's stance on the proposal to send a bishop to America?

➤ At first glance, "The Bostonians in Distress" seems sympathetic toward the colonists, caged as a consequence of the Coercive Acts (1774). What does a closer look suggest? How does the artist depict the colonists? What aspects of the picture suggest that the men in the cage do not deserve respect?

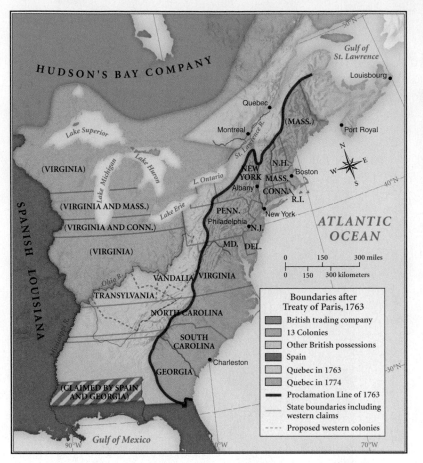

MAP 5.4   British Western Policy, 1763–1774

Despite the Proclamation of 1763, which restricted white settlement west of the Appalachian Mountains, Anglo-Americans settlers and land speculators proposed two new colonies in the West, Vandalia and Transylvania. But the Quebec Act of 1774 designated most western lands as Indian reserves and, by vastly enlarging the boundaries of Quebec, eliminated the sea-to-sea land claims of many seaboard colonies. The act also angered New England Protestants, who condemned its provisions allowing French residents to practice Catholicism, and colonial political leaders, who condemned its failure to provide a representative assembly there.

colonies and to recognize the Continental Congress as a lawful body. In return for these concessions, he suggested, the Congress should acknowledge parliamentary supremacy and grant a continuing revenue to help defray the British national debt.

The British ministry rejected Chatham's plan. Twice it had backed down in the face of colonial resistance; a third retreat was impossible. The honor of the nation was at stake. Branding the Continental Congress an illegal assembly, the ministry also ruled out Lord Dartmouth's proposal to send commissioners to America to negotiate a settlement. Instead, Lord North set stringent terms: Americans must pay for their own defense and administration, and must acknowledge Parliament's authority to tax them. To put teeth in these demands, North imposed a naval blockade on American trade with foreign nations and ordered General Gage to suppress dissent in Massachusetts. "Now the case seemed desperate," the prime minister told Thomas Hutchinson, whom the Patriots had forced into exile in London. "Parliament would not—could not—concede. For aught he could see it must come to violence."

The Countryside Rises Up

Ultimately, the success of the urban-led Patriot movement would depend on the large rural population. Most farmers had little interest in imperial affairs. Their lives were deeply rooted in the soil, and their prime allegiance was to family and community. But imperial policies increasingly intruded into the isolated world of farm families taking their sons for military duty and raising their taxes. Before the outbreak of the French and Indian War in 1754, farmers on Long Island had paid an average of 10 shillings a year in taxes; by 1756, their taxes had jumped to 30 shillings. Peace brought little relief: The British-imposed Quartering Act kept taxes high, an average of 20 shillings a year. These levies, though much less than the taxes most Britons paid, angered American farmers.

The Patriot Movement Expands. The urban-led boycotts of 1765 and 1768 raised the political consciousness of rural Americans. When the First Continental Congress placed a new ban on British goods in 1774, it easily established a rural network of committees of safety and inspection to enforce it. Appealing to rural thriftiness, the Congress discouraged the wearing of expensive imported clothes to funerals, suggesting instead "a black crape or ribbon on the arm or hat for gentlemen, and a black ribbon and necklace for ladies." In Concord, Massachusetts, 80 percent of the male heads of families and a number of single women signed a "Solemn League and Covenant" supporting nonimportation. In other towns, men blacked their faces, disguised themselves in blankets "like Indians," and threatened violence against shopkeepers who traded "in rum, molasses, & Sugar, &c." in violation of the boycott.

Patriots also appealed to the yeoman tradition of landownership, which was everywhere under threat. In long-settled communities, arable land was now scarce and expensive; and in new communities, merchants were seizing farmsteads as payment for delinquent debts. Money was always in short supply in rural households, and, complained the town meeting of Petersham, Massachusetts, new British taxes would further drain "this People of the Fruits of their Toil." "The duty on tea," warned a Patriot pamphlet, "was only a prelude to a window-tax, hearth-tax, land-tax, and poll-tax, and these were only paving the way for reducing the country to lordships." By the 1770s, many northern yeomen felt personally threatened by British imperial policy (Table 5.2).

Despite their higher standard of living, southern slave owners had similar fears. Many Virginia Patriots—including Patrick Henry, George Washington, and Thomas Jefferson—speculated in western lands, and they reacted angrily when first the Proclamation of 1763 and then the Quebec Act of 1774 invalidated their claims. Moreover, many Chesapeake planters lived extravagantly and were indebted to British merchants. A debt of £1,000 had once been considered excessive, a planter observed in 1766, but "ten times that sum is now spoke of with indifference and thought no great burthen on Some Estates." Although many planters faced financial disaster, George Washington noted, they were determined to live "genteely and hospitably" and were "ashamed" to adopt frugal ways. Accustomed to being absolute masters on their slave-labor plantations, they resented their financial dependence and dreaded the prospect of political subservience. After Parliament used the Coercive Acts to subdue Massachusetts, the planters feared Virginia would be next. The ministry might dissolve Virginia's representative assembly and judicial institutions, and allow British merchants to seize their debt-burdened property. That is why the Patriot gentry supported demands by yeomen farmers to close the law courts. Now, farmers and planters alike could bargain with merchants over debts without the threat of legal action. "The spark of liberty is not yet extinct among our people," declared one planter, "and if properly fanned by the Gentlemen of influence will, I make no doubt, burst out again into a flame."

Loyal Americans

Although many wealthy planters and affluent merchants joined the Patriot cause, other prominent Americans worried that resistance to Britain would destroy respect for all political institutions and end in mob rule. Their fears increased when the Sons of Liberty upheld the boycotts by intimidation and force. One well-to-do New Yorker complained, "No man can be in a more abject state of bondage than he whose Reputation, Property and Life are exposed to the discretionary violence ... of the community." As the crisis continued, these men rallied to the support of the royal governors.

Other social groups also refused to endorse the Patriot movement. In Pennsylvania and New Jersey, many Quakers and Germans tried to remain neutral because they held pacifist beliefs and because they feared political change. In regions where many wealthy landowners became Patriots—the Hudson River Valley of New York, for example—tenant farmers supported the king because they hated their landlords. Similar social divisions prompted some Regulators in the North Carolina backcountry and many farmers in eastern Maryland to oppose the Patriots there. And enslaved blacks had even less reason to support the cause of their Patriot masters. In November 1774, James Madison reported that some Virginia slaves planned to escape from their Patriot owners "when the English troops should arrive."

To mobilize support for the king, prominent American Loyalists—mostly royal officials, merchants with military contracts, clergy of the Church of England, and well-established lawyers—denounced the Patriot leaders and accused them of working toward independence. These Loyalists formed an articulate pro-British party, but one that remained small and ineffective. A Tory association started by Governor Benning Wentworth of New Hampshire enrolled just fifty-nine members, fourteen of whom were his relatives. At this crucial juncture, Americans who supported resistance to British rule commanded the allegiance—or at least the acquiescence—of the majority of white Americans.

Compromise Fails

When the Continental Congress met in September 1774, Massachusetts was already in open defiance of

The Debate over Representation and Sovereignty

Before 1763, Benjamin Franklin told the House of Commons, Americans had paid little attention to the question of Parliament's "right to lay taxes and duties" in the colonies. The reason was simple, Franklin said: "A right to lay internal taxes was never supposed to be in Parliament, as we are not represented there." Franklin recognized that representation was central to the imperial debate. As the following selections show, the failure to solve this problem—and the closely related issue of parliamentary sovereignty—led to the American rebellion.

JARED INGERSOLL
Report on the Debates in Parliament (1765)

Jared Ingersoll was a Connecticut lawyer who served as that colony's agent, or lobbyist, in Britain. In this letter written to the governor of Connecticut in 1765, Ingersoll summarizes the debate in Parliament over the Stamp Act. When the act passed, he accepted a commission as the stamp distributor in Connecticut. A mob forced him to resign that post. Ingersoll later served as a Vice Admiralty judge in Philadelphia and, during the revolution, remained loyal to Britain.

The principal Attention has been to the Stamp bill that has been preparing to Lay before Parliament for taxing America. The Point of the Authority of Parliament to impose such Tax I found on my Arrival here was so fully and Universally yielded, that there was not the least hopes of making any impressions that way.

I beg leave to give you a Summary of the Arguments which are made use of in favour of such Authority. The House of Commons, say they, is a branch of the supreme legislature of the Nation, and which in its Nature is supposed to represent, or rather to stand in the place of, the Commons, that is, of the great body of the people, who are below the dignity of peers. . . .

That this house of Commons, therefore, is now fixt and ascertained and is a part of the Supreme unlimited power of the Nation, as in every State there must be some unlimited Power and Authority. . . .

They say a Power to tax is a necessary part of every Supreme Legislative Authority, and that if they have not that Power over America, they have none, and then America is at once a Kingdom of itself.

On the other hand those who oppose the bill say, it is true the Parliament have a supreme unlimited Authority over every Part and Branch of the Kings dominions and as well over Ireland as any other place.

Yet [they say] we believe a British parliament will never think it prudent to tax Ireland [or America]. Tis true they say, that the Commons of England and of the British Empire are all represented in and by the house of Commons, but this representation is confessedly on all hands by Construction and Virtual [because most British subjects] . . . have no hand in choosing the representatives. . . .

[They say further] that the Effects of this implied Representation here and in America must be infinitely different in the Article of Taxation. . . . By any Mistake an act of Parliament is made that prove injurious and hard the Member of Parliament here sees with his own Eyes and is moreover very accessible to the people. . . . [Also,] the taxes are laid equally by one Rule and fall as well on the Member himself as on the people. But as to America, from the great distance in point of Situation [they are not represented in the same way]. . . .

[Finally, they say] we already by the Regulations upon their trade draw from the Americans all that they can spare, at least they say this Step [of taxation] should not take place until or unless the Americans are allowed to send Members to Parliament.

Thus I have given you, I think, the Substance of the Arguments on both sides of that great and important Question of the right and also of the Expediency of taxing America by Authority of Parliament. . . . However, . . . upon a Division of the house upon the Question, there was about 250 to about 50 in favour of the Bill. . . .

SOURCE: New Haven Colonial Historical Society, *Papers* (1918), 9: 306–315.

JOSEPH GALLOWAY
Plan of Union (1775)

Joseph Galloway, a lawyer, was Speaker of the Pennsylvania assembly and a delegate to the First Continental Congress.

At the Congress, he proposed a plan that addressed the issue of representation. The colonies would remain British territories, but would operate under a continental government with the power to veto parliamentary laws that affected America adversely. Radical Patriots in the Congress, who favored independence, prevented a vote on Galloway's plan and suppressed mention of it in the records. Galloway remained loyal to Britain, fought on the British side in the war, and moved to England in 1778.

If we sincerely mean to accommodate the difference between the two countries, . . . we must take into consideration a number of facts which led the Parliament to pass the acts complained of . . . . [You will recall] the dangerous situation of the Colonies from the intrigues of France, and the incursions of the Canadians and their Indian allies, at the commencement of the last war. . . . Great-Britain sent over her fleets and armies for their protection. . . .

In this state of the Colonies, it was not unreasonable to expect that Parliament would have levied a tax on them proportionate to their wealth, . . . Parliament was naturally led to exercise the power which had been, by its predecessors, so often exercised over the Colonies, and to pass the Stamp Act. Against this act, the Colonies petitioned Parliament, and denied its authority. . . . The petitions rested in a declaration that the Colonies could not be represented in that body. This justly alarmed the British Senate. It was thought and called by the ablest men and Britain, a clear and explicit declaration of the American Independence, and compelled the Parliament to pass the Declaratory Act, in order to save its ancient and incontrovertible right of supremacy over all the parts of the empire. . . .

Having thus briefly stated the arguments in favour of parliamentary authority, and considered the state of the Colonies, I am free to confess that the exercise of that authority is not perfectly constitutional in respect to the Colonies. We know that the whole landed interest of Britain is represented in that body, while neither the land nor the people of America hold the least participation in the legislative authority of the State. Representation, or a participation in the supreme councils of the State, is the great principle upon which the freedom of the British Government is established and secured.

I wish to see . . . the right to participate in the supreme councils of the State extended, in some form . . . to America . . . [and therefore] have prepared the draught of a plan for uniting America more intimately, in constitutional policy, with Great-Britain. . . . I am certain when dispassionately considered, it will be found to be the most perfect union in power and liberty with the Parent State, next to a representation in Parliament, and I trust it will be approved of by both countries.

The Plan
That the several [colonial] assemblies shall [form an American union and] choose members for the grand council. . . .

That the Grand Council . . . shall hold and exercise all the like rights, liberties and privileges, as are held and exercised by and in the House of Commons of Great-Britain. . . .

That the President-General shall hold his office during the pleasure of the King, and his assent shall be requisite to all acts of the Grand Council, and it shall be his office and duty to cause them to be carried into execution. . . .

That the President-General, by and with the advice and consent of the Grand-Council, hold and exercise all the legislative rights, powers, and authorities, necessary for regulating and administering all the general police and affairs of the colonies. . . .

That the said President-General and the Grand Council, be an inferior and distinct branch of the British legislature, united and incorporated with it, . . . and that the assent of both [Parliament and the Grand Council] shall be requisite to the validity of all such general acts or statutes [that affect the colonies].

SOURCE: Joseph Galloway, *Historical and Political Reflections on the Rise and Progress of the American Rebellion* (1780), 70.

ANALYZING THE EVIDENCE

➤ According to Ingersoll, what were the main arguments of those in Parliament who opposed the Stamp Act? Did they agree with the act's supporters that Parliament had the right to tax the colonies?

➤ How did Galloway's plan solve the problem of colonial representation in Parliament? How do you think ministers who advocated parliamentary supremacy would have reacted to the plan?

➤ The framers of the U.S. Constitution addressed the problem of dividing authority between state governments and the national government by allowing the state governments to retain legal authority over most matters and delegating only limited powers to the national government (see Chapter 6). Do you think this type of solution could have been implemented in the British empire? Why or why not?

TABLE 5.2	Patriot Resistance, 1762–1776	
Date	**British Action**	**Patriot Response**
1762	Revenue Act	Merchants complain privately
1763	Proclamation Line	Land speculators voice discontent
1764	Sugar Act	Merchants and Massachusetts legislature protest
1765	Stamp Act	Sons of Liberty riot; Stamp Act Congress; first boycott of British goods
1765	Quartering Act	New York assembly refuses to fund until 1767
1767–1768	Townshend Act; military occupation of Boston	Second boycott of British goods; harassment of pro-British merchants
1772	Royal commission to investigate *Gaspée* affair	Committees of correspondence form
1773	Tea Act	Widespread resistance; Boston Tea Party
1774	Coercive Acts; Quebec Act	First Continental Congress; third boycott of British goods
1775	British raids near Boston; king's Proclamation for Suppressing Rebellion and Sedition	Armed resistance; Second Continental Congress; invasion of Canada; cut off of colonial exports
1776	Military attacks by royal governors in South	Paine's *Common Sense;* Declaration of Independence

British authority. In August, 150 delegates to an extralegal Middlesex County Congress advised Patriots to close the royal courts of justice and to transfer their political allegiance to the popularly elected House of Representatives. Following the Middlesex congress, armed crowds harassed Loyalists and ensured Patriot rule in most of New England.

General Thomas Gage, now the military governor of Massachusetts, tried desperately to maintain imperial power. In September, he ordered British troops in Boston to seize Patriot armories and storehouses in nearby Charlestown and Cambridge. In response, twenty thousand colonial militiamen mobilized to safeguard other military supply depots. The Concord town meeting raised a defensive force, the famous **Minutemen**, to "Stand at a minutes warning in Case of alarm." Increasingly, Gage's authority was limited to Boston, where it rested primarily on the bayonets of his 3,500 troops. Meanwhile, the Patriot-controlled Massachusetts House met in defiance of Parliament, collected taxes, bolstered the militia, and assumed the responsibilities of government.

In London, the colonial secretary, Lord Dartmouth, proclaimed Massachusetts to be in "open rebellion" and ordered Gage to march quickly against the "rude rabble." On the night of April 18, 1775, Gage dispatched seven hundred soldiers to capture colonial leaders and supplies at Concord.

Paul Revere and two other Bostonians warned the Patriots; and at dawn, local militiamen met the British troops first at Lexington and then at Concord. A handful of men lost their lives in the skirmishes. But as the British retreated to Boston, militiamen from neighboring towns repeatedly ambushed them. By the end of the day, 73 British soldiers were dead, 174 wounded, and 26 missing. British fire had killed 49 Americans and wounded 39. Too much blood had been spilled to allow another compromise. Twelve years of economic conflict and constitutional debate had ended in civil war.

The Second Continental Congress Organizes for War

In May 1775, Patriot leaders gathered in Philadelphia for the Second Continental Congress. Soon after the Congress opened, three thousand British troops attacked American fortifications on Breed's Hill and Bunker Hill overlooking Boston. After three assaults and one thousand casualties, they finally dislodged the Patriot militia. Inspired by his countrymen's valor, John Adams exhorted the Congress to rise to the "defense of American liberty" by creating a continental army and nominated George Washington to lead it. After bitter debate, the Congress approved the proposals, but, Adams lamented, only "by bare majorities."

Political Propaganda: The Empire Strikes Back

A British cartoon satirizes the women of Edenton, North Carolina, for supporting the boycott of British trade by hinting at their sexual lasciviousness and — by showing an enslaved black woman holding an inkstand for these supposed advocates of liberty — their moral hypocrisy. Library of Congress.

A SOCIETY of PATRIOTIC LADIES, AT EDENTON in NORTH CAROLINA.

Plate V.

Congress Versus the King. Despite the bloodshed in Massachusetts, a majority in the Congress still hoped for reconciliation. Led by John Dickinson of Pennsylvania, these moderates won approval of a petition expressing loyalty to George III and asking for repeal of oppressive parliamentary legislation. But Samuel Adams, Patrick Henry, and other zealous Patriots drummed up support for a much stronger statement, the Declaration of the Causes and Necessities of Taking Up Arms. Americans dreaded the "calamities of civil war," the declaration asserted, but were "resolved to die Freemen rather than to live [as] slaves." George III failed to exploit the divisions among the Patriots; instead, in August 1775, he issued the Proclamation for Suppressing Rebellion and Sedition.

Even before the king's proclamation reached America, the radicals in the Congress had won support for an invasion of Canada. They hoped to unleash an uprising among the French inhabitants and add a fourteenth colony to the rebellion. Patriot forces easily defeated the British forces at Montreal; but in December 1775, they failed to capture Quebec City. Meanwhile, American merchants waged financial warfare by carrying out the promise of the First Continental Congress to cut off all exports to Britain and its West Indian sugar islands. Parliament retaliated with the Prohibitory Act, which outlawed all trade with the rebellious colonies.

Rebellion in the South. Skirmishes between Patriot and Loyalist forces broke out in many areas. In Virginia, the Patriot-dominated House of Burgesses forced the royal governor, Lord Dunmore, to take refuge on a British warship in Chesapeake Bay. Branding the Patriots "traitors," the governor organized two military forces—one white, the Queen's Own Loyal Virginians, and one black, the

Drawn by Earl & engraved by A.Doolittle in 1775   Re-Engraved by A.Doolittle and J.W.Barber in 1832

BATTLE OF LEXINGTON.

The Confrontation on Lexington Green

Amos Doolittle's engraving accurately depicts the events of April 19, 1775. When British troops arrived in Lexington, a British officer recalled, they "found on a green close to the road a body of the country people drawn up in military order, with arms and accoutrements." When someone fired a shot, the British soldiers let loose a volley. The provincial militiamen scattered, finding cover behind nearby stone walls, and then returned fire. Library of Congress.

Ethiopian Regiment, which enlisted some one thousand slaves who had fled their Patriot owners. In November 1775, Dunmore issued a controversial proclamation promising freedom to slaves and indentured servants who joined the Loyalist cause. White planters denounced this "Diabolical scheme," claiming it "point[ed] a dagger to their Throats." Faced with black unrest and pressed by yeoman and tenant farmers demanding independence, Patriot planters called for a final break with Britain.

In North Carolina, too, military clashes prompted demands for independence. Early in 1776, Josiah Martin, the colony's royal governor, journeyed to the backcountry, where he raised a Loyalist force of 1,500 Scottish Highlanders. In response, Patriots mobilized the low-country militia and, in February, defeated Martin's army at the Battle of Moore's Creek Bridge, capturing more than 800 Highlanders. Following this victory, radical Patriots turned the North Carolina assembly into an independent provincial congress, which instructed its representatives in Philadelphia "to concur with the Delegates of other Colonies in declaring Independence, and forming foreign alliances." In May, Virginia Patriots followed suit: Led by James Madison, Edmund Pendleton, and Patrick Henry, they met in convention and resolved unanimously to support independence.

Thomas Paine's *Common Sense*

As Patriots edged toward independence, many colonists retained a deep loyalty to the crown. Joyous crowds had toasted the health of George III when he ascended the throne in 1760 and again in 1766, when his ministers repealed the Stamp Act. Their loyalty to the king stemmed in part from the character of social authority in the patriarchal family. As the Stonington (Connecticut) Baptist Association put it, every father was "a king, and governor in his family." Just as the settlers obeyed elders in town meetings and ministers in churches, so they should obey the king, their imperial "father."

George III, 1771

King George III (b. 1738) was a young man when the American troubles began in 1765. Six years later, as this portrait by Johann Zoffany suggests, the king had aged. Initially, George was headstrong, trying to impose his will on Parliament, but he succeeded only in generating political confusion and inept policy. He did strongly support Parliament's attempts to tax the colonies, and continued the war with the colonies long after most of his ministers agreed that it had been lost. The Royal Collection. © Her Majesty Queen Elizabeth II.

Denial of the king's legitimacy might disrupt the social order.

But by 1775, many Americans had turned against the monarch. As military conflicts escalated, they accused George III of supporting oppressive legislation and ordering armed retaliation against them. Surprisingly, agitation became especially intense in Quaker-dominated Philadelphia, the largest — but hardly the most radical — seaport city. Many Philadelphia merchants harbored Loyalist sympathies and had been slow to join the boycott against the Townshend duties. However, artisans, who made up about half of Philadelphia's workers, had become a powerful force in the Patriot movement. Worried that British imports threatened their small-scale manufacturing enterprises, they organized a Mechanics Association to protect America's "just Rights and Privileges." By February 1776, forty artisans sat with forty-seven merchants on the Philadelphia Committee of Resistance, the extralegal body that enforced the trade boycott in the city.

Scots-Irish artisans and laborers became Patriots for cultural and religious reasons. They came from Presbyterian families that had fled British-controlled Ireland to escape economic and religious discrimination, and many of them had embraced the egalitarian message preached by Gilbert Tennent and other New Light ministers (see Chapter 4). As pastor of Philadelphia's Second Presbyterian Church, Tennent had told his congregation that all men and women were equal before God. Applying that idea to politics, New Light Presbyterians shouted in street demonstrations that they had "no king but King Jesus." Republican ideas derived from the European Enlightenment also circulated freely in Pennsylvania among artisans and political leaders. Patriot leaders Benjamin Franklin and Dr. Benjamin Rush questioned not only the wisdom of George III but the very idea of monarchy.

With popular sentiment in flux, a single pamphlet tipped the balance toward the Patriots. In January 1776, Thomas Paine published *Common Sense*, a rousing call for independence and a republican form of government. Paine had served as a minor bureaucrat in the customs service in England and was fired for protesting low wages. He found his way to London, where he wangled a meeting with Benjamin Franklin. In 1774, Paine migrated to Philadelphia, where he met Rush and other Patriots who shared his republican sentiments.

In *Common Sense*, Paine launched an assault on the traditional political order in language that stirred popular emotions. "Monarchy and hereditary succession have laid the world in blood and ashes," Paine proclaimed, leveling a personal attack at George III, "the hard hearted sullen Pharaoh of England." Mixing insults with biblical quotations, Paine blasted the British system of "mixed government" among the three estates of king, lords, and commoners. "That it was noble for the dark and slavish times in which it was created," Paine granted, but now it yielded only "monarchical tyranny in the person of the king" and "aristocratical tyranny in the persons of the peers."

Paine also made a compelling case for American independence. Turning the traditional metaphor of patriarchal authority on its head, he asked, "Is it the interest of a man to be a boy all his life?" Within six months, *Common Sense* had gone through twenty-five editions and reached hundreds of thousands of people throughout the colonies. "There is great talk of independence," a worried New York Loyalist noted, "and the unthinking multitude are mad for it. ... A pamphlet called Common Sense has carried off ... thousands." Paine called on Americans to reject the king and Parliament and create independent republican states. "A government of our own is our natural right, 'TIS TIME TO PART" (see Voices from Abroad, "Thomas Paine: *Common Sense*," p. 164).

Thomas Paine

Common Sense

Thomas Paine was a sharp critic and an acute observer. Before arriving in Philadelphia from his native England in mid-1774, Paine had rejected the legitimacy of monarchy. He quickly came to understand that American politics was republican in spirit and could easily be adapted to create independent governments that might change the course of history. In his widely read political pamphlet, Common Sense *(1776), he showed the colonists that American independence was "natural" and simply "common sense."*

In the following pages I offer nothing more than simple facts, plain arguments, and common sense. . . . The sun never shined on a cause of greater worth. 'Tis not the affair of a city, a country, a province, or a kingdom, but of a continent—of at least one eighth part of the habitable globe. 'Tis not the concern of a day, a year, or an age; posterity are virtually involved in the contest, and will be more or less affected, even to the end of time. . . .

We have boasted the protection of Great-Britain, without considering, that her motive was *interest* not *attachment;* that she did not protect us from *our enemies* on *our account,* but from *her enemies* on *her own account.* . . . Our plan is commerce, and that, well attended to, will secure us the peace and friendship of all Europe; because, it is the interest of all Europe to have America a *free port.* Her trade will always be a protection, and her barrenness of gold and silver secure her from invaders. I challenge the warmest advocate for reconciliation, to shew, a single advantage that this continent can reap, by being connected with Great Britain. . . . Our corn will fetch its price in any market in Europe, and our imported goods must be paid for buy them where we will.

Every thing that is right or natural pleads for separation. The blood of the slain, the weeping voice of nature cries, 'TIS TIME TO PART. Even the distance at which the Almighty hath placed England and America, is a strong and natural proof, that the authority of the one, over the other, was never the design of Heaven. . . . There is something very absurd, in supposing a continent to be perpetually governed by an island. In no instance hath nature made the satellite larger than its primary planet, and as England and America, with respect to each other, reverses the common order of nature, it is evident they belong to different systems: England to Europe, America to itself.

But the most powerful of all arguments, is, that nothing but independence, i.e. a continental form of government, can keep the peace of the continent and preserve it inviolate from civil wars. . . . If there is any true cause of fear respecting independence, it is because no plan is yet laid down. Men do not see their way out—Wherefore, . . . I offer the following hints. . . .

Let the assemblies [of the former colonies] be annual, with a President only . . . their business wholly domestic, and subject to the authority of a Continental Congress.

Let each colony be divided into six, eight, or ten convenient districts, each district to send a proper number of delegates to Congress, so that each colony send at least thirty. The whole number in Congress will be at least 390. . . .

But where, say some, is the King of America? I'll tell you. Friend, he reigns above, and doth not make havoc of mankind like the Royal Brute of Britain. Yet that we may not appear to be defective even in earthly honors, let a day be solemnly set apart for proclaiming the charter [of the new Continental republic]; let it be brought forth placed on the divine law, the word of God; let a crown be placed thereon, by which the world may know . . . that in America the LAW IS KING. For as in absolute governments the King is law, so in free countries the law ought to be King; and there ought to be no other. . . . Let the crown at the conclusion of the ceremony, be demolished, and scattered among the people whose right it is. A government of our own is our natural right. . . .

O ye that love mankind! Ye that dare oppose, not only the tyranny, but the tyrant, stand forth! Every spot of the old world is overrun with oppression. Freedom hath been hunted round the globe. Asia, and Africa, have long expelled her. — Europe regards her like a stranger, and England hath given her warning to depart. O! receive the fugitive, and prepare in time an asylum for mankind.

SOURCE: Thomas Paine, *Common Sense* (Philadelphia, 1776).

ANALYZING THE EVIDENCE

➤ On what grounds does Paine argue for American independence? Where do you see the influence of Enlightenment thinking in his argument?

➤ Given that all European nations pursued mercantilist policies, was Paine correct in thinking they would welcome America as "a free port"? How were Europe's monarchies likely to respond to American independence?

➤ How could Paine celebrate America as a land of freedom and "an asylum for mankind" given the importance of slavery and indentured servitude to the economy there? What sort of liberty was Paine championing?

➤ Why do you think *Common Sense* struck such a chord with Americans throughout the colonies?

Independence Declared

Inspired by Paine's arguments and beset by armed Loyalists, Patriot conventions throughout the colonies urged a break from Britain. In June 1776, Richard Henry Lee presented the Virginia convention's resolution to the Continental Congress: "That these United Colonies are, and of right ought to be, free and independent states . . . absolved from all allegiance to the British Crown." Faced with certain defeat, staunch Loyalists and anti-independence moderates withdrew from the Congress, leaving committed Patriots to take the fateful step. On July 4, 1776, the Congress approved the Declaration of Independence (see Documents, p. D-1).

The main author of the Declaration was Thomas Jefferson, a young planter from Virginia. As a member of the Virginia legislature, Jefferson had mobilized resistance to the Coercive Acts with the pamphlet *A Summary View of the Rights of British America* (1774). To persuade Americans and foreign observers to support independence and a republican form of government, Jefferson vilified George III: "He has plundered our seas, ravaged our coasts, burned our towns, and destroyed the lives of our people. . . . A prince, whose character is thus marked by every act which may define a tyrant," Jefferson concluded, conveniently ignoring his own actions as a slave owner, "is unfit to be the ruler of a free people."

Independence Declared

In this painting by John Trumbull, Thomas Jefferson and the other drafters (John Adams of Massachusetts, Roger Sherman of Connecticut, Robert Livingston of New York, and Benjamin Franklin of Pennsylvania) present the Declaration of Independence to John Hancock, the president of the Second Continental Congress. When the Declaration was read at a public meeting in New York City on July 10, one Patriot reported, a massive statue of George III was "pulled down by the Populace" and its four thousand pounds of lead melted down to make "Musquet balls" for use against the British troops massed on Staten Island.
Yale University Art Gallery, Mabel Brady Garven Collection.

Employing the ideas of the European Enlightenment, Jefferson proclaimed a series of "self-evident" truths: "that all men are created equal"; that they possess the "unalienable rights" of "Life, Liberty, and the pursuit of Happiness"; that government derives its "just powers from the consent of the governed" and can rightly be overthrown if it "becomes destructive of these ends." By linking these doctrines of individual liberty, **popular sovereignty**, and republican government with American independence, Jefferson established them as the defining values of the new nation.

For Jefferson, as for Paine, the pen proved mightier than the sword. In rural hamlets and seaport cities, crowds celebrated the Declaration by burning effigies of George III and toppling statues of the king. These acts of destruction broke the Patriots' psychological ties to the father-monarch and established the legitimacy of republican state governments. On July 8, 1776, in Easton, Pennsylvania, a "great number of spectators" heard a reading of the Declaration, "gave their hearty assent with three loud huzzahs, and cried out, 'May God long preserve and unite the Free and Independent States of America.'"

➤ Why did the Patriot movement wane in the early 1770s? Why did the Tea Act reignite colonial resistance?

➤ Why did the leaders of the mainland colonies and of Britain fail to reach a political compromise to save the empire?

SUMMARY

In this chapter we have focused on a short span of time—a mere decade and a half—and laid out the plot of a political drama in three acts. In Act I, British political leaders begin to implement a program of imperial reform and taxation. Act II is full of dramatic action, as colonial mobs riot, Patriot writers articulate ideologies of resistance, and British ministers search for compromise between claims of parliamentary sovereignty and claims of colonial autonomy. Act III takes the form of tragedy: The once-proud British empire dissolves into civil war, an imminent nightmare of death and destruction.

Why did this happen? More than two centuries later, the answers still are not clear. Certainly, the lack of astute leadership in Britain was a major factor. But British leaders had to contend with circumstances that constrained their freedom to act: a huge national debt and a deeply held belief in the absolute authority of Parliament. Moreover, in America, decades of salutary neglect strengthened Patriots' demands for political autonomy, as did the fears and aspirations of artisans and farmers. The trajectory of their histories placed Britain and its American possessions on course for a disastrous—and fatal—collision.

Connections: Government

It is impossible to understand the Patriot resistance movement without understanding political developments during the colonial era. As we noted in the part opener (p. 135), after 1689,

> local governments and representative assemblies became more important and created a tradition of self-rule that would spark demands for political independence from Britain.

As we have seen in Chapter 5, and will see again in Chapter 6, the tradition of local self-rule retained its vitality. During the War of Independence, local communities equipped and supplied militia units. State legislatures not only raised money and men for the Continental army but also devised new republican constitutions. The states assumed the status of sovereign entities, subject only to the will of their voting citizens. Local, state-based political power was now a matter of constitutional law.

In fact, the tradition of local rule was so strong that it was only with great difficulty that nationalist-minded politicians were able to secure ratification of the Constitution of 1787, which restored a measure of political centralization to America. Even then, most Americans looked first to their local and state governments. Having resisted and fought a distant British regime, they were not eager to place control of their lives in the hands of a remote national government.

CHAPTER REVIEW QUESTIONS

➤ Trace the key events in both Britain and America from 1763 to 1776 that forged the Patriot movement. Why did those in Parliament believe that the arguments of the rebellious colonists were not justified? How did the Patriots gain the widespread support of the colonists?

➤ The narrative suggests that the war for American independence was not inevitable, that the British empire could have been saved. Do you agree? Was there a point during the imperial crisis at which peaceful compromise was possible?

TIMELINE

1756–1763	Great War for Empire
	British national debt almost doubles
1760	George III becomes king
1762	Revenue Act reforms customs service
	Royal Navy arrests smugglers
1763	Treaty of Paris ends Great War for Empire
	Proclamation Line restricts white settlement west of Appalachians
	George Grenville becomes Britain's prime minister
1764	Parliament passes Sugar Act and Currency Act
	Colonists oppose vice-admiralty courts
1765	Stamp Act imposes direct tax on colonists
	Quartering Act provides barracks for British troops
	Sons of Liberty riot throughout colonies
	Stamp Act Congress meets in New York City
	First American boycott of British goods begins
1766	First compromise: Parliament repeals Stamp Act but passes Declaratory Act
1767	Townshend duties on certain colonial imports
	Restraining Act suspends New York assembly
1768	Second American boycott of British goods begins
	Daughters of Liberty make "homespun" cloth
	British army occupies Boston
1770	Second compromise: Parliament repeals Townshend Act but retains tax on tea
	Boston Massacre
1772	Committees of correspondence form
1773	Tea Act assists British East India Company
	Boston Tea Party
1774	Coercive Acts punish Massachusetts
	Quebec Act angers Patriots
	First Continental Congress meets in Philadelphia
	Third American boycott of British goods begins
	Loyalists organize
1775	General Thomas Gage marches to Lexington and Concord
	Second Continental Congress meets in Philadelphia and creates Continental army
	Lord Dunmore promises freedom to slaves who join Loyalists
	American invasion of Canada
	Patriots and Loyalists skirmish in South
1776	Thomas Paine publishes *Common Sense*
	Declaration of Independence

FOR FURTHER EXPLORATION

Jack P. Greene and J. R. Pole, eds., *The Blackwell Encyclopedia of the American Revolution* (1991), illuminate many aspects of the Revolutionary era, as do the personal testimonies in Barbara DeWolfe, *Discoveries of America: Personal Accounts of British Emigrants to North America During the Revolutionary Era* (1997). A suspenseful journalistic account that focuses on leading men, A. J. Langguth's *Patriots: The Men Who Started the American Revolution* (1988), should be read in conjunction with Gary B. Nash's *The Unknown American Revolution: The Unruly Birth of Democracy* (2005).

Edmund Morgan and Helen Morgan tell the story of *The Stamp Act Crisis* (1953), and Philip Lawson's *George Grenville* (1984) offers a sympathetic portrait of a reform-minded prime minister. Benjamin Labaree's *The Boston Tea Party* (1979) shows how one "small" event altered the course of history; and David Hackett Fischer explains the rise of the radical Patriots in *Paul Revere's Ride* (1994). For events in Virginia, see the probing study by Woody Holton, *Forced Founders: Indians, Debtors, Slaves, & the Making of the American Revolution in Virginia* (1999).

Liberty! The American Revolution (6 hours), a PBS video, describes the main events of the era and has a fine Web site (**www.pbs.org/ktca/liberty/**). For a British perspective, see "The Sceptered Isle: Empire" (**www.bbc.co.uk/radio4/history/empire/regions/americas.shtml**).

Two fine collections of pamphlets and images of the revolutionary era are available at **odur.let.rug.nl/~usa/D/index.htm** and **www.research.umbc.edu/~bouton/Revolution.links.htm**. On its Web site (**www.nga.gov**), the National Gallery of Art shows American paintings of the colonial and Revolutionary periods. In *Angel in the Whirlwind: The Triumph of the American Revolution* (1997), Benson Bobrick narrates a grand epic that stretches from the French and Indian War to Washington's inauguration. For a more complex narrative, see John Ferling, *A Leap in the Dark: The Struggle to Create the American Republic* (2003). A compelling fictional account of Thomas Paine's life is Howard Fast, *Citizen Tom Paine* (1943). Pauline Maier, *American Scripture: Making the Declaration of Independence* (1997), explains the background of the Declaration and how it has been redefined over the past two-plus centuries. The Continental Congress Broadside Collection at the Library of Congress (**memory.loc.gov/ammem/collections/continental/**) contains early versions of the Declaration and many other documents.

TEST YOUR KNOWLEDGE

To assess your command of the material in this chapter, see the Online Study Guide at **bedfordstmartins.com/henretta**.

For Web sites, images, and documents related to topics and places in this chapter, visit **bedfordstmartins.com/makehistory**.

BOSTON

CHARLES TOWN

6

Making War and Republican Governments

1776–1789

W HEN THE PATRIOTS OF FREDERICK COUNTY, Maryland, demanded allegiance to the American cause in 1776, Robert Gassaway would have none of it. "It was better for the poor people to lay down their arms and pay the duties and taxes laid upon them by King and Parliament," he told the local committee of safety, "than to be brought into slavery and commanded and ordered about [by you]." The story was much the same in Farmington, Connecticut, where Patriot officials imprisoned Nathaniel Jones and seventeen other men for "remaining neutral." Throughout the colonies, the events of 1776 forced families to choose the Loyalist or the Patriot side.

Because Patriots controlled most local governments, they had an edge in the battle for the hearts and minds of ordinary men and women. Patriot leaders organized their neighbors into militia units and recruited volunteers for the Continental army, a ragtag force that held its own on the battlefield. "I admire the American troops tremendously!" exclaimed a French officer. "It is incredible that soldiers composed of every age, even children of fifteen, of whites and blacks, almost naked, unpaid, and rather poorly fed, can march so well and withstand fire so steadfastly."

Military mobilization created political commitment. To encourage Americans to support the war — as soldiers, taxpayers, and republican

◄ **The Battle of Bunker Hill**

As British warships and artillery lob cannon balls at Patriot positions, British redcoats advance up the steep slope of Bunker Hill (to the right). It took three assaults and one thousand casualties before they finally dislodged the Patriot militia. The British bombardment ignited fires in nearby Charlestown, which burns in the background. *Attack on Bunker's Hill, with the Burning of Charles Town,* American 18th Century, Gift of Edgar William and Bernice Chrysler Garbisch, Image © 2005 Board of Trustees, National Gallery of Art, Washington, D.C.

citizens—Patriot leaders encouraged them to take an active role in government. And as the common people exerted their influence, the character of politics changed. "From subjects to citizens the difference is immense," remarked South Carolina Patriot David Ramsay. "Each citizen of a free state contains . . . as much of the common sovereignty as another." By raising a democratic army and repudiating aristocratic and monarchical rule, the Patriots launched the age of republican revolution that would soon sweep the Americas and throw Europe into turmoil.

The Trials of War, 1776–1778

The Declaration of Independence coincided with a full-scale British military assault. For two years, British forces manhandled the Continental army. A few inspiring American victories kept the rebellion alive, but during the winters of 1776 and 1777, the Patriot cause hung in the balance.

War in the North

Once the British resorted to military force, few European observers gave the rebels a chance. Great Britain had a great demographic advantage: 11 million people compared to the colonies' 2.5 million, 20 percent of whom were enslaved Africans. Britain also had access to the immense wealth generated by the South Atlantic System and the emerging Industrial Revolution. Its financial resources paid for the most powerful navy in the world, a standing army of 48,000 Britons, and thousands of German (Hessian) soldiers. In addition, Britain had an experienced officer corps and the support of thousands of American Loyalists and many Indian tribes (Map 6.1). The Cherokees in the Carolinas were firmly committed to the British, as were four of the six Iroquois Nations of New York—the Mohawks, Senecas, Cayugas, and Onondagas—who were led by the pro-British Mohawk chief Joseph Brant.

By contrast, the Americans were economically and militarily weak. They had no strong central government to raise revenues, and the new Continental army, commanded by General George Washington, consisted of about 18,000 poorly trained recruits hastily assembled in Virginia and New England. The Patriots could field thousands more militiamen but only near their own farms. Although many American officers had served in the military during the Great War for Empire, they had never commanded a large force or faced a disciplined European army.

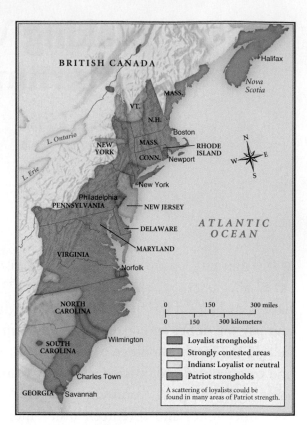

MAP 6.1 Patriot and Loyalist Strongholds

Patriots were in the majority in most of the thirteen mainland colonies and used their control of local governments to funnel men, money, and supplies to the rebel cause. Although Loyalists could be found in every colony, their strongholds were limited to Nova Scotia, eastern New York, New Jersey, and certain areas in the South. However, most Native American peoples favored the British cause and bolstered the power of Loyalist militias in central New York (see Map 6.3) and in the Carolina backcountry.

To exploit this military advantage, Britain's prime minister, Lord North, assembled a large invasion force under the command of General William Howe. North ordered Howe to capture New York City and seize control of the Hudson River, which would isolate the radical Patriots in New England from the colonies to the south. As the Second Continental Congress was declaring independence in Philadelphia in July 1776, Howe landed 32,000 troops—British regulars and German mercenaries—outside New York City, about 100 miles to the north.

British military superiority was immediately apparent. In August 1776, Howe defeated the Americans in the Battle of Long Island and forced their retreat to Manhattan Island. There, Howe outflanked Washington's troops and nearly trapped them. Outgunned and outmaneuvered, the

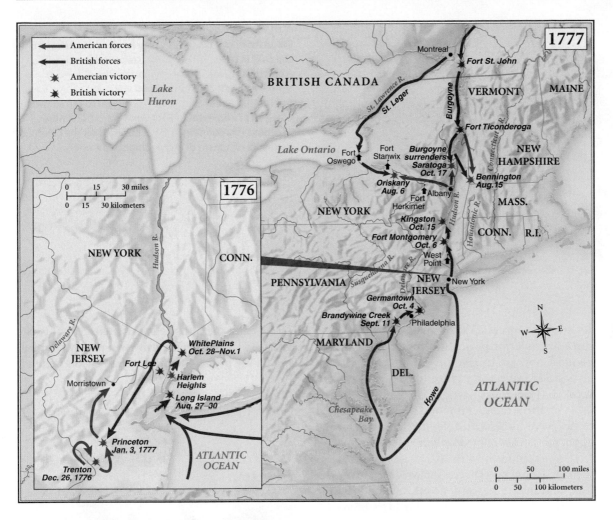

MAP 6.2   The War in the North, 1776–1777

In 1776, the British army drove Washington's forces across New Jersey into Pennsylvania. The Americans counterattacked successfully at Trenton and Princeton and then set up winter headquarters in Morristown. In 1777, British forces stayed on the offensive. General Howe attacked the Patriot capital, Philadelphia, from the south and captured it in early October. Meanwhile, General Burgoyne and Colonel St. Leger launched simultaneous invasions from Canada. With the help of thousands of New England militiamen, American troops commanded by General Horatio Gates defeated Burgoyne in August at Bennington, Vermont, and, in October 1777, at Saratoga, New York, the military turning point in the war.

Continental army again retreated, eventually crossing the Hudson River to New Jersey. By December, the British army had pushed the rebels across New Jersey and over the Delaware River into Pennsylvania.

From the Patriots' perspective, winter came just in time. Following eighteenth-century military custom, the British halted their campaign for the cold months, allowing the Americans to catch them off guard. On Christmas night 1776, Washington led his troops back across the Delaware River and staged a surprise attack on Trenton, New Jersey, where he forced the surrender of one thousand German soldiers. And in early January 1777, the

Continental army won a small victory at nearby Princeton (Map 6.2). Bright stars in a dark sky, these minor triumphs could not mask British military superiority. These are the times, wrote Tom Paine, that "try men's souls."

Armies and Strategies

Thanks in part to General Howe's tactical decisions, the Continental army remained intact and the rebellion survived. Howe had opposed the Coercive Acts of 1774, and he still hoped for a political compromise. He did not want to pursue the retreating

A British Camp, c. 1778

While American troops at Valley Forge took shelter from the cold in tents, British troops stationed just outside New York City (on upper Manhattan Island) lived in simple but well-constructed and warm log cabins. Each hut housed either a few officers or eight to ten soldiers of the 17th Regiment of Foot. John Ward Dunsmore executed this painting in 1915, basing it on the careful fieldwork of a team of archaeologists. New-York Historical Society.

American army and destroy it; he simply wanted to show his superior power and convince the Continental Congress to give up the struggle. Howe's tactics also reflected eighteenth-century military practice: Win the surrender of opposing forces, don't destroy them. Although Howe's restrained tactics were understandable, they cost Britain the opportunity to nip the rebellion in the bud.

Howe's failure to win a decisive victory was paralleled by Washington's success at avoiding a major defeat. Washington proceeded with caution, advising Congress, "On our Side the War should be defensive." His strategy was to draw the British away from the seacoast, extend their lines of supply, and sap their morale while keeping the Continental army intact.

Congress had promised Washington a regular force of 75,000 men, but the Continental army never reached a third of that number. Yeomen farmers wanted to plant and harvest their crops and so chose to serve in their local militia; consequently, most Continental army recruits were propertyless farmers and laborers. The Continental soldiers drawn from the state of Maryland and commanded by General William Smallwood were either poor American-born youths or older foreign-born men — often British ex-convicts and former indentured servants. They enlisted primarily for the bonus of $20 in cash (about $2,000 today) and the promise of 100 acres of land. Molding these recruits into a fighting force took time. Many men panicked in the face of a British artillery bombardment or flank attack; hundreds deserted, unwilling to submit to the discipline of military life. The soldiers who stayed resented the contempt their officers had for the "camp followers," the women who fed and cared for the troops.

Actually, the camp followers were crucial to the cause. The Continental army was poorly supplied and faintly praised. Radical Whig Patriots believed

American Militiamen

Beset by continuing shortages of cloth, the Patriot army dressed in a variety of uniforms and fabrics. This German engraving, based on a drawing by a Hessian officer, shows two barefoot American militiamen wearing hunting shirts and trousers made of ticking, a strong linen fabric that often was used to cover mattresses and pillows. Anne S. K. Brown Military Collection, Brown University.

a standing army was a threat to liberty; even in wartime, they preferred militias to a professional force. General Philip Schuyler of New York complained that his troops were "weak in numbers, dispirited, naked, destitute of provisions, without camp equipage, with little ammunition, and not a single piece of cannon." Given these handicaps, Washington was fortunate to have escaped sudden and overwhelming defeat.

Victory at Saratoga

Howe's failure to achieve a quick and total victory dismayed Lord North and his colonial secretary, Lord George Germain. But accepting the challenge of a long-term military commitment, the ministry increased the British land tax and used the funds to mount a major military campaign in 1777.

The isolation of New England remained Britain's primary goal. To achieve it, Germain planned a three-pronged attack converging on Albany, New York. General John Burgoyne would lead a large contingent of British regulars south from Quebec to Albany. Colonel Barry St. Leger and a force of Iroquois warriors would attack from the west, and General Howe would dispatch a force northward from New York City (see Map 6.2, p. 171).

Howe had a different plan, and it led to a disastrous result. He wanted to attack Philadelphia, the home of the Continental Congress, and end the rebellion with a single victory over Washington's army. Apparently with Germain's approval, Howe set his plan in motion — but very slowly. Instead of marching quickly through New Jersey, British troops sailed south from New York and then up the Chesapeake Bay to attack Philadelphia from the south. The strategy worked brilliantly. Howe's troops easily outflanked the American positions along Brandywine Creek in Delaware and, in late September, marched triumphantly into Philadelphia. Howe expected the capture of the rebels' capital would end the uprising, but the members of the Continental Congress, determined to continue the struggle, fled into the interior.

Howe's slow attack against Philadelphia contributed directly to the defeat of Burgoyne's army. Burgoyne's troops had advanced quickly from Quebec, crossing Lake Champlain, overwhelming the American defenses at Fort Ticonderoga in early July, and driving toward the upper reaches of the Hudson River. Then they stalled. Burgoyne fought with style — he was called "Gentleman Johnny" — stopping early each day to pitch comfortable tents and consume ample stocks of food and wine. The American troops led by General

Joseph Brant

Mohawk chief Thayendanegea, known to whites as Joseph Brant, was a devout member of the Church of England; later he helped translate the Bible into the Iroquois language. An influential man, Brant persuaded four of the six Iroquois Nations to support Britain in the war. In 1778 and 1779, he led Iroquois warriors and Tory rangers in devastating attacks on American settlements in the Wyoming Valley of Pennsylvania and Cherry Valley in New York. In this painting from 1797, Charles Willson Peale portrayed Brant with European features.
Independence National Historic Park, Philadelphia.

Horatio Gates further slowed Burgoyne's progress by felling huge trees and raiding his long supply lines to Canada.

By summer's end, Burgoyne's army of six thousand British and German troops and six hundred Loyalists and Indians was bogged down near Saratoga, New York. Desperate for food and horses, the British raided nearby Bennington, Vermont, but were beaten back by two thousand American militiamen. Patriot forces in the Mohawk Valley also forced St. Leger and the Iroquois to retreat. To make matters worse, the British commander in New York City recalled four thousand troops he had sent toward Albany and dispatched them to Philadelphia to bolster Howe's force. While Burgoyne waited in vain for help, thousands of Patriot militiamen from Massachusetts, New Hampshire, and New York joined Gates's forces. They "swarmed around the army like birds of prey," reported an alarmed English sergeant, and in October 1777 they forced Burgoyne to surrender

Saratoga Camp

The Generals in America doing nothing, or worse than nothing.

Losing the War of Public Opinion

The American victory at Saratoga shocked the British public. Opposition politicians heaped blame on the generals, many of whom had close ties to the ruling ministry. This political cartoon shows General Burgoyne abjectly surrendering to the Americans at Saratoga while General Howe, who failed to dispatch a supporting army from Philadelphia, sleeps outside his tent, oblivious to the situation. Library of Congress.

(see Voices from Abroad, "Baroness Von Riedesel: The Surrender of Burgoyne, 1777," p. 175).

The battle at Saratoga proved to be the turning point of the war. The Patriots captured more than five thousand British troops and their equipment. Equally important, the victory ensured the success of American diplomats, who were in Paris seeking a military alliance with France.

Social and Financial Perils

The Patriots' celebration of the triumph at Saratoga was tempered by wartime difficulties. A British naval blockade had cut supplies of European manufactures and disrupted the New England fishing industry; and the British occupation of Boston, New York, and Philadelphia had reduced domestic trade and manufacturing. As unemployed shipwrights, dock laborers, masons, coopers, and bakers moved to the countryside, New York City's population declined from 21,000 in 1774 to fewer than 10,000 three years later. In the Chesapeake, the British blockade cut tobacco exports and forced planters to grow grain that could be sold to the contending armies. All across the land, farmers and artisans adapted to a war economy.

With goods in short supply, government officials requisitioned military supplies directly from the people. In 1776, Connecticut officials asked the citizens of Hartford to provide 1,000 coats and 1,600 shirts, and they assessed smaller towns proportionately. The following year, they again pressed the citizenry to provide shirts, stockings, and shoes for the state's Continental units. Soldiers added personal pleas. After losing "all the shirts except the one on my back" during the Battle of Long Island, Captain Edward Rogers told his wife that "the making of cloath . . . must go on. . . . I must have shirts and stockings & a jacket sent me as soon as possible & a blankit."

Women and Household Production. Patriot women responded by increasing their output of homespun cloth. One Massachusetts town produced 30,000 yards of homespun, while women in Elizabeth, New Jersey, promised "upwards of 100,000 yards of linnen and woolen cloth." Other women assumed the burdens of farmwork while their men were away at war. Some went into the fields, plowing, harvesting, and loading grain, while others supervised laborers and acquired a taste for decision making. "We have sow'd our oats as you desired," Sarah Cobb Paine wrote to her absent husband. "Had I been master I should have planted it to Corn." Their self-esteem boosted by their wartime activities, some women expected greater legal rights in the new republican society.

Despite the women's efforts, goods remained scarce and prices rose sharply. Hard-pressed consumers decried merchants and traders as "enemies, extortioners, and monopolizers" and called for government regulation. But when a convention of New England states imposed price ceilings in 1777, many farmers and artisans refused to lower their prices. In the end, a government official admitted, consumers had to pay the higher market prices "or submit to starving."

Even more frightening, the fighting exposed tens of thousands of civilians to deprivation, displacement, and death. "An army, even a friendly one, are a dreadful scourge to any people," a Connecticut soldier wrote from Pennsylvania. "You cannot imagine what devastation and distress mark their steps." British and American armies marched back and forth across New Jersey, forcing Patriot and Loyalist families to flee their homes to escape arrest — or worse. Soldiers and partisans looted farms for food, and disorderly troops harassed and raped women and girls. When British warships sailed up the Potomac River, women and children

Baroness Von Riedesel

The Surrender of Burgoyne, 1777

Frederika Charlotte Louise, Baroness Von Riedesel, was the wife of General Friedrich Von Riedesel, commander of the Hessian soldiers in Burgoyne's army. An intrepid woman, the baroness was an eyewitness to the Saratoga campaign and a forthright critic of "Gentleman Johnny" Burgoyne. After Burgoyne's surrender, she, her husband, and their three children (ages six, three, and one) were held as prisoners of war, first in Massachusetts and then in Virginia.

We were halted at six o'clock in the morning [of October 9, 1777], to our general amazement. General Burgoyne ordered the artillery to be drawn up in a line, and to have it counted. This gave much dissatisfaction, as a few marches more would have ensured our safety. . . . At length we recommenced our march; but scarcely an hour had elapsed, before the army was again halted, because the enemy was in sight. They were but two hundred in number, who came to reconnoitre, and who might easily have been taken, had not general Burgoyne lost all his presence of mind. The rain fell in torrents. . . . On the 9th, it rained terribly the whole day; nevertheless we kept ourselves ready to march. The savages [Native Americans in Burgoyne's force] had lost their courage, and they walked off in all directions. The least untoward event made them dispirited, especially when there was no opportunity for plunder. . . .

We reached Saratoga about dark, which was but half an hour's march from the place where we had spent the day. I was quite wet, and was obliged to remain in that condition, for want of a place to change my apparel. I seated myself near the fire, and undressed the children, and we then laid ourselves upon some straw. — I asked general Phillips, who came to see how I was, why we did not continue our retreat, my husband having pledged himself to cover the movement, and to bring off the army in safety. "My poor lady," said he, "you astonish me. Though quite wet, you have so much courage as to wish to go farther in this weather. What a pity it is that you are not our commanding general! He complains of fatigue, and has determined upon spending the night here, and giving us a supper."

It is very true, that General Burgoyne liked to make himself easy, and that he spent half his nights in singing and drinking, and diverting himself. . . . I refreshed myself at 7 o'clock, the next morning, (the 10th of October,) with a cup of tea, and we all expected that we should soon continue our march. About 2 o'clock [the next day] we heard again a report of muskets and cannon, and there was much alarm and bustle among our troops. My husband sent me word, that I should immediately retire into a house which was not far off. Soon after our arrival, a terrible cannonade began, and the fire was principally directed against the house, where we had hoped to find a refuge, probably because the enemy inferred, from the great number of people who went towards it, that this was the headquarters of the generals, while, in reality, none were there except women and crippled soldiers. We were at last obliged to descend into the cellar, where I laid myself in a corner near the door. My children put their heads upon my knees. An abominable smell, the cries of the children, and my own anguish of mind, did not permit me to close my eyes, during the whole night.

On the next morning, the cannonade begun anew, but in a different direction. . . . Eleven cannon-balls passed through the house, and made a tremendous noise. A poor soldier, who was about to have a leg amputated, lost the other by one of these balls. All his comrades ran away at that moment, and when they returned, they found him in one corner of the room, in the agonies of death. . . .

The want of water continuing to distress us, we could not but be extremely glad to find a soldier's wife so spirited as to fetch some from the river, an occupation from which the boldest might have shrunk, as the Americans shot every one who approached it. They told us afterwards that they spared her on account of her sex. . . .

On the 17th of October, the capitulation was carried into effect. The generals waited upon the American general Gates, and the troops surrendered themselves prisoners of war and laid down their arms.

SOURCE: Madame de Riedesel, *Letters and Memoirs Relating to the War of American Independence, and the Capture of the German Troops at Saratoga* (New York, 1827), 173–183.

ANALYZING THE EVIDENCE

➤ What light, if any, does Von Riedesel's account shed on the Battle of Saratoga? How reliable a witness was she?

➤ What does the presence of the baroness, her children, and the wives of several British officers suggest about the nature of eighteenth-century warfare?

fled from Alexandria, Virginia, and "stowed themselves into every Hut they can get, out of the reach of the Enemys canon" and troops.

The war divided many communities. Patriots formed committees of safety that collected taxes to support the Continental army, and imposed fines or jail sentences on those who refused to pay. In New England, mobs of Patriot farmers beat suspected Tories and destroyed their property. "Every Body submitted to our Sovereign Lord the Mob," a Loyalist preacher lamented. In some areas of Maryland, the number of "nonassociators" — those who refused to join either side — was so large that they successfully defied Patriot organizers. "Stand off you dammed rebel sons of bitches," Robert Davis of Anne Arundel County shouted, "I will shoot you if you come any nearer."

Financial Crisis. Such defiance exposed the weakness of the new state governments. Most governments were afraid to raise taxes, forcing Patriot officials to pay war expenses by borrowing gold or silver currency from wealthy individuals. When those funds ran out, individual states printed paper money: Eventually, they issued $260 million in currency. Because the new currency was printed in huge quantities and was not backed by gold, tax revenues, or mortgages on land, many Americans refused to accept it at face value. North Carolina's paper money came to be worth so little that even the state's tax collectors refused it.

The finances of the Continental Congress collapsed too, despite the efforts of Philadelphia merchant Robert Morris, the government's chief treasury official. Because Congress lacked the authority to impose taxes, Morris relied on funds requisitioned from the states, but they paid late or not at all. So the treasury looked to France and Holland for loans, and encouraged wealthy Americans to purchase Continental bonds. Eventually, Congress followed the lead of the states and printed $191 million in currency and bills of credit, which also fell quickly in value. In 1778, a family needed $7 in Continental bills to buy goods worth $1 in gold or silver. As the rate of exchange between paper currency and specie rose — to 42 to 1 in 1779, 100 to 1 in 1780, and 146 to 1 in 1781 — it sparked social upheaval. In Boston, a mob of women accosted merchant Thomas Boyleston, "seazd him by his Neck," and forced him to sell his wares at traditional prices. In rural Ulster County, New York, women demanded that the local committee of safety lower food prices; otherwise, they said, "their husbands and sons shall fight no more." Civilian and military morale crumbled, and some Patriot leaders doubted the rebellion could succeed.

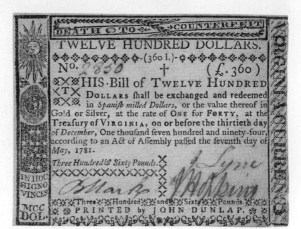

Paper Currency

To symbolize their independent status, the new state governments printed their own currency. Rejecting the English system of pounds and shillings, Virginia used the Spanish gold dollar as its basic unit of currency, although the currency also showed the equivalent in English pounds. Initially, $1,200 was equal to £360 — a ratio of 3.3 to 1. By 1781, Virginia had printed so much paper money to pay its soldiers and wartime expenses that the value of its currency had depreciated. It now took $40 in Virginia currency to buy the same amount of goods as £1 sterling. American Numismatic Society, New York City.

Valley Forge. Fears reached their peak during the winter of 1777. While Howe's army partook of warm lodgings and ample food in Philadelphia, Washington's army retreated 20 miles to the west to Valley Forge, where 12,000 soldiers and hundreds of camp followers suffered horribly. "The army . . . now begins to grow sickly," a surgeon confided to his diary. "Poor food — hard lodging — cold weather — fatigue — nasty clothes — nasty cookery. . . . Why are we sent here to starve and freeze?" Nearby farmers refused to help. Some were pacifists, Quakers and German sectarians unwilling to support either side. Others looked out for their families by refusing to sell grain for worthless Continental currency, accepting only the gold and silver offered by British quartermasters. "Such a dearth of public spirit, and want of public virtue," Washington lamented. By spring, one thousand hungry soldiers had vanished into the countryside, and another three thousand had died from malnutrition and disease. One winter at Valley Forge took as many American lives as had two years of fighting.

In this dark hour, Baron von Steuben raised the self-respect and readiness of the American army. A former Prussian military officer, von Steuben was one of a handful of republican-minded foreign aristocrats who helped the American cause. To counter falling morale, he instituted a strict system of drill and encouraged officers to become more professional. Thanks to von Steuben, the smaller Continental army that emerged from Valley Forge in the spring of 1778 was a much tougher and better-disciplined force.

➤ Why were British forces militarily superior to American forces in the first years of the war? How did the Americans sustain the Revolution between 1776 and 1778?

➤ Who was most to blame for Britain's failure to win a quick victory over the American rebels — General Howe, General Burgoyne, or the ministers in London? Explain your answer.

➤ What were the most important economic and fiscal problems facing the Patriots at the outset of the war? How successful were they in addressing them?

The Path to Victory, 1778–1783

Wars are often won by astute diplomacy, and that was the case with the War of Independence. The Patriots' prospects improved dramatically in 1778, when the Continental Congress concluded a military alliance with France, the most powerful nation in Europe. The alliance gave the Americans a source of desperately needed money, supplies, and, eventually, troops. Equally important, it confronted Britain with an international war that challenged its domination of the Atlantic world.

The French Alliance

France and America were unlikely partners. France was Catholic and a monarchy; the United States was Protestant and a federation of republics. From 1689 to 1763, the two peoples had been enemies: New Englanders had brutally expelled the French population from Acadia (Nova Scotia); and the French, with the help of Indian allies, had organized raids of British settlements. But the Comte de Vergennes, the French foreign minister, was determined to avenge the loss of Canada to Britain in the Great War for Empire. He persuaded King Louis XVI to provide the rebellious colonies with a secret loan and much-needed

gunpowder, and he opened contact with American diplomats. When news of the rebel victory at Saratoga reached Paris in December 1777, Vergennes sought a formal alliance.

Negotiating the Treaty. Benjamin Franklin and other American diplomats craftily exploited France's rivalry with Britain to win an explicit commitment to American independence. The Treaty of Alliance of February 1778 specified that once France entered the war, neither partner would sign a separate peace without the "liberty, sovereignty, and independence" of the United States. In return, the Continental Congress agreed to recognize any French conquests in the West Indies.

The alliance gave new life to the Patriots' cause. "There has been a great change in this state since the news from France," a Patriot soldier reported from Pennsylvania. Farmers — "mercenary wretches," he called them — "were as eager for Continental Money now as they were a few weeks ago for British gold." Its confidence bolstered by the alliance, the Continental Congress addressed the financial demands of the officer corps. Most officers came from the upper ranks of society, equipped themselves, and often served without pay; in return, they insisted on lifetime military pensions at half pay. John Adams condemned the officers for "scrambling for rank and pay like apes for nuts," but General Washington urged Congress to grant the pensions and warned the lawmakers that "the salvation of the cause depends upon it." Congress reluctantly granted the officers half pay, but only for seven years.

The British Response. Meanwhile, the war was becoming increasingly unpopular in Britain. Radical Whig politicians and republican-minded artisans supported American demands for autonomy and campaigned for domestic political reforms, among them greater representation for cities in Parliament and the elimination of the rotten boroughs. The gentry protested increases in the land tax, and merchants condemned new levies on carriages, wine, and imported goods. "It seemed we were to be taxed and stamped ourselves instead of inflicting taxes and stamps on others," a British politician complained.

At first, George III remained committed to crushing the rebellion. If America won independence, he warned Lord North, "the West Indies must follow them. Ireland would soon follow the same plan and be a separate state, then this island would be reduced to itself, and soon would be a poor island indeed." Stunned by the British defeat at

Saratoga, the king changed his mind. To prevent an American alliance with France, he authorized North to seek a negotiated settlement. In February 1778, North persuaded Parliament to repeal the Tea and Prohibitory acts and, in an amazing concession, to renounce its power to tax the colonies. Opening discussions with the Continental Congress, the prime minister proposed a return to the constitutional "condition of 1763," before the Sugar and Stamp acts. But the Patriots, now allied with France and committed to independence, rejected North's overture.

War in the South

The French alliance did not bring a rapid end to the war. When French forces entered the conflict in June 1778, they were sent to capture Barbados or Jamaica or another rich sugar island. Spain, which joined the war against Britain in 1779, wanted to regain Florida and the fortress of Gibraltar at the entrance to the Mediterranean Sea. As the agendas of France and Spain turned the war into a worldwide conflict, the British ministry revised its military strategy in America and shifted the main theater of war to the South.

Britain's Southern Strategy. Rather than using their army to isolate New England, British ministers turned their attention to the rich tobacco- and rice-growing colonies — Virginia, the Carolinas, and Georgia. They planned to win these areas and then rely on local Loyalists to hold them. In the Carolinas, the British counted on the allegiance of Scottish Highlanders. They hoped to recruit other Loyalists from the ranks of the Regulators, the enemies of the low-country Patriot planters (see Chapter 4), and to mobilize the Cherokees and other Indian peoples against the land-hungry Americans (Map 6.3). The ministry also planned to exploit racial divisions in the South. In 1776, more than one thousand slaves had fought for Lord Dunmore under the banner "Liberty to Slaves!"; a British invasion might prompt thousands more to flee their Patriot owners. South Carolina whites knew that slavery was a double-edged sword, a source of wealth in peacetime but a danger in war. The state could not raise an army, its representative told the Continental Congress, "by reason of the great proportion of citizens necessary to remain at home to prevent insurrection among the Negroes."

Implementing Britain's southern military strategy became the responsibility of Sir Henry Clinton. Moving the main British army to secure quarters in New York City, Clinton ordered a seaborne attack on Savannah, Georgia; troops under the command of Colonel Archibald Campbell captured the town in December 1778. Mobilizing hundreds of blacks to unload and transport supplies, Campbell moved inland and captured Augusta early in 1779. By year's end, Clinton's forces and local Loyalists controlled coastal Georgia, and 10,000 troops were poised for an assault on South Carolina.

During most of 1780, British forces in the South marched from victory to victory (Map 6.4). In May, Clinton laid siege to Charleston, South Carolina, and forced the surrender of General Benjamin Lincoln and his garrison of 5,000 troops. Then Lord Cornwallis assumed control of the British forces and marched into the countryside. In August, at the Battle of Camden, Cornwallis defeated an American force commanded by General Horatio Gates, the hero of Saratoga. Only 1,200 Patriot militiamen joined Gates at Camden — a fifth of the number at Saratoga — and many of them panicked. As Cornwallis took control of South Carolina, hundreds of African Americans fled to freedom in British-controlled Florida, while hundreds more found refuge with the British army.

Then the tide of battle turned. The Dutch declared war against Britain, and France finally dispatched troops to the American mainland. The French decision was in part the work of the Marquis de Lafayette, a republican-minded aristocrat who had long supported the American cause. In 1780, Lafayette persuaded Louis XVI to send General Comte de Rochambeau and 5,500 men to Newport, Rhode Island, where they threatened British forces in New York City.

Partisan Warfare in the Carolinas. Meanwhile, Washington dispatched General Nathanael Greene to recapture the Carolinas. Greene faced a difficult task. His troops, he reported, "were almost naked and we subsist by daily collections and in a country that has been ravaged and plundered by both friends and enemies." To make use of local militiamen, who were "without discipline and addicted to plundering," Greene placed them under strong leaders and unleashed them on less-mobile British forces. In October 1780, a militia of Patriot farmers defeated a regiment of Loyalists at King's Mountain, South Carolina, taking about one thousand prisoners. Led by the "Swamp Fox," General Francis Marion, American guerrillas won a series of small but fierce battles in South Carolina. Then, in January 1781, General Daniel Morgan led another American force to a bloody victory at Cowpens, South Carolina. But Loyalist garrisons and militia

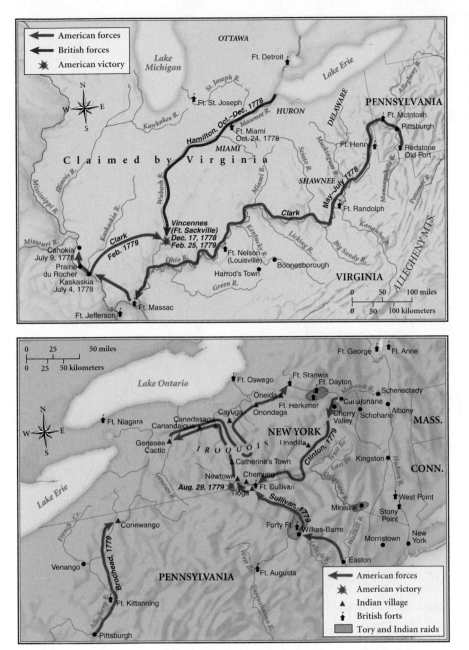

MAP 6.3 Native Americans and the War in the West, 1778–1779

Many Indian peoples remained neutral, but some, fearing land-hungry Patriot farmers, used British-supplied guns to raid American settlements. To thwart attacks by militant Shawnees, Cherokees, and Delawares, a Patriot militia led by George Rogers Clark captured the British fort and supply depot at Vincennes on the Wabash River in February 1779. To the north, Patriot generals John Sullivan and James Clinton defeated pro-British Indian forces near Tioga (on the New York–Pennsylvania border) in August 1779 and then systematically destroyed villages and crops throughout the Iroquois' lands.

units remained powerful, helped by the well-organized Cherokees, who were determined to protect their lands from American settlers and troops. "We fight, get beaten, and fight again," General Greene declared doggedly. In March 1781, Greene's soldiers fought Cornwallis's seasoned army to a draw at North Carolina's Guilford Court House. Weakened by this **war of attrition**, the British general decided to concede the Carolinas to Greene and seek a decisive victory in Virginia.

Benedict Arnold and Conflicting Loyalties. In the summer of 1781, Cornwallis invaded the Tidewater region of Virginia. He was joined there by British

reinforcements from New York under the command of General Benedict Arnold. Arnold was born in Connecticut and had joined the War of Independence on the American side. Troops under his command captured Fort Ticonderoga for the Patriots in 1775 and then launched an unsuccessful assault on Quebec City. In that battle, Arnold stormed over a barricade and took a musket ball through his leg. At Saratoga, he led an attack against the center of the British line and was again wounded in the leg. Admiring Arnold's boldness and courage, General Washington appointed him to various commands, including the important Hudson River fort at West Point. There, Arnold turned against his country.

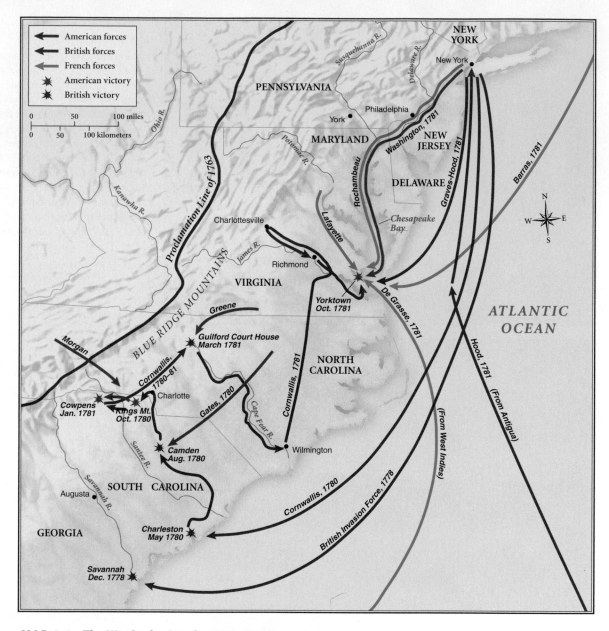

MAP 6.4   The War in the South, 1778–1781

Britain's southern strategy started well. British forces captured Savannah in December 1778, took control of Georgia during 1779, and vanquished Charleston in May 1780. Over the next eighteen months, brutal warfare between British and Loyalist units and the American army and militia raged in the interior of the Carolinas and ended in a stalemate. Hoping to break the deadlock, British general Charles Cornwallis carried the battle into Virginia in 1781. A Franco-American army led by Washington and Lafayette, with the help of the French fleet under Admiral de Grasse, surrounded Cornwallis's forces on the Yorktown Peninsula and forced their surrender.

Facing ruin because of shady financial dealings, uncertain of future promotion because of his reputation for arrogance and avarice, and disgusted with congressional politics, Arnold promised to deliver West Point and its three thousand defenders to the British for £20,000 sterling (about $1 million today). When his plan was exposed, Arnold became a British brigadier general and served George III with the same skill and enthusiasm he had shown in the Patriot cause. Supporting Cornwallis, he led raiding parties along the James River and, in a daring attack on Richmond, destroyed large stocks of munitions and grain.

Britain Defeated. While troops led by Arnold and Cornwallis sparred near the York Peninsula with an American force commanded by Lafayette, France ordered its fleet from the West Indies to North America. Emboldened by the French naval forces, Washington launched a well-coordinated attack. Feinting an assault on New York City, he secretly marched General Rochambeau's army from Rhode Island to Virginia, where it joined his Continental forces. Simultaneously, the French fleet massed off the coast, taking control of Chesapeake Bay. By the time the British discovered Washington's audacious plan, Cornwallis was surrounded—his 9,500-man army outnumbered 2 to 1 on land and cut off from reinforcement or retreat by sea. In a hopeless position, Cornwallis surrendered at Yorktown in October 1781.

The Franco-American victory at Yorktown broke the resolve of the British government. "Oh God! It is all over!" Lord North exclaimed when he heard the news. Isolated diplomatically in Europe, stymied militarily in America, and lacking public support at home, the British ministry gave up active prosecution of the war.

The Patriot Advantage

Angry members of Parliament demanded an explanation. How could mighty Britain, victorious in the Great War for Empire, be defeated by a motley rebel army? The ministry blamed the military leadership, pointing with some justification to a series of blunders. Why had Howe not ruthlessly pursued Washington's army in 1776? Why had Howe and Burgoyne failed to coordinate the movement of their armies in 1777? Why had Cornwallis marched deep into the Patriot-dominated state of Virginia in 1781?

Although historians acknowledge British blunders, most agree that the decisive factor in the rebels' victory was the broad support in America for their cause. At least a third of the white colonists were zealous Patriots, and another third supported the war effort by paying taxes and joining the militia. Moreover, the Patriots were led by experienced politicians who commanded public support. And then there was George Washington. Washington emerged as an inspired military leader and an astute politician. By deferring to the civil authorities, he won the support of the Continental Congress and the state governments. Confident of his military leadership, he acted decisively. When unruly troops stationed at Morristown, New Jersey, mutinied because of low pay and sparse rations, Washington ordered the execution of several soldiers. At

Benedict Arnold, 1776

Arnold first captured British attention because of his daring assault on Quebec City, which is pictured in the background of this painting. But the portrait is imaginary, the creation of a London bookseller eager to capitalize on British interest in the American revolt. After Arnold defected to the crown in 1780, British engravers usually portrayed him in profile, a pose traditionally reserved for those of noble character. Anne S. K. Brown Military Collection, Brown University.

the same time, he urged Congress to pacify the troops with back pay and new clothing. Later in the war, the American general thwarted a dangerous challenge to Congress's authority by discontented officers at Newburgh, New York. Finally, Washington had a greater margin for error than the British generals did because the Patriots controlled local governments. At crucial moments, he was able to get those governments to mobilize rural militias to reinforce the Continental army. Alone, Patriot militias lacked the weapons and tactical knowledge needed to defeat the British army. However, in combination with Continental forces, they provided the margin of victory at Saratoga in 1777 and forced Cornwallis from the Carolinas in 1781. Once the rebels had French support, they could reasonably hope for a decisive triumph, as happened at Yorktown.

In the end, it was the American people who decided the outcome of the war. Preferring Patriot rule, they refused to support the British army or accept occupation by Loyalist forces. Most

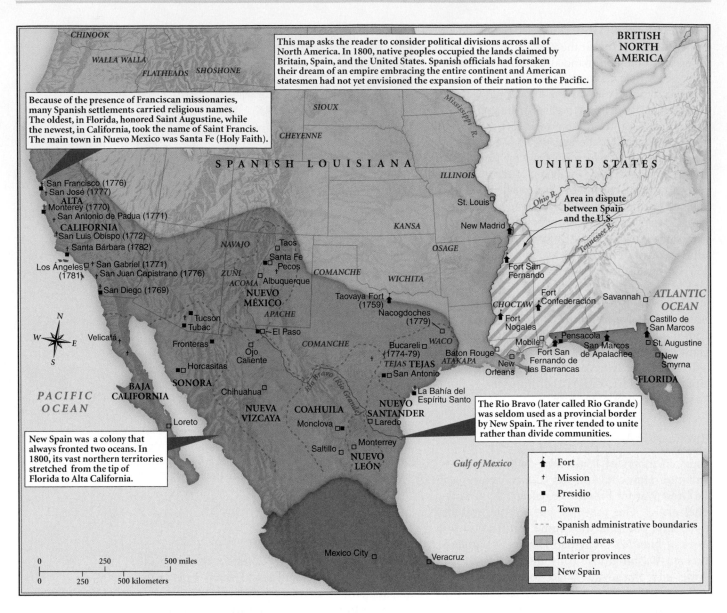

This map asks the reader to consider political divisions across all of North America. In 1800, native peoples occupied the lands claimed by Britain, Spain, and the United States. Spanish officials had forsaken their dream of an empire embracing the entire continent and American statesmen had not yet envisioned the expansion of their nation to the Pacific.

Because of the presence of Franciscan missionaries, many Spanish settlements carried religious names. The oldest, in Florida, honored Saint Augustine, while the newest, in California, took the name of Saint Francis. The main town in Nuevo Mexico was Santa Fe (Holy Faith).

New Spain was a colony that always fronted two oceans. In 1800, its vast northern territories stretched from the tip of Florida to Alta California.

The Rio Bravo (later called Rio Grande) was seldom used as a provincial border by New Spain. The river tended to unite rather than divide communities.

MAP 6.5 New Spain's Northern Empire, 1763–1800

After it acquired Louisiana from France in 1763, Spain tried to create a great northern empire. It established missions and forts (presidos) in California (such as that at Monterey), expanded its settlements in New Mexico, and, by allying with France during the War of Independence, won the return of Florida from Britain. By the early nineteenth century, however, Spain's dream of a northern empire had been shattered by Indian uprisings in California and Texas, Napoleon's seizure of Louisiana, and the Americans' imminent takeover of Florida.

important, they endured the inflation that placed most of the costs of the war on their shoulders. Tens of thousands of farmers and artisans accepted Continental bills in payment for supplies, and thousands of soldiers took them as pay—even as the currency literally depreciated in their pockets. Every paper dollar held for a week lost value, imposing a hidden "currency tax" on those who accepted payment in the paper currency. Each individual tax was small—a few pennies on each

dollar. But as millions of dollars changed hands multiple times, these currency taxes paid the huge cost of the American military victory.

Diplomatic Triumph

After Yorktown, diplomats took two years to end the war. Peace talks began in Paris in April 1782, but the French and Spanish stalled because they still hoped for a major naval victory or territorial conquest. Their delaying tactics infuriated the American diplomats — Benjamin Franklin, John Adams, and John Jay. Fearing that France might sacrifice American interests, the Patriot diplomats negotiated secretly with the British, prepared if necessary to ignore the Treaty of Alliance and sign a separate peace. British ministers were eager for a quick settlement because Parliament no longer supported the war and because they feared the loss of a rich West Indian sugar island.

Exploiting this situation, the American diplomats secured peace on very favorable terms. In the Treaty of Paris, signed in September 1783, Great Britain formally recognized the independence of the rebel colonies. While retaining Canada, Britain relinquished its claims to lands south of the Great Lakes and east of the Mississippi River, and promised to withdraw British garrisons from this trans-Appalachian region "with all convenient speed." Leaving its native allies to their fate, the British negotiators did not insist on a separate Indian territory. "In endeavouring to assist you," a Wea Indian complained to a British general, "it seems we have wrought our own ruin."

Other provisions of the treaty were equally favorable to the Americans. The treaty granted Americans fishing rights off Newfoundland and Nova Scotia, prohibited the British from "carrying away any negroes or other property," and guaranteed freedom of navigation on the Mississippi to American citizens "forever." In return, the American government allowed British merchants to pursue legal claims for prewar debts and agreed to encourage the state legislatures to return confiscated property to Loyalists and grant them citizenship.

In the Treaty of Versailles, signed simultaneously, Britain made peace with France and Spain. Neither American ally gained very much. Spain reclaimed Florida from Britain (Map 6.5), but failed to win back the strategic fortress at Gibraltar. France gained control of the Caribbean island of Tobago, small consolation for a war that sharply raised taxes and quadrupled the national debt. Just six years later, cries for tax relief and political liberty would spark the French Revolution. Only the Americans profited handsomely from the treaties, which gave them independence from Britain and opened the trans-Appalachian west for settlement.

➤ Why did Britain switch to a southern military strategy? Why did that strategy ultimately fail?

➤ How did the French alliance ensure the success of the American rebellion?

➤ The text argues that "it was the American people who decided the outcome of the war." Based on the evidence presented in the chapter, do you agree? Why or why not?

Creating Republican Institutions, 1776–1787

When the Patriot leaders declared independence at the beginning of the war, they had to decide how to allocate political power among themselves. "Which of us shall be the rulers?" asked a Philadelphia newspaper. The question was multifaceted: Where would power reside, in the national government or the states? Who would control the new republican institutions, traditional elites or average citizens? Would women have greater political and legal rights? And what about the slaves? What would their status be in the new republic? Many of the answers to these questions began to emerge from Americans' wartime experience.

The State Constitutions: How Much Democracy?

In May 1776, the Second Continental Congress urged Americans to reject royal authority and establish republican governments. Most states quickly complied. Within six months, Virginia, Maryland, North Carolina, New Jersey, Delaware, and Pennsylvania had written new constitutions, and Connecticut and Rhode Island had revised their colonial charters by deleting references to the king. "Constitutions employ every pen," an observer noted.

Americans Define Popular Sovereignty. Republicanism meant more than ousting the king. The Declaration of Independence had stated the principle of popular sovereignty: that governments derive "their just powers from the consent of the governed." In the heat of revolution, many Patriots gave this clause a democratic twist. In North Carolina, the backcountry farmers of Mecklenburg County instructed their delegates to the state's constitutional convention to "oppose everything that leans to aristocracy or power in the hands of the rich and chief men exercised to the oppression of the poor." In Virginia, voters elected a new

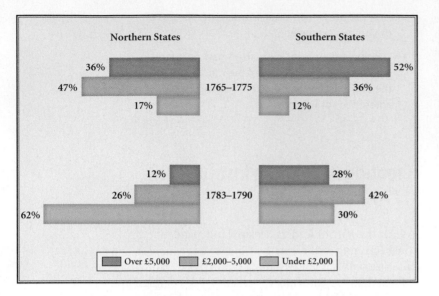

Northern States   **Southern States**

1765–1775

1783–1790

Over £5,000   £2,000–5,000   Under £2,000

FIGURE 6.1 Middling Men Enter the Halls of Government, 1765–1790

Before the Revolution, wealthy men dominated most colonial assemblies, particularly in the southern colonies. In the new American republic, the proportion of middling legislators (yeoman farmers and others of little wealth, as measured by tax lists and probate records) increased dramatically, especially in the northern states. SOURCE: Adapted from Jackson T. Main, "Government by the People: The American Revolution and the Democratization of the Legislatures," *William and Mary Quarterly*, 3d ser., vol. 23 (1966).

assembly that, an eyewitness remarked, "was composed of men not quite so well dressed, nor so politely educated, nor so highly born" as colonial-era legislatures (Figure 6.1).

This democratic impulse achieved its fullest expression in Pennsylvania, thanks to a coalition of Scots-Irish farmers, Philadelphia artisans, and Enlightenment-influenced intellectuals. The Pennsylvania Constitution of 1776 abolished property ownership as a test of citizenship and granted tax-paying men the right to vote and hold office. It also created a unicameral (one-house) legislature with complete power. There was no upper house, and no governor who exercised veto power. Other provisions mandated an extensive system of elementary education and protected citizens from imprisonment for debt.

John Adams and Conservative Republicanism.
Pennsylvania's democratic constitution alarmed many leading Patriots. From Boston, John Adams denounced the unicameral legislature as "so democratical that it must produce confusion and every evil work." "Remember," Adams continued, invoking history as his guide, "democracy never lasts long. It soon wastes, exhausts, and murders itself." Along with other conservative Patriots, Adams believed office holding should be restricted to "men of learning, leisure and easy circumstances" and feared that ordinary citizens would use their larger numbers to tax the rich: "If you give [democrats] the command or preponderance in the . . . legislature, they will vote all property out of the hands of you aristocrats."

To counter the appeal of the Pennsylvania Constitution, Adams published *Thoughts on Government* (1776). In this treatise, he adapted the British Whig theory of mixed government (in which power is shared by the monarch and Houses of Lords and Commons) to a republican society. To disperse authority and preserve liberty, he assigned the different functions of government—lawmaking, administering, and judging—to separate institutions. Legislatures would make the laws, the executive would administer them, and the judiciary would enforce them. Adams also called for a bicameral (two-house) legislature with an upper house, its members substantial property owners, that would check the power of popular majorities in the lower house. As a further curb on democracy, he proposed an elected governor with the power to veto laws and an appointed—not elected—judiciary to review them.

Conservative Patriots endorsed Adams's scheme for a bicameral legislature because it preserved representative government while restricting popular power. But they hesitated to give the veto power to governors because they recalled the arbitrary conduct of royal governors and feared executive authority. Most states did follow Adams's suggestion about retaining traditional property qualifications for voting. Under the terms of the New York Constitution of 1777, for example, 80 percent of white men had enough property to vote in elections for the assembly, but only 40 percent could vote for the governor and the upper house. The most flagrant use of property to retain power for the wealthy was in South Carolina, where the 1778 constitution required candidates for governor to have a debt-free estate of £10,000 (about $700,000 today), senators to be worth £2,000, and assemblymen to own property valued at £1,000. These provisions ruled out office holding for about 90 percent of white men.

John and Abigail Adams

Both Adamses had strong personalities and often disagreed in private about political and social issues. In 1794, John playfully accused his wife of being a "Disciple of Wollstonecraft," but Abigail's commitment to legal equality for women long predated Mary Wollstonecraft's treatise, *A Vindication of the Rights of Woman* (1792). Boston Athenaeum; New York State Historical Association, Cooperstown.

The political legacy of the Revolution was complex. Only in Pennsylvania and Vermont were radical Patriots able to take power and create truly democratic institutions. Yet everywhere, representative legislatures had acquired more power, and the day-to-day politics of electioneering and interest-group bargaining had become much more responsive to average citizens.

Women Seek a Public Voice

The extraordinary excitement of the Revolutionary era tested the dictum that only men could engage in politics. Although men controlled all public institutions—legislatures, juries, government offices—upper-class women entered political debate and, defying male opposition, filled their letters, diaries, and conversations with opinions on public issues. "The men say we have no business [with politics]," Eliza Wilkinson of South Carolina complained in 1783. "They won't even allow us liberty of thought, and that is all I want."

These American women did not insist on civic equality with men; but they did insist on ending various restrictive customs and laws. Abigail Adams, for example, demanded equal legal rights for married women, who under common law could not own property, enter into contracts, or initiate lawsuits. "Men would be tyrants" if they continued to hold such power over women, Adams declared to her husband, criticizing him and other Patriots for "emancipating all nations" from monarchical despotism while "retaining absolute power over Wives."

Most men ignored women's requests, and most husbands remained patriarchs who dominated their household. Even young men who embraced the republican ideal of "companionate marriage" (see Chapter 8) did not support legal equality or a public role for their wives and daughters. With the exception of New Jersey, which until 1807 allowed unmarried and widowed female property holders to vote, women remained disenfranchised.

The republican belief in an educated citizenry created opportunities for at least some American women. In her 1779 essay "On the Equality of the Sexes," Judith Sargent Murray argued that men and women had an equal capacity for memory and that women had a superior imagination. She conceded that most women were inferior to men in judgment and reasoning, but insisted that was only because they had not been trained: "We can only reason from what we know," she argued, and most women had

Judith Sargent (Murray), Age Nineteen

The well-educated daughter of a wealthy Massachusetts merchant, Judith Sargent enjoyed a privileged childhood. As an adult, however, she endured a difficult seventeen-year marriage to John Stevens, who ultimately went bankrupt, fled from his creditors, and died in the West Indies. In 1788, she married John Murray, a minister who became a leading American Universalist. Her portrait, painted around 1771 by John Singleton Copley, captures the young woman's skepticism, which enabled her to question customary gender roles. Terra Museum of American Art, Chicago, Illinois. Daniel J. Terra Collection.

been denied "the opportunity of acquiring knowledge." That began to change in the 1790s, when the attorney general of Massachusetts declared that girls had an equal right to schooling under the state constitution. With greater access to public elementary schools and the rapid growth of girls' academies (private high schools), many young women became literate and knowledgeable. By 1850, the literacy rates of women and men in the northeastern states would be much the same, and educated women would again challenge their subordinate legal and political status (see Reading American Pictures, "Did the Revolution Promote Women's Rights?" p. 187).

The Loyalist Exodus

The creation of republican institutions was greatly helped by the voluntary exodus of 100,000 supporters of the monarchy. Departing Loyalists usually

suffered severe financial losses. John Tabor Kempe, the last royal attorney general of New York, wanted £65,000 sterling (about $4.5 million today) from the British government to compensate for Patriot land seizures; he received £5,000. Refugees often suffered psychologically too. Prominent Loyalists who fled to England found little happiness there; many complained of "their uneasy abode in this country of aliens." Among the great mass of Loyalist evacuees who moved to Canada or the West Indies, many lamented the loss of their old lives. Watching "sails disappear in the distance," wrote an exiled woman in Nova Scotia, "[I had] such a feeling of loneliness . . . I sat down on the damp moss with my baby on my lap and cried bitterly."

Some Patriots demanded that the state governments seize all Loyalist property and distribute it to needy Americans; but most Patriot leaders argued that confiscation would violate republican principles. In Massachusetts, officials cited the state's constitution of 1780, which declared that every citizen should be protected "in the enjoyment of his life, liberty, and property, according to the standing laws." So the new republican governments confiscated only a small amount of Loyalist property and usually sold it to the highest bidder, more likely a wealthy Patriot than a yeoman farmer or a propertyless foot soldier. In a few cases, confiscation did produce a democratic result: In North Carolina, about half the new owners of Loyalist lands were small-scale farmers; in New

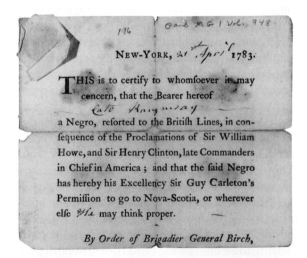

A Black Loyalist Pass, 1783

White Patriots claimed their freedom by fighting *against* the British; thousands of black slaves won liberty by fighting *for* them. This pass certifies that Cato Rammsay, "a Negro," supported the Loyalist cause in New York and is now free "to go to Nova-Scotia, or wherever else He may think proper." Nova Scotia Archives and Record Management, Halifax.

Did the Revolution Promote Women's Rights?

Frontispiece from *Lady's Magazine,* 1792. The Library Company of Philadelphia.

"Keep Within Compass," c. 1785. Henry Francis du Pont Winterthur Museum, Winterthur, Delaware.

According to the text, the republican revolution forced Americans to examine the meaning of equality. One question centered on women's rights: Did the doctrine of popular sovereignty apply to women as well as to men? These two engravings, both published in American magazines, are evidence that the question was the subject of public debate. Pictures like these pose a twofold challenge to historians — to see them as contemporaries did, and, with the power of hindsight, to understand them in their historical context. How do these pictures help us understand the status of women in the young republic?

ANALYZING THE EVIDENCE

➤ The illustration on the left appeared at the front of *The Lady's Magazine and Repository of Entertaining,* which was published in Philadelphia in 1792. The magazine contained excerpts from Mary Wollstonecraft's *A Vindication of the Rights of Woman* (1792), which explicitly linked the republican ideology of the American and French revolutions with women's rights. What sort of clothing are the women wearing? Whom do they represent? Do you think this imagery was empowering to women at the time? Why or why not?

➤ The engraving on the right urges women to "Keep Within Compass." What does the phrase mean? What does it mean in the context of the picture? Look at the smaller pictures on the lower left and lower right corners. What do they suggest might happen to women who challenge their place in society?

York, the state government seized the Philipse manor (see p. 107) and sold its farmsteads to the tenants. When Frederick Philipse III tried to reclaim his estate, former tenants replied that they had "purchased it with the price of their best blood" and "will never become your vassals again." In general, though, the Revolution did not drastically alter the structure of rural society.

Social turmoil was greater in the cities, where Patriot merchants replaced Tories at the top of the economic ladder. In Massachusetts, the Lowell, Higginson, Jackson, and Cabot families moved their trading enterprises to Boston to fill the vacuum created by the departure of the Loyalist Hutchinson and Apthorp clans. In Philadelphia, small-scale Patriot traders stepped into the vacancies created by the collapse of Anglican and Quaker mercantile firms. The War of Independence replaced a traditional economic elite — one that invested its profits from trade in real estate and became landlords — with a group of republican entrepreneurs who promoted new trading ventures and domestic manufacturing. This shift helped ensure America's rapid economic development in the years to come.

The Articles of Confederation

As the Patriots moved toward independence in 1776, they envisioned a central government with limited powers. Carter Braxton of Virginia thought the Continental Congress should have the power to "regulate the affairs of trade, war, peace, alliances, &c." but "should by no means have authority to interfere with the internal police [governance] or domestic concerns of any Colony."

That thinking — that the powers of the central government should be limited — informed the Articles of Confederation, which were passed by the Continental Congress in November 1777. The first national constitution, the Articles provided for a loose confederation — "The United States of America" — in which "each state retains its sovereignty, freedom, and independence." Still, the Articles gave the Confederation government considerable authority: It could declare war and peace, make treaties with foreign nations, adjudicate disputes between the states, borrow and print money, and requisition funds from the states "for the common defense or general welfare." These powers would be exercised by a central legislature, the Congress, in which each state had one vote regardless of its population or wealth. Important laws needed the approval of at least nine of the thirteen states, and changes in the Articles required the consent of all states. In the Confederation government, there was neither a separate executive nor a judiciary.

Disputes over western lands delayed ratification of the Articles until 1781. Many states — including Virginia, Massachusetts, and Connecticut — claimed that their royal charters gave them boundaries that stretched to the Pacific Ocean. States without western claims — Maryland and Pennsylvania — refused to accept the Articles until the land-rich states relinquished their claims. Threatened by Cornwallis's army in 1781, Virginia agreed to give up its land claims, and Maryland, the last holdout, finally ratified the Articles (Map 6.6).

Ongoing Fiscal Crisis. Formal ratification of the Articles was anticlimactic. Over the previous four years, Congress had exercised de facto constitutional authority — raising the Continental army, negotiating foreign treaties, and financing the war through loans and requisitions. The Confederation did have a major weakness though: It lacked the authority to tax either the states or the people. Indeed, by 1780, the central government was nearly bankrupt, and General Washington was calling urgently for a national system of taxation, warning Patriot leaders that otherwise "our cause is lost."

In response, nationalist-minded members of Congress tried to expand the Confederation's authority. Robert Morris, who became superintendent of finance in 1781, persuaded Congress to charter the Bank of North America, a private institution in Philadelphia, arguing that its notes would stabilize the inflated Continental currency. Morris also set up a comprehensive financial system to handle army expenditures, apportion war expenses among the states, and centralize the foreign debt. He hoped that the existence of a "national" debt would underline the Confederation's need for an import duty to pay it off. However, Rhode Island and New York rejected Morris's proposal for a tax of 5 percent on imports. New York's representative told Morris that his state had opposed British-imposed duties and would not accept them from Congress.

The Organization of the Southwest. To raise revenue, Congress looked to the sale of western lands, which were coveted by farmers and speculators. In 1783, it opened negotiations with Native American peoples, arguing that the recently signed Treaty of Paris had extinguished the Indians' land rights. Congress also sought payment from squatters — "white savages," John Jay called them — who had illegally settled on frontier tracts. In 1784, settlers in what is now eastern Tennessee organized a new state, gave it the name Franklin, and sought admission to the Confederation. To preserve its authority over the West, Congress refused to recognize Franklin and gave Virginia control over the region. Subsequently,

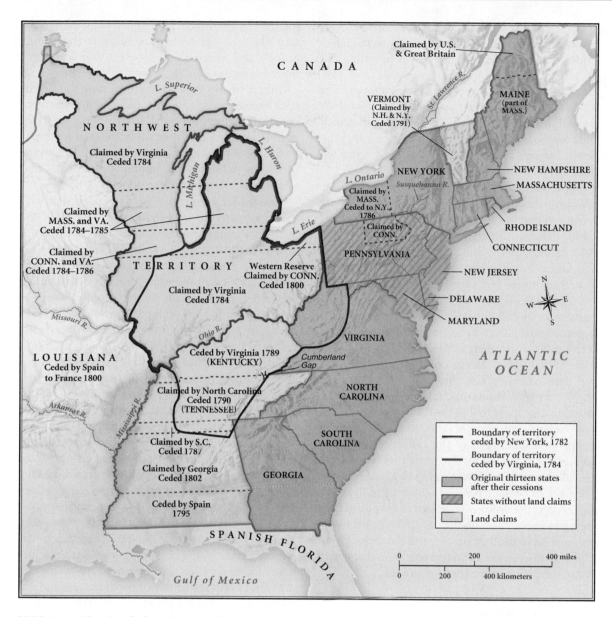

MAP 6.6   The Confederation and Western Land Claims, 1781–1802

The Congress of the Confederation inherited the conflicting claims of the states to western lands. For example, notice the huge — and overlapping — territories claimed by New York and Virginia on the basis of their royal charters. Between 1781 and 1802, the Confederation Congress and, after 1789, the U.S. Congress persuaded all of the states to cede their claims, creating a "national domain" open to all citizens. In the Northwest Ordinances, the Congress divided the domain north of the Ohio River into territories and set up democratic procedures by which they could join the Union. South of the Ohio River, the Congress allowed the existing southern states to play a substantial role in the settling of the ceded lands.

Congress created the Southwest Territory, the future states of Alabama and Mississippi, on lands ceded by North Carolina and Georgia. Because these cessions carried the stipulation that "no regulation . . . shall tend to emancipate slaves," the states that eventually formed in the Southwest Territory (and the entire region south of the Ohio River) allowed slavery.

The Northwest Territory. The Confederation Congress did ban slavery north of the Ohio River. Between 1784 and 1787, it issued three important ordinances organizing the "Old Northwest." The Ordinance of 1784, written by Thomas Jefferson, divided the region into territories that would become states when their population equaled that of the smallest existing state. The Land Ordinance of 1785 promoted settlement by mandating a rectangular-grid system of surveying that could be completed quickly, and by encouraging large-scale land purchases. The ordinance specified a minimum price of $1 an acre and required that half of the townships be sold in single blocks of 23,040 acres each, which only large-scale speculators could afford, and the rest in parcels of 640 acres each, which restricted their sale to well-to-do farmers (Map 6.7).

The Northwest Ordinance of 1787 put the finishing touches on the settlement plans. It created the territories that would eventually become the states of Ohio, Indiana, Illinois, Michigan, and Wisconsin. And, in line with the Enlightenment beliefs of Jefferson and other Patriots, the ordinance prohibited slavery in those territories and earmarked funds from land sales for the support of schools. The ordinance also specified that Congress would appoint a governor and judges to administer each new territory until the population reached 5,000 free adult men; at that point, the citizens could elect a territorial legislature. When the population reached 60,000, the legislature could ratify a republican constitution and apply to join the Confederation.

The land ordinances of the 1780s were a great and enduring achievement of the Confederation Congress. They provided for the orderly settlement and the admission of new states on the basis of equality; there would be no dependent "colonies" in the West. But even as the ordinances helped to transform thirteen governments along the eastern seaboard into a national republic, they perpetuated the geographical division between slave and free territories that would haunt the nation in the coming decades.

Shays's Rebellion

However bright the future of the West, postwar conditions in the East were grim. Peace brought economic recession, not a return to prosperity. The war had destroyed many American merchant ships and disrupted the export of tobacco, rice, and wheat. The British Navigation Acts, which had nurtured colonial commerce, now barred Americans from legal trade with the British West Indies. Moreover, low-priced British manufactures were flooding American markets, driving urban artisans and wartime textile firms out of business.

The economic condition of the state governments was equally fragile, a function of political conflicts over large war debts. On one side were speculators — mostly wealthy merchants and landowners — who had purchased huge quantities of state debt certificates from farmers and soldiers for far less than their face value. They demanded that the state governments redeem the bonds quickly and at full value, a policy that would require high taxes. On the other side were the elected members of the state legislatures, now the dominant branch of government. Because the new state constitutions apportioned seats on the basis of population, they increased the number of representatives from rural and western communities, many of whom were men of "middling circumstances" who knew "the wants of the poor."

Indeed, by the mid-1780s, middling farmers and urban artisans controlled the lower houses of the legislature in most northern states and formed a sizable minority in southern assemblies (see Figure 6.1 on p. 184). Their representatives opposed the collection of back taxes and other measures that tended "toward the oppression of the people." Pressure from western farmers prompted some legislatures to move the state capital from merchant-dominated seaports like New York City, Philadelphia, and Charleston, to inland cities like Albany, Harrisburg, and Columbia. And when yeomen farmers and artisans demanded tax relief, most state legislatures reduced levies and refused to redeem the war bonds held by speculators. State legislatures also printed paper currency and enacted laws allowing debtors to pay their private creditors in installments. Although wealthy men deplored these measures, claiming they destroyed "the just rights of creditors," the measures probably prevented a major social upheaval.

A case in point was Massachusetts, where lawmakers did not enact debtor-relief legislation. Instead, merchants and creditors persuaded the legislature to impose high taxes to pay off the state's war debt, and to cut the supply of paper currency to deter inflation. When cash-strapped farmers could not pay their debts, creditors threatened them with lawsuits. Debtor Ephraim Wetmore heard that merchant Stephan Salisbury "would have my Body Dead or Alive in case I did not pay." To protect their farms, residents of inland counties called extralegal conventions. The conventions protested the tax increases and property seizures and demanded the abolition of debtors' prisons, property qualifications for office holding, and the elitist upper house of the state legislature. Then mobs of angry farmers — including men of status and substance — closed the courts by force. "[I] had no Intensions to Destroy the Publick Government," declared Captain Adam Wheeler, a former town selectman; he had joined the mob to prevent "Valuable and Industrious members of Society [being] dragged from their families to prison [because of their debts], to the great damage . . . of the Community

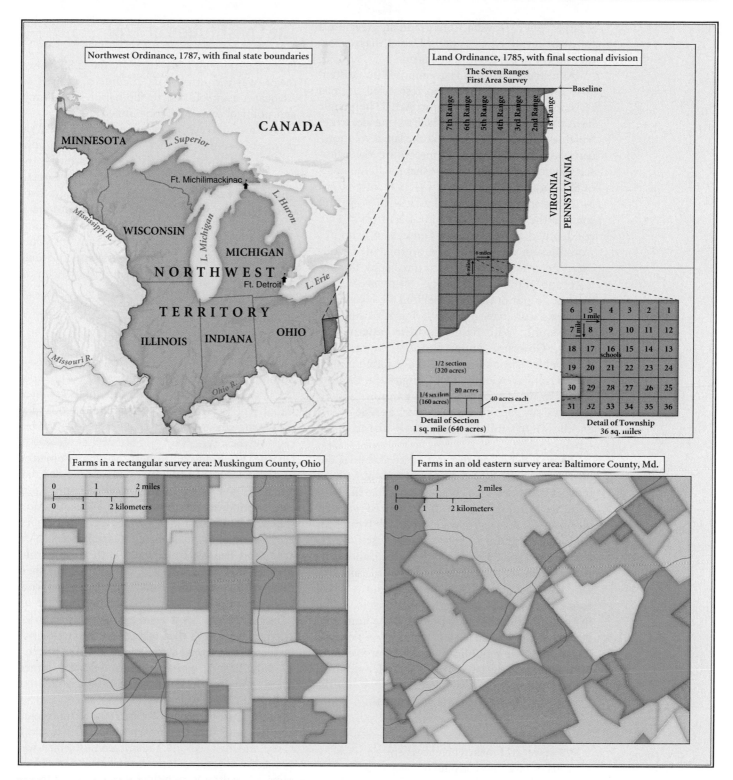

MAP 6.7   Land Division in the Northwest Territory

Throughout the Northwest Territory, government surveyors imposed a rectangular grid on the landscape, regardless of the local topography, so that farmers bought neatly defined tracts of land. The right-angled property lines in Muskingum County, Ohio (lower left), contrasted sharply with those in Baltimore County, Maryland (lower right), where — as in most of the eastern and southern states — boundaries followed the contours of the land.

at large." These crowd actions gradually grew into a full-scale revolt led by Captain Daniel Shays, a former officer in the Continental army.

As a struggle against taxes imposed by a distant government, Shays's Rebellion resembled colonial resistance to the British Stamp Act. "The people have turned against their teachers the doctrines which were inculcated to effect the late revolution," complained Fisher Ames, a conservative Massachusetts lawmaker. To drive home that point, members of Shays's army placed pine twigs in their hats, just as troops in the Continental army had done. But some of the men who were radical Patriots in 1776 condemned the Shaysites: "Those Men, who . . . would lessen the Weight of Government lawfully exercised must be Enemies to our happy Revolution and Common Liberty," charged Samuel Adams. To put down the rebellion, the Massachusetts legislature passed the Riot Act, outlawing illegal assembly. With financing from eastern merchants, Governor James Bowdoin equipped a formidable fighting force and called for additional troops from the Continental Congress. In the end, Shays's army fell victim to freezing weather and inadequate supplies during the winter of 1786–1787, and Bowdoin's military force easily dispersed the rebels.

Shays's Rebellion did not succeed; but it did provide proof that the costs of war and the fruits of independence were not being evenly shared. Middling Patriot families who had endured wartime sacrifices felt they had exchanged British tyrants for American oppressors. Angry Massachusetts voters turned Governor Bowdoin out of office, and debt-ridden farmers in New York, northern Pennsylvania, Connecticut, and New Hampshire closed courthouses and demanded economic relief. British officials in Canada predicted the imminent demise of the United States, and many Americans feared for their republican experiment. Events in Massachusetts, declared nationalist Henry Knox, formed "the strongest arguments possible" for the creation of "a strong general government."

> ➤ What were the main differences between conservative state constitutions, like that of Massachusetts, and more-democratic constitutions, like Pennsylvania's?

> ➤ Was there a consensus among different social groups about the meaning of America's republican revolution? What evidence does the chapter provide?

> ➤ What were the causes of Shays's Rebellion?

The Constitution of 1787

From the moment of its creation, the U.S. Constitution was a controversial document, praised by advocates as a solution to the nation's economic and political woes and condemned by critics as a perversion of republican principles. The main point at issue was whether republican institutions were suited only to small political units—the states—or could govern a vast nation? The Constitution addressed this question by creating a two-level republican government, national and state, both elected by the people. In this composite political system, the new national government would exercise limited, delegated powers, and the state governments would retain legal authority in all other matters.

The Rise of a Nationalist Faction

Money questions—debts, taxes, and tariffs—dominated the postwar political agenda. Those political leaders who had served the Confederation as military officers, officials, and diplomats looked at these problems from a national perspective and became advocates of a stronger central government. George Washington, Robert Morris, Benjamin Franklin, John Jay, and John Adams demanded that the states give Congress the power to control foreign commerce and impose tariffs. However, most state legislators wanted to manage their own affairs. For example, lawmakers in Massachusetts, New York, and Pennsylvania, states with strong commercial traditions, insisted on controlling their own tariffs so that they could protect artisans from low-cost imports while limiting the burden on their merchants. Most southern planters opposed any tariffs because they wanted to import British textiles and ironware at the lowest possible prices.

Nonetheless, some southern planters joined the nationalist faction because of the economic policies of the legislatures in their states. During the economic recession of the 1780s, lawmakers in Virginia and other southern states had lowered taxes and delayed the redemption of state war bonds. Such actions, lamented Charles Lee of Virginia, a wealthy bondholder, led taxpayers to believe that they would "never be compelled to pay" the public debt. Creditors had similar complaints about state laws that "stayed" (delayed) the payment of mortgages and other private debts. "While men are madly accumulating enormous debts, their legislators are making provisions for their non-payment," complained a South Carolina merchant. To these procreditor nationalists, the democratic majorities in the state legislatures constituted a grave threat to republican government.

In 1786, James Madison and other nationalists persuaded the Virginia legislature to invite all the states to a convention to discuss tariff and taxation policies. Only five state governments sent delegates to the meeting, which took place in Annapolis, Maryland. Ignoring their small number, the delegates called for another meeting in Philadelphia to undertake a broad review of the Confederation. Spurred on by Shays's Rebellion, nationalists in Congress secured a resolution calling for a revision of the Articles of Confederation and endorsing the Philadelphia convention. "Nothing but the adoption of some efficient plan from the Convention," a fellow nationalist wrote to James Madison, "can prevent anarchy first & civil convulsions afterwards."

The Philadelphia Convention

In May 1787, fifty-five delegates arrived in Philadelphia. They came from every state except Rhode Island, where the legislature opposed any increase in central authority. Most of the delegates were men of property: merchants, slaveholding planters, or "monied men." There were no artisans, backcountry settlers, or tenants, and there was only a single yeoman farmer.

Some delegates, among them Benjamin Franklin, had been early advocates of independence. Others, including George Washington and Robert Morris, had risen to prominence during the war. A number of longtime Patriots missed the convention. John Adams and Thomas Jefferson were abroad, serving as American ministers to Britain and France, respectively. The Massachusetts General Court did not send Samuel Adams because he favored a strictly limited national government, and his fellow firebrand from Virginia, Patrick Henry, refused to attend because he "smelt a rat."

The absence of these experienced leaders allowed capable young nationalists to set the agenda. Arguing that the convention would "decide for ever the fate of Republican Government," James Madison insisted on an increase in national authority. Alexander Hamilton of New York also demanded a strong central government that would protect the republic from "the imprudence of democracy."

James Madison and the Virginia Plan. The delegates elected Washington as their presiding officer and, to prevent popular interference with their deliberations, met in secret. They ignored their mandate to revise the Articles of Confederation and instead considered the Virginia Plan, a scheme for a powerful national government devised by James Madison.

Just thirty-six years old, Madison had arrived in Philadelphia determined to fashion new political institutions and to populate the government with men of high character. A graduate of Princeton, he had read classical and modern political theory and served in both the Confederation Congress and the Virginia assembly. Once an optimistic Patriot, Madison had become discouraged by the "narrow ambition" and outlook of many state officials.

Madison's Virginia Plan differed from the Articles of Confederation in three crucial respects. First, the plan rejected state sovereignty in favor of the "supremacy of national authority." The central government would have the power not only to "legislate in all cases to which the separate States are incompetent" but also to overturn state laws. Second, the plan called for a national government to be established by the people as a whole and to have direct authority over them. As Madison explained, national laws would bypass the state governments and operate directly "on the individuals composing them." Third, the plan created a three-tier election

James Madison, Statesman

Throughout his long public life, Madison kept the details of his private life to himself. His biography, he believed, should be a record of his public accomplishments. Future generations celebrated him not as a great man (like Hamilton or Jefferson) or as a great president (like Washington), but as an original and incisive political thinker. The chief architect of the U.S. Constitution and the Bill of Rights, Madison was the preeminent republican political theorist of his generation. Library of Congress.

system that would reduce popular power. Citizen voters would elect only the lower house of the national legislature. The lower house would name the members of the upper house, and then both houses would choose the executive and judiciary.

From a political perspective, Madison's plan had two fatal flaws. First, the provision allowing the national government to veto state laws was unacceptable to most state politicians and to many ordinary citizens. Second, the power accorded to the lower house of the legislature, in which states were represented on the basis of their population, would enhance the influence of the large states. Small-state delegates immediately rejected this provision. According to a Delaware delegate, Madison's scheme would allow the populous states to "crush the small ones whenever they stand in the way of their ambitious or interested views."

The Challenge of the New Jersey Plan. Small-state delegates rallied behind a plan devised by William Paterson of New Jersey. The New Jersey Plan gave the Confederation the power to raise revenue, control commerce, and make binding requisitions on the states. But it preserved the states' control of their own laws and guaranteed their equality: Each state would have one vote in a unicameral legislature, the form in use in the Confederation. Delegates from the populous states vigorously opposed this provision. Finally, after a month of debate, a bare majority of the states agreed to take Madison's Virginia Plan as the basis of discussion.

This decision raised the prospect of a dramatically different constitutional system, so different that two New York representatives accused the delegates of exceeding their mandate and left the convention. During the hot humid summer of 1787, the remaining delegates met six days a week, debating high principles and discussing practical details. Experienced politicians, they knew that their plan had to be acceptable to existing political interests and powerful social groups. Pierce Butler of South Carolina invoked a classical Greek precedent: "We must follow the example of Solon, who gave the Athenians not the best government he could devise but the best they would receive."

Compromise over Representation. Representation of large and small states remained the central problem. To satisfy both large and small states, the Connecticut delegates suggested that the upper chamber, the Senate, have two members from each state, while seats in the lower chamber, the House of Representatives, be apportioned by population (determined every ten years by a national census). After bitter debate, this "Great Compromise" was accepted, but only reluctantly; to at least some delegates from populous states, it seemed less a compromise than a victory for the small states.

Other state-related issues were quickly settled by restricting (or leaving ambiguous) the extent of central authority. A number of delegates opposed a national system of courts, warning "the states will revolt at such encroachments" on their judicial authority. So the convention defined the judicial power of the United States in broad terms, vesting it "in one supreme Court" and leaving the new national legislature to decide whether to establish lower courts within the states. The convention also refused to require that voters in national elections be landowners. "Eight or nine states have extended the right of suffrage beyond the freeholders," George Mason of Virginia pointed out. "What will people there say if they should be disfranchised?" Finally, the convention placed the selection of the president in an electoral college chosen on a state-by-state basis, and specified that state legislatures would elect members of the U.S. Senate. By giving states and their legislatures important roles in the new constitutional system, the delegates hoped their citizens would accept a reduction in state sovereignty.

Gouverneur Morris and the Debate over Slavery. Slavery hovered in the background of the debates, and Gouverneur Morris of New York brought it to the fore. Born into the comfortable world of the New York aristocracy, Morris initially opposed independence out of fear it would result in the "domination of a riotous mob." Becoming a Patriot and a nationalist, he came to the Philadelphia convention convinced that the protection of "property was the sole or primary object of Government & Society." To safeguard property rights, Morris demanded life terms for senators, a property qualification for voting in national elections, and a strong president with veto power. Still, despite his conservative politics, Morris rejected the legitimacy of two traditional types of property—the feudal dues claimed by aristocratic landowners and the ownership of slaves. An advocate of **free markets** and personal liberty, he condemned slavery as "a nefarious institution" and called for its end "so that in future ages, every human being who breathes the air . . . shall enjoy the privileges of a freeman."

Southern delegates joined together to defend slavery, citing its long history and continuing economic importance; but they disagreed on the issue of the Atlantic slave trade. George Mason called for an end to that trade. He was representing planters in the Chesapeake region, who already owned ample numbers of slaves. Rice planters from South Carolina and Georgia, however, argued that slave

Gouverneur Morris, Federalist Statesman

When the war with Britain broke out, Morris had debated joining the Loyalist cause: He was a snob who liked privilege and feared the common people. ("The mob begins to think and reason," he once noted with disdain.) He became a Federalist for much the same reasons. He helped write the Philadelphia constitution and, after 1793, strongly supported the Federalist Party.

National Portrait Gallery, Smithsonian Institution/Art Resource, New York.

imports must continue; otherwise, their states "shall not be parties to the Union." At their insistence, the delegates denied Congress the power to regulate immigration—and so the slave trade—until 1808 (see Comparing American Voices, "The First National Debate over Slavery," pp. 196–197).

To preserve national unity, the delegates also treated other slavery-related issues as political rather than moral questions. To satisfy southern slave owners, they agreed to a "fugitive" clause that allowed masters to reclaim enslaved blacks (or white indentured servants) who fled to other states. Acknowledging the antislavery sentiments of Morris and other northerners, the delegates refused to mention slavery explicitly in the Constitution, which spoke instead of citizens and "all other Persons." They also compromised on the issue of counting slaves in determining a state's representation in Congress. Because slaves could not vote, antislavery delegates did not want to count them in apportioning the national legislature; southerners, on the other hand, demanded they be counted as full citizens. Ultimately, the delegates agreed to count each slave as three-fifths of a free person for purposes of representation and taxation, a compromise that helped the South dominate the national government until 1860.

National Power. Having allayed the concerns of small states and slave states, the delegates created a powerful procreditor national government. The finished document made the Constitution and all national legislation the "supreme" law of the land. It gave the national government broad powers over taxation, military defense, and external commerce, as well as the authority to make all laws "necessary and proper" to implement those and other provisions. To protect creditors and establish the fiscal integrity of the new government, the Constitution mandated that the United States honor the existing national debt. Moreover, it restricted the ability of state governments to help debtors by forbidding the states to issue money or enact "any Law impairing the Obligation of Contracts."

The proposed constitution was not a "perfect production," Benjamin Franklin admitted on September 17, 1787, as he urged the forty-one delegates still present to sign it. But the great statesman confessed his astonishment at finding "this system approaching so near to perfection as it does." His colleagues apparently agreed; all but three signed the document.

The People Debate Ratification

The procedures for ratifying the new constitution were as controversial as its contents. The delegates refused to submit the Constitution to the state legislatures for their unanimous consent, as required by the Articles of Confederation, because they knew that Rhode Island (and perhaps a few other states) would reject it. So they arbitrarily specified that the Constitution would go into effect when ratified by special conventions in nine states. Because of its nationalist sympathies, the Confederation Congress winked at this extralegal procedure; surprisingly, so, too, did most state legislatures, which promptly called ratification conventions.

Federalists Versus Antifederalists. As the great constitutional debate began, the nationalists seized the initiative with two bold moves. First, they called themselves **Federalists**, suggesting that they supported a federal union—a loose, decentralized system—obscuring their commitment to a strong national authority. Second, they launched a coordinated campaign in pamphlets and newspapers touting the proposed constitution.

The opponents of the Constitution, the Antifederalists, had diverse backgrounds and motives. Some, like Governor George Clinton of New York,

The First National Debate over Slavery

In Part Two of the text, "The New Republic," we trace the impact of republican ideology on American politics and society. What happened when republicanism collided head-on with the well-established practice of slavery? After the Revolution, the Massachusetts courts abolished slavery (see Chapter 8). But in 1787, in the rest of the Union, slavery was legal; and in the southern states, it was the bedrock of both the social order and agricultural production. A look at the debates on the issue of the African slave trade at the Philadelphia convention and in a state ratifying convention tells us how divisive an issue slavery already was at the birth of the nation, a dark cloud threatening the bright future of the young republic.

The Constitutional Convention

Slavery was not a major topic of discussion in Philadelphia, but it surfaced a number of times, notably in the important debate over representation (which produced the three-fifths clause). The discussion of the Atlantic slave trade began when Luther Martin, a delegate from Maryland, proposed changing a clause to allow Congress to impose a tax on or prohibit the importation of slaves.

Mr. Martin proposed to vary article 7, sect. 4 so as to allow a prohibition or tax on the importation of slaves. . . . [He believed] it was inconsistent with the principles of the Revolution, and dishonorable to the American character, to have such a feature [promoting the slave trade] in the Constitution.

Mr. [John] Rutledge [of South Carolina] did not see how the importation could be encouraged by this section . . . . [Moreover,] religion and humanity had nothing to do with this question. Interest alone is the governing principle with nations. The true question at present is whether the Southern states shall or shall not be parties to the Union. . . .

Mr. [Oliver] Ellsworth [of Connecticut] was for leaving the clause as it stands. Let every state import what it pleases. The morality or wisdom of slavery are considerations belonging to the states themselves. . . . The old Confederation had not meddled with this point, and he did not see any greater necessity for bringing it within the policy of the new one.

Mr. [Charles C.] Pinckney [said] South Carolina can never receive the plan if it prohibits the slave trade. In every proposed extension of the powers of Congress, that state has expressly and watchfully excepted that of meddling with the importation of Negroes. . . .

Mr. [Roger] Sherman [of Connecticut] was for leaving the clause as it stands. He disapproved of the slave trade; yet, as the states were now possessed of the right to import slaves, . . . and as it was expedient to have as few objections as possible to the proposed scheme of government, he thought it best to leave the matter as we find it.

Col. [George] Mason [of Virginia stated that] this infernal trade originated in the avarice of British merchants. The British government constantly checked the attempts of Virginia to put a stop to it. The present question concerns not the importing states alone, but the whole Union. . . . Maryland and Virginia, he said, had already prohibited the importation of slaves expressly. North Carolina had done the same in substance. All this would be in vain if South Carolina and Georgia be at liberty to import. The Western people are already calling out for slaves for their new lands, and will fill that country with slaves, if they can be got through South Carolina and Georgia. Slavery discourages arts and manufactures. The poor despise labor when performed by slaves. They prevent the immigration of whites, who really enrich and strengthen a country. . . .

Every master of slaves is born a petty tyrant. They bring the judgment of Heaven on a country. As nations cannot be rewarded or punished in the next world, they must be in this. By an inevitable chain of causes and effects, Providence punishes national sins by national calamities. . . . He held it essential, in every point of view, that the general government should have power to prevent the increase of slavery.

Mr. Ellsworth, as he had never owned a slave, could not judge of the effects of slavery on character. He said, however, that if it was to be considered in a moral light, we ought to go further, and free those already in the country. . . . Let us not intermeddle. As population increases, poor laborers will be so plenty as to render slaves useless. Slavery, in time, will not be a speck in our country. . . .

Gen. [Charles C.] Pinckney [argued that] South Carolina and Georgia cannot do without slaves. As to Virginia, she will gain by stopping the importations. Her slaves will rise in value, and she has more than she wants. It would be unequal to require South Carolina and Georgia to confederate on such unequal terms. . . . He contended that the importation of slaves would be for the interest of the whole Union. The more slaves, the more produce to employ the carrying trade; the more consumption also; and the more of this, the more revenue for the common treasury. . . . [He] should consider a rejection of the [present] clause as an exclusion of South Carolina from the Union.

SOURCE: Max Farrand, ed., *The Records of the Federal Convention of 1787* (New Haven: Yale University Press, 1911), 2: 364–365, 369–372.

The Massachusetts Ratifying Convention

In Philadelphia, the delegates agreed on a compromise: They gave Congress the power to tax or prohibit slave imports, as Luther Martin had proposed, but withheld that power for twenty years. In the Massachusetts convention, the delegates split on this issue and on many others. They eventually did ratify the Constitution but by a narrow margin, 187 to 168.

Mr. Neal (from Kittery) [an Antifederalist] went over the ground of objection to . . . the idea that slave trade was allowed to be continued for 20 years. His profession, he said, obliged him to bear witness against any thing that should favor the making merchandize of the bodies of men, and unless his objection was removed, he could not put his hand to the constitution. Other gentlemen said, in addition to this idea, that there was not even a proposition that the negroes ever shall be free: and Gen. Thompson exclaimed— "Mr. President, shall it be said, that after we have established our own independence and freedom, we make slaves of others? Oh! Washington . . . he has immortalized himself! but he holds those in slavery who have a good right to be free as he is. . . ."

On the other side, gentlemen said, that the step taken in this article, towards the abolition of slavery, was one of the beauties of the constitution. They observed, that in the confederation there was no provision whatever for its ever being abolished; but this constitution provides, that Congress may after twenty years, totally annihilate the slave trade. . . .

Mr. Heath (Federalist): . . . I apprehend that it is not in our power to do any thing for or against those who are in slavery in the southern states. No gentleman within these walls detests every idea of slavery more than I do: it is generally detested by the people of this commonwealth, and I ardently hope that the time will soon come, when our brethren in the southern states will view it as we do, and put a stop to it; but to this we have no right to compel them.

Two questions naturally arise: if we ratify the Constitution, shall we do any thing by our act to hold the blacks in slavery or shall we become the partakers of other men's sins? I think neither of them: each state is sovereign and independent to a certain degree, and they have a right, and will regulate their own internal affairs, as to themselves appears proper. . . . We are not in this case partakers of other men's sins, for nothing do we voluntarily encourage the slavery of our fellow men. . . .

The federal convention went as far as they could; the migration or immigration &c. is confined to the states, now existing only, new states cannot claim it. Congress, by their ordnance for erecting new states, some time since, declared that there shall be no slavery in them. But whether those in slavery in the southern states, will be emancipated after the year 1808, I do not pretend to determine: I rather doubt it.

SOURCE: Jonathan Elliot, ed., *The Debates . . . on the Adoption of the Federal Constitution* (Philadelphia: J. B. Lippincott, 1863), 1: 103–105, 107, 112, 117.

ANALYZING THE EVIDENCE

➤ At the Constitutional Convention in Philadelphia, what were the main arguments for and against federal restrictions on the Atlantic slave trade? How do you explain the position taken by the Connecticut delegates in Philadelphia and Mr. Heath in the Massachusetts debate?

➤ Why did George Mason, a Virginia slave owner, demand a prohibition of the Atlantic slave trade?

➤ What evidence of regional tensions do you see in the documents? Several men from different states — Mason from Virginia, Ellsworth from Connecticut, and Heath from Massachusetts — offered predictions about the future of slavery. How accurate were they?

feared that state governments would lose power. Rural democrats protested that the proposed constitution, unlike most state constitutions, lacked a declaration of individual rights. These smallholding farmers were concerned that the central government would be run by wealthy men. "Lawyers and men of learning and monied men expect to be managers of this Constitution," worried a Massachusetts farmer, "and get all the power and all the money into their own hands and then they will swallow up all of us little folks . . . just as the whale swallowed up Jonah." Giving political substance to these fears, Melancton Smith of New York argued that the large electoral districts prescribed by the Constitution would bring wealthy upper-class men into office, whereas the smaller districts used in state elections usually produced legislatures "composed principally of respectable yeomanry."

Well-educated Americans with a traditional republican outlook also opposed the new system. To keep government "close to the people," they wanted the nation to remain a collection of small sovereign republics tied together only for trade and defense — not the "United States" but the "States United." Citing French political philosopher Montesquieu, the Antifederalists argued that republican institutions were best suited to cities or small states, a localist perspective that shaped American political thinking well into the twentieth century. "No extensive empire can be governed on republican principles," declared James Winthrop of Massachusetts. Patrick Henry predicted the Constitution would recreate the worst features of British rule: high taxes, an oppressive bureaucracy, a standing army, and a "great and mighty President . . . supported in extravagant munificence."

The Federalist Papers. In New York, where ratification was hotly contested, James Madison, John Jay, and Alexander Hamilton countered the arguments against a strong national government in a series of eighty-five essays collectively called *The Federalist*. Although the essays were not widely read outside New York City — only a few were reprinted in newspapers elsewhere — *The Federalist* came to be recognized as an important statement of republican political doctrine. Its authors stressed the need for a strong national government to conduct foreign affairs, and they denied that a centralized government would foster domestic tyranny. Drawing on Montesquieu's theory of mixed government and John Adams's *Thoughts on Government*, Madison, Jay, and Hamilton pointed out that authority would be divided among an executive (the president), a bicameral legislature, and a judiciary. Each branch of government would "check and balance" the others and so preserve liberty.

In "Federalist No. 10," Madison made a significant contribution to political thought by challenging the traditional belief that republican governments were suited only to cities or small states. Rather, large states would better protect republican liberty. It was "sown in the nature of man," Madison wrote, that individuals would seek power and form factions to advance their interests. Indeed, "a landed interest, a manufacturing interest, a mercantile interest, a moneyed interest, with many lesser interests, grow up of necessity in civilized nations." He argued that a free society should not suppress those groups but rather prevent any one of them from becoming dominant — an end best achieved in a large republic. "Extend the sphere," Madison concluded, "and you take in a greater variety of parties and interests; you make it less probable that a majority of the whole will have a common motive to invade the rights of other citizens."

The Ratification Conventions. The delegates who debated these issues in the state ratification conventions were a diverse group. They included untutored farmers and middling artisans as well as educated gentlemen. Generally, backcountry delegates were Antifederalists, while those from the coast were Federalists. In Pennsylvania, Philadelphia merchants and artisans combined with commercial farmers to ratify the Constitution. Other early Federalist successes came in four less-populous states — Delaware, New Jersey, Georgia, and Connecticut — where delegates hoped a strong national government would offset the power of large neighboring states (Map 6.8).

The Constitution's first real test came in January 1788 in Massachusetts, a populous state filled with Antifederalists. Influential Patriots, including Samuel Adams and Governor John Hancock, opposed the new constitution, as did many admirers of Daniel Shays. But Boston artisans, who wanted tariff protection from British imports, supported ratification. To win the votes needed for ratification, Federalist leaders assured the convention that they would enact a national bill of rights to protect individuals from possible oppression by the new government. That promise swayed some delegates. By a close vote of 187 to 168, the Federalists carried the day.

Spring brought Federalist victories in Maryland and South Carolina. When New Hampshire narrowly ratified the Constitution in June, the required nine states had approved it. Still, the essential states of Virginia and New York had not yet acted. It took the powerful arguments advanced in *The Federalist* and the promise of a bill of rights to secure the Constitution's adoption. It won ratification in Virginia by 10 votes, 89 to 79; and that success carried the Federalists to victory — by just 3 votes, 30 to 27 — in

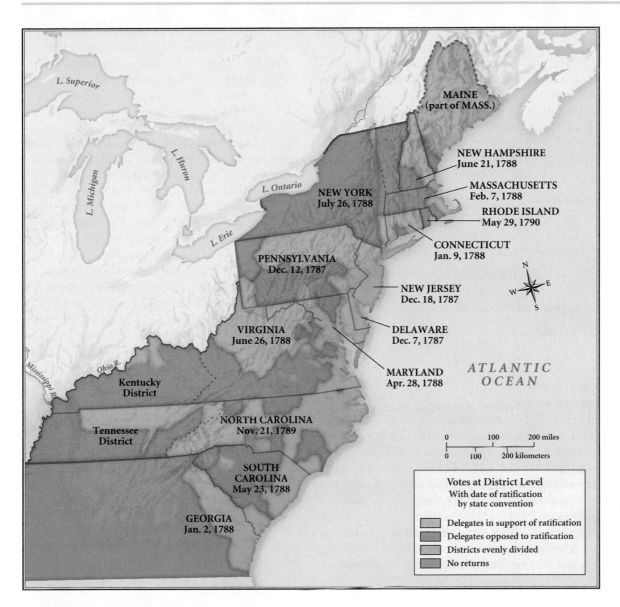

MAP 6.8   Ratifying the Constitution of 1787

In 1907, geographer Owen Libby mapped the votes of members of the state conventions that ratified the Constitution. His map showed that most delegates from seaboard or commercial farming districts, which sent many delegates to the conventions, supported the Constitution, while those from sparsely represented backcountry areas opposed it. Subsequent research has confirmed Libby's socioeconomic interpretation of the voting patterns in North and South Carolina and in Massachusetts. However, other factors influenced delegates in other states. For example, in Georgia, delegates from all regions voted for ratification.

New York. Suspicious of centralized power, voters in North Carolina did not ratify the Constitution until 1789; and voters in Rhode Island held out until 1790.

Testifying to their respect for popular sovereignty and majority rule, most Americans accepted the verdict of the ratifying conventions. The Antifederalist movement withered away, and state legislatures and politicians accepted the Constitution. "A decided majority" of the New Hampshire as-

sembly had opposed the "new system," reported Joshua Atherton, but now they said, "It is adopted, let us try it." In Virginia, Patrick Henry vowed to "submit as a quiet citizen" and fight for amendments "in a constitutional way."

Working against great odds, the Federalists had created a national republic and partly restored an elitist system of political authority. Federalists celebrated their triumph by organizing great processions in the seaport cities. By marching in an orderly fashion—in conscious contrast to the riotous Revolutionary mobs—Federalist-minded citizens affirmed their allegiance to a self-governing republican community. The marchers carried a copy of the Constitution on an "altar of liberty." By invoking sacred symbolism, Federalists hoped to endow the new regime with moral legitimacy and to create an enduring **civil religion** based on national political institutions and principles.

> ➤ What were the central problems of the Articles of Confederation and how did the delegates to the Philadelphia convention address them?

> ➤ How did the Philadelphia convention resolve three contentious political issues: the representation of large and small states, slavery, and state sovereignty?

> ➤ Why did the Antifederalists oppose the Constitution?

SUMMARY

In this chapter, we examined the unfolding of two important and related sets of events. The first was the war between Britain and its rebellious colonies that began in 1776 and ended in 1783. Two great battles determined the outcome of that conflict, Saratoga in 1777 and Yorktown in 1781. Surprisingly, given the military might of the British empire, both were American victories. These triumphs stand as testimony to the determination and resilience of George Washington and the Continental army and to the broad support for the Patriot cause of thousands of local militia units and tens of thousands of taxpaying citizens.

This popular support reflected the Patriots' success in building effective institutions of republican government. These institutions had their origins in the colonial period, in the town meetings and assemblies that were responsive to popular pressure and increasingly independent of imperial control. They took on new meaning between 1776 and 1781 in the state constitutions that made British subjects into American citizens, and in the first national constitution, the Articles of Confederation. Despite the challenges of the postwar economy, these fledgling political institutions laid the foundation for the Constitution of 1787, the national charter that endures today.

Connections: Diplomacy

In the essay that introduces Part Two (p. 135), we pointed out that

to create and preserve their new republic, Americans of European descent had to fight two wars against Great Britain, an undeclared war against France, and many battles with Indian peoples and confederations.

As Chapter 6 has revealed, American success in the War of Independence was the result, in substantial measure, of French assistance. The French first provided secret monetary and material aid; then, after 1778 and the formal Treaty of Alliance, French military and naval forces helped the Patriots secure their great victory at Yorktown. It was astute American diplomacy by Benjamin Franklin and others that obtained this French assistance and that negotiated a favorable peace at the end of the war. As we will see in Chapter 7, subsequent American diplomatic efforts produced mixed results: The United States nearly went to war with France in 1798, failed to force the British and French to lift restrictions on American merchant vessels in 1807, and maneuvered itself into a second, nearly disastrous, war with Great Britain in 1812. Only the purchase of Louisiana from France in 1803 stands out as an unblemished American diplomatic triumph.

Still, the number and form of these diplomatic initiatives point out the crucial importance of relationships with foreign nations and, to a lesser extent, Indian peoples during the era of the early American republic. European entanglements—diplomatic, military, commercial, and ideological—stood at the center of American history during these years and are a major focus of our discussion in the chapters that follow.

CHAPTER REVIEW QUESTIONS

> ➤ The text states that Saratoga was the turning point of the War of Independence. Do you agree? Explain your answer.

> ➤ How revolutionary was the American Revolution? What political, social, and economic changes did it produce? What stayed the same?

> ➤ Why was the Constitution a controversial document even as it was being written?

> ➤ Both the Federalists and the Antifederalists claimed to represent the true spirit of the Revolution. Which group do you think was right? Why?

TIMELINE

1776	Second Continental Congress declares independence
	Howe forces Washington to retreat from New York and New Jersey
	Pennsylvania approves a democratic state constitution
	John Adams publishes *Thoughts on Government*
1777	Articles of Confederation
	Patriot women become important in war economy
	Howe occupies Philadelphia (September)
	Gates defeats Burgoyne at Saratoga (October)
	Severe inflation of paper currency begins
1778	Franco-American alliance (February)
	Lord North seeks political settlement; Congress rejects negotiations
	British adopt southern strategy; capture Savannah (December)
1779	British and American forces battle in Georgia
1780	Sir Henry Clinton seizes Charleston (May)
	French troops land in Rhode Island
1781	Lord Cornwallis invades Virginia (April); surrenders at Yorktown (October)
	States finally ratify Articles of Confederation
	Large-scale Loyalist emigration
1783	Treaty of Paris (September 3) officially ends war
1784–1785	Congress enacts political and land ordinances for new states
1786	Nationalists hold convention in Annapolis, Maryland
	Shays's Rebellion roils Massachusetts
1787	Congress passes Northwest Ordinance
	Constitutional Convention in Philadelphia
1787–1788	Jay, Madison, and Hamilton write *The Federalist*
	Eleven states ratify U.S. Constitution

FOR FURTHER EXPLORATION

For vivid accounts of the war, see John C. Dann, ed., *The Revolution Remembered: Eyewitness Accounts of the War for Independence* (1980). "The Virtual Marching Tour" at **www.ushistory .org/brandywine/index.html** offers an interesting multimedia view of Howe's attack on Philadelphia. For a fascinating analysis of espionage during the Revolution, prepared by the Central Intelligence Agency, see **www.odci.gov/cia/publications/ warindep/frames.html.**

Colin G. Calloway, *The American Revolution in Indian Country* (1995), traces the Revolution's impact on Native peoples, while Robin Blackburn, *The Overthrow of Colonial Slavery, 1776–1848* (1988), studies its impact on racial bondage in the Western Hemisphere. Sylvia R. Frey, *Water from the Rock* (1991), shows how African Americans absorbed and used republican ideology and Christian beliefs. A data-rich source on the black experience is "Africans in America: Revolution" (**www.pbs.org/wgbh/ aia/part2/title.html**). Two Canadian Web sites, "Black Loyalists: Our History, Our People" (**collections.ic.gc.ca/blackloyalists/ wireframe.htm**) and "Remembering Black Loyalists, Black Communities in Nova Scotia" (**museum.gov.ns.ca/blackloyalists/**), provide vivid accounts of African American refugees.

Two important studies of women are Mary Beth Norton, *Liberty's Daughters: The Revolutionary Experience of American Women, 1750–1800* (1980), and Carol Berkin, *Revolutionary Mothers: Women in the Struggle for America's Independence* (2005). Also see Cynthia Kierner, *Southern Women in Revolution, 1776–1800: Personal and Political Narratives* (1998), and the analysis of women's political activism during the Revolution at the Women and Social Movements Web site (**womhist. binghamton.edu/amrev/abstract.htm**).

For a dramatic retelling of the Constitutional Convention, see Catherine Drinker Bowen's *Miracle at Philadelphia* (1966). Jack Rakove's *Original Meanings: Politics and Ideas in the Making of the Constitution* (1996) offers a more complex analysis of the Framers. Saul Cornell, *The Other Founders: The Antifederalists and the American Dissenting Tradition* (1999), addresses opposition to the Constitution; and Michael Kammen, *A Machine That Would Go by Itself* (1986), explains its changing reputation. David Waldstreicher's *In the Midst of Perpetual Fetes: The Making of American Nationalism, 1776–1820* (1997) is a fascinating analysis of public celebrations. Also see the Library of Congress site, "Religion and the Founding of the American Republic" (**www.loc.gov/exhibits/religion/rel03.html**). For music of the period, see "Folk Music of the American Revolution" (**members.aol.com/bobbyj164/mrev.htm**).

TEST YOUR KNOWLEDGE

To assess your command of the material in this chapter, see the Online Study Guide at **bedfordstmartins.com/henretta.**

For Web sites, images, and documents related to topics and places in this chapter, visit **bedfordstmartins.com/makehistory.**

7

Politics and Society in the New Republic

1787–1820

Lᴀ ᴀɴ ᴇᴀʀᴛʜǫᴜᴀᴋᴇ, ᴛʜᴇ ᴀᴍᴇʀɪᴄᴀɴ Revolution shook the foundations of the European monarchical order, and its aftershocks reverberated far into the nineteenth century. By "creating a new republic based on the rights of the individual, the North Americans introduced a new force into the world," eminent German historian Leopold von Ranke explained to the king of Bavaria in 1854. In the end, Ranke warned, American republicanism might cost the monarch his throne. Before the Revolution, "a king who ruled by the grace of God had been the center around which everything turned. Now the idea emerged that power should come from below [from the people]."

Other republican revolutions — England's Puritan Commonwealth of the 1640s and 1650s and the French Revolution of 1789 — had ended in political chaos and military rule. A similar fate would befall many of the republics in Latin America that would achieve independence from Spain in the early nineteenth century. But somehow the American states escaped a military dictatorship. When the War of Independence ended and General George Washington left public life in 1783 to return to his plantation, Europeans were astonished. "Tis a Conduct so novel," American painter John Trumbull reported from London, that it is "inconceivable to People [here]." Washington's voluntary retirement both preserved

◄ **American Commerce, c. 1800**

In 1800, when Thomas Birch painted this view of shipping along the Delaware River, Philadelphia was still the nation's largest and wealthiest seaport. The city's merchants were especially active in the Caribbean sugar and coffee trade and in the importation of mahogany and other valuable woods from Central America. Notice the presence of several black longshoremen, members of the city's substantial African American population. Rare Book Department, The Free Library of Philadelphia.

and bolstered the authority of the elected Patriot leaders, who were fashioning representative republican governments.

This great task absorbed the energy and intellect of an entire generation. As Americans wrote new state and federal constitutions, some political leaders worried that the new constitutions—state and national—were too democratic. When a bill was introduced into a state legislature, grumbled Connecticut conservative Ezra Stiles, every elected official "instantly thinks how it will affect his constituents" rather than its impact on the public as whole. What Stiles criticized as the irresponsible pursuit of self-interest, most Americans welcomed. The interests of ordinary citizens had taken center stage in the halls of government, and the monarchs of Europe trembled.

The Political Crisis of the 1790s

The final decade of the eighteenth century brought fresh political challenges. The Federalists divided into two irreconcilable factions, first over financial policy and then over the French Revolution. During these struggles, Alexander Hamilton and Thomas Jefferson offered contrasting visions of the future. Would the United States remain, as Jefferson hoped, an agricultural nation governed by local and state officials? Or would Hamilton's vision of a strong national government and an economy based on manufacturing become reality?

The Federalists Implement the Constitution

The Constitution expanded the dimensions of American political life. Previously voters had elected local and state officials; now, they chose national leaders as well. The Federalists swept the election of 1788, winning forty-four seats in the first House of Representatives; only eight Antifederalists won election. As expected, members of the Electoral College chose George Washington as president. John Adams received the second highest number of electoral votes, and he became vice president.

Once the military savior of his country, Washington now became its political father. At fifty-seven, the first president was a man with great personal dignity. Recognizing that he would be setting precedents for his successors, Washington proceeded cautiously (see Reading American Pictures, "Creating a National Political Tradition" p. 205). He adopted many of the administrative practices of the Confederation and asked Congress to reestablish the existing

executive departments: Foreign Affairs (State), Finance (Treasury), and War. He did introduce one important innovation: The Constitution specified that the president needed the consent of the Senate to appoint major officials, but Washington insisted that only he—not the Senate—could remove them, ensuring the president's control over the executive bureaucracy. To head the Department of State, Washington chose Thomas Jefferson, a fellow Virginian and an experienced diplomat. For secretary of the treasury, he turned to Alexander Hamilton, a lawyer and his military aide during the war. Then the new president designated Jefferson, Hamilton, and Secretary of War Henry Knox as his cabinet, or advisory body.

The Constitution had created a supreme court but left to Congress the task of establishing the rest of the national court system. Because the Federalists wanted strong national institutions, they enacted the far-reaching Judiciary Act in 1789. The act established a federal district court in each state and provided three circuit courts to hear appeals from the districts, with the Supreme Court having the final say. The Judiciary Act also allowed appeals to the Supreme Court of federal legal issues that arose in the courts of the various states. This provision ensured that national judges would have the final say on the meaning of the Constitution.

The Federalists kept their promise to add a declaration of rights to the Constitution. James Madison, now a member of the House of Representatives, submitted a list of nineteen amendments to the First Congress; ten were approved by Congress and ratified by the states in 1791. These ten amendments, known as the Bill of Rights, safeguard fundamental personal rights, including freedom of speech and religion, and mandate trial by jury and other legal procedures that protect individual citizens (see Documents, p. D-x). By easing Antifederalists' concerns about an oppressive national government, the amendments secured the legitimacy of the Constitution. However, they did not resolve the core issue of federalism—the proper balance between national and state power. That issue would divide the nation until the Civil War, and it remains important today.

Hamilton's Financial Program

George Washington's most important decision was his choice of Alexander Hamilton as secretary of the treasury. An ambitious self-made man of great charm and intelligence, Hamilton married into the Schuyler family, rich and influential Hudson River Valley landowners, and became a prominent lawyer in New York City. As a delegate to the Philadelphia convention, Hamilton took a strongly conservative

Creating a National Political Tradition

Washington's Journey from Mount Vernon.
The City of New York, The Harry T. Peters Collection (56.300.847).

"Independence Declared 1776. The Union Must Be Preserved." Library of Congress.

"Four score and seven years ago our fathers brought forth, upon this continent, a new nation. . . ." So Abraham Lincoln began his famous address at Gettysburg in 1863. Although a new republic was founded in 1776, it became a *nation*, with a sense of national consciousness, only in subsequent decades. How did America's nationhood develop? Graphic evidence like these engravings played an important role in the process of reaching a national consensus on the meaning of being an American. By carefully interpreting the symbols in pictures like these, historians broaden our understanding of the past.

ANALYZING THE EVIDENCE

➤ George Washington had a lot to do with creating America's sense of nationhood. How is Washington portrayed in the image on the left, a depiction of his journey from Virginia to New York in 1789 to assume the presidency? What symbols does the artist use? What do these symbols suggest about Washington? About the presidency? How might those interpretations conflict with America's republican self-image?

➤ In the Gettysburg Address, Lincoln speaks reverently of "our fathers." The banner in the engraving of Washington, which was created in 1845, reads: "THE DEFENDER OF THE MOTHERS WILL BE THE PROTECTOR OF THE DAUGHTERS." What is the significance of the use of family imagery by Lincoln and the engraver? How does this imagery "make personal" the abstract concept of the nation?

➤ The engraving on the right, from 1839, supports the incumbent president, Martin Van Buren (see Chapter 10). He firmly clasps the hand of Andrew Jackson, his predecessor, political ally, and the author of the famous toast "The Union Must Be Preserved." What use does the engraver make of Washington and the presidents who followed him? How do you think this imagery might have helped create a national political tradition?

stance. He condemned the "amazing violence and turbulence of the democratic spirit" and called for an authoritarian government headed by a president with near-monarchical powers.

As treasury secretary, Hamilton devised bold policies to enhance national authority and to favor wealthy financiers and merchants. He outlined his plans in three groundbreaking reports to Congress: on public credit (January 1790), on a national bank (December 1790), and on manufactures (December 1791). These reports laid out a program of national mercantilism, a system of state-assisted economic development.

"Report on the Public Credit."

The financial and social implications of Hamilton's "Report on the Public Credit" made it instantly controversial. Hamilton called on Congress to redeem at face value the millions of dollars in securities issued by the Confederation (Figure 7.1). He reasoned that, as an underdeveloped nation, the United States was heavily dependent on Dutch and British loans and needed good credit to survive. However, the redemption plan would also ensure enormous profits to speculators and that offended a majority of Americans, who had yet to accept the inequalities inherent in a full-fledged capitalist economy. For example, a Massachusetts merchant firm, Burrell & Burrell, had paid $600 for Confederation notes with a face value of $2,500; it stood to reap a profit of $1,900 (about $38,000 today). Equally controversial, Hamilton proposed to pay the Burrells and other Confederation noteholders with new government-issued, interest-bearing securities, thereby creating a permanent **national debt** owned mostly by wealthy families.

Hamilton's plan for a national debt reawakened the fears of Radical Whigs and "Old Republicans." Speaking for the Virginia House of Burgesses, Patrick Henry condemned this plan "to erect, and concentrate, and perpetuate a large monied interest" and warned that it would prove "fatal to the existence of American liberty." James Madison challenged the morality of Hamilton's redemption proposal. Madison demanded that Congress help the original owners of Confederation securities — the thousands of shopkeepers, farmers, and soldiers who had been paid with the securities during the dark days of the war and later sold them to speculators. However, it would have been difficult to find the original owners; moreover, nearly half the members of the House of Representatives owned Confederation securities and would profit personally from Hamilton's plan. Melding practicality with self-interest, the House rejected Madison's suggestion.

Hamilton then proposed that the national government enhance the public credit by assuming the war debts of the states. This plan also would favor wealthy creditors. In fact, it unleashed a flurry of speculation and government corruption. Knowing Hamilton's intentions, Assistant Secretary of the Treasury William Duer and his associates bought

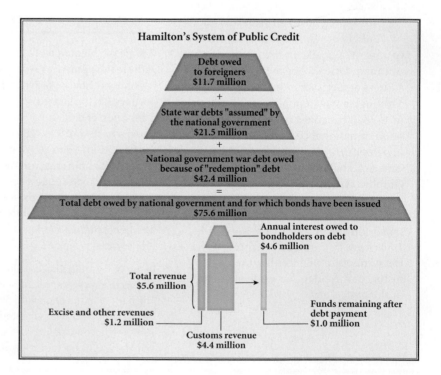

FIGURE 7.1 Hamilton's Fiscal Structure, 1792

As treasury secretary, Alexander Hamilton established a national debt by redeeming Confederation securities and assuming the states' war debts. He then used the revenue from excise taxes and customs duties to defray the annual interest on the national debt. Hamilton deliberately did not pay off the debt because he wanted to tie wealthy American bondholders to the new national government.

up the war bonds of southern states at cheap rates. Members of Congress condemned that speculation. They also pointed out that some states had already paid off their war debts, an argument Hamilton countered by modifying his plan to include reimbursement of the states. Representatives from Virginia and Maryland worried that assumption would enhance the already excessive financial sway of the national government. To quiet their fears, the treasury chief agreed to locate the permanent national capital along the banks of the Potomac, where suspicious southerners could easily watch its operations. This kind of astute political bargaining gave Hamilton the votes he needed to enact both his redemption and assumption plans.

A National Bank. In December 1790, Hamilton issued a second report, which asked Congress to charter the Bank of the United States. The bank would be jointly owned by private stockholders and the national government. Hamilton argued that the bank, by making loans to merchants, handling government funds, and issuing bills of credit, would provide financial stability and a respected currency for the specie-starved American economy. These potential benefits persuaded Congress to charter Hamilton's bank — for a period of twenty years — and send the legislation to the president for approval.

At this critical juncture, Secretary of State Thomas Jefferson joined ranks with James Madison against Hamilton's financial initiatives. Jefferson had condemned the "corrupt squadron of paper dealers" who speculated in southern war bonds. Now he charged that Hamilton's scheme for a national bank was unconstitutional. "The incorporation of a Bank," Jefferson told President Washington, was not a power expressly "delegated to the United States by the Constitution." Jefferson's argument rested on a strict interpretation of the national charter. In response, Hamilton devised a loose interpretation of the Constitution, stating that Article 1, Section 8, empowered Congress to make "all Laws which shall be necessary and proper" to carry out the provisions of the Constitution. Agreeing with his treasury secretary, Washington signed the legislation.

Revenue and Tariffs. Hamilton turned now to the final element of his financial system: revenue to pay the annual interest on the national debt. At Hamilton's insistence, Congress imposed a number of domestic excise taxes, including a duty on whiskey distilled in the United States. These taxes would yield $1 million a year. To raise another $4 million to $5 million, the treasury secretary proposed higher tariffs on foreign imports (see Figure 7.1).

Although Hamilton's "Report on Manufactures" (1791) urged the nation to become self-sufficient in manufacturing, he did not support high **protective tariffs** that would exclude competing foreign products. Instead, he advocated **revenue tariffs** that would pay the interest on the debt and defray the expenses of the national government.

Hamilton's scheme worked brilliantly. As American trade increased, customs revenue rose steadily and allowed the treasury to implement the redemption and assumption programs. Tariffs also had the unexpected effect of encouraging rapid settlement of the West, an outcome opposed by Hamilton and favored by his political opponents. Because import duties brought in 90 percent of the U.S. government's income from 1790 to 1820, the government was able to sell lands in the national domain at ever-lower prices. All in all, Hamilton had devised a strikingly modern fiscal system that provided the new national government with financial flexibility.

Jefferson's Agrarian Vision

Hamilton paid a high political price for his success. Even before Washington began his second four-year term in 1793, Hamilton's financial measures had split the Federalists into two irreconcilable factions. Most northern Federalists adhered to the political alliance led by Hamilton, while most southern Federalists joined a rival group headed by Madison and Jefferson. By the elections of 1794, the two factions had acquired names. Hamilton's supporters retained the original name: Federalists. Madison and Jefferson's allies called themselves Democratic Republicans or simply Republicans.

Thomas Jefferson spoke for the southern planters and western farmers who rejected Hamilton's economic and social policies. Well-read in architecture, natural history, agricultural science, and political theory, Jefferson embraced the optimistic spirit of the Enlightenment. He firmly believed in the "improvability of the human race" and so deplored the corrupt financial practices and emerging social divisions that threatened its achievement. Having seen the poverty of factory laborers in the manufacturing regions of Britain, Jefferson doubted that wageworkers had the economic and political independence necessary to sustain a republic.

Jefferson's democratic vision of America, then, was of an agricultural society based on free labor. Although he had grown up (and remained) a slave owner, Jefferson pictured the West settled by productive farm families. "Those who labor in the earth are the chosen people of God," he wrote in *Notes on the State of Virginia* (1785). The grain and

meat from their farms would feed European nations, which "would manufacture and send us in exchange our clothes and other comforts." Jefferson's notion of an international division of labor was similar to that proposed by Scottish economist Adam Smith in *The Wealth of Nations* (1776).

Turmoil in Europe brought Jefferson's vision closer to reality by creating new opportunities for American farmers. The French Revolution began in 1789; four years later, France's republican government went to war against a British-led coalition of monarchies. As warfare disrupted European farming, wheat prices leaped from 5 to 8 shillings a bushel and remained high for twenty years, bringing substantial profits to Chesapeake and Middle Atlantic farmers. Simultaneously, a boom in the export of raw cotton, fueled by the invention of the cotton gin and the mechanization of cloth production in Britain (see Chapter 9), boosted the economies of Georgia and South Carolina. As Jefferson had hoped, European markets brought prosperity to American farmers and planters.

The French Revolution Divides Americans

American merchants profited even more handsomely from the European war. In 1793, President Washington issued a Proclamation of Neutrality, which allowed U.S. citizens to trade with both sides. As neutral carriers, American merchants were initially able to pass their ships through the British naval blockade of French ports; soon they dominated the lucrative sugar trade between France and its West Indian islands. Commercial earnings rose spectacularly, averaging $20 million annually in the 1790s—twice the value of cotton and tobacco exports. As the American merchant fleet increased

dramatically, from 355,000 tons in 1790 to more than 1.1 million tons in 1808, northern shipowners provided work for thousands of shipwrights, sailmakers, laborers, and seamen. Hundreds of carpenters, masons, and cabinetmakers in the major seaports of Boston, New York, and Philadelphia found work building warehouses and fashionable "Federal-style" town houses for newly affluent merchants. In Philadelphia, a European visitor reported, "a great number of private houses have marble steps to the street door, and in other respects are finished in a style of elegance."

Ideological Conflicts. Even as they profited from the European struggle, Americans argued passionately over its ideologies. Most Americans had welcomed the French Revolution of 1789 because it abolished feudalism and established a constitutional monarchy. There was much less consensus, however, in 1792, when the French formed a democratic republic. Many Americans applauded the downfall of the French monarchy. Urban artisans were particularly taken with the egalitarianism of the Jacobins, a radical French group, and followed their example— addressing one another as "citizen" and starting democratic political clubs. Conversely, American with strong religious beliefs condemned the new French government because it rejected Christianity and closed many churches, instead promoting a "rational" religion based on "natural morality." Wealthy Americans also condemned Robespierre and his radical republican followers for executing King Louis XVI, three thousand of the king's aristocratic supporters, and fourteen thousand other citizens (see Voices from Abroad, "William Cobbett: Peter Porcupine Attacks Pro-French Americans," p. 210).

These ideological conflicts sharpened the debate over Hamilton's economic policies and helped to foment a domestic insurrection. In 1794, farmers in western Pennsylvania mounted the Whiskey Rebellion to protest Hamilton's excise tax on spirits, which had raised the price — and cut the demand — for the corn whiskey they bartered for eastern manufactures. Like the Sons of Liberty in 1765 and the Shaysites in 1786, the Whiskey Rebels attacked both local tax collectors and the authority of a distant government. They also waved banners proclaiming the French revolutionary slogan "Liberty, Equality, and Fraternity!" To uphold national authority and deter secessionist movements along the frontier, President Washington raised an army of twelve thousand troops and dispersed the Whiskey rebels.

Jay's Treaty. Britain's maritime strategy widened the political divisions in America. In November 1793, the Royal Navy began to stop American ships carrying French sugar, eventually seizing more than 250 vessels. Hoping to protect American property rights though diplomacy, President Washington dispatched John Jay to Britain. Jay returned with a controversial treaty that acknowledged Britain's right to remove French property from neutral ships, rejecting American merchants' claim that "free ships make free goods." The treaty also required the U.S. government to make "full and complete compensation" to British merchants for pre–Revolutionary War debts owed by American citizens who refused to pay them. In return, the agreement allowed American merchants to submit claims of illegal seizure to arbitration and, more important, required the British to remove their military garrisons from the Northwest Territory and to end their alliance with the Indians there. Jefferson and other Republicans attacked the treaty for being too conciliatory, but the Senate ratified it in 1795, albeit by the bare two-thirds majority required by the Constitution. As long as Hamilton and his Federalist allies were in power, the United States would have a pro-British foreign policy.

The Rise of Political Parties

The appearance of Federalists and Republicans marked a new stage in American politics, the rise of what historians call the First Party System. Although colonial legislatures had often divided temporarily into factions based on family, ethnicity, or region, they did not form organized political parties. The new state and national constitutions made no provision for political societies. In fact, most Americans thought parties were unnecessary and even dangerous to the government; they had little notion of a "loyal opposition." Following classical republican principles, American leaders maintained that voters and legislators should act independently in the interest of the public as a whole. Senator Pierce Butler of South Carolina criticized his congressional colleagues as "men scrambling for partial advantage, State interests, and in short, a train of narrow, impolitic measures."

Federalist Gentry

A prominent New England Federalist, Oliver Ellsworth served as chief justice of the United States from 1796 to 1800. His wife, Abigail Wolcott Ellsworth, was the daughter of a Connecticut governor. In 1792, portraitist Ralph Earl captured the aspirations of the Ellsworths by painting them as aristocrats and prominently displaying their mansion (in the window). Like other Federalists who tried to reconcile their wealth and social authority with republican values, Ellsworth dressed with restraint and his manners, remarked Timothy Dwight, were "wholly destitute of haughtiness and arrogance."
Wadsworth Atheneum, Hartford.

William Cobbett

Peter Porcupine Attacks Pro-French Americans

The Democratic Republican follow-ers of Thomas Jefferson declared that "he who is an enemy to the French Revolution, cannot be a firm republi-can." William Cobbett, a British jour-nalist who settled in Philadelphia and wrote under the pen name "Peter Porcupine," contested this definition of republicanism. A strong supporter of the Federalist Party, Cobbett regularly attacked its opponents in caustic and widely read pamphlets and newspaper articles like this one, which was pub-lished in 1796.

France is a republic, and the decrees of the Legislators were necessary to maintain it a republic. This word out-weighs, in the estimation of some persons (I wish I could say they were few in number), all the horrors that have been and that can be committed in that country. One of these modern republicans will tell you that he does not deny that hundreds of thousands of innocent persons have been mur-dered in France; that the people have neither religion nor morals; that all the ties of nature are rent asunder; ... that its riches, along with millions of the best of the people, are gone to en-rich and aggrandize its enemies; that its commerce, its manufactures, its sciences, its arts, and its honour, are no more; but at the end of all this, he will tell you that it must be happy, be-cause it is a republic. I have heard more than one of these republican zealots declare, that he would sooner

see the last of the French extermi-nated, than see them adopt any other form of government. Such a senti-ment is characteristic of a mind locked up in a savage ignorance.

Shall we say that these things never can take place among us? ... We are not what we were before the French revolution. Political projectors from every corner of Europe, trou-blers of society of every description, from the whining philosophical hyp-ocrite to the daring rebel, and more daring blasphemer, have taken shelter in these States.

We have seen the guillotine toasted to three times three cheers. ... And what would the reader say, were I to tell him of a Member of Congress, who wished to see one of these mur-derous machines employed for lop-ping off the heads of the French, permanent in the State-house yard of the city of Philadelphia?

If these men of blood had suc-ceeded in plunging us into a war; if they had once got the sword into their hands, they would have mowed us down like stubble. The word Aristo-crat would have been employed to as good account here, as ever it had been in France. We might, ere this, have seen our places of worship turned into stables; we might have seen the banks of the Delaware, like those of the Loire, covered with human car-casses, and its waters tinged with blood: ere this we might have seen our parents butchered, and even the head of our admired and beloved President rolling on a scaffold.

I know the reader will start back with horror. His heart will tell him that it is impossible. But, once more, let him look at the example before us. The attacks on the character and con-duct of the aged Washington, have been as bold, if not bolder, than those which led to the downfall of the un-fortunate French Monarch [Louis

XVI, executed in 1793]. Can it then be imagined, that, had they possessed the power, they wanted the will to dip their hands in his blood?

SOURCE: William Cobbett, *Peter Porcupine in America,* ed. David A. Wilson (Ithaca: Cornell University Press, 1994), 150–154.

ANALYZING THE EVIDENCE

➤ What horrors does Cobbett de-scribe? Why does he believe a simi-lar fate could befall the United States?

➤ By 1796, Americans had a long tra-dition of popular protests. Which of those protests gave credence to Cobbett's warning that a blood-bath might "take place among us"?

➤ Why do you think Americans gen-erally were able to resolve their po-litical disputes peacefully, while the French took up arms to do so?

Still, the conflict in the 1790s over fiscal policies divided America's legislators, and popular sovereignty, which drew average citizens into politics, accentuated the division. Most merchants, creditors, and urban artisans supported Federalist policies, as did wheat-exporting slaveholders in the Tidewater districts of the Chesapeake. The emerging Republican coalition was more diverse. It included not only southern tobacco and rice planters and debt-conscious western farmers but also Germans and Scots-Irish in the southern backcountry and subsistence farmers in the Northeast.

Party identity crystallized in 1796. To prepare for the presidential election, Federalist and Republican leaders called caucuses in Congress and conventions in the states to discuss policies and nominate candidates. The parties organized the citizenry through public festivals and processions: The Federalists celebrated Washington's birthday in February, and the Republicans honored the Declaration of Independence on July Fourth.

Federalist candidates triumphed in the national elections of 1796, winning a majority in Congress and electing John Adams to the presidency. Adams continued Hamilton's pro-British foreign policy and reacted sharply to seizures of American merchant ships by the French navy. When the French foreign minister Talleyrand solicited a loan and a bribe from American diplomats to stop the seizures, Adams charged that Talleyrand's agents, whom he dubbed X, Y, and Z, had insulted America's honor. Responding to the XYZ Affair, the Federalist-controlled Congress cut off trade with France in 1798 and authorized American privateers to seize French ships. The party conflict that had begun over Hamilton's financial policies now extended to foreign affairs.

Constitutional Crisis, 1798–1800

Ominously, the controversial foreign policy of the Federalists prompted domestic protest and governmental repression. As the United States fought an undeclared maritime war against France, immigrants from Ireland vehemently attacked Adams's pro-British foreign policy. A Federalist pamphleteer in Philadelphia responded in kind: "Were I president, I would hang them for otherwise they would murder me." To silence their critics, the Federalist-controlled Congress enacted three coercive laws that threatened individual rights and the fledgling party system. The Naturalization Act lengthened the residency requirement for American citizenship — and so the right to vote — from five to fourteen years; the Alien Act authorized the deportation of foreigners; and the Sedi-

tion Act prohibited the publication of insults or malicious attacks on the president or members of Congress. "He that is not for us is against us," thundered the Federalist *Gazette of the United States*. It was the Sedition Act that generated the most controversy. Prosecutors arrested more than twenty Republican newspaper editors and politicians, accused them of sedition, and convicted and jailed a number of them.

What ensued was a constitutional crisis. With justification, Republicans charged that the Sedition Act violated the First Amendment's prohibition against "abridging the freedom of speech, or of the press." They did not appeal to the Supreme Court because the Court's power to review congressional legislation was uncertain and because most of the justices were Federalists. Instead, Madison and Jefferson looked to the state legislatures for a remedy. At their urging, the Kentucky and Virginia legislatures issued resolutions in 1798 declaring the Alien and Sedition Acts to be "unauthoritative, void, and of no force." The resolutions set forth a **states' rights** interpretation of the Constitution, asserting that the states had a "right to judge" the legitimacy of national laws.

The debate over the Sedition Act set the stage for the presidential election of 1800. Jefferson, once opposed in principle to political parties, now saw them as a valuable way "to watch and relate to the people" the activities of an oppressive government. With Republicans strongly supporting Jefferson's bid for the presidency, President Adams reevaluated his foreign policy. Adams was a complicated man: He was easily offended but had great personal strength and determination. Rejecting Hamilton's advice to declare war against France (and so benefit from an upsurge in patriotism), Adams put country ahead of party and entered into diplomatic negotiations that ended the fighting.

Despite Adams's statesmanship, the campaign of 1800 degenerated into name-calling. The Federalists attacked Jefferson's values, branding him an irresponsible pro-French radical and, because he opposed state support of religion in Virginia, "the arch-apostle of irreligion and free thought." And both parties changed state election laws to favor their candidates. In fact, tensions ran so high that there were rumors the Federalists were planning a military coup and civil war.

The election did not end these worries. Thanks to a low Federalist turnout in Virginia and Pennsylvania and the three-fifths rule (which boosted electoral votes in the southern states), Jefferson won a narrow 73 to 65 victory over Adams in the Electoral College. However, the Republican electors also gave 73 votes to Aaron Burr of New York, who was Jefferson's vice presidential running mate (Map 7.1).

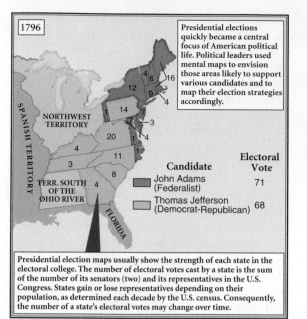

Presidential election maps usually show the strength of each state in the electoral college. The number of electoral votes cast by a state is the sum of the number of its senators (two) and its representatives in the U.S. Congress. States gain or lose representatives depending on their population, as determined each decade by the U.S. census. Consequently, the number of a state's electoral votes may change over time.

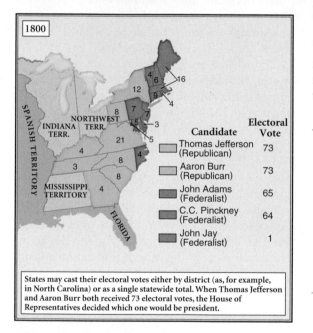

States may cast their electoral votes either by district (as, for example, in North Carolina) or as a single statewide total. When Thomas Jefferson and Aaron Burr both received 73 electoral votes, the House of Representatives decided which one would be president.

MAP 7.1 The Presidential Elections of 1796 and 1800

Both elections pitted Federalist John Adams of Massachusetts against Republican Thomas Jefferson of Virginia, and both saw voters split along regional lines. Adams carried every New England state and, reflecting Federalist strength in maritime and commercial areas, the eastern districts of the Middle Atlantic states; Jefferson won most of the agricultural-based states of the South and West (Kentucky and Tennessee). New York was the pivotal swing state. It gave its twelve electoral votes to Adams in 1796 and, thanks to the presence of Aaron Burr on the Republican ticket, to Jefferson in 1800.

The Constitution specified that in the case of a tie vote, the House of Representatives would choose the president. For thirty-five ballots, Federalists in the House blocked Jefferson's election, prompting a new rumor that Virginia was raising a military force to put Jefferson into office.

Ironically, it was arch-Federalist Alexander Hamilton who ushered in a more democratic era by supporting Jefferson. Calling Burr an "embryo Caesar" and the "most unfit man in the United States for the office of president," he persuaded key Federalists to allow Jefferson's election. The Federalists' concern for political stability also played a role. As Senator James Bayard of Delaware explained, "It was admitted on all hands that we must risk the Constitution and a Civil War or take Mr. Jefferson."

Jefferson called the election the "Revolution of 1800," and so it was. The bloodless transfer of power demonstrated that governments elected by the people could be changed in an orderly way, even in times of bitter partisan conflict. In his inaugural address in 1801, Jefferson praised this achievement, declaring, "We are all Republicans, we are all Federalists." Defying the predictions of European conservatives, the republican experiment of 1776 had survived a quarter-century of economic and political turmoil.

➤ What was Hamilton's vision of the future? What policies did he advocate to achieve it? How was Jefferson's vision different?

➤ What were the consequences of the French Revolution in America? How did it affect the development of American politics?

➤ Do you agree with Jefferson that the election of 1800 was a revolution? Explain your answer.

The Westward Movement and the Jeffersonian Revolution

"It is a country in flux," a French aristocrat observed of the United States in 1799, and "that which is true today as regards its population, its establishments, its prices, its commerce will not be true six months from now." Indeed, the American republic was poised to begin a period of dynamic westward expansion. Beginning in the 1780s, thousands of extraordinarily self-confident farm families began to trek into the interior. George Washington, himself a western land speculator, noted that the Sons of

Liberty had become "the lords and proprietors of a vast tract of continent." Unfortunately for Washington's Federalist Party, most western farmers supported Thomas Jefferson's Republicans.

The Expanding Republic and Native American Resistance

In the Treaty of Paris of 1783, Great Britain relinquished its claims to the trans-Appalachian region and, as one British diplomat put it, left the Indian nations "to the care of their [American] neighbours." *Care* was hardly the right term: Many white Americans, including a number of influential men, wanted to destroy native communities and even the native peoples themselves. "Cut up every Indian Cornfield and burn every Indian town," proclaimed William Henry Drayton, a congressman from South Carolina, so that their "nation be extirpated and the lands become the property of the public." Other leaders, including Henry Knox, Washington's first secretary of war, favored assimilating the Indians into Euro-American society. Knox proposed the division of commonly held tribal lands among individual Indian families, who would become citizens of the various states. This debate among whites over the fate of Native Americans would hold an important place on the nation's agenda until 1900, and continues even today.

Conflict over Land Rights. Not surprisingly, the major struggle between Indians and whites centered on land. Invoking the Treaty of Paris and classifying Britain's Indian allies as conquered peoples, the U.S. government asserted its ownership of the trans-Appalachian west. Native Americans rejected that claim, insisting that they had not signed the Paris treaty and had not been conquered. Brushing aside those arguments, U.S. commissioners used the threat of military action to force the pro-British Iroquois peoples—the Mohawks, Onondagas, Cayugas, and Senecas—to relinquish much of their land in New York and Pennsylvania in the Treaty of Fort Stanwix (1784). New York officials and land speculators used liquor and bribes to take title to millions of additional acres, confining the once powerful Iroquois to relatively small tribal reservations.

American negotiators used similar tactics to grab western lands. In 1785, they persuaded the Chippewas, Delawares, Ottawas, and Wyandots to sign away most of the future state of Ohio. The tribes quickly repudiated the agreements, justifiably claiming they were made under duress. To defend their lands, they joined with the Shawnee, Miami, and Potawatomi peoples in the Western Confederacy. Led by Miami chief Little Turtle, confederacy warriors crushed American expeditionary forces sent by President Washington in 1790 and 1791.

Fearing an alliance between the Western Confederacy and the British in Canada, Washington doubled the size of the U.S. Army and ordered General "Mad Anthony" Wayne to lead a new expedition. In August 1794, Wayne defeated the Indians in the Battle of Fallen Timbers (near present-day Toledo, Ohio), but the resistance continued. In the Treaty of Greenville (1795), American negotiators acknowledged Indian ownership of the land; in return, the Indian peoples ceded most of Ohio and various strategic areas along the Great Lakes, including Detroit and the future site of Chicago (Map 7.2). The members of the Western Confederacy also agreed to place themselves "under the protection of the United States, and no other Power whatever." These American advances prompted Britain to change its policies in North America: It reduced its trade with the Indian peoples and, following Jay's Treaty (1795), began to remove its military garrisons from the region.

The Greenville Treaty sparked a wave of white migration. By 1805, Ohio, a state for just two years, had more than 100,000 residents. Thousands more farm families moved into the future states of Indiana and Illinois, sparking new conflicts with native peoples over land and hunting rights. Declared one Delaware Indian: "The Elks are our horses, the buffaloes are our cows, the deer are our sheep, & the whites shan't have them."

Assimilation Proposed and Rejected. To alleviate these tensions, the U.S. government encouraged Native Americans to assimilate into white society. The goal, as one Kentucky Protestant minister put it, was to make the Indian "a farmer, a citizen of the United States, and a Christian." But most Indians rejected assimilation. Even those who embraced Christian teachings held to many of their ancestral values. To think of themselves as individuals or even as members of a nuclear family, as white Americans were demanding, meant repudiating the clan, the very essence of Indian life. To preserve their traditional cultures, many Indian communities expelled white missionaries and forced Christianized Indians to participate in tribal rites. As a Munsee prophet put it, "There are two ways to God, one for the whites and one for the Indians."

A few Indian leaders tried to find a middle path. Among the Senecas, the prophet Handsome Lake encouraged traditional animistic ceremonies that gave thanks to the sun, the earth, water, plants, and animals. But he also included some Christian ele-

Treaty Negotiations at Greenville, 1795

In 1785, a number of Indian tribes formed the Western Confederacy to prevent white settlement north of the Ohio River. The American victory at the Battle of Fallen Timbers (1794) opened up the region for white farmers. Peace came the following year with the Treaty of Greenville. That treaty recognized many Indian rights because it was negotiated between relative equals. The artist suggests this equality: Notice the height and stately bearing of the Indian leaders and their placement slightly in front of the American officers.
Unknown, *Treaty of Greenville*, n.d., Chicago Historical Society.

ments in his teachings — the concepts of heaven and hell, for example — to deter his followers from alcohol, gambling, and witchcraft. Handsome Lake's doctrines divided the tribe into hostile factions. More conservative Senecas, led by Chief Red Jacket, condemned Indians who accepted white ways and demanded a return to ancestral customs.

Most Indians also rejected the efforts of American missionaries to turn warriors into farmers and women into domestic helpmates. Among eastern woodland peoples, women were primarily responsible for growing staple foods; as a result, women controlled cultivation rights — they passed through the female line — and exercised considerable political power, which they were eager to retain. Nor were Indian men interested in becoming farmers. When war raiding and hunting were no longer possible, they turned to grazing cattle and sheep.

Migration and the Changing Farm Economy

Native American resistance slowed the advance of white farmers and planters but did not stop it. Between 1790 and 1820, settlers continued to pour across the Appalachian Mountains and to move southward along the Atlantic coastal plain (Map 7.3). This migratory surge transformed America's farm economy.

Movement out of the South. Between 1790 and 1820, two great streams of migrants moved out of the southern states. One stream, composed primarily of white tenant farmers and struggling yeomen families, flocked through the Cumberland Gap into Kentucky and Tennessee. "Boundless settlements open a door for our citizens to run off and leave us," a worried

MAP 7.2 Indian Cessions and State Formation, 1776–1840

By virtue of the Treaty of Paris (1783) with Britain, the United States claimed sovereignty over the entire trans-Appalachian west. The Western Confederacy contested this claim, but the U.S. government upheld it with military force. By 1840, armed diplomacy had forced most Native American peoples to move west of the Mississippi River. White settlers occupied their lands, formed territorial governments, and eventually entered the Union as members of separate — and equal —states. Gradually, the trans-Appalachian region emerged as an important economic and political force.

eastern landlord lamented in the *Maryland Gazette*, "depreciating all our landed property and disabling us from paying taxes." In fact, many migrants were fleeing from this planter-controlled society: They wanted more freedom and hoped to prosper by growing cotton and hemp, which were in great demand.

But many of the settlers in Kentucky and Tennessee lacked ready cash to buy land. These settlers invoked the principle articulated in the 1770s by the North Carolina Regulators, that poor settlers had a customary right to occupy "back waste vacant Lands" sufficient "to provide a subsistence for themselves and their posterity." Virginia, which administered the Kentucky Territory, had a more elitist vision. Although it allowed poor settlers to purchase up to 1,400 acres of land at reduced prices, it also sold or granted estates of 20,000 to 200,000 acres to scores of wealthy slave owners and land speculators. When Kentucky became a state in 1792, a handful of speculators owned one-fourth of the state, while half the white men there owned no land and lived as squatters or tenant farmers.

Widespread landlessness — and opposition to slavery — prompted a new migration across the Ohio River into the future states of Ohio, Indiana, and Illinois. In a free community, thought Peter Cartwright, a Methodist lay preacher from southwestern Kentucky who moved to Illinois, "I would be entirely clear of the evil of slavery . . . [and] could raise my children to work where work was not thought a degradation."

Meanwhile, a second stream of southern migrants from the Carolinas, dominated by slave-owning planters and their enslaved African Americans, moved along the coastal plain toward the Gulf of Mexico. The planters set up new cotton plantations in the interior of Georgia and South Carolina. Then they moved into the Old Southwest, the future states of Alabama, Mississippi, and Louisiana. "The Alabama Feaver rages here with great violence," a North Carolina planter remarked, "and has carried off vast numbers of our Citizens." To cultivate their cotton crop, the planters bought more slaves: They imported about 115,000 Africans between 1776 and 1808, when Congress cut off the Atlantic slave trade. The black population in

Chief Red Jacket, or Sagoyewatha, c. 1828
Like most Senecas, Sagoyewatha fought for the British during the American War of Independence. In fact, he was called Red Jacket for the red coat a British officer had given him. In 1792, Red Jacket journeyed to Philadelphia as a member of a delegation that ceded Iroquois lands to the United States. There he met with President Washington, who presented him with a silver peace medal. Later Red Jacket would strongly oppose Christian missionary efforts and would call for a return to the traditional Indian way of life. This painting by an unknown artist is based on a portrait by Robert W. Weir painted around 1828. Fenimore Art Museum/© New York State Historical Association, Cooperstown.

America grew even more through reproduction, increasing from 500,000 in 1775 to 1.8 million in 1820.

Beginning around 1750, water-powered spinning jennies, weaving mules, and other technological innovations boosted textile production in Europe, greatly increasing the demand for raw wool and cotton. Responding to that demand, South Carolina and Georgia planters began growing cotton, and American inventors—including Connecticut-born Eli Whitney—built machines (called gins) that efficiently extracted seeds from strands of cotton. The cotton boom financed the rapid settlement of Mississippi and Alabama—in a single year, a government land office in Huntsville, Alabama, sold $7 million of uncleared land—and the two states entered the Union in 1817 and 1819, respectively.

Exodus from New England. As southern whites and blacks moved across the Appalachians and along the Gulf Coast, a third stream of migrants flowed out of the overcrowded communities of New England. Previous generations of farm families from Massachusetts and Connecticut had moved north and east, settling New Hampshire, Vermont, and Maine. Now farmers throughout New England were on the move, this time to the west. Seeking land for their children, thousands of parents packed their wagons with tools and household goods and migrated to New York. By 1820, almost 800,000 New England migrants lived in a string of settlements that stretched from Albany to Buffalo, and many others had moved on to Ohio and Indiana.

This vast migration was organized by the settlers themselves, who often moved in large family or religious groups. One traveler reported from central New York: "The town of Herkimer is entirely populated by families come from Connecticut. We stayed at Mr. Snow's who came from New London with about ten male and female cousins." When 176 residents of Granville, Massachusetts, relocated to Ohio,

MAP 7.3 Regional Cultures Move West, 1790–1820

By 1790, four core cultures had developed in the long-settled states along the Atlantic seaboard. Between 1790 and 1820, residents of these four regions migrated into the trans-Appalachian west, carrying their cultures with them. New England customs and institutions were a dominant influence in upstate New York and along the Great Lakes, while the Lower South's hierarchical system of slavery and heavy concentration of African Americans shaped the culture of the new states along the Gulf of Mexico. The pattern of cultural diffusion was more complex in the Ohio and Tennessee river valleys, which were settled by migrants from various core regions.

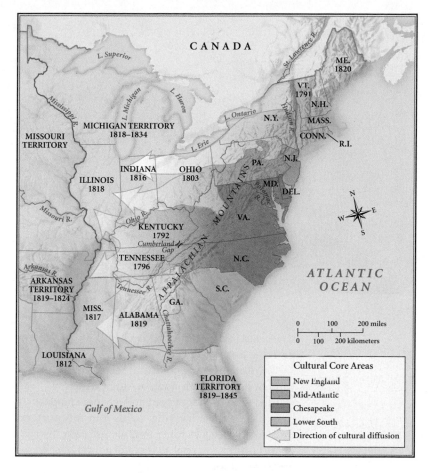

they were led by the minister and elders of their Congregational church. Throughout the Northwest Territory, many new communities were actually old New England communities that had moved inland.

In New York, as in Kentucky, well-connected speculators snapped up much of the best land. In the 1780s, financier Robert Morris acquired 1.3 million acres in the Genesee region of central New York. The Wadsworth family also bought thousands of acres and tried to set up a manorial system like the one in the Hudson River Valley. To attract tenants, the Wadsworths leased farms rent-free for the first seven years, after which they charged rents. Many New England farm families chose instead to sign agreements with the Holland Land Company, a Dutch-owned syndicate of speculators, which allowed settlers to buy the land as they worked it. But high interest rates and, at least initially, a lack of markets for their crops mired thousands of these aspiring freeholders in debt.

Agricultural Change in the East. To pay their debts, farmers in central New York exported wheat to the east, forcing major changes in agriculture there. Unable to compete with low-priced New York grains, farmers in New England switched to potatoes, which were high yielding and nutritious. To compensate for the labor of sons and daughters who had moved inland, Middle Atlantic farmers bought more efficient farm equipment. For example, they replaced metal-tipped wooden plows with cast-iron models that dug deeper and required a single yoke of oxen instead of two or three. This advance in technology kept production high even with fewer workers.

Easterners also took advantage of the progressive farming methods touted by British agricultural reformers. "Improvers" in Pennsylvania doubled their average yield per acre by rotating their crops and planting nitrogen-rich clover to offset nutrient-hungry wheat and corn. Yeomen farmers diversified production by raising sheep and selling the wool to textile manufacturers. Many farmers adopted a year-round planting cycle, sowing wheat in early winter for market and corn in the spring for animal fodder. Women and girls milked the family

Hop Picking, 1801

Farm labor was nothing new for rural women and children, who had always worked about the farm. What was different after 1800 was the growing number of outworkers, landless or poor families who labored for wages paid by shopkeepers and manufacturers. In this somewhat romanticized watercolor by Lucy Sheldon, a Connecticut schoolgirl at the Litchfield Female Academy, a young couple and their children pick hops, which they will deliver to a storekeeper or local brewer to be made into beer. Litchfield Historical Society.

cows and made butter and cheese to sell in the growing towns and cities nearby.

In this new agricultural economy, families worked harder and longer, but their efforts were rewarded with higher output and a better standard of living. Whether hacking fields out of western forests or carting manure to replenish eastern soils, farm families increased their productivity. Westward migration had boosted the farming economy throughout the country.

The Jeffersonian Presidency

From 1801 to 1825, three Republicans from Virginia — Thomas Jefferson, James Madison, and James Monroe — served two terms each as president. Supported by farmers in the South and West and strong Republican majorities in Congress, this "Virginia Dynasty" completed what Jefferson had called the Revolution of 1800. It reversed many Federalist policies and actively supported westward expansion.

When Jefferson took office in 1801, he became the first chief executive to live in the White House in the District of Columbia, the new national capital. His administration began with an international crisis inherited from the Federalists. During the 1790s, the Barbary States of North Africa had systematically raided merchant ships in the Mediterranean and, like many European states, the United States had paid an annual bribe to protect its vessels. Jefferson refused to pay this "tribute"; and when the Barbary pirates renewed their raids, he ordered the U.S. Navy to retaliate. The president did not want all-out war, which would have

increased taxes and the national debt, so he negotiated a settlement that restored the tribute but at a lower rate.

At home, Jefferson inherited a national judiciary filled with Federalist appointees, including the formidable John Marshall of Virginia, the new chief justice of the Supreme Court. Marshall had been appointed by President Adams at the end of his term and quickly confirmed by the Federalist-controlled Senate. To add more Federalists to the court system, the outgoing Congress had also passed the Judiciary Act of 1801. The act created sixteen new judgeships and six additional circuit courts, which Adams filled with "midnight appointees" just before he left office. The Federalists "have retired into the judiciary as a stronghold," Jefferson complained, "and from that battery all the works of Republicanism are to be beaten down and destroyed."

Jefferson's fears were soon realized. When Republican legislatures in Kentucky and Virginia repudiated the Alien and Sedition Acts and claimed the authority to determine the constitutionality of national laws, the Federalist judiciary responded quickly. The Constitution stated that "the judicial Power shall extend to all Cases . . . arising under this Constitution [and] the Laws of the United States," which implied that the Supreme Court held the power of constitutional review. This important issue came to the fore when James Madison, the new secretary of state, refused to deliver the commission of William Marbury, one of Adams's midnight appointees. Marbury petitioned the Supreme Court to compel delivery under the terms of the Judiciary Act of 1789. In *Marbury v. Madison* (1803),

BOMBARDMENT OF TRIPOLI.

America in the Middle East, 1804

To protect American merchants from capture and captivity in the Barbary States, President Thomas Jefferson sent in the U.S. Navy. This 1846 lithograph, created by the famous firm of Currier & Ives, depicts the attack on the North African port of Tripoli by Commodore Edward Preble in August 1804 and his intentional destruction of the *USS Philadelphia,* which had been captured by the Tripolians. The Granger Collection, New York.

Marshall wrote that although Marbury had the right to the appointment, the Court did not have the power under the Constitution to enforce it. In defining the authority of the Court, Marshall had voided a section of the Judiciary Act of 1789, in effect asserting the Court's power to review congressional legislation and decide the meaning of the constitution. "It is emphatically the province and duty of the judicial department to say what the law is," the chief justice declared, directly challenging the Republican view, outlined in the Virginia and Kentucky resolutions of 1798, that the state legislatures had authority to interpret the constitution.

Implementing the Revolution of 1800. Ignoring this setback, Jefferson and the Republicans turned their attention to reversing Federalist policies. When the Alien Act and the Sedition Act expired in 1801, Congress branded them political and unconstitutional, and refused to reenact them. It also amended the Naturalization Act to allow resident aliens to become citizens after five years, the original waiting period. Charging the Federalists with grossly expanding the national government's size and power, Jefferson mobilized the Republican Congress to shrink it. He abolished all internal taxes, including the excise tax that had sparked the Whiskey Rebellion of 1794. Addressing "Old Republican" fears of a military coup, Jefferson reduced the size of the permanent army. He also secured repeal of the Judiciary Act of 1801, thereby ousting forty of Adams's midnight appointees.

But Jefferson governed tactfully. He allowed competent Federalist bureaucrats to retain their jobs. Apart from the midnight appointees, he removed only 69 of 433 Federalist officeholders during his eight years as president. He also tolerated the economically important Bank of the United States, which he had condemned as unconstitutional in 1791. He chose as his secretary of the treasury Albert Gallatin, a fiscal conservative who believed that the national debt was "an evil of the first magnitude." By carefully controlling expenditures and using customs revenues to redeem government bonds, Gallatin reduced the debt from $83 million in 1801 to $45 million in 1808. With Jefferson and Gallatin at the helm, the nation was no longer run in the interests of northeastern creditors and merchants.

Jefferson and the West

Long before he became president, Jefferson championed settlement of the West. He celebrated the yeoman farmer in *Notes on the State of Virginia*, wrote one of the Confederation's western land ordinances, and strongly supported Thomas Pinckney's treaty (1795), which allowed settlers in the Mississippi River Valley to export crops by way of the river and Spanish-held New Orleans.

As president, Jefferson pursued similar policies. In 1796, the Federalist-dominated Congress had doubled the minimum price of land in the national domain to $2 per acre. In response, Republican congresses passed a series of laws that made it easier for farm families to acquire land. By 1820, a farmer needed only $100 in cash to buy eighty acres. Inspired by Jeffersonian policies, subsequent congresses reduced the price still further and eventually, in the Homestead Act of 1862, gave farmsteads to settlers at no cost.

The Louisiana Purchase. International events challenged Jefferson's vision of westward expansion. In 1799, Napoleon Bonaparte seized power in France and began an ambitious campaign to establish a French empire in Europe and in America. In 1801, he coerced Spain into signing a secret treaty that returned Louisiana to France. A year later, he directed Spanish officials in Louisiana to restrict American access to New Orleans, violating the terms of Pinckney's Treaty. Meanwhile, Napoleon planned an invasion to restore French rule in Haiti (then called Saint-Domingue), a rich sugar island seized in 1793 by rebellious black slaves led by Toussaint L'Ouverture.

Napoleon's aggression prompted Jefferson to question his party's pro-French foreign policy. "The day that France takes possession of New

Toussaint L'Ouverture, Haitian Revolutionary and Statesman

The American Revolution represented a victory for republicanism; the Haitian revolt represented a triumph of liberty and a demand for racial equality. After leading the black army that ousted French planters and British invaders from Haiti, Toussaint formed a constitutional government in 1801 that gave him great authority. A year later, he negotiated a treaty with the French, who had invaded the island; the treaty halted Haitian resistance in exchange for a promise that the French would not reinstate slavery. Subsequently, the French seized Toussaint and sent him to France, where he died in a prison in 1803. Snark/Art Resource, New York.

Orleans," the president warned, "we must marry ourselves to the British fleet and nation." Jefferson feared that the French might close the Mississippi River to western farmers, threatening his vision of an expanding yeoman republic. He instructed Robert Livingston, the American minister in Paris, to negotiate the purchase of New Orleans. Simultaneously, Jefferson sent James Monroe to Britain to negotiate an alliance in case of war with France.

Jefferson's diplomacy yielded a magnificent prize: the entire territory of Louisiana. By 1802, the French invasion of Haiti was faltering in the face of disease and determined black resistance, a new war threatened in Europe, and Napoleon feared an American invasion of Louisiana. Acting with characteristic decisiveness, the French ruler offered to sell not only New Orleans but the entire territory of Louisiana for $15 million (about $500 million today). "We have lived long," Livingston remarked to Monroe as they concluded the Louisiana Purchase in 1803, "but this is the noblest work of our lives."

The Louisiana Purchase forced the president to reconsider his strict interpretation of the Constitution. Jefferson had always maintained that the national government possessed only the powers "expressly" delegated to it in the Constitution, but there was no constitutional provision for adding new territory. In this instance, a pragmatic Jefferson accepted a loose interpretation of the Constitution, using the treaty-making powers authorized there to complete the deal with France.

A scientist as well as a statesman, Jefferson wanted detailed information about the physical features of the new territory, its plant and animal life, and its Native peoples. In 1804, he sent his personal secretary, Meriwether Lewis, to explore the region with William Clark, an army officer. With the help of Indian guides, Lewis and Clark and their party of American soldiers and frontiersmen traveled up the Missouri River, across the Rocky Mountains, and, venturing beyond the bounds of the Louisiana Purchase, down the Columbia River to the Pacific Ocean. After two years, they returned with the first maps of the immense wilderness and vivid accounts of its natural resources and inhabitants (Map 7.4).

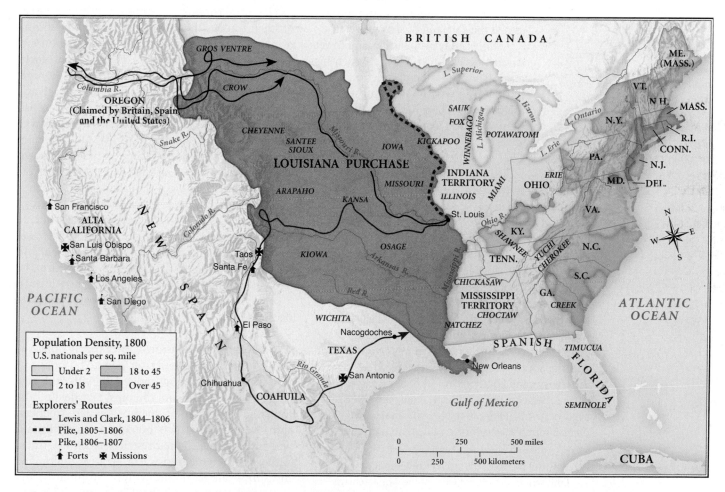

MAP 7.4 U.S. Population Density in 1803 and the Louisiana Purchase

When the United States purchased Louisiana from France in 1803, much of the land between the Appalachian Mountains and the Mississippi River remained in Indian hands: Only a few residents were of European or African descent. The vast lands beyond the Mississippi were virtually unknown, even after the epic explorations of Meriwether Lewis and William Clark, and Zebulon Pike. Still, President Jefferson predicted quite accurately that the vast Mississippi River Valley "from its fertility . . . will ere long yield half of our whole produce, and contain half of our whole population."

Aaron Burr, Man of Ambition

Burr came from distinguished stock. His maternal grandfather was the great revivalist Jonathan Edwards; his father, the president of Princeton. In this portrait of Burr as young man, artist Gilbert Stuart captures his remarkable hazel eyes, handsome features, and compelling charm. After dedicated service in the army during the revolution, Burr became a lawyer, a leading Republican politician, and, from 1801 to 1805, vice president of the United States. From the Collections of the New Jersey Historical Society, Newark, New Jersey.

Threats to the Union: Aaron Burr. Although the Louisiana Purchase was a stunning accomplishment that doubled the size of the nation, it created a new threat. New England Federalists, fearing that western expansion would diminish the power of their states and their party, were talking openly of leaving the Union. Alexander Hamilton refused to support their plan for a northern confederacy, so the secessionists turned to Aaron Burr, the ambitious vice president. When Hamilton accused Burr of participating in a conspiracy to destroy the Union, Burr challenged him to a pistol duel, which was illegal in most northern states. To uphold his aristocratic sense of "honor," Hamilton accepted the dare and died by gunshot.

This tragedy propelled Burr into yet another secessionist scheme. When his term as vice president ended in 1805, Burr moved west to avoid prosecution for dueling. There he conspired with General James Wilkinson, the military governor of the Louisiana Territory. Their plan remains a mystery, but it probably involved either the capture of territory in New Spain or a rebellion to establish Louisiana as a separate nation headed by Burr. But Wilkinson betrayed Burr: He arrested the former vice president as he led an armed force down the Ohio River. In a highly politicized trial presided over by Chief Justice John Marshall, the jury acquitted Burr of treason. Ultimately, the verdict was less important than the dangers to national unity that the trial revealed. The Republicans' policy of western expansion had increased party conflict and generated secessionist schemes in both New England and the Southwest. In the coming decades, regional differences and conflicts would continue to complicate American politics and challenge Madison's argument in "Federalist No. 10" that a large and diverse republic was more stable than a small one.

> ➤ Why did the Western Indian Confederacy fail to limit white settlement west of the Appalachians?

> ➤ How did Jeffersonian policy encourage expansion westward? Why did Jefferson and other expansionists believe the West was crucial to the well-being of the republic?

> ➤ Why did easterners leave their communities and move to the trans-Appalachian west?

The War of 1812 and the Transformation of Politics

Trouble was also brewing in Europe, where war had broken out again in 1802. For the next decade, American politicians tried to safeguard national interests while avoiding war. When this effort finally failed, it set in motion a series of dramatic political changes that destroyed the Federalist Party and split the Republicans into National and Jeffersonian factions.

Conflict in the Atlantic and the West

The Napoleonic Wars that ravaged Europe between 1802 and 1815 endangered American commerce. As Napoleon conquered European countries, he cut off their trade with Britain and ordered the seizure of neutral merchant ships that had stopped there. The British ministry responded with a naval blockade that stopped ships carrying goods to Europe, including American vessels filled with sugar and molasses from the French West Indies. The British navy also searched American merchant ships ostensibly for British deserters; in reality, the navy used these raids to replenish its forces, a practice known as impressment. Between 1802 and 1811, British officers seized nearly eight thousand sailors, including many American citizens. In 1807, American anger over these seizures turned to outrage when a British warship attacked the U.S. Navy vessel *Chesapeake,* killing three, wounding eighteen, and seizing four alleged deserters. "Never since the battle of Lexington have I seen this country in such a state of exasperation as at present," Jefferson declared.

The Embargo. To protect American interests while avoiding war, Jefferson pursued a policy of peaceful coercion. Working closely with Secretary of State James Madison, the president devised the Embargo Act of 1807, which prohibited American ships from leaving their home ports until Britain and France repealed their restrictions on U.S. trade. Although the embargo was a creative diplomatic measure — an economic weapon inspired by the successful boycotts of the 1760s and 1770s — it overestimated the dependence of Britain and France on American shipping, and it underestimated the resistance of New England merchants, who feared it would ruin them.

In fact, the embargo was a disaster for the American economy. Exports plunged from $108 million in 1806 to $22 million in 1808, which hurt farmers as well as merchants and prompted widespread demands for repeal. "Would to God," exclaimed one Federalist, "that the Embargo had done as little evil to ourselves as it has done to foreign nations."

Despite discontent over the embargo, voters elected Republican James Madison to the presidency in 1808. A powerful advocate for the Constitution, the architect of the Bill of Rights, and a prominent congressman and party leader, Madison had served the nation well. However, John Beckley, a loyal Republican, worried that Madison was "too timid and indecisive as a statesman." Events would prove Beckley right. Acknowledging the embargo's failure, Madison replaced it with a series of new economic restrictions, none of which persuaded Britain or France to respect American interests. "The Devil himself could not tell which government, England or France, is the most wicked," an exasperated congressman declared.

Tenskwatawa and Tippecanoe. Republican congressmen from the West had no doubts: For them, Britain was the primary offender. In particular, they pointed to its continued assistance to the Indians in the Ohio River Valley, a violation of the Treaty of Paris. In 1809, bolstered by British guns and supplies, the Shawnee war chief Tecumseh [*ta-KUM-sa*] and his brother, the prophet Tenskwatawa [*tens-QUA-ta-wa*], revived the Western Confederacy. As a young man, Tenskwatawa was known as Lalawethika ("Rattle" or "Noisemaker") because of his boastful ways and blatant alcoholism. In 1805, at age thirty, he had a profound emotional experience: He lapsed into unconsciousness; and when he awoke, he claimed to have visited the Master of Life, the main Shawnee god. Taking the name Tenskwatawa ("The One Who Opens the Door"), he preached a nativist message, urging his followers to shun Americans, "the children of the Evil Spirit . . . who have taken away your lands"; renounce alcohol; and return to

Tenskwatawa, "The Prophet," 1836

Tenskwatawa added a spiritual dimension to Native American resistance by urging a holy war against the invading whites and by calling for a return to sacred ancestral ways. His dress reflects his teachings: Note the animal skin shirt and the heavily ornamented ears. Tenskwatawa's religious message transcended the cultural differences among Indian peoples and helped his brother, Tecumseh, create a formidable political and military alliance. Smithsonian American Art Museum, Washington, D.C./Art Resource.

traditional ways. When Tenskwatawa founded a holy village, Prophetstown, near the juncture of the Tippecanoe and Wabash rivers in the Indiana Territory, he attracted warriors and wise men from many peoples — Kickapoo, Potawatomi, Winnebago, Ottawa, and Chippewa.

Inspired by the prophet's teachings, Tecumseh mobilized the western Indian peoples for war. Realizing the threat to American settlers, William Henry Harrison, the governor of the territory, decided on a preemptive strike. Taking advantage of Tecumseh's absence in the South (where he was seeking the support of the Chickasaws, Choctaws, and Creeks), Harrison mobilized one thousand troops and militiamen. Fending off the confederacy's warriors at the Battle of Tippecanoe, he burned Prophetstown to the ground In November 1811.

Republican War Hawks. With Britain helping the Indians in the West and seizing American ships and sailors in the Atlantic, Henry Clay of Kentucky, the new Speaker of the House of Representatives, and John C. Calhoun, a rising young congressman from South Carolina, pushed Madison toward war. Like other Republican war hawks from the West and South, they supported the acquisition of territory in British Canada and Spanish Florida. With national elections approaching, Madison demanded British respect for American sovereignty in the West and neutral rights on the Atlantic. When the British were slow to respond, Madison asked Congress for a declaration of war. In June 1812, a sharply divided Senate voted 19 to 13 for war, and the House of Representatives concurred, 79 to 49.

The underlying causes of the War of 1812 have been much debated. Officially, the United States went to war because of violations of its neutral rights: the seizure of merchant ships and the impressment of American sailors. But the Federalists who represented merchants' and seamen's interests in Congress voted against the war; and in the election of 1812, voters in New England and the Middle Atlantic states cast their ballots (and 89 electoral votes) for the Federalist candidate for president, De Witt Clinton of New York. Madison amassed most of his 128 electoral votes in the South and West, where voters strongly supported the war. Because of this regional split, many historians argue that the conflict was actually "a western war with eastern labels" (see Comparing American Voices, "Factional Politics and the War of 1812," pp. 226–227).

The War of 1812

The War of 1812 was a near disaster for the United States, both militarily and politically. Predictions of an easy advance into British Canada quickly proved wrong when an American invasion force had to retreat to Detroit. But Americans stayed on the offensive in the West: In April 1813, an American expedition burned York (present-day Toronto) before withdrawing. In September 1813, Commodore Oliver Hazard Perry defeated a small British flotilla on Lake Erie. And the next month, General William Henry Harrison led an expedition into Canada and triumphed over a British and Indian force at the Battle of the Thames. In that battle, Harrison's forces killed Tecumseh, who had become a general in the British army.

Political divisions prevented a major invasion of Canada in the East. New England Federalists opposed the war and prohibited their states' militias from attacking Canada. Boston merchants and banks refused to lend money to the federal government, making the war difficult to finance. In Congress, Daniel Webster, a dynamic young representative from New Hampshire, led Federalist opposition to higher taxes and tariffs and to the national conscription of state militiamen.

These domestic political conflicts contributed to the tide of battle gradually turning in Britain's favor. When the war began, American privateers had quickly captured scores of British merchant vessels but the Royal Navy soon seized the initiative. By 1813, a flotilla of British warships was harassing American ships and threatening seaports along the Atlantic coast. In 1814, a British fleet sailed up Chesapeake Bay. In August, British troops stormed ashore to attack Washington City and burn U.S. government buildings, including the Capitol. After two years of warfare, the United States was stalemated along the Canadian frontier and on the defensive in the Atlantic, and its new capital city was in ruins. The only positive news came from the Southwest. There a rugged slave-owning planter named Andrew Jackson led a force of militiamen from Tennessee to victory over the British-supported Creek Indians in the Battle of Horseshoe Bend (1814) and forced the Indians to cede 23 million acres of land (Map 7.5).

American military setbacks strengthened opposition to the war in New England. In 1814, Massachusetts Federalists called for a convention "to lay the foundation for a radical reform in the National Compact," and New England Federalists met in Hartford, Connecticut, to discuss strategy.

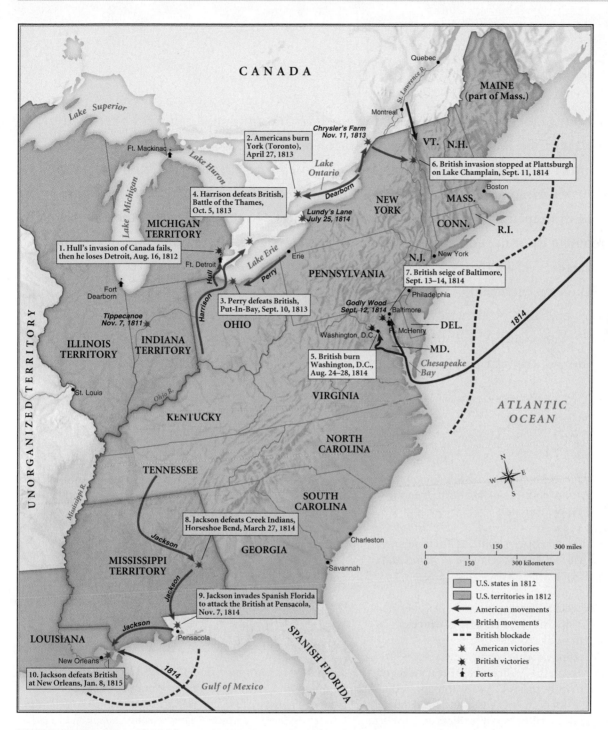

MAP 7.5   The War of 1812

Unlike the War of Independence, the War of 1812 had few large-scale military campaigns. In 1812 and 1813, most of the fighting took place along the Canadian border, as American armies and naval forces attacked British targets with mixed success (#1–4). The British took the offensive in 1814, launching a successful raid on Washington, but their attack on Baltimore failed; and they suffered heavy losses when they invaded the United States along Lake Champlain (#5–7). Near the Gulf of Mexico, American forces moved from one success to another: General Andrew Jackson defeated the pro-British Creek Indians at the Battle of Horseshoe Bend, won a victory in Pensacola, and, in the single major battle of the war, routed an invading British army at New Orleans (#8–10).

Factional Politics and the War of 1812

In the quarter-century following the ratification of the U.S. Constitution, American leaders had to deal with the wars of the French Revolution and Napoleon. These European conflicts posed two dangers to the United States. First, the naval blockades imposed by the British and the French raised the prospect of an American military response. Second, the ideological and political struggles in Europe threatened to deepen party conflicts in the United States. On three occasions, the danger to the American republic from the combination of an external military adversary and internal political turmoil loomed large. In 1798, the Federalist administration of John Adams almost went to war with France to help American merchants and undermine support for the Republican Party. In 1807, Thomas Jefferson's embargo on American commerce shocked Federalists and sharply increased political tensions. And, as the second and third of the following selections show, these political divisions became so acute during the War of 1812 that they threatened the existence of the American republic.

GEORGE WASHINGTON
Farewell Address, 1796

Washington's support for Alexander Hamilton's economic policies promoted the growth of political factionalism. Ignoring his own role in creating that political divide, Washington spoke out about the dangers of factionalism and, as his presidency proceeded, tried to stand above party conflicts. In his farewell address, Washington warned Americans to stand united and avoid the "Spirit of Party."

A solicitude for your welfare [prompts me] . . . to offer . . . the disinterested warnings of a parting friend, who can possibly have no personal motive to bias his counsels. . . .

The Unity of Government which constitutes you one people . . . is a main Pillar in the Edifice of your real independence . . . your tranquility at home; your peace abroad. . . . But it is easy to foresee, that, from different causes, and from different quarters, much pains will be taken, many artifices employed, to weaken in your minds the conviction of this truth. . . .

I have already intimated to you the danger of parties in the State, with particular reference to founding them on geographical discriminations. Let me now take a more comprehensive view, and warn you, in the most solemn manner, against the baneful effects of the Spirit of Party, generally.

This spirit, unfortunately, is inseparable from our nature, having its root in the strongest passions of the human mind. It exists under different shapes, in all governments, more or less stifled, controlled or repressed; but in those of the popular form, it is seen in its greatest rankness, and is truly their worst enemy.

The alternate dominion of one faction over another, sharpened by the spirit of revenge. . . , is itself a frightful despotism; but this leads at length to a more formal and permanent despotism.

SOURCE: James D. Richardson, ed., *A Compilation of the Messages and Papers of the Presidents, 1789–1896* (Washington, D.C.: U.S. Government Printing Office, 1896), 1: 213–215.

JOSIAH QUINCY ET AL.
Federalists Protest "Mr. Madison's War"

Washington's warning was to no avail. The parties—and the nation—divided sharply over the War of 1812. As Congress debated the issue of going to war against Great Britain, Josiah Quincy and other antiwar Federalist congressmen published a manifesto that asked a series of probing questions about the justifications for the war offered by President Madison and the military strategy proposed by Republican war hawks.

How will war upon the land [an invasion of British Canada] protect commerce upon the ocean? What balm has Canada for wounded honor? How are our mariners benefited by a war which exposes those who are free, without promising release to those who are impressed?

But it is said that war is demanded by honor. Is national honor a principle which thirsts after vengeance, and is appeased only by blood? . . . If honor demands a war with England, what opiate lulls that honor to sleep over the wrongs done us by France? On land, robberies, seizures, imprisonments, by French authority; at sea, pillage, sinkings, burnings, under French orders. These are notorious. Are they unfelt because they are French? . . .

There is . . . a headlong rushing into difficulties, with little calculation about the means, and little concern about the consequences. With a navy comparatively [small], we are about to enter into the lists against the greatest marine [power] on the globe. With a commerce unprotected and spread over every ocean, we propose to make a profit by privateering, and for this endanger the wealth of which we are honest proprietors. An invasion is threatened of the colonies [in Canada] of a power which, without putting a new ship into commission, or taking another soldier into pay, can spread alarm or desolation along the extensive range of our seaboard. . . .

What are the United States to gain by this war? Will the gratification of some privateersmen compensate the nation for that sweep of our legitimate commerce by the extended marine of our enemy which this desperate act invites? Will Canada compensate the Middle states for [the loss of] New York; or the Western states for [the loss of] New Orleans?

Let us not be deceived. A war of invasion may invite a retort of invasion. When we visit the peaceable, and as to us innocent, colonies of Great Britain with the horrors of war, can we be assured that our own coast will not be visited with like horrors?

SOURCE: *Annals of Congress*, 12th Cong., 1st sess., vol. 2, cols. 2219–2221.

HEZEKIAH NILES
A Republican Defends the War

During 1814, what the Federalists feared had come to pass: British ships blockaded American ports, and British troops invaded American territory. In January 1815, Republican editor Hezekiah Niles used the pages of his Baltimore newspaper, Niles's Weekly Register, to explain current Republican policies and blame the Federalists for American reverses.

It is universally known that the causes for which we declared war are no obstruction to peace. The practice of blockade and impressment having ceased by the general pacification of Europe, our government is content to leave the principle as it was. . . .

We have no further business in hostility, than such as is purely defensive; while that of Great Britain is to humble or subdue us. The war, on our part, has become a contest for

life, liberty and property—on the part of our enemy, of revenge or ambition. . . .

What then are we to do? Are we to encourage him by divisions among ourselves—to hold out the hope of a separation of the states and a civil war—to refuse to bring forth the resources of the country against him? . . . I did think that in a defensive war—a struggle for all that is valuable—that all parties would have united. But it is not so—every measure calculated to replenish the treasury or raise men is opposed as though it were determined to strike the "star spangled banner" and exalt the bloody cross. Look at the votes and proceedings of congress—and mark the late spirit [to secede from the Union] . . . that existed in Massachusetts, and see with what unity of action every thing has been done [by New England Federalists] to harass and embarrass the government. Our loans have failed; and our soldiers have wanted their pay, because those [New England merchants] who had the greater part of the monied capital covenanted with each other to refuse its aid to the country. They had a right, legally; to do this; and perhaps, also, by all the artifices of trade or power that money gave them, to oppress others not of their "stamp" and depress the national credit—but history will shock posterity by detailing the length to which they went to bankrupt the republic. . . .

To conclude—why does the war continue? It is not the fault of the government—we demand no extravagant thing. I answer the question, and say—*it lasts because Great Britain depends on the exertions of her "party" in this country to destroy our resources, and compel "unconditional submission."*

Thus the war began, and is continued, by our divisions.

SOURCE: *Niles Weekly Register*, January 28, 1815.

ANALYZING THE EVIDENCE

➤ According to Washington, what is the ultimate cause of political factionalism? Why might he believe that factionalism is most dangerous in "popular"—that is, republican—governments?

➤ What specific dangers did Josiah Quincy and the Federalists foresee with regard to Republican war policies? Read the section on the War of 1812 in the text, and then discuss the accuracy of their predictions. Why might New England Federalists oppose an imperialistic war that would add western states to the Union?

➤ According to Hezekiah Niles, by 1815, what were the war goals of the Republican administration? How had those goals changed since the start of the war? Niles charged the Federalists and their supporters with impeding the American war effort. What were his specific charges? Did they have any merit?

Some delegates to the Hartford convention proposed secession, but most wanted to revise the Constitution instead. To end Virginia's domination of the presidency, the delegates proposed a constitutional amendment that would limit the office to a single four-year term and rotate it among citizens from different states. They also suggested amendments restricting commercial embargoes to sixty days and requiring a two-thirds majority in Congress to declare war, prohibit trade, or admit a new state to the Union.

As a minority party in Congress and the nation, the Federalists could prevail only if the war was going badly—a very real prospect. Britain's triumph over Napoleon in Europe, Albert Gallatin warned Henry Clay in May, meant that a "well organized and large army is [now] . . . ready together with a super abundant naval force, to act immediately against us." As the British took the offensive late in the summer of 1814, only an American naval victory on Lake Champlain averted an invasion of the Hudson River Valley. A few months later, thousands of seasoned British troops landed outside New Orleans, threatening American control of the Mississippi River. The United States was under military pressure from both north and south. Given the "hostile attitude" of New England, Gallatin feared that "a continuance of the war might prove vitally fatal to the United States."

Fortunately for the young American republic, Britain wanted peace. The twenty-year war with France in Europe had sapped its wealth and energy, and so it entered into negotiations with the United States in Ghent, Belgium. At first the American commissioners—John Quincy Adams, Gallatin, and Clay—demanded territory in Canada and Florida, and British diplomats insisted on an Indian buffer state between the United States and Canada. Ultimately, both sides realized that these objectives were not worth the costs of prolonged warfare. The Treaty of Ghent, signed on Christmas Eve 1814, retained the prewar borders of the United States.

The result hardly justified three years of fighting, but a final military victory lifted Americans' morale. Before news of the Treaty of Ghent reached the United States, newspaper headlines proclaimed an "ALMOST INCREDIBLE VICTORY!! GLORIOUS NEWS": On January 8, 1815, General Jackson's troops (including a contingent of French-speaking black Americans, the Corps d'Afrique) crushed the British forces attacking New Orleans. The Americans fought from carefully constructed breastworks and rained "grapeshot and cannister bombs" on the massed British formations. The British lost seven hundred men, and two thousand more were wounded or taken prisoner. By contrast, just thirteen Americans died, and only fifty-eight were wounded. The victory made Jackson a national hero and redeemed the nation's battered pride. The war had increased regional tensions, but the peace undercut the Hartford convention's demands for a significant revision of the Constitution.

The Federalist Legacy

The War of 1812 ushered in a new phase of the Republican political revolution. Before the conflict, Federalists had strongly supported Alexander Hamilton's program of national mercantilism—a funded debt, a central bank, and tariffs—while Jeffersonian Republicans opposed Hamilton's program. After the war, the Republicans split into two factions. Henry Clay led the National Republicans. In 1816, he pushed through legislation creating the Second Bank of the United States and, in part because of the difficulties in financing the War of 1812, President Madison signed it. The following year, Clay won passage of the Bonus Bill, sponsored by Representative Calhoun of South Carolina, which established a national fund for roads and other internal improvements. Madison vetoed it: Along with many other Jeffersonian Republicans, he believed that funding internal improvements by the national government was contrary to the Constitution.

Meanwhile, the Federalist Party was in severe decline. Nationalist Republicans had won the allegiance of many Federalist voters in the East, and the profarmer policies of Jeffersonian Republicans maintained their party's dominance in the South and West. "No Federal character can run with success," Gouverneur Morris of New York lamented. The election of 1818 bore out his pessimism: Following the election Republicans outnumbered Federalists 37 to 7 in the Senate and 156 to 27 in the House. Westward expansion and the success of Jefferson's Revolution of 1800 had ended both the Federalists and the First Party System.

John Marshall's Jurisprudence. Although the Federalists were no more, their policies remained very much in evidence because of John Marshall's long tenure on the Supreme Court. Appointed chief justice by President John Adams in January 1801, Marshall, a committed Federalist, dominated the Court until 1822 and strongly influenced its deliberations until his death in 1835. Marshall's success reflected the power of his logic and the

Battle of New Orleans, by Jean Hyacinthe de Laclotte (detail)

As their artillery (right center) bombarded the American lines, British troops attacked the center of General Andrew Jackson's troops. At the same time, a column of redcoats (foreground) tried to turn the right flank of the American fortifications. Secure behind their battlements, Jackson's forces repelled the assaults, leaving the ground littered with British casualties and taking thousands of prisoners. New Orleans Museum of Art, gift of Edgar William and Bernice Chrysler Garbisch.

force of his personality. By winning the support of Joseph Story and other Nationalist Republican justices on the Court, Marshall shaped the evolution of the Constitution.

Three principles informed Marshall's jurisprudence: He was committed to judicial authority, the supremacy of national laws, and traditional property rights (Table 7.1). After Marshall claimed the right of judicial review for the Court in 1803, in *Marbury v. Madison,* the doctrine evolved slowly. The Supreme Court did

not void another congressional law until the *Dred Scott* decision in 1857 (see Chapter 13). But the Marshall Court frequently overturned state laws that infringed on the U.S. Constitution, as it did in the important case of *McCulloch v. Maryland* (1819). When Congress created the Second Bank of the United States in 1816, it allowed the bank to set up branches in the states. To preserve the competitive position of its state-chartered banks, the Maryland legislature imposed an annual tax of $15,000 on notes issued by the Baltimore

John Marshall, **by Chester Harding, c. 1830**

Even at the age of seventy-five, John Marshall (1755–1835) had a commanding personal presence. After he became chief justice of the U.S. Supreme Court in 1801, Marshall elevated the Court from a minor department of the national government to a major institution in American legal and political life. His decisions on judicial review, contract rights, the regulation of commerce, and national banking permanently shaped the character of American constitutional law. Boston Athenaeum.

branch of the Second Bank. The Second Bank immediately protested that the Maryland law infringed on the powers of the national government and was therefore unconstitutional. In response, lawyers for the state of Maryland invoked Jefferson's argument that Congress lacked the constitutional authority to charter a national bank. Even if a national bank was legitimate, the lawyers argued, Maryland had a right to tax its activities within the state.

Marshall and the Nationalist Republicans on the Court firmly rejected both arguments. The Second Bank was constitutional, said the chief justice, because it was "necessary and proper" given the national government's responsibility to control currency and credit. Like Alexander Hamilton, Marshall adopted a loose construction of the Constitution. If the goal of a law is "legitimate [and] . . . within the scope of the Constitution," he wrote, then "all means which are appropriate" to secure that goal are also constitutional. The chief justice also argued that "the power to tax involves the power to destroy" and suggested that Maryland's bank tax would render the national government

TABLE 7.1	Major Decisions of the Marshall Court	
Date	**Case**	**Significance of Decision**
1803	*Marbury v. Madison*	Asserts principle of judicial review
1810	*Fletcher v. Peck*	Protects property rights through broad reading of Constitution's contract clause
1819	*Dartmouth College v. Woodward*	Safeguards property rights, especially of chartered corporations
1819	*McCulloch v. Maryland*	Interprets Constitution to give broad powers to national government
1824	*Gibbons v. Ogden*	Gives national government jurisdiction over interstate commerce

"dependent on the states," an outcome that "was not intended by the American people" who ratified the Constitution.

The Marshall Court again asserted the dominance of national statutes over state legislation in *Gibbons v. Ogden* (1824). The decision struck down a monopoly that the New York legislature had granted Aaron Ogden for steamboat passenger service across the Hudson River to New Jersey. Asserting that the Constitution gave the federal government the authority to regulate interstate commerce, the chief justice sided with Thomas Gibbons, who held a federal license to transport people and goods between the two states.

Property Rights. Marshall also used the Constitution to uphold Federalist notions of property rights. During the 1790s, Thomas Jefferson and other Republicans had celebrated the primacy of statutes enacted by "the will of THE PEOPLE." In response, Federalist politicians warned that popular sovereignty would lead to "tyranny of the majority" if state legislatures enacted statutes that infringed on the property rights of wealthy citizens, and Federalist judges vowed to void those laws.

Marshall was no exception. He was determined to protect individuals' property from laws passed by the state legislatures, and he invoked the contract clause of the Constitution to do it. The contract clause (in Article 1, Section 10) prohibits the states from passing any law "impairing the obligation of contracts." The delegates at the Philadelphia convention included the clause to prevent state legislation that kept creditors from seizing the lands and goods of debtors. In *Fletcher v. Peck* (1810), Marshall expanded the clause by broadly defining *contract* to include the grants and charters made by state governments. The case involved a large grant of land made by the Georgia legislature to the Yazoo Land Company. When a new legislature canceled the grant, alleging fraud and bribery, speculators who had already purchased Yazoo lands appealed to the Supreme Court to uphold their titles. Marshall ruled that the legislative grant was a contract that could not subsequently be changed. This far-reaching decision safeguarded vested property rights and, by protecting out-of-state investors, promoted the development of a national capitalist economy.

The Court extended its defense of vested property rights in *Dartmouth College v. Woodward* (1819). Dartmouth College was a private institution established by a charter granted by King George III. In 1816, New Hampshire's Republican legislature enacted a statute that converted the school into a public university. The Dartmouth trustees opposed the legislation and hired Daniel Webster to plead their case. A renowned constitutional lawyer, as well as a leading Federalist, Webster cited the Court's decision in *Fletcher v. Peck* and argued that the royal charter constituted a contract that could not be altered by the state legislature. The Supreme Court agreed and upheld the rights of the college.

The Rise of John Quincy Adams. Even as Marshall incorporated the important Federalist principles of judicial review, the primacy of national law, and corporate property rights into the American legal system, the political elite and the voting citizenry embraced the outlook of the Republican party. The career of John Quincy Adams was a case in point. Although he was the son of President John Adams, a Federalist, John Quincy had joined the Republican Party before the War of 1812. He came to national attention for his role in negotiating the Treaty of Ghent, which ended the war.

Adams then served brilliantly as secretary of state for two terms under President James Monroe (1817–1825). Ignoring traditional Republican antagonism toward Great Britain, in 1817 Adams negotiated the Rush-Bagot Treaty, which limited American and British naval forces on the Great Lakes. The following year, he concluded another agreement with Britain that set the forty-ninth parallel as the border between Canada and the lands of the Louisiana Purchase. In the Adams-Onís Treaty of 1819, the secretary persuaded Spain to cede Florida to the United States (Map 7.6). In return, the American government took responsibility for its citizens' financial claims against Spain, renounced Jefferson's earlier claim that Spanish

Texas was part of the Louisiana Purchase, and agreed on a compromise boundary between New Spain and the state of Louisiana, which had entered the Union in 1812.

Finally, Adams persuaded President Monroe to articulate American national policy with respect to the Western Hemisphere. At Adams's behest, Monroe warned Spain and other European powers in 1823 to keep their hands off the Spanish colonies in Latin America that had fought for and established independent republics. The American continents were not "subject for further colonization," the president declared—a policy that thirty years later became known as the Monroe Doctrine. In return, Monroe pledged that the United States would not "interfere in the internal concerns" of European nations. Thanks to Adams, the United States had asserted diplomatic leadership of the Western Hemisphere and gained international acceptance of its claims to nearly all the lands

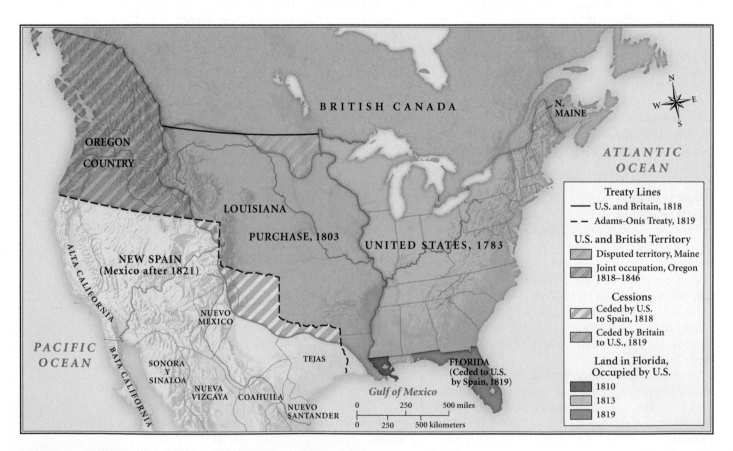

MAP 7.6 Defining the National Boundaries, 1800–1820

After the War of 1812, American diplomats negotiated treaties with Great Britain and Spain that defined the boundaries of the Louisiana Purchase, with British Canada to the north and New Spain (which in 1821 became the independent nation of Mexico) to the south and west. These treaties eliminated the threat of border wars with neighboring states for a generation, giving the United States a much-needed period of peace and security.

The American Eagle Over New Orleans

Jefferson's purchase of Louisiana made New Orleans part of the United States, but many districts in the city retained their French look (note the steeply pitched roofs on the right) and culture for decades. A traveler noted that "the great enmity existing between the Creoles [the French settlers] . . . and the Americans results in fights and Challenges — there are some of both sides in jail. This *View of New Orleans Taken from the Plantation of Marigny* was painted by John L. Boqueto de Woiserie in 1803. Chicago Historical Society.

south of the forty-ninth parallel and east of the Rocky Mountains.

The appearance of a national consensus after two decades of bitter party politics prompted observers to dub James Monroe's presidency the "Era of Good Feeling." The political harmony was real; but it was also transitory. The Republican Party was increasingly divided between the National faction, led by Clay and Adams, and the Jeffersonian faction, soon to be led by Martin Van Buren and Andrew Jackson. The two groups differed sharply over many issues, including federal support for internal improvements like roads and canals. As the aging Jefferson himself complained about the National Republicans, "You see so many of these new republicans main-

taining in Congress the rankest doctrines of the old federalists." This division in the ranks of the Republican Party and the disappearance of the Federalists would soon produce a Second Party System, in which new parties — national-minded Whigs and state-focused Democrats — faced off against each other (see Chapter 10). By the early 1820s, one cycle of American politics and economic debate had ended, and another was about to begin.

> ➤ What were the causes of the War of 1812? Where did Republicans and Federalists stand on declaring and then fighting the war? What regional tensions did the war expose?

➤ How did the decisions of the Supreme Court between 1801 and 1820 affect the nation's understanding of the Constitution? How did they change American society?

SUMMARY

In this chapter, we have traced three interrelated themes: public policy, westward expansion, and party politics. We began by examining the contrasting public policies advocated by Alexander Hamilton and Thomas Jefferson. A Federalist, Hamilton supported a strong national government and created a fiscal infrastructure (the national debt, tariffs, and a national bank) to spur economic development in trade and manufacturing. By contrast, Jefferson wanted to preserve the authority of state governments; and he envisioned an America enriched by farming rather than industry.

The westward movement promoted by Jefferson and his Republican Party changed many aspects of American life. As hundreds of thousands of yeomen farmers, southern planters, and enslaved Africans moved west, they sparked new conflicts with the Indian peoples and transformed the agricultural economy by dramatically increasing the market sale of farm produce. Expansion westward also shaped American diplomacy: The Louisiana Purchase, the War of 1812, and many of the treaties negotiated by John Quincy Adams were a response, at least in part, to the American drive west.

Finally, there was the unexpected rise of the First Party System and its equally unexpected decline. As Hamilton's policies split the political elite, the French Revolution divided Americans into hostile ideological groups. The result was two decades of bitterness over controversial measures — the Federalists' Sedition Act, the Republicans' Embargo Act, and Madison's decision to go to war with Britain. Although the Federalist Party faded away, it left as its enduring legacy Hamilton's financial innovations and John Marshall's constitutional jurisprudence. Tempered by war and political factions, a new generation of Republican leaders would face the task of devising their own vision of America's future. As Chapter 8 will show, mounting regional tensions over a number of issues — most important, the future of slavery — would cloud this vision.

Connections: Economy and Society

Before the American Revolution, both northern and southern colonies had different types of farming economies: one characterized by yeoman families' raising grain; the other, by large planters, who relied on enslaved laborers to grow tobacco and rice for export. After the Revolution, the two economies began to diverge in other ways. As we pointed out in the essay that began Part Two (p. 135):

> Beginning in the 1780s, northern merchants financed a banking system and organized a rural system of manufacturing. . . . Meanwhile, southern planters continued their dependence on enslaved African Americans and began to export a new staple crop — cotton — to markets in the North and in Europe.

In Chapter 8, we will explore the creation of a capitalist commonwealth — an increasingly urban, commercial society — in the North. And we will show how life in this society fostered a democratic republican culture that encouraged social mobility for men and new marriage rules and child-rearing practices. In Chapter 8, we also will probe the nature of the aristocratic republican culture that continued to characterize the slave-based society of the South, and we will examine the Missouri crisis of 1819–1821, the first major conflict between these two increasingly distinct societies.

In the part opening, we also noted that "many yeomen farm families migrated to the West to grow grain." As we will see in Chapter 8, these families were particularly affected by the Second Great Awakening, the religious revival that fundamentally changed American culture.

CHAPTER REVIEW QUESTIONS

➤ Explain the rise and fall of the First Party System. How did the policies pursued by Republican presidents between 1801 and 1825 differ from those implemented by Hamilton and the Federalists during the 1790s? Why did the Federalist agenda fall out of favor? What legacy did the Federalists leave?

➤ What impact did the two great developments of this period — the French Revolution and war in Europe, and westward expansion in the United States — have on each other?

TIMELINE

1783	Treaty of Paris opens access to the west
1784	Iroquois peoples cede lands in New York
1787	Northwest Ordinance
1789	Judiciary Act establishes federal court system Outbreak of French Revolution
1790	Hamilton wins public credit system
1790–1791	Western Confederacy defeats American armies
1791	Bill of Rights ratified Bank of the United States is chartered
1792	Kentucky joins Union; Tennessee follows (1796) French Republic formed
1793	King Louis XVI executed Madison and Jefferson found Republican Party War between Britain and France; Washington's Proclamation of Neutrality
1794	Whiskey Rebellion in western Pennsylvania Battle of Fallen Timbers
1795	Jay's Treaty with Great Britain Pinckney's Treaty with Spain Treaty of Greenville recognizes Indian land rights
1798	XYZ Affair cuts off trade with France Alien, Sedition, and Naturalization Acts Kentucky and Virginia resolutions
1800	Jefferson elected in "Revolution of 1800"
1801	John Marshall heads Supreme Court
1801–1807	Gallatin reduces national debt
1802–1807	France and Britain seize American ships
1803	Louisiana Purchase *Marbury v. Madison* asserts judicial review
1804–1806	Lewis and Clark explore West
1807	Embargo Act cripples American shipping
1808	Madison elected president
1811	Battle of Tippecanoe
1812–1815	War of 1812
1817–1825	Era of Good Feeling
1819	Adams-Onís Treaty *McCulloch v. Maryland* *Dartmouth College v. Woodward*

FOR FURTHER EXPLORATION

In *American Politics in the Early Republic* (1993), James Roger Sharp describes the near disintegration of the new nation. One cause was the Whiskey Rebellion, the subject of a probing study by Thomas P. Slaughter (1986). For the impact of the French Revolution on the Atlantic world, see "Liberty, Equality, Fraternity: Exploring the French Revolution" (**chnm.gmu.edu/revolution/**). Women are the subject of Rosemarie Zagarri, *A Woman's Dilemma: Mercy Otis Warren and the American Revolution* (1995), and Linda Kerber, *No Constitutional Right to Be Ladies: Women and the Obligations of Citizenship* (1999).

Washington's strong leadership is a central theme of William Martin's fictionalized biography, *Citizen Washington* (1999). For a sense of Washington's personality, read his correspondence, available at **www.virginia.edu/gwpapers/**. Abundant material on Thomas Jefferson's life can be accessed online at **www.pbs.org/jefferson**; Jefferson's ideas "On Politics & Government" are available at **etext.virginia.edu/jefferson/quotations**. David McCullough's highly readable biography, *John Adams* (2001), draws material from **www.masshist.org/digitaladams/aea**. For Alexander Hamilton, see Ron Chernow, *Alexander Hamilton* (2004), and **www.alexanderhamilton exhibition.org/**. On the tumultuous election of 1800, see John Ferling, *Adams vs. Jefferson* (2004).

For the explorations of the West, visit **www.pbs.org/lewisandclark** and **www.americanjourneys.org/**. Gregory Evans Dowd, *A Spirited Resistance: The North American Indian Struggle for Unity, 1745–1815* (1992), describes the Indian Resistance, as does the "Chickasaw Historical Research Page" (**home.flash.net/~kma/**). Two fine studies of cultural interactions between native peoples and white Americans are Theda Perdue, *Cherokee Women: Gender and Culture Change, 1700–1835* (1998), and William G. McLoughlin, *Cherokee Renascence in the New Republic* (1986).

Ralph Louis Ketcham's *Presidents Above Party: The First American Presidency, 1789–1829* (1984) probes the political ideology of the early republic; Gore Vidal's *Burr: A Novel* (1973) offers an entertaining narrative of the life of Aaron Burr. See "A Century of Lawmaking for a New Nation" (**memory.loc.gov/ammem/amlaw/lawhome.html**) for the text of congressional documents and debates. The site also contains information about and maps of Indian land cessions between 1784 and 1894. Donald R. Hickey, *The War of 1812: A Forgotten Conflict* (1989), places that struggle in its economic and diplomatic context. Also see "The War of 1812" (**members.tripod.com/~war1812/**).

TEST YOUR KNOWLEDGE

To assess your command of the material in this chapter, see the Online Study Guide at **bedfordstmartins.com/henretta.**

For Web sites, images, and documents related to topics and places in this chapter, visit **bedfordstmartins.com/makehistory.**

8 Creating a Republican Culture

1790–1820

B Y THE 1820S, A SENSE of optimism pervaded white American society. "The temperate zone of North America already exhibits many signs that it is the promised land of civil liberty, and of institutions designed to liberate and exalt the human race," declared a Kentucky judge in a Fourth of July speech. White Americans had good reason to feel fortunate. They lived under a representative republican government, free from arbitrary taxation and the oppression of an established church.

Inspired by their political freedom, these Americans sought to extend republican principles throughout their society. However, they did not agree on what those principles were. For entrepreneurial-minded merchants, farmers, and political leaders, republicanism meant **capitalism**: They wanted to use the power of republican government to solidify capitalist cultural values and create a dynamic market economy. Invoking the assistance of state governments, they advocated mercantilist policies that would assist private businesses to enhance the "common-wealth." Other citizens celebrated republican social values. In the North, they championed a democratic republicanism, an equality in family and social relationships. In the South, where class and race sharply divided society, politicians and political writers devised an aristocratic republicanism that stressed liberty for whites rather than equality for all. Yet

◀ **The Fourth of July in Philadelphia, c. 1811**

By the early nineteenth century, the Fourth of July had become a popular holiday celebrating America's republican government. This detail from a painting by John Lewis Krimmel links the new nation to the Greek and Roman republics through architecture (the building and the statue), notes its social diversity (by including blacks as well as whites), and hints at the tenor of its social life. The young man buying an alcoholic drink and flirting with the young mother may well engage in some rowdy behavior before Independence Day is over. Pennsylvania Academy of the Fine Arts, Philadelphia. Pennsylvania Academy Purchase (from the estate of Paul Beck, Jr.).

another vision of American republicanism that attracted adherents in all regions emerged during the Second Great Awakening, the massive religious revival that swept the nation during the first half of the nineteenth century. For the many Americans who embraced this religious vision, the United States was both a great experiment in republican government and the seedbed of a new Christian civilization that would redeem the world—a moral mission that, for better or worse, would inform American diplomacy in the centuries to come.

The Capitalist Commonwealth

"If movement and the quick succession of sensations and ideas constitute life," observed a French visitor to the United States, "here one lives a hundred fold more than elsewhere; here, all is circulation, motion, and boiling agitation." Circulation and motion were especially evident in the Northeast, where republican state legislatures actively promoted banking and commerce. "Experiment follows experiment; enterprise follows enterprise," a European traveler noted, and "riches and poverty follow." Of the two, riches were the more apparent. Beginning around 1800, the per capita income of Americans increased by more than 1 percent a year, more than 30 percent in a single generation.

Banks, Manufacturing, and Markets

America was "a Nation of Merchants," a British visitor reported from Philadelphia in 1798, "keen in the pursuit of wealth in all the various modes of acquiring it." And acquire it they did, exploiting the opportunities to make spectacular profits from the wars (1793-1815) triggered by the French Revolution. Fur trader John Jacob Astor and merchant Robert Oliver became the nation's first millionaires. Oliver began his career working for an Irish linen firm in Baltimore and then started trading on his own in West Indian coffee and sugar. Astor, who migrated from Germany to New York in 1784, became wealthy carrying furs from the Pacific Northwest to markets in China.

Banking and Credit. To finance mercantile enterprises, Americans needed a banking system. Before the Revolution, farmers relied on government-sponsored land banks for loans, while merchants arranged partnerships or obtained credit from

A Cloth Merchant, 1789

Elijah Boardman (1760–1832) was a prosperous storekeeper in New Milford, Connecticut, who eventually became a U.S. senator. Like other American traders, he imported huge quantities of cloth from Britain. When the wars of the 1790s cut off trade, some merchants financed the domestic production of textiles. Others, including Boardman, turned to land speculation. In 1795, he joined the Connecticut Land Company and bought huge tracts in Connecticut's Western Reserve, including the present towns of Medina, Palmyra, and Boardman, Ohio. Ralph Earl painted this portrait in 1789. Elijah Boardman, the Metropolitan Museum of Art, New York, Bequest of Susan W. Tyler, 1979.

British suppliers. To facilitate commercial transactions, Philadelphia merchants persuaded the Confederation Congress to charter the Bank of North America in 1781, and traders in Boston and New York soon founded similar lending institutions. "Our monied capital has so much increased from the Introduction of Banks, & the Circulation of the Funds," Philadelphia merchant William Bingham boasted in 1791, "that the Necessity of Soliciting Credits from England will no longer exist."

That same year, Federalists in Congress chartered the First Bank of the United States. The Bank

The China Trade

Following the Revolution, New England merchants took an active role in the long-standing European trade with China. In this painting by George Chinnery (1774–1852), the American flag flies prominently in front of the warehouse district in Canton. There, merchants exchanged bundles of American furs for cargoes of Chinese silks and porcelain plates, cups, and serving dishes. Bridgeman Art Library Ltd.

issued notes and made commercial loans. Its profits averaged a handsome 8 percent annually; and by 1805, the bank had branches in eight major cities. However, Jeffersonian Republicans opposed the Bank: They claimed it was unconstitutional and potentially oppressive, and that it encouraged "a consolidated, energetic government supported by public creditors, speculators, and other insidious men lacking in public spirit of any kind." When the bank's twenty-year charter expired in 1811, it was not renewed. To fill the gap, merchants, artisans, and farmers petitioned their state legislatures to charter banks. By 1816, when Congress chartered the Second Bank of the United States, there were 246 state-chartered banks with $68 million in banknotes in circulation. But many of these state banks were shady operations that issued notes without adequate specie reserves and made ill-advised loans to insiders.

State banking policies and those of the Second Bank were a factor in the Panic of 1819. But the primary cause of the financial crisis was an abrupt 30 percent drop in world agricultural prices. As their income plummeted, many planters and farmers could not pay their debts to storekeepers, wholesale merchants, and banks, sending those businesses into bankruptcy. By 1821, the state banks that were still solvent had just $45 million in circulation. The panic gave Americans their first taste of a **business cycle,** the periodic expansion and contraction of production and employment that are inherent to a market economy. And it left a legacy of popular hostility to banks that would prove a political force in the coming decades.

Rural Manufacturing. The Panic of 1819 also revealed that artisans and yeomen as well as

The Yankee Peddler, c. 1830

Even in 1830, most Americans lived too far from a market town to go there regularly to buy goods. Instead, they purchased their tinware, clocks, textiles, and other manufactures from peddlers, often from New England, who traveled far and wide in small horse-drawn vans like the one pictured in the doorway. Courtesy IBM Corporation, Armonk, New York.

merchants now depended for their prosperity on the market economy. Before 1800, most artisans in New England worked part-time and sold their handicrafts locally. In central Massachusetts, a French traveler found many houses "inhabited by men who are both cultivators and artisans; one is a tanner, another a shoemaker, another sells goods, but all are farmers." In the Middle Atlantic region, artisans bartered products with neighbors. Clock-maker John Hoff of Lancaster, Pennsylvania, exchanged his fine, wooden-cased instruments for a dining table, a bedstead, and labor on his small farm. By 1820, many artisans — shipbuilders in seacoast towns, ironworkers in Pennsylvania and Maryland, and shoemakers in Massachusetts — had expanded their reach and were selling their products in regional and national markets.

By 1800, American entrepreneurs had developed a rural manufacturing network similar to the European outwork system (see Chapter 1). Enterprising merchants bought raw materials, hired workers in farm families to process them, and sold the finished manufactures in regional or national markets. "Straw hats and Bonnets are manufactured by many families," an official in Maine noted in the 1810s, while another observer estimated that "probably 8,000 females" in the vicinity of Foxborough, Massachusetts, braided rye straw into hats for market sale. Merchants shipped these products — shoes, brooms, palm-leaf hats, and cups, baking pans, and other tin utensils — to seaport cities, and New England peddlers, equipped "with a horse and a cart covered with a box or with a wagon," carried them to the rural South, where they earned the dubious reputation of being crafty, hard-bargaining Yankees.

This expansion of household production and the market economy reflected innovations in the organization of production and in marketing rather than in technology. American manufacturers only gradually adopted water-powered machines, the technology that triggered the Industrial Revolution in Britain. As early as the 1780s, merchants in New England and the Middle Atlantic states built small mills with water-powered machines that carded and combed wool—and later cotton—into long strands. But until the 1820s, they used the household-based outwork system for the next steps in the textile manufacturing process: They paid women and children on farms to spin the strands into thread and yarn on foot-driven spinning wheels, and men in other households to use foot-powered looms to weave the yarn into cloth. In his "Letter on Manufactures" (1810), Secretary of the Treasury Albert Gallatin estimated that there were 2,500 outwork weavers in New England. A decade later, more than 12,000 household workers were weaving woolen cloth, which was then pounded flat and given a smooth finish in water-powered fulling mills. Even before production was centralized in factories, then, America had a profitable and expanding system of textile manufacturing in the Northeast (see Chapter 9).

The penetration of the market economy into rural areas offered new opportunities—and new risks—to farmers. Ambitious farm families switched from growing crops for subsistence to raising livestock for sale. They sold meat, butter, and cheese to city markets and cattle hides to the booming shoe industry. "Along the whole road from Boston, we saw women engaged in making cheese," a Polish traveler reported from central Massachusetts. Other farm families raised sheep and sold raw wool to textile manufacturers. Processing these raw materials brought new businesses to many farming towns. In 1792, Concord, Massachusetts, had one slaughterhouse and five small tanneries; a decade later, the town boasted eleven slaughterhouses and six large tanneries.

The Environmental Impact of Early Industry. As the rural economy churned out more goods, it significantly altered the environment. Foul odors from stockyards and tanning pits wafted over Concord and many other leather-producing towns. In addition, tanners, who used hemlock bark to process hides into leather, cut down thousands of acres of trees each year. The multiplication of livestock—dairy cows, cattle, and especially sheep—brought the destruction of even more trees, felled to create vast pastures and meadows. By the mid-nineteenth century, most of the forests in southern New England and eastern New York were gone: "The hills had been stripped of their timber," New York's *Catskill Messenger* noted, "so as to present their huge, rocky projections." Scores of textile milldams dotted New England's rivers, altering

their flow and making it difficult for fish to reach their upriver spawning grounds. Even as the income of many farmers rose, the quality of their natural environment deteriorated.

The new capitalist-run market economy had other drawbacks, too. Rural parents and their children worked longer and harder, making yarn, hats, and brooms during the winter and then doing their regular farming chores during the warmer seasons. More important, these farm families lost a measure of their economic independence as they toiled as part-time wage earners and bought the textiles, shoes, and hats they had once made for themselves. At the same time the new market economy was making families and communities more productive and prosperous, it was reducing their self-sufficiency.

Transportation Bottlenecks and Government Initiatives

America's very size threatened to stifle its economic growth. Water transport was the quickest and cheapest way to get goods to market, but most new settlements were not near navigable streams. Consequently, improved overland trade became a high priority for the new state governments. Between 1793 and 1812, the Massachusetts legislature granted charters to more than one hundred private turnpike companies. These charters gave the companies special legal status and often included monopoly rights to a transportation route. Pennsylvania issued fifty-five charters, including one to the Lancaster Turnpike Company. The company quickly built a graded gravel road between Lancaster and Philadelphia, a distance of 65 miles. The venture was expensive—investors saw only modest profits—but it gave an enormous boost to the regional economy. "The turnpike is finished," a farm woman noted, "and we can now go to town at all times and in all weather." A boom in turnpike construction soon connected dozens of inland market centers to seaport cities.

Meanwhile, state governments and private entrepreneurs improved water transport by dredging rivers to make them navigable and by constructing canals to bypass waterfalls or rapids. But there was no water route through the Appalachian Mountains until the 1820s, when New York built the Erie Canal to connect the state's central and western counties to the Hudson River (see Chapter 9). Until then, settlers in Kentucky, Tennessee, and the southern regions of Ohio, Indiana, and Illinois paid premium prices for land near the tributaries of the great Ohio and Mississippi

View of Cincinnati, **by John Casper Wild, c. 1835**

Thanks to its location on the Ohio River, Cincinnati quickly became one of the major processing centers for grain and hogs in the trans-Appalachian west. By the 1820s, passenger steamboats and freight barges connected the city with Pittsburgh to the north and the ocean port of New Orleans far to the south.   Museum of Fine Arts, Boston.

rivers, and speculators bought up property in the cities along their banks: Cincinnati, Louisville, Chattanooga, and St. Louis. Farmers and merchants built barges to carry cotton, surplus grain, and meat downstream to New Orleans, which by 1815 was handling about $5 million in agricultural products yearly.

Public Policy: The Commonwealth System

Legislative support for road and canal companies was part of a broad system of state mercantilism known as the Commonwealth system. Just as the British Parliament had enacted the Navigation Acts to spur trade and manufacturing, so the American state legislatures passed measures they

thought would be "of great public utility" and increase the "common wealth." These laws generally took the form of special charters to corporate enterprises, and often included grants of limited liability, which made it easier to attract investors: If a business failed, the shareholders' personal assets could not be seized to pay the corporation's debts. And most transportation charters included the valuable power of eminent domain, which allowed turnpike, bridge, and canal corporations to force the sale of privately owned land along their routes. State legislatures also aided capitalist flour millers and textile manufacturers, who often had to flood adjacent farmland when they constructed dams to power their water-driven machinery. In Massachusetts, the Mill Dam Act of 1795 deprived farmers of their traditional right under common law to stop the flooding and forced them to accept "fair compensation" for their lost acreage.

Critics condemned these grants of special rights to private enterprises as violations of republican principles. The award of "peculiar privileges" to corporations, they argued, not only violated the "equal rights" of all citizens but also restricted the sovereignty of the people. As a Pennsylvanian put it, "Whatever power is given to a corporation, is just so much power taken from the State" and its citizens. Nonetheless, judges in state courts, following the lead of John Marshall's Supreme Court (see Chapter 7), consistently upheld corporate charters and routinely approved grants of eminent domain to private transportation corporations. "The opening of good and easy internal communications is one of the highest duties of government," declared a New Jersey judge.

State mercantilism soon encompassed much more than transportation. Following Jefferson's embargo of 1807, which cut off goods and credit from Europe, the New England states awarded charters to two hundred iron-mining, textile-manufacturing, and banking companies, and Pennsylvania granted more than eleven hundred. By 1820, innovative state governments had created a republican political economy: a Commonwealth system that funneled state aid to private businesses whose projects would improve the general welfare.

➤ How did the development of a market economy change the lives of artisans and farm families?

➤ What challenges did the promoters of the Commonwealth system face? How did they use government at state and national levels to promote economic growth and the market economy?

➤ Why did many Americans believe that the grant of special privileges and charters to private businesses was in conflict with republican principles?

Toward a Democratic Republican Culture

After independence, many Americans in the northern states embraced a democratic republicanism that celebrated political equality and social mobility, at least for white males. These citizens, primarily members of the emerging **middle class,** also redefined the nature of the family and of education by seeking more egalitarian marriages and more affectionate ways of rearing and educating their children.

Social and Political Equality for White Men

Between 1780 and 1820, hundreds of well-educated Europeans visited the United States and agreed, almost unanimously, that the American republic embodied a genuinely new social order. In his famous *Letters from an American Farmer* (1782), French-born essayist J. Hector St. Jean de Crèvecoeur wrote that European society was composed "of great lords who possess everything, and of a herd of people who have nothing." America, by contrast, had "no aristocratical families, no courts, no kings, no bishops."

The absence of a hereditary aristocracy encouraged Americans to condemn inherited social privilege and to extol the republican principle of legal equality for all free men. "The law is the same for everyone both as it protects and as it punishes," noted one European traveler. Yet Americans willingly accepted social divisions that reflected personal achievement. As individuals used their "talents, integrity, and virtue" to amass wealth, their social standing rose—a phenomenon that astounded some Europeans. "In Europe to say of someone that he rose from nothing is a disgrace and a reproach," remarked an aristocratic Polish visitor. "It is the opposite here. To be the architect of your own fortune is honorable. It is the highest recommendation."

Some Americans from long-distinguished families questioned the morality of a system of status based on financial success. "The aristocracy of Kingston [New York] is more one of money than any village I have ever seen," complained Nathaniel Booth, whose family had once ruled the small port town along the Hudson River. "Man is estimated by dollars," he lamented; "what he is worth determines his character and his position." However, for most white men, such a merit-based system meant the opportunity to better themselves.

Cultural rules—and new laws—continued to deny that opportunity to most women and African American men. As the republican doctrine of equality gained acceptance, it raised the prospect of voting rights for all citizens (see Map 8.1). To limit those rights to white men, legislators explicitly wrote race or gender restrictions into the law. In 1802, Ohio disfranchised African Americans, and the New York constitution of 1821 required blacks (but not whites) to meet a property-holding requirement to vote. The most striking case of explicit racial and sexual discrimination occurred in

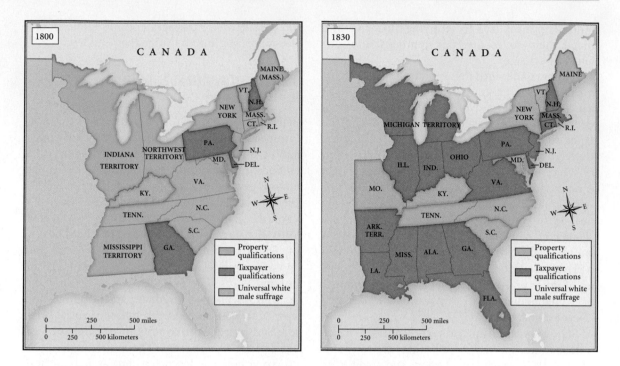

MAP 8.1   The Expansion of Voting Rights for White Men, 1800 and 1830

Between 1800 and 1830, the United States moved steadily toward political equality for white men. Many existing states revised their constitutions and replaced a property qualification for voting with a less-restrictive criterion (the voter must pay taxes or have served in the militia). Some new states in the West extended the suffrage for all adult white men. As parties sought votes from a broader electorate, the tone of politics became more open and competitive — swayed by the interests and values of ordinary people.

New Jersey, where the state constitution of 1776 had granted **suffrage** to all property holders. After 1800, as Federalists and Republicans competed for votes, they challenged political custom by encouraging voting by property-owning single women and widows. Sensing a threat to the male-centered political world, in 1807 the New Jersey legislature limited voting rights to white men only. To justify the exclusion of women, legislators invoked both biology and custom. As one letter to a newspaper put it, "Women, generally, are neither by nature, nor habit, nor education, nor by their necessary condition in society fitted to perform this duty with credit to themselves or advantage to the public."

Toward a Republican System of Marriage

The controversy over women's political rights mirrored a debate over authority within the household. British and American husbands had long dominated their wives and controlled their family's property. But as John Adams lamented in 1776, the republican doctrine of political equality had "spread where it was not intended," encouraging some white women to speak out on public matters and to demand control of their finances. These women insisted that their subordinate social position was at odds with the republican ideology of equal natural rights. Patriarchy was not a "natural" rule but a social contrivance, argued Patriot author and historian Mercy Otis Warren; placing men at the head of households was justified only "for the sake of order in families."

Economic and cultural changes also eroded customary paternal authority over children and their marriages. In colonial America, most property-owning parents had arranged their children's marriages. To ensure the welfare of the entire family, they tended to place the highest priority on the personal character and financial resources of a prospective son- or daughter-in-law; the physical attraction between the young people and their emotional compatibility were secondary considerations. However, as land holdings shrank in long-settled rural communities, many yeomen fathers could no longer leave substantial farms to their children and so could no longer select their spouses. Young men and women began to choose their own partners, influenced by a new cultural attitude, **sentimentalism**.

The Wedding, 1805

Bride and groom stare intently into each other's eyes as they exchange vows, suggesting that their union was a love match, not a marriage based on economic calculation. Given the plain costumes of the guests and the sparse furnishings of the room, the unknown artist may have provided us with a picture of a rural Quaker wedding. Philadelphia Museum of the Fine Arts.

The Effects of Sentimentalism. Sentimentalism originated in Europe as part of the Romantic movement of the late eighteenth century; it came to America in the early nineteenth century and spread quickly through all classes of society. Rejecting the Enlightenment's emphasis on rational thought, sentimentalism celebrated the importance of "feeling" — a physical, sensuous appreciation of God, nature, and other human beings. This new sensibility dripped from the pages of German and English literary works, fell from the lips of actors in popular melodramas, and infused the emotional rhetoric of revivalist preachers.

As the hot sentimental passions of the heart overwhelmed the cool rational logic of the mind, a new marriage system appeared. Around 1800, magazines began to encourage marriages "contracted from motives of affection, rather than of interest," and many young people looked for a spouse who was, as Eliza Southgate of Maine put it, "calculated to promote my happiness." As young people fell in love and married, many fathers saw their roles change

from authoritarian patriarchs to watchful paternalists, from dictating their children's behavior to protecting them from the consequences of their behavior. To guard against a free-spending son-in-law, for example, a wealthy father might place his daughter's inheritance in a legal trust, where her husband could not get at it. Wrote one Virginia planter to his lawyer: "I rely on you to see the property settlement properly drawn before the marriage, for I by no means consent that Polly shall be left to the Vicissitudes of Life."

As voluntary agreements between individuals, love-marriages conformed more closely to republican principles than did arranged matches. And, in theory, **companionate marriages** gave wives "true equality, both of rank and fortune" with their husbands, as one Boston man suggested. In practice, though, husbands continued to dominate most marriages, both because male authority was deeply ingrained in cultural mores and because husbands controlled the family's property under English and American common law. Moreover, the new love-based marriage system discouraged parents

The Trials of Married Life

As the text explains, the ideal American marriage of the early nineteenth century was republican (a contract between equals) and romantic (a match in which mutual love was foremost). Were these ideals attainable, given the social authority of men and the volatility of human passions? These selections from a variety of American women offer insights into the new system of marriage. Letters, memoirs, and diaries are excellent sources for understanding historical change at the personal level. They provide a window through which we can see changes in cultural values intersecting with individual lives.

EMMA HART WILLARD
The Danger of High Expectations

Born in Connecticut in 1787, Emma Hart married John Willard in 1809. An early proponent of advanced education for women, she founded Female Seminaries in Middlebury, Vermont, in 1814 and in Troy, New York, in 1821. She wrote this letter to her sister, Almira Hart, in 1815.

You think it strange that I should consider a period of happiness as more likely than any other to produce future misery. I know I did not sufficiently explain myself. Those tender and delicious sensations which accompany successful love, while they soothe and soften the mind, diminish its strength to bear or to conquer difficulties. It is the luxury of the soul; and luxury always enervates. . . . This life is a life of vicissitude. . . .

[Suppose] you are secured to each other for life. It will be natural that, at first, he should be much devoted to you; but, after a while, his business must occupy his attention. While absorbed in that he will perhaps neglect some of those little tokens of affection which have become necessary to your happiness. His affairs will sometimes go wrong, . . . and he may sometimes hastily give you a harsh word or a frown.

But where is the use, say you, of diminishing my present enjoyment by such gloomy apprehensions? Its use is this, that, if you enter the marriage state believing such things to be absolutely impossible, if you should meet them, they would come upon you with double force.

CAROLINE HOWARD GILMAN
Female Submission in Marriage

Caroline Howard was born in Boston in 1794 and moved to Charleston, South Carolina, with her husband, Samuel Gilman, a Unitarian minister. A novelist, she published Recollections of a Housekeeper *(1835), a portrait of domestic life in New England, and* Recollections of a Southern Matron *(1838), from which this selection is taken.*

The planter's bride, who leaves a numerous and cheerful family in her paternal home, little imagines the change which awaits her in her own retired residence. She dreams of an independent sway over her household, devoted love and unbroken intercourse with her husband, and indeed longs to be released from the eyes of others, that she may dwell only beneath the sunbeam of his. And so it was with me. . . .

There we were together, asking for nothing but each other's presence and love. At length it was necessary for him to tear himself away to superintend his interests. . . . But the period of absence was gradually protracted; then a friend sometimes came home with him, and their talk was of crops and politics, draining the fields and draining the revenue. . . . A growing discomfort began to work upon my mind. I had undefined forebodings; I mused about past days; my views of life became slowly disorganized; my physical powers enfeebled; a nervous excitement followed: I nursed a moody discontent. . . .

If the reign of romance was really waning, I resolved not to chill his noble confidence, but to make a steadier light rise on his affections. . . .This task of self-government was not easy. To repress a harsh answer, to confess a fault . . . in gentle submission, sometimes requires a struggle like life and death; but these . . . efforts are the golden threads with which domestic happiness is woven. . . . How clear is it, then, that woman loses by petulance and recrimination! Her first study must be self-control, almost to hypocrisy. A good wife must smile amid a thousand perplexities.

MARTHA HUNTER HITCHCOCK
Isolation, Unmentionable Sorrows, and Suffering

Martha Hunter Hitchcock married a doctor in the U.S. Army. These letters to her cousins Martha and Sarah Hunter describe her emotional dependence on her husband and her unhappy life. The letters are in the collection of the Virginia Historical Society.

To Martha Hunter, 1840:

If I had never married how much of pain, and dissatisfaction, should I have escaped—at all events I should never have known what jealousy is. You must not betray me, dear cousin, for despite all my good resolutions, I find it impossible always to struggle against my nature—the school of indulgence, in which I was educated, was little calculated to teach me, those lessons of forbearance, which I have had to practice so frequently, since my marriage—it is ungrateful in me to murmur, if perchance a little bitter is mingled in my cup of life.

To Sarah Hunter, 1841:

I have lived so long among strangers since my marriage, that when I contrast it with the old warm affection, in which I was nurtured, the contrast is so tremble, that I cannot refrain from weeping at the thought of it—I hope my dear cousin, that yours, will be a happier destiny than mine, in that respect—only think of it! Nearly a year and a half have passed away, since I have seen, a single relation!

To Martha Hunter, 1845:

Uneasiness about [my daughter] Lillie, and very great sorrows of my own, which I cannot commit to paper, have almost weighed me down to the grave; and indeed, without any affectation, I look forward to that, as the only real rest, I shall ever know.

To Martha Hunter, 1846:

Lillie had the scarlet fever, during our visit to Alabama, and she has never recovered from the effects of it—My life is a constant vigil—and there is nothing which wearies mind, and body, so much, as watching a sickly child. . . . All this I have to endure, and may have to suffer more for I know not, what Fate may have in store for me.

ELIZABETH SCOTT NEBLETT
"My Seasons of Gloom and Despondency"

Elizabeth Scott Neblett lived with her husband and children in Navarro County, Texas. In 1860, she reflected on eight years of marriage in her diary.

It has now been almost eight years since I became a married woman. Eight years of checkered good and ill, and yet thro' all it seems the most of the ill has fallen to my lot, until now my poor weak cowardly heart sighs only for its final resting place, where sorrow grief nor pain can never reach it more.

I feel that I have faithfully discharged my duty towards you and my children, but for this I know that I deserve no credit nor aspire to none; my affection has been my prompter, and the task has proven a labor of love. You have not rightly understood me at all times, and being naturally very hopeful you could in no measure sympathize with me during my seasons of gloom and despondency. . . . But marriage is a lottery and that your draw proved an unfortunate one on your part is not less a subject of regret with me than you. . . .

It is useless to say that during these eight years I have suffered ten times more than you have and ten times more than I can begin to make you conceive of, but of course you can not help the past, nor by knowing my suffering relieve it, but it might induce you to look with more kindness upon [my] faults. . . . The 17th of this month I was 27 years old and I think my face looks older than that, perhaps I'll never see an other birth day and I don't grieve at the idea.

SOURCE: All of the selections are abridged versions of materials in Anya Jabour, ed., *Major Problems in the History of American Families and Children* (Boston: Houghton Mifflin, 2005), 108–113.

ANALYZING THE EVIDENCE

➤ What problems do these women share? How might their problems be related to larger social and economic changes in the nineteenth century?

➤ Was Emma Willard correct? Did the emotional problems experienced by these women stem, at least in part, from their overly optimistic expectations of love-based marriage? Or was something else the cause of their unhappiness?

➤ What was Caroline Gilman's advice to wives? Did the other women follow her advice?

➤ Do these selections prove that most American women had unfulfilled marriages? Or were these isolated cases? Would you expect to find more records of unhappy marriages than happy ones?

from protecting the interests of young wives, and governments refused to prevent domestic tyranny. Women who would rather "starve than submit" to the orders of their husbands, a lawyer noted, were left to their fate. The marriage contract "is so much more important in its consequences to females than to males," a young man at the Litchfield Law School in Connecticut astutely observed in 1820, "for besides leaving everything else to unite themselves to one man, they subject themselves to his authority. He is their all — their only relative — their only hope" (see Comparing American Voices, "The Trials of Married Life," pp. 246–247).

Young adults who chose partners unwisely were severely disappointed when their spouses failed as providers or faithful companions. Divorces were very difficult to obtain and, before 1800, were only granted in cases of neglect, abandonment, or adultery — serious offenses against the moral order of society. After 1800, most divorce petitions cited emotional grounds. One woman complained that her husband had "ceased to cherish her," while a man grieved that his wife had "almost broke his heart." In response to changes in cultural values, several states expanded the legal grounds for divorce to include drunkenness and personal cruelty.

Republican Motherhood

Traditionally, most American women spent their time on family duties: working in the home or on the farm and bearing and nurturing children. But by the 1790s, the birthrate in the northern seaboard states was dropping dramatically. In the farming village of Sturbridge in central Massachusetts, women who had married before 1750 gave birth, on average, to eight or nine children; in contrast, women who married around 1810 had an average of six children. In the growing seaport cities, native-born white women bore an average of only four children.

The United States was one of the first countries in the world to experience a sharp decline in birthrate — what historians call a demographic transition. There were several causes. Beginning in the 1790s, thousands of young men migrated to the trans-Appalachian west; their departure left some women without partners for life and delayed marriage for many more. Women who married later in life had fewer children. In addition, thousands of white couples in the increasingly urban middling classes deliberately limited the size of their families. Fathers favored smaller families so that they could provide their children with an adequate inheritance;

and mothers, influenced by new ideas of individualism and self-achievement, refused to spend all of their active years bearing and rearing children. After having four or five children, these couples used birth control or abstained from sexual intercourse.

Women's lives changed as well because of new currents in Christian social thought. Traditionally, most religious writers had argued that women were morally inferior to men, that they were dangerous sexual temptresses or witches. By 1800, Protestant ministers were blaming men for sexual and social misconduct and claiming that modesty and purity were inherent in women's nature. Soon political leaders were echoing that thinking, calling on women to become dedicated "republican wives" and "republican mothers" to shape the character of American men. In his *Thoughts on Female Education* (1787), Philadelphia physician Benjamin Rush argued that a young woman should receive intellectual training so that she would be "an agreeable companion for a sensible man" and ensure "his perseverance in the paths of rectitude." Rush also called for loyal "republican mothers" who would instruct "their sons in the principles of liberty and government."

Christian ministers readily embraced the idea of **republican motherhood.** "Preserving virtue and instructing the young are not the fancied, but the real 'Rights of Women,'" Reverend Thomas Bernard told the Female Charitable Society of Salem, Massachusetts. He urged his audience to dismiss the public roles for women — for example, voting and holding office — that English feminist Mary Wollstonecraft had advocated in *A Vindication of the Rights of Woman* (1792). Instead, women should care for their children, a responsibility that gave them "an extensive power over the fortunes of man in every generation." A few religious leaders expanded Bernard's argument and suggested a different public role for women as purveyors of republican ethics. "Give me a host of educated pious mothers and sisters and I will revolutionize a country, in moral and religious taste," declared South Carolina minister Thomas Grimké.

Raising and Educating Republican Children

Republican values also altered assumptions about inheritance and child rearing. Under English common law, property owned by a father who died without a will passed to his eldest son, a practice known as primogeniture (see Chapter 1).

After the Revolution, most state legislatures enacted statutes that required that such estates be divided equally among all the offspring. Most American parents applauded these statutes because they had already begun to treat their children equally.

Encouraging Independence. Many European visitors believed that republican parents gave their children too much freedom. Because of the "general ideas of Liberty and Equality engraved on their hearts," suggested a Polish aristocrat who traveled around the United States in 1800, American children had "scant respect" for their parents. Several decades later, a British traveler stood dumbfounded as an American father excused his son's "resolute disobedience" with a smile and the remark "A sturdy republican, sir." The traveler guessed that American parents encouraged their children to be independent to help the young people "go their own way" in the world.

Permissive child rearing was not universal. Foreign visitors interacted primarily with well-to-do Americans, who were mostly members of Episcopal or Presbyterian churches. These parents often followed the teachings of rationalist religious writers influenced by John Locke and other Enlightenment thinkers. According to these authors, children were "rational creatures" who should be encouraged to act appropriately by means of advice and praise. The parents' role was to develop their child's conscience and self-discipline so that the child would be able to control his or her own behavior and act responsibly. This rationalist method of child rearing was widely adopted by families in the rapidly expanding middle class.

By contrast, many yeomen and tenant farmers, influenced by the Second Great Awakening, raised their children with authoritarian methods. Evangelical Baptist and Methodist writers insisted that children were "full of the stains and pollution of sin" and needed strict rules and harsh discipline. Fear was a "useful and necessary principle in family government," John Abbott, a minister, advised parents; a child "should submit to your authority, not to your arguments or persuasions." Abbott told parents to instill humility in children and to teach them to subordinate their personal desires to God's will (see Reading American Pictures, "Changing Middle-Class Families: Assessing the Visual Record," p. 250).

Expanding Education. The values transmitted within families were crucial because most education still took place within the household. In New England, locally funded public schools provided most boys and some girls with basic instruction in reading and writing. However, there were few publicly funded schools in other regions: About 25 percent of the boys and perhaps 10 percent of the girls attended private institutions or had personal tutors. Even in New England, only a small percentage of young men and almost no young women went on to grammar school (high school today). And only 1 percent of men attended college.

In the 1790s, Bostonian Caleb Bingham, an influential textbook author, called for "an equal distribution of knowledge to make us emphatically a 'republic of letters.'" Both Thomas Jefferson and Benjamin Rush proposed an ambitious scheme for a comprehensive system of primary and secondary schooling, followed by college for bright young men. They also advocated the establishment of a

The Battle over Education

The artist is poking fun at a tyrannical schoolmaster and, indirectly, at the evangelicals' strict approach to child rearing. The students' faces reflect the artist's own rationalist outlook. One minister who had been influenced by the Enlightenment suggested that we see in young children's eyes "the first dawn of reason, beaming forth its immortal rays." Copyright The Frick Collection, New York City.

Changing Middle-Class Families: Assessing the Visual Record

Throughout the text, we have discussed and analyzed American families—yeoman families, black slave families, and now republican families. These images allow us to compare two families of similar status—a middle-class eighteenth-century family typical of the colonial era, the Cheneys (top), with a nineteenth-century family, the Caverlys (bottom). Because families are the basic social unit in all societies, comparing paintings of family scenes helps us see change over time and understand how change in daily lives and relationships alters the nature of society.

The Cheneys, c. 1795. National Gallery of Art, Washington, Gift of Edgar William and Bernice Chrysler Garbisch.

ANALYZING THE EVIDENCE

➤ Count the number of children in each painting and look closely at their mothers. Given the decline in birthrates discussed in the text, how many more children is Mrs. Caverly likely to bear? Why?

➤ How are the children posed in each painting? What do their poses reveal about how adults thought of children? In the paintings, is there evidence of change in that thinking from the colonial era to the nineteenth century?

➤ Mrs. Caverly is depicted with a Bible, and her husband is reading a newspaper. What do these clues suggest about the roles of women and men in the 1830s? From your reading of the text, how does this symbolism reflect important social and cultural changes at the time?

➤ Whom do you see first when you look at the painting of the Cheneys? Is there a similar visual center in the image of the Caverlys? Notice the differences in the physical settings and in the placement of the family members. Compare the two backgrounds: Why is one plain and gray, and the other decorated and filled with objects? What do the differences tell you about the changing values of the American middle class?

The Caverlys, 1836. New York State Historical Society, Cooperstown.

Women's Education

Even in education-conscious New England, few girls attended free public primary schools for more than a few years. After 1800, as this scene from *A Seminary for Young Ladies* (c. 1810–1820) indicates, some girls stayed in school into their teenage years and studied a wide variety of subjects, including geography. Many graduates of these female academies became teachers, a new field of employment for women. St. Louis Art Museum.

university in which distinguished scholars would lecture on law, medicine, theology, and political economy.

To ordinary citizens, talk of secondary and college education smacked of elitism. Farmers, artisans, and laborers wanted elementary schools that would instruct their children in the "three Rs": reading, 'riting, and 'rithmetic. Because their teenage children had to work, they generally refused to fund secondary schools or colleges. "Let anybody show what advantage the poor man receives from colleges," an anonymous "Old Soldier" wrote to the *Maryland Gazette*. "Why should they support them, unless it is to serve those who are in affluent circumstances, whose children can be spared from labor, and receive the benefits?"

Although many state constitutions encouraged legislatures to support education, few legislatures acted until the 1820s, when a new generation of reformers, primarily merchants and manufacturers, successfully campaigned to raise educational standards by certifying qualified teachers and appointing statewide superintendents of schools. To encourage self-discipline and individual enterprise in students, the reformers chose textbooks like *The Life of George Washington* (c. 1800) — an account embellished by the author, Parson Mason Weems, to praise honesty and hard work and to condemn gambling, drinking, and laziness. Believing that patriotic instruction would foster shared cultural ideals, they also required the study of American history. Thomas Low recalled his days as a New Hampshire schoolboy: "We were taught every day and in every way that ours was the freest, the happiest, and soon to be the greatest and most powerful country of the world."

Promoting Cultural Independence. Writer Noah Webster believed education should develop the American intellect. Asserting that "America must be as independent in *literature* as she is in politics," he called on his fellow citizens to detach themselves "from the dependence on foreign opinions and manners, which is fatal to the efforts of genius in this country." Webster's *Dissertation on the English Language* (1789) helpfully defined words according to American usage. It less successfully proposed that words be spelled as they were pronounced, that *labour* (British spelling), for example, be spelled *labur*. Still, Webster's famous "blue-back speller," a compact textbook first published in 1783, sold 60 million copies over the next half-century and helped give Americans of all backgrounds a common vocabulary and grammar. "None of us was 'lowed to see a book," an enslaved African American recalled, "but we gits hold of that Webster's old blue-back speller and we . . . studies [it]."

Despite Webster's efforts, a republican literary culture was slow to develop. Ironically, the most accomplished and successful writer in the new republic was Washington Irving, an elitist-minded Federalist. His essays and histories, including *Salmagundi* (1807) and *Dietrich Knickerbocker's History of New York* (1809), which told the tales of "Rip Van Winkle" and "The Legend of Sleepy Hollow," sold well in America and won praise abroad. Impatient with the slow pace of American literary development, Irving lived for seventeen years in Europe, where he reveled in its aristocratic culture and intense intellectual life.

Apart from Irving, no American author was well known in Europe or, indeed, in the United States. "Literature is not yet a distinct profession with us," Thomas Jefferson told an English friend. "Now and then a strong mind arises, and at its intervals from business emits a flash of light. But the first object of young societies is bread and covering." Not until the 1830s and 1840s would American authors achieve a professional identity and, in the works of Ralph Waldo Emerson and novelists of the **American Renaissance,** make a significant contribution to the great literature of Western society (see Chapter 11).

➤ In what ways did American culture become more democratic in the early nineteenth century? How did the social and political status of women and African Americans change in relation to the status of white males?

➤ How did republican ideas shape marital relations and expectations?

➤ How did the nature of fathering change in the period? Why did it change?

Symbols of Slavery — and Freedom

The scar on the forehead of this black woman, who was widely known as "Mumbet," underlined the cruelty of slavery. Winning emancipation through a legal suit in Massachusetts, she chose a name befitting her new status: Elizabeth Freeman. This watercolor, by Susan Sedgwick, was painted in 1811. Massachusetts Historical Society, Boston.

Aristocratic Republicanism and Slavery

Republicanism in the South differed significantly from that in the North. Enslaved Africans constituted one-third of the South's population and exposed an enormous contradiction in white Americans' ideology of freedom and equality. "How is it that we hear the loudest yelps for liberty among the drivers of Negroes?" British author Samuel Johnson had chided the American rebels in 1775, a point some Patriots took to heart. "I wish most sincerely there was not a Slave in the province," Abigail Adams confessed to her husband, John. "It always appeared a most iniquitous Scheme to me — to fight ourselves for what we are daily robbing and plundering from those who have as good a right to freedom as we have."

The Revolution and Slavery, 1776–1800

In fact, the whites' struggle for independence raised the prospect of freedom for blacks. As the war began, a black preacher in Georgia told his fellow slaves that King George III "came up with the Book [the Bible], and was about to alter the World, and set the Negroes free." Similar rumors, probably prompted by Governor Dunmore's proclamation of 1775 (see Chapter 5), circulated among slaves in Virginia and the Carolinas and prompted thousands of African Americans to flee behind British lines. Two neighbors of Richard Henry Lee, the

Virginia Patriot, lost "every slave they had in the world," as did many other planters. In 1781, when the British army evacuated Charleston, more than six thousand former slaves went with them; another four thousand left from Savannah. All told, thirty thousand blacks may have fled their owners. Hundreds of freed black Loyalists settled permanently in Canada. More than a thousand others, poorly treated by British officials in Nova Scotia, sought a better life in Sierra Leone, West Africa, a settlement established by English antislavery organizations.

Yet thousands of African Americans supported the Patriot cause. Eager to raise their social status, free blacks in New England volunteered for military service in the First Rhode Island Company and the Massachusetts "Bucks." In Maryland, a significant number of slaves took up arms for the rebels in return for the promise of freedom. Slaves in Virginia struck informal bargains with their Patriot masters, trading loyalty in wartime for the promise of liberty. In 1782, the Virginia assembly passed a **manumission** act, which allowed individual owners to free their slaves; and within a decade, planters had released ten thousand slaves.

Quakers took the lead in condemning slavery. Beginning in the 1750s, Quaker evangelist John

Woolman urged Friends to free their slaves, and, during the war, many did so. Rapidly growing evangelical Christian churches, notably the Methodists and the Baptists, also advocated emancipation and admitted both enslaved and free blacks to their congregations. In 1784, a conference of Virginia Methodists declared that slavery was "contrary to the Golden Law of God on which hang all the Law and Prophets."

Enlightenment philosophy also undermined the widespread belief among whites that Africans were inherently inferior to Europeans. John Locke had argued that ideas were not innate, that they stemmed from a person's experiences in the world. Accordingly, Enlightenment thinkers suggested that the oppressive conditions of captivity accounted for the debased situation of blacks: "A state of slavery has a mighty tendency to shrink and contract the minds of men." Anthony Benezet, a Quaker philanthropist who funded a school for blacks in Philadelphia, defied popular opinion when he declared that African Americans were "as capable of improvement as White People."

These new religious and intellectual currents sparked legal change. In 1784, judicial rulings abolished slavery in Massachusetts; and, over the next twenty years, every state north of Delaware enacted legislation to end slavery (Map 8.2). Emancipation itself was gradual: The laws compensated white owners by requiring years—even decades—of continuing servitude. For example, the New York Emancipation Act of 1799 granted freedom to slave children only when they reached the age of twenty-five. As late as 1810, almost thirty thousand blacks in the northern states—nearly a fourth of the African Americans living there—were still enslaved. Two other factors contributed to the slow pace of emancipation in the North: competition for jobs and the fear of racial melding. Massachusetts addressed the racial issue in 1786 by reenacting an old law that prohibited whites from marrying blacks, mulattos, or Indians.

The tension in American republican ideology between respect for liberty and respect for property rights was greatest in the South, where slaves represented a huge financial investment. Some Chesapeake tobacco planters, moved by religious principles or an oversupply of workers, allowed blacks to buy their freedom through paid work as artisans or laborers. Manumission and self-purchase gradually brought freedom to one-third of the African American residents of Maryland. However, in 1792, the Virginia legislature made manumission more difficult. Following the lead of Thomas Jefferson, who owned more than one

Captain Absalom Boston

Absalom Boston was born in 1785 on the island of Nantucket, Massachusetts, the heart of America's whaling industry. A member of a community of free African American whalers manumitted from slavery by their Quaker owners, Boston went to sea at age fifteen. By the age of thirty, he had used his earnings to become the proprietor of a public inn. In 1822, Boston became the first black master with an all-black crew to undertake a whaling voyage from Nantucket. Later he served as a trustee of the island's African School. Nantucket Historical Association.

hundred slaves, the Virginia legislators argued that slavery was a "necessary evil" required to maintain white supremacy and the luxurious planter lifestyle. Resistance to black freedom was even greater in North Carolina, where the legislature condemned Quaker manumissions as "highly criminal and reprehensible." The slave-hungry rice-growing states of South Carolina and Georgia rejected emancipation out of hand. In fact, between 1776 and 1809, merchants and planters in the Lower South imported about 115,000 Africans—nearly half the number introduced into Britain's mainland settlements during the entire colonial period (Table 8.1).

The debate over emancipation among southern whites ended in 1800, when Virginia authorities thwarted an uprising planned by Gabriel Prosser,

TABLE 8.1	African Slaves Imported into the United States, by Ethnicity, 1776–1809		
African Region of Departure	**Ethnicity**	**Number**	**Percentage of Imported Slaves**
Senegambia	Mandinka, Fulbe, Serer, Jola, Wolof, and Bambara	8,000	7
Sierra Leone	Via, Mende, Kpelle, and Kru	18,300	16
Gold Coast	Ashanti and Fanit	15,000	13
Bight of Benin; Bight of Biafra	Ibo and Ibibio	5,700	5
West Central Africa	Kongo, Tio, and Matamba	37,800	33
Southeast Africa	Unknown	1,100	1
Other or unknown		28,700	25
Total		**114,600**	**100**

NOTE: Recent research suggests that 433,000 enslaved Africans arrived in British North America and the United States between 1607 and 1820: 33,200 before 1700; 278,400 from 1700 to 1775; 114,600 from 1776 to 1809; and 7,000 from 1810 to 1819. The numbers in this table are based on known voyages of 65,000 Africans.

SOURCE: Aaron S. Fogleman, "From Slaves, Convicts, and Servants to Free Passengers: The Transformation of Immigration in the Era of the American Revolution," *Journal of American History,* June 1998, table 1 and table A.6.

an enslaved artisan, and hanged him and thirty of his followers. "Liberty and equality have brought the evil upon us," a letter to the *Virginia Herald* proclaimed; such doctrines are "dangerous and extremely wicked in this country, where every white man is a master, and every black man is a slave." To preserve their privileged social position, southern whites redefined republicanism so that its principles of individual liberty and legal equality applied only to members of the "master race" — creating what historians call a *herrenvolk* (master people) republic.

The North and South Grow Apart

European visitors to the United States agreed that the South formed a distinct society, and many cast doubts on its character. New England was home to religious "fanaticism," according to a British observer, but "the lower orders of citizens" there had "a better education, are more intelligent, and better informed" than those he met in the South. "The state of poverty in which a great number of white people live in Virginia" surprised the Marquis de Chastellux, and other visitors to the South commented on the rude manners, heavy drinking, and weak work ethic of its residents. White tenant farmers and small freeholders seemed only to have a "passion for gaming at the billiard table, a cock-fight or cards," and many planters squandered their wealth on extravagant lifestyles while their slaves suffered in bitter poverty.

Some southerners admitted that human bondage corrupted their society and induced ignorance and poverty among whites as well as blacks. A South Carolina merchant observed, "Where there are Negroes a White Man despises to work, saying what, will you have me a Slave and work like a Negroe?" For their part, wealthy planters wanted a compliant labor force that was content with the drudgery of agricultural work. Consequently, they trained most of their slaves as field hands (allowing only a few to learn the arts of the blacksmith, carpenter, or bricklayer), and did little to provide ordinary whites with elementary instruction in reading or arithmetic. In 1800, the political leaders of Essex County, Virginia, spent about 25 cents per person for local government, including schooling, while their counterparts in Acton, Massachusetts, expended about $1 per person. This difference in support for education mattered: By the 1820s, nearly all native-born men and women in New England could read and write; more than one-third of white southerners lacked these basic intellectual skills.

Slavery and National Politics. As the northern states ended human bondage, the South's continuing

MAP 8.2 The Status of Slavery, 1800

In 1775, racial slavery was legal in all of the British colonies in North America. By the time the states achieved their independence in 1783, most African Americans in New England had also been freed. By 1800, all of the states north of Maryland had provided for the gradual abolition of slavery, but the process was not completed until the 1830s. Some slave owners in the Chesapeake region also manumitted their slaves, leaving only the whites of the Lower South firmly committed to racial bondage.

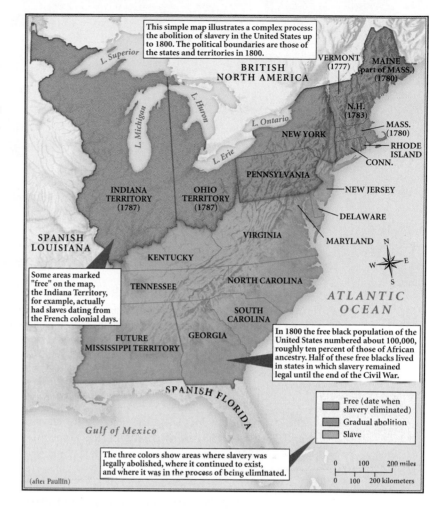

This simple map illustrates a complex process: the abolition of slavery in the United States up to 1800. The political boundaries are those of the states and territories in 1800.

Some areas marked "free" on the map, the Indiana Territory, for example, actually had slaves dating from the French colonial days.

In 1800 the free black population of the United States numbered about 100,000, roughly ten percent of those of African ancestry. Half of these free blacks lived in states in which slavery remained legal until the end of the Civil War.

Free (date when slavery eliminated)
Gradual abolition
Slave

The three colors show areas where slavery was legally abolished, where it continued to exist, and where it was in the process of being eliminated.

(after Paullin)

commitment to slavery became a political issue. At the Philadelphia convention in 1787, northern and southern delegates had compromised. Northerners accepted clauses guaranteeing the return of fugitive slaves and allowing slave imports from Africa to continue for twenty years; in return, southerners agreed that Congress could end the Atlantic slave trade after 1807 (see Chapter 6). Seeking a protection for their "peculiar institution," southerners in the new national legislature won approval of James Madison's resolution that "Congress have no authority to interfere in the emancipation of slaves, or in the treatment of them within any of the States."

Nonetheless, slavery remained a contested issue. The successful slave revolt in Haiti in the 1790s brought a flood of white refugees to the United States and prompted congressional debates about diplomatic relations with the island's new black government. Simultaneously, northern politicians assailed the British impressment of American sailors as just "as oppressive and tyrannical as the slave trade" and demanded the end of both. When Congress outlawed American participation in the Atlantic slave trade in 1808, some northern representatives called for a similar prohibition on the interstate trade in black labor. In response, southern leaders mounted a defense of their slave society. "A large majority of people in the Southern states do not consider slavery as even an evil," declared one congressman. The South's political clout—especially its domination of the presidency and the Senate—ensured that the national government would continue to protect slavery. During the War of 1812, American diplomats vigorously, and successfully, demanded compensation for slaves freed by the British; subsequently, Congress enacted legislation upholding the property rights of slave owners in the District of Columbia.

Political conflict over slavery increased as the South expanded its slave-based agricultural economy into the lower Mississippi Valley. Antislavery advocates had hoped that African bondage would "die a natural death" following the end of the Atlantic slave trade and with the decline of the tobacco economy. Their hopes quickly faded as

The Reverend Richard Allen and the African Methodist Episcopal Church

One of the best known African Americans in the early republic, Allen founded a separate congregation for Philadelphia's black Methodists, the Bethel Church. Working with other ministers in 1816, Allen created the first independent black religious denomination in the United States — the African Methodist Episcopal (AME) Church — and became its first bishop. Library of Congress; Bethel AME Church, Philadelphia.

the cotton boom increased the demand for slaves, and Louisiana (1812), Mississippi (1817), and Alabama (1819) joined the Union with state constitutions permitting slavery.

Richard Allen Responds to Colonization Proposals. In 1817, influential Americans who were worried about the impact of slavery and race on society founded the American Colonization Society. According to Henry Clay, the Speaker of the House of Representatives and a slave owner, racial bondage had placed his state, Kentucky, "in the rear of our neighbors . . . in the state of agriculture, the progress of manufactures, the advance of improvement, and the general prosperity of society." Slavery had to end, and, members of the society argued, freed blacks had to be sent back to Africa. Emancipation without removal, Clay predicted, "would be followed by instantaneous collisions between the two races, which would break out into a civil war that would end in the extermination or subjugation of the one race or the other." To prevent racial chaos, the society planned to encourage planters to emancipate their slaves, who now numbered almost 1.5 million people; then, it would resettle them in Africa.

The society's plan was a dismal failure. Few planters freed their slaves, and the organization raised only enough money to purchase freedom for

a few hundred slaves. Equally important, most free blacks rejected colonization. They agreed with Bishop Richard Allen of the African Methodist Episcopal Church that "this land which we have watered with our tears and our blood is now our mother country." Allen knew of what he spoke. Born into slavery in Philadelphia in 1760 and sold to a farmer in Delaware, Allen had lived in bondage. In 1777, Freeborn Garretson, an itinerant preacher, converted Allen to Methodism and convinced his owner that on Judgment Day slaveholders would be "weighted in the balance, and . . . found wanting." Allowed to buy his freedom, Allen raised the money by working for years sawing cordwood and loading wagons. He then enlisted in the Methodist cause, becoming a "licensed exhorter" and then a regular minister in Philadelphia. In 1795, he formed a separate black congregation, the Bethel Church; and in 1816, he became the first bishop of a new denomination, the African Methodist Episcopal Church. Two years later, three thousand African Americans met in Allen's church to condemn colonization and to claim citizenship. Echoing the principles of democratic republicanism, they vowed to defy racial prejudice and advance in American society using "those opportunities . . . which the Constitution and the laws allow to all."

Lacking significant support from white slave owners and from free blacks like Richard Allen, the

American Colonization Society transported only six thousand African Americans to Liberia, a colony it established on the west coast of Africa.

The Missouri Crisis, 1819–1821

The failure of colonization set the stage for a new political conflict over slavery. In 1818, Congressman Nathaniel Macon of North Carolina warned slave owners that radical members of the "colonizing bible and peace societies" hoped to use the national government "to try the question of emancipation." In fact, a major national struggle erupted even more quickly than Macon had anticipated. When Missouri applied for admission to the Union in 1819 with a constitution that allowed slavery, Congressman James Tallmadge of New York proposed a ban on the importation of slaves into Missouri and the gradual emancipation of its black residents. Missouri whites rejected Tallmadge's proposals, and the northern majority in the House of Representatives responded by blocking the territory's admission to the Union.

White southerners were horrified. "It is believed by some, & feared by others," Alabama senator John Walker reported from Washington, that Tallmadge's amendment was "merely the entering wedge and that it points already to a total emancipation of the blacks." "You conduct us to an awful precipice, and hold us over it," Mississippi congressman Christopher Rankin warned his northern colleagues. To underline their commitment to slavery, southerners used their power in the Senate — where they held half the seats — to withhold statehood from Maine, which was seeking to separate itself from Massachusetts.

In the ensuing debate over slavery, southerners advanced three constitutional arguments. First, raising the principle of "equal rights," they argued that Congress could not impose conditions on Missouri that it had not imposed on other territories seeking statehood. Second, they maintained that slavery fell under the sovereignty of the state governments: Under the Constitution, states exercised control over their internal affairs and domestic institutions, including slavery and marriage. Finally, they insisted that Congress had no authority to infringe on the property rights of individual slaveholders. Going beyond these constitutional issues, southern leaders reaffirmed their commitment to a slave society. Abandoning their Revolutionary-era argument that slavery was a "necessary evil," they now relied on religion to champion it as a "positive good." "Christ himself gave a sanction to slavery," declared Senator William Smith of South Carolina. "If it be offensive and sinful to own slaves," a prominent Mississippi Methodist added, "I wish someone would just put his finger on the place in Holy Writ."

Controversy raged in Congress and newspapers for two years before Henry Clay put together a series of political agreements known collectively as the Missouri Compromise. Faced with unwavering southern opposition to Tallmadge's plan, a group of northern congressmen deserted the antislavery coalition. They accepted a deal that allowed Maine to enter the Union as a free state in 1820 and Missouri to follow as a slave state in 1821. By admitting both states, the agreement preserved a balance in the Senate between North and South and set a precedent for future additions to the Union. For their part, southern senators accepted the prohibition of slavery in the vast northern section of the Louisiana Purchase, the lands north of latitude 36°30′ (the southern boundary of Missouri) (Map 8.3).

As they had in the Constitutional Convention of 1787 (see Chapter 6), white politicians once again preserved the Union by compromising over slavery. But the task had become more difficult. The delegates in Philadelphia had resolved their sectional differences in two months; it took Congress two years to work out the Missouri Compromise, and even then the agreement did not command universal support. "If we yield now, beware," the *Richmond Enquirer* warned as southern congressmen agreed to exclude slavery from most of the Louisiana Purchase. "What is a *territorial* restriction today becomes a *state* restriction tomorrow." The fate of the western lands, the black race, and the Union itself were now inextricably entwined — an ominous conjuncture that raised the specter of civil strife, the dissolution of the Union, and the end of the American experiment in republican government. As the aging Thomas Jefferson exclaimed in the midst of the Missouri crisis, "This momentous question, like a fire-bell in the night, awakened and filled me with terror."

➤ How did the aristocratic republicanism of the South differ from the democratic republicanism of the North? How did slavery affect the culture and values of the white population of the South?

➤ What compromises over slavery did the members of Congress make to settle the Missouri crisis? How did the compromises over slavery in 1820–1821 compare with those made by the delegates to the Constitutional Convention in 1787?

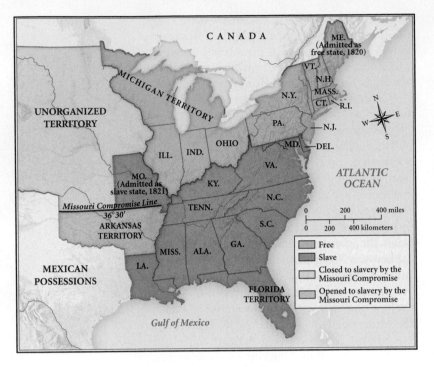

MAP 8.3 The Missouri Compromise, 1820–1821

The Missouri Compromise resolved for a generation the issue of slavery in the lands of the Louisiana Purchase. The agreement prohibited slavery north of the Missouri Compromise line (36°30′ north latitude), with the exception of the state of Missouri. To maintain an equal number of senators from free and slave states in the U.S. Congress, the compromise provided for the nearly simultaneous admission to the Union of Maine and Missouri.

Protestant Christianity as a Social Force

Throughout the colonial era, religion played a significant role in American life. Beginning in 1790, a series of religious revivals planted the values of Protestant Christianity deep in the national character, giving a spiritual definition to American republicanism. These revivals especially changed the lives of blacks and of women. Thousands of African Americans absorbed the faith of white Baptists and Methodists and created a distinctive and powerful institution—the black Christian church. Evangelical Christianity also created new public roles for women, especially in the North, and set in motion a long-lasting movement for social reform.

A Republican Religious Order

The demand for greater liberty unleashed by the republican revolution of 1776 forced American lawmakers to devise new relationships between church and state. Previously, only the Quaker- and Baptist-controlled governments of Pennsylvania and Rhode Island had repudiated the idea of an **established church**. Then, in 1776, James Madison and George Mason used Enlightenment principles to undermine the legal status of the Anglican Church in Virginia. They persuaded the state's constitutional convention to issue a declaration guaranteeing all Christians the "free exercise of religion." To win Presbyterian and Baptist support for the War of Independence, Virginia's Anglican elite accepted the legitimacy of the churches they had previously persecuted. In fact, in 1778, Virginia Anglicans launched their own revolution by severing ties with the hierarchy of the Church of England and founding the Protestant Episcopal Church of America.

Following independence, an established church and compulsory religious taxes were no longer the norm in the United States. Baptists, in particular, opposed the use of taxes to support religion. In Virginia, the Baptists' political influence prompted lawmakers to reject a bill, supported by George Washington and Patrick Henry, that would have imposed a general tax to fund all Christian churches. Instead, in 1786, the Virginia legislature enacted Thomas Jefferson's Bill for Establishing Religious Freedom, which made all churches equal before the law and granted direct financial support to none.

In New York and New Jersey, the sheer number of churches—Episcopalian, Presbyterian, Dutch Reformed, Lutheran, and Quaker, among others—prevented lawmakers from agreeing on an established church or compulsory religious taxes. Congregationalism remained the official state church in New England until the 1830s, but members of other denominations could pay taxes to their own churches.

TABLE 8.2	Number of Church Congregations by Denomination, 1780 and 1860		
	Number of Congregations		**Increased roughly by a factor of:**
Denomination	**1780**	**1860**	
Anglican/Episcopalian	406	2,100	5
Baptist	457	12,150	26
Catholic	50	2,500	50*
Congregational	742	2,200	3
Lutheran	240	2,100	9
Methodist	50	20,000	400
Presbyterian	495	6,400	13

NOTE: The increase in Catholic congregations occurred mostly after 1840, as the result of immigration from Ireland and Germany. See Chapter 9.

Even in Jefferson's Virginia, the separation of church and state was not complete. Many influential Americans believed that such ties promoted morality and respect for authority. "Pure religion and civil liberty are inseparable companions," a group of North Carolinians advised their minister. "It is your particular duty to enlighten mankind with the unerring principles of truth and justice, the main props of all civil government." Accepting this premise, most state governments provided churches with indirect aid by exempting their property and ministers from taxation.

Freedom of conscience proved equally difficult to achieve. In Virginia, Jefferson's Bill for Establishing Religious Freedom prohibited religious requirements for holding public office, but other states discriminated against those who dissented from the doctrines of Protestant Christianity. The North Carolina Constitution of 1776 disqualified from public employment any citizen "who shall deny the being of God, or the Truth of the Protestant Religion, or the Divine Authority of the Old or New Testament." New Hampshire's constitution contained a similar provision until 1868.

Americans influenced by Enlightenment deism and by Evangelical Protestantism condemned these religious restrictions. Leading American intellectuals, including Jefferson and Benjamin Franklin, argued that God had given humans the power of reason so that they could determine moral truths for themselves. To protect society from "ecclesiastical tyranny," they demanded complete freedom of conscience. Many evangelical Protestants also demanded religious liberty; their goal was to protect their churches from an oppressive

government. Isaac Backus, a New England minister, warned Baptists not to incorporate their churches or accept public funds because that might lead to state control. In Connecticut, a devout Congregationalist welcomed voluntarism, the voluntary funding of churches by their members, because it allowed the laity to control the clergy, thereby furthering self-government and "the principles of republicanism."

The Second Great Awakening

Overshadowing this debate was a decades-long series of religious revivals — the Second Great Awakening — that made the United States a Christian society. The churches that prospered during the revivals were those that preached spiritual equality and governed themselves democratically. Because bishops and priests dominated the Roman Catholic Church, it attracted few Protestants, who preferred Luther's doctrine of the priesthood of all believers. The unchurched — the great number of Americans who ignored religion — likewise shunned Catholicism because they feared its clergy's power. Few Americans joined the Episcopal Church (the successor to the Church of England) because it also had a hierarchical structure and was dominated by its wealthiest members (Table 8.2). The Presbyterian Church attracted more members, in part because its members elected laymen to the synods, the church congresses that determined doctrine and practice. Evangelical Methodist and Baptist churches were by far the most popular. The Baptists boasted a republican church organization, with self-governing congregations. In common with

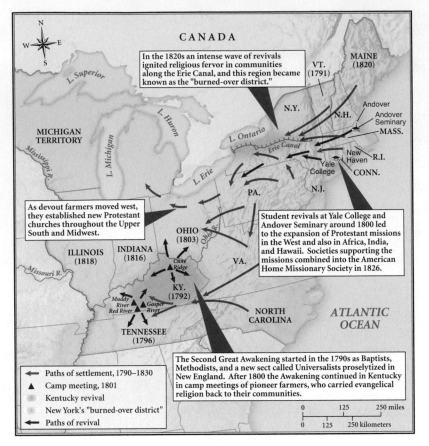

CANADA

L. Superior

MICHIGAN
TERRITORY

L. Huron

L. Michigan

Mississippi R.

In the 1820s an intense wave of revivals ignited religious fervor in communities along the Erie Canal, and this region became known as the "burned-over district."

N.Y.

VT.
(1791)

MAINE
(1820)

N.H.

Andover
Andover
Seminary

MASS.

L. Ontario

Erie Canal

New
Haven

R.I.

Yale
College

CONN.

L. Erie

PA.

N.J.

As devout farmers moved west, they established new Protestant churches throughout the Upper South and Midwest.

OHIO
(1803)

Ohio R.

Student revivals at Yale College and Andover Seminary around 1800 led to the expansion of Protestant missions in the West and also in Africa, India, and Hawaii. Societies supporting the missions combined into the American Home Missionary Society in 1826.

ILLINOIS
(1818)

INDIANA
(1816)

Cane
Ridge

VA.

Missouri R.

KY.
(1792)

Muddy
River
Red River

Gasper
River

NORTH
CAROLINA

ATLANTIC
OCEAN

TENNESSEE
(1796)

The Second Great Awakening started in the 1790s as Baptists, Methodists, and a new sect called Universalists proselytized in New England. After 1800 the Awakening continued in Kentucky in camp meetings of pioneer farmers, who carried evangelical religion back to their communities.

◄— Paths of settlement, 1790–1830
▲   Camp meeting, 1801
●   Kentucky revival
●   New York's "burned-over district"
◄— Paths of revival

0   125   250 miles
0   125   250 kilometers

MAP 8.4 The Second Great Awakening, 1790–1860

The awakening lasted for decades and invigorated churches in every part of the nation. The revivals in Kentucky and New York State, though, were particularly influential. As thousands of farm families migrated to the west, they carried with them the fervor generated by the Cane Ridge revival in Kentucky in 1801. And, between 1825 and 1835, the area along the Erie Canal in New York witnessed so many revivals that it came to be known as the Burned-over District.

Methodists, they developed an egalitarian religious culture marked by communal singing and emotional services.

The Revivalist Impulse. The revivalist movement that began in the 1790s was much broader than the First Great Awakening of the 1740s. Baptists and Methodists evangelized in the cities and the backcountry of New England. A new sect of Universalists, who repudiated the Calvinist doctrine of predestination and preached universal salvation, gained thousands of converts, especially in Massachusetts and northern New England. After 1800, enthusiastic camp meetings swept the frontier regions of South Carolina, Tennessee, Ohio, and Kentucky. The largest gathering, at Cane Ridge in Kentucky in 1801, lasted for nine electrifying days and nights, and attracted almost 20,000 people (Map 8.4).

Through these revivals, Baptist and Methodist preachers reshaped the spiritual landscape of the South and the Old Southwest. Offering a powerful emotional message and the promise of religious fellowship, revivalists attracted both unchurched individuals and pious families searching for social ties

in their new frontier communities (see Voices from Abroad, "Frances Trollope: A Camp Meeting in Indiana," p. 262).

The Second Great Awakening changed the denominational makeup of American religion. The most important churches of the colonial period—the Congregationalists, Episcopalians, and Quakers—grew slowly from the natural increase of their members. The Methodist and Baptist churches expanded in spectacular fashion by winning converts, and soon were the largest denominations. In the urbanized Northeast, pious Methodist and Baptist women aided their ministers by holding prayer meetings and providing material aid to members in need. In the rural South and West, Methodist preachers followed a circuit, "riding a hardy pony or horse . . . with . . . Bible, hymnbook, and Discipline," and visiting existing congregations on a regular schedule. They established new churches by searching out devout families, bringing them together for worship, and then appointing lay elders to lead the congregation and enforce moral discipline.

Evangelical ministers copied the "practical preaching" techniques of George Whitefield and

Women in the Awakening

The Second Great Awakening was a pivotal moment in the history of American women. In this detail from *Religious Camp Meeting,* painted by J. Maze Burbank in 1839, all the preachers are men, but women fill the audience and form the majority of those visibly "awakened." By transforming millions of women into devout Christians, the Awakening provided Protestant churches with dedicated workers, teachers, and morality-minded mothers. When tens of thousands of these women also joined movements for temperance, abolition, and women's rights, they spurred a great wave of social reform. Old Dartmouth Historical Society/New Bedford Whaling Museum, New Bedford, Massachusetts.

other eighteenth-century revivalists (see Chapter 4). To attract converts, preachers spoke from memory in plain language but with theatrical gestures and flamboyance. "Preach without papers" and emphasize piety rather than theology, advised one minister, "seem earnest & serious; & you will be listened to with Patience, & Wonder."

Black Protestantism. In the South, evangelical religion was initially a disruptive force because it spoke of spiritual equality and criticized slavery.

Husbands and planters grew angry when their wives became more assertive and when blacks were welcomed into their congregations. To retain white men in their churches, Methodist and Baptist preachers gradually adapted their religious message to justify the authority of yeomen patriarchs and slave-owning planters. A Baptist minister declared that a man was naturally at "the head of the woman," while a Methodist conference proclaimed, "We hold that a Christian slave must be submissive, faithful, and obedient."

Frances Trollope

A Camp Meeting in Indiana

Frances Trollope, a successful English author and the mother of novelist Anthony Trollope, lived for a time in Cincinnati, where she owned a bazaar that sold imported goods from Europe. Unsuccessful as a storekeeper, she won great acclaim as a social commentator. Her critical and at times acerbic Domestic Manners of the Americans (1832) was a best-seller in both Europe and the United States. Here she provides her readers with a vivid description of a revivalist meeting in Indiana around 1830.

The prospect of passing a night in the back-woods of Indiana was by no means agreeable, but I screwed my courage to the proper pitch, determined to see with my own eyes, and hear with my own ears, what a camp meeting really was. . . . We reached the ground about an hour before midnight, and the approach to it was highly picturesque. The spot chosen was the verge of an unbroken forest, where a space of about twenty acres appeared to have been partially cleared for the purpose. Tents of different sizes were pitched very near together in a circle round the cleared space. . . .

Four high frames, constructed in the form of altars, were placed at the four corners of the inclosure; on these were supported layers of earth and sod, on which burned immense fires of blazing pine-wood. On one side a rude platform was erected to accommodate the preachers, fifteen of whom attended this meeting, and with very short intervals for necessary refreshment and private devo-

tion, preached in rotation, day and night, from Tuesday to Saturday.

When we arrived, the preachers were silent; but we heard issuing from nearly every tent mingled sounds of praying, preaching, singing, and lamentation. . . . The floor [of one of the tents] was covered with straw, which round the sides was heaped in masses, that might serve as seats, but which at that moment were used to support the heads and arms of the close-packed circle of men and women who kneeled on the floor.

Out of about thirty persons thus placed, perhaps half a dozen were men. One of these [was] a handsome-looking youth of eighteen or twenty. . . . His arm was encircling the neck of a young girl who knelt beside him, with her hair hanging dishevelled upon her shoulders, and her features working with the most violent agitation; soon after they both fell forward on the straw, as if unable to endure in any other attitude the burning eloquence of a tall grim figure in black, who, standing erect in the center, was uttering with incredible vehemence an oration that seemed to hover between praying and preaching; his arms hung stiff and immoveable by his side, and he looked like an ill-constructed machine, set in action by a movement so violent as to threaten its own destruction, so jerkingly, painfully, yet rapidly, did his words tumble out; the kneeling circle ceasing not to call, in every variety of tone, on the name of Jesus. . . .

One tent was occupied exclusively by Negroes. They were all full-dressed, and looked exactly as if they were performing a scene on a stage. One woman wore a dress of pink gauze trimmed with silver lace; another was dressed in pale yellow silk; one or two had splendid turbans; and all wore a profusion of ornaments. The men were in snow white pantaloons, with gay colored linen jackets. One of these, a youth of coal-black

comeliness, was preaching with the most violent gesticulations. . . .

At midnight, a horn sounded through the camp, which, we were told, was to call the people from private to public worship; and we presently saw them flocking from all sides to the front of the preacher's stand. . . . There were about two thousand persons assembled.

One of the preachers began in a low nasal tone, and, like all other Methodist preachers, assured us of the enormous depravity of man. . . . Above a hundred persons, nearly all females, came forward, uttering howlings and groans so terrible that I shall never cease to shudder when I recall them. They appeared to drag each other forward, and on the word being given, "let us pray," they fell on their knees . . . and they were soon all lying on the ground in an indescribable confusion of heads and legs.

SOURCE: Frances Trollope, *Domestic Manners of the Americans* (London: Whittaker, Treacher, 1832), 139–142.

ANALYZING THE EVIDENCE

➤ What is Trollope's opinion about what she witnessed "in the back-woods of Indiana"? Did she see what she expected to see? What clues does the narrative provide?

➤ Who attended the camp meeting? How would you explain the different dress and deportment of the African American believers?

➤ How did the worship at this nineteenth-century camp meeting differ from that in, say, a New England Congregational church in the eighteenth century? How do you explain the difference?

➤ How does Trollope describe the words of the Methodist preacher? How did the Methodists' theology differ from that of earlier Calvinists?

Other evangelists ignored the objections of slave owners and carried the teachings of Protestant Christianity to enslaved African Americans. For much of the eighteenth century, most blacks had maintained the religious practices of their African homelands, giving homage to African gods and spirits or practicing Islam. "At the time I first went to Carolina," remembered Charles Ball, an escaped slave, "there were a great many African slaves in the country. . . . Many of them believed there were several gods [and] I knew several . . . Mohamedans [Muslims]." Then, in the mid-1780s, Protestant evangelists converted hundreds of African Americans along the James River in Virginia and throughout the Chesapeake region.

Subsequently, black preachers adapted the teachings of the white Protestant churches to their own needs. Black Christians generally ignored the doctrines of original sin and Calvinist predestination as well as biblical passages that encouraged unthinking obedience to authority. Some African American converts envisioned the Christian God as a warrior who had liberated the Jews. Their "cause was similar to the Israelites," Martin Prosser, Gabriel's brother and a preacher, told his fellow slaves as they plotted rebellion in Virginia in 1800. "I have read in my Bible where God says, if we worship him, . . . five of you shall conquer a hundred and a hundred of you a hundred thousand of our enemies." Confident of a special relationship with God, Christian slaves prepared themselves spiritually for emancipation, the first step in their journey to the Promised Land.

New Religious Thought and Institutions. Influenced by republican ideology, whites also rejected the Calvinist preoccupation with human depravity and weakness, embracing instead Christian doctrines that focused on human ability and free will. In New England, many educated and affluent Congregationalists placed increasing emphasis on the power of human reason. Discarding the concept of the Trinity—Father, Son, and Holy Spirit—they worshiped an indivisible and "united" God; hence they took the name Unitarians. "The ultimate reliance of a human being is, and must be, on his own mind," argued William Ellery Channing, the famous Unitarian minister, "for the idea of God is the idea of our own spiritual nature, purified and enlarged to infinity."

Other New England Congregationalists reinterpreted Calvinist doctrines. Lyman Beecher, the preeminent Congregationalist clergyman of the early nineteenth century, retained the traditional Christian belief that people had a natural tendency to sin; but, rejecting predestination, he affirmed the capacity of all men and women to choose God. In accepting the doctrines of free will and universal salvation, Beecher testified to the growing belief that people could shape their destiny.

Reflecting this optimism, Reverend Samuel Hopkins linked individual salvation to religious benevolence—the practice of disinterested virtue. As the Presbyterian minister John Rodgers explained, fortunate individuals who had received God's grace had a duty "to dole out charity to their poorer brothers and sisters." Heeding this message, pious merchants in New York founded the Humane Society and other charitable organizations. By the 1820s, so many devout Protestant men and women had embraced benevolent reform that conservative church leaders warned them not to neglect spiritual matters. Still, improving society was a key element of the new religious thought. Said Lydia Maria Child, a devout Christian social reformer: "The only true church organization [is] when heads and hearts unite in working for the welfare of the human-race."

By the 1820s, Protestant Christians were well positioned to undertake that task. Unlike the First Great Awakening, which split churches into warring factions, the Second Great Awakening fostered cooperation among denominations. Religious leaders founded five interdenominational societies: the American Education Society (1815), the Bible Society (1816), the Sunday School Union (1824), the Tract Society (1825), and the Home Missionary Society (1826). Although based in eastern cities—New York, Boston, and Philadelphia—the societies ministered to a national congregation, dispatching hundreds of missionaries to western regions and distributing tens of thousands of religious pamphlets.

Increasingly, Protestant ministers and laypeople saw themselves as part of a united religious movement that could change the course of history. "I want to see our state evangelized," declared a pious churchgoer near the Erie Canal (where the fires of revivalism were so hot that it was known as the "Burned-over District"): "Suppose the great State of New York in all its physical, political, moral, commercial, and pecuniary resources should come over to the Lord's side. Why it would turn the scale and could convert the world. I shall have no rest until it is done."

Because the Second Great Awakening aroused such enthusiasm, religion became an important force in political life. On July 4, 1827, Reverend Ezra

Republican Motherhood

Art often revels much of the cultural values of the time. In this 1795 painting, the artist James Peale, brother of the famous portraitist Charles Willson Peale, depicts himself with his wife and children. The mother stands in the foreground, offering advice to her eldest daughter, while her husband stands to the rear, pointing to the other children. The father, previously the center of attention in family protraits during the colonial era, now gives pride of place to his wife and offspring (see also Reading American Pictures, "Changing Middle-Class Families," p. 250). Pennsylvania Academy of the Fine Arts, Philadelphia.

Stiles Ely called on the members of the Seventh Presbyterian Church in Philadelphia to begin a "Christian party in politics." Ely's sermon, "The Duty of Christian Freemen to Elect Christian Rulers," proclaimed a religious goal for the American republic — an objective that Thomas Jefferson and John Adams would have found strange and troubling. The two founders had died the same day, July 4, 1826, on the fiftieth anniversary of the Declaration of Independence, and had gone to their graves believing that America's mission was to spread political republicanism. In contrast, Ely urged the United States to become an evangelical Christian nation dedicated to religious conversion at home and abroad: "All our rulers ought in their official capacity to serve the Lord Jesus Christ." Similar calls for a union of church and state would arise again during the Third (1880–1900) and Fourth (1970–present) Great Awakenings among American Christians.

Women's New Religious Roles

The upsurge in religious enthusiasm allowed women to demonstrate their piety and even to found new sects. Mother Ann Lee organized the Shakers in Britain and then, in 1774, migrated to America, where she attracted numerous recruits; by the 1820s, Shaker communities dotted the American countryside from New Hampshire to Indiana

(see Chapter 11). Jemima Wilkinson, a young Quaker woman in Rhode Island, founded a more controversial sect. Stirred by reading George Whitefield's sermons, Wilkinson had a vision that she had died and been reincarnated as Christ. Repudiating her birth name, Wilkinson declared herself the "Publick Universal Friend," dressed in masculine attire, and preached a new gospel. Her teachings blended the Calvinist warning of "a lost and guilty, gossiping, dying World" with Quaker-inspired plain dress, pacifism, and abolitionism. Wilkinson's charisma initially won scores of converts, but her radical lifestyle and the challenge she presented to traditional gender roles aroused hostility, and her sect dwindled away.

Increasing Public Activities. These female-led religious experiments were less significant than the activities of thousands of women in mainstream churches. To give but a few examples: Women in New Hampshire managed more than fifty local "cent" societies that raised funds for the Society for Promoting Christian Knowledge; New York City women founded the Society for the Relief of Poor Widows; and young Quaker women in Philadelphia ran the Society for the Free Instruction of African Females.

Women took charge of religious and charitable enterprises both because they were excluded from other public roles and because ministers relied increasingly on them to do the work of the church. After 1800, more than 70 percent of the members of New England Congregational churches were female, which prompted ministers to end long-standing practices like gender-segregated prayer meetings. In fact, evangelical Methodist and Baptist preachers encouraged mixed praying. "Our prayer meetings have been one of the greatest means of the conversion of souls," a minister in central New York reported in the 1820s, "especially those in which brothers and sisters have prayed together."

Far from leading to promiscuity, as critics feared, mixing the sexes promoted greater self-discipline. Believing in female virtue, many young women and the men who courted them now postponed sexual intercourse until after marriage — previously a rare form of self-restraint. In Hingham, Massachusetts, and many other New England towns, more than 30 percent of the women who married between 1750 and 1800 bore a child within eight months of their wedding day; by the 1820s, the rate had dropped to 15 percent.

As women claimed new spiritual authority, men tried to curb their power. Evangelical Baptist churches that had once advocated spiritual equality now denied women the right to vote on church matters or to offer testimonies of faith before the congregation. Those activities, declared one layman, were "directly opposite to the apostolic command in Cor[inthians] XIV, 34, 35, 'Let your women learn to keep silence in the churches.'" "Women have a different *calling*," claimed another. "That they *be chaste, keepers at home* is the Apostle's direction." Combining that injunction with the concept of republican motherhood, mothers throughout the United States founded maternal associations to encourage Christian child rearing. By the 1820s, *Mother's Magazine* and other newsletters, widely read in hundreds of small towns and villages, were giving women a sense of shared purpose and identity.

Women's Education. Religious activism advanced female education. Churches established scores of seminaries and academies where, girls from the middling classes received sound intellectual and moral instruction. Emma Willard, the first American advocate of higher education for women, opened the Middlebury Female Seminary in Vermont in 1814 and later founded girls' schools in Waterford and Troy, New York. Beginning in the 1820s, women educated in these seminaries and academies displaced men as public-school teachers.

Because educated women had few other opportunities for paid employment, they accepted lower pay than men would. Female schoolteachers earned from $12 to $14 a month with room and board — less than a farm laborer. But as schoolteachers, women had an acknowledged place in public life, a goal that had been beyond their reach in colonial and Revolutionary times.

Just as the ideology of democratic republicanism had expanded voting rights and the political influence of ordinary men in the North, so the values of Christian republicanism had bolstered the public authority of middling women. The Second Great Awakening made Americans a fervently Protestant people. Along with the values of republicanism and capitalism, this religious impulse formed the core of an emerging national identity. This identity would be tested in the decades to come, when fundamental economic changes and the growing sectional conflict over slavery would divide the nation along economic and sectional lines.

> ➤ How did republicanism affect the organization, values, and popularity of American churches?

> ➤ Why did Protestant Christianity and Protestant women emerge as forces for social change? In what areas did women become active?

SUMMARY

Like all important ideologies, republicanism has many facets, and we have explored three of them in this chapter. We saw how state legislatures created a capitalist commonwealth, a political economy that encouraged government support of private business. This republican-inspired policy of state mercantilism remained dominant until the 1840s, when it was replaced by classical liberal doctrines (see Chapter 10).

We also saw how republicanism gradually changed social and family values. The principle of legal equality encouraged social mobility among white men and prompted both men and women to seek companionate marriages. Republicanism likewise encouraged parents to provide their children with equal inheritances and to allow them to choose their marriage partners. In the South, republican doctrines of liberty and equality coexisted uneasily with slavery, and ultimately were restricted to the white population.

Finally, we observed the complex interaction of republicanism and religion. Stirred by republican principles, many citizens joined denominations with democratic forms of governance and egalitarian religious cultures, like the Methodist and Baptist churches. Inspired by "benevolent" ideas and the enthusiastic preachers of the Second Great Awakening, many churchgoers joined reformist organizations and infused the emergent republican society with religious values. The result of all these initiatives — in economic policy, social relations, and religious institutions — was the creation of a distinctive American republican culture.

Connections: Culture

In 1763, the year in which Part Two begins, the residents of British North America had little in common. Over the next six decades, they began to create a common culture, an emerging sense of American nationality that would flower in the nineteenth century. As we suggested in the essay that opened Part Two (p. 135),

> by 1820, to be an American meant, for many members of the dominant white population, to be a republican, a Protestant, and an enterprising individual in a capitalist-run market system.

This process of creating a national culture took place in stages. As we saw in Chapter 5, the Patriot movement generated a sense of American identity — as opposed to a Virginian or New York identity — and the republican revolution of 1776 gave it ideological content. And as we noted in Chapter 6, the creation of a national government, first in the Articles of Confederation and then in the Constitution of 1787, greatly augmented that political identity.

As people began to think of themselves as American citizens, they acted purposefully to create a dynamic market-based economy. As we pointed out in Chapter 7 both the state and the national governments took an active role in the development of a capitalist economy. Simultaneously, the intense focus on financial gain by tens of thousands of entrepreneurial farmers, planters, artisans, and merchants shaped a culture that placed high value on hard work and economic achievement. Those characteristics emerged as markers of American identity.

Finally, as we noted in this chapter, the Revolution dramatically increased the commitment to religious liberty on the part of people and government, and set in motion the revivalism that added a Christian component to the emergent American identity.

In 1820, many Americans — blacks, women, laborers, native peoples, the unchurched — either refused to embrace some or all of these values or were denied full membership in republican governments, religious institutions, and business organizations. However, in subsequent decades, these American values — republicanism, capitalism, and Protestantism — would become more widely shared. At the same time, as we will see in Part Three, "Economic Revolution and Sectional Strife, 1820–1876," they become more complex and a source of deep conflict.

CHAPTER REVIEW QUESTIONS

➤ Explain how the republican ideas of the Revolutionary era shaped American society and culture in the late eighteenth and early nineteenth centuries. What regional differences in the social development of republicanism emerged? How can we account for these differences?

➤ Trace the relationship between America's republican culture and the surge of evangelism called the Second Great Awakening. In what ways are the goals of the two movements similar? How are they different?

➤ The text argues that by 1820, a distinct American identity had begun to emerge. How would you describe this identity? What were the forces for unity? And what were the points of contention?

TIMELINE

1782	St. Jean de Crèvecoeur publishes *Letters from an American Farmer*
	Virginia passes law allowing manumission (reversed in 1792)
1783	Noah Webster publishes his "blue-back" speller
1784	Slavery abolished in Massachusetts; other northern states legislate gradual emancipation
1787	Benjamin Rush writes *Thoughts on Female Education*
1790s	States grant corporations charters and special privileges
	Private companies build roads and canals to facilitate trade
	Merchants develop rural outwork system
	Chesapeake blacks adopt Protestant beliefs
	Parents limit family size as farms shrink
	Second Great Awakening expands church membership
1791	Congress charters First Bank of the United States
1792	Mary Wollstonecraft, *A Vindication of the Rights of Woman*
1795	Massachusetts Mill Dam Act promotes textile industry
1800	Gabriel Prosser plots slave rebellion in Virginia
1800s	Rise of sentimentalism and of companionate marriages
	Women's religious activism; founding of female academies
	Religious benevolence sparks social reform
1801	Cane Ridge revival in Kentucky
1807	New Jersey excludes propertied women from suffrage
1816	Congress charters Second Bank of the United States
1817	American Colonization Society is founded
1819	Plummeting agricultural prices set off panic
1819–1821	Missouri Compromise
1820s	States begin reforming public education
	Women become schoolteachers in increasing numbers

FOR FURTHER EXPLORATION

R. Kent Newmyer, *The Supreme Court Under Marshall and Taney* (1968), concisely analyzes constitutional development; Jeffrey L. Pasley, Andrew W. Robertson, and David Waldstreicher, eds. *Beyond the Founders: New Approaches to the Political History of the Early American Republic* (2004), show how ordinary citizens promoted a democratic polity. Jack Larkin, *The Reshaping of Everyday Life, 1790–1840* (1997), explores changes in material culture, as do two excellent Web sites: **memorialhall.mass.edu/collection/index.html** and **memorialhall.mass.edu/activities/turns_activities/index.html**.

Nancy Cott analyzes changing marriage rules in *Public Vows: A History of Marriage and the Nation* (2000); an interview with the author can be heard at **www.npr.org/templates/story/story.php?storyId=1054009**. For an intimate portrayal of family life on the Maine frontier, see Laurel Thatcher Ulrich, *A Midwife's Tale: The Life of Martha Ballard* (1990), the subject of a PBS documentary. Additional materials on Ballard's experiences are available on the Web at **www.pbs.org/amex/midwife** and **www.DoHistory.org**.

Jan Lewis's *The Pursuit of Happiness: Family and Values in Jefferson's Virginia* (1983) explores the lives of the paternalistic slave-owning gentry of the Upper South; James David Miller, *South by Southwest: Planter Emigration and Identity in the Slave South* (2002), discusses their subsequent migration to the Mississippi Valley. For analyses of slavery and the slave trade, see Ira Berlin, *Generations of Captivity: A History of African-American Slaves* (2003); Douglas R. Egerton, *Gabriel's Rebellion: The Virginia Slave Conspiracies of 1800 and 1802* (1995); and the rich Web site at **dpls.dacc.wisc.edu/slavedata/index.html**.

In *The Democratization of American Christianity* (1987), Nathan Hatch traces the impact of evangelical Protestantism. Other fine overviews of American religion are Mark A. Noll, *America's God: From Jonathan Edwards to Abraham Lincoln* (2003), and Bernard Weisberger, *They Gathered at the River* (1958).

TEST YOUR KNOWLEDGE

To assess your command of the material in this chapter, see the Online Study Guide at **bedfordstmartins.com/henretta.**

For Web sites, images, and documents related to topics and places in this chapter, visit **bedfordstmartins.com/makehistory.**

Economic Revolution and Sectional Strife

PART THREE

1820–1877

	ECONOMY	SOCIETY	GOVERNMENT	CULTURE	SECTIONALISM
	The economic revolution begins	**A new class structure emerges**	**Creating a democratic polity**	**Reforming people and institutions**	**From compromise to Civil War and Reconstruction**
1820	▶ Waltham textile factory opens (1814) ▶ Erie Canal completed (1825) ▶ Market economy expands nationwide ▶ Cotton belt emerges in South ▶ Protective tariffs passed (1824, 1828)	▶ Business class emerges ▶ Rural women and girls recruited as factory workers ▶ Mechanics form craft unions	▶ Spread of universal white male suffrage ▶ Rise of Andrew Jackson and Democratic Party ▶ Anti-Masonic Party rises and declines	▶ American Colonization Society (1817) ▶ Benevolent reform movements ▶ Revivalist Charles Finney	▶ Missouri Crisis and Compromise (1819–1821) ▶ David Walker's *Appeal… to the Colored Citizens of the World* (1829) ▶ Domestic slave trade moves African Americans west
1830	▶ Protective tariff (1832) triggers nullification crisis ▶ Panic of 1837 ▶ U.S. textile makers outcompete British	▶ Depression (1839–1843) shatters labor movement ▶ New urban popular culture appears	▶ Whig Party forms (1834) ▶ Second Party System emerges	▶ Joseph Smith founds Mormonism ▶ Female Moral Reform Society (1834) ▶ Temperance crusade expands	▶ Ordinance of Nullification (1832) and Force Bill (1833) ▶ W. L. Garrison forms American Anti-Slavery Society (1833)
1840	▶ Irish immigrants join labor force ▶ *Commonwealth v. Hunt* (1842) legalizes unions in Massachusetts	▶ Working-class districts emerge in cities ▶ Irish and German immigration accelerates	▶ Log cabin campaign (1840) mobilizes voters ▶ Antislavery parties: Liberty (1840) and Free-Soil (1848)	▶ Fourierist and other communal settlements founded ▶ Seneca Falls Women's Rights convention (1848)	▶ Texas annexation (1845), Mexican War (1846–1848), and Wilmot Proviso (1846) increase sectional conflict
1850	▶ Surge of cotton output in South and of railroads in North and Midwest ▶ Manufacturing expands ▶ Panic of 1857	▶ Expansion of farm society into Midwest and Far West ▶ Free-labor ideology justifies inequality	▶ Whig Party disintegrates ▶ Republican Party founded (1854) ▶ Third Party System begins	▶ Harriet Beecher Stowe's *Uncle Tom's Cabin* (1852) ▶ Anti-immigrant nativist movement and Know-Nothing Party	▶ Compromise of 1850 ▶ Kansas-Nebraska Act (1854) and "Bleeding Kansas" ▶ *Dred Scott* decision (1857)
1860	▶ Republicans enact policy agenda: Homestead Act (1862), railroad aid, high tariffs, and national banking	▶ Emancipation Proclamation (1863) ▶ Free blacks in the South struggle for control of land	▶ Thirteenth Amendment (1865) ends slavery ▶ Fourteenth Amendment (1868) extends legal and political rights	▶ U.S. Sanitary Commission founded (1861)	▶ South Carolina leads secession movement (1860) ▶ Confederate States of America (1861–1865)
1870	▶ Panic of 1873	▶ Rise of sharecropping in the South	▶ Fifteenth Amendment (1870) extends vote to black men	▶ Freed African Americans create schools and churches	▶ Compromise of 1877 ends Reconstruction

In America, a French visitor remarked in 1839, "all is circulation, motion, and boiling agitation. Enterprise follows enterprise [and] riches and poverty follow." Indeed, as we shall see in Part Three, American society was rapidly changing in basic ways. In 1820, the United States was predominately an agricultural nation; by 1877, it boasted one of the world's most powerful industrial economies. Two other sets of dramatic events marked this era. The first was the creation of a genuinely modern polity: a democratic political system with competitive political parties. Second, many Americans developed a complex social identity that was both staunchly nationalistic and resolutely sectional. These profound transformations affected every aspect of life in the northern and midwestern states and brought important changes in the South as well. Here, in brief, is an outline of that story.

ECONOMY An economic revolution, powered by advances in industrial production and a vast expansion in the market system, transformed the nation's economy. Factory owners used high-speed machines and a new system of labor discipline to boost the output of goods dramatically. Simultaneously, enterprising merchants made use of a new network of canals and railroads to create a vast national market. Manufacturers produced 5 percent of the country's wealth in 1820 but more than 30 percent in 1877, and now sold their products throughout the nation.

SOCIETY The new economy created a class-based society in the North and Midwest. A wealthy elite of merchants, manufacturers, bankers, and entrepreneurs struggled to the top of the social order. Once in charge, they tried to maintain social stability through a paternalistic program of benevolent reform. However, a rapidly growing urban middle class created a distinct material and religious culture and spearheaded movements for radical

social reform. Moreover, a mass of propertyless workers, many of them impoverished immigrants from Germany and Ireland, joined labor unions to win better wages and working conditions. Thanks to the interstate slave trade, Southern planters extended the plantation society of the Chesapeake and Carolinas as far south and west as Texas.

GOVERNMENT The rapid growth of political parties sparked the creation of a democratic polity open to many social groups. Between 1790 and 1830, farmers, workers, and entrepreneurs persuaded governments to improve transportation, shorten workdays, and award valuable corporate charters. Catholic immigrants from Ireland and Germany entered the political arena to protect their religion and cultures from restrictive legislation advocated by Protestant nativists and reformers.

With Andrew Jackson at its head, the Democratic Party advanced the interests of southern planters, farmers, and urban workers. In the 1830s and 1840s, the Jacksonians led a political and constitutional revolution that cut government aid to financiers, merchants, and corporations. To contend with the Democrats, the Whig Party (and, in the 1850s, the Republican Party) devised a competing program that stressed economic development, moral reform, and individual social mobility. This party competition engaged the energies of the electorate and helped unify a fragmented social order.

CULTURE Between 1820 and 1860, a series of reform movements, many with religious roots and goals, swept across America. Dedicated men and women preached the gospel of temperance, Sunday observance, prison reform, and dozens of other causes. Some Americans pursued their social dreams in isolated utopian communities, but most reformers worked within society. Two interrelated groups — abolitionists and women's rights activists — demanded

radical changes: the immediate end of slavery and the overthrow of the patriarchal legal and political order. As southern planters increasingly defended slavery as a "positive good," antislavery advocates turned to political action. During the 1840s and 1850s, they demanded free soil in the western territories and charged that a "slave power conspiracy" threatened free labor and republican values throughout the nation.

SECTIONALISM The economic revolution and social reform sharpened sectional divisions: The North developed into an urban industrial society based on free labor, whereas the South remained a rural agricultural society dependent on slavery. Following the Mexican War (1846–1848), northern and southern politicians struggled bitterly over the expansion of slavery into the vast territories seized from Mexico and the lands of the Louisiana Purchase. The election of Republican Abraham Lincoln in 1860 prompted the secession of the South from the Union and the onset of sectional warfare. The conflict became a total war, a struggle between two societies as well as two armies. And because of new technology and the mobilization of huge armies, the two sides endured unprecedented casualties and costs.

The fruits of victory for the North were substantial. During Reconstruction, the Republican Party ended slavery, imposed its economic policies and constitutional doctrines, and extended full democratic rights to former slaves. In the face of massive resistance from white Southerners, northern leaders gradually abandoned the effort to secure African Americans the full benefits of freedom. These decades, which began with great optimism and impressive achievements, thus ended on the bitter notes of a costly war, an acrimonious peace, and a half-won freedom.

ART IS THE HANDMAID OF HUMAN GOOD. · LOWELL. ·

Economic Transformation

1820–1860

IN 1804, LIFE TURNED GRIM FOR eleven-year-old Chauncey Jerome of Connecticut. His father died suddenly, and Jerome faced indentured servitude on a nearby farm. Knowing that few farmers "would treat a poor boy like a human being," Jerome bought out his indenture by making dials for clocks and eventually ended up a journeyman clockmaker for Eli Terry. A manufacturing wizard, Terry had designed an enormously popular desk clock with brass parts; his business turned Litchfield, Connecticut, into the clock-making center of the United States. Jerome followed in Terry's footsteps and in 1816 set up his own clock factory. By organizing work more efficiently and using new machines that made interchangeable metal parts, Jerome drove down the price of a simple clock from $20 to $5 and then to less than $2. By the 1840s, he was selling his clocks in England, the hub of the Industrial Revolution; two decades later, his workers were turning out 200,000 clocks a year, clear testimony to American enterprise and the American economic transformation. By 1860, the United States was not only the world's leading exporter of cotton and wheat but also the third-ranked manufacturing nation behind Britain and France.

"Business is the very soul of an American: the fountain of all human felicity," Francis Grund, a European immigrant, observed shortly after

◄ **Technology Celebrated**

Artists joined with manufacturers in praising the new industrial age. In this 1836 image, a cornucopia (horn of plenty) spreads its bounty over the city of Lowell, Massachusetts. The bales of raw cotton in the foreground will be transformed in the water-powered textile factories into smooth cloth, for shipment to far-flung markets via the new railroad system. The image of prosperity was deceptive. Two years earlier, two thousand women textile workers had gone on strike in Lowell, claiming that their wages failed to provide a decent standard of living. Private Collection.

his arrival. "It is as if all America were but one gigantic workshop, over the entrance of which there is the blazing inscription, 'No admission here, except on business.'" As the editor of *Niles' Weekly Register* in Baltimore put it, there was an "almost universal ambition to get forward." Stimulated by the entrepreneurial culture of early-nineteenth-century America, thousands of artisan-inventors like Eli Terry and Chauncey Jerome and thousands of merchants and traders propelled the country into a new economic era. Two great changes defined that era: the growth and mechanization of industry, the Industrial Revolution, and the expansion and integration of markets, the **Market Revolution**.

Not all Americans embraced the new ethic of enterprise, and many of the most ambitious failed to share in the new prosperity. The spread of industry and commerce created a class-divided society that challenged the founders' vision of an agricultural republic with few distinctions of wealth. As the philosopher Ralph Waldo Emerson warned in 1839: "The invasion of Nature by Trade with its Money, its Credit, its Steam, [and] its Railroad threatens to . . . establish a new, universal Monarchy."

The American Industrial Revolution

Industrialization came to the United States between 1790 and 1820, as merchants and manufacturers reorganized work routines and built factories. The rapid construction of turnpikes, canals, and railroads by state governments and private entrepreneurs, working together in the Commonwealth system (see Chapter 8) allowed manufactures to be sold throughout the land, and goods that once had been luxury items became part of everyday life (Table 9.1).

The Division of Labor and the Factory

Rising living standards stemmed initially from changes in the organization of work. Consider the shoe industry. Traditionally, New England shoemakers worked in small wooden shacks called "ten-footers," where they controlled the pace of work as they turned leather hides into finished shoes and boots. During the 1820s and 1830s, the merchants and manufacturers of Lynn, Massachusetts, gradually took over the shoe industry by increasing efficiency through an outwork system and a **division of labor**. The employers hired semiskilled journeymen and set them to work in large shops cutting leather into soles and uppers. They sent out the upper sections to dozens of rural Massachusetts towns, where women binders sewed in fabric linings. The manufacturers then had other journeymen attach the uppers to the soles and return the shoes to the central shop for inspection, packing, and sale. The new system turned employers into powerful "shoe bosses" and eroded workers' control of their labor. Whatever the cost to workers, the division of labor dramatically increased the output of shoes and cut their price.

| **TABLE 9.1** | Leading Branches of Manufacture, 1860 |

Item	Number of Workers	Value of Product (millions)	Value Added by Manufacture (millions)	Rank by Value Added
Cotton textiles	115,000	$107.3	$54.7	1
Lumber	75,600	$104.9	$53.8	2
Boots and shoes	123,000	$91.9	$49.2	3
Flour and meal	27,700	$248.6	$40.1	4
Men's clothing	114,800	$80.8	$36.7	5
Iron (cast, forged, etc.)	49,000	$73.1	$35.7	6
Machinery	41,200	$52.0	$32.5	7
Woolen goods	40,600	$60.7	$25.0	8
Leather	22,700	$67.3	$22.8	9
Liquors	12,700	$56.6	$22.5	10

SOURCE: Adapted from Douglass C. North, *Growth and Welfare in the American Past*, 2nd ed. (Paramus, NJ: Prentice Hall, 1974), table 6.1.

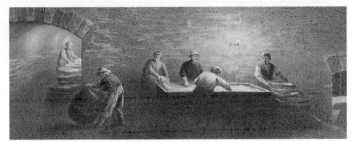

Pork Packing in Cincinnati

The only modern technology in this Cincinnati pork-packing plant was the overhead pulley that carried hog carcasses past the workers. The plant's efficiency came from its organization, a division of labor in which each worker performed a specific task. Plants like this pioneered the design of the moving assembly line, which would reach a high level of sophistication in the early twentieth century, in Henry Ford's automobile factories. Cincinnati Historical Society.

For products that were not suited to the out-work system, manufacturers created the modern **factory**, which concentrated production under one roof. For example, in the 1830s, Cincinnati merchants built large slaughterhouses that processed thousands of hogs every month. A simple system of overhead rails moved the hog carcasses past workers who performed specific tasks. One worker split the animals, another removed various organs, and still others trimmed the carcasses into pieces. Packers then stuffed the cuts of pork into barrels and pickled them to prevent spoilage. The Cincinnati system was so efficient and quick — processing 60 hogs an hour — that by the 1840s, the city was known as "Porkopolis." By 1850, factories in the city were slaughtering hogs in even greater volume — 334,000 a year. Reported Frederick Law Olmsted:

We entered an immense low-ceiling room and followed a vista of dead swine, upon their backs, their paws stretching mutely toward heaven. Walking down to the vanishing point, we found there a sort of human chopping-machine where the hogs were converted into commercial pork. . . . Plump falls the hog upon the table, chop, chop; chop, chop; chop, chop, fall the cleavers. . . . We took out our watches and counted thirty-five seconds, from the moment when one hog touched the table until the next occupied its place.

Some factories boasted impressive new technology. As early as the 1780s Oliver Evans, a prolific Delaware inventor, built a highly automated flour mill driven by waterpower. His machinery lifted the wheat to the top of the mill, cleaned the grain as it fell into hoppers, ground it into flour, conveyed the flour back to the top of the mill, and then cooled the flour as it was poured into barrels. Evans's factory, remarked one observer, "was as full of machinery as the case of a watch." It needed only six men to mill 100,000 bushels of wheat a year—perhaps ten times as much as they could grind in a traditional flour mill.

By the 1830s, factory owners were using newly improved stationary steam engines to power their mills, which now manufactured a wide array of products. Previously, most factories processed agricultural goods: pork, leather, wool, and cotton; by the 1830s and 1840s, they were fabricating metal goods. Cyrus McCormick of Chicago used power-driven machines to make parts for reaping machines, which workers assembled on a power-driven conveyor belt (see Reading American Pictures, "How Did Americans Dramatically Increase Farm Productivity?" p. 275). In Hartford, Connecticut, Samuel Colt built an assembly line to produce his invention—the six-shooter revolver, as it became known. These technological advances alarmed a team of British observers: "The contriving and making of machinery has become so common in this country, and so many heads and hands are at work with extraordinary energy, that . . . it is to be feared that American manufacturers will become exporters not only to foreign countries, but even to England."

The Textile Industry and British Competition

British textile manufacturers were particularly worried about American competition. To protect its industrial leadership, the British government prohibited the export of textile machinery and the emigration of **mechanics** who knew how to build it. Lured by high wages or offers of partnerships, though, thousands of British mechanics disguised themselves as ordinary laborers and set sail for the United States. By 1812, there were at least three hundred British mechanics at work in the Philadelphia area alone.

Samuel Slater was the most important of them. Slater came to America in 1789 after working for Richard Arkwright, who invented the most advanced British machinery for spinning cotton. Slater reproduced Arkwright's innovations in merchant Moses Brown's cotton mill in Providence, Rhode Island; its opening in 1790 marks the start of the Industrial Revolution in America.

American and British Advantages. In competing with British mills, American manufacturers had the advantage of an abundance of natural resources. The nation's farmers produced a wealth of cotton and wool, and its fast-flowing rivers provided a cheap source of energy. As rivers cascaded down from the Appalachian foothills to the Atlantic coastal plain, they were easily harnessed to power machinery. From Massachusetts to Delaware, these waterways became dotted with industrial villages and towns dominated by massive textile mills, some as large as 150 feet long, 40 feet wide, and four stories high (Map 9.1).

Still, British textile producers easily undersold their American competitors. Thanks to cheap transatlantic shipping and low interest rates in Britain, they could import raw cotton from the United States, manufacture it into cloth, ship the cloth to America, and sell it there at a bargain price. Moreover, well-established British companies could engage in cutthroat competition, slashing prices to drive fledgling American firms out of business. The most important British advantage was cheap labor: Britain had a larger population—about 12.6 million in 1810 compared to 7.3 million Americans—and thousands of landless laborers who were willing to take low-paying factory jobs.

To offset these British advantages, American entrepreneurs won help from the federal government. In 1816 Congress passed a tariff that protected textile manufacturers from low-cost imports of cotton cloth. In 1824 a new tariff levied a tax of 35 percent on higher-grade woolen and cotton textiles, imported iron goods, and various agricultural products; in 1828 the textile duty rose to 50 percent. But in 1833, under pressure from southern planters, western farmers, and urban consumers—who wanted inexpensive imports—Congress began to reduce the tariffs (see Chapter 10), a decision that led to hard times and even bankruptcy for some American textile companies.

Improved Technology and Women Workers. American producers used two other strategies to compete with their British rivals. First, they improved on British technology. In 1811, Francis Cabot Lowell, a wealthy Boston merchant, toured British textile mills. A charming young man, he flattered his hosts by asking many questions; he also duped them, secretly making detailed drawings of their power machinery. Paul Moody, an experienced American mechanic, then copied the machines and refined them. In 1814, Lowell joined with merchants Nathan Appleton and Patrick Tracy Jackson to form the Boston Manufacturing Company. Raising the staggering sum of $400,000, they built a textile plant on the Charles River in Waltham, Massachusetts. The Waltham factory was

How Did Americans Dramatically Increase Farm Productivity?

Acentral aspect of the economic transformation during the mid-nineteenth century was the increased productivity brought about by harnessing machinery to human power. It is easy to understand how the use of water to power spinning and weaving machines increased output in factories. But what impact did machines have on farming, the dominant occupation in the United States at the time? Did farmers' productivity improve?

ANALYZING THE EVIDENCE

➤ The picture on the top shows the wheat harvest at Bishop Hill, a commune founded in Illinois in 1848 by Swedish Pietists (see Chapter 11 for a discussion of rural communes). What tools are the men using to cut the wheat? What are the women's tasks? Do you think these communalists harvested wheat significantly more efficiently than individual farm families had done for a hundred years?

➤ Now look at the picture of McCormick's reaper, taken from an advertisement. Using this machine, the farmer and his son could harvest as much in a day as the nineteen workers at Bishop Hill. How did it achieve such a dramatic increase in productivity?

➤ Look closely at the reaper in the advertisement. What is the purpose of the letters inscribed on each part of the machine? What does this tell you about the standardization of parts that was crucial to the Industrial Revolution?

Why do you think the manufacturer provided this information to potential buyers?

Wheat Farming at Bishop Hill, Illinois. Bishop Hill Historic Site/Illinois Historic Preservation Agency.

Diagram of McCormick's Reaper from *The Cultivator*, May 1846. Wisconsin Historical Society.

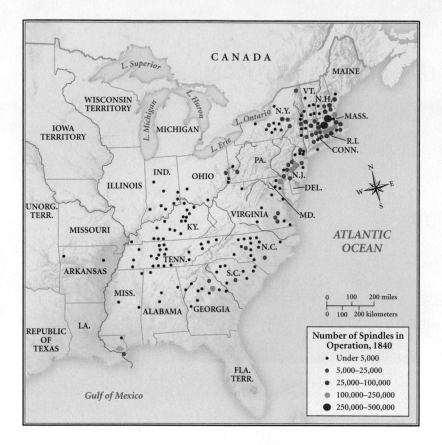

MAP 9.1 New England's Dominance in Cotton Spinning, 1840

Although the South grew the nation's cotton, it did not process it. Entrepreneurs in Massachusetts and Rhode Island built most of the factories that spun and wove raw cotton into cloth. The new factories made use of the abundant waterpower available in New England and the area's surplus labor force. Initially, factory managers hired young farm women to work the machines; later, they would rely on immigrants from Ireland and French-speaking regions of Canada.

the first in America to perform all the operations of cloth making under one roof. Thanks to Moody's improvements, Waltham's power looms operated at higher speeds than British looms and needed fewer workers.

The second American strategy was to tap a new, and cheaper, source of labor. In the 1820s, the Boston Manufacturing Company pioneered a labor system that became known as the Waltham plan. The company recruited thousands of young women from farm families to work in its textile factories. To lure the women, it provided them with rooms in boardinghouses and with evening lectures and other cultural activities. To reassure their parents about their daughters' moral welfare, the mill owners enforced strict curfews, prohibited alcoholic beverages, and required regular church attendance. At Lowell (1822), Chicopee (1823), and other sites in Massachusetts and New Hampshire, the company built new cotton factories modeled on the Waltham plan; other Boston-based companies quickly followed suit.

By the early 1830s, more than 40,000 New England women were working in textile mills. As an observer noted, the wages were "more than could be obtained by the hitherto ordinary occupation of housework," and the living conditions were often better than those in crowded farmhouses. Lucy

Larcom became a textile operative at age eleven so that she could support herself and not be "a trouble or burden or expense" to her widowed mother. Other women operatives used their wages to pay off their father's farm mortgages, send their brothers to school, or accumulate a dowry for themselves.

A few operatives just had a good time. Susan Brown, a Lowell weaver, spent half of her earnings on food and lodging and the rest on plays, concerts, lectures, and a two-day excursion to Boston. Like most textile workers, Brown soon tired of the monotony and rigor of factory work and the never-ceasing clatter of the machinery, which ran twelve hours a day, six days a week. After eight months, she quit, lived at home for a spell, and then moved to another mill. Whatever the hardships, waged work gave young women a new sense of freedom and autonomy. "Don't I feel independent!" a woman mill worker wrote to her sister. "The thought that I am living on no one is a happy one indeed to me."

The owners of the Boston Manufacturing Company were even happier. By combining tariff protection with improved technology and female labor, they could undersell their British rivals. Their textiles were also cheaper than those manufactured in New York and Pennsylvania, where farmworkers were better paid than in New England and textile wages consequently were higher. Manufacturers in

Mill Girl, c. 1850

This fine daguerreotype (an early photograph) shows a neatly dressed textile worker of about twelve. The harsh working conditions in the mill have taken a toll on her spirit and body: The girl's eyes and mouth show little joy or life, and her hands are rough and swollen. She probably worked either as a knotter, tying broken threads on spinning jennies, or a warper, straightening out the strands of cotton or wool as they entered the loom. Jack Naylor Collection.

those states remained in business by using advanced technology to produce higher-quality cloth. Even Thomas Jefferson, the great champion of yeoman farming, was impressed. "Our manufacturers are now very nearly on a footing with those of England," he boasted in 1825.

American Mechanics and Technological Innovation

By the 1820s, American-born artisans had replaced British immigrants at the cutting edge of technological innovation. Although few of these mechanics had a formal education, they now claimed respect as "men professing an ingenious art." In the Philadelphia region, the most important inventors came from the remarkable Sellars family. Samuel Sellars Jr. invented a machine for twisting worsted woolen yarn to give it an especially smooth surface. His son John devised more efficient ways of using waterpower to run the family's sawmills and built a machine to weave wire sieves. John's sons and grandsons built machine shops that turned out riveted leather fire hoses, papermaking equipment, and eventually locomotives. In 1824, the Sellars family joined with other mechanics to found the Franklin Institute in Philadelphia. Named after Benjamin Franklin, whom the mechanics admired for his scientific accomplishments and idealization of hard work, the Franklin Institute published a journal; provided high-school-level instruction in mechanics, chemistry, mathematics, and mechanical drawing; and organized annual fairs to exhibit new products. Craftsmen in Ohio and many other states established their own mechanics' institutes, which disseminated technical knowledge and encouraged innovation. Around 1820, the U.S. Patent Office was issuing about two hundred patents for new inventions each year, mostly to gentlemen and merchants. By 1860, the office was awarding four thousand patents annually, mostly to mechanics from modest backgrounds.

Eli Whitney and Machine Tools. American craftsmen facilitated the rapid spread of the Industrial Revolution by pioneering the development of

Eli Whitney

Eli Whitney posed for this portrait in the 1820s, when he had achieved both prosperity and social standing as the inventor of the cotton gin and other machines. Whitney's success prompted the artist, his young New Haven, Connecticut, neighbor Samuel F. B. Morse, to turn his creative energies from painting to industrial technology. By the 1840s, Morse had devised the first successful commercial telegraph. Yale University Art Gallery, Gift of George Hoadley, BA 1801.

An Early Cotton Gin

This picture shows the bottom part of a cotton gin, which contained the moving parts. The worker fed the bolls of cotton into the bottom comparment in the front of the machine (to your right) and turned the crank. The toothed cylinder caught the fibers and pulled them from the seeds; the revolving brushes then removed the fibers from the cylinder and pushed them out of the gin, either through the rear or the top. The gin processed cotton quickly and cheaply, and thereby facilitated the dramatic expansion of the cotton textile industry. Over the years, inventors devised much larger gins, powered by water and steam, to process huge bales of raw cotton. Smithsonian Institution, Washington, D.C.

machine tools—machines that made parts for other machines. The key innovator was Eli Whitney (1765–1825), the son of a middling New England farm family. At the age of fourteen, Whitney began manufacturing nails and knife blades and, later, women's hatpins and men's walking sticks. Aspiring to wealth and high social status, Whitney won admission to Yale College and subsequently became a tutor on a Georgia cotton plantation. Using his expertise in making hatpins, he built a simple machine that separated the seeds from the delicate cotton fibers. Although Whitney patented his cotton "engine" (or "gin," as it became known), other manufacturers improved on his design and captured the market.

To restore his finances, Whitney decided in 1798 to manufacture military weapons, a product with a guaranteed government market. With the help of Secretary of the Treasury Oliver Wolcott, he won a U.S. government contract to manufacture 10,000 muskets within twenty-eight months.

Although Whitney failed to meet the deadline, he eventually designed and built machine tools that could rapidly produce interchangeable musket parts. This success won him new contracts for weapons during the War of 1812, and the wealth, social position, and fame as an inventor that he had long craved. After Whitney's death, his partner John H. Hall, an engineer at the federal armory in Harpers Ferry, Virginia (now West Virginia), built lathes to fashion gun stocks and an array of machine tools to work metal: turret lathes, milling machines, and precision grinders.

Entrepreneurial Energy Unleashed. Technological innovation now swept through the rest of American manufacturing. Mechanics in the textile industry invented lathes, planers, and boring machines that turned out standardized parts for new spinning jennies and weaving looms. Although produced in large numbers, these jennies and looms were precise enough in design and construction to operate at higher speeds than British equipment. In 1837, Richard Garsed fashioned improvements that nearly doubled the speed of the power looms in his father's factory in Delaware. Garsed also patented a cam and harness device that allowed machines to weave damask and other fabrics with elaborate designs. Meanwhile, the mechanics employed by Samuel W. Collins in his Connecticut ax-making company built a vastly improved die-forging machine, a device that pressed and hammered hot metal into dies, or cutting forms. Using this machine, a worker could make three hundred ax heads a day—versus twelve using the traditional method. In Richmond, Virginia, Welsh- and American-born mechanics made similar technical advances at the Tredegar Iron Works. Soon, many manufacturers were using machine tools to produce complicated manufacturing equipment with great speed, at low cost, and in large quantities. As a team of British observers noted with admiration, many American products were made "with machinery applied to almost every process . . . all reduced to an almost perfect system of manufacture."

With the expanded availability of machines, the American Industrial Revolution came of age. The sheer volume of output elevated some products—Remington rifles, Singer sewing machines, and Yale locks—into household names in the United States and abroad. After showing their machine-tooled goods at the Crystal Palace Exhibition in London in 1851, the first major international display of industrial goods, Remington, Singer, and other American businesses built factories in Great Britain and soon dominated many European markets.

Wageworkers and the Labor Movement

As the Industrial Revolution gathered momentum, it changed the nature of work and of workers' lives. By the early nineteenth century, many American **craft workers** had developed an "artisan republican ethic" — a collective identity based on the principles of liberty and equality. They saw themselves as small-scale producers, equal to one another and free to work for themselves. The poet Walt Whitman summed up their outlook: "Men must be masters, under themselves."

However, as the outwork and factory systems spread, more and more workers took jobs as wage earners. They no longer labored "under themselves" but under the control and direction of their employers. Unlike women, who embraced factory work because it freed them from parental control and domestic service, men often bridled at their status as wageworkers. To maintain a sense of their personal independence, most male wageworkers repudiated the traditional terms *master* and *servant*; instead, they used the Dutch *boss* to refer to their employer. But as *hired hands*, they received meager wages and had little job security. The artisan-republican ideal, a by-product of the American Revolution, was giving way to the harsher reality of the waged work force in an industrializing capitalist society.

The Emergence of Unions. Some wageworkers labored as journeymen carpenters, stonecutters, masons, and cabinetmakers, traditional crafts that required specialized skills and so generated a strong sense of identity. Both factors enabled these workers to form unions and bargain with their master-artisan employers. The journeymen's main concern was the increasing length of the workday, which kept them from their families and from educational opportunities. Before 1800, the workday in the building trades averaged about twelve hours, including breaks for meals. By the 1820s, masters were demanding a longer day during the summer, when it stayed light longer, while paying journeymen the old daily rate. In response, six hundred carpenters in Boston went on strike in 1825, demanding a ten-hour workday, 6 A.M. to 6 P.M., with an hour each for breakfast and lunch. Although the Boston protest failed, journeymen carpenters in Philadelphia won a similar strike in 1827. By the mid-1830s, building-trades workers had won a ten-hour workday from many employers and from the federal government at the Philadelphia navy yard.

Artisans whose occupations were threatened by industrialization were less successful in preserving

Woodworker, c. 1850

Skilled furniture makers took great pride in their work, which was often intricately designed and beautifully executed. To underline the dignity of his occupation, this woodworker poses in formal dress and proudly displays the tools of his craft. A belief in the value of labor was an important ingredient of the artisan-republican ideology held by many workers. Library of Congress.

their living standards. As aggressive entrepreneurs and machine technology changed the nature of production, shoemakers, hatters, printers, furniture makers, and weavers faced falling income, unemployment, and loss of status. To avoid the regimentation of factory work, some artisans in these trades moved to small towns or set up specialized shops. In New York City, 800 highly skilled cabinetmakers owned small shops that made fashionable or custom-made furniture. In status and income, they outranked a much larger group of 3,200 semitrained workers — derogatively called "botches" — who labored for wages in factories making cheap mass-produced tables and chairs. The new industrial system had divided the traditional artisan class into two groups: self-employed craftsmen and wage-earning workers.

In many industries, wage earners banded together to form unions and bargain for better pay and working conditions. However, under English and American common law, unions were illegal. As a Philadelphia judge put it, unions were "a government unto themselves," and unlawfully interfered with an employer's authority over his "servant" and with workers who wanted to bargain for their own wages and working conditions. Despite the legal obstacles, unions sprang up. In 1830, journeymen shoemakers founded a mutual benefit society in Lynn, Massachusetts, and similar organizations soon appeared in other shoemaking centers. "The division of society into the producing and non-producing classes," the journeymen explained, had made workers like themselves into a mere "commodity" whose labor could be bought and sold without regard for their welfare. As another group of workers put it, "The capitalist has no other interest in us, than to get as much labor out of us as possible. We are hired men, and hired men, like hired horses, have no souls." Indeed, we are "slaves in the strictest sense of the word," declared various groups of Lynn shoemakers and Lowell textile workers. But one Lowell worker pointed out, "We are not a quarter as bad off as the slaves of the south. . . . They can't vote nor complain and we can." To exert more pressure on their capitalist employers, in 1834, local unions from Boston to Philadelphia formed the National Trades' Union, the first regional union of different trades.

Labor Ideology and Strikes. Union leaders criticized the new industrial order by endorsing and expanding **artisan republicanism** to include waged laborers. Pointing out that wage earners were becoming "slaves to a monied aristocracy," they condemned the new outwork and factory systems in which "capital and labor stand opposed." To restore a just society in which artisans and waged workers could "live as comfortably as others," they advanced a **labor theory of value**. This theory, or standard, proposed that the price of a good should reflect the labor required to make it and that most of the money from its sale should go to the individual or individuals who produced it—not to factory owners, middlemen, or storekeepers. Appealing to the spirit of the American Revolution, which had destroyed the aristocracy of birth, union publicists called for a new revolution to destroy the aristocracy of capital. In 1836, armed with this artisan-republican ideology, unionized men organized nearly fifty strikes for higher wages.

Women textile operatives were equally active. Competition in the woolen and cotton textile industries was fierce because the output of textiles was growing faster than demand, causing prices to fall. As their profits declined, employers reduced workers' wages and imposed more-stringent work rules. In 1828, women mill workers in Dover, New Hampshire, struck against new rules and won some

relief; six years later, more than eight hundred Dover women walked out to protest wage cuts. In Lowell, two thousand women operatives backed a strike by withdrawing their savings from an employer-owned bank. "One of the leaders mounted a pump," the *Boston Transcript* reported, "and made a flaming . . . speech on the rights of women and the iniquities of the 'monied aristocracy.'" When conditions did not improve, young women in New England refused to enter the mills, and impoverished Irish (and later French Canadian) immigrants took their places.

By the 1850s, many industrial workers were facing the threat of unemployment. As machines produced more goods, the supply of manufactures exceeded the demand for them and prompted employers to lay off workers. In 1857, overproduction coincided with a financial panic that was sparked by speculative investments in railroads that went bankrupt. The result was a major economic recession. Unemployment rose to 10 percent, reminding Americans of the social costs of the new—and otherwise very successful—system of industrial production.

➤ How did American textile manufacturers compete with British manufacturers? How successful were they?

➤ In what ways did the emerging industrial economy conflict with artisan republicanism?

➤ How did wage laborers respond to the new economy?

The Market Revolution

As American factories and farms turned out more goods, businessmen and legislators created faster and cheaper ways to get those products to consumers. Beginning in the late 1810s, they constructed a massive system of canals and roads that linked the states along the Atlantic coast with one another and with the new states in the trans-Appalachian west. This transportation system set in motion both a market revolution and a great migration of people. By 1860, nearly one-third of the nation's citizens lived in the Midwest (the five states carved out of the Northwest Territory—Ohio, Indiana, Illinois, Michigan, and Wisconsin—along with Missouri, Iowa, and Minnesota), where they created a complex society and economy that increasingly resembled the Northeast.

The Transportation Revolution Forges Regional Ties

With the Indian peoples in retreat, slave-owning planters from the Lower South settled in Missouri (admitted to the Union in 1821), and pushed on to Arkansas (1836). Simultaneously, yeomen farm families from the Upper South joined migrants from New England and New York in taking control of the fertile farmlands of the Great Lakes basin. Once Indiana and Illinois were settled, land-hungry farmers poured into Michigan (1837), Iowa (1846), and Wisconsin (1848) (see Voices from Abroad, "Ernst Stille: German Immigrants in the Midwest," p. 282). In 1820, to meet the demand for cheap farmsteads, Congress reduced the price of federal land from $2.00 an acre to $1.25 — just enough to cover the cost of the survey and sale. For $100, a farmer could buy eighty acres, the minimum required under federal law. By 1840, this generous land-distribution policy had lured about 5 million people to states and territories west of the Appalachians (Map 9.2).

To link these settlers to one another, state governments chartered private companies to build toll roads, or turnpikes. In 1806, Congress approved funds for the construction of the National Road, which would tie the Midwest to the seaboard states. The project began in Cumberland in western Maryland in 1811; reached Wheeling, Virginia (now West Virginia), in 1818; crossed the Ohio River in 1833; and ended in Vandalia, Illinois, in 1839. The National Road and other interregional highways carried migrants and their heavily loaded wagons westward; along the way, they passed herds of livestock destined for eastern markets.

Canals. Long-distance travel overland was slow and expensive. To carry people, crops, and manufactures to and from the Midwest, public and private sectors developed a water-borne transportation system of unprecedented size, complexity, and cost. The key event was the decision of the New York legislature in 1817 to build the Erie Canal, a 364-mile waterway from Lake Erie to the Hudson River. It was

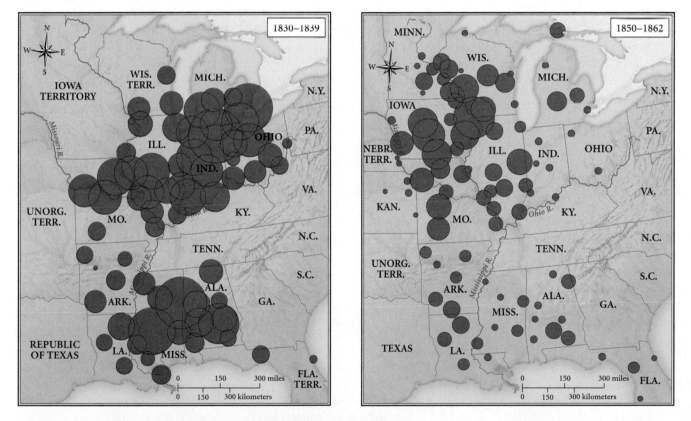

MAP 9.2   Western Land Sales, 1830–1839 and 1850–1862

The federal government set up land offices to sell farmsteads to settlers. During the 1830s, the offices sold huge amounts of land in the corn and wheat belt of the Old Northwest (Ohio, Indiana, Illinois, and Michigan) and the cotton belt of the Old Southwest (especially Alabama and Mississippi). By the 1850s, most sales of government land were in the upper Mississippi River Valley (particularly Iowa and Wisconsin). Each circle centers on a government land office and indicates the relative amount of land sold at that office.

Ernst Stille

German Immigrants in the Midwest

*B*etween *1830 and 1860, Germans flooded into the midwestern states. Among them were twenty-three members of the interrelated Stille and Krumme families from the Prussian province of Westphalia in northwestern Germany. Most of the migrating Stilles and Krummes were younger sons and daughters, who could not hope to inherit farms or make good marriages if they stayed in Westphalia. The letters of Ernst Stille reveal the economic opportunities—and the hardships—of working life in America during the Market Revolution.*

Cincinäti, May 20th 1847

Dearest friends and relatives,

I can't neglect sending a short letter from a foreign country to you in the Fatherland.... We went from Bremen to Neu Orleans in 2 months.... The trip from Neu Orleans to Cincinäti took 12 days. When I got here there was little work and wage in the city since it was the worst time of the whole year that there is, but I was lucky enough to get a job with Fr. Lutterbeck from Ladbergen [a village near his home in Prussia].... In April all the brickmakers started to work again, many Germans work this trade and earn a good wage and I set to work at this too and earn a dollar a day, of that I have to pay 7 dollars a month for board and washing.... We make 8,500 bricks a day and it's hard work but when we start at 4 o'clock in the morning we can be finished by 3 o'clock, if I can stay healthy I will keep working here since if you're healthy and can stand the work, it pays the best.

The only people who are really happy here are those who were used to work in Germany and with toil and great pains could hardly earn their daily bread. When people like that come here, even if they don't have any money, they can manage, they rent a room and the husband goes to work, earns his dollar a day and so he can live well and happily, with a wife and children. But a lot of people come over here who were well off in Germany but were enticed to leave their fatherland by boastful and imprudent letters from their friends or children and thought they could become rich in America, this deceives a lot of people, since what can they do here, if they stay in the city they can only earn their bread at hard and unaccustomed labor? If they want to live in the country and don't have enough money to buy a piece of land that is cleared and has a house then they have to settle in the wild bush and have to work very hard to clear the trees out of the way so they can sow and plant, but people who are healthy, strong and hard-working do pretty well. Here in Cincinati I know a lot of people who have made it by working hard, like Ernst Lots for example he does very well he also owns a brickyard and earns good money....

Cincinäti, July 10th 1848

At the beginning of April, I started working for Ernst Lots in the brickyard.... In the winter no one can work at this trade because of the snow and ice, then there's a huge number of idle people. The main work in the winter is with fat livestock, brought in from the country in large herds, on the outer edge of the city there are large buildings where about 1000 a day are slaughtered and cleaned, then they're brought into the city where they are cut up and salted and put in barrels that's how they're sent from here to other countries. This is a pretty hard and dirty job, that's why most people would rather do nothing for ¼ year than do this, but if you want to put up with this you can earn 1 to 1½ dollars a day.

I also want to let you know that I got married on the 4th of May of this year, to Heinriette Dickmans, the daughter of one of Dieckman's tenants in Leeden [another village near his Prussian home]. She is 20 years old, left on the same day from Bremerhafen as we went on board but she went via Baltimore. I didn't know her before, neither in Germany nor here, but I got to know her this spring through her uncle Rudolph Expel from Lienen, a good friend of mine who also works for Ernst Lots, who is his son-in-law.

My plan is if I stay in good health for the next couple of years to buy a piece of land and live there, since from my childhood I've been used to farming, I'd rather do that than stay in the city all my life, you can't start very well unless you have 300 dollars.

SOURCE: Walter D. Kamphoefner, Wolfgang Helbid, and Ulrike Sommer, eds., *News from the Land of Freedom: German Immigrants Write Home,* trans. Susan Carter Vogel (Ithaca, NY: Cornell University Press, 1991), 83–87.

ANALYZING THE EVIDENCE

► What does it suggest about the immigrant experience that so many people from a cluster of villages in Prussia ended up in contact with one another in Cincinnati, Ohio?

► What is Ernst Stille's opinion about what it takes to be successful in America? What will be the key factors in determining whether he achieves his dream of owning a farm?

Building the Erie Canal

By 1860, the success of the Erie Canal had prompted the construction of a vast system of canals, an infrastructure that was as important to the nation as the railroad network of the late nineteenth century, and the interstate highway and airport transportation systems of the late twentieth century. Tens of thousands of workers — many of them Irish immigrants and free blacks — dug out thousands of miles of canals by hand and, with the aid of the simple hoists shown here, built hundreds of stone locks. The unknown artist who sketched this scene focused on the scale of the project, leaving faceless the laborers who undertook this dangerous work. In the marshes near Syracuse, New York, one thousand workers fell ill with fever, and many died. Miriam and Ira D. Wallach Division of Art, Prints and Photographs. The New York Public Library. Astor, Lenox and Tilden Foundations.

an ambitious undertaking. At the time, the longest artificial waterway in the United States was just 28 miles long — a reflection of the huge capital cost of canals and the lack of American engineering expertise. The New York project did have three things in its favor: the vigorous support of New York City's merchants, who wanted access to western markets; the backing of New York's governor, De Witt Clinton, who persuaded the legislature to finance the waterway from tax revenues, tolls, and bond sales to foreign investors; and the relative gentleness of the terrain west of Albany. Even so, the task was enormous. Workers — many of them Irish immigrants — had to dig out millions of cubic yards of soil, quarry thousands of tons of rock to build the huge locks that raised and lowered the boats, and construct vast reservoirs to ensure a steady supply of water.

The first great engineering project in American history, the Erie Canal altered the ecology and the economy of an entire region. As farming communities and market towns sprang up along the waterway, settlers cut down millions of trees to provide wood for building and heating, and land for growing crops and grazing animals. Cows and sheep foraged on pastures recently occupied by deer and bears, and spring rains caused massive erosion of the denuded landscape.

Whatever its ecological consequences, the Erie Canal was an instant economic success. The first section, a stretch of 75 miles, opened in 1819 and immediately generated enough revenue to repay its cost. When the canal was completed in 1825, a 40-foot-wide ribbon of water stretched 364 miles from Buffalo, on the eastern shore of Lake Erie, to

Albany, where it joined the Hudson River for a 150-mile trip to New York City. After an excursion on the canal, novelist Nathaniel Hawthorne suggested that its water "must be the most fertilizing of all fluids, for it causes towns with their masses of brick and stone, their churches and theaters, their business and hubbub, their luxury and refinement, their gay dames and polished citizens, to spring up."

The Erie Canal brought prosperity to the farmers of central and western New York by carrying wheat, flour, and meat to eastern cities and from there to foreign markets. One-hundred-ton freight barges, each pulled by two horses, moved along the canal at a steady 30 miles a day, cutting transportation costs and greatly accelerating the flow of goods. In 1818, the mills in Rochester had processed 26,000 barrels of flour; ten years later, their output had soared to 200,000 barrels; and by 1840, it was at 500,000 barrels. Northeastern manufacturers used the canal to ship clothing, boots, and agricultural equipment to farm families throughout the Great Lakes basin and the Ohio River Valley. In payment, the farmers sent grain, cattle, and hogs as well as raw materials (leather, wool, and hemp, for example) to the East.

The spectacular benefits of the Erie Canal prompted a national canal boom. Civic and business leaders in Philadelphia and Baltimore proposed waterways to link their cities to the West. Implementing New York's fiscal innovations, they persuaded their state governments to invest directly in canal companies or to force state-chartered banks to do so. They also won state guarantees for

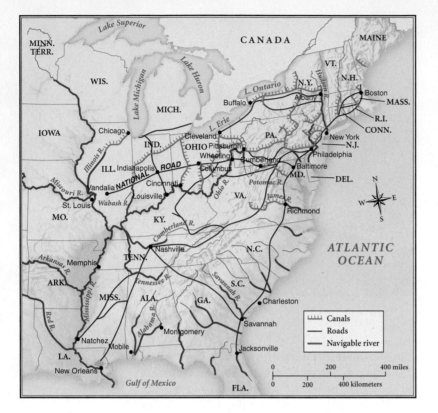

MAP 9.3 The Transportation Revolution: Roads and Canals, 1820–1850

By 1850, the United States had an efficient transportation system with three distinct parts. One system, composed of short canals and navigable rivers, carried cotton, tobacco, and other products from the countryside of the southern seaboard states into the Atlantic commercial system. A second system, centered on the Erie, Chesapeake and Ohio, and Pennsylvania Mainline canals, linked the major seaport cities of the Northeast to the vast trans-Appalachian region. Finally, a set of regional canals in the Old Northwest connected most of the Great Lakes region to the Ohio and Mississippi rivers and the port of New Orleans.

canal bonds to encourage British and Dutch investors to buy them. In fact, foreign investors provided almost three-quarters of the $400 million invested in canals by 1840. Waterways connected the farms and cities of the Great Lakes region with the great port cities of New York, Philadelphia, and Baltimore (via the Erie, Pennsylvania, and Chesapeake and Ohio canals) and with New Orleans (via the Ohio and Mississippi Rivers). In 1848, the completion of the Michigan and Illinois Canal, which linked Chicago to the Mississippi River, completed an inland all-water route from New York City to New Orleans (Map 9.3).

Steamboats Improve Interregional Transportation. The steamboat, another product of the industrial age, ensured the economic success of the river-borne transportation system of the Midwest. Engineer-inventor Robert Fulton had built the first American steamboat, the *Clermont*, which he navigated up the Hudson River in 1807. However, the first steamboats could not navigate shallow western rivers. During the 1820s, engineers broadened the hulls of the steamboats to reduce their draft and enlarge their cargo capacity. The improved steamboats halved the cost of upstream river transport and, along with the canals, dramatically increased the flow of goods, people, and news to the Midwest.

In 1830, a traveler or a letter from New York could go by water to Buffalo or Pittsburgh in less than a week, and to Detroit or St. Louis in two weeks. Thirty years earlier, the same journeys had taken twice as long.

The states and the national government played key roles in the development of this interregional system of transportation and communication. Working through the Commonwealth system, state governments subsidized the canals. For its part, the national government created a vast postal system, the first network for the exchange of information. Following passage of the Post Office Act of 1792, the mail system grew rapidly—to eight hundred post offices by 1800 and to more than eight thousand by 1830—and safely carried thousands of letters and millions of dollars of banknotes from one end of the country to the other. The U.S. Supreme Court, headed by John Marshall, likewise encouraged interstate trade by striking down state restrictions on commerce. In *Gibbons v. Ogden* (1824), the Court voided a New York law that created a monopoly on steamboat travel into New York City, establishing the authority of the federal government over interstate commerce (see Chapter 7). That decision meant that no local or state monopolies—or tariffs—would impede the flow of goods, services, and news across the nation.

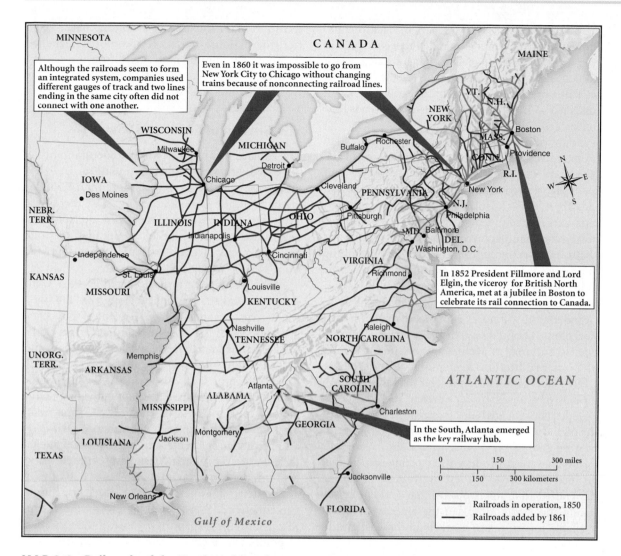

MINNESOTA

Although the railroads seem to form an integrated system, companies used different gauges of track and two lines ending in the same city often did not connect with one another.

Even in 1860 it was impossible to go from New York City to Chicago without changing trains because of nonconnecting railroad lines.

CANADA

MAINE

In 1852 President Fillmore and Lord Elgin, the viceroy for British North America, met at a jubilee in Boston to celebrate its rail connection to Canada.

In the South, Atlanta emerged as the key railway hub.

ATLANTIC OCEAN

Gulf of Mexico

Railroads in operation, 1850
Railroads added by 1861

MAP 9.4   Railroads of the North and South, 1850 and 1861

In the decade before the Civil War, entrepreneurs in the Northeast and the Midwest laid thousands of miles of new railroad lines, creating an extensive and dense transportation system that stimulated economic development. The South built a more limited system of railroads. In all regions, railroad companies used different track gauges, which hindered the efficient flow of traffic.

Railroads and Regional Ties. By the 1850s, another product of industrial technology—the railroad—linked the Northeast and the Midwest and soon replaced the canals as the center of the national transportation system (Map 9.4). To capture the market in midwestern grain, capitalists in Boston and New York invested heavily in transportation routes on or near the Great Lakes. In 1852, the canals of the region carried twice the tonnage transported by railroads; within a decade, railroads became the main carriers of wheat and freight. Serviced by a vast network of locomotive and freight-car repair shops, the Erie Railroad, the Pennsylvania Railroad, the New York Central

Railroad, and the Baltimore and Ohio Railroad connected the Atlantic ports—New York, Philadelphia, and Baltimore—with the rapidly expanding Great Lakes cities of Cleveland and Chicago.

Moreover, the railroad boom of the 1850s opened up the vast territory south and west of Chicago. Trains carried large quantities of lumber from Michigan to the treeless prairies of Indiana, Illinois, Iowa, and Missouri, where settlers built 250,000 new farms (covering 19 million acres) and hundreds of small towns. The rail lines moved millions of bushels of wheat to Chicago, for transport by boat or rail to eastern markets. Increasingly, they also carried hogs and cattle to Chicago's growing stockyards. A farmer in Jacksonville, Illinois, reported that he intended to feed his entire corn crop of 1,500 bushels "to hogs & cattle, as we think it is more profitable than to sell the corn." "In ancient times," boasted a Chicago newspaper, "all roads led to Rome; in modern times all roads lead to Chicago."

Many of the first migrants to the Midwest relied on manufactured goods made in Britain or in the Northeast. They bought high-quality shovels and spades fabricated at the Delaware Iron Works and the Oliver Ames Company in Easton, Massachusetts; axes forged in Connecticut factories; and steel horseshoes manufactured in Troy, New York. By the 1840s, midwestern entrepreneurs were beginning to produce these and other manufactures: machine tools, hardware, furniture, and especially agricultural implements. Working as a blacksmith in Grand Detour, Illinois, John Deere made his first steel plow out of old saws in 1837; ten years later, he opened a factory in Moline, Illinois, that made use of **mass production** to manufacture the plows. Deere's steel plows were stronger than the cast-iron models developed earlier in New York by Jethro Wood; they allowed midwestern farmers to cut through the thick sod of the prairies. Other midwestern companies—McCormick and Hussey, for example—mass-produced self-raking reapers that enabled a farmer to harvest twelve acres of grain a day (rather than the two acres that could be cut by hand) and vastly increased the amount of wheat available for export to markets in the East and in Europe.

Extraregional trade also linked southern planters to northeastern textile plants and foreign markets. This commerce bolstered the wealth of the South but did not transform the economic and social order there as it did in the Midwest. Southern investors continued to commit their capital to land and slaves, which yielded high profits and provided impressive increases in output (see Chapter 12). By the 1840s, the South produced more than two-thirds of the world's cotton and accounted for almost two-thirds of American exports. With the exception of Richmond, Virginia, and a few other places, though, planters did not invest their cotton profits in manufacturing. Lacking cities, factories, and highly trained workers, the South remained an agricultural economy that provided high living standards only to the 25 percent of the white population that owned plantations and slaves. By 1860, the southern economy generated an average annual per capita income of $103, while the more productive economic system of the Northeast yielded an average income of $141. By facilitating the transport of the staple crops of cotton, tobacco, and rice, the national system of commerce deepened the South's commitment to agriculture and slavery, even as it promoted diversified economies in the Northeast and Midwest.

The Growth of Cities and Towns

The expansion of industry and trade dramatically increased America's urban population. In 1820, there were only 58 towns with more than 2,500 inhabitants in the United States; by 1840, there were 126 urban centers, located mostly in the Northeast and Midwest. During those two decades, the total number of city dwellers grew more than fourfold, from 443,000 to 1,844,000.

The most rapid growth occurred in the new industrial towns that sprang up along the "fall line," where rivers began their rapid descent to the coastal plain. In 1822, the Boston Manufacturing Company expanded north from its base in Waltham and built a complex of mills in the sleepy Merrimack River village of East Chelmsford, Massachusetts, and quickly transformed it into the bustling textile factory town of Lowell. Hartford, Connecticut; Trenton, New Jersey; and Wilmington, Delaware, also became urban centers as mill owners exploited the waterpower of their rivers and recruited workers from the countryside.

Western commercial cities like Pittsburgh, Cincinnati, and New Orleans grew almost as rapidly. These cities expanded because of their location at points where goods were transferred from one mode of transport to another—canal boats or farmers' wagons, for example, to steamboats or sailing vessels. As the midwestern population grew during the 1830s and 1840s, St. Louis, Detroit, and especially Buffalo and Chicago emerged as dynamic centers of commerce. "There can be no two places in the world," journalist and author Margaret Fuller wrote from Chicago in 1843, "more completely thoroughfares than this place and Buffalo. They are the correspondent valves that open and shut all the time, as the life-blood rushes from east to west, and back again from west to east." To a German visitor, the city seemed "for the most part to consist of shops . . . [as if] people came here merely to trade, to make money, and not to live" (see Chapter 18). Chicago's merchants and bankers developed the marketing, provisioning, and financial services that were essential to farmers and small-town merchants in the surrounding countryside. "There can be no better [market] any where in the Union," declared a farmer in Paw Paw, Illinois.

MAP 9.5 The Nation's Major Cities, 1840

By 1840, the United States boasted three major conglomerations of cities. The oldest ports on the Atlantic — from Boston to Baltimore — served as centers for import merchants, banks, insurance companies, and manufacturers of ready-made clothing, and their reach extended far into the interior — nationwide in the case of New York City. A second group of cities stretched along Lake Erie and included the wholesale distribution hubs of Buffalo, Detroit, and Chicago, as well as the manufacturing center of Cleveland. A third urban system extended along the Ohio River, comprising the industrial cities of Pittsburgh and Cincinnati and the wholesale centers of Louisville and St. Louis.

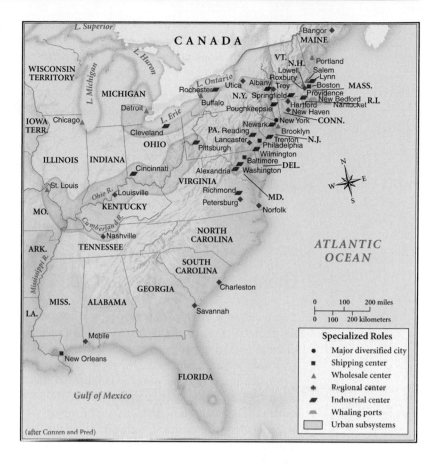

The midwestern commercial hubs quickly became manufacturing centers as well. Maximizing the cities' locations as key junctions for railroad lines and steamboats, entrepreneurs built docks, warehouses, flour mills, and packing plants, creating work for hundreds of artisans and factory laborers. In 1846, Cyrus McCormick moved his reaper factory from western Virginia to Chicago to be closer to his midwestern customers. By 1860, St. Louis and Chicago had become the nation's third and fourth largest cities, respectively, after New York and Philadelphia (Map 9.5).

The old Atlantic seaports — Boston, Philadelphia, Baltimore, Charleston, and especially New York City — remained important for their foreign commerce and, increasingly, as centers of finance and manufacturing. New York City and nearby Brooklyn grew at a phenomenal rate: Between 1820 and 1860, its population quadrupled to nearly one million as tens of thousands of German and Irish immigrants poured into the city. Drawing on the abundant supply of labor, New York became a center of small-scale manufacturing and the ready-made clothing industry, which relied on the labor of thousands of low-paid seamstresses. "The

wholesale clothing establishments are . . . absorbing the business of the country," a "Country Tailor" complained to the *New York Tribune*, "casting many an honest and hardworking man out of employment [and allowing] . . . the large cities to swallow up the small towns."

New York's growth stemmed primarily from its dominant position in foreign and domestic trade. It had the best harbor in the United States and, thanks to the Erie Canal, was the best gateway to the West for immigrants and manufactures and the best outlet for shipments of western grain. Exploiting the city's prime location, in 1818, four Quaker merchants founded the Black Ball Line, which carried cargo, people, and mail on a regular schedule between New York and the European ports of Liverpool, London, and Le Havre. New York merchants likewise dominated trade with the newly independent South American nations of Brazil, Peru, and Venezuela. New York–based traders took over the cotton trade by offering finance, insurance, and shipping to export merchants in southern ports. By 1840, the port of New York handled almost two-thirds of foreign imports into the United States, almost half of all foreign trade, and much of the immigrant traffic.

➤ What roles did government — state and national — play in the development of America's transportation networks?

➤ From the evidence provided in the text, could it be argued that the construction of the Erie Canal was the central economic event of the first half of the nineteenth century? Why or why not?

➤ Describe the different types of cities that emerged in the United States in the first half of the nineteenth century. How do you explain the differences in their development?

Changes in the Social Structure

The Industrial and Market revolutions improved the material lives of many Americans by enabling them to live in larger houses, cook on iron stoves, and wear better-made clothes. But especially in the cities, the new economic order led to distinct social classes: a wealthy industrial and commercial elite, a substantial middle class, and a mass of propertyless wage earners. By creating a class-divided society, industrialization posed a momentous challenge to America's republican ideals.

The Business Elite

Before industrialization, white Americans thought of their society in terms of rank: That is, "notable" families had higher status than families of the "lower orders." Yet in most rural areas, people in the different ranks shared a common culture: Gentlemen farmers talked easily with yeomen about crop yields, while their wives conversed about the art of quilting. In the South, humble tenants and aristocratic slave owners shared the same amusements: gambling, cockfighting, and horse racing. Rich and poor attended the same Quaker meetinghouse or Presbyterian church. "Almost everyone eats, drinks, and dresses in the same way," a European visitor to Hartford, Connecticut, reported in 1798, "and one can see the most obvious inequality only in the dwellings."

The Industrial Revolution shattered this agrarian social order and created a fragmented society composed of distinct regions, classes, and cultures. The new economic system pulled many Americans into large cities, thereby accentuating the differences between rural and urban life. Moreover, it made a few city residents — the merchants, manufacturers, bankers, and landlords who comprised the business elite — very rich. In 1800, the top 10 percent of the nation's families owned about 40 percent of the wealth; by 1860, the richest 10 percent owned nearly 70 percent of the wealth. In large cities like New York, Chicago, Baltimore, and New Orleans, the superrich — the top 1 percent — owned more than 40 percent of all tangible property (land and buildings, for example) and an even higher share of intangible property (stocks and bonds).

Government tax policies facilitated the accumulation of wealth. In an era before federal taxes on individual and corporate income, the U.S. Treasury raised most of its revenue from tariffs — taxes on textiles and other imported goods that were purchased mostly by ordinary citizens. State and local governments also favored the wealthier classes. They usually taxed real estate (farms, city lots, and buildings) and tangible personal property (furniture, tools, and machinery) but almost never taxed the stocks and bonds owned by the rich or the inheritances they passed on to their children.

Cities that were once relatively homogenous took on an increasingly fragmented character. Over time, the wealthiest families consciously set themselves apart. They dressed in well-tailored clothes, rode in fancy carriages, and lived in expensively furnished houses tended by butlers, cooks, and other servants. The women no longer socialized with those of lesser wealth, and the men no longer labored side by side with their journeymen. Instead, they became managers and directors and relied on trusted subordinates to issue orders to hundreds of factory operatives. Increasingly, merchants, manufacturers, and bankers, searching for privacy, chose to live in separate neighborhoods, often at the edge of the city. The reclusiveness of privileged families and the massive flow of immigrants into other districts divided cities geographically along lines of class, race, and ethnicity.

The Middle Class

Standing between wealthy owners at one end of the urban social spectrum and propertyless wage earners at the other was a growing middle class — the social product of the economic revolution. As a Boston printer explained, the bulk of the "middling class" was made up of "the farmers, the mechanics, the manufacturers, the traders, who carry on professionally the ordinary operations of buying, selling, and exchanging merchandize." Other members of the middle class came from various professional groups — building contractors, lawyers, and surveyors — who suddenly found their services in great demand and financially profitable. Middle-class business owners, employees, and professionals were most numerous in the Northeast, where in the 1840s they numbered about 30 percent of the population. But they also could be found in the agrarian South: In 1854, Oglethorpe, Georgia (population 2,500), a cotton boomtown, had eighty "business houses" and eight hotels.

The growing size, wealth, and cultural influence of the middle class reflected a dramatic rise in urban prosperity. Between 1830 and 1857, the per capita income of Americans increased by about 2.5 percent a year, a remarkable rate never since matched. This surge in income, along with the availability of inexpensive mass-produced goods, facilitated the emergence of a distinct middle-class urban culture. Middle-class husbands earned enough to support their families and to save about 15 percent of their income, which they used to buy a well-built house in a "respectable part of town." They purchased handsome clothes and drove about town in smart carriages. Relieved from the burden of labor, their wives became purveyors of genteel culture, buying books, pianos, lithographs, and commodious furniture for their front parlors. Instead of hiring Irish or African Americans to perform menial tasks, some middle-class families relied on the new industrial technology. They outfitted their residences with furnaces that heated water for bathing and for radiators that warmed entire rooms; they bought cooking stoves with ovens and treadle-operated sewing machines. Well-to-do urban families now kept their perishable food in iceboxes, which ice-company wagons filled periodically, and bought many varieties of packaged goods. As early as 1825, the Underwood Company of Boston was marketing well-preserved Atlantic salmon in jars.

If material comfort was one distinguishing mark of the middle class, moral and mental discipline was another. Middle-class writers denounced the black-led festivals of Election Day and Pinkster as a "chaos of sin and folly, of misery and fun," and, by the 1830s, had secured their suppression. Ambitious parents were equally concerned with their children's moral character and stressed discipline, integrity, and hard work. To ensure their success, middle-class parents usually provided their offspring with a high school education (in an era when most white children received only five years of schooling). Many American Protestants had long believed that diligent work in an earthly "calling" was a duty owed to God. Now the business elite and the middle class gave this idea a secular twist. They celebrated work as the key to a higher standard of living for the nation and to social mobility for the individual.

Benjamin Franklin gave classical expression to the secular work ethic in his *Autobiography*, which was published in full in 1818 (almost thirty years after Franklin died) and immediately found a huge audience. Heeding Franklin's suggestion that an industrious man would become a rich one, tens of thousands of young American men worked hard, saved their money, adopted temperate habits, and practiced honesty in their business dealings. Countless magazines, children's books, self-help manuals, and novels taught the same lessons. The **self-made man** became a central theme of American popular culture. Knowing that many affluent families had risen from modest beginnings, middle-class men and women took them as models. Just as the rural-producer ethic had united the social ranks in pre-1800 America, personal achievement linked the upper and middle classes of the new industrializing society.

Urban Workers and the Poor

As thoughtful business leaders surveyed their industrializing society, they concluded that the yeoman and artisan-republican's ideal — a society of independent producers — was no longer possible. "Entire independence ought not to be wished for," Ithamar A. Beard, the paymaster of the Hamilton Manufacturing Company, told a mechanics' association in 1827. "In large manufacturing towns, many more must fill subordinate stations and must be under the immediate direction and control of a master or superintendent, than in the farming towns."

Wageworkers Increase. Beard had a point. In 1840, all of the nation's slaves and about half of its native-born free workers were laboring for others. The bottom 10 percent of white wage earners consisted of casual workers — those hired on a short-term basis for the most arduous jobs. Poor women washed clothes, while their husbands and sons carried lumber and bricks for construction projects, loaded ships, and dug out dirt and stones to build canals. When they could find work, these men earned "their dollar *per diem*," an "Old Inhabitant" wrote to the *Baltimore American*, but he cautioned that those workers could never save enough "to pay rent, buy fire wood and eatables" when the harbor froze up. During business depressions, they bore the brunt of unemployment; and even in the best of times, their jobs were temporary and dangerous.

Other laborers had greater security of employment, but few were prospering. In Massachusetts in 1825, the daily wage of an unskilled worker was about two-thirds that of a mechanic; two decades later it was less than half as much. The 18,000 native-born and immigrant women who made men's clothing in New York City in the 1850s earned a few pennies a day, less than $80 a year. Those meager wages barely paid for food and rent, which meant that many wage earners were unable to take advantage of the rapidly falling prices of manufactured goods. Only the most fortunate working-class families could afford to educate their children, buy an apprenticeship for their sons, or accumulate small dowries so that their daughters could marry men with better prospects. Most families sent their ten-year-old children out to work, and the death of a parent often threw the survivors into dire poverty. As a charity worker noted, "What can a bereaved widow do, with 5 or 6 little children, destitute of every means of support but what her own hands can furnish (which in a general way does not amount to more than 25 cents a day)."

The Lives of the Poor. Over time, their poverty forced these urban workers to move into dilapidated housing or bad neighborhoods. Single men and women lived in crowded boardinghouses, while families jammed themselves into tiny apartments in the basements and attics of small houses. As immigrants poured into the nation after 1840, urban populations soared, and developers squeezed more and more dwellings and foul-smelling outhouses onto a single lot. Venturing into the slums of New York City in the 1850s, shocked state legislators found gaunt shivering people with "wild ghastly faces" living amid "hideous squalor and deadly effluvia, the dim, undrained courts oozing with pollution, the dark, narrow stairways, decayed with age, reeking with filth, overrun with vermin."

Many wage earners sought solace in alcohol. Beer and rum had long been standard fare in many American rituals: patriotic ceremonies, work breaks, barn raisings, and games. But during the 1820s and 1830s, the consumption of intoxicating beverages and alcoholism throughout the population reached new heights. Heavy drinking killed Daniel Tomkins, vice president under James Monroe, and undermined Henry Clay's bid for the presidency. It had a devastating impact on urban wage earners. Although Methodist artisans and ambitious craft workers "swore off" liquor to protect their work skills, health, and finances, other workers began to drink heavily on the job — not just during the traditional 11 A.M. and 4 P.M. "refreshers." A baker recalled how "one man was stationed at the window to watch, while the rest drank." Long before the arrival of spirit-drinking Irish and beer-drinking German immigrants, there were grogshops on almost every block in working-class districts. These saloons became focal points of disorder. Unrestrained drinking by young men led to fistfights, brawls, and robberies; and the urban police, mostly low-paid watchmen and untrained constables, were unable to contain the lawlessness.

The Benevolent Empire

The disorder among native-born urban wage earners alarmed the rising middle class, who profited from their labors but feared their potential power. Many upwardly mobile men and women embraced the principle of religious benevolence and now used it to spearhead a movement of conservative social reform. In the 1820s, they joined with their Congregational and Presbyterian ministers and launched programs of social reforms that historians refer to collectively as the **Benevolent Empire**. The purpose of the reforms, announced Lyman Beecher, a minister who spoke out loudly against intemperance and poverty, was to restore "the moral government of God." The reformers introduced new forms of moral discipline into their own lives and tried to infuse them into the lives of working people as well. They would regulate popular behavior — by persuasion if possible, by law if necessary.

Although the Benevolent Empire targeted age-old evils like drunkenness, adultery, prostitution, and crime, its methods were new. Instead of relying on church sermons and the suasion of community leaders, the reformers set out to institutionalize charity and systematically combat evil. They established large-scale organizations — the Prison Discipline Society and the American Society for the Promotion of Temperance, among many others. Each organization had a managing staff, a network of hundreds of chapters, thousands of volunteer members, and a newspaper.

Often working in concert, these benevolent groups wanted to improve society. First, they encouraged people to lead well-disciplined lives by campaigning for temperance (moderation or even abstention from alcohol) and "regular habits." They persuaded local governments to ban the carnivals of drink and dancing, such as Negro Election Day (mock festivities in which African Americans symbolically took over the government), which had been enjoyed by whites as well as blacks. Second, they devised new institutions to help those in need and to control those they considered threats to society. Reformers provided homes of refuge for abandoned children and asylums for insane individuals, who previously had been confined by their families in

Five Points, New York City, 1827

To upper-class New Yorkers, like the top-hatted gentleman at the center of the picture, Five Points was a frightening slum. Indeed, the neighborhood of overcrowded tenement buildings filled with impoverished Irish immigrants and African Americans had all too much physical violence and early death. Still, it was home to thousands of working-class New Yorkers, who created a rich social life in local taverns and markets. *Valentine's Manual, 1855.*

attics and cellars. They campaigned to end corporal punishment and to rehabilitate criminals in new penitentiaries designed to modify criminal behavior.

Women were a crucial part of the Benevolent Empire. Since the 1790s, upper-class women had sponsored charitable organizations like the Society for the Relief of Poor Widows with Small Children, which was founded in New York by Isabella Graham, a devout Presbyterian widow. Her daughter Joanna Bethune set up other charitable institutions, including the Orphan Asylum Society and the Society for the Promotion of Industry, which found jobs for hundreds of poor women as spinners and seamstresses.

Some reformers believed that the greatest threat to the "moral government of God" was the decline of the traditional Sabbath. As commerce increased, merchants and storekeepers conducted business on Sundays, and urban saloons provided drink and entertainment. To halt these activities, in 1828, Lyman Beecher and other ministers formed the General Union for Promoting the Observance of the Christian Sabbath. General Union chapters — replete with women's auxiliaries — sprang up from Maine to the Ohio River Valley. To rally Christians to its cause, the General Union demanded repeal of a law Congress had enacted in 1810 allowing mail to be transported — though not delivered — on

An Inside View of the Benevolent Empire

Early-nineteenth-century reformers condemned corporal punishment for criminals. So they built prisons designed to rehabilitate offenders and turn them into responsible citizens. As this folk painting by a prisoner at a Massachusetts penitentiary suggests, prison officials imposed tight discipline on inmates. The inmates marched in silence: In line with the latest penal theories, prisoners were not allowed to speak with one another, the silence key to their reflection on their crimes and ultimate penitence. David A. Schorsch.

Sunday. Its members also boycotted shipping companies that did business on the Sabbath and campaigned for municipal laws forbidding games and festivals on the Lord's day.

The Benevolent Empire's efforts to enforce the Sabbath aroused controversy. Many men who labored twelve or fourteen hours a day for six days a week refused to spend their one day of leisure in meditation and prayer. Shipping company managers demanded that the Erie Canal provide lockkeepers on Sundays and joined those Americans who argued that using laws to enforce a particular set of moral beliefs was "contrary to the free spirit of our institutions." When some evangelical reformers proposed to teach Christianity to slaves, many white southerners were outraged. This kind of popular resistance limited the success of the Benevolent Empire.

Charles Grandison Finney: Revivalism and Reform

Presbyterian minister Charles Grandison Finney found a new way to propagate religious values

among Americans. Finney was not part of the traditional religious elite. Born into a poor farming family in Connecticut, he planned to become a lawyer and rise into the middle class. But in 1823, Finney underwent an intense conversion experience and chose the ministry as his career. Beginning in towns along the Erie Canal, the young minister conducted emotional revival meetings that stressed conversion rather than instruction and discipline. Repudiating traditional Calvinist beliefs, he maintained that God would welcome any sinner who submitted to the Holy Spirit. Finney's ministry drew on — and greatly accelerated — the Second Great Awakening, the wave of Protestant revivalism that had begun after the Revolution (see Chapter 8).

Evangelical Ideology. Finney's central message was that "God has made man a moral free agent" who could choose salvation. This doctrine of free will was particularly attractive to members of the new middle class, who had already chosen to improve their material lives. But Finney also had great

Charles Grandison Finney, Evangelist (1792–1875)

When an unknown artist painted this flattering portrait in 1834, Finney was forty-two years old and at the height of his career as an evangelist. Handsome and charismatic, Finney had just led a series of enormously successful revivals in Rochester, New York, and other cities along the Erie Canal. In 1835, he established a theology department at newly founded Oberlin College in Ohio, where he trained a generation of ministers and served as president from 1851 to 1866. Oberlin College Archives.

success in converting those at the ends of the social spectrum: the haughty rich, who had placed themselves above God, and the abject poor, who seemed lost to drink and sloth. Finney celebrated their common fellowship in Christ and identified them spiritually with pious middle-class respectability.

Finney's most spectacular triumph came in 1830, when he moved his revivals from small towns to Rochester, New York, now a major milling and commercial city on the Erie Canal. Preaching every day for six months and promoting group prayer meetings in family homes, he won over the influential merchants and manufacturers of Rochester, who pledged to reform their lives and those of their workers. They promised to attend church, give up intoxicating beverages, and work hard. To encourage their employees to follow suit, wealthy businessmen founded a Free Presbyterian church — "free" because members did not have to pay for pew space. Other evangelical Protestants founded similar churches to serve transient canal laborers,

and pious businessmen set up a savings bank to encourage thrift among the working classes. Meanwhile, Finney's wife, Lydia, and other pious middle-class women carried the Christian message to the wives of the unconverted, set up Sunday schools for poor children, and formed the Female Charitable Society to assist the unemployed.

Finney's efforts to create a harmonious community of morally disciplined Christians were not completely successful. Skilled workers who belonged to strong craft organizations — boot makers, carpenters, stonemasons, and boatbuilders — argued that they needed higher wages and schools more urgently than sermons and prayers. Poor people ignored Finney's revival, as did the Irish Catholic immigrants who had recently begun arriving in Rochester and other northeastern cities, bringing with them a hatred of Protestants as both religious heretics and political oppressors.

Ignoring this resistance, revivalists from New England to the Midwest copied Finney's evangelical message and techniques. In New York City, wealthy silk merchants Arthur and Lewis Tappan founded a magazine, *The Christian Evangelist*, which promoted Finney's ideas. The revivals swept through Pennsylvania, North Carolina, Tennessee, and Indiana, where, a convert reported, "you could not go upon the street and hear any conversation, except upon religion." The success of the revivals "has been so general and thorough," concluded a Presbyterian general assembly, "that the whole customs of society have changed."

The Temperance Crusade. The **temperance movement** proved to be the most effective arena for evangelical social reform. In 1832, evangelicals gained control of the American Temperance Society; soon the society boasted two thousand chapters and more than 200,000 members. The society employed the methods that had worked so well in the revivals — group confession and prayer, a focus on the family and the spiritual role of women, and sudden emotional conversion — and took them to every northern town and southern village. On one day in New York City in 1841, more than 4,000 people took the temperance "pledge." Throughout America, the consumption of spirits fell dramatically, from an average of five gallons per person in 1830 to two gallons in 1845.

Evangelical reformers celebrated religion as the moral center of the temperance movement and the foundation of the American work ethic. Laziness and drinking could not be cured by Benjamin Franklin's method of self-discipline, they argued; instead, people had to experience a profound

The Drunkard's Progress: From the First Glass to the Grave

This 1846 lithograph, published by N. Currier, depicts the inevitable fate of those who drink. The drunkard's descent into "Poverty and Disease" ends with "Death by suicide," leaving a grieving and destitute wife and child. Temperance reformers urged Americans to take "The Cold Water Cure," to drink water instead of liquor. To promote abstinence among the young, Reverend Thomas Hunt founded the Cold Water Army, an organization that grew to embrace several hundred thousand children, all of whom pledged "perpetual hate to all that can Intoxicate." Library of Congress.

change of heart through religious conversion. This evangelical message fostered individual enterprise and moral discipline not only among middle-class Americans but also among many wage earners. Thus, religion and the ideology of social mobility served as powerful cement that held society together in the face of the divisions created by industrialization, the market economy, and increasing cultural diversity.

Immigration and Cultural Conflict

Cultural diversity stemmed in part from a vast wave of immigrants. Between 1840 and 1860, about 2 million Irish, 1.5 million Germans, and 750,000 Britons poured into the United States. They were a diverse lot. The British migrants were primarily Protestant and relatively prosperous; their ranks included many trained professionals, propertied farmers, and skilled workers. Many

German immigrants also came from property-owning farming and artisan families and had the resources to move to the midwestern states of Wisconsin, Iowa, and Missouri. Other Germans and most of the Irish settled in the Northeast, where by 1860 they accounted for nearly one-third of white adults. Most immigrants avoided the South because they opposed slavery or feared competition from enslaved workers.

Irish Immigration. The poorest migrants were Irish peasants and laborers, who were fleeing a famine caused by severe overpopulation and a devastating blight on the potato crop. Arriving in dire poverty, the Irish settled mostly in the cities of New England and New York; the men took low-paying jobs as factory hands, construction workers, and canal diggers, while the women took positions as domestic servants in middle- and upper-class homes. Irish families crowded into cheap tenement buildings with primitive sanitation systems and were the first to die when disease struck. In the summer of 1849, a cholera epidemic took the lives of thousands of poor immigrants in St. Louis and New York City.

In times of hardship and sorrow, immigrants turned to their churches. Many Germans and virtually all the Irish were Catholics, and they fueled the growth of the Catholic Church. In 1840, there were sixteen Catholic dioceses and seven hundred churches in the United States; by 1860, there were forty-five dioceses and twenty-five hundred churches. Under the guidance of their priests and bishops, Catholics built an impressive network of institutions — charitable societies, orphanages, militia companies, parochial schools, and political organizations — that helped them maintain both their religion and their German or Irish identity.

Nativism and Anti-Catholicism. The Protestant fervor stirred up by the Second Great Awakening meant that a rash of anti-Catholic publications greeted the immigrants (see Comparing American Voices, "A Debate over Catholic Immigration," pp. 296–297). One of the most militant critics of Catholicism was artist and inventor Samuel F. B. Morse. In 1834, Morse published *Foreign Conspiracy Against the Liberties of the United States*, which warned of a Catholic threat to American republican institutions. Morse believed that Catholic immigrants would obey the dictates of Pope Gregory XVI, who in an encyclical in 1832 had condemned liberty of conscience, freedom of publication, and the separation of church and state, and had urged Catholics to repudiate republicanism and acknowledge the "submission due to princes." Republican-minded Protestants of many denominations shared Morse's fears, and *Foreign Conspiracy* became their textbook.

The social tensions stemming from industrialization also intensified anti-Catholic sentiment. During business recessions, unemployed Protestant mechanics and factory workers joined mobs that attacked Catholics, accusing them of taking jobs and driving down wages. These cultural conflicts inhibited the creation of a unified labor movement. Many Protestant wage earners felt they had more in common with their Protestant employers than with their Catholic coworkers. Other Protestants organized nativist clubs, which called for limits on immigration, the restriction of public office to native-born citizens, and the exclusive use of the Protestant version of the Bible in public schools. Benevolent-minded Protestant reformers supported the anti-Catholic movement for reasons of public

Anti-Catholic Riots

When riots against Irish Catholics broke out in Philadelphia in 1844, the governor of Pennsylvania called out the militia to protect Catholic churches and residential neighborhoods. In the foreground, two Protestant rioters, depicted by the artist as well-dressed gentlemen, attack an Irish family with sticks; in the background, militiamen fire on other members of the mob. Library Company of Philadelphia.

policy. As crusaders for public education, they opposed the diversion of tax resources to Catholic schools; as advocates of a civilized society, they condemned the rowdyism of drunken Irish men.

In many northeastern cities, religious and cultural conflicts led to violence. In 1834, in Charlestown, Massachusetts, a quarrel between Catholic laborers repairing a convent owned by the Ursuline order of nuns and Protestant workers in a neighboring brickyard turned into a full-scale riot and led to the destruction of the convent. In Philadelphia, violence erupted in 1844, when the Catholic bishop persuaded public-school officials to use both Catholic and Protestant versions of the Bible. Anti-Irish rioting incited by the city's nativist clubs lasted for two months and escalated into open warfare between Protestants and the Pennsylvania militia. Even as economic revolution brought prosperity to many Americans and attracted millions of immigrants, it divided the society along the lines of class, ethnicity, and religion.

➤ Identify the social classes created by the economic revolution, and describe their defining characteristics.

➤ What were the main goals of the Benevolent Empire? To what extent were they achieved?

A Debate over Catholic Immigration

Between 1776 and 1830, relatively few Europeans immigrated to the United States. Then, as the text explains, population growth and poverty sparked the migration of increasing numbers of Germans (mostly Protestants) and Irish Catholics. The arrival of hundreds of thousands of foreign Catholics in the midst of the Second Great Awakening led to riots, the formation of the American Party, and debates in the public press. By using contemporary newspapers and other writings as a source, historians come to understand the public rhetoric (and often the private passions) of the time.

LYMAN BEECHER
Catholicism Is Incompatible with Republicanism

Lyman Beecher (1775–1863) was one of the leading Protestant ministers of his generation and the father of a family of Christian social reformers and well-known authors: minister Henry Ward Beecher, Harriet Beecher Stowe (Uncle Tom's Cabin), and Catherine Beecher (A Treatise on Domestic Economy). In A Plea for the West *(1835), Beecher alerted his fellow Protestants to the centralized power of the Roman Catholic Church and its opposition to republican institutions. That opposition was formalized in papal encyclicals issued by Pope Gregory XVI (Mirari Vos, 1832) and Pope Pius IX (Quanta Cura, 1864), both of which condemned republicanism and freedom of conscience as false political ideologies.*

Since the irruption of the northern barbarians, the world has never witnessed such a rush of dark-minded population from one country to another, as is now leaving Europe, and dashing upon our shores. . . .

They come, also, not undirected. There is evidently a supervision abroad—and one here—by which they come, and set down together, in city or country, as a Catholic body, and are led or followed quickly by a Catholic priesthood, who maintain over them in the land of strangers and unknown tongues an [absolute] ascendancy. . . .

The ministers of no Protestant sect could or would dare to attempt to regulate the votes of their people as the Catholic priests can do, who at the confessional learn all the private concerns of their people, and have almost unlimited power over the conscience as it respects the performance of every civil or social duty.

There is another point of dissimilarity of still greater importance. The opinions of the Protestant clergy are congenial with liberty—they are chosen by the people who have been educated as freemen, and they are dependent on them for patronage and support. The Catholic system is adverse to liberty, and the clergy to a great extent are dependent on foreigners [the Pope and church authorities in Rome] opposed to the principles of our government.

Nor is this all—the secular patronage at the disposal of an associated body of men, who under the influence of their priesthood may be induced to act as one . . . would enable them to touch far and wide the spring of action through our cities and through the nation. . . . How many mechanics, merchants, lawyers, physicians, in any political crisis, might they reach and render timid . . .? How will [the priesthood's] power extend and become omnipresent and resistless as emigration shall quadruple their numbers and action on the political and business men of the nation?

A tenth part of the suffrage of the nation, thus condensed and wielded by the Catholic powers of Europe, might decide our elections, perplex our policy, inflame and divide the nation, break the bond of our union, and throw down our free institutions. . . .

[Catholicism is] a religion which *never prospered but in alliance with despotic governments, has always been and still is the inflexible enemy of Liberty of conscience and free inquiry, and at this moment is the main stay of the battle against republican institutions.*

SOURCE: Lyman Beecher, *A Plea for the West* (Cincinnati: Truman & Smith, 1835), 72–73, 126, 59–63, 85–86, 59.

ORESTES BROWNSON

Catholicism as a Necessity for Popular Government

Like Lyman Beecher, Orestes Brownson was born into the Presbyterian Church, but he quickly grew dissatisfied with its doctrines. After experimenting with Unitarianism, communalism, socialism, and transcendentalism (see Chapter 11), Brownson converted to Catholicism in 1844. A zealous convert, Brownson defended Catholicism with rigorous, logical, and provocative arguments in this article, "Catholicity Necessary to Sustain Popular Liberty" (1845).

Without the Roman Catholic religion it is impossible to preserve a democratic government, and secure its free, orderly, and wholesome action.... The theory of democracy is, Construct your government and commit it to the people to be taken care of ... as they shall think proper.

It is a beautiful theory, and would work admirably, if it were not for one little difficulty, namely, the people are fallible, both individually and collectively, and governed by their passions and interests, which not unfrequently lead them far astray, and produce much mischief.

We know of but one solution of the difficulty, and that is in RELIGION. There is no foundation for virtue but in religion, and it is only religion that can command the degree of popular virtue and intelligence requisite to insure to popular government the right direction.... But what religion? It must be a religion which is above the people and controls them, or it will not answer the purpose. It cannot be Protestantism, ... for Protestantism assumes as its point of departure that Almighty God has indeed given us a religion, but has given it to us not to take care of us, but to be taken care of by us.

[However,] Protestant faith and worship tremble as readily before the slightest breath of public sentiment, as the aspen leaf before the zephyr. The faith and discipline of a sect take any and every direction the public opinion of that sect demands. All is loose, floating, — is here to-day, is there tomorrow, and, next day, may be nowhere. The holding of slaves is compatible with Christian character south of the geographical line, and incompatible north; and Christian morals change according to the prejudices, interests, or habits of the people....

Here, then, is the reason why Protestantism, though it may institute, cannot sustain popular liberty. It is itself subject to popular control, and must follow in all things the popular will, passion, interest, ignorance, prejudice, or caprice.

If Protestantism will not answer the purpose, what religion will? The Roman Catholic, or none. The Roman Catholic religion assumes, as its point of departure, that it is instituted not to be taken care of by the people, but to take care of the people; not to be governed by them, but to govern them. The word is harsh in democratic ears, we admit; but it is not the office of religion to say soft or pleasing words.... The people need governing, and must be governed, or nothing but anarchy and destruction await them. They must have a master....

Quote our expression, THE PEOPLE MUST HAVE A MASTER, as you doubtless will; hold it up in glaring capitals, to excite the unthinking and unreasoning multitude, and to doubly fortify their prejudices against Catholicity; be mortally scandalized at the assertion that religion ought to govern the people, and then go to work and seek to bring the people into subjection to your banks or moneyed corporations....

The Roman Catholic religion, then, is necessary to sustain popular liberty, because popular liberty can be sustained only by a religion free from popular control, above the people, speaking from above and able to command them, and such a religion is the Roman Catholic.

SOURCE: Orestes A. Brownson, *Essays and Reviews, Chiefly on Theology, Politics, and Socialism* (New York: D. & J. Sadlier, 1852), 368–370, 372–373, 376, 379–381.

ANALYZING THE EVIDENCE

➤ According to Beecher, what specific dangers does Catholicism pose to American republican institutions? Why would he argue that Protestant churches do not pose the same dangers?

➤ Does Brownson disagree with Beecher's criticism of the social and political impact of Catholicism? Or does he simply think it is good and necessary, while Beecher believes it is dangerous? Explain your answer.

➤ Given Brownson's statement that "the people must have a master," what would be his view of democracy and popular government?

➤ Do you think the leaders of the Benevolent Empire would agree with any parts of Brownson's social and political philosophy? Why or why not?

SUMMARY

In this chapter, we examined the causes and consequences of the economic transformation that marked the first half of the nineteenth century. That transformation had two facets: the increase in production known as the Industrial Revolution, and the expansion of commerce known as the Market Revolution. Water and steam were crucial ingredients in both revolutions—driving factory machinery, carrying goods to market in canals and rivers, and propelling steamboats and railroad engines.

We also explored the many important results of the economic transformation: the rise of an urban society, the regional similarity of the East and Midwest and their difference from the South, and the creation of a class-divided society. Responding to these changes, benevolent reformers and evangelical revivalists worked to instill middle-class and Christian values in the entire population. However, other social groups—artisan republicans, unionized workers, Irish and German immigrants—accepted only those beliefs that were compatible with their own economic or cultural goals. The result was a fragmented society. Differences of class and culture now split the North just as race and class had long divided the South. As we will see in the next chapter, to address these divisions, Americans looked to the political system, which was becoming increasingly democratic. The resulting tension between social inequality and political democracy would become a troubling, and enduring, part of American life.

Connections: Economy and Society

In 1820, most Americans lived in a rural, agricultural society that was similar to the world of their parents and grandparents. Then, as we noted in the opening essay for Part Three (p. 269), came dramatic changes that "affected every aspect of life in the northern and midwestern states and brought important changes in the South as well." In this chapter, we have described the industrial and market factors that played a major role in creating a new economy and a new society in the Northeast and the Midwest. Our analysis of this economic and social transformation in the South will continue in Chapter 12, where we assess the causes and consequences of the enormous expansion in plantation agriculture and cotton production between 1820 and 1860 and the devastating impact of the domestic slave trade on the lives of millions of African Americans.

In the opening essay, we also observed that the new economy created a class-based society in the North and Midwest. A wealthy elite of merchants, manufacturers, bankers, and entrepreneurs struggled to the top of the social order. Once in charge, they tried to maintain social stability through a paternalistic program of benevolent reform.

This discussion of social reform continues in Chapter 11, which describes how advocates of temperance, religious utopianism, abolitionism, and women's rights took the reform movement in new directions. Their radical outlooks and activities were the result, in part, of the overthrow of the traditional political system and the rise of Jacksonian democracy, the subjects of Chapter 10.

CHAPTER REVIEW QUESTIONS

➤ Weigh the relative importance of the Industrial and Market revolutions in changing the American economy. In what ways was the economy different in 1860 from what it had been in 1800? How would you explain those differences?

➤ What was the impact of the economic revolution on the lives of women in various social groups and classes?

➤ Did the Industrial and Market revolutions make America a more or less republican society? How so?

TIMELINE

1782	Oliver Evans develops automated flour mill
1790	Samuel Slater opens spinning mill in Providence, Rhode Island
1792	Congress passes the Post Office Act
1793	Eli Whitney manufactures cotton gins
1800–1830	Entrepreneurs take over shoe industry, introduce division of labor
1807	Robert Fulton launches the *Clermont*, the first American steamboat
1814	Boston Manufacturing Company opens cotton mill in Waltham, Massachusetts
1816–1828	Congress passes series of protective tariffs on textiles and other imports
1817	Erie Canal begun (completed in 1825)
1820	Minimum federal land price reduced to $1.25 per acre
1820–1840	Urban population in Northeast and Midwest increases more than fourfold
1820s	New England women begin working in textile factories
	Rise of Benevolent Empire leads to conservative social reform
1824	*Gibbons v. Ogden* promotes interstate trade
1830s	Emergence of western commercial cities
	Labor movement gains strength
	Cities begin to segregate by class
	Middle-class culture emerges
	Growth of temperance movement
1830	Charles Grandison Finney begins Rochester revivals
1834	Local unions form National Trades' Union
	John Deere invents steel plow
1840s	Irish and German immigration sparks ethnic riots
	Rise of machine-tool industry
1848	Michigan and Illinois Canal completes inland water route from New York City to New Orleans
1850s	Expansion of railroads in Northeast and Midwest
1857	Overproduction and speculation trigger a financial panic

FOR FURTHER EXPLORATION

Stuart Bruchey, *Enterprise: The Dynamic Economy of a Free People* (1990), offers a panoramic history; Charles G. Sellers, *The Market Revolution: Jacksonian America, 1815–1846* (1991), focuses on the social and cultural aspects of economic change. Scott A. Sandage, *Born Losers: A History of Failure in America* (2005), explores the fate of unsuccessful entrepreneurs. David Freeman Hawke, *Nuts and Bolts of the Past: A History of American Technology, 1776–1860* (1988), offers an entertaining account of eccentric inventors and technical progress. A Web site that explores the impact of technology is "The Eli Whitney Museum & Workshop" (**www.eliwhitney.org/**).

Stephen Aron, *How the West Was Lost: The Transformation of Kentucky from Daniel Boone to Henry Clay* (1996), explores economic and political conflict in the trans-Appalachian west; Peter Way, *Common Labor: Workers and the Digging of North American Canals, 1780–1860* (1993), describes the hard lives of the men who dug the canals. For New York's Erie Canal, go to **www.canals.state.ny.us/cculture/index.html**. First-person accounts, biographies, and promotional literature about the settlement of Michigan, Minnesota, and Wisconsin (1820–1910) are online at "Pioneering the Upper Midwest" (**memory.loc.gov/ammem/umhtml/umhome.html**).

Stuart M. Blumin's *The Emergence of the Middle Class: Social Experience in the American City, 1760–1900* (1989), discusses urban class formation; Stephen P. Rice, *Minding the Machine: Languages of Class in Early Industrial America* (2004), traces the middle-class triumph in the culture wars of the early nineteenth century. A fine study of urban disorder is David Grimsted, *American Mobbing* (1998). In *Home and Work* (1990), Jeanne Boydston takes a critical look at the impact of the market and the city on women's lives. For a woman textile operative's first-hand account of mill life, see **www.fordham.edu/halsall/mod/robinson-lowell.html**.

In *The Democratization of American Christianity* (1987), Nathan Hatch traces the impact of Evangelical Protestantism; for dramatic portraits of revivals and revivalists, consult Mark A. Noll, *America's God: From Jonathan Edwards to Abraham Lincoln* (2003), and Bernard Weisberger's classic study, *They Gathered at the River* (1958). The Library of Congress offers a fine collection on "Religion and the Founding of the American Republic" at **www.loc.gov/exhibits/religion/**. An important recent study is William R. Hutchison, *Religious Pluralism in America: The Contentious History of a Founding Ideal* (2003).

TEST YOUR KNOWLEDGE

To assess your command of the material in this chapter, see the Online Study Guide at **bedfordstmartins.com/henretta**.

For Web sites, images, and documents related to topics and places in this chapter, visit **bedfordstmartins.com/makehistory**.

10

A Democratic Revolution
1820–1844

EUROPEAN VISITORS TO THE UNITED STATES during the 1820s and 1830s generally praised America's republican society, but they found little to celebrate in its political parties and politicians. "The gentlemen spit, talk of elections and the price of produce, and spit again," Frances Trollope reported in *Domestic Manners of the Americans* (1832). In her view, American politics was the sport of party hacks who reeked of "whiskey and onions." Other Europeans lamented the low intellectual level of political debates and their bombastic character. The "clap-trap of praise and pathos" uttered by a leading Massachusetts politician "deeply disgusted" Harriet Martineau, while Basil Hall could only shake his head in astonishment at the shallow arguments, the "conclusions in which nothing was concluded," that were advanced by the inept "farmers, shopkeepers, and country lawyers" who sat in the New York assembly.

The verdict was unanimous and negative. "The most able men in the United States are very rarely placed at the head of affairs," French aristocrat Alexis de Tocqueville observed in *Democracy in America* (1835). Tocqueville ascribed this unhappy result to the character of democracy itself. Ordinary citizens ignored important issues of policy, refused to elect their intellectual superiors to office, and willingly assented to "the

◄ **The Inauguration of President William Henry Harrison, March 4, 1841**

After being sworn into office, President Harrison stands on the steps of the U.S. Capitol (in the box on the left) reviewing a parade of military units. The short balding man to Harrison's right is Martin Van Buren, the departing president. Although they could not vote, many women attended the ceremony, both to enjoy the festivities and to indicate their support for the Whig Party's policies of social and moral reform. Anne S. K. Brown Military Collection, Brown University.

clamor of a mountebank [a charismatic fraud] who knows the secret of stimulating their tastes."

The European visitors were witnesses to the unfolding of the American Democratic Revolution. In the early decades of the American republic, men of great ability had sat in the seats of government, and the prevailing ideology had been republicanism, rule by property-owning "men of TALENTS and VIRTUE." By the 1820s and 1830s, the watchword was *democracy*, which in practice meant rule by popularly elected party politicians. "That the majority should govern was a fundamental maxim in all free governments," declared Martin Van Buren, the most talented of the new breed of middle-class professional politicians who had taken over the halls of government and who would soon build America's Second Party System. The new party politicians often pursued selfish goals; but by uniting ordinary Americans in "election fever" and party organizations, they held together a social order increasingly fragmented by economic change and cultural diversity.

The Rise of Popular Politics, 1820–1829

Expansion of the **franchise** was the most dramatic symbol of the Democratic Revolution. As early as the 1810s, some states had extended the right to vote to almost all white men, bringing many farmers and wage earners into the political arena by ending traditional property qualifications for voting. Nowhere else in the world did ordinary men have so much power. In England, for example, the Reform Bill of 1832 extended the vote to only 600,000 out of 6 million English men — a mere 10 percent.

The Decline of the Notables and the Rise of Parties

The American Revolution weakened the deferential society of the colonial era, but it did not overthrow it. Only two state constitutions — those of Pennsylvania and Vermont — allowed all male taxpayers to vote; and even in those states, families in the low and middle ranks continued to accept the leadership of their social "betters." Consequently, wealthy notable men — northern landlords, slave-owning planters, and seaport merchants — continued to dominate the political system in the first decades of the republic. And rightly so, thought the first chief justice of the Supreme Court, John Jay. As he put it in 1810, "Those who own the country are the most fit persons to participate in the government of it." Local notables managed elections by building up an "interest": lending money to small farmers, giving business to storekeepers, and treating their tenants to rum at election time. An outlay of $20 for refreshments, remarked one poll watcher, "may produce about 100 votes." This gentry-dominated system excluded men without wealth and powerful family connections from running for office.

The Advance of Democracy. The struggle to expand the suffrage began in the 1810s. Reformers in Maryland challenged local notables in the language of Revolutionary-era republicans, condemning property qualifications as a "tyranny" that endowed "one class of men with privileges which are denied to another." To defuse this criticism and deter migration to the West, notables in Maryland and other seaboard state legislatures grudgingly accepted a broader franchise. The new voters changed the tone of politics. They refused to support politicians who flaunted their high social status by wearing "top boots, breeches, and shoe buckles," their hair in "powder and queues." Instead, they elected men who dressed simply and endorsed democracy, even if those politicians favored policies that benefited those with substantial wealth.

Smallholding farmers and ambitious laborers in the Midwest and Southwest pushed forward this challenge to the traditional hierarchical social and political order. In Ohio, a traveler reported, "no white man or woman will bear being called a servant." The constitutions of the new states of Indiana (1816), Illinois (1818), and Alabama (1819) prescribed a broad male franchise, and voters usually elected middling men to local and state offices. A well-to-do migrant in Illinois noted with surprise that the man who plowed his fields "was a colonel of militia, and a member of the legislature." Once in public office, men from modest backgrounds enacted laws that restricted imprisonment for debt, kept taxes low, and allowed farmers to claim squatters' rights to unoccupied land.

By the mid-1820s, only a few states—North Carolina, Virginia, and Rhode Island — required the ownership of freehold property for voting. Many states had instituted universal white male suffrage, and others — Ohio and Louisiana, for example — excluded only the relatively few men who did not pay taxes or serve in the militia. Moreover, between 1818 and 1821, Connecticut, Massachusetts, and

New York wrote new constitutions that reapportioned legislative districts on the basis of population and made local governments more democratic by mandating the election, rather than the appointment, of judges and justices of the peace.

Democratic politics was contentious and, because it was run by men on the make, often corrupt as well. Powerful entrepreneurs and speculators — both notables and self-made men — demanded government assistance for their business enterprises and paid bribes to get it. To secure charters or increase interest rates, bankers distributed shares of stock to key legislators, while speculators won land grants by paying off the members of key committees. And legislators soon found ways to help themselves directly. When the Seventh Ward Bank of New York City received a charter in 1833, the supervising commissioners appointed by the legislature set aside one-third of the bank's 3,700 shares of stock for themselves and their friends, and almost two-thirds for their political allies holding state offices, leaving just 40 shares for public sale.

Other Americans turned to politics to advance the religious and cultural agenda advocated by the benevolent reformers (see Chapter 9). The result of this crusade was political controversy. When evangelical Presbyterians in Utica, New York, called for a town ordinance in 1828 to restrict Sunday entertainment, a member of the local Universalist church — Universalism is a freethinking Protestant denomination — denounced the coercive reforms and called for "Religious Liberty."

Martin Van Buren and the Rise of Parties. The appearance of political parties encouraged debate on issues of government policy. Revolutionary-era Americans had condemned political "factions" and "parties" as antirepublican; consequently, neither the national nor the state constitutions gave parties a role in the governing process. But as the power of notables waned, political parties became more prominent. By the 1820s, parties in a number of states were highly disciplined organizations managed by professional politicians, often middle-class lawyers and journalists. One observer noted that the parties were like a well-designed textile loom, "machines" that wove the diverse interests of various social and economic groups into the elaborate tapestry of a coherent legislative program.

Martin Van Buren of New York was the chief architect of the emerging system of party government, first at the state and then at national level. The son of a tavernkeeper, Van Buren grew up in the landlord-dominated society of the Hudson River Valley. He relied on the powerful Van Ness clan to get his training as a lawyer; then, to avoid becoming the dependent "Tool" of this notable family, he repudiated their tutelage and set out to create a new political order. Van Buren rejected the traditional republican belief that political parties were dangerous and argued that the opposite was true: "All men of sense know that political parties are inseparable from free government" because they check the government's "disposition to abuse power . . . [and curb] the passions, the ambition, and the usurpations" of potential tyrants.

Having defended the legitimacy of political parties, Van Buren undertook to create one of his own. Between 1817 and 1821, he turned his "Bucktail" supporters (so called because they wore a deer's tail on their hats) into the first statewide **political machine**, the Albany Regency. Purchasing a newspaper, the *Albany Argus*, Van Buren used its pages to promote a platform and get out the vote. **Patronage** was an even more important tool. When Van Buren and the Regency won control of the New York legislature in 1821, they acquired a political "interest" much greater than that of the notables — the power to appoint some six thousand of their followers to positions in New York's legal bureaucracy of judges, justices of the peace, sheriffs, deed commissioners, and coroners. This **spoils system** was fair, Van Buren suggested, for it "would operate sometimes in favour of one party, and sometimes of another." And it was thoroughly republican because it was based on rule by the majority. To ensure the passage of important legislation, Van Buren insisted on party discipline and required elected officials to follow the dictates of the **party caucus**. On one crucial occasion, the "Little Magician" — a nickname that acknowledged both Van Buren's height (or lack of it) and his political dexterity — persuaded seventeen New York legislators "magnanimously [to] sacrifice individual preferences for the general good" and lauded them at a banquet with "something approaching divine honors."

The Election of 1824

The advance of political democracy and party government in the states undermined the old consensus system of national politics and the power of the notables who ran it. After the War of 1812, the aristocratic Federalist Party virtually disappeared, and the Republican Party broke up into competing factions (see Chapter 7). As the election of 1824 approached, no fewer than five candidates, all calling themselves Republicans, campaigned for the presidency. Three were veterans of President James Monroe's cabinet: Secretary of State John Quincy Adams, the son of former president John Adams; Secretary of War John C. Calhoun; and Secretary of the Treasury William H. Crawford. The fourth candidate was Henry Clay of Kentucky, the dynamic Speaker of the House of Representatives; and the fifth was General Andrew Jackson, now a senator from Tennessee.

When a caucus of Republicans in Congress selected Crawford as the party's official nominee, the other candidates refused to withdraw. Instead, they introduced competition to national politics by seeking popular support. Democratic reforms in eighteen of the twenty-four states required popular elections (rather than a vote of the state legislature) to choose members of the Electoral College from their states. The battle was closely fought. Thanks to his diplomatic successes as secretary of state (see Chapter 7), John Quincy Adams enjoyed national recognition; and his Massachusetts origins gave him the electoral votes of New England. Henry Clay framed his candidacy around domestic issues. As a congressman, Clay promoted the **American System**, an integrated program of national economic development similar to the Commonwealth policies pursued by state governments. Clay wanted the Second Bank of the United States to regulate state banks and advocated the use of tariff revenues to build roads and canals. His nationalistic program was popular in the West, which needed transportation improvements, but was sharply criticized in the South, which relied on rivers to carry its cotton to market and did not have manufacturing industries to protect. William Crawford of Georgia, an ideological heir of Thomas Jefferson, spoke for the South. Fearing the "consolidation" of political power in Washington, Crawford and other Old Republicans denounced the American System. Recognizing Crawford's appeal in the South, John C. Calhoun of South Carolina withdrew from the presidential race and endorsed Andrew Jackson.

As the hero of the Battle of New Orleans, Jackson benefited from the wave of patriotism that flowed from the War of 1812. Born in the Carolina backcountry, Jackson had settled in Nashville, Tennessee, where he formed ties to influential families through marriage and his career as an attorney and slave-owning cotton planter. His rise from common origins fit the tenor of the new democratic age, and his reputation as a "plain solid republican" attracted voters in all regions.

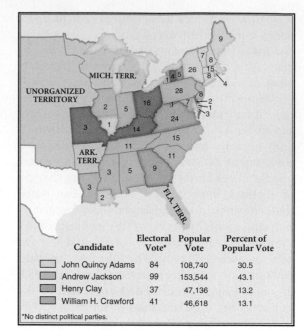

Candidate	Electoral Vote*	Popular Vote	Percent of Popular Vote
John Quincy Adams	84	108,740	30.5
Andrew Jackson	99	153,544	43.1
Henry Clay	37	47,136	13.2
William H. Crawford	41	46,618	13.1

*No distinct political parties.

MAP 10.1 The Presidential Election of 1824

Regional voting was the dominant factor in 1824. John Quincy Adams captured every electoral vote in New England and most of those in New York. Henry Clay carried Ohio and Kentucky, the most populous trans-Appalachian states; and William Crawford took the southern states of Virginia and Georgia. Only Andrew Jackson claimed a national constituency, winning Pennsylvania and New Jersey in the East, Indiana and most of Illinois in the Midwest, and much of the South. Only 356,000 Americans voted, about 27 percent of the eligible electorate.

Still, Jackson's strong showing in the election surprised most political leaders. The Tennessee senator received 99 votes in the Electoral College; Adams garnered 84 votes; Crawford, who suffered a stroke during the campaign, won 41; and Clay finished with 37 (Map 10.1). Because no candidate received an absolute majority, the decision fell to the House of Representatives, as it had in the election of 1800. The Twelfth Amendment to the Constitution (ratified in 1804) specified that the House would choose the president from among the three leading contenders. This procedure hurt Jackson because many congressmen did not want a rough-hewn "military chieftain" in the White House, worried he might become a tyrant. Personally out of the race, Henry Clay used his influence as Speaker to thwart Jackson's election. When the House met in February 1825, Clay assembled a coalition of congressmen from New England and the Ohio River Valley that voted Adams into the presidency.

Adams showed his gratitude by appointing Clay his secretary of state, then the traditional stepping-stone to the presidency.

Clay's appointment was a politically fatal mistake for both men. John C. Calhoun accused Adams of abusing the power of the presidency to thwart the popular will. Along with other Jackson supporters, Calhoun suspected that Clay had made a deal with Adams to become secretary of state. Condemning this "corrupt bargain," they vowed that Clay would never become president.

The Last Notable President: John Quincy Adams

As president, Adams called for bold national leadership. "The moral purpose of the Creator," he told Congress, was to use the president and every other public official to "improve the conditions of himself and his fellow men." Adams called for the establishment of a national university in Washington, extensive scientific explorations in the Far West, and a uniform standard of weights and measures. Most important, he endorsed Henry Clay's American System of national economic development and its three key elements: protective tariffs to stimulate manufacturing, federally subsidized roads and canals to facilitate commerce, and a national bank to control credit and provide a uniform currency.

Resistance to the American System. Manufacturers, entrepreneurs, and growers in the Northeast and Midwest welcomed Adams's policies. But those policies won little support in the South, where planters opposed protective tariffs because they raised the price of manufactures, and smallholders feared powerful banks that could force them into bankruptcy. From his deathbed, Thomas Jefferson condemned Adams for promoting "a single and splendid government of [a monied] aristocracy . . . riding and ruling over the plundered ploughman and beggared yeomanry."

Other politicians objected to the American System on constitutional grounds. In 1817, President Madison had vetoed the Bonus Bill, which would have used the national government's income from the Second Bank of the United States to fund improvement projects in the states. These kinds of projects, Madison had argued, were the sole responsibility of the states, a sentiment that was widely shared among Old Republicans. After a trip to Monticello to meet Thomas Jefferson, his longtime hero, Martin Van Buren declared his allegiance to the constitutional "doctrines of the Jefferson School." Now a member of the U.S.

John Quincy Adams

This famous daguerreotype of the former president, taken about 1843 by Philip Haas, conveys his rigid personality and high moral standards. Although these personal attributes contributed to Adams's success as an antislavery congressman from Massachusetts in the 1830s and 1840s, they hindered his effectiveness as the nation's chief executive. Metropolitan Museum of Art, New York. Gift of I. N. Phelps Stokes, Edward S. Hawes, Alice Mary Hawes, Marion Augusta Hawes.

Senate, Van Buren joined the Old Republicans in defeating most national subsidies for roads and canals. Congress approved only a few of Adams's proposals for internal improvements, among them the short extension of the National Road from Wheeling, Virginia, into Ohio.

The Tariff Battle. The most far-reaching battle of the Adams administration came over tariffs. The Tariff of 1816 placed relatively high duties on imports of cheap English cotton cloth, allowing New England textile producers to dominate that market. In 1824, Adams and Clay secured a new tariff that protected manufacturers in New England and Pennsylvania against imports of iron goods and more-expensive woolen and cotton textiles. When Van Buren and his Jacksonian allies won control of Congress in the election of 1826, they proposed higher tariffs on wool, hemp, and other imported

A CARTOON COMPARING CONDITIONS UNDER FREE TRADE AND
PROTECTIVE TARIFF

From "The United States Weekly Telegram," November 5, 1832.

The "Tariff of Abominations"

Political cartoons enjoyed wide use in eighteenth-century England and became popular in the United States during the political battles of the First Party system (1794–1815). By the 1820s, American newspapers, most of which were subsidized by political parties, published cartoons on a daily basis. This political cartoon attacks the tariffs of 1828 and 1832 as hostile to the interests and prosperity of the South. The gaunt figure on the left represents a southern planter, starved by exactions of the tariff, while the northern textile manufacturer has grown stout feasting on the bounty of protectionism. Corbis-Bettmann.

raw materials. Their goal was to win the support of wool- and hemp-producing farmers in New York, Ohio, and Kentucky for Jackson's presidential candidacy in 1828. The tariff had become a prisoner of politics. "I fear this tariff thing," remarked Thomas Cooper, the president of the College of South Carolina and an advocate of free trade, "by some strange mechanical contrivance ... it will be changed into a machine for manufacturing Presidents, instead of broadcloths, and bed blankets." Disregarding southern protests, northern Jacksonians joined with Adams and Clay's supporters to enact the Tariff of 1828, which significantly raised duties on raw materials, textiles, and iron goods.

The new tariff enraged the South. As the world's cheapest producer of raw cotton, the South did not need a tariff to protect its main industry. Moreover, by raising the price of manufactures, the tariff cost southern planters about $100 million a year. Planters had the unpleasant choice of buying either higher-cost American textiles and iron goods, thus enriching northeastern businesses and workers, or highly dutied British imports, thus paying the cost of the national government. The new tariff was "little less than legalized pillage," an Alabama legislator declared, calling it a "Tariff of Abominations."

Ignoring the Jacksonians' support for the Tariff of 1828, most southerners blamed President Adams for the new act. They also criticized Adams's Indian policy. A deeply moral man, the president had supported the land rights of Native Americans against expansionist whites in the South. In 1825, U.S. commissioners had secured a treaty from one Creek faction that would have ceded the tribe's lands in Georgia to the United States, for eventual sale to the citizens of that state. When the Creek National Council repudiated the treaty, claiming it was fraudulent, Adams called for new negotiations. Eager to acquire the Creeks' land, Georgia governor George M. Troup attacked the president as a "public enemy . . . the unblushing ally of the savages." Joining forces with Georgia's representatives in Congress, Troup persuaded the national legislature to enact a measure that extinguished the Creeks' land titles and forced most Creeks to leave the state.

Elsewhere in the nation, Adams's primary weakness was his increasingly out-of-date political style. The last notable to serve in the White House, he acted the part: aloof, moralistic, and paternalistic. When Congress rejected his activist economic policies, Adams questioned the wisdom of the people and advised elected officials not to be "palsied by the will of our constituents." Ignoring his waning popularity, the president did not use patronage to reward his supporters and allowed hostile federal officials to remain in office. Rather than "run" for reelection in 1828, Adams "stood" for it, telling supporters, "If my country wants my services, she must ask for them."

"The Democracy" and the Election of 1828

Martin Van Buren and the professional politicians handling Andrew Jackson's campaign had no reservations about running for the presidency or any other elected office. To recreate the national political coalition first formed by Thomas Jefferson, Van Buren championed policies that appealed both to northern farmers and artisans (whom he called the "plain Republicans of the North") and to southern slave owners and smallholders who had voted for the Virginia Dynasty. John C. Calhoun, Jackson's vice presidential running mate, brought his South Carolina allies into Van Buren's party, and Jackson's close friends in Tennessee rallied voters there and throughout the states of the Old Southwest. By creating a national political party, Jackson's friends hoped to overcome the diversity of economic and social "interests" that, as James Madison had noted in "Federalist No. 10," would inevitability arise in a large republic.

At Van Buren's direction, his Jacksonian allies orchestrated a massive publicity campaign. In New York, fifty newspapers declared their support for Jackson on the same day. Elsewhere, Jacksonians organized mass meetings, torchlight parades, and barbecues to celebrate their candidate's frontier origin and his rise to fame. They praised "Old Hickory"— the name they gave Jackson saying he was as hard as hickory wood—as a "natural" aristocrat, a self-made man. "Jackson for ever!" was their cry.

Initially, the Jacksonians called themselves Democratic Republicans; but as the campaign wore on, they became Democrats or "the Democracy," names that conveyed their egalitarian message. As Jacksonian Thomas Morris told the Ohio legislature, he and his party believed that the republic had been corrupted by legislative gifts of corporate charters that gave "a few individuals rights and privileges not enjoyed by the citizens at large." Morris promised that the Democracy would destroy such "artificial distinction in society." And Jackson himself declared that "equality among the people in the rights conferred by government" was the "great radical principle of freedom."

Jackson's message of equal rights and popular rule appealed to many social groups. His hostility to business corporations and to Clay's American System won support among northeastern artisans and workers who felt threatened by industrialization. Jackson also won the votes of Pennsylvania ironworkers and New York farmers who had been enriched by the controversial Tariff of Abominations. Yet, by astutely declaring his personal preference for a "judicious"

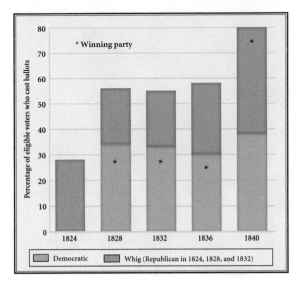

Figure 10.1 Changes in Voting Patterns, 1824–1840

Voter participation soared in 1828 and again in 1840 as competition heated up between Democrats and Whigs, who advocated different policies and philosophies of government.

tariff that would balance regional interests, Jackson remained popular in the South as well. In the Southeast and the Midwest, Old Hickory garnered votes because his well-known hostility toward Native Americans reassured white farmers who wanted the Indians removed from their ancestral lands.

The Democrats' celebration of popular rule carried Jackson into office. In 1824, little more than a quarter of the eligible electorate had voted; in 1828, more than half of all potential voters went to the polls, and 56 percent cast their ballots for the senator from Tennessee (Figure 10.1). Jackson received 178 of 261 electoral votes and became the first president from a trans-Appalachian state (Map 10.2). As the president-elect traveled to Washington, he cut a dignified figure. According to an English observer, he "wore his hair carelessly but not ungracefully arranged, and in spite of his harsh, gaunt features looked like a gentleman and a soldier." However, the outpouring of popular enthusiasm for Jackson frightened men of wealth. As Senator Daniel Webster of Massachusetts, a former Federalist Congressman from New Hampshire and now a corporate lawyer in Boston, warned his clients, the new president would "bring a breeze with him. Which way it will blow, I cannot tell [but] . . . my fear is stronger than my hope." Supreme Court Justice Joseph Story and other influential observers shared Webster's apprehensions. Watching an unruly crowd clamber over the elegant

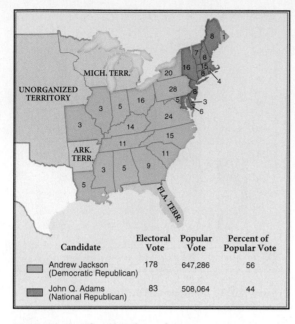

MAP 10.2   The Election of 1828

As he did in 1824, John Quincy Adams carried all of New England and some of the Mid-Atlantic states. However, Andrew Jackson swept the rest of the nation and won a resounding victory in the Electoral College. More than 1.1 million American men cast ballots in 1828, more than three times the number who voted in 1824.

Candidate	Electoral Vote	Popular Vote	Percent of Popular Vote
Andrew Jackson (Democratic Republican)	178	647,286	56
John Q. Adams (National Republican)	83	508,064	44

furniture in the White House to shake the hand of the newly inaugurated president, Story lamented that "the reign of King 'Mob' seemed triumphant."

> ➤ Was there necessarily a connection between the growth of democracy and the emergence of disciplined political parties? Or did they just happen at the same time? Explain your answer.

> ➤ How do you explain John Quincy Adams's great success as secretary of state (see Chapter 7) and his relative lack of success as president?

The Jacksonian Presidency, 1829–1837

American-style political democracy—a broad franchise, a disciplined political party, and policies that addressed the interests of specific social groups—ushered Andrew Jackson into office. Subsequently, Jackson used his popular mandate to transform the presidency and the policies of the national government. During his two terms in office, he enhanced the authority of the president over that of Congress, destroyed the nationalistic American System, and ordained a new ideology for the Democracy. An Ohio supporter summarized Jackson's vision this way: "the Sovereignty of the People, the Rights of the States, and a Light and Simple Government."

Jackson's Agenda: Rotation and Decentralization

Although Jackson had a formal cabinet, for policy-making he relied primarily on an informal group of advisors that came to be known as the Kitchen Cabinet. Its most influential members were Francis Preston Blair of Kentucky, who edited the Democracy's main newspaper, the *Washington Globe*; Amos Kendall, also from Kentucky, who helped Jackson write his speeches; Roger B. Taney of Maryland, who became attorney general, treasury secretary, and then chief justice of the United States; and, most important, Secretary of State Martin Van Buren.

Following Van Buren's example in New York, Jackson used patronage to create a loyal and disciplined national party. He insisted on rotation in office: When an administration was voted out of office, the officials it had appointed would have to leave government service. Dismissing the argument that rotation would lessen expertise, Jackson suggested that most public duties were "so plain and simple that men of intelligence may readily qualify themselves for their performance." William L. Marcy, a New York Jacksonian, put it more bluntly: Government jobs were like the spoils of war, and "to the victor belong the spoils of the enemy." Using the spoils system, Jackson dispensed government jobs to help his friends and to win support for his legislative program.

Jackson's priority was to destroy the centralized plan of economic development known as the American System. As Henry Clay noted apprehensively, the new president wanted "to cry down old constructions of the Constitution . . . to make all Jefferson's opinions the articles of faith of the new Church." Declaring that the "voice of the people" called for "economy in the expenditures of the Government," Jackson rejected national support for transportation projects, which he also opposed on constitutional grounds. In 1830, he vetoed four internal improvement bills, including an extension of the National Road, because they amounted to "an infringement of the reserved powers of states."

President Andrew Jackson, 1830

The new president came to Washington with a well-deserved reputation as an aggressive Indian fighter and dangerous military leader. But in this official portrait, he looks "presidential"—his dress and posture, and the artist's composition, created the image of a calm deliberate statesman. Subsequent events would show that Jackson had not lost his hard-edged authoritarian personality. Library of Congress.

Then Jackson turned his attention to two complex and equally controversial parts of the American System: protective tariffs and the national bank.

The Tariff and Nullification

The Tariff of 1828 had helped Jackson win the presidency, but it saddled him with a major political crisis. Fierce opposition to high protective tariffs arose in South Carolina, where white planters suffered from chronic insecurity. South Carolina was the only state with an African American majority—56 percent of the population in 1830—and its slave owners, like the white sugar planters in the West Indies, lived in fear of a black rebellion. They also worried about the legal abolition of slavery. The British Parliament had promised to end slavery in the West Indies and did so in

August 1833; remembering the northern effort to prohibit bondage in Missouri (see Chapter 8), South Carolina planters worried that the U.S. government might do the same. To limit the powers of the central government, South Carolina politicians launched an attack against protective tariffs.

The crisis began in 1832, when high-tariff congressmen ignored southern warnings that they were "endangering the Union" and passed new legislation that retained the high rates of the Tariff of Abominations. In response, leading South Carolinians called a state convention in November, which boldly adopted the Ordinance of Nullification. The ordinance declared the tariffs of 1828 and 1832 to be null and void, prohibited the collection of those duties in South Carolina after February 1, 1833, and threatened secession if federal officials tried to collect them.

South Carolina's act of **nullification** rested on the constitutional arguments developed in *The South Carolina Exposition and Protest* (1828). Written anonymously by Vice President John C. Calhoun, the *Exposition* gave a localist interpretation to the federal union. Because each region had distinct interests, localists argued, protective tariffs and other national legislation that operated unequally on the various states lacked both fairness and legitimacy—in fact, they were unconstitutional. Obsessively determined to protect the economic interests of the white South, Calhoun exaggerated the frequency and extent of such legislation, declaring: "Constitutional government and the government of a majority are utterly incompatible."

To develop an alternative interpretation of the Constitution, Calhoun turned to the arguments first advanced by Jefferson and Madison in the Kentucky and Virginia resolutions of 1798. Because the U.S. Constitution had been ratified by conventions in the various states, the resolutions suggested, sovereignty lay in the states, not in the people. From this dubious proposition, Calhoun developed a states' rights interpretation of the Constitution. He also advanced the even more dubious claim that a state convention could decide if a congressional law was unconstitutional and declare it null and void within the state's borders. Replying to this argument, which had no basis in the text of the Constitution, Daniel Webster articulated a nationalist construction that endorsed popular sovereignty and celebrated the frequent success of Congress in securing the "general welfare."

Jackson hoped to find a middle path. Although he wanted to limit the reach and power of the

Fashion and Fear in South Carolina, 1831

This painting, executed by South Carolina artist S. Bernard around the time of the nullification crisis, shows fashionably dressed whites strolling along the East Battery of Charleston. To the left, two black boys are fighting, while other African Americans sit and watch. Although the scene is tranquil, many whites feared an uprising by enslaved blacks, who formed a majority of the state's population. Yale University Art Gallery.

national government, he denounced Calhoun's radical doctrine of localist federalism. The Constitution clearly gave the federal government the authority to establish tariffs, and, whatever the costs, Jackson would enforce that power. The president's response to South Carolina's Ordinance of Nullification was direct: Jackson declared that nullification violated the Constitution and was "unauthorized by its spirit . . . and destructive of the great object for which it was formed." "Disunion by armed force is treason," he warned. At Jackson's request, Congress passed the Force Bill early in 1833, which authorized the president to use military force to compel South Carolina to obey national laws. Simultaneously, Jackson addressed the South's objections to high import duties by winning passage of an act that gradually reduced tariff rates. By 1842, tariffs would revert to the modest levels of 1816,

thereby eliminating another part of Clay's American System.

The compromise worked. Having won a gradual reduction in duties, the South Carolina convention rescinded its nullification of the tariff (although it defiantly nullified the Force Bill). Jackson was satisfied. He had addressed the economic demands of the South while upholding the constitutional principle that no state could nullify a law of the United States — a principle that Abraham Lincoln would embrace in defense of the Union during the secession crisis of 1861.

The Bank War

In the middle of the tariff crisis, Jackson faced another major challenge, this time from the political supporters of the Second Bank of the United States.

The Great Webster-Hayne Debate, 1830

The Tariff of Abominations sparked one of the greatest debates in American history. When Senator Robert Y. Hayne of South Carolina (seated in the middle of the picture, with his legs crossed) opposed the federal levies by invoking the doctrines of states' rights and nullification, Daniel Webster rose to the defense of the Union. Speaking for two days to a spellbound Senate, Webster delivered an impassioned oration that celebrated the unity of the American people as the key to their freedom. His parting words—"Liberty *and* Union, now and forever, one and inseparable!"—quickly became part of the national memory.

Webster's Reply to Hayne, by G. P. A. Healy. City of Boston Art Commission.

Founded in Philadelphia in 1816 (see Chapter 7), the bank was a privately managed institution that held a twenty-year charter from the federal government, which owned 20 percent of its stock. The bank's most important role was to stabilize the nation's money supply. Most American money consisted of notes and bills of credit—in effect, paper money—issued by state-chartered banks. The banks promised to redeem the notes on demand with "hard" money—that is, gold or silver coins (also known as specie). By collecting those notes and regularly demanding specie, the Second Bank kept the state banks from issuing too much paper money.

During the prosperous 1820s, the Second Bank maintained monetary stability by closing reckless state banks and restraining expansion-minded bankers in the western states. This tight-money policy pleased bankers and entrepreneurs in Boston, New York, and Philadelphia, whose capital investments were underwriting economic development. However, most ordinary Americans did not understand the regulatory role the Second Bank played; they were simply worried about the national bank's ability to force bank closures, which left them holding worthless paper notes. Some politicians opposed the Second Bank because of the financial clout wielded by its arrogant president, Nicholas Biddle. "As to mere power," Biddle boasted, "I have been for years in the daily exercise of more personal authority than any President habitually enjoys." Fearing Biddle's influence, bankers in New York and other states wanted the specie owned by the federal government to be deposited in their institutions rather than in the

Second Bank. Other bankers, including friends of Jackson's in Nashville, wanted to escape supervision by any central bank.

Jackson Vetoes the Rechartering Bill. Although the Bank had many enemies, it was a political miscalculation by its friends that brought its downfall. In 1832, Jackson's opponents in Congress, led by Henry Clay and Daniel Webster, persuaded Biddle to seek an early extension of the bank's charter. They commanded enough votes in Congress to enact the required legislation and hoped to lure Jackson into a veto that would split the Democrats just before the 1832 elections.

Jackson turned the tables on Clay and Webster. He did veto the bill that rechartered the bank, and he did so with a masterful veto message that blended constitutional arguments with class rhetoric and patriotic fervor. Adopting Jefferson's position, Jackson declared that Congress had no constitutional authority to charter a national bank, which was "subversive of the rights of the States." Using the populist republican rhetoric of the American Revolution, he then attacked the Second Bank as "dangerous to the liberties of the people." He called it a nest of special privilege and monopoly power that promoted "the advancement of the few at the expense of . . . farmers, mechanics, and laborers." Finally, the president evoked nationalism and patriotism by pointing out that British aristocrats owned much of the bank's stock; any such powerful institution should be "purely American," he declared.

Jackson's attack on the bank carried him to victory in the election of 1832. Prior to the election Calhoun had resigned as vice president in order to advance Southern interests as a senator from South Carolina. As his new running mate, Jackson chose his longtime political ally Martin Van Buren. Together Old Hickory and "Little Van" overwhelmed Henry Clay, who headed the National Republican ticket, by 219 to 49 electoral votes. Jackson's most fervent supporters were eastern workers and western farmers, whose lives had been disrupted by falling wages or price fluctuations, and who blamed their fate on the Second Bank. "All the flourishing cities of the West are mortgaged to this money power," charged Senator Thomas Hart Benton, a Jacksonian from Missouri. "They may be devoured by it at any moment." But many Jackson supporters had prospered during a decade of strong economic growth. Along with thousands of middle-class Americans—lawyers, clerks, shopkeepers, artisans—they wanted equal opportunity to rise in the world and cheered Jackson's attacks on privileged corporations.

The Bank Destroyed. Early in 1833, Jackson called on Roger B. Taney to launch an assault on the Second Bank, which still had four years left on its original charter. A strong opponent of corporate privilege, Taney assumed control of the Treasury Department and promptly withdrew the government's gold and silver from the Second Bank. He deposited the specie in various state banks, which critics called Jackson's "pet banks." To justify this abrupt (and probably illegal) transfer, Jackson claimed that his reelection represented "the decision of the people against the bank" and gave him a mandate to destroy it. This occasion was the first in which a president claimed that victory at the polls allowed him to pursue a controversial policy or to act independently of Congress.

The "bank war" escalated into an all-out political battle. In March 1834, Jackson's opponents in the Senate passed a resolution written by Henry Clay that censured the president and warned of executive tyranny: "We are in the midst of a revolution, hitherto bloodless, but rapidly descending towards a total change of the pure republican character of the Government, and the concentration of all power in the hands of one man." Jackson was not deterred by these charges or the widespread opposition in Congress to his policies. "The Bank is trying to kill me but I will kill it," he vowed to Van Buren. And so he did. When the Second Bank's national charter expired in 1836, Jackson prevented its renewal.

Jackson had destroyed both national banking—the creation of Alexander Hamilton—and the American System of protective tariffs and internal improvements instituted by Henry Clay and John Quincy Adams. The result was a profound reduction in the economic activities and the creative energy of the national government. "All is gone," observed a Washington newspaper correspondent. "All is gone, which the General Government was instituted to create and preserve."

Indian Removal

The status of Native American peoples posed an equally complex political problem. By the late 1820s, white voices throughout the states and territories of the South and Midwest were calling for the Indian peoples to be moved and resettled west of the Mississippi River. Many easterners who were sympathetic to Native Americans also favored resettlement. Removal to the West seemed the only way to protect Indian societies from alcohol, financial exploitation, and the loss of their culture.

Most Indians, however, did not want to leave their ancestral lands. The Old Southwest was home to the so-called Five Civilized Tribes: the Cherokees and Creeks in Georgia, Tennessee, and Alabama; the Chickasaws and Choctaws in Mississippi and Alabama; and the Seminoles in Florida. During the War of 1812, Andrew Jackson had forced the Creeks to relinquish millions of acres of land, but Indian peoples still controlled vast tracts. Moreover, the mixed-blood offspring of white traders and Indian women had now assumed the leadership of many tribes. Growing up in a bicultural world, mixed-bloods knew the political ways of whites; most of them strongly resisted removal, and some favored assimilation into white society.

Actually, a number of prominent Indians had adopted the institutions and the lifestyle of southern planters. James Vann, a Georgia Cherokee, owned more than twenty black slaves, two trading posts, and a gristmill. Forty other mixed-blood Cherokee families owned twenty or more African American slaves. To protect their property and the lands of their people, the mixed-bloods promoted a strong Indian identity. For example, Sequoyah, a mixed-blood, spent years developing a system of writing for the Cherokee language that he perfected in 1821; and in 1827, mixed-blood Cherokees introduced a new charter of government modeled directly on the U.S. Constitution. Full-blood Cherokees, who made up 90 percent of the population, resisted many of the mixed-bloods' cultural and political innovations but were equally determined to retain their ancestral lands. "We would not receive money for land in which our fathers and friends are buried," one full-blood chief declared. "We love our land; it is our mother" (see Comparing American Voices, "The Cherokees Debate Removal to the Indian Territory," pp. 314–315).

What the Cherokees wanted carried no weight with the Georgia legislature. In 1802, Georgia had given up its western land claims in return for a federal promise to extinguish Indian landholdings in the state. Now it demanded fulfillment of that pledge. Having spent his military career fighting Indians and seizing their lands, Andrew Jackson gave his full support to Georgia. On assuming the presidency, he withdrew the federal troops that had protected Indian enclaves there and in Alabama and Mississippi. The states, he declared, were sovereign within their borders.

Jackson then pushed the Indian Removal Act of 1830 through Congress. The act granted money and land in present-day Oklahoma and Kansas to Native American peoples who would give up their ancestral holdings. To persuade Indians to move, government officials promised that they could live on the new lands, "they and all their children, as long as grass grows and water runs." When Chief Black Hawk and his Sauk and Fox followers refused to move from rich farmland in western Illinois in 1832, Jackson sent troops to expel them. Rejecting Black Hawk's offer to surrender, the American army pursued him into the Wisconsin Territory and, in the brutal eight-hour Bad Axe Massacre, killed 850 of Black Hawk's 1,000 warriors. Over the next five years, American diplomatic

Black Hawk

This portrait of Black Hawk (1767–1838), by Charles Bird King, shows the Indian leader as a young warrior, wearing a medal commemorating an early-nineteenth-century agreement with the U.S. government. Later, in 1830, when Congress approved Andrew Jackson's Indian Removal Act, Black Hawk mobilized Sauk and Fox warriors to protect their ancestral lands in Illinois. "It was here, that I was born—and here lie the bones of many friends and relatives," the aging chief declared. "I . . . never could consent to leave it." Newberry Library, Chicago.

The Cherokees Debate Removal to the Indian Territory

President Jackson's policy of Indian removal divided many native peoples. Because some influential Cherokee leaders were literate in English, historians know the most about their debate over removal. The selections here focus on the Treaty of New Echota (1835), which traded the Cherokees' land east of the Mississippi for new land in the Indian Territory (in present-day Oklahoma and Kansas). Most full-blood Cherokees never accepted the legitimacy of the treaty, and some sought revenge. When Elias Boudinot, one of the Cherokees who signed the treaty, settled in the Indian Territory in 1839, members of the antitreaty faction labeled him a traitor and stabbed him to death.

JOHN ROSS
"A Fraud upon the Cherokee People," July 2, 1836

John Ross was the public voice of the antitreaty faction, writing petitions to Congress and publishing various letters, such as the one below, to marshal support for his position. Ross had fought as an officer under General Andrew Jackson against the Creeks in 1813. Now he vigorously opposed Jackson's removal policy, in part because he owned a three-hundred-acre cotton plantation in Georgia, which was worked by twenty African American slaves. Following the death of his Cherokee wife, Quatie, during the Trail of Tears (the forced march westward), Ross set up a new cotton plantation in the Indian Territory, which was worked by slaves he brought from Georgia. He continued to lead his people until his death in 1866.

I believe, the document [the Treaty of New Echota] signed by unauthorized individuals at Washington, will never be regarded by the Cherokee nation as a Treaty. The delegation appointed by the people to make a Treaty, have protested against that instrument "as deceptive to the world and a fraud upon the Cherokee people." . . .

Suppose we are to be removed through it from a home, by circumstances rendered disagreeable and even untenable, to be secured in a better home, where nothing can disturb or dispossess us. *Here is the great mystification.* We are not secured in the new home promised to us. We are exposed to precisely the same miseries, from which, if this measure is enforced, the United States' power professes to relieve us, but does so entirely by the exercise of that power, against our will.

One impression concerning us, is, that though we object to removal, as we are equally averse to becoming citizens of the United States, we ought to be forced to remove; to be tied hand and foot and conveyed to the extreme western frontier, and then turned loose among the wild beasts of the wilderness. Now, the fact is, we never have objected to become citizens of the United States and to conform to her laws; but in the event of conforming to her laws, we have required the protection and privileges of her laws to accompany that conformity on our part. We have asked this repeatedly and repeatedly has it been denied. . . .

In conclusion I would observe, that I still strongly hope we shall find ultimate justice from the good sense of the administration and of the people of the United States. . . . I am persuaded they have erred only in ignorance, and an ignorance forced upon them by the misrepresentation and artifices of the interested.

ELIAS BOUDINOT
Removal as "the Only Practicable Remedy," 1837

Elias Boudinot was born Gallegina ("Buck") Watie to Cherokee parents in Georgia in 1804. His father sent him to a local Moravian missionary school. In 1817, Gallegina transferred to a religious academy in Connecticut and took the name of one of its patrons, New Jersey lawyer and congressman Elias Boudinot (1740–1821). Returning to Georgia, Boudinot became the editor of the bilingual Cherokee Phoenix, *the first Native American newspaper, in 1828. His belief that removal was "the only practicable remedy" was at odds with the Cherokee government and led to his resignation from the newspaper in 1832. The selection here was a response to John Ross's writings on the Treaty of New Echota.*

What is to be done?" was a natural inquiry, after we found that all our efforts to obtain redress from the General Government, on the land of our fathers, had been of no avail. The first rupture among ourselves was the moment we presumed to answer that question. To a portion of the Cherokee people it early became evident that the interest of their countrymen and the happiness of their posterity depended upon an entire change of policy. Instead of contending uselessly against superior power, the only course left, was, to yield to circumstances over which they had no control.

In all difficulties of this kind, between the United States and the Cherokees the only mode of settling them has been by treaties; consequently, when a portion of our people became convinced that no other measures would avail, they became the *advocates of a treaty*, as the only means to extricate the Cherokees from their perplexities; hence they were called *the treaty party*. Those who maintained the old policy were known as the *anti-treaty party*. At the head of the latter has been Mr. John Ross. . . . To advocate a treaty was to declare war against the established habits of thinking peculiar to the aborigines. It was to come in contact with settled prejudices with the deep rooted attachment for the soil of our forefathers. Aside from these natural obstacles, the influence of the chiefs, who were ready to take advantage of the well known feelings of the Cherokees in reference to their lands was put in active requisition against us. . . .

It is with sincere regret that I notice you [here, Boudinot is addressing John Ross directly] say little or nothing about the moral condition of this people, as affected by present circumstances. . . . Look at the mass, look at the entire population as it now is, and say, can you see any indication of a progressing improvement, anything that can encourage a philanthropist? You know that it is almost a dreary waste. I care not if I am accounted a slanderer of my country's reputation; every observing man in this nation knows that I speak the words of truth and soberness. . . . I say their condition is wretched. Look, my dear sir, around you, and see the progress that vice and immorality have already made! See the spread of intemperance and the wretchedness and misery it has already occasioned! I need not reason with a man of your sense and discernment, and of your observation, to show the debasing character of that vice to our people; you will find an argument in every tippling shop in the country; you will find its cruel effects in the bloody tragedies that are frequently occurring in the frequent convictions and executions for murders, and in the tears and groans of the widows and fatherless, rendered homeless, naked, and hungry, by this vile curse of our race. And has it stopped its cruel ravages with the lower or poorer classes of our people? Are the

higher orders, if I may so speak, left untainted? . . . It is not to be denied that, as a people, we are making a rapid tendency to a general immorality and debasement. . . .

If the dark picture which I have here drawn is a true one, and no candid person will say it is an exaggerated one, can we see a brighter prospect ahead? In another country, and under other circumstances, there is a *better* prospect. Removal, then, is the only remedy, the only *practicable* remedy. By it there *may be* finally a renovation; our people *may* rise from their very ashes, to become prosperous and happy, and a credit to our race. . . . My language has been; "fly for your lives"; it is now the same. I would say to my countrymen, you among the rest, fly from the moral pestilence that will finally destroy our nation.

What is the prospect in reference to your plan of relief, if you are understood at all to have any plan? It is dark and gloomy beyond description. Subject the Cherokees to the laws of the States in their present condition? . . . Instead of remedying the evil you would only rivet the chains and fasten the manacles of their servitude and degradation. . . . May God preserve us from such a destiny.

SOURCE: Both selections are taken from Theda Perdue and Michael D. Green, eds., *The Cherokee Removal: A Brief History with Documents*, 2d ed. (Boston: Bedford/St. Martin's, 2005), 147–151, 153–159.

ANALYZING THE EVIDENCE

➤ What are John Ross's main arguments against removal? What alternative does he implicitly propose?

➤ Why does Elias Boudinot believe that removal is the best alternative? In what ways is he hopeful that it will improve the lives of the Cherokees?

➤ Suppose that Boudinot and his associates had not signed the Echota Treaty. Would anything have turned out differently for the Cherokees?

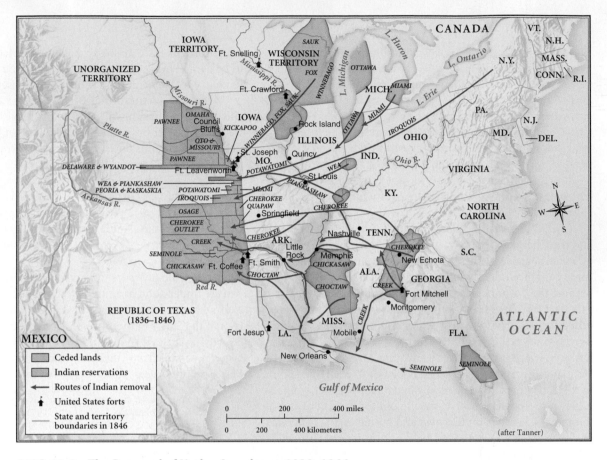

MAP 10.3   The Removal of Native Americans, 1820–1846

Beginning in the 1820s, the U.S. government forced scores of native American peoples to sign treaties that exchanged Indian lands in the East for money and designated reservations west of the Mississippi River. Then, in the 1830s, the government used military force to expel the Cherokees, Chickasaws, Choctaws, Creeks, and many Seminoles from their ancestral homes in the Old Southeast and to resettle them in the Indian Territory, land in the present-day states of Oklahoma and Kansas.

pressure and military power forced seventy Indian peoples to sign treaties and move west of the Mississippi (Map 10.3).

In the meantime, the Cherokees had carried their case to the Supreme Court, where they claimed the status of a "foreign nation." In *Cherokee Nation v. Georgia* (1831), Chief Justice John Marshall, writing for the majority, denied the Cherokees' claim of independence, declaring that Indian peoples were "domestic dependent nations." However, in *Worcester v. Georgia* (1832), Marshall and the court sided with the Cherokees against Georgia. Voiding Georgia's extension of state law over the Cherokees, they held that Indian nations were "distinct political communities, having territorial boundaries, within which their authority is exclusive [and this is] guaranteed by the United States."

Instead of guaranteeing the Cherokees' territory, the U.S. government took it from them. After

negotiating a removal treaty with a minority Cherokee faction in 1835—the Treaty of New Echota—American officials insisted that all Cherokees abide by it. When only two thousand of seventeen thousand Cherokees had moved west by the deadline, May 1838, President Martin Van Buren ordered General Winfield Scott to enforce the treaty. Scott's army rounded up some fourteen thousand Cherokees and forcibly marched them 1,200 miles to the Indian Territory, an arduous journey they described as the Trail of Tears. Along the way, three thousand Indians died of starvation and exposure.

After the Creeks, Chickasaws, and Choctaws moved west of the Mississippi, the Seminoles were the only numerically significant Indian people remaining in the Old Southwest. With the aid of runaway slaves who had married into the tribe, the Seminoles fought a successful guerrilla war against the U.S. Army during the 1840s and retained their

Raising Public Opinion Against the Seminoles

During the eighteenth century, hundreds of black slaves fled South Carolina and Georgia, and found refuge in Spanish Florida, where they lived among and intermarried with the Seminole people. This color engraving from the 1830s — showing red and black Seminoles butchering respectable white families — was intended to bolster political support for the forced removal of the Seminoles to the Indian Territory. By the mid-1840s, after a decade of warfare, the U.S. army had forced 2,500 Seminoles to migrate to Oklahoma. However, another 2,500 Seminoles continued their armed resistance and eventually won a new treaty allowing them to live in Florida. Granger Collection.

lands in Florida, which was still a sparsely settled frontier region. The Seminoles were an exception. The national government had forced the removal of most eastern Indian peoples.

The Jacksonian Impact

Jackson's legacy, like that of every great president, is complex and rich. On the institutional level, he permanently expanded the potential authority of the nation's chief executive by identifying it with the voice of the people. As Jackson put it, "The President is the direct representative of the American people." Assuming that role during the nullification crisis, he upheld national authority by threatening the use of military force, laying the foundation for Lincoln's defense of the Union a generation later. At the same time (and somewhat contradictorily), Jackson purposefully curbed the reach of the national government. By undermining Henry Clay's American System of national banking, protective tariffs, and internal improvements, he reinvigorated the Jeffersonian tradition of a limited and frugal central government.

Roger B. Taney and the Court. Jackson also undermined the constitutional jurisprudence of John Marshall by appointing Roger B. Taney as Marshall's successor. During his long tenure as chief justice from 1835 to 1864, Taney partially reversed the na-

tionalist and property-rights decisions of the Marshall Court and gave constitutional legitimacy to Jackson's policies endorsing states' rights and free enterprise. In the landmark case *Charles River Bridge Co. v. Warren Bridge Co.* (1837), Taney declared that a legislative charter — in this case, to build and operate a toll bridge — did not necessarily bestow a monopoly, and that a legislature could charter a competing bridge to promote the general welfare: "While the rights of private property are sacredly guarded, we must not forget that the community also has rights." This decision directly challenged Marshall's interpretation of the contract clause of the Constitution in *Dartmouth College v. Woodward* (1819), which had stressed the binding nature of public charters (see Chapter 7). By limiting the property claims of existing canal and turnpike companies, the decision opened the way for legislatures to charter railroads that would provide cheaper and more-efficient transportation.

Other decisions by the Taney Court placed limits on Marshall's nationalistic interpretation of the commerce clause by enhancing the regulatory role of state governments. For example, in *Mayor of New York v. Miln* (1837), the Taney Court ruled that New York State could use its "police power" to inspect the health of arriving immigrants. The Court also restored to the states some of the economic powers they had exercised before 1787. In *Briscoe v. Bank of Kentucky* (1837), for example, the justices found that when it issued currency, a bank owned by the state of Kentucky did not violate the provision of the U.S. Constitution (Article 1, Section 10) that prohibits states from issuing "bills of credit."

States Embrace Classical Liberal Doctrines. Inspired by Jackson and Taney's example, Democrats in the various states mounted their own constitutional revolutions. Between 1830 and 1860, twenty states called conventions to write new constitutions that would extend democracy. The revised constitutions were more democratic because they usually gave the vote to all white men and reapportioned state legislatures on the basis of population. They also brought government "near to the people" by mandating the election, rather than the appointment, of most public officials, including sheriffs, justices of the peace, and judges.

Most of the new constitutions also introduced the principles of **classical liberalism**, or **laissez-faire**—that the government's role in the economy should be limited. (Twentieth-century social-welfare liberalism endorses the opposite principle, that government should intervene in economic and social life. See Chapter 24.) As president, Jackson had destroyed the American system and its program of national government subsidies; now his disciples in the states set out to undermine the Commonwealth philosophy, the use of chartered corporations and state funds to promote economic development. Most Jackson-era constitutions prohibited states from granting exclusive charters to corporations or extending loans and credit guarantees to private businesses. "If there is any danger to be feared in . . . government," declared a New Jersey Democrat, "it is the danger of associated wealth, with special privileges." The revised state constitutions also protected taxpayers by setting strict limits on state debt and encouraging judges to enforce them. Said one New York reformer: "We will not trust the legislature with the power of creating indefinite mortgages on the people's property."

"The world is governed too much," the Jacksonians proclaimed as they condemned government-granted special privileges and embraced a small-government, laissez-faire outlook. The first American populists, they celebrated the power of ordinary people to make decisions in the marketplace and the voting booth.

➤ What were Andrew Jackson's policies on banking and tariffs? How did they evolve? Do you think those policies helped or hurt the American economy? Why?

➤ Why did Jackson support Indian removal? Did removal help to preserve, or to destroy, Native American culture? Explain your answer.

➤ How did the constitutional interpretations of the Taney Court differ from those of the Marshall Court? What changed as a result of the Taney Court's decisions?

Class, Culture, and the Second Party System

The rise of the Democracy and Jackson's tumultuous presidency sparked the creation in the mid-1830s of a second national party—the **Whigs**—and a new party system. For the next two decades, Whigs and Democrats competed fiercely for votes. Each party appealed to different cultural groups: Many evangelical Protestants became Whigs, while most Catholic immigrants and traditional Protestants joined the Democrats. By debating issues of economic policy, class power, and moral reform, party politicians offered Americans a clear choice between competing programs and political leaders. "Of the two great parties," remarked philosopher and essayist Ralph Waldo Emerson, the Democracy "has the best cause . . . for free trade, for wide suffrage." The Whig party, he said, "has the best men."

The Whig Worldview

The Whig Party began in 1834, when a group of congressmen banded together to oppose Andrew Jackson's policies and his high-handed, "kinglike" conduct. They took the name *Whigs* to identify themselves with the pre-Revolutionary American and British parties—also called Whigs—that had opposed the arbitrary actions of British monarchs. The Whigs accused "King Andrew I" of violating the Constitution by creating a "spoils system" and increasing presidential authority. Jackson's "executive usurpation," they charged, undermined government by elected legislators, who were the true representatives of the sovereign people (see Reading American Pictures, "Politics and the Press: Cartoonists Take Aim at Andrew Jackson," p. 319).

Whig Ideology. Initially, the Whigs were a diverse group, a "heterogeneous mass" drawn from various political factions and outlooks. However, under the leadership of Senators Webster of Massachusetts, Clay of Kentucky, and Calhoun of South Carolina, the Whigs gradually articulated a distinct vision.

Politics and the Press: Cartoonists Take Aim at Andrew Jackson

The Rats Leaving a Falling House, 1831. Library of Congress.

King Andrew the First, 1832. New-York Historical Society.

The 1830s witnessed the rise of the Second Party System, in which Whigs and Democrats competed fiercely for power and patronage. They also witnessed an expansion of the franchise. These two factors — party conflict and democratic suffrage — produced an outpouring of political literature, especially in party-subsidized newspapers. Cartoons quickly became a staple of democratic politics because their use of simple terms and caricature appealed to ordinary voters. Cartoons like these — and thousands more — give us insight into the partisan political culture of the era.

ANALYZING THE EVIDENCE

➤ The cartoon on the left was inspired by Edward Williams Clay (no relation to Henry Clay), a Philadelphia portrait painter and engraver who was also a great cartoonist. In 1831, President Jackson's critics printed 10,000 copies of "The Rats Leaving a Falling House." Why was this cartoon so popular? What does the use of rats suggest about the tone of politics in the 1830s? What other visual clues reveal the artist's political grievances?

➤ In the image to the right, how does the cartoonist depict the threat Jackson poses to the republic? Based on the material in this chapter, do you think there was any justification for the artist's point of view?

➤ Do these cartoons suggest why Andrew Jackson became a prime target of cartoonists? What was there about his personality, appearance, or political style that made him especially vulnerable to caricature?

➤ Why were cartoons like the two here particularly effective as political weapons in the early nineteenth century? How do they work as propaganda? In what ways do they try to persuade their audience?

Their goal, like that of the Federalists of the 1790s, was a political world dominated by men of ability and wealth; unlike the Federalists, though, the Whig elite would be chosen by talent, not birth.

The Whigs celebrated the entrepreneur and the enterprising individual: "This is a country of self-made men," they boasted, pointing to the relative absence of permanent distinctions of class and status among the white citizens of the United States. Embracing the Industrial Revolution, northern Whigs welcomed the investments of "moneyed capitalists," which provided workers with jobs and so "bread, clothing and homes." Whig congressman Edward Everett told a Fourth of July crowd in Lowell, Massachusetts, that there should be a "holy alliance" among laborers, owners, and governments. Many workers agreed, especially those who held jobs in the New England textile factories and Pennsylvania iron mills that benefited from government subsidies and protective tariffs. To ensure continued economic progress, Everett and other northern Whigs called for a return to the American System.

Support for the Whigs in the South rested on the appeal of specific policies and politicians rather than agreement with the Whigs' social vision. Some southern Whigs were wealthy planters who invested in railroads and banks or sold their cotton to New York merchants. Most were yeomen whites who wanted to break the grip over state politics held by low-country planters, most of whom were Democrats. In addition, some states' rights Democrats in Virginia and South Carolina became Whigs because, like John C. Calhoun, they condemned Andrew Jackson's crusade against nullification.

Like Calhoun, most southern Whigs did not share the Whig Party's enthusiasm for high tariffs for industry and social mobility for individual Americans. Calhoun was extremely conscious of class divisions in society. He maintained that the northern Whig ideal of equal opportunity was contradicted not only by slavery, which he considered a fundamental American institution, but also by the wage-labor system of industrial capitalism. "There is and always has been in an advanced state of wealth and civilization a conflict between labor and capital," Calhoun declared in 1837. He urged slave owners and factory owners to unite against their common foe: a working class comprised of enslaved blacks and propertyless whites.

Most northern Whigs rejected Calhoun's class-conscious social ideology. "A clear and well-defined line between capital and labor" might fit the slave South or class-ridden European societies, Daniel Webster conceded, but in the North "this distinction grows less and less definite as commerce advances." Ignoring the ever-increasing mass of propertyless immigrants, Webster focused on the growing size and affluence of the northern middle class, whose members became strong supporters of Whig candidates. In fact, in the election of 1834, the Whigs won a majority in the House of Representatives by appealing to evangelical Protestants and the upwardly mobile — prosperous farmers, small-town merchants, and skilled industrial workers in New England, New York, and the new communities along the Great Lakes.

Anti-Masonic Influence. Many of these Whig voters had previously supported the Anti-Masons, a powerful but short-lived political party that formed in the late 1820s. As their name implies, Anti-Masons opposed the Order of Freemasonry, a republican organization that began in eighteenth-century Europe. The order was a secret society of men, its rituals closely guarded. New members had to be vouched for by a Mason and profess a belief in a supreme being. Freemasonry spread rapidly in America and attracted political leaders — including George Washington, Henry Clay, and Andrew Jackson — and ambitious businessmen. By the mid-1820s, there were twenty thousand Masons in New York State, organized into 450 local lodges. Following the kidnapping and murder in 1826 of William Morgan, a New York Mason who had threatened to reveal the order's secrets, the Freemasons fell into disrepute. Thurlow Weed, a Rochester newspaper editor, spearheaded the Anti-Masonic Party, which attacked the order for being a secret aristocratic fraternity and ousted its members from local and state offices.

The Whigs recruited Anti-Masons to their party by endorsing the Anti-Masons' support for temperance, equality of opportunity, and evangelical moralism. Throughout the Northeast and Midwest, Whig politicians advocated legal curbs on the sale of alcohol and supported local bylaws to preserve Sunday as a day of worship. The Whigs also won congressional seats in the Ohio and Mississippi valleys, where farmers, bankers, and shopkeepers favored Henry Clay's advocacy of government subsidies for roads, canals, and bridges. For these citizens of the growing Midwest, the Whigs' program of nationally subsidized transportation projects was as important as their moral agenda.

The Election of 1836. In the election of 1836, the Whig Party faced Martin Van Buren, the architect of the Democratic Party and Jackson's handpicked successor. Van Buren denounced the American System

Celebrating a Political Triumph, 1836

To commemorate Martin Van Buren's election in 1836 and to reward friends for their support, the Democratic Party distributed thousands of snuff boxes inscribed with the new president's portrait. By using gifts and other innovative measures to enlist the loyalty of voters, Van Buren and his allies transformed American politics from an upper-class avocation to a democratic contest for votes and power. Collection of Janice L. and David J. Frent.

and warned that its revival would undermine the rights of the states and create an oppressive system of "consolidated government." Positioning himself as a defender of individual rights, Van Buren also opposed the efforts of Whigs and moral reformers to use state laws to impose temperance and national laws to restrict or abolish slavery. "The government is best which governs least" became his motto in economic, cultural, and racial matters.

To oppose Van Buren, the Whigs ran four candidates, each of whom had a strong regional reputation. Their plan was to garner enough electoral votes to throw the contest into the House of Representatives. However, the Whig tally—73 electoral votes collected by William Henry Harrison of Ohio, 26 by Hugh L. White of Tennessee, 14 by Daniel Webster of Massachusetts, and 11 by W. P. Magnum of Georgia—fell far short of Van Buren's 170 votes. Still, the size of the popular vote for the four Whig candidates—49 percent of the total—showed that the party's message of economic and moral improvement appealed not only to middle-class Americans but also to farmers and workers with little or no property (see Voices from Abroad, "Alexis de Tocqueville: Parties in the United States," p. 323).

Labor Politics and the Depression of 1837–1843

As the Democrats struggled to maintain their national political supremacy, they faced a challenge on the local level from a new political party made up primarily of artisans and laborers. Market expansion and urban growth had swelled the number of nonfarm workers, and these workers were demanding attention to their economic and political needs (see Chapter 9).

Working Men's Parties and Unions. In 1827, artisans and workers in Philadelphia organized the Mechanics' Union of Trade Associations, a group of fifty unions with ten thousand members. The following year, they founded a Working Men's Party to secure "a just balance of power . . . between all the various classes." The new party campaigned for the abolition of banks, fair taxation, and universal public education. Equally important, it blazed the trail for similar organizations: By 1833, laborers had established Working Men's Parties in fifteen states.

The new parties had a clear agenda. The economic transformation had brought prosperity to bankers and entrepreneurs, but rising prices and stagnant wages had lowered the standard of living of many urban artisans and wage earners. These contradictory trends exposed what workers called "the glaring inequality of society" and prompted them to organize for political action. "Past experience teaches us that we have nothing to hope from the aristocratic orders of society," declared the New York Working Men's Party. It vowed "to send men of our own description, if we can, to the Legislature at Albany" and to win the passage of laws that would put an end to private banks, chartered monopolies, and debtors' prisons. In Philadelphia, the Working Men's Party demanded higher taxes on the wealthy and, in 1834, persuaded the Pennsylvania legislature to authorize tax-supported schools to educate workers' children.

Artisan republicanism—workers' independence—was the core ideology of the working men's parties. According to radical thinker Orestes Brownson, their goal was a society without dependent wage earners: "All men will be independent proprietors, working on their own capitals, on their own farms, or in their own shops." This ideal prompted many artisan republicans to join Jacksonian Democrats in demanding equal rights and attacking chartered corporations. "The only safeguard against oppression," argued William Leggett, a leading member of the New York Loco-Foco (Equal Rights) Party, "is a system of legislation

Frances Wright: Radical Reformer

Wright (1795–1852) grew up in a wealthy, republican-minded merchant family in Scotland. After a sojourn in the United States, she published *Views of Society and Manners in America* (1821), which won her the friendship of Lafayette and Jefferson. In 1825, she founded a utopian community of whites and freed slaves at Nashoba in western Tennessee. Three years later, Wright took New York by storm, lecturing to large audiences that a "monied aristocracy" of bankers and a "professional aristocracy" of ministers and lawyers were oppressing the "laboring class." She set up a reading room and medical dispensary and won a following among artisans and journeymen, some of whom turned to politics and energized the Working Men's Party. This portrait, painted at Nashoba in 1826, relays a subversive message. Wright is wearing pantaloons covered by a tunic. Compounding that masculine imagery, she is standing next to a horse, a traditional symbol of virility. Miriam and Ira D. Wallach Division of Art, Prints and Photographs. The New York Public Library. Astor, Lenox and Tilden Foundations.

which leaves to all the free exercise of their talents and industry." Working Men's candidates initially won office in many cities, but divisions over policy and the parties' weakness in statewide contests soon took a toll. By the mid-1830s, most politically active workers had joined the Democratic Party, which already had a strong base in the dominant farm population, and urged that party to enact legislation to eliminate protective tariffs and to tax the stocks and bonds of wealthy capitalists.

As they campaigned for a more egalitarian society, workers formed unions to bargain for higher wages for themselves. Employers responded by attacking the union movement. In 1836, clothing manufacturers in New York City agreed to dismiss workers who belonged to the Society of Journeymen Tailors and circulated a list—a so-called **blacklist**—of the society's members. The employers also brought lawsuits to overturn **closed-shop agreements** that required them to hire only union members. They argued that these contracts violated both the common law and legislative statutes that prohibited "conspiracies" in restraint of trade.

Judges usually sided with the employers. In 1835, the New York Supreme Court found that a shoemakers' union in Geneva had illegally caused "an industrious man" to be "driven out of employment" because he would not join the union. "It is important to the best interests of society that the price of labor be left to regulate itself," the court declared. When a court in New York City upheld a conspiracy verdict against a tailors' union, a crowd of 27,000 people denounced the decision in a mass meeting, and tailors circulated handbills proclaiming that the "Freemen of the North are now on a level with the slaves of the South." Juries were more

Alexis de Tocqueville

Parties in the United States

In Democracy in America (1835), Alexis de Tocqueville presented both a philosophical analysis of the society of the United States and an astute description of its political institutions. Here the republican-minded French aristocrat explains the role of lawyers in American politics, why "great political parties" are not to be found in the United States, and how regional interests and political ambition threaten the stability of the political system.

In visiting the Americans and studying their laws, we perceive that the authority they have entrusted to the members of the legal profession, and the influence that these individuals exercise in the government, are the most powerful existing security against the excesses of democracy.... Men who have made a special study of the laws derive from [that] occupation certain habits of order, a taste for formalities, and a kind of instinctive regard for the regular connection of ideas, which naturally render them very hostile to the revolutionary spirit and the unreflecting passions of the multitude.... Lawyers belong to the people by birth and interest, and to the aristocracy by habit and taste; they may be looked upon as the connecting link between the two great classes of society....

The political parties that I style great are those which cling to principles rather than to their consequences; to general and not to special cases; to ideas and not to men.... In them private interest, which always plays the chief part in political passions, is more studiously veiled under the pretext of the public good....

Great political parties ... are not to be met with in the United States at the present time. Parties, indeed, may be found which threaten the future of the Union; but there is none which seems to contest the present form of government or the present course of society. The parties by which the Union is menaced do not rest upon principles, but upon material interests. These interests constitute, in the different provinces of so vast an empire, rival nations rather than parties. Thus, upon a recent occasion [the Tariff of 1832 and the nullification crisis in South Carolina] the North contended for the system of commercial prohibition, and the South took up arms in favor of free trade, simply because the North is a manufacturing and the South an agricultural community; and the restrictive system that was profitable to the one was prejudicial to the other.

In the absence of great parties the United States swarms with lesser controversies.... The pains that are taken to create parties are inconceivable, and at the present day it is no easy task. In the United States there is no religious animosity, ... no jealousy of rank, ... no public misery.... Nevertheless, ambitious men will succeed in creating parties.... A political aspirant in the United States begins by discerning his own interest [and] then contrives to find out some doctrine or principle that may suit the purposes of this new organization, which he adopts in order to bring forward his party and secure its popularity....

The deeper we penetrate into the inmost thought of these parties, the more we perceive that the object of the one [the Whigs] is to limit and that of the other [the Democrats] to extend the authority of the people. I do not assert that the ostensible purpose or even that the secret aim of American parties is to promote the rule of aristocracy or democracy in the country; but I affirm that aristocratic or democratic passions may easily be detected at the bottom of all parties....

To quote a recent example, when President Jackson attacked the Bank of the United States, the country was excited, and parties were formed; the well-informed classes rallied round the bank, the common people round the President. But it must not be imagined that the people had formed a rational opinion upon a question which offers so many difficulties to the most experienced statesmen. By no means. The bank is a great establishment, which has an independent existence; and the people ... are startled to meet with this obstacle to their authority [and are] led to attack it, in order to see whether it can be shaken, like everything else.

SOURCE: Alexis de Tocqueville, *Democracy in America* (1835; New York: Random House, 1981), 1: 94–99.

ANALYZING THE EVIDENCE

➤ Based on your understanding of the Second Party System, was Tocqueville correct in arguing that American parties were the creation of "ambitious" men? How does Tocqueville characterize the Whigs and Democrats? Do you think he is accurate?

➤ Tocqueville claims that there was "no religious animosity" in American society and politics. Do you agree? What was the position of the parties with respect to the legal enforcement of morality?

likely to reflect public opinion, which opposed conspiracy prosecutions. In 1836, local juries acquitted shoemakers in Hudson, New York, carpet makers in Thompsonville, Connecticut, and plasterers in Philadelphia of similar conspiracy charges.

The Panic of 1837 and the Depression. At this juncture, the Panic of 1837 threw the American economy—and the union movement—into disarray. The panic began when the Bank of England, hoping to boost the faltering British economy, sharply curtailed the flow of money and credit to the United States. Over the previous decade and a half, British manufacturers and investors had extended credit to southern planters to expand cotton production and had purchased millions of dollars of the canal bonds issued by northern states. Suddenly deprived of British funds, American planters, merchants, and canal corporations had to withdraw specie from domestic banks to pay their commercial debts and interest on their foreign loans. Moreover, because the Bank of England refused credit to British cotton brokers, the price of raw cotton in the South collapsed, plummeting from 20 cents a pound to 10 cents or less.

The drain of gold and silver to Britain and falling cotton prices set off a financial panic. On May 8, the Dry Dock Bank of New York City closed its doors. Worried depositors quickly withdrew more than $2 million in gold and silver coins from other New York banks, forcing them to suspend all specie payments. Within two weeks, every bank in the United States stopped trading specie and curtailed credit. These measures turned a financial panic into an economic crisis because many businesses had to curtail production. "This sudden overthrow of the commercial credit and honor of the nation" had a "stunning effect," observed Henry Fox, the British minister in Washington. "The conquest of the land by a foreign power could hardly have produced a more general sense of humiliation and grief."

A second, longer-lasting downturn began in 1839. To revive the economy after the Panic of 1837, state governments increased their investments in canals and other transportation ventures. As they issued more and more bonds to finance these ventures, bond prices fell sharply in Europe, sparking a four-year-long international financial crisis. The crisis engulfed state governments in America, which were unable to meet the substantial interest payments on their bonds. Nine states defaulted on their obligations to foreign creditors, which, in turn, undermined the confidence of European investors and cut the flow of capital to the United States. Bumper crops drove down cotton prices even further, bringing more bankruptcies.

The American economy fell into a deep depression. By 1843, canal construction had dropped by 90 percent, and prices by nearly 50 percent. Unemployment reached almost 20 percent of the workforce in seaports and industrial centers. Minister Henry Ward Beecher described a land "filled with lamentation . . . its inhabitants wandering like bereaved citizens among the ruins of an earthquake, mourning for children, for houses crushed, and property buried forever."

The Fate of the Labor Movement. By creating a surplus of unemployed workers, the depression devastated the labor movement. In 1837, six thousand masons, carpenters, and other building-trades workers lost their jobs in New York City, depleting unions' rosters and destroying their bargaining power. By 1843, most local unions and all the national labor organizations had disappeared, along with their newspapers.

However, two events in this dismal period improved the long-term prospects of the labor movement. The first was a major legal victory. In *Commonwealth v. Hunt* (1842), the Massachusetts Supreme Judicial Court upheld the rights of workers to form unions. Chief Justice Lemuel Shaw, one of the great jurists of the nineteenth century, overturned common-law precedents, ruling that a union was not an inherently illegal organization and could strike to enforce a closed-shop agreement. Courts in many states accepted Shaw's opinion, but Whigs on the bench—and there were many of them—found other ways to deter unions. For example, some courts issued injunctions, orders that prohibited workers from picketing or striking. Labor's second success was political. Continuing Jackson's effort to recruit workers to the Democratic Party, President Van Buren signed an executive order in 1840 setting a ten-hour day for federal employees. This victory showed that the outcome of workers' struggles—like conflicts over tariffs, banks, and internal improvements—depended not only on economic factors but also on political decisions.

"Tippecanoe and Tyler Too!"

The depression had a major impact on politics because many Americans blamed the Democrats for their economic woes. In particular, they derided Jackson for destroying the Second Bank and for issuing the Specie Circular of 1836, which had

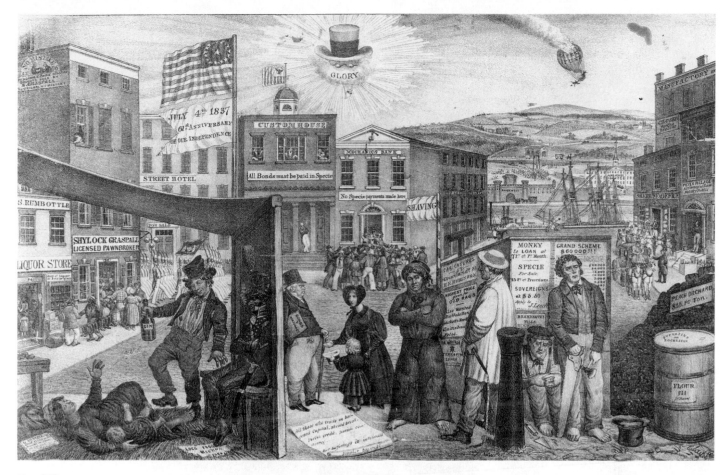

Hard Times

The Panic of 1837 struck Americans hard. As this anti-Democratic political cartoon suggests, unemployed workers turned to drink; women and children begged in the streets; and fearful depositors tried to withdraw funds before banks collapsed. As the plummeting hot-air balloon in the background symbolized, the rising "Glory" of America had come crashing to earth. Library of Congress.

required western settlers to use gold and silver coins to pay for land purchases from the federal government. Not realizing that specie shipments to Britain were the main cause of the financial panic, the Whigs—and many voters—blamed Jackson's policies.

The public turned its anger on Van Buren, who took office just as the panic struck. Ignoring the pleas of influential bankers, the new president refused to revoke the Specie Circular or take other actions that might have reversed the downturn. Holding to his philosophy of limited government, Van Buren advised Congress that "the less government interferes with private pursuits the better for the general prosperity." As the depression deepened in 1839, this laissez-faire policy commanded less and less political support. Worse, Van Buren's major piece of economic legislation, the Independent

Treasury Act of 1840, actually delayed recovery. The act pulled federal specie out of Jackson's pet banks (which had used it to back loans) and placed it in government vaults, where it did no economic good at all.

The Election of 1840. Determined to exploit Van Buren's weakness, the Whigs organized their first national convention in 1840 and nominated William Henry Harrison of Ohio for president and John Tyler of Virginia for vice president. A military hero of the Battle of Tippecanoe and the War of 1812, Harrison was well advanced in age (sixty-eight) and had little political experience. But the Whig leaders in Congress, Clay and Webster, simply wanted a president who would rubber-stamp their program for protective tariffs and a national bank. An unpretentious, amiable man, Harrison told

The Log Cabin Campaign, 1840

During the Second Party system, politics became more responsive to the popular will as ordinary people voted for candidates who shared their values and lifestyles. The barrels of hard cider framing this homemade campaign banner evoke the drink of the common man, while the central image falsely portrays William Henry Harrison as a poor and simple frontier farmer. New-York Historical Society, New York City.

voters that Whig policies were "the only means, under Heaven, by which a poor industrious man may become a rich man without bowing to colossal wealth."

Panic and depression stacked the political cards against Van Buren, although the contest turned as much on style as on substance. It became the great "log cabin campaign"—the first time two well-organized parties competed for the loyalties of a mass electorate through a new style of campaigning. Whig songfests, parades, and well-orchestrated mass meetings drew new voters into the political arena. Whig speakers assailed "Martin Van Ruin" as a manipulative politician with aristocratic tastes—a devotee of fancy wines and elegant clothes, as indeed he was. Less truthfully, they portrayed Harrison as a self-made man who would have been happy living in a log cabin and drinking hard cider, a drink of the common people. In fact, Harrison's father was a wealthy Virginia planter who had signed the Declaration of Independence.

The Whigs boosted their electoral hopes by welcoming women to campaign festivities. Previously,

President John Tyler (1790–1862)

Both as an "accidental" president and as a man, Tyler left his mark upon the world. His initiative to annex Texas made the election of 1844 a crucial contest and helped to trigger war with Mexico in 1846. His first wife, Letitia, gave birth to eight children before dying in the White House in 1842. Two years later, Tyler married 24-year-old Julia Gardiner, who bore him seven more children. White House Historical Association (White House Collection).

women had been excluded not only from voting and jury duty but also from marching in political parades. Jacksonian Democrats, in particular, thought of politics as a "manly" affair. They denounced women who ventured into the political arena, likening them to "public" women, the prostitutes who plied their trade in theaters and other public places. The Whigs recognized that women from Yankee families, a key Whig constituency, had already entered American public life through religious revivalism, the temperance movement, and other benevolent activities. In October 1840, Daniel Webster addressed a meeting of twelve hundred Whig women, praised their support for moral reform, and urged them to back Whig candidates. "This way of making politicians of their women is something new under the sun," noted one Democrat, worried that it would bring more Whig men to the polls. And it did: More than 80 percent of the eligible male voters cast ballots in 1840 (up from less than 60 percent in 1832 and 1836; see Figure 10.1, p. 307). Heeding the Whig slogan "Tippecanoe and Tyler Too," they voted Harrison into the White House — he won 53 percent of the popular vote and 80 percent of the electoral vote — and gave the Whigs a majority in Congress.

John Tyler versus the Whigs. Led by Clay and Webster, the Whigs in Congress were poised to reverse Jacksonian policies. Their anticipation was short-lived, though; barely a month after his inauguration, Harrison died of pneumonia, and the nation got "Tyler Too." But in what capacity, as acting president or as president? The Constitution was silent on the issue. Ignoring his Whig associates in Congress, who feared a strong president like Jackson, Tyler not only took the presidential oath of office but also declared his intention to govern as he pleased.

And that would not be like a Whig. Tyler had served in the House and the Senate as a Jeffersonian Democrat, firmly committed to slavery and states' rights. He had joined the Whigs only to protest Jackson's stance against nullification. On economic issues, Tyler shared Jackson's hostility to the Second Bank and the American System. And so the new president vetoed Whig bills that would have raised tariffs and created a new national bank. Disgusted, most of the members of Tyler's cabinet resigned in 1842, and the Whigs expelled him from their party. "His Accidency," as he was called by his critics, was now a president without a party.

The split between Tyler and the Whigs allowed the Democrats to regroup. The party vigorously recruited supporters among subsistence farmers in the North, smallholders in the South, and former members of the Working Men's parties in the cities. It also won success among Irish and German Catholic immigrants — whose numbers had increased during the 1830s — by supporting their demands for religious and cultural freedom. In time, this pattern of **ethnocultural politics**, as historians refer to the practice of voting along ethnic and religious lines, became a prominent feature of American life. Thanks to these urban and rural recruits, the Democrats remained the majority party in most parts of the nation. Their program of equal rights, states' rights, and cultural liberty was more attractive than the Whig platform of economic nationalism, moral reform, and individual mobility.

➤ How did the ideology of the Whigs differ from that of the Working Men's Party? From that of the Jacksonian Democrats?

➤ Why did the Democrats win the election of 1836 but lose the election of 1840?

SUMMARY

In this chapter, we have examined the causes and the consequences of the democratic political revolution that went hand in hand with the economic transformation of the early nineteenth century. We saw that the expansion of the franchise weakened the political system run by notables of high status. In its place emerged a system managed by professional politicians, men like Martin Van Buren, who were mostly of middle-class origin.

We also witnessed a revolution in government policy, as Andrew Jackson and his Democratic party dismantled the political foundation of the mercantilist system. On the national level, Jackson destroyed Henry Clay's American System; on the state level, Democrats wrote new constitutions that ended the Commonwealth system of government charters and subsidies to private businesses.

Finally, we watched the emergence of the Second Party System. In the aftermath of the fragmentation of the Republican Party during the election of 1824, two new parties—the Democrats and the Whigs—appeared on the national level and eventually absorbed the members of two other political movements, the Anti-Masonic and Working Men's parties. The new party system continued to deny women, Native Americans, and most African Americans a voice in public life, but it established universal suffrage for white men and a mode of representative government that was responsive to ordinary citizens. In their scope and significance, these political innovations matched the economic advances of the Industrial and Market revolutions.

Connections: Government

In this chapter, we witnessed the process that transformed the republican polity and culture described in Chapters 7 and 8 into a new, democratic political culture and the Second Party System of Whigs and Democrats. As we observed in the essay that opened Part Three (p. 269):

> The rapid growth of political parties sparked the creation of a democratic polity open to many social groups. . . . Party competition engaged the energies of the electorate and provided unity to a fragmented social order.

We continue the story of America's political development in Chapter 13, which covers the years between 1844 and 1860. There we will watch the disintegration of the Second Party System over the issue of slavery. The political problems posed by the westward expansion of plantation slavery were not new; as the discussion in Chapter 8 showed, the North and the South quarreled bitterly between 1819 and 1821 over the extension of slavery into Missouri. At that time, notable politicians raised in the old republican culture resolved the issue through compromise. Would democratic politicians be equally adept at fashioning a compromise over slavery in the territories seized from Mexico in 1848? Even more important, would their constituents accept that compromise? These questions are difficult to answer because, by 1848, the United States had become a more complex and contentious society, a change that at least in part stemmed from the appearance of new cultural movements and radical reform organizations, which are the subject of Chapter 11.

CHAPTER REVIEW QUESTIONS

➤ In what respects did the Jackson era fundamentally change the American economy, public policy, and society?

➤ Explain the rise of the Second Party System. How would you characterize American politics in the early 1840s?

➤ The chapter argues that a democratic revolution swept America in the decades after 1820. What evidence does the text present to support this argument? How persuasive is the evidence?

TIMELINE

1810s	State constitutions begin expanding voting rights for white men Martin Van Buren creates a disciplined party in New York
1825	John Quincy Adams is elected president by House and adopts Henry Clay's American System
1828	Artisans and laborers in Philadelphia organize Working Men's Party Tariff of Abominations raises duties on imported goods and manufactures Andrew Jackson is elected to first term as president *The South Carolina Exposition and Protest* challenges national legislation and majority rule
1830	Jackson vetoes extension of National Road Congress enacts Jackson's Indian Removal Act
1831	*Cherokee Nation v. Georgia* denies Indians' claim of national independence
1832	American troops kill 850 Sauk and Fox warriors in Bad Axe Massacre President Jackson vetoes renewal of the Second Bank's charter South Carolina adopts Ordinance of Nullification *Worcester v. Georgia* upholds political autonomy of Indian peoples
1833	Congress passes Force Bill and compromise tariff
1834	Whig Party formed by Henry Clay, John C. Calhoun, and Daniel Webster
1835	Roger Taney named Supreme Court chief justice
1836	Martin Van Buren elected president
1837	*Charles River Bridge Co. v. Warren Bridge Co.* weakens legal position of chartered monopolies Panic of 1837 ends long period of economic expansion and derails labor movement
1838	Thousands of Cherokees die on forced march (Trail of Tears) to Indian Territory
1839–1843	American loans spark international financial crisis and four-year economic depression
1840	Whigs win victory in log cabin campaign
1841	John Tyler succeeds William Henry Harrison as president
1842	*Commonwealth v. Hunt* legitimizes trade unions

FOR FURTHER EXPLORATION

George Dangerfield, *The Era of Good Feelings* (1952), remains the classic study of American politics between 1815 and 1828. For a new synthesis, see Sean Wilentz, *The Rise of American Democracy: Jefferson to Lincoln* (2005). Two concise surveys of the Jackson era are Harry L. Watson, *Liberty and Power: The Politics of Jacksonian America* (1990), which emphasizes republican ideology and the Market Revolution, and Daniel Feller, *The Jacksonian Promise: America, 1815–1840* (1995), which underlines the tremendous optimism of the time. In *The Idea of a Party System* (1969), Richard Hofstadter lucidly explains the triumphant entry of parties into America politics. The Internet Public Library (**www.ipl.org/div/potus/jqadams.html**) covers the election of 1824 and the administration of John Quincy Adams. For an audio account of the election of 1824, go to **www.albany.edu/talkinghistory/arch2000july-december.html**, and listen to the interview with Professor Paul Finkelman.

Robert V. Remini, *The Life of Andrew Jackson* (1988), highlights Jackson's triumphs without neglecting his shortcomings. For a brief treatment of Jackson's life and some of his important state papers, log on to **odur.let.rug.nl/~usa/P/aj7/aj7.htm**. The brutal impact of Jackson's Indian policy is brought to life in Robert J. Conley, *Mountain Windsong: A Novel of the Trail of Tears* (1992), and in two studies by historians: Sean Michael O'Brien, *In Bitterness and in Tears: Andrew Jackson's Destruction of the Creeks and Seminoles* (2003), and John Buchanan, *Jackson's Way: Andrew Jackson and the People of the Western Waters* (2001). For material on the Cherokees, see the Web site maintained by Ken Martin, a member of the Cherokee Nation of Oklahoma, **cherokeehistory.com/**. Also see **www.rosecity.net/tears/**, which has links to articles, primary sources, and other Web sites.

Major L. Wilson, *The Presidency of Martin Van Buren* (1984), provides a shrewd assessment of the man and his policies. The best treatment of leading Whigs is Merrill D. Peterson's *The Great Triumvirate: Webster, Clay, and Calhoun* (1987). For the ideology and politics of artisans and laborers, see Sean Wilentz, *Chants Democratic: New York City and the Rise of the American Working Class, 1788–1850* (1986).

Alexis de Tocqueville's classic, *Democracy in America* (1835), has wonderful insights into the character of American society and political institutions in the early nineteenth century. It is available online, along with an excellent exhibit and collection of essays at **xroads.virginia.edu/~hyper/detoc/home.html**. For ordinary and outrageous political cartoons, go to "American Political Prints, 1766–1876" at **loc.harpweek.com/**.

TEST YOUR KNOWLEDGE

To assess your command of the material in this chapter, see the Online Study Guide at **bedfordstmartins.com/henretta**.

For Web sites, images, and documents related to topics and places in this chapter, visit **bedfordstmartins.com/makehistory**.

11 Religion and Reform
1820–1860

"THE SPIRIT OF REFORM IS in every place," the children of legal reformer David Dudley Field wrote in their handwritten monthly *Gazette* in 1842:

> The labourer with a family says "reform the common schools"; the merchant and the planter say, "reform the tariff"; the lawyer "reform the laws," the politician "reform the government," the abolitionist "reform the slave laws," the moralist "reform intemperance," . . . the ladies wish their legal privileges extended, and in short, the whole country is wanting reform.

Like many Americans, the young Fields sensed that the political whirlwind of the 1830s had transformed the way people thought about themselves as individuals and as a society. Suddenly, thousands of men and women, inspired by the economic progress and democratic spirit of the age and the religious optimism of the Second Great Awakening believed they could improve not just their personal lives but society as a whole. Some dedicated themselves to the cause of reform. William Lloyd Garrison started out as an antislavery advocate, and then went on to embrace women's rights, pacifism, and the abolition of prisons. Such obsessive individuals, warned the Unitarian minister Henry W. Bellows, were pursuing "an object, which in its very nature is unattainable — the perpetual improvement of the outward condition."

◄ **"Pieties Quilt," by Maria Cadman Hubbard, 1848**

Maria Hubbard may have been a Quaker: "No Cross, No Crown" (a pious saying stitched on the far right) was the title of a pamphlet William Penn wrote in the 1670s attacking the Church of England. Whatever Hubbard's affiliation, she used her skills as a quilt maker to express deeply held religious beliefs. By stitching her name and age on the quilt, she created a cultural artifact that would perpetuate both her memory and the religious spirit of her era. Unlike most women (and men), she would not vanish from the record of the past. Museum of American Folk Art. Gift of Cyril Irwin Nelson in loving memory of his parents, Cyril Arthur and Elise Mary Nelson.

Reform was complex and contradictory. Some reformers vowed to improve society by preventing people from behaving in ways the reformers considered dangerous or simply wrong. Indeed, the first wave of American reformers, the benevolent religious improvers of the 1820s, advocated the extension of discipline to all phases of life. To solve the nation's ills, they championed regular church attendance, temperance, and the strict moral codes of the evangelical churches. Their righteousness prompted one critic to protest, "A peaceable man can hardly venture to eat or drink, . . . to correct his child or kiss his wife, without obtaining the permission . . . of some moral or other reform society."

A second wave of reformers, which emerged during the 1830s and 1840s, was more intent on liberating people from archaic customs and encouraging them to devise new lifestyles. These new reformers were mostly middle-class northerners and midwesterners. They propounded a bewildering assortment of radical ideals—extreme individualism, common ownership of property, the immediate emancipation of slaves, and sexual equality—and demanded prompt action to satisfy their visions. Although their numbers were small, these reformers launched an intellectual and cultural debate that won the attention, and often the horrified opposition, of the majority of Americans. As one fearful southerner saw it, the goal of these reformers was a chaotic world in which there would be "No-Marriage, No-Religion, No-Private Property, No-Law and No-Government."

The Founder of Transcendentalism

As this painting of Ralph Waldo Emerson by an unknown artist indicates, the young philosopher was an attractive man, his face brimming with confidence and optimism. With his radiant personality and incisive intellect, Emerson deeply influenced dozens of influential writers, artists, and scholars, and enjoyed great success as a lecturer to the emerging middle class. The Metropolitan Museum of Art, bequest of Chester Dale, 1962 [64.97.4].

Individualism

Those fears were not exaggerated. Rapid economic development and geographical expansion had weakened many traditional institutions and social rules, forcing individuals to fend for themselves. In 1835, Alexis de Tocqueville coined a new word, *individualism,* to describe the social world of native-born white Americans. Americans were "no longer attached to each other by any tie of caste, class, association, or family," and so lived more solitary lives than most Europeans did. Unlike Tocqueville, an aristocrat who feared the disintegration of society, the New England transcendentalist Ralph Waldo Emerson (1803–1882) celebrated the liberation of the individual from traditional constraints. Emerson's vision of individual freedom influenced thousands of ordinary Americans and a generation of important artists.

Ralph Waldo Emerson and Transcendentalism

Emerson was the leading voice of **transcendentalism**, an intellectual movement rooted in the religious soil of New England. Its first advocates were spiritual young men, often Unitarian ministers from well-to-do New England families, who questioned the constraints of their Puritan heritage (see Chapter 8). For inspiration, they turned to Europe and a new conception of self and society known as romanticism. Romantic thinkers, like German philosopher Immanuel Kant and English poet Samuel Taylor Coleridge, rejected the ordered, rational world of the eighteenth-century Enlightenment. They wanted to capture the passionate aspects of the human spirit and so gain deeper insight into the mysteries of existence. By tapping their intuitive powers, the young Unitarians believed, people could transcend the limits of ordinary existence and come to know the infinite and the eternal.

As a Unitarian minister, Emerson already stood outside the mainstream of American Protestantism. Unlike most Christians, Unitarians believed that God was a single being, not a trinity of Father, Son, and Holy Spirit. In 1832, Emerson took a more radical step by resigning his Boston pulpit and rejecting all organized religion. He moved to Concord, Massachusetts, and gradually articulated the philosophy of transcendentalism. In a series of influential essays, Emerson focused on what he called "the infinitude of the private man," the idea of the radically free individual.

The young philosopher argued that people were trapped by inherited customs and institutions. They wore the ideas of earlier times — the tenets of New England Calvinism, for example — as a kind of "faded masquerade"; and they needed to shed those values and practices. "What is a man born for but to be a Reformer, a Remaker of what man has made?" he asked. For Emerson, an individual could be remade only by discovering his or her own "original relation with Nature," an insight that would produce a mystical union with the "currents of Universal Being." The ideal setting for this kind of transcendent discovery: under an open sky, in solitary communion with nature.

Emerson's genius lay in his capacity to translate his abstract ideas into examples that made sense to middle-class Americans. His essays and lectures suggested that all nature was saturated with the presence of God, a pantheistic spiritual outlook that departed from traditional Christian doctrine. Emerson also warned his readers that the new market society was diverting the nation's spiritual energy, that the preoccupation with work, profits, and the consumption of factory-made goods would hurt Americans spiritually and physically (Figure 11.1). "Things are in the saddle," he wrote, "and ride mankind."

The transcendentalist message of self-realization reached hundreds of thousands of people, primarily through Emerson's writings and lectures. Public lectures had become a spectacularly successful way of spreading information and fostering discussion among the middle classes. Beginning in 1826, the Lyceum movement promoted "the general diffusion of knowledge," organizing lecture tours by hundreds of poets, preachers, scientists, and reformers. (A *lyceum* is a public hall; the word derives from the name of the place where the ancient Greek philosopher Aristotle taught.) The lyceum became an important cultural institution in the North and Midwest — but not in the South, where popular education was a lower priority and apologists for slavery discouraged the open discussion of controversial ideas. In 1839, nearly 150 local lyceums in Massachusetts invited lecturers to speak to more than 33,000 subscribers. The most popular speaker on the circuit was Emerson, who gave fifteen hundred lectures in more than three hundred towns in twenty states.

Emerson celebrated individuals who rejected traditional social restraints but retained both self-discipline and civic responsibility. In fact, his words

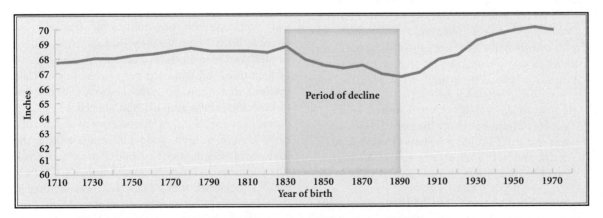

FIGURE 11.1 Environment and Health: Average Height of Native-born Men, by Year of Birth, 1710–1970

The transcendentalists sensed that the new urban and industrial society would damage people's health and welfare, and modern research suggests they were right. The average height of men born in America from the 1830s to the 1890s (as recorded in military records and other sources) was significantly lower than that of men born between 1710 and 1830. Researchers attribute the phenomenon to the men's childhood experiences: less-adequate nutrition and greater exposure to infectious diseases, especially in urban areas. SOURCE: Richard Steckel, "Health and Nutrition in the Preindustrial Era" (Working Paper 8452, National Bureau of Economic Research, Cambridge, Mass., 2001), fig. 3.

spoke directly to the personal experience of many mid-nineteenth-century middle-class Americans, who had left family farms and made their own way in the urban world. The great revivalist Charles Grandison Finney published an account of his religious conversion that underscored the influence of Emerson's ideas and values. Finney pictured his conversion as the mystical union of an individual, alone in the woods, with God. Like Emerson, Finney stressed the need to transcend the constraints and doctrines of the past. He taught that "God has made man a moral free agent," endowing individuals with the ability—and the responsibility—to determine their spiritual fate.

Emerson's Literary Influence

Emerson took as one of his tasks the remaking of American literature. In an address entitled "The American Scholar" (1837), the philosopher issued a literary declaration of independence from the "courtly muse" of Old Europe. He urged American writers to celebrate democracy and individual freedom and to find inspiration in ordinary human experiences: "the ballad in the street; the news of the boat; the glance of the eye; the form and gait of the body."

Henry David Thoreau and Margaret Fuller. One young New England intellectual, Henry David Thoreau (1817–1862), heeded Emerson's call by turning to the American environment for inspiration. In 1845, depressed by his beloved brother's death, Thoreau turned away from society and embraced the natural world. He built a cabin at the edge of Walden Pond near Concord, Massachusetts, and lived alone there for two years. In 1854, he published *Walden, or Life in the Woods*, an account of his search for meaning beyond the artificiality of "civilized" life:

> I went to the woods because I wished to live deliberately, to front only the essential facts of life, and see if I could not learn what it had to teach, and not, when I came to die, discover that I had not lived.

Although Thoreau's book had little impact during his lifetime, *Walden* has become an essential text of American literature and an inspiration to those who reject the dictates of society. Its most famous metaphor provides an enduring justification for independent thinking: "If a man does not keep pace with his companions, perhaps it is because he hears a different drummer." Beginning from this premise, Thoreau advocated social nonconformity and civil disobedience against unjust laws.

As Thoreau was seeking independence and self-realization for men, Margaret Fuller (1810–1850)

Margaret Fuller, 1848

At thirty-eight, Fuller moved to Italy, where she worked as a correspondent for a New York newspaper and reported on the Revolution of 1848. There, too, she fell in love with Thomas Hicks (1823–1890), a much younger American artist. Hicks rebuffed Fuller's advances but painted this flattering portrait, softening her features and giving her a pensive look. Fuller married a Roman nobleman, Giovanni Angelo, Marchese d'Ossoli, and gave birth to a son in September 1848. Two years later, the entire family died in shipwreck. Constance Fuller Threinen.

was exploring the possibilities of freedom for women. Born into a wealthy Boston family, Fuller mastered six languages, read broadly in classic works of literature, and educated her four siblings. While teaching in a school for girls, she became interested in Emerson's ideas and, in 1839, started a transcendental "conversation," or discussion group, for educated Boston women. Soon Fuller was editing the leading transcendentalist journal, *The Dial.* In 1844, she published *Woman in the Nineteenth Century,* which proclaimed that a "new era" was coming in the relationships between men and women.

Fuller's philosophy began with the transcendental belief that women, like men, had a mystical relationship with God that gave them identity and dignity. Every woman, therefore, deserved psychological and social independence—the ability "to grow, as an intellect to discern, as a soul to live freely and unimpeded." "We would have every arbitrary barrier thrown down," she wrote, and "every path laid open to Woman as freely as to Man." Embracing that vision, Fuller became the literary critic of the *New York Tribune* and traveled to Italy to report on the Revolution of 1848. Her adventurous life led to an early death; in 1850 she drowned in a shipwreck while returning to the United States. Fuller's life and writings inspired a rising generation of women writers and reformers.

Walt Whitman. Another writer who responded to Emerson's call was the poet Walt Whitman (1819–1892). When Whitman first met Emerson, he had been "simmering, simmering"; then Emerson "brought me to a boil." Whitman worked as a teacher, a journalist, an editor of the *Brooklyn Eagle*, and an influential publicist for the Democratic Party. But poetry was the "direction of his dreams." In *Leaves of Grass,* a wild, exuberant poem first published in 1855 and constantly revised and expanded, Whitman recorded in verse his efforts to pass a number of "invisible boundaries": between solitude and community, between prose and poetry, even between the living and the dead. At the center of *Leaves of Grass* is the individual — the figure of the poet, "I, Walt." He begins alone: "I celebrate myself, and sing myself." But because he has an Emersonian "original relation" with nature, Whitman claims perfect communion with others: "For every atom belonging to me as good belongs to you." Whitman celebrates democracy as well as himself by seeking a profoundly intimate, mystical relationship with a mass audience. For Emerson, Thoreau, and Fuller, the individual had a divine spark; for Whitman, the individual had expanded to become divine, and democracy assumed a sacred character.

The transcendentalists were optimistic but not naive. Whitman wrote about human suffering with passion, and Emerson laced his accounts of transcendence with twinges of anxiety. "I am glad," he once said, "to the brink of fear." Thoreau was gloomy about everyday life: "The mass of men lead lives of quiet desperation." Still, dark murmurings remain muted in their work, overshadowed by assertions that nothing was impossible for the individual who could break free from tradition, law, and other social restraints.

Darker Visions: Nathaniel Hawthorne and Herman Melville. Emerson's writings also influenced two great novelists, Nathaniel Hawthorne and Herman Melville, who had more pessimistic worldviews. Both sounded powerful warnings that unfettered egoism could destroy individuals and those around them. Hawthorne brilliantly explored the theme of excessive individualism in his novel *The Scarlet Letter* (1850). The two main characters, Hester Prynne and Arthur Dimmesdale, challenge their seventeenth-century New England community in the most blatant way — by committing adultery

and producing a child. Their choice to ignore social restraints is not liberation but degradation; it earns them a profound sense of guilt and the condemnation of the community.

Herman Melville explored the limits of individualism in even more extreme and tragic terms and emerged as a scathing critic of transcendentalism. He made his most powerful statement in *Moby Dick* (1851), the story of Captain Ahab's obsessive hunt for a mysterious white whale that ends in death for Ahab and all but one member of his crew. Here the quest for spiritual meaning in nature brings death, not transcendence, because Ahab, the liberated individual, lacks inner discipline and self-restraint.

Moby Dick was a commercial failure. The middle-class audience that was the primary target of American publishers refused to follow Melville into the dark, dangerous realm of individualism gone mad. Readers also lacked enthusiasm for Thoreau's advocacy of civil disobedience during the U.S. war with Mexico (see Chapter 13) and Whitman's boundless claims of a mystical union between the man of genius and the democratic masses. What middle-class readers emphatically preferred were the more modest examples of individualism offered by Emerson and Finney — personal improvement through spiritual awareness and self-discipline.

Brook Farm

To escape the constraints of America's emerging market society, transcendentalists and other radical reformers created ideal communities, or utopias. They hoped that these planned societies, which organized life in new ways, would allow their members to realize their spiritual and moral potential. The most important transcendentalist communal experiment was Brook Farm, founded just outside Boston in 1841. The intellectual life at Brook Farm was electric. Hawthorne lived there for a time and later used the setting for his novel *The Blithedale Romance* (1852). All the major transcendentalists, including Emerson, Thoreau, and Fuller, were residents or frequent visitors. A former member recalled that they "inspired the young with a passion for study, and the middle-aged with deference and admiration, while we all breathed the intellectual grace that pervaded the atmosphere."

Whatever its spiritual rewards, Brook Farm was an economic failure. The residents hoped to escape the ups and downs of the market economy by becoming self-sufficient in food and exchanging their surplus milk, vegetables, and hay for nonagricultural goods. However, most members were ministers, teachers, writers, and students who had few farming skills; only the cash contributions of affluent residents kept the enterprise afloat. And after a devastating fire in 1846, the organizers disbanded the community and sold the farm.

With Brook Farm a failure, the Emersonians abandoned their quest for a new system of social organization. They accepted the brute reality of the emergent industrial order and tried to reform it, especially through the education of workers. The passion of the transcendentalists for individual freedom and social progress lived on, though, in the movement to abolish slavery, which many of them actively supported.

> ➤ What were the main beliefs of transcendentalism? How was transcendentalism an expression of the social changes sweeping nineteenth-century society?

> ➤ How does transcendentalism embody American individualism? What was the relationship between transcendentalism and social reform?

Rural Communalism and Urban Popular Culture

Even as Brook Farm collapsed, thousands of Americans were joining communal settlements in rural areas of the Northeast and Midwest (Map 11.1).

Many communalists were farmers and artisans seeking refuge and security during the seven-year economic depression that began with the Panic of 1837. However, these rural utopias were also symbols of social protest and experimentation. By prescribing the common ownership of property and unconventional forms of marriage and family life, communalist leaders and their followers challenged the legitimacy of capitalist values and traditional gender roles.

Simultaneously, tens of thousands of rural Americans and immigrants poured into the larger cities of the United States. There they created a popular culture that repudiated customary sexual norms, reinforced traditional racist feelings, and encouraged new styles of dress and behavior.

Mother Ann Lee and the Shakers

The Shakers were the first successful American communal movement. In 1770, Ann Lee Stanley (Mother Ann), a young cook in Manchester, England, had a vision that she was an incarnation of Christ and that Adam and Eve had been banished from the Garden of Eden because of their sexual lust. Four years later, she led a band of eight followers to America, where they established a church near Albany, New York. Because of the ecstatic dances that were part of their worship, the sect became known as the Shakers (see Voices from Abroad, "The Mystical World of the Shakers," p. 337).

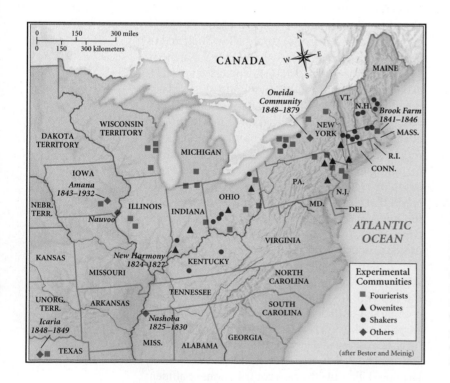

MAP 11.1 Major Communal Experiments Before 1860

Some experimental communities settled along the frontier, but the vast majority chose relatively secluded areas in well-settled regions of the North and Midwest. Because of their opposition to slavery, communalists usually avoided the South. Most secular experiments failed within a few decades, as the founders lost their reformist enthusiasm or died off; religious communities — like those of the Shakers and the Mormons (see Map 11.2 on p. 342) — were longer-lived.

The Mystical World of the Shakers

Foreigners were both attracted to, and distressed by, the strange religious practices they observed in the United States. In either case, they made certain to include reports of revivals and communal settlements in their letters and journals. In a book recounting his travels in America in the 1830s, an anonymous British visitor describes a Shaker dance and the sect's intimate contact with spiritual worlds inaccessible to those without faith.

At half past seven P.M. on the dancing days, all the members retired to their separate rooms, where they sat in solemn silence, just gazing at the stove, until the silver tones of the small tea-bell gave the signal for them to assemble in the large hall. Thither they proceeded in perfect order and solemn silence. Each had on dancing shoes; and on entering the door of the hall they walked on tip-toe, and took up their positions as follows: the brothers formed a rank on the right, and the sisters on the left, facing each other, about five feet apart. After all were in their proper places the chief Elder stepped into the center of the space, and gave an exhortation for about five minutes, concluding with an invitation to them all to "go forth, old men, young men and maidens, and worship God with all [your] might in the dance." . . .

First they formed a procession and marched around the room in double-quick time, while four brothers and sisters stood in the center singing for them. . . . They commenced dancing, and continued it until they were pretty well tired.

During the dance the sisters kept on one side, and the brothers on the other, and not a word was spoken by any one of them. . . . [Then] each one took his or her place in an oblong circle formed around the room, and all waited to see if anyone had received a "gift," that is, an inspiration to do something odd. Then two of the sisters would commence whirling round like a top, with their eyes shut; and continued this motion for about fifteen minutes. . . .

On some occasions when a sister had stopped whirling, she would say, "I have a communication to make"; . . . The first message I heard was as follows. "Mother Ann has sent two angels to inform us that a tribe of Indians has been round here two days, and want the brothers and sisters to take them in. They are outside the building there, looking in at the windows." I shall never forget how I looked round at the windows, expecting to see the yellow faces, when this announcement was made; but I believe some of the old folks who eyed me, bit their lips and smiled. It caused no alarm to the rest, but the first Elder exhorted the brothers "to take in the poor spirits and assist them to get salvation." He afterward repeated more of what the angels had said, viz., "that Indians were a savage tribe who had all died before Columbus discovered America, and had been wandering about ever since. Mother Ann wanted them to be received into the meeting tomorrow night."

The next dancing night we again assembled in the same manner as before. . . . The elder then urged upon the members the duty of "taking them in." Whereupon eight or nine sisters became possessed of the spirits of Indian squaws, and about six of the brethren became Indians. Then ensued a regular pow-wow, with whooping and yelling and strange antics, such as would require a Dickens to describe. . . . These performances continued till about ten o'clock: then the chief Elder requested the Indians to go away, telling them they would find someone waiting to conduct them to the Shakers in the heavenly world. . . .

At one of the meetings . . . two or three sisters commenced whirling . . . and revealed to us that Mother Ann was present at the meeting, and that she had brought a dozen baskets of spiritual fruit for her children; upon which the Elder invited all to go forth to the baskets in the center of the floor, and help themselves. Accordingly they all stepped forth and went through the various motions of taking fruit and eating it. You will wonder if I helped myself to the fruit, like the rest. No; I had not faith enough to see the baskets or the fruit.

SOURCE: Noel Rae, ed., *Witnessing America* (New York: Penguin Press, 1966), 372–373.

ANALYZING THE EVIDENCE

➤ Why do you think the author — a visitor from England — was fascinated with the Shakers and their ceremonies?

➤ How might the episode with the Indians be explained? What was the policy of state and federal governments toward the Indians in the 1830s? Do you think that policy had any bearing on the Shakers' worship? Explain your answer.

➤ How would you characterize the roles ascribed to men and women? Were the Shakers' ideas about gender typical of communal movements? Were their ideas more radical or more conservative than those of the society at large?

After Mother Ann's death in 1784, the Shakers honored her as the Second Coming of Christ, withdrew from the profane world, and formed disciplined religious communities. Members embraced the common ownership of property, accepted the strict oversight of church leaders, and pledged to abstain from alcohol, tobacco, politics, and war. Shakers also repudiated marriage and sexual pleasure. Their commitment to celibacy followed Mother Ann's testimony against "the lustful gratifications of the flesh as the source and foundation of human corruption."

The Shakers' theology was as radical as their social thought. They held that God was "a dual person, male and female," and that Mother Ann represented God's female component. These doctrines underpinned their efforts to eliminate arbitrary distinctions of authority between the sexes. They placed community governance in the hands of both women and men — the Eldresses and the Elders — but maintained a traditional division of labor between the sexes.

Beginning in 1787, Shakers founded twenty communities, mostly in New England, New York, and Ohio. Their agriculture and crafts, especially furniture making, acquired a reputation for quality that made most Shaker communities self-sustaining and even comfortable. Because the Shakers did not engage in sexual intercourse and had no children of their own, they relied on conversions and the adoption of thousands of young orphans to increase their numbers. During the 1830s, three thousand adult converts joined the Shakers, attracted by the sect's economic success and ideology of sexual equality. Women converts outnumbered men more than two to one, and included blacks as well as whites. To Rebecca Cox Jackson, an African American seamstress from Philadelphia, the Shakers seemed to be "loving to live forever." As the supply of orphans dried up during the 1840s and 1850s (with the increase in publicly and privately funded orphanages), Shaker communities stopped growing and eventually began to decline. By 1900, the Shakers had virtually disappeared, leaving as their material legacy a distinctive plain-but-elegant style of wood furniture.

Arthur Brisbane and Fourierism

As the number of Shakers leveled off during the 1840s, the American Fourierist movement was rapidly expanding. Charles Fourier (1777–1837) was a French reformer who devised an eight-stage theory of social evolution that predicted the imminent decline of individualism and capitalism. According to Arthur Brisbane, Fourier's leading disciple in America, Fourierism would free workers from the "menial and slavish system of Hired Labor or Labor for Wages," just as republicanism ("our great political movement of 1776") had freed Americans from the slavish monarchical system of government. The new order replaced capitalism with **socialism**. Instead of working for themselves or for employers, men and women would work for the community, in cooperative groups called phalanxes. The members of a phalanx would be its shareholders; they would own all its property in common, including stores and a bank, a school, and a library.

Fourier and Brisbane saw the phalanx as a humane system that would liberate women as well as men. "In society as it is now constituted," Brisbane wrote, individual freedom was possible only for men, while "woman is subjected to unremitting and slavish domestic duties." In the "new Social Order . . . based upon Associated households," men would share women's domestic labor and thereby increase sexual equality.

Brisbane skillfully promoted Fourier's ideas in his influential book *The Social Destiny of Man* (1840), a regular column in Horace Greeley's *New York Tribune,* and hundreds of lectures, many of them in towns along the Erie Canal. Fourierist ideas found a receptive audience among educated farmers and craftsmen, who yearned for economic stability and communal solidarity in the wake of the Panic of 1837. During the 1840s, Brisbane and his followers started nearly one hundred cooperative communities, mostly in western New York and in the Midwest (see Map 11.1). However, most of the communities collapsed within a decade or two because of disputes over work responsibilities and social policies. If the rise of Fourierism testified to the social impact of the depression, then its decline showed the difficulty of establishing a utopian community in the absence of a charismatic leader or a compelling religious vision.

John Humphrey Noyes and the Oneida Community

John Humphrey Noyes (1811–1886) was both charismatic and deeply religious. He ascribed the failure of the Fourierists to their secular outlook and took as his model the pious Shakers, the true "pioneers of modern Socialism." The Shakers' marriageless society also appealed to Noyes, and inspired him to create a community that defined sexuality and gender roles in radically new ways.

Shakers at Prayer

Most Americans viewed the Shakers with a mixture of fascination and distaste. They feared the sect's commitment to celibacy and communal property and considered the Shakers' dancing more an invitation to debauchery than a form of prayer. Those apprehensions surfaced in this engraving, which expresses both the powerful intensity and the menacing character of the Shaker ritual. © Bettmann/Corbis.

Noyes was a well-to-do graduate of Dartmouth College who became a minister after hearing Charles Grandison Finney preach. Dismissed as the pastor of a Congregational church for holding unorthodox beliefs, Noyes turned to perfectionism. Perfectionism was an evangelical Protestant movement of the 1830s that attracted thousands of religious New Englanders who had moved to New York and Ohio. Perfectionists believed that Christ had returned to earth (the Second Coming) and that people could therefore aspire to sinless perfection in their earthly lives. Unlike most perfectionists, who lived conventional personal lives, Noyes believed that the major barrier to achieving this ideal state was marriage, which did not exist in heaven and should not exist on earth. "Exclusiveness, jealousy, quarreling have no place at the marriage supper of the Lamb," Noyes wrote. Like the Shakers, Noyes wanted to liberate individuals from sin by reforming relationships between men and women. But instead of the Shakers' celibacy, Noyes and his followers embraced "complex marriage"—all the members of the community were married to one another.

Noyes's marriage system reflected the growing debate over the legal and cultural constraints on women's lives. He rejected monogamy in order to free women from being regarded as the property of their husbands, as they were by custom and by

"Bloomerism — An American Custom"

The hippies of the 1960s weren't the first to draw attention to themselves with their dress (sloppy) and smoking (marijuana). Independent women of the 1850s took to wearing bloomers and puffing on cigars, behaviors that elicited disapproving stares from matrons and verbal and physical assaults from street urchins. Both movements questioned existing cultural norms and sought to expand the boundaries of personal freedom. This cartoon appeared in 1851 in *Harper's New Monthly Magazine*, a major periodical of the time. *Harper's New Monthly Magazine* (August 1851)/Picture Research Consultants & Archives.

common law. To give women the time and energy to become full participants in the community, Noyes urged them to avoid multiple pregnancies. He asked men to assist in this effort by avoiding orgasm during intercourse. To raise the children of his followers, Noyes set up communal nurseries run by both men and women. To symbolize sexual equality, Noyes's women followers cut their hair short and wore pantaloons under calf-length skirts.

In 1839, Noyes established a Perfectionist community near his hometown, Putney, Vermont, and introduced the practice of complex marriage in the mid-1840s. When the community's unorthodox sexual practices aroused opposition, Noyes moved his followers to an isolated area near Oneida, New York. By the mid-1850s, the Oneida settlement had two hundred residents; it became financially self-sustaining when the inventor of a highly successful steel animal trap joined the community. With the profits acquired by making traps, the Oneidians

diversified into the production of silverware. When Noyes fled to Canada in 1879 to avoid prosecution for adultery, the community abandoned complex marriage but retained its cooperative spirit. Its members founded Oneida Community, Ltd., a jointly owned, silverware-manufacturing company that remained an independent and prosperous enterprise until the end of the twentieth century.

The historical significance of the Oneidians, Shakers, and Fourierists does not lie in their numbers, which were small, or in their fine crafts. These groups were important because their members, in a dramatically more radical fashion than Emerson and the transcendentalists, repudiated both traditional sexual norms and the principles and class divisions of the emergent capitalist society. Their utopian communities stood as countercultural blueprints of a more egalitarian social and economic order.

A Mormon Man and His Wives

The practice of polygamy split the Mormon community and, because it deviated from traditional religious principles, enraged other Christian denominations. This Mormon household, pictured in the late 1840s, was unusually prosperous, partly because of the labor of the husband's multiple wives. Although the cabin provides cramped quarters for such a large family, it boasts a brick chimney and — a luxury for any pioneer home — a glass window.
Library of Congress.

Joseph Smith and the Mormon Experience

The Shakers and the Oneidians were radical utopians because they challenged marriage and family life, two deeply rooted institutions. However, their communities remained small and consequently aroused relatively little hostility. The Mormons, members of the Church of Jesus Christ of Latter-day Saints, were utopians with a much more conservative social agenda — perpetuating the traditional patriarchal family. But because of their cohesive organization and substantial numbers, the Mormons provoked more animosity than the radical utopians did.

Joseph Smith. Like many social movements of the era, Mormonism emerged from the religious ferment among families of Puritan descent who lived along the Erie Canal. The founder of the Mormon Church was Joseph Smith Jr. (1805–1844). Smith was born in Vermont to a poor farming and shop-keeping family, which then migrated to Palmyra in central New York. In a series of religious experiences that began in 1820, Smith came to believe that God had singled him out to receive a special revelation of divine truth. In 1830, he published *The Book of Mormon,* which he claimed to have translated from ancient hieroglyphics on gold plates shown to him by an angel named Moroni. *The Book of Mormon* told the story of ancient civilizations from the Middle East that had migrated to the Western Hemisphere and of the visit of Jesus Christ, soon after the Resurrection, to one of them. Smith's account provided an explanation of the presence of native peoples in the Americas and integrated them into the Judeo-Christian tradition.

Smith proceeded to organize the Church of Jesus Christ of Latter-day Saints. Seeing himself as a prophet in a sinful, excessively individualistic society, Smith revived traditional social doctrines, among them patriarchal authority within the family. Like many Protestant ministers, he encouraged practices that were central to individual success in the age of capitalist markets and factories — frugality, hard work, and enterprise. But Smith also placed great emphasis on communal discipline that would safeguard the Mormon "New Jerusalem" from individualism and rival religious doctrines. His goal was a church-directed society that would inspire moral perfection.

Smith struggled for years to establish a secure home for his new religion. Constantly harassed by hostile anti-Mormons, Smith and his growing congregation trekked west and eventually settled in Nauvoo, Illinois, a town they founded on the Mississippi River (Map 11.2). By the early 1840s, Nauvoo had become the largest utopian community in the United States, with 30,000 inhabitants. The rigid discipline and secret rituals of the Mormons — along with their prosperity, hostility toward other sects, and bloc voting in Illinois elections — fueled resentment among their neighbors. This resentment turned to overt hostility when Smith refused to abide by any Illinois law of which he disapproved, asked Congress to turn Nauvoo into a separate federal territory, and declared himself a candidate for president of the United States.

Moreover, Smith claimed to have received a new revelation that justified polygamy, the practice of a man's having more than one wife at one time. When leading Mormon men took several wives, they sparked a contentious debate within the Mormon community and enraged Christians in neighboring

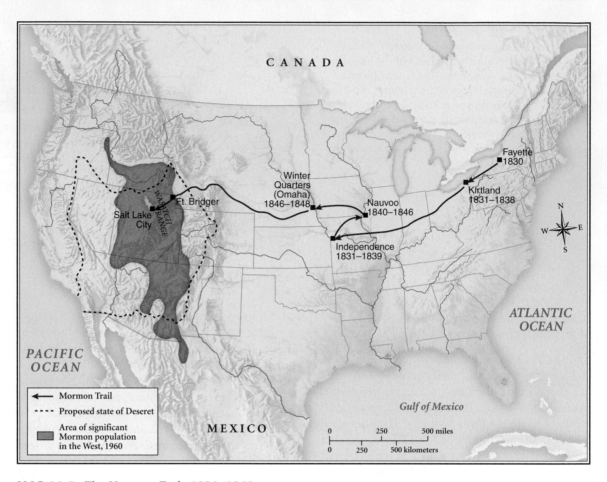

MAP 11.2 The Mormon Trek, 1830–1848

Because of their unorthodox religious views and communal solidarity, Mormons faced hostility first in New York and then in Missouri and Illinois. After founder Joseph Smith Jr. was murdered, Brigham Young led the polygamist faction of Mormons into lands thinly populated by Native American peoples. From Omaha, the migrants followed the path of the Oregon Trail to Fort Bridger and then struck off to the southwest. In 1847, they settled along the Wasatch Mountains in the basin of the Great Salt Lake, in Indian lands that were part of Mexico and are now in Utah.

towns and villages. In 1844, Illinois officials arrested Smith and charged him with treason for allegedly conspiring with foreign powers to create a Mormon colony in Mexican territory. An anti-Mormon mob stormed the jail in Carthage, Illinois, where Smith and his brother were being held, and murdered them.

Brigham Young and Utah. Led by Brigham Young, Smith's leading disciple and an energetic missionary, a large contingent of Mormons fled the United States. Beginning in 1847, approximately 10,000 people crossed the Great Plains into Mexican territory, where they settled in the Great Salt Lake Valley in present-day Utah. Using cooperative labor and an elaborate irrigation system based on com-

munal water rights, the Mormon pioneers transformed the region. They quickly spread planned agricultural communities along the base of the Wasatch mountain range. Many Mormons who rejected polygamy remained in the United States. Under the leadership of Smith's son, Joseph Smith III, they formed the Reorganized Church of Jesus Christ of Latter-day Saints and settled throughout the Midwest.

When the United States acquired title to Mexico's northern territories in 1848 (see Chapter 13), the Salt Lake Mormons petitioned Congress to create a vast new state, Deseret, which would stretch from present-day Utah to the Pacific coast. Instead, Congress set up the much smaller Utah Territory in 1850 and named Brigham Young its governor. In

1858, President James Buchanan responded to pressure from Protestants to eliminate polygamy by removing Young from the governorship and sending a small army to Salt Lake City. However, the "Mormon War" proved bloodless. Fearing that the forced abolition of polygamy would serve as a precedent for ending slavery, the pro-South Buchanan withdrew the troops. (To win support for Utah's bid to join the Union in 1896, its citizens ratified a constitution that "forever" banned the practice of polygamy, but the state government has never strictly enforced that ban.)

Mormons had succeeded even as other social experiments and utopian communities had failed. By endorsing the private ownership of property and encouraging individual enterprise, they became prosperous contributors to the new market society. However, Mormon leaders resolutely used strict religious controls to create patriarchal families and disciplined communities, reaffirming traditional eighteenth-century values. This blend of economic innovation, social conservatism, hierarchical leadership, in combination with a strong missionary impulse, created a wealthy and expansive church, which now claims a worldwide membership of about 12 million people.

Urban Popular Culture

As utopian reformers organized new communities on the land, rural migrants and foreign immigrants created a new culture in the cities. In 1800, American cities were overgrown towns: New York had only 60,000 residents, and Philadelphia 41,000. Then urban growth accelerated. By 1840, New York's population had ballooned to 312,000; Philadelphia and its suburbs had 150,000 residents; and three other cities—New Orleans, Boston, and Baltimore—each had about 100,000. By 1860, New York had become a metropolis with more than 1 million residents: 813,000 in Manhattan and another 266,000 in the adjacent community of Brooklyn.

These new cities, particularly New York, generated a new urban culture. At its center were thousands of young men and women from rural areas, who flocked to the city in search of fortune and adventure. Many found only hard work and a hard life. Young men labored for meager wages on the construction crews that erected thousands of new buildings each year. Or they worked as low-paid operatives or clerks in hundreds of mercantile and manufacturing firms. The young women were even worse off. Thousands toiled as live-in domestic servants, ordered about by the mistress of the household and often sexually abused by their well-to-do masters (see Reading American Pictures, "Looking for Clues in Art About Women's Lives," p. 344). Thousands more scraped out a bare living as needlewomen in New York's booming clothes manufacturing industry. Unable to abide the humiliations of domestic service or the subsistence wages of the needlewoman, thousands of young girls turned to prostitution. In the 1850s, Dr. William Sanger's careful survey in New York City found six thousand women engaged in commercial sex. Three-fifths of them were native-born Americans, and most were young—between fifteen and twenty years old. Half were or had been domestic servants, half had children, and half were infected with syphilis.

Sex and Dress. Commercialized sex—and sex in general—formed one facet of the new urban culture. "Sporting men" engaged freely in sexual conquests; respectable married men kept mistresses in handy apartments; and working men frequented bawdy houses in the city. In New York City there were some two hundred brothels in the 1820s and five hundred in the 1850s. Prostitutes openly advertised their wares on Broadway, the city's fashionable thoroughfare, and welcomed clients on the infamous "Third Tier" of the theaters. This illicit sexuality was widely considered by men as their right. "Man is endowed by nature with passions that must be gratified," declared the *Sporting Whip*, a working-class magazine. Reverend William Berrian, pastor of the ultrarespectable Trinity Episcopal Church, did not disagree; he remarked from the pulpit that he had resorted to "a house of ill-fame" a mere ten times.

Prostitution formed only the tip of the urban sexual mountain. Freed from family oversight, the young men and women in the city pursued romantic adventure and sexual pleasure. Many moved from partner to partner until they chanced on an ideal mate. To enhance their attractiveness, they dressed in the latest fashions: elaborate bonnets and silk dresses for young women; flowing capes, leather boots, and silver-plated walking sticks for young men. Rivaling the elegant style on Broadway was the colorful style visible on the Bowery, the broad avenue that ran up the east side of lower Manhattan. By day, the "Bowery Boy" worked as an apprentice or journeyman; by night, he prowled the streets a "consummate dandy," his hair cropped at the back of his head "as close as scissors could cut," with long front locks "matted by a lavish application of *bear's grease*, the ends tucked under so as to form a roll and brushed until they shone like glass bottles." The "B'hoy," as he was called, cut a dashing figure, as he

Looking for Clues in Art About Women's Lives

A Nineteenth-Century Job Interview. © Collection of the New-York Historical Society.

This rather somber painting, *The Intelligence Office,* by William Henry Burr (1849), depicts a scene at an urban employment agency. The woman sitting to the right, dressed formally in green satin, is deciding whether to hire the two standing women as domestic servants. What does this picture tell us about social relations in nineteenth-century America? Burr's work refers to various hallmarks of the new age: contractual labor relations, then-current forms of communication, and the intensification of class identity. Look closely. Do you see them?

ANALYZING THE EVIDENCE

➤ Study the applicants' clothing. How does their garb differ from that of the employer? Look carefully at their faces and posture. Does the expression on the face of the seated woman in the dark outfit suggest her anxiety about finding a position? And how do you interpret the attitude of the standing girl, facing outward, looking down?

➤ Suppose Burr had been painting in 1749, a century earlier. How would a wealthy village squire or a prosperous merchant go about hiring domestic help? What had changed over the decades? Why did an employer in 1849 need the services of a professional agent? What clues in the painting point to those changes?

➤ How did the women applicants come to use the agent's services? What clues has the artist placed in the picture that suggest an answer?

Night Life in Philadelphia

This watercolor by Russian painter Pavel Svinin (1787–1839) captures the diversity and allure of urban America. A respectable gentleman relishes the delicacies sold by a black oysterman. Meanwhile, a young woman — probably a prostitute — engages the attention of two well-dressed young "swells" outside the Chestnut Street Theatre. The Metropolitan Museum of Art, Rogers Fund, 1942 (42.95.18). Photograph © 1989 The Metropolitan Museum of Art.

walked along, often with a "Bowery Gal" in a striking dress and shawl: "a light pink contrasting with a deep blue" or "a bright yellow with a brighter red."

Racism and Nativism. Popular entertainment was a third facet of the new urban culture in New York. Workingmen could partake of traditional rural blood sports — rat and terrier fights — at Sportsmen Hall, or they could crowd into the pit of the Bowery Theatre to see the "Mad Tragedian," Junius Brutus Booth, deliver a stirring performance of Shakespeare's *Richard III.* Middle-class couples could venture out to the huge Broadway Tabernacle to listen to an abolitionist lecture and see the renowned Hutchinson Family Singers of New Hampshire lead the audience in a spirited, roof-raising rendition of their antislavery anthem, "Get Off the Track." Or they could visit the museum of oddities (and hoaxes) created by P. T. Barnum, the great cultural entrepreneur and founder of the Barnum & Bailey Circus.

But the most popular and most original theatrical entertainments were the minstrel shows. Performed by white actors in blackface, minstrel shows were a complex blend of racist caricature and social criticism. Minstrelsy began around 1830, when a few individual actors put on blackface and performed comic song-and-dance routines. The most famous was John Dartmouth Rice, whose "Jim Crow" blended a weird shuffle-dance-and-jump with unintelligible lyrics delivered in "Negro dialect." By the 1840s, there were hundreds of minstrel troupes, whose members sang rambling improvisational songs. The actor-singers poked racist fun at the African Americans they depicted, portraying them as lazy, sensual, and irresponsible, while using them as a vehicle for social criticism. The minstrels also ridiculed the drinking habits of Irish immigrants, parodied the speech of recent German arrivals, denounced women's demands for political rights, and mocked the arrogance of upper-class men.

Rampant Racism

Minstrel shows and music were immensely popular among whites and immensely damaging to the status and self-respect of blacks. Still, minstrelsy had so much appeal that a group of black entertainers, Gavitt's Original Ethiopian Serenaders, joined the circuit. "It is something gained when the colored man in any form can appear before a white audience," black abolitionist Frederick Douglass remarked after watching the group perform, "but they must represent the colored man rather as he is, than as Ethiopian Minstrels usually represent him to be. They will *then* command the respect of both races; whereas *now* they only shock the taste of the one, and provoke the disgust of the other." Courtesy The Library Company of Philadelphia.

Still, by performing in blackface, the minstrels declared the importance of being white. The shows' racism allowed Irish and German immigrants to identify with the dominant native-born white culture and eased their entry into New York society. By the 1830s, most new residents in New York City were foreign-born; by 1855, 200,000 Irish men and women lived in the city, along with 110,000 Germans (Figure 11.2). German-language shop signs dominated entire sections of the city, and German foodways (sausages, hamburgers, sauerkraut, and beer) became part of the city's culture. The mass of impoverished Irish migrants, fleeing the potato famine, found allies in the American Catholic Church, which soon became an Irish-dominated institution, and the Democratic Party, which gave them a foothold in the political process.

Many native-born New Yorkers denounced this ethnic diversity, creating a nativist movement that was the final aspect of the new urban culture. Beginning in the mid-1830s, nativists opposed further immigration and mounted a cultural and political assault on foreign-born residents (see Chapter 9). Gangs of B'hoys assaulted Irish youth in the streets, employers hired Irish workers for only the most menial jobs, and temperance reformers denounced the German fondness for beer.

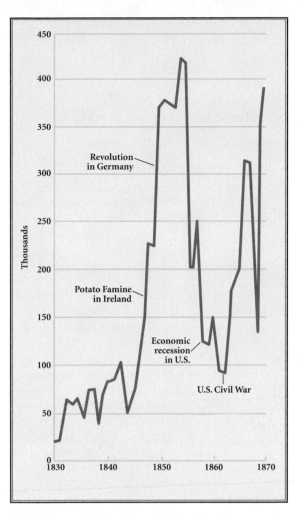

FIGURE 11.2 The Surge in Immigration, 1842–1855

The failure of the potato crop prompted the wholesale migration of peasants from the overcrowded farms of western Ireland. Population pressure likewise spurred the migration of tens of thousands of German peasants, while the failure of the liberal republican political revolution of 1848 prompted hundreds of prominent German politicians and intellectuals to settle in the United States.

In 1844, the American Republican Party, with the endorsement of the Whigs, swept to victory in the city elections by focusing on the emotional issues of temperance and anti-Catholic nativism (see Comparing American Voices, "Saving the Nation from Drink," pp. 348–349).

In the city, as in the countryside, a struggle to define a new society and culture was under way. The sexual freedom advocated by Noyes at Oneida had its counterpart in the commercialized sex and male promiscuity in New York City. Similarly, the disciplined rejection of tobacco and alcohol by the Shakers and the Mormons found a parallel in the Washington

Temperance Society and other urban reform organizations. American society was in ferment, and the outcome was far from clear.

➤ How do you explain the proliferation of rural utopian communities in the nineteenth century? What made some more successful than others? Why were gender relationships so prominent in their beliefs?

➤ In what respects were the new cultures of the mid-nineteenth century — those of utopian communalists and of urban residents — different from the mainstream culture described in Chapters 8 and 9? How were they alike?

Abolitionism

Like other reform movements, abolitionism drew on the religious energy and ideas generated by the Second Great Awakening. Early-nineteenth-century reformers had argued that human bondage was contrary to republicanism and liberty. Abolitionists condemned slavery as a sin, and took it as their moral duty to end this violation of God's law. Their demands for the immediate end to slavery led to fierce political debates, urban riots, and sectional conflicts.

Black Social Thought: Uplift, Race Equality, Rebellion

Beginning in the 1790s, leading African Americans in the North advocated a strategy of social uplift. They encouraged free blacks to "elevate" themselves through education, temperance, moral discipline, and hard work. By securing "respectability," they argued, blacks could assume a position of equality with whites. To promote that goal, black leaders — men like James Forten, a Philadelphia sailmaker; Prince Hall, a Boston barber; and ministers Hosea Easton and Richard Allen (see Chapter 8) — founded an array of churches, schools, and self-help associations. Capping off this effort in 1827, John Russwurm and Samuel D. Cornish of New York published the first African American newspaper, *Freedom's Journal*.

The black quest for respectability elicited a violent response from whites in Boston, Pittsburgh, and many other northern cities, who refused to accept African Americans as their social equals. "I am Mr. ____'s *help*," a white maid informed a British

Saving the Nation from Drink

The temperance crusade was the first and greatest antebellum reform movement. It mobilized more than a million supporters from all sections of the country and significantly lowered the consumption of alcoholic beverages. Like other reform efforts, the crusade divided over questions of strategy and tactics. The following passages, taken from the writings of leading temperance advocates, show that some reformers favored legal regulation while others preferred voluntary restraint.

LYMAN BEECHER
"Intemperance Is the Sin of Our Land"

A leading Protestant minister and spokesman for the Benevolent Empire, Lyman Beecher conceived of drunkenness as a sin. His Six Sermons on . . . Intemperance (1829) had one message for temperate members of the middle class and a very different one for working-class drunkards.

Intemperance is the sin of our land, and, with our boundless prosperity, is coming in upon us like a flood; and if anything shall defeat the hopes of the world, which hang upon our experiment of civil liberty, it is that river of fire. . . .

In every city and town the poor-tax, created chiefly by intemperance, is augmenting. . . . The frequency of going upon the town [relying on public welfare] has taken away the reluctance of pride, and destroyed the motives to providence which the fear of poverty and suffering once supplied. The prospect of a destitute old age, or of a suffering family, no longer troubles the vicious portion of our community. They drink up their daily earnings, and bless God for the poorhouse, and begin to look upon it as, of right, the drunkard's home. . . . Every intemperate and idle man, whom you behold tottering about the streets and steeping himself at the stores, regards your houses and lands as pledged to take care of him, puts his hands deep, annually, into your pockets. . . .

What then is this universal, natural, and national remedy for intemperance? IT IS THE BANISHMENT OF ARDENT SPIRITS FROM THE LIST OF LAWFUL ARTICLES OF COMMERCE, BY A CORRECT AND EFFICIENT PUBLIC SENTIMENT; SUCH AS HAS TURNED SLAVERY OUT OF HALF OUR LAND, AND WILL YET EXPEL IT FROM THE WORLD.

We are not therefore to come down in wrath upon the distillers, and importers, and venders of ardent spirits. None of us are enough without sin to cast the first stone. . . . It is the buyers who have created the demand for ardent spirits, and made distillation and importation a gainful traffic. . . .

Let the temperate cease to buy—and the demand for ardent spirits will fall in the market three fourths, and ultimately will fail wholly, as the generation of drunkards shall hasten out of time. . . .

This however cannot be done effectually so long as the traffic in ardent spirits is regarded as lawful, and is patronized by men of reputation and moral worth in every part of the land. Like slavery, it must be regarded as sinful, impolitic, and dishonorable. That no measures will avail short of rendering ardent spirits a contraband of trade, is nearly self-evident.

ABRAHAM LINCOLN
"A New Class of Champions"

In Baltimore in 1840, a group of reformed drunkards formed the Washington Temperance Society, which turned the movement in a new direction. By relating their personal experience of alcoholic decline and spiritual recovery, they inspired thousands of men to "sign the pledge" of total abstinence. In 1842, Lincoln, a teetotaler, and an ambitious lawyer and member of the Illinois legislature at the time, spoke to the Washingtonian Society of Springfield, Illinois.

Although the temperance cause has been in progress for near twenty years, it is apparent to all that it is just now being crowned with a degree of success hitherto unparalleled. The list of its friends is daily swelled by the additions of fifties, of hundreds, and of thousands.

The warfare heretofore waged against the demon intemperance has somehow or other been erroneous. . . . [Its] champions for the most part have been preachers, lawyers, and hired agents. Between these and the mass of mankind there is a want of approachability. . . .

But when one who has long been known as a victim of intemperance bursts the fetters that have bound him, and appears before his neighbors "clothed and in his right mind," . . . to tell of the miseries once endured, now to be endured no more . . . there is a logic and an eloquence in it that few with human feelings can resist. . . .

In my judgment, it is to the battles of this new class of champions that our late success is greatly, perhaps chiefly, owing. . . . [Previously,] too much denunciation against dram-sellers and dram-drinkers was indulged in. This I think was both impolitic and unjust. . . . When the dram-seller and drinker were incessantly told . . . . in the thundering tones of anathema and denunciation . . . that their persons should be shunned by all the good and virtuous, as moral pestilences . . . they were slow, very slow, to . . . join the ranks of their de-nouncers in a hue and cry against themselves.

By the Washingtonians this system of consigning the ha-bitual drunkard to hopeless ruin is repudiated. They adopt a more enlarged philanthropy. . . . They teach hope to all—despair to none. As applying to their cause, they deny the doctrine of unpardonable sin. . . .

If the relative grandeur of revolutions shall be estimated by the great amount of human misery they alleviate, and the small amount they inflict, then indeed will this be the grandest the world shall ever have seen. Of our political rev-olution of '76 we are all justly proud. It has given us a degree of political freedom far exceeding that of any other nation of the earth. . . . But, with all these glorious results, past, present, and to come, it had its evils too. It breathed forth famine, swam in blood, and rode in fire; and long, long after, the orphan's cry and the widow's wail continued to break the sad silence that ensued. These were the price, the inevitable price, paid for the blessings it brought.

Turn now to the temperance revolution. In it we shall find a stronger bondage broken, a viler slavery manumitted, a greater tyrant deposed; in it, more of want supplied, more disease healed, more sorrow assuaged. By it no orphans starving, no widows weeping.

Glorious consummation! Hail, fall of fury! Reign of reason, all hail!

AMERICAN TEMPERANCE MAGAZINE
"You Shall Not Sell"

In 1851, the Maine legislature enacted a statute prohibiting the sale of alcoholic beverages in the state. The Maine Supreme Court upheld the statute declaring the legislature's "right to regulate by law the sale of any article, the use of which would be detrimental of the morals of the people." As this article from 1852 shows, American Temperance Magazine *became a strong advocate of legal prohibition and, within four years, had won passage of "Maine Laws" in twelve other states (see Chapter 9).*

This is a utilitarian age. The speculative has in all things yielded to the practical. Words are mere noise unless they are things.

In this sense, moral suasion is moral balderdash. "Words, my lord, words" . . . are a delusion. . . . The drunkard's mental and physical condition pronounces them an absurdity. He is ever in one or other extreme — under the excitement of drink, or in a state of morbid collapse. . . . Reason with a man when all reason has fled, and it is doubtful whether he or you is the greater fool. . . . Moral suasion! Bah!

Place this man we have been describing out of the reach of temptation. He will have time to ponder. His mind and frame recover their native vigor. The public-house does not beset his path. . . . Thus, and thus only, will reformation and temperance be secured. And how is this accomplished? Never except through the instrumentality of the law. If it were possible to reason the drunkard into sobriety, it would not be possible to make the rumseller forego his filthy gains. Try your moral suasion on him. . . . The only logic he will comprehend, is some such ordinance as this, coming to him in the shape and with the voice of law — you shall not sell.

SOURCE: All three selections are from David Brion Davis, *Antebellum American Culture: An Interpretive Anthology* (University Park: Pennsylvania State University Press, 1997), 395–398, 403–409.

ANALYZING THE EVIDENCE

➤ What does Lincoln's address to the Washingtonians tell us about his general political philosophy?

➤ Compare Lincoln's position to Beecher's. In what ways are they similar? How are they different?

➤ Where in these selections do you see the influence of the Sec-ond Great Awakening, especially the evangelical message of Charles Grandison Finney? Where do you see the influence of the Market Revolution and the middle-class values of the market economy? Do all of the selections take the same position concerning the role of government in regulating morality?

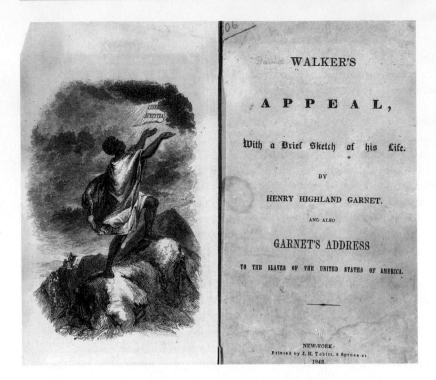

visitor, "I am no *sarvant*; none but *negers* are *sarvants*." This racial contempt led white mobs to terrorize black communities. The attacks in Cincinnati were so violent and destructive that several hundred African Americans fled to Canada for safety.

Responding to the attacks, David Walker published a stirring pamphlet: *An Appeal . . . to the Colored Citizens of the World* (1829). Walker was a free black from North Carolina who had moved to Boston, where he sold secondhand clothes and *Freedom's Journal*. A self-educated critic of racial slavery, Walker devoured volumes of history as well as the writings and speeches of Thomas Jefferson. His *Appeal* ridiculed the religious pretensions of slaveholders, justified slave rebellion, and in biblical language warned white Americans that slaves would revolt if justice were delayed. "We must and shall be free," he told white Americans. "And woe, woe, will be it to you if we have to obtain our freedom by fighting. . . . Your DESTRUCTION is at hand, and will be speedily consummated unless you REPENT." Within a year, Walker's pamphlet had gone through three printings and, carried by black merchant seamen, had begun to reach free African Americans in the South.

In 1830, Walker and other African American activists called a national convention in Philadelphia. The delegates refused to endorse Walker's radical call for a slave revolt; they also refused to restrict their focus to the welfare and uplift of free blacks.

Instead, this new generation of African American leaders demanded freedom and equality for all members of their race. To attain what they called "race-equality," they urged free blacks to use every legal means, including petitions and other forms of political protest, to break "the shackles of slavery."

As Walker threatened violence in Boston, Nat Turner, a slave in Southampton County, Virginia, staged a bloody revolt—a coincidence that had far-reaching consequences. As a child, Turner had taught himself to read and had hoped for emancipation, but a new owner forced him to work in the fields, and another new owner separated him from his wife. Turner became deeply spiritual and, in a religious vision, "the Spirit" told him that "Christ had laid down the yoke he had borne for the sins of men, and that I should take it on and fight against the Serpent, for the time was fast approaching when the first should be last and the last should be first." Taking an eclipse of the sun as an omen, Turner and a handful of relatives and friends decided to meet the masters' terror with their own. In August 1831, Turner and his followers rose in rebellion and killed at least fifty-five white men, women, and children. Turner hoped that a vast army of slaves would rally to his cause, but he mustered only sixty men. The white militia quickly dispersed his poorly armed force and then took their revenge. One company of cavalry killed forty blacks in two days, and put the heads of fifteen on poles to warn "all those who should undertake a similar plot."

Captured after two months in hiding, Turner died by hanging, still identifying his mission with that of his Savior. "Was not Christ crucified?" he asked.

Deeply shaken by Turner's Rebellion, the Virginia assembly debated a bill providing for gradual emancipation and colonization. When the representatives rejected the bill by a vote of 73 to 58, the possibility that southern planters would legislate an end to slavery was gone. Instead, the southern states toughened their slave codes, limited the movement of blacks, and prohibited anyone from teaching slaves to read. They would meet Walker's radical *Appeal* with radical measures of their own.

Evangelical Abolitionism

Concurrently, a cadre of evangelical Christians in the North and Midwest launched a moral crusade to abolish slavery. Many Quakers—and some pious Methodists and Baptists—had already freed their slaves; they advocated the gradual emancipation of all blacks. But in 1831, radical Christian abolitionists demanded that southerners free their slaves immediately. The issue was absolute: If the slave owners did not allow slaves their God-given status as free moral agents, they faced revolution in this world and damnation in the next.

William Lloyd Garrison and the American Anti-Slavery Society. The most uncompromising abolitionist was William Lloyd Garrison (1805–1879). A Massachusetts-born printer, Garrison had worked in Baltimore during the 1820s with Quaker Benjamin Lundy, the publisher of the *Genius of Universal Emancipation*. In 1830, Garrison went to jail, convicted of libeling a New England merchant engaged in the domestic slave trade. The following year, Garrison moved to Boston, started his own anti-slavery weekly, *The Liberator,* and founded the New England Anti-Slavery Society.

From the outset, *The Liberator* demanded the immediate abolition of slavery without compensation to slaveholders. In pursuing this goal, Garrison declared, "I will not retreat a single inch—AND I WILL BE HEARD." Indeed, Garrison was heard, accusing the American Colonization Society (see Chapter 8) of perpetuating slavery because of its voluntary and gradual approach, and assailing the U.S. Constitution as "a covenant with death and an agreement with Hell" because of its implicit acceptance of racial bondage.

In 1833, Garrison met with Theodore Dwight Weld and sixty other abolitionists, black and white, and established the American Anti-Slavery Society. The society received financial support from Arthur

William Lloyd Garrison, c. 1835

As this portrait suggests, William Lloyd Garrison was an intense and righteous man. In 1831, his hatred of slavery prompted Garrison to demand an immediate end to it, which marked the beginning of the abolitionist movement. Believing that the U.S. Constitution upheld slavery, Garrison publicly burned a copy of the document, declaring, "So perish all compromises with tyranny." From slavery, Garrison moved on to attack other institutions and cultural practices that prevented individuals—whites as well as blacks, women as well as men—from achieving their full potential and enjoying civic equality. Trustees of the Boston Public Library.

and Lewis Tappan, wealthy silk merchants in New York City. Women abolitionists established separate organizations, including the Philadelphia Female Anti-Slavery Society, founded by Lucretia Mott in 1833, and the Anti-Slavery Conventions of American Women, formed by a network of local societies in the late 1830s. The women's societies raised money for *The Liberator* and carried the movement to the farm villages of the Midwest, where they distributed abolitionist literature and collected tens of thousands of signatures on anti-slavery petitions.

Abolitionist leaders developed a three-pronged plan of attack. One prong consisted of an appeal to religious Americans. In 1837, Weld published *The Bible Against Slavery,* which used passages from Christianity's holiest book to discredit slavery. Two

AN AFFECTING SCENE IN KENTUCKY.

The Complexities of Race

This cartoon takes aim at Richard Mentor Johnson of Kentucky, pictured here as a distraught man being comforted by a black and an abolitionist. Surprisingly, Johnson was the Democrats' vice presidential candidate in 1836. Although the party stood for the South and slavery — and condemned mixed-race unions — Johnson lived openly with an enslaved woman, Julia Chinn, whose portrait is held by his mixed-race daughters. Future Supreme Court justice John Catron noted with disgust that Johnson "endeavored often to force his daughters into society," and that they and their mother "rode in carriages, and claimed equality." Racial prejudice cost Johnson some votes; but, he won a plurality in the electoral college, and, on a party-line vote, Democrats in the Senate elected him Martin Van Buren's vice president. Library of Congress.

years later, Weld teamed up with the Grimké sisters — Angelina, whom he married, and Sarah. The Grimkés had left their father's plantation in South Carolina, converted to Quakerism, and taken up the abolitionist cause in Philadelphia. In *American Slavery as It Is: Testimony of a Thousand Witnesses* (1839), Weld and the Grimkés addressed a simple question: "What is the actual condition of the slaves in the United States?" Using reports from southern newspapers and firsthand testimony, they presented a mass of incriminating evidence. In her testimonial, Angelina Grimké told of a treadmill that South Carolina slave owners used for punishment:

> One poor girl, [who was] sent there to be flogged, and who was accordingly stripped naked and whipped, showed me the deep gashes on her back — I might have laid my whole finger in them — large pieces of flesh had actually been cut out by the torturing lash.

The book sold more than 100,000 copies the year it was published.

To distribute their message, the abolitionists used the latest techniques of mass communication. With the help of new steam-powered printing presses, the American Anti-Slavery Society distributed thousands of pieces of literature in 1834. In 1835, the society launched its "great postal campaign," which flooded the nation, including the South, with a million pamphlets.

The abolitionists' second tactic was to help African Americans who had fled from slavery. Blacks who lived near a free state had the greatest chance of success, but fugitives from plantations deeper in the South received aid from the Underground Railroad, an informal network of whites and free blacks in Richmond, Charleston, and other southern cities (Map 11.3). In Baltimore, a free African American sailor lent his identification papers to future abolitionist Frederick Douglass, who

used them to escape to New York. Some runaway slaves, among them Harriet Tubman, risked reenslavement or death by returning repeatedly to the South to help others escape. "I should fight for . . . liberty as long as my strength lasted," Tubman explained, "and when the time came for me to go, the Lord would let them take me." Thanks to the Railroad, each year about a thousand African Americans reached freedom in the North.

There they faced an uncertain future because most whites did not favor civic equality for African Americans. In fact, voters in six northern and midwestern states adopted constitutional amendments that denied or limited the franchise for free blacks. "We want no masters," declared a New York artisan, "and least of all no negro masters." Moreover, the Fugitive Slave Law (1793) allowed owners and their hired slave catchers to

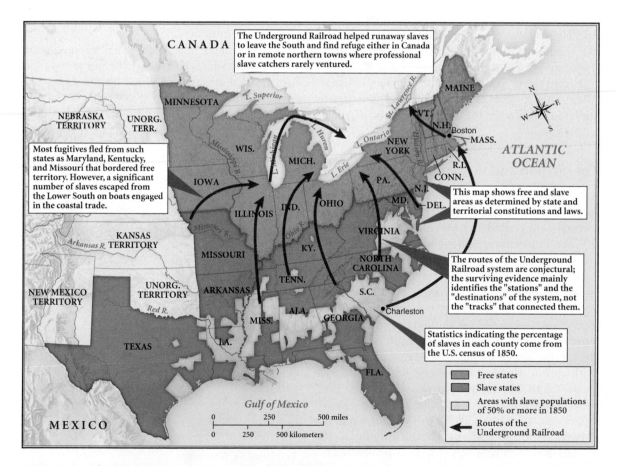

MAP 11.3   The Underground Railroad in the 1850s

Before 1840, most blacks who fled slavery did so on their own or with the help of family and friends. Thereafter, they could count on support from members of the Underground Railroad. Provided with food, directions, and free black guides in the South, fugitive slaves crossed into free states. There, they received protection and shelter from sympathetic men and women who arranged for their transportation to Canada or to "safe" American cities and towns.

seize suspected runaways and carry them back to bondage. To thwart these efforts, white abolitionists and free blacks in northern cities formed mobs that seized recaptured slaves and drove slave catchers out of town.

The third element of the abolitionists' program was an appeal to state and national legislators. In 1835, members of the American Anti-Slavery Society bombarded Congress with petitions demanding the abolition of slavery in the District of Columbia, an end to the interstate slave trade, and a ban on admission to the Union of new slave states. By 1838, petitions with close to 500,000 signatures had arrived in Washington.

This protest activity drew thousands of deeply religious farmers and small-town proprietors to abolitionism. The number of local abolitionist societies grew from two hundred in 1835 to two thousand by 1840, with nearly 200,000 members, including many leading transcendentalists. Emerson condemned American society for tolerating slavery, and Thoreau was even more assertive. Claiming that the Mexican War was an attempt to extend slavery, Thoreau refused to pay his taxes in 1846 and submitted to arrest. Two years later, Thoreau published "Resistance to Civil Government," an essay urging individuals to resist the state and follow a higher moral law.

Opposition and Internal Conflict

Still, abolitionists remained a small minority. Perhaps 10 percent of northerners and midwesterners strongly supported the movement, and another 20 percent were sympathetic to its goals. Its opponents were more numerous and equally aggressive. Men of wealth feared that the attack on slave property might become a general assault on all property rights; conservative clergymen condemned the public roles assumed by abolitionist women; and northern merchants and textile manufacturers supported the southern planters who supplied them with cotton. Northern wage earners, who already described themselves as "white slaves" to their employers, feared that freed blacks would work for lower wages and take their jobs. Finally, whites almost universally opposed "amalgamation," the racial mixing and intermarriage that Garrison seemed to support by encouraging meetings of black and white abolitionists of both sexes.

Antiabolitionist Mobs. Motivated by racial fears, white workers in the North periodically took part in violent mob actions. They attacked places of dubious reputation where blacks and whites mixed,

including taverns and brothels; they also attacked "respectable" African American institutions: churches, temperance halls, and orphanages. In 1833, a mob of fifteen hundred New Yorkers stormed a church in search of Garrison and Arthur Tappan. Another white mob swept through Philadelphia's African American neighborhoods, clubbing and stoning residents and destroying homes and churches. "Gentlemen of property and standing" led some of these riots. In 1835, a group of lawyers, merchants, and bankers broke up an abolitionist convention in Utica, New York, and beat several delegates. Two years later, in Alton, Illinois, a mob shot and killed Elijah P. Lovejoy, editor of the abolitionist *Alton Observer*. By pressing the issues of emancipation and equality, the abolitionists revealed the extent of racial prejudice in the North and the near impossibility of creating a biracial middle class of respectable whites and blacks. In fact, the abolitionist crusade had heightened race consciousness and encouraged whites — and blacks — to identify across class lines with those of their own race.

Racial solidarity was especially strong in the South, where whites banned abolitionist groups and demanded that northern states do the same. The Georgia legislature offered a $5,000 reward to anyone who would kidnap Garrison and bring him south to be tried for inciting rebellion. In Nashville, vigilantes whipped a northern college student for distributing abolitionist pamphlets; in Charleston, a mob attacked

Retribution, Southern Style

Jonathan Walker, a Massachusetts shipwright, paid for his abolitionist activities by being branded, as this daguerreotype shows. Captured off the coast of Florida in 1844 while trying to smuggle seven slaves to freedom in the Bahama islands, Walker had the initials *SS* (for "slave stealer") burned into his hand. Massachusetts Historical Society.

the post office and destroyed sacks of abolitionist mail. After 1835, southern postmasters simply refused to deliver mail suspected to be of abolitionist origin.

Politicians also joined the fray. President Andrew Jackson, a longtime slave owner, asked Congress in 1835 to restrict the use of the mails by abolitionist groups. Congress did not comply; but in 1836, the House of Representatives adopted the so-called gag rule. Under this informal rule, which remained in force until 1844, antislavery petitions were automatically tabled so that they could not become the subject of debate in the House, thus keeping the explosive issue of slavery off the national stage.

The Fight over Gender Splits the Abolitionist Movement.

Assailed by racists from the outside, abolitionists fought among themselves over gender issues. Many antislavery clergymen opposed an activist role for women and condemned the Grimké sisters for lecturing to mixed-sex audiences. But Garrison had broadened his reform agenda to include pacifism, the abolition of prisons, and women's rights. Arguing that "our object is universal emancipation, to redeem women as well as men from a servile to an equal condition," he demanded that the American Anti-Slavery Society support women's rights. In 1840, that demand split the abolitionist movement. Abby Kelley, Lucretia Mott, Elizabeth Cady Stanton, and other women's rights advocates remained with Garrison in the American Anti-Slavery Society and proclaimed the common interests of enslaved blacks and free white women.

Garrison's opponents founded a new organization, the American and Foreign Anti-Slavery Society, which focused its energies on ending slavery. Some of its members mobilized their churches to oppose racial bondage; others established the Liberty Party, the first antislavery political party. In 1840, the new party nominated James G. Birney, a former Alabama slave owner, for president. Birney and the Liberty Party argued that the Constitution did not recognize slavery and, consequently, that slaves automatically became free when they entered areas of federal authority, including the District of Columbia and the national territories. However, Birney won few votes in the election, and the future of political abolitionism appeared dim.

Coming hard on the heels of popular violence in the North and government suppression in the South, schisms and electoral failure stunned the abolitionist movement. By melding the energies and ideas of evangelical Protestants, moral reformers, and transcendentalists, it had raised the banner of antislavery to new heights. Indeed, it was the growing visibility of the abolitionist movement that had sparked a hostile backlash. "When we first unfurled the banner of *The Liberator*," Garrison admitted, "it did not occur to us that nearly every religious sect and every political party would side with the oppressor."

➤ What were the origins of the abolitionist movement?

➤ How did black social thought change over the first half of the nineteenth century? What role did black activists play in the abolitionist movement?

➤ How did the abolitionists' proposals and methods differ from those of earlier antislavery movements (see Chapter 8)? Why did those proposals and methods arouse such hostility in the South and in the North?

The Women's Rights Movement

The prominence of women among the abolitionists reflected a broad shift in American culture. By joining religious revivals and reform movements like the temperance crusade and the abolitionist movement, women had entered public life. Their activism caused issues of gender — sexual behavior, marriage, family authority — to become subjects of debate. In 1848, the debate entered a new phase, when some reformers turned their advocacy toward women's rights and demanded complete equality with men.

Origins of the Women's Movement

"Don't be afraid, not afraid, fight Satan; stand up for Christ; don't be afraid." So spoke Mary Walker Ostram on her deathbed in 1859. Her religious convictions were as firm at the age of fifty-eight as they had been in 1816, when she helped found the first sabbath school in Utica. Married to a lawyer-politician but childless, Ostram had devoted her life to evangelical Presbyterianism and its program of benevolent social reform. Her minister, Philemon Fowler, celebrated Ostram in his eulogy of her as a "living fountain" of faith, an exemplar of "Women's Sphere of Influence" in the world.

Transcending the "Separate Sphere."

A public presence for women was hard won and still contested. Even as Reverend Fowler heaped praise on Ostram, he reiterated the Revolutionary-era precept that women should limit their political role to that of "republican mother," instructing "their sons in the principles of liberty and government." According to Fowler, women inhabited a "**separate sphere**" and had no place in "the markets of trade, the scenes of politics and popular agitation, the courts of justice and the halls of legislation. Home is her peculiar sphere and members of her family her peculiar care."

Ostram and many other middle-class women had transcended these rigid boundaries by joining in the Second Great Awakening. Their spiritual activities bolstered their authority within the household and allowed them to influence many areas of family life, including the timing of pregnancies. Publications like *Godey's Lady's Book* and Catharine Beecher's *Treatise on Domestic Economy* (1841) taught women how to make their homes examples of middle-class efficiency and domesticity. Women in propertied farm families were equally vigilant. To protect their homes and husbands from alcoholic excess, they joined the Independent Order of Good Templars, a family-oriented temperance organization that granted them full membership.

Some women used their religious activities to enhance the position of their gender. In 1834, a group of middle-class women in New York City founded the Female Moral Reform Society and elected Lydia Finney, the wife of revivalist Charles Grandison Finney, as its president. The society's goals were to end the prostitution that was so prevalent in New York City and to protect the city's single women from moral corruption. Rejecting the sexual double standard, its members demanded chastity for men as well as for women. By 1840, the Female Moral Reform Society had grown into a national association, with 555 chapters and 40,000 members throughout the North and Midwest. Employing only women as agents, the society provided moral guidance for young women working in factories, as seamstresses, or as servants and living away from their families. Society members visited brothels, where they sang hymns, offered prayers, searched for runaway girls, and noted the names of clients. They also founded homes of refuge for prostitutes, and won the passage of laws in Massachusetts and New York regulating men's sexual behavior by making seduction a crime.

Dorothea Dix and Institutional Reform.

Other women turned their energies to the improvement of public institutions, and Dorothea Dix (1801–1887) was their model. Dix's paternal grandparents were prominent Bostonians, but her father, a Methodist minister, ended up an impoverished alcoholic. Poor and emotionally abused as a child, Dix grew up to become a compassionate young woman with a strong sense of moral purpose. She used her grand-

Dorothea Dix

This daguerreotype captures Dix's firm character, which helped her endure emotional abuse as a child and achieve great success as a social reformer. Her call for government action to address social problems anticipated twentieth-century reform and social-welfare measures. Boston Athenaeum.

parents' resources to set up charity schools to "rescue some of America's miserable children from vice." While teaching, Dix became a successful author and a public figure. By 1832, she had published seven books, including *Conversations on Common Things* (1824), an enormously successful treatise on natural science and moral improvement.

In 1841, Dix took up a new cause. Discovering that insane women were jailed alongside male criminals, she persuaded Massachusetts lawmakers to enlarge the state hospital to accommodate indigent mental patients. Exhilarated by that success, Dix began a national movement to establish separate, well-funded state hospitals for those with mental illness. By 1854, she had traveled more than 30,000 miles and visited eighteen state penitentiaries, three hundred county jails and houses of correction, and more than five hundred almshouses in addition to innumerable hospitals. Issuing dozens of reports, she aroused public support and prompted many states to expand their state hospitals and improve their prisons.

Both as reformers and as teachers, other northern women transformed public education. From Maine

MAP 11.4 Women and Antislavery, 1837–1838

Beginning in the 1830s, abolitionists and antislavery advocates dispatched dozens of petitions to Congress demanding an end to slavery. Women accounted for two-thirds of the 67,000 signatures on the petitions submitted in 1837–1838, a fact that suggests not only the influence of women in the antislavery movement but also the extent of female organizations and social networks. Lawmakers, eager to avoid sectional conflict, had an informal agreement to table the petitions without discussion.

to Wisconsin, women vigorously supported the movement led by Horace Mann to increase the number of elementary schools and improve their quality. As secretary of the Massachusetts Board of Education from 1837 to 1848, Mann lengthened the school year; established teaching standards in reading, writing, and arithmetic; and improved instruction by recruiting well-educated women as teachers. The intellectual leader of the new corps of women educators was Catharine Beecher, who founded academies for young women in Hartford and Cincinnati. In widely read publications, Beecher argued that "energetic and benevolent women" were better qualified than men were to impart moral and intellectual instruction to the young. By the 1850s, most teachers were women both because local school boards heeded Beecher's arguments and because women could be paid less than men.

Abolitionist Women

Women had long been active in the antislavery movement. During the Revolutionary era, Quaker women in Philadelphia established schools for freed slaves, and Baptist and Methodist women in the Upper South endorsed religious arguments against slavery. One of the first abolitionists recruited by William Lloyd Garrison was Maria W. Stewart, an African American, who spoke to mixed audiences of men and women in Boston in the early 1830s. As the abolitionist movement mushroomed, scores of white women delivered lectures condemning slavery, and thousands more made home "visitations" to win converts to their cause (Map 11.4).

Women abolitionists were particularly aware of the special horrors of slavery for their sex. In her autobiography, *Incidents in the Life of a Slave Girl*, black abolitionist Harriet Jacobs described being forced to have sexual relations with her white owner: "I cannot tell how much I suffered in the presence of these wrongs." According to Jacobs and the other female slaves who testified, the sexual assaults were compounded by the cruel treatment they suffered at the hands of their owners' wives, who were enraged by their husbands' promiscuity. In her best-selling novel, *Uncle Tom's Cabin* (1852), Harriet Beecher Stowe charged that among the greatest moral failings of slavery was the degradation of slave women.

As abolitionist women attacked slavery and sexual oppression, many men challenged their right to participate in public debate. In response, women activists rejected the subordinate status of their sex. The most famous advocates were Angelina and Sarah Grimké, who had become antislavery lecturers. When some Congregationalist clergymen demanded in 1836 that they stop lecturing to mixed

Sojourner Truth

Few women had as interesting a life as Sojourner Truth. Born "Isabella" in Dutch-speaking rural New York about 1797, she labored as a slave until 1827. Following a religious vision, Isabella moved to New York City, learned English, and worked for deeply religious — and ultimately fanatical — Christian merchants. In 1843, in search of further spiritual enlightenment, she took the name "Sojourner Truth" and left New York. After briefly joining the Millerites (who believed the world would end in 1844), Truth became famous as a forceful speaker on behalf of abolitionism and women's rights. This illustration, showing Truth addressing an antislavery meeting, suggests her powerful personal presence.
Miriam and Ira D. Wallach Division of Art, Prints and Photographs. The New York Public Library.

male and female audiences, Sarah Grimké turned to the Bible for justification: "The Lord Jesus defines the duties of his followers in his Sermon on the Mount . . . without any reference to sex or condition," she wrote. "Men and women are CREATED EQUAL! They are both moral and accountable beings and whatever is right for man to do is right for woman." In a debate with Catharine Beecher (who believed that women should exercise power primarily as wives, mothers, and schoolteachers), Angelina Grimké pushed the argument beyond religion, invoking Enlightenment principles to claim equal civic rights for women:

> It is a woman's right to have a voice in all the laws and regulations by which she is governed,

whether in Church or State. . . . The present arrangements of society, on these points are a violation of human rights, a rank usurpation of power, a violent seizure and confiscation of what is sacredly and inalienably hers.

By 1840, female abolitionists were asserting that traditional gender roles amounted to the "domestic slavery" of women. "How can we endure our present marriage relations," asked Elizabeth Cady Stanton, relations that gave a woman "no charter of rights, no individuality of her own?" Said another female reformer: "The radical difficulty . . . is that women are considered as *belonging* to men." Drawn into public life by abolitionism, thousands of northern women now advocated greater rights not only for enslaved African Americans but also for themselves.

The Program of Seneca Falls and Beyond

During the 1840s, women's rights activists devised a pragmatic program of reform. They did not challenge the institution of marriage or even the conventional division of labor within the family. Instead, they tried to strengthen the legal rights of married women, especially with respect to property. This initiative won crucial support from affluent men, who wanted to protect their wives' assets in case their own businesses went into bankruptcy in the volatile new market economy. By ensuring that their married daughters had property rights, fathers also hoped to protect them (and their inheritances) from spendthrift sons-in-law. These considerations prompted legislatures in three states — Mississippi, Maine, and Massachusetts — to enact married women's property acts between 1839 and 1845. In New York, women activists won a more comprehensive statute (1848), which gave women full legal control over the property they brought to a marriage and became the model for similar laws in fourteen other states.

To advance the nascent women's movement, Elizabeth Cady Stanton and Lucretia Mott organized a gathering in the small town of Seneca Falls in central New York in 1848. Seventy women and thirty men attended the meeting, which issued a rousing manifesto for women's equality. Taking the Declaration of Independence as a model, the attendees explicitly extended its republican ideology to women. "All men and women are created equal," the Declaration of Sentiments declared. Yet, "the history of mankind is a history of repeated injuries and usurpations on the part of man toward woman, having in direct object the establishment

Crusading Women Reformers

Elizabeth Cady Stanton (1815–1902) and Susan B. Anthony (1820–1906) were a dynamic duo of social reformers. Stanton was the well-educated daughter of a prominet New York judge and an early supporter of the abolitionist movement. In 1840 she married abolitionist lawyer Henry Stanton, by whom she had seven children. Anthony was raised as a Quaker, worked for ten years as a teacher, and then became a temperance activist. After meeting in 1851, Stanton and Anthony became intimate friends and successful reformers and organizers. From 1854 to 1860, they led a successful struggle to expand the New York's Married Women's Property Law of 1848. During the Civil War, they set up the Women's Loyal National League, which supported the Union war effort and helped to win passage of the Thirteenth Amendment. In 1866, they helped to found the American Equal Rights Association, which demanded the vote for all women as well as African American men. Corbis/Bettman.

of an absolute tyranny over her." To persuade Americans to right this long-standing wrong, the activists resolved to "use every instrumentality within our power . . . [to] employ agents, circulate tracts, petition the State and National legislatures, and endeavor to enlist the pulpit and the press on our behalf." By staking out claims for equality for women in public life, the Seneca Falls reformers repudiated the idea that the natural order of society demanded separate spheres for men and women.

Most men dismissed the Seneca Falls declaration as nonsense, and many women repudiated the activists and their message. Writing in her diary, one small-town mother and housewife lashed out at the female reformer who "aping mannish manners . . . wears absurd and barbarous attire, who talks of her wrongs in harsh tone, who struts and strides, and thinks that she proves herself superior to the rest of her sex."

Still, the women's rights movement attracted a growing number of supporters. In 1850, delegates to the first national women's rights convention in Worcester, Massachusetts, hammered out a program of action. The women called on churches to revise concepts of female inferiority in their theology. Addressing state legislatures, they proposed laws to guarantee the custody rights of mothers in the event of divorce or a husband's death, and to allow married women to institute lawsuits and testify in court. Finally, and above all else, they began a concerted campaign to win the vote for women. The national women's rights convention of 1851 declared that suffrage was "the corner-stone of this enterprise, since we do not seek to protect woman, but rather to place her in a position to protect herself."

The activists' legislative campaign required leaders who had talents as organizers and lobbyists. The most prominent political operative was Susan B. Anthony (1820–1906). Anthony came from a Quaker family and as a young woman participated in the temperance and antislavery movements. That experience, Anthony explained, had taught her "the great evil of woman's utter dependence on man" and led her to the women's rights movement. Working closely with Stanton, Anthony created a network of political "captains," all women, who relentlessly lobbied the legislature in New York and other states. In 1860, her efforts culminated in a New York law granting women the right to collect and spend their own wages (which fathers or husbands had previously controlled), own property acquired by "trade, business, labors, or services," and, if widowed, to assume sole guardianship of their children. These successes laid the foundation for more-aggressive attempts at reform after the Civil War.

> Why did religious women like Mary Walker Ostram and the Grimké sisters become social reformers?

> What were the principles and the goals of the women's rights movement? Why did they arouse intense opposition?

SUMMARY

In this chapter, we have examined four major intellectual and cultural movements of the mid-nineteenth century and explored the character of the new popular culture in New York City. One focus of our discussion of the transcendentalists was the influence of Ralph Waldo Emerson on the great literary figures of the era; we also linked transcendentalism to the rise of individualism and the character of middle-class culture.

Our analysis of communal movements had a different thrust. It probed the efforts of communalists to devise new rules for sexual behavior, gender relationships, and property ownership. We saw that successful communal experiments—Mormonism, for example—began with a charismatic leader and a religious foundation, and endured through the development of strong, authoritarian institutions.

We also traced the extremely close connections between the abolitionist and women's rights movements. Personal and ideological factors linked the two causes. Lucretia Mott, Elizabeth Cady Stanton, and the Grimké sisters began as antislavery advocates; but, denied access to lecture platforms by male abolitionists, they gradually became staunch defenders of women's rights. This transition was a logical one: Both enslaved blacks and married women were "owned" by men, either as property or as their legal dependents. In fact, the efforts of women's rights advocates to abolish the legal prerogatives of husbands were as controversial as the abolitionists' efforts to end the legal ownership of human property. As reformers took aim at these deeply rooted institutions and customs, many Americans feared that their activism would not perfect society but destroy it.

Connections: Culture

Before 1800, the United States contained a variety of regional cultures in New England, the Middle Atlantic region, and the Chesapeake Bay area. Mixed in with these English cultures, were a variety of eighteenth-century immigrant cultures, primarily African, German, and Scots-Irish. As we saw in Chapter 8, between 1790 and 1820, the immigrant societies slowly became more American in character, while the regional cultures acquired distinct republican outlooks and a strong religious impulse.

Then, as we observed in the essay opening Part Three, (p. 269), beginning in the 1820s,

> a series of reform movements, many with religious roots and goals, swept across America. Dedicated men and women preached the gospel of temperance, Sunday observance, prison reform, and dozens of other causes.

The reform movements sparked a series of culture wars, as temperance advocates won laws regulating drink, Sabbatarians tried to curtail work and entertainment on Sundays, white mobs rioted against abolitionists, and community hostility forced Mormons westward. The sudden appearance of millions of new Catholic migrants from Germany and Ireland sparked more cultural conflicts. These confrontations caused some observers to worry that American society, particularly in the Northeast and Midwest, was coming apart at the seams. Meanwhile, in the South, a vast movement of peoples—white and black—into the lower Mississippi Valley disrupted the traditional English- and African-based cultures of the Chesapeake states and the Carolinas. The creation of a new "cotton states" culture is the subject of the next chapter.

CHAPTER REVIEW QUESTIONS

➤ Did the era of reform increase or decrease the belief in and practice of liberty in American society?

➤ Explain the relationship between individualism and communalism as presented in the chapter. How were these movements related to the social and economic changes in America in the decades after 1820?

➤ Explain the relationship between religion and reform in the decades from 1820 to 1860. Why did many religious people feel compelled to remake society? What was their motivation? How successful were they? Do you see any parallels with social movements today?

➤ What was the relationship between the abolitionist and women's rights movements?

➤ Why did women's issues suddenly become so prominent in American culture?

TIMELINE

1826	Lyceum movement begins
1829	David Walker's *Appeal . . . to the Colored Citizens of the World*
1830	Joseph Smith publishes *The Book of Mormon*
1830s	Emergence of minstrelsy shows Nativist movement mounts assault on immigrants and immigration
1831	William Lloyd Garrison founds *The Liberator* Nat Turner's uprising in Virginia
1832	Ralph Waldo Emerson rejects organized religion and begins defining transcendentalism
1833	Garrison organizes American Anti-Slavery Society
1834	New York activists create Female Moral Reform Society
1835	Abolitionists launch mail campaign; antiabolitionists riot against them
1836	House of Representatives adopts gag rule on antislavery petitions Grimké sisters defend public roles for women
1840	Liberty Party runs James G. Birney for president
1840s	Fourierist communities arise in Midwest Commercialized sex flourishes in New York City
1841	Transcendentalists found Brook Farm Dorothea Dix promotes hospitals for the insane
1844	Margaret Fuller publishes *Woman in the Nineteenth Century*
1845	Henry David Thoreau withdraws to Walden Pond
1846	Mormon followers of Brigham Young reach Salt Lake
1848	John Humphrey Noyes founds Oneida Community Seneca Falls convention proposes women's equality
1850	Nathaniel Hawthorne publishes *The Scarlet Letter*
1851	Herman Melville issues *Moby Dick*
1852	Harriet Beecher Stowe writes *Uncle Tom's Cabin*
1855	Walt Whitman issues first edition of *Leaves of Grass*
1858	"Mormon War" over polygamy

FOR FURTHER EXPLORATION

Ronald Walters, *American Reformers, 1815–1860* (1978), offers a succinct discussion of the major antebellum reform movements, while Robert H. Abzug, *Cosmos Crumbling: American Reform and the Religious Imagination* (1994), demonstrates their religious roots. David S. Reynolds, *Walt Whitman's America: A Cultural Biography* (1995), is a fine study of the poet and his society. Charles Capper, *Margaret Fuller: An American Romantic Life* (1992), illuminates her intellectual milieu. Fuller inspired the character of Zenobia in Nathaniel Hawthorne's *The Blithedale Romance* (1852), which reflects his life at Brook Farm. Peter S. Field, in *Ralph Waldo Emerson: The Making of a Democratic Individual* (2003), offers a convincing profile. For fine Web sites on transcendentalism and other American religious sects, go to **www.vcu.edu/engweb/transcendentalism/** and **religiousmovements.lib.virginia.edu/**. For religious utopianism gone mad, read Paul E. Johnson and Sean Wilentz, *The Kingdom of Matthias: A Story of Sex and Salvation in Nineteenth-Century America* (1995).

James B. Stewart, *Holy Warriors: The Abolitionists and American Slavery* (1976), places Garrison's movement in a broad social context. Also see Mark Perry, *Lift Up Thy Voice: The Grimké Family's Journey* (2001). Stephen B. Oates, *The Fires of Jubilee: Nat Turner's Fierce Rebellion* (1975), explores the life of the insurrectionist; the text of *The Confessions of Nat Turner* (1831) is available at **docsouth.unc.edu/turner/menu.html**. *The Narrative of the Life of Frederick Douglass, an American Slave, Written by Himself* (1845), is a literary masterpiece. John Stauffer, *The Black Hearts of Men* (2001), is a fine collective biography of Douglass and other abolitionists. Important new biographies of Harriet Tubman are Kate Clifford Larson, *Bound for the Promised Land* (2004), and Catherine Clinton, *Harriet Tubman: The Road to Freedom* (2004). For antiabolitionism, see Leonard L. Richards, *"Gentlemen of Property and Standing": Anti-Abolition Mobs in Jacksonian America* (1970), and David Roediger, *The Wages of Whiteness* (1995). For many resources on slavery and abolition, consult the PBS "Africans in America" site (**www.pbs.org/wgbh/aia/ part4/**).

Anne M. Boylan, *The Origins of Women's Activism . . . 1797–1840* (1992), and Mary Ryan, *Women in Public . . . 1825–1880* (1990), explore women's civic activities. Also see Eleanor Flexner, *Century of Struggle* (1959); the PBS video directed by Ken Burns, "Not for Ourselves Alone: The Story of Elizabeth Cady Stanton and Susan B. Anthony" (3 hours); and the National Park Service Web site for Seneca Falls (**www.nps.gov/wori/home.htm**).

TEST YOUR KNOWLEDGE

To assess your command of the material in this chapter, see the Online Study Guide at **bedfordstmartins.com/henretta**.

For Web sites, images, and documents related to topics and places in this chapter, visit **bedfordstmartins.com/makehistory**.

12 The South Expands: Slavery and Society

1820–1860

L IFE IN SOUTH CAROLINA HAD been good to James Lide. A slave-owning planter who lived near the Pee Dee River, Lide and his wife had raised twelve children and lived in relative comfort. Content with his lot, Lide had long resisted the "Alabama Fever" that had prompted thousands of Carolina families to move west. Finally, at age sixty-five, probably seeking land for his many offspring, he moved his slaves and family — including six children and six grandchildren — to a plantation near Montgomery, Alabama. There, the family took up residence in a squalid double log cabin with airholes but no windows; still, Lide's daughter Maria remarked, "Our house is considered quite a comfortable one for this country." Even as their living conditions improved, the Lides' family life remained unsettled. "Pa is quite in the notion of moving somewhere," Maria reported a few years later, "his having such a good crop seems to make him more anxious to move." Although James Lide lived out his years in Alabama, many of his children did not. In 1854, at the age of fifty-eight, Eli Lide moved to Texas, telling his father, "Something within me whispers onward and onward."

The story of the Lide family was the story of American society. Between 1800 and 1860, white planters from the South and yeomen farmers from the North were moving west. As historian James Oakes

◄ **Generations in Slavery**

In 1862, a traveling photographer, Timothy O'Sullivan, took this picture at the Beaufort, South Carolina, plantation of J. J. Smith. It shows four — perhaps five — generations of a slave family, all of whom were born on the plantation. As you read this chapter, consider whether the experience of this African American family was the exception or the rule. Who might be missing from this family photograph? For example, what happened to the brothers and sisters of the man standing in the back? Library of Congress.

has suggested, the South's "master class was one of the most mobile in history." The southerners' goal was to make the West into a "slave society" similar to the one their fathers and grandfathers had built in Virginia and South Carolina. Using their own muscles and those of thousands of enslaved African Americans, the planters rapidly cultivated millions of acres of land. By 1840, the South was at the cutting edge of the American Market Revolution. It annually produced and exported 1.5 million bales of raw cotton — over two-thirds of the world's supply — and its economy was larger and richer than that of most nations. "Cotton is King," boasted the *Southern Cultivator,* the leading Georgia farm journal, "and wields an astonishing influence over the world's commerce."

No matter how rich they were, few cotton planters in the southwestern states of Alabama, Mississippi, and Texas lived in elegant houses or led cultured lives. The slave owners of the Cotton South largely abandoned the aristocratic gentility characteristic of the Chesapeake region and the Carolinas. The goal of these agricultural capitalists was to make money. "To sell cotton in order to buy negroes — to make more cotton to buy more negroes, 'ad infinitum,' is the aim . . . of the thorough-going cotton planter," a New England traveler reported from Mississippi in 1835. "His whole soul is wrapped up in the pursuit." A generation later, Frederick Law Olmsted found that little had changed: "The plantations are all large" in Mississippi, but their owners do not live well, he observed; "the greater number have but small and mean residences." Plantation women were especially aware of the loss of genteel surroundings and polite society. Raised in North Carolina, where she was "blest with every comfort, & even luxury," a "discontented" Mary Drake found Mississippi and Alabama "a dreary waste."

Tens of thousands of enslaved African Americans in the Lower Mississippi River Valley knew what "dreary waste" really was: unremitting toil, poverty, and profound sadness. Sold south from Maryland, where his family had lived for generations, Charles Ball's father became "gloomy and morose" and, when threatened again with sale, ran off and disappeared. With good reason. On cotton plantations, slaves labored from "sunup to sundown" and from one end of the year to the other. As one field hand put it, there was "no time off [between] de change of de seasons. . . . Dey was allus clearin' mo' lan' or sump'." Day by day, the forced labor of unwilling migrants extracted the great wealth of the Cotton South from its bountiful lands. And wanting more, southern planters and politicians plotted to extend the sway of slave property rights across the continent.

Creating the Cotton South

American slavery began on the tobacco plantations of the Chesapeake and in the rice fields of the Carolina Low Country. It grew to maturity on the sugar fields of Louisiana, the hemp farms of Kentucky and Tennessee, and especially on the cotton plantations of the states bordering the Gulf of Mexico: Alabama, Mississippi, and Texas (Figure 12.1). The transplantation of slavery to these new lands brought vast changes to the lives of enslaved blacks, slave-owning planters, and white farmers. Beyond that, it led planters to believe that American slavery could and should continue to expand — across the continent or to the Caribbean. "We want land, and have a right to it," declared a Georgia planter on the eve of the Civil War.

The Domestic Slave Trade

By 1817, when the American Colonization Society announced its plan to return freed blacks to Africa (see Chapter 8), the southern plantation system was rapidly expanding, as was the demand for slave labor. In 1790, the western boundary of the plantation system ran through the middle of Georgia; by 1830, it stretched through western Louisiana; by 1860, the slave frontier extended far into Texas. (Map 12.1).

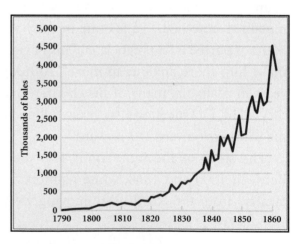

FIGURE 12.1 The Surge in Cotton Production, 1835–1860

Between 1835 and the mid-1840s, southern planters doubled their output of 500-pound bales of cotton from 1 million per year to 2 million. Another dramatic rise came in the 1850s, as production doubled again — reaching 4 million bales per year by the end of the decade. Because the price of raw cotton rose slightly (from about 11 cents a pound in the 1830s to 13 cents in the 1850s), planters reaped substantial profits, an economic incentive that reinforced their commitment to the slave system. SOURCE: Robert William Fogel and Stanley L. Engerman, *Time on the Cross* (Boston: Little, Brown, 1974), fig. 25.

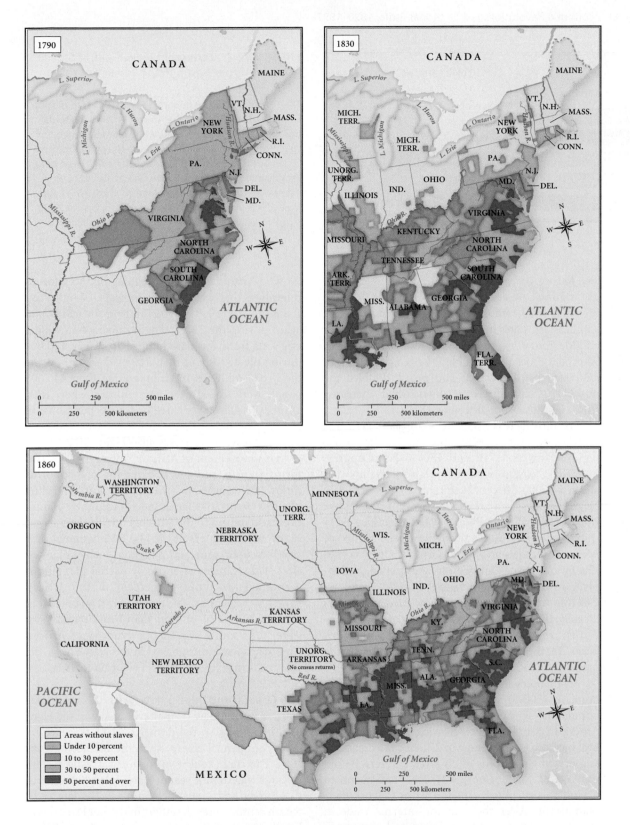

MAP 12.1 Distribution of the Slave Population in 1790, 1830, and 1860

The cotton boom shifted many African Americans to the Old Southwest. In 1790, most slaves lived and worked on the tobacco plantations of the Chesapeake and in the rice and indigo areas of South Carolina. By 1830, hundreds of thousands of enslaved blacks were laboring on the cotton and sugar lands of the Lower Mississippi Valley and on cotton plantations in Georgia and Florida. Three decades later, the centers of slavery lay along the Mississippi River and in an arc of fertile cotton land — the "black belt" — sweeping from Mississippi through Georgia.

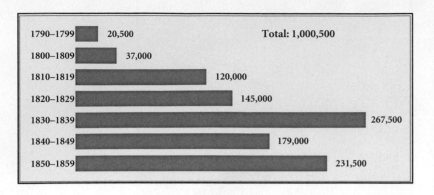

1790–1799	20,500
1800–1809	37,000
1810–1819	120,000
1820–1829	145,000
1830–1839	267,500
1840–1849	179,000
1850–1859	231,500

Total: 1,000,500

FIGURE 12.2   Estimated Movement of Slaves from the Upper South to the Lower South, 1790–1860

The cotton boom that began in the 1810s set in motion a great redistribution of the African American population. Between 1790 and 1860, white planters moved or sold more than a million slaves from the Upper to the Lower South, a process that broke up families and long-established black communities. SOURCE: Based on data in Robert William Fogel and Stanley L. Engerman, *Time on the Cross* (Boston: Little, Brown, 1974); and Michael Tadman, *Speculators and Slaves: Masters, Traders, and Slaves in the Old South* (Madison: University of Wisconsin Press, 1996).

The federal government played a major role in this expansion of slavery by securing Louisiana from the French in 1803, removing Native Americans from the southeastern states in the 1830s, and annexing Texas and Mexican territories in the 1840s. That advance of 900 miles more than doubled the geographical area cultivated by slave labor and nearly doubled the number of southern slave states, which increased from eight in 1800 to fifteen by 1850.

To cultivate this vast area, white planters turned first to Africa for slaves and then to the Chesapeake region. Between 1776 and 1809, when Congress outlawed the Atlantic slave trade, planters imported about 115,000 Africans (see Table 8.1, p. 254). "The Negro business is a great object with us," one slave trader declared, "the Planter will . . . sacrifice every thing to attain Negroes." Despite the influx of Africans, the demand for labor on the new cotton plantations in the Gulf region far exceeded the supply. Consequently, planters in the Cotton South began importing thousands of new African workers illegally, through the Spanish colony of Florida until 1819 and then through the Mexican province of Texas. Yet these Africans were too few to satisfy the demand for labor.

So planters looked to the Chesapeake region, home in 1800 to nearly half of the country's black population. Throughout the Old South, the African American population was growing rapidly from natural increase—an average of 27 percent a decade—and creating a surplus of enslaved laborers. Before the War of 1812, "Georgia traders" had begun to exploit this surplus by buying slaves to work their plantations. After the war, the internal trade in slaves expanded vastly in scope and size. Each decade, planters and slave traders moved to the rich soils of the Cotton South about 10 percent of the African Americans who lived in the main exporting states of the Upper South—Maryland and Virginia before 1820, plus the Carolinas by 1830, plus Kentucky by 1840.

The "mania for buying negroes" led to a forced migration that was massive in scale. Seventy-five thousand slaves left Virginia during the 1810s and again during the 1820s. The number of unwilling migrants from the state jumped to nearly 120,000 during the 1830s and then averaged 85,000 during the 1840s and 1850s. In Virginia alone, then, 440,000 people were ripped from communities where their families had lived for three or four generations. In all, by 1860, more than 1 million slaves had been forced to leave the Upper South (Figure 12.2).

This movement of African Americans took two forms: transfer and sale. Looking for new opportunities, thousands of Chesapeake and Carolina planters—men like James Lide—sold their plantations and moved to the Southwest with their slaves. Many other planters in the Old South signed over slaves to their sons and daughters, who migrated west. This transfer of entire or partial plantations accounted for about 40 percent of the African Americans migrants. The rest—about 60 percent of the total migration of more than 1 million slaves—were "sold south." By 1860 a majority of African Americans lived and worked in the New South, the vast lands that stretched from Georgia to Texas.

The Coastal and Inland Networks. Just as the Atlantic slave trade was a major industry in the eighteenth century, so the domestic slave trade was a great commercial enterprise in the nineteenth century. The trade took two forms: a coastal system through the Atlantic seaports and inland commerce using river and roads. Beginning in the late eighteenth century, French settlers in the hot lowlands of Louisiana set up sugar plantations; and even before Louisiana became a state in 1812, hundreds of American planters had joined them. Sugar was a "killer" crop, and Louisiana (like the West Indies) soon had a reputation among African Americans "as a place of slaughter," where hundreds of field workers died each year. Moreover, the ratio of men

The Internal Slave Trade

Mounted whites escort a convoy of slaves from Virginia to Tennessee in Lewis Miller's *Slave Trader, Sold to Tennessee* (1853). For white planters, the interstate trade in slaves was lucrative; it pumped money into the declining Chesapeake economy and provided young workers for the expanding plantations of the cotton belt. For blacks it was a traumatic journey, a new Middle Passage that broke up their families and communities. Abby Aldrich Rockefeller Folk Art Center, Williamsburg, VA. Gift of Dr. and Mrs. Richard M. Kain in memory of George Hay Kain.

to women was severely skewed — with 130 men for every 100 women — and slave fertility remained low. Planters constantly needed new workers.

To meet the insatiable demand for male labor in the sugar fields, slave traders developed a coastal network. They scoured the countryside near the port cities of the Chesapeake and the Carolinas — Baltimore, Alexandria, Richmond, Charleston — searching, as one of them put it, for "likely young men such as I think would suit the New Orleans market." Each year, hundreds of young muscular slaves passed through the auction houses of the port cities bound for the massive trade mart in New Orleans. Because this traffic in laborers was highly visible, it elicited widespread condemnation by northern abolitionists.

The inland trade in slaves for the Cotton South was less visible but much more extensive. To some extent, it also relied on professional slave traders, who went from one rural village to another buying "young and likely Negroes." The traders then marched their purchases in coffles — columns of slaves bound to one another — to Alabama, Mississippi, and Missouri in the 1830s and to Arkansas and Texas in the 1850s. One slave described the arduous journey: "Dem Speculators would put the chilluns in a wagon usually pulled by oxens and de older folks was chained or tied together sos dey could not run off." Once a coffle reached its destination, the trader would offer slaves for sale "at every village in the county."

Established Chesapeake and Carolina planters provided the inland slave trade with its human cargo. Some planters sold slaves when poor management or their "own extravagances" threw them into debt. "Trouble gathers thicker and thicker around me," Thomas B. Chaplin of South Carolina lamented in his diary, "I will be compelled to send about ten prime Negroes to Town on next Monday, to be sold." Many more planters speculated in slaves: They earned substantial profits by traveling south to sell some of their slaves and those of their neighbors. As prices soared during the cotton boom of the 1850s, one owner noted, a slave that "wouldn't bring over $300, seven years ago, will fetch $1000, cash, quick, this year." Exploiting this demand for laborers, Thomas Weatherly of South Carolina drove his surplus slaves to Hayneville, Alabama, where he lived "in his tents" and "sold ten negroes last week at fair prices." Colonel E. S. Irvine, a member of the South Carolina legislature and "a highly respected gentleman" in white circles, likewise traveled frequently "to the west to sell a drove of Negroes."

The domestic slave trade was crucial to the prosperity of the southern economy. Obviously, it provided tens of thousands of workers to carve new cotton plantations out of the forests of the Gulf states. But equally important, the trade bolstered the economy of the Upper South. By selling their surplus workers, tobacco, rice, and grain planters in the Chesapeake and Carolinas added about 20 percent to their income from the sale of agricultural goods. The domestic trade in slaves, remarked a Maryland newspaper, served as "an almost universal resource to raise money."

The Impact on Slave Families. For African American families, the domestic slave trade was a disaster that accentuated their status — and vulnerability — as property. On this issue, black and white commentators were in full agreement As W. C. Pennington,

The Business of Slavery

In the 1850s, Virginia slaves were still being "sold South." The painting above, *Slave Auction in Richmond, Virginia* (1852), captures the pensive and apprehensive emotions of the enslaved women and the discontent of the man, none of whom can control their fate. Whites — plantation overseer, slave trader, top-hatted aristocratic planter — lurk in the background, where they are completing the commercial transaction. The illustration to the right, a public notice for a slave auction to be held in Iberville, Louisiana, advertises "24 Head of Slaves" as if they were cattle — a striking statement on the business of slavery. The Granger Collection, New York / Library of Congress.

a former slave, reflected, "The being of slavery, its soul and its body, lives and moves in the chattel principle, the property principle, the bill of sale principle." The slave's earnings "belong to *me*," a South Carolina master boasted, "because I bought him." There was an "immense amount of capital which is invested in slave property," declared Henry Clay in 1839. "It is owned by widows and orphans, by the aged and infirm, as well as the sound and vigorous. It is the subject of mortgages, deeds of trust, and family settlements." The Whig politician concluded: "I know that there is a visionary dogma, which holds that negro slaves cannot be the subject of property. I shall not dwell long on this speculative abstraction. That is property which the law declares to be property."

As a slave owner, Clay knew that property rights were key to slave discipline. As one master put it, "I govern them . . . without the whip by stating . . . that I should sell them if they do not conduct themselves as I wish." The threat was effective. "The Negroes here dread nothing on earth so much as this," an observer in Maryland noted. "They regard the south with perfect horror, and to be sent there is considered as the worst punishment that could be inflicted on them."

The sheer size of the domestic trade meant that it touched thousands of families and destroyed about one in every four slave marriages. "I am Sold to a man by the name of Peterson a trader," lamented a Georgia slave. "My Dear wife for you and my Children my pen cannot Express the griffe I feel to be parted from you all." And the

BY HEWLETT & RASPILLER,

On Saturday, 14th April, inst.

At 1-2 12 o'clock, at Hewlett's Exchange,

WILL BE SOLD,

24 HEAD OF SLAVES,

Lately belonging to the Estate of Jno. Erwin, of the parish of Iberville. These Slaves have been for more than 10 years in the country, and are all well acclimated, and accustomed to all kinds of work on a Sugar Plantation. There are among them a first rate cooper, a first rate brick maker, and an excellent hostler and coachman. They will be sold chiefly in families.

TERMS.----One year's credit, payable in notes endorsed to the satisfaction of the vendor, and bearing mortgage until final payment. Sales to be passed before Carlisle Pollock, Esq. at the expense of the purchasers.

Fielding, aged 27 years, field hand,
Sally, aged 24 do. field hand and cook,
Levi, aged 26 years, cooper and field hand,
Aggy, do. 24 do. house servant and field hand.
James, do. 6 do.
Emeline, do. 8 do.
Stephen, do. 3 do.
Priscilly, do. 1 do.
Bill, aged 24 years, field hand,
Leah, do. 22 do. field hand,
Rosette, do. 3 do.
Infant child.
Alfred, aged 22 years, brick maker, servant and field hand,
Charlotte, do. 20 years, house servant and field hand,
Infant.
Forrester, aged 41 years, hostler, house servant and field hand,
Mary, aged 22 years, field hand and cook.
Infant.
Harry, aged 24 years, field hand,
Charity, aged 24 years, field hand,
Polly, aged 22 years, house servant and seamstress,
Sam, aged 2 years.
Bedford, aged 14 years, field hand,
Mahaly, aged 12 years, field hand,

---

trade was not limited to adults: Planters sold many slaves as they reached maturity, separating them forever from their families. "Dey sole my sister Kate," Anna Harris remembered decades later, "and I ain't seed or heard of her since." The trade also separated almost a third of all slave children under the age of fourteen from one or both of their parents. Sarah Grant remembered, "Mamma used to cry when she had to go back to work because she was always scared some of us kids would be sold while she was away." Well she might worry, for slave traders worked quietly and fast. "One night I lay down on de straw mattress wid my mammy," Vinny Baker recalled, "an' de nex' mo'nin I woke up an' she wuz gone." When their owner sold seven-year-old Laura Clark and ten other children from their plantation in North Carolina, Clark sensed that she would see her mother "no mo' in dis life."

Despite these sales, 80 percent of slave marriages remained unbroken, and the majority of children lived with one or both parents until puberty. Consequently, the sense of family among African Americans remained strong. Sold from Virginia to Texas in 1843, Hawkins Wilson carried with him a detailed mental picture of his

family and kin. Twenty-five years later and now a freedman, Wilson set out to find his "dearest relatives" in Virginia. "My sister belonged to Peter Coleman in Caroline County and her name was Jane. . . . She had three children, Robert Charles and Julia, when I left — Sister Martha belonged to Dr. Jefferson. . . . Sister Matilda belonged to Mrs. Botts."

During the intervening quarter century, Laura Clark, Hawkins Wilson, and thousands of other African Americans constructed new lives for themselves in the Mississippi River Valley. Undoubtedly, many of these forced migrants did so with a sense of foreboding: They knew from experience that at any moment, their lives could be shaken to the core. Like Charles Ball, some "longed to die, and escape from the bonds of my tormentors." Even moments of joy were shadowed by the darkness of slavery. When enslaved men and women married in a Christian ceremony, the rites rarely ended with the customary phrase "until death do you part." Knowing that sales often ended slave marriages, a white minister blessed one couple "for so long as God keeps them together."

That a substantial majority of African American marriages endured allowed slave owners to see themselves as benevolent masters, committed to the welfare of "my family, black and white." Some masters gave substance to this paternalist ideal by treating with kindness various "loyal and worthy" slaves — the drivers, the mammy who raised their children, and trusted house servants. By safeguarding the families of these slaves from sale, many planters convinced themselves that they "sold south" only "coarse" troublemakers and uncivilized slaves who had "little sense of family." Other owners were more honest about the impact of their pursuit of economic gain. "Tomorrow the negroes are to get off" to Kentucky, a slave-owning woman in Virginia wrote to a friend, "and I expect there will be great crying and mourning, with children Leaving there mothers, mothers there children, and women there husbands."

Whether or not they acknowledged the slaves' pain, few southern whites questioned the morality of the domestic trade in slaves. As a committee of the Charleston City Council declared in response to abolitionist criticism, slavery was completely consistent "with moral principle and with the highest order of civilization," as was "the removal of slaves from place to place, and their transfer from master to master, by gift, purchase, or otherwise."

The Dual Cultures of the Planter Elite

Westward movement had a profound impact on the small elite of extraordinarily wealthy planter families who stood at the top of southern society. These families — about three thousand in number — each owned more than one hundred slaves and huge tracts of the most fertile lands. Their ranks included many of the richest families in the entire United States. On the eve of the Civil War, nearly two-thirds of all American men with wealth of $100,000 or more were southern plantation owners.

The plantation elite consisted of two distinct groups: the traditional aristocrats in the Old South, who had grown rich planting tobacco and rice and who lived in large and impressive mansions; and the market-driven entrepreneurs in the New South, whose wealth came from the booming cotton industry and who usually lived in relatively modest houses.

Slave-owning Aristocrats. With the increase in tobacco and rice production that occurred around 1700, a wealthy planter elite came to dominate the social and political life of the Tidewater region of the Chesapeake and the low country of South Carolina and Georgia. During the eighteenth century, these planters adopted the manners and values of the English landed gentry (see Chapter 3), and their aristocratic culture survived the republican revolution of 1776. Classical republican theorists had long identified political tyranny as a major threat to liberty, and southern aristocrats, who feared government interference with their property in slaves, embraced this ideological outlook. To prevent despotic rule by democratic demagogues or radical legislatures, planters demanded that authority rest in the hands of incorruptible men of "virtue."

Indeed, affluent planters cast themselves as the embodiment of this ideal — a republican aristocracy (see Chapter 8). "The planters here are essentially what the nobility are in other countries," declared James Henry Hammond of South Carolina. "They stand at the head of society & politics . . . [and form] an aristocracy of talents, of virtue, of generosity and courage." Most of these planters criticized the increasingly democratic polity and egalitarian society, especially as they were developing in the Northeast and Midwest. "Inequality is the fundamental law of the universe," declared one would-be aristocrat. Others condemned professional politicians as "a set of demagogues" and questioned the legitimacy of universal suffrage. "Times are sadly different now to what they were when I was a boy," lamented South Carolinian

David Gavin. Then, the "Sovereign people, alias mob" had little power; now they vied for power with the elite. How can "I rejoice for a freedom," Gavin demanded to know, "which allows every bankrupt, swindler, thief, and scoundrel, traitor and seller of his vote to be placed on an equality with myself?"

To maintain their exclusivity, their very identity, aristocratic planters married their sons and daughters to one another and taught them to follow in their footsteps — the men working as planters, merchants, lawyers, newspaper editors, and ministers, and the women hosting plantation balls and church bazaars. To confirm their social preeminence, they lived extravagantly and entertained graciously. James Henry Hammond built a Greek Revival mansion with a center hall 53 feet by 20 feet, its floor embellished with stylish Belgian tiles and expensive Brussels carpets. "Once a year, like a great feudal landlord," a guest recounted, Hammond "gave a fete or grand dinner to all the country people."

As the nineteenth century progressed, rice planters remained at the apex of the plantation aristocracy. In 1860, the fifteen proprietors of the vast plantations in All Saints Parish in the Georgetown District of South Carolina owned 4,383 slaves, who annually grew and processed 14 million pounds of rice. As cheaper rice from Asia entered the world market and cut the profit margins of Carolina planters, they sold some slaves and worked the others harder — two strategies that allowed them to sustain their luxurious lifestyle. The "hospitality and elegance" of Charleston and Savannah greatly impressed savvy English traveler John Silk Buckingham. Buckingham likewise found "polished" families among long-established French Catholic planters in New Orleans and along the Mississippi River. There, "the sugar and cotton planters live in splendid edifices, and enjoy all the luxury that wealth can impart" (see Voices from Abroad, "Bernhard, Duke of Saxe-Weimar-Eisenach: The Racial Complexities of Southern Society," p. 372).

In tobacco-growing regions, the lives of the planter aristocracy followed a different course, in part because of the widespread diffusion of slave ownership. In the 1770s, about 60 percent of white families in the Chesapeake region owned at least one African American slave. The subsequent westward migration of thousands of wealthy planters and their slaves created a tobacco-growing economy in which families that owned between five and twenty slaves played an increasingly important role. The descendants of the old planter aristocracy remained influential in the Chesapeake, but increasingly as slave-owning grain farmers, lawyers,

A Louisiana Plantation, 1861

This view of a southern Louisiana plantation by Marie Adrien Persac, a French-born artist, presents an exquisitely detailed but romanticized vision of the planter lifestyle. Well-dressed slaves stand amid neatly spaced rows of cotton as the women of the household prance by on well-groomed horses. Off to the right, smoke rises from the chimneys of a small mill, probably used to process the sugarcane grown elsewhere on the plantation. Louisiana State University Museum of Art.

merchants, industrialists, and politicians. Those slaves they didn't need for their own businesses, they hired out, sold, or allowed to purchase their freedom.

Although this genteel planter aristocracy flourished primarily around the periphery of the South — in Virginia, South Carolina, and Louisiana, its members took the lead in defending slavery as a benevolent social system. Ignoring the old Jeffersonian defense of slavery as a "necessary evil" (see Chapter 8), southern apologists now maintained that slavery was a "positive good" that allowed a civilized lifestyle for whites and provided tutelage for genetically inferior Africans. "As a race, the African is inferior to the white man," declared Alexander Stephens, the future vice president of the Confederacy. "Subordination to the white man, is his normal condition." Stephens and other apologists depicted planters and their wives as aristocratic models of "disinterested benevolence," who provided food and housing for their workers and cared for them in old age. Declared one wealthy Georgian: "Plantation government should be eminently patriarchal"; the planter, as "the *pater-familias*, or head of the family, should, in one sense, be the father of the whole concern, negroes and all."

Taking this ideology to heart, many planters intervened increasingly in the lives of their slaves. Some built cabins for their workers and insisted they be whitewashed regularly. Many others supervised the religious activities of their laborers. They welcomed evangelical preachers, built churches on

Bernhard, Duke of Saxe-Weimar-Eisenach

The Racial Complexities of Southern Society

In 1825 and 1826, Bernhard, Duke of the German principality of Saxe-Weimar-Eisenach, traveled throughout the United States; and in 1828, he published an account of his adventures. Subsequently, Bernhard compiled a distinguished military record in the service of the king of the Netherlands and then ruled his principality from 1853 until his death in 1862. In this selection from his Travels, Bernhard notes the migration to the cotton belt and describes the racial intricacies of New Orleans society.

[On our way to New Orleans] we met several parties of emigrants from the eastern sections of Georgia on their way to Butler County in Alabama. They proposed to settle on lands that they had acquired very cheaply from the federal government. The number of their Negroes, horses, wagons, and cattle showed that these wanderers were well off.

In New Orleans we were invited to a subscription ball. These affairs are held twice a week, on Tuesdays and Fridays, in the same hall, the French theater. Only good society is invited to these balls. The first to which we came was not very well attended; but most of the ladies were very nice looking and well turned out in the French manner. Their clothing was elegant after the latest Paris fashions. They danced very well and did credit to their French dancing masters. Dancing and some music are the main branches of the education of a Creole woman. . . .

The native men are far from matching the women in elegance. And they stayed only a short time, preferring to escape to a so-called "Quarterons Ball" which they find more amusing and where they do not have to stand on ceremony. There were, as a result, soon many more women than men.

A "quarteron" (octoroon) is the offspring of a mestizo mother and a white father, just as the mestizo is the child of a mulatto and a white man. The "quarterons" are almost completely white. There would be no way of recognizing them by their complexion, for they are often fairer than the Creoles. Black hair and eyes are generally the signs of their status, although some are quite blond. The ball is attended by the free "quarterons." Yet the deepest prejudice reigns against them on account of their colored origin; the white women particularly feel or affect to feel a strong repugnance to them.

Marriage between colored and white people is forbidden by the laws of the state. Yet the "quarterons," for their part, look upon the Negroes and mulattoes as inferiors and are unwilling to mix with them. The girls therefore have no other recourse than to become the mistresses of white men. The "quarterons" regard such attachment as the equivalent of marriage. They would not think of entering upon it other than with a formal contract in which the man engages to pay a stipulated sum to the mother or father of the girl. The latter even assumes the name of her lover and regards the affair with more faithfulness than many a woman whose marriage was sealed in a church.

Some of these women have inherited from their fathers and lovers, and possess considerable fortunes. Their status is nevertheless always very depressed. They must not ride in the street in coaches, and their lovers can bring them to the balls in their own conveyances only after nightfall. They must never sit opposite a white lady, nor may they enter a room without express permission. . . . But many of these girls are much more carefully educated than the whites, behave with more polish and more politeness, and make their lovers happier than white wives their husbands. And yet the white ladies speak of these unfortunate depressed creatures with great disdain, even bitterness. Because of the depth of these prejudices, many fathers send their daughters, conceived after this manner, to France where good education and wealth are no impediments to the attainment of a respectable place.

SOURCE: C. J. Jeronimus, ed., Travels by His Highness Duke Bernhard of Saxe-Weimar-Eisenach Through North America in the Years 1825 and 1826, trans. William Jeronimus (Lanham, Md.: University Press of America, 2001), 296–297, 343, 346–347.

ANALYZING THE EVIDENCE

➤ What does this passage suggest about the effect of racial slavery on white marriages?

➤ Why were France and French fashions so important in the lives of the white and "quarteron" population of New Orleans?

➤ How does Bernhard's account help explain the values and outlook of the free black population in the Slave South?

their plantations, and often required their slaves to attend services. A few encouraged African Americans with spiritual "gifts" to serve as exhorters and deacons. The motives of the planters were mixed. Some acted from sincere Christian belief, while others wanted to counter abolitionist criticism or to use religious teachings to control their workers.

Southern apologists also sought religious justification for human bondage. Protestant ministers pointed out that the Hebrews, God's chosen people, had owned slaves and that Jesus Christ had never condemned slavery. As Hammond told a British abolitionist in 1845: "What God ordains and Christ sanctifies should surely command the respect and toleration of man." Many apologists and wealthy planters lived in towns or were absentee landlords, and rarely glimpsed the day-to-day brutality of the slave regime. "I was at the plantation last Saturday and the crop was in fine order," an absentee's son wrote to his father, "but the negroes are most brutally scarred & several have run off."

Slave-owning Entrepreneurs. There was much less hypocrisy and far less elegance among the entrepreneurial slave owners of the Cotton South. "The glare of expensive luxury vanishes" in the black soil regions of Alabama and Mississippi, John Silk Buckingham noted as his travels took him to inland areas, and so, too, did aristocratic paternalism. A Mississippi planter put it plainly: "Everything has to give way to large crops of cotton, land has to be cultivated wet or dry, negroes [must] work, hot or cold." Angry at being separated from their kinfolk and pressed to hard labor, many slaves grew "mean" and stubborn. Those who would not labor were subject to the lash. "Whiped all the hoe hands," Alabama planter James Torbert wrote matter-of-factly in his journal. Overseers pushed their workers equally hard because their salaries usually depended on the quantity of cotton they were able "to make for the market." "When I wuz so tired I cu'dnt hardly stan'," a Mississippi slave recalled, "I had to spin my cut of cotton befor' I cu'd go to sleep. We had to card, spin, an' reel at nite."

Cotton was a demanding crop because of its long growing season. Slaves plowed the land in March, dropped seeds into the ground in early April, and, once the plants began to grow, continually chopped away the surrounding grasses. In between these tasks, they planted the corn and peas that would provide food for them and the plantation's hogs and chickens. When the cotton bolls ripened in late August, the long four-month picking season began. Slaves in the Cotton South, concluded traveler Frederick Law Olmsted, worked

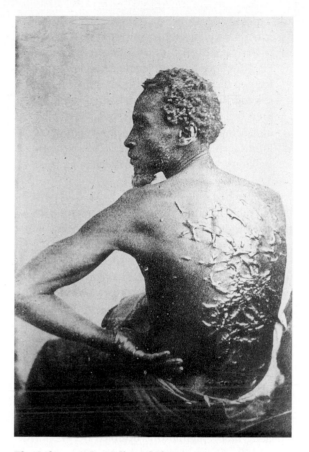

The Inherent Brutality of Slavery

Like all systems of forced labor, American racial slavery relied on physical coercion. Slave owners and overseers routinely whipped slaves who worked slowly or defied their orders. On occasion, they applied the whip with such ferocity that the slave died or was permanently injured. This photograph of a slave named Gordon stands as graphic testimony to the inherent brutality of the system. National Archives.

"much harder and more unremittingly" than those in other regions. Moreover, their labor demanded fewer skills: No coopers were needed to make casks for tobacco or sugar; no engineers to build the irrigation systems for the rice fields.

To increase the output of their enslaved workers, profit-conscious cotton planters began during the 1820s to use a rigorous **gang-labor system**. Previously, many planters had either supervised their workers sporadically, or assigned them random jobs and let them work at their own pace. Now masters with twenty or more slaves organized disciplined teams, or "gangs," supervised by black drivers and white overseers. They instructed drivers and overseers to use the lash to work the gangs at a steady pace, clearing and plowing land or hoeing and picking cotton. A traveler in Mississippi described two gangs returning from work:

> First came, led by an old driver carrying a whip, forty of the largest and strongest women I ever saw together; they were all in a simple uniform dress of a bluish check stuff, the skirts reaching little below the knee; . . . they carried themselves loftily, each having a hoe over the shoulder, and walking with a free, powerful swing.

Next marched the plow hands with their mules, "the cavalry, thirty strong, mostly men, but a few of them women." Finally, "a lean and vigilant white overseer, on a brisk pony, brought up the rear."

The cotton planters' quest for profits and their use of gang labor to expand cotton production had mixed results. Cotton monoculture and the failure to rotate crops quickly depleted the nutrients in the soil and gradually reduced the output per acre. Still, because slaves working in gangs finished as much work in thirty-five minutes as yeomen farmers or enslaved blacks did in an hour when working in the traditional way, the new system produced impressive profits and became ever more prevalent. In one Georgia county, the percentage of slaves working on gang-labor plantations doubled between 1830 and 1850. Their increased productivity brought great wealth to the planter class as the demand for, and the price of, raw cotton surged after 1846. During the 1850s, the number of planters using gang labor increased by 70 percent and their wealth soared. And no wonder: Nearly 2 million enslaved African Americans now labored on the plantations of the Cotton South which annually produced 4 million bales of the valuable fiber.

Planters, Smallholding Yeomen, and Tenants

Despite the fact that the South was a "slave society" — that is, the institution of slavery affected all aspects of life there — most white southerners did not own slaves. The absolute number of slave owners increased constantly between 1800 and 1860; however, the white population of the South rose even faster. Consequently, the percentage of white families who held blacks in bondage continually went down — from 36 percent in 1830, to 31 percent in 1850, to about 25 percent a decade later. There were significant variations among the regions in most states. In some cotton-rich counties, 40 percent or more of the white families owned slaves; in the hill country near the Appalachian Mountains, the proportion dropped to 10 percent.

Among the privileged minority of 395,000 families who owned slaves in 1860, there was a strict hierarchy. The top one-fifth of these families — a planter elite that constituted just 5 percent of the South's white population — owned twenty or more slaves; together, they owned over 50 percent of the entire slave population of 4 million, and their plantations grew 50 percent of the South's cotton crop. These planters had an average wealth of $56,000; by contrast, the average southern yeoman or northern farmer owned property worth $3,200.

A group of substantial proprietors, another fifth of the slave-owning population, held title to six to twenty bondsmen and -women. These "middle-class" planters played a substantial role in the slave society: They owned almost 40 percent of the slave population and produced more than 30 percent of the cotton. Many of these planters pursued dual careers as skilled artisans or professional men. Thus, many of the fifteen slaves owned by Samuel L. Moore worked in his brick factory; the others labored on his Georgia farm. In Macon County, Alabama, James Tolbert owned a plantation that yielded 50 bales of cotton a year; but Tolbert also ran a sawmill, "which pays as well as making Cotton." Dr. Thomas Gale used the income from his medical practice to buy a Mississippi plantation that annually produced 150 bales of cotton. In Alabama, a young lawyer named Benjamin Fitzpatrick invested the profits from his law office to buy ten slaves.

Many other lawyers joined Fitzpatrick as slave-owning planters, and some became influential politicians. Scattered widely among the small towns of the Cotton South, lawyers became wealthy by handling the legal affairs of elite planters, representing merchants and storekeepers in suits for debt, and settling disputes over property. They also became well known by helping smallholders and tenants register their deeds and contracts. Standing at the legal crossroads of their small towns and personally known by many of the residents, lawyers regularly won election to public office. Less than 1 percent of the male population, lawyers made up 16 percent of the Alabama legislature in 1828 and an astounding 26 percent in 1849.

Less visible than the wealthy grandees and the prominent middle-class lawyer-planters were the smallholders who made up the majority of slave owners. Because they worked the land themselves, they were similar in many respects to the yeomen in the North. These slave owners held from one to five black laborers in bondage and claimed title to a few hundred acres of land. Some smallholders were well-connected young men, who would rise to wealth when the death of a father or another benefactor blessed them with more land and slaves. Others were poor men trying to pull themselves up by their bootstraps, often with the encouragement of elite planters and proslavery advocates. "Ours is a pro-slavery form of Government, and the pro-slavery element should be increased," declared a Georgia newspaper. "We would like to see every white man at the South the owner of a family of negroes."

Taking this advice to heart, ambitious men saved or borrowed enough to acquire more land and more laborers. Many achieved modest prosperity. One German settler in Alabama reported in 1855 that "nearly all his countrymen" who emigrated with him were now slaveholders. "They were poor on their arrival in the country; but no sooner did they realize a little money than they invested it in slaves" and grew rich from their labors.

Influenced by the patriarchal ideology of the planter class, these yeomen farmers ruled their smallholdings with a firm hand. According to a South Carolina judge, the male head of the household had authority over all the dependents — wives, children, and slaves — and the legal right on his property "to be as churlish as he pleases." The wives of southern yeomen had very little power. Like women in the North, they lost their legal identity when they married and had many fewer legal rights than male citizens did. Looking for ways to express their concerns and interests, southern women turned to religion in huge numbers, and regularly outnumbered male church members by a margin of two to one. Many welcomed the message of spiritual equality preached in evangelical Baptist and Methodist churches; they hoped that the church communities would hold their husbands to the same standards of Christian faith and action to which they themselves were held. Still, most churches supported patriarchal rule and encouraged their female members to continue in "wifely obedience," whatever the behavior of their husbands. Thus, the Gum Branch Baptist Church refused to aid a member who "wished to attend church but . . . was prevented . . . by her husband."

Whatever the extent of their authority within the household, most yeomen lived and died hardscrabble farmers. They worked alongside their slaves in the fields, struggled to make ends meet as their families grew, and moved regularly in search of opportunity. Thus, in 1847, James Buckner Barry left North Carolina with his new wife and two slaves to settle in Bosque County, Texas. There he worked part-time as an Indian fighter while his slaves toiled on his drought-ridden farm and barely kept the family in food. In South Carolina, W. J. Simpson struggled for years planting cotton on his small farm before he gave up. He hired out one of his two slaves and went to work as an overseer on his father's farm.

Other smallholders fell from the privileged ranks of the slave-owning classes. Selling their land and slaves to pay off debts, they joined the large group of propertyless tenants who farmed the estates of wealthy landlords. In 1860, in Hancock County, Georgia, there were fifty-six slave-owning planters and three hundred propertyless white farm laborers and factory workers; in Hart County, 25 percent of the white farmers were tenants. Across the South, about 40 percent of the white population worked as tenants or farm laborers; as the *Southern Cultivator* noted, they had "no legal right nor interest in the soil [and] no homes of their own."

Propertyless whites enjoyed few of the benefits of slavery and suffered many of its ill consequences. Because hard labor was deemed fit only for enslaved blacks, white workers received little respect. Nor could they hope for a better life for their children because planters refused to pay taxes to fund public schools. Moreover, wealthy slave owners bid up the price of slaves, depriving white laborers and tenants of easy access to the slave labor required to accumulate wealth. Finally, planter-dominated legislatures forced all white men — whether they owned slaves or not — to serve in the patrols and militias that deterred black uprisings. For their sacrifices, poor whites gained only the psychological satisfaction that they ranked above blacks. In the words of Alfred Iverson, a U.S. senator from Georgia, a white man "walks erect in the dignity of his color and race, and feels that he is a superior being, with the more exalted powers and privileges than others." Hoping to reinforce this sense of racial and social superiority, planter James Henry Hammond told his poor white neighbors, "In a slave country every freeman is an aristocrat."

Rejecting that half-truth, many southern whites fled planter-dominated counties and sought farms in the Appalachian hill country and beyond — in western Virginia, Kentucky, Tennessee, Missouri, and the southern regions of Illinois and Indiana. There they took up lives as yeomen farmers, using family labor to grow foodstuffs for sustenance. To obtain cash or store credit to buy agricultural implements, cloth, shoes, salt, and other necessities, yeomen families sold their surplus crops, raised hogs for market sale, and — when the price of cotton rose sharply in the 1850s — a few bales of cotton. Their goals were modest: On the family level, they wanted to preserve their holdings and secure enough new land to set up all of

Starting Out in Texas

Thousands of white farmers, some owning a few slaves, moved onto small farms in Texas and Arkansas during the 1840s and 1850s. They lived in crudely built log huts; owned a few cows, horses, and oxen; and eked out a meager living by growing a few acres of cotton in addition to their corn crops. Their aspirations were simple: to achieve modest prosperity during their lives and to leave their property to their children. Daughters of the Republic of Texas Library.

their children as small-scale farmers. As citizens, these smallholders wanted to control local governments by electing men of their own kind to public office. Thoughtful yeomen knew, and others sensed, that the cotton revolution of the nineteenth century had undercut the democratic potential of the Revolutionary era and sentenced independent family farmers of the South to a subordinate place in the social and political order. They could hope for a life of independence and dignity only by moving north or farther west, where labor was "free" and hard work was considered respectable.

The Politics of Democracy

Despite their economic and social prominence, the slave-owning elite did not dominate the political life of the Cotton South. Unlike the planter-aristocrats of the eighteenth century, they lived in a republican society with democratic institutions. The Alabama Constitution of 1819 granted suffrage to all white men; it also provided for a **secret ballot**, apportionment based on population, and the election of county supervisors, sheriffs, and clerks of court. Given this democratic ethos, political factions in Alabama had to compete with one another for popular favor. When a Whig newspaper sarcastically asked whether the state's policies should "be governed and controlled by the whim and caprice of the majority of the people," Democrats immediately stood forth as champions of the common folk. They called on "Farmers, Mechanics, laboring men" to repudiate Whig "aristocrats . . . the soft handed and soft headed gentry."

Cultivating Popular Support. To curry favor among voters, Alabama Democrats nominated candidates and endorsed low taxes and other policies that would command popular support. The Whigs, their opponents in the Second Party System, continued to advocate government support for banks, canals, roads, and other internal improvements; but they also turned to candidates who appealed to the common people. Most candidates from both parties were men of wealth and high status. In the early 1840s, nearly 90 percent of Alabama's legislators owned slaves, testimony to the power of the slave-owning minority. Still, relatively few lawmakers — only about 10 percent — were rich planters, a group voters by and large distrusted. "A rich man cannot sympathize with the poor," declared one candidate. Consequently, the majority of elected state officials, like most county officials in the Cotton South, came from the ranks of middle-class planters and planter-lawyers.

Whatever their social rank, Alabama's legislators usually enacted policies that reflected the interests of the slave-owning population. Still, they were careful not to alienate the mass of yeomen farmers and propertyless whites by proposing too many of the expensive public works projects favored by the Whig Party. "Voting against appropriations is the safe and popular side," one senator declared, and his colleagues agreed; until the 1850s, they rejected most of the bills that would have granted subsidies to railroads, canals, and banks. They also took care not to lay "oppressive" taxes on the people, particularly the poor white majority, those who owned no slaves. Between 1830 and 1860, the Alabama legislature extracted about 70 percent of the state's revenue from taxes on slaves and on land. Another 10 to 15 percent came from levies on carriages, gold watches, and other luxury goods, and on the capital invested in banks, transportation companies, and manufacturing enterprises.

Taxes in Alabama had a democratic thrust and placed the burden on those best able to pay; but the policies pursued by other southern states divided the white population along lines of class and geography. In some states, wealthy planters used their political influence to exempt slave property from taxation. They shifted the tax burden to backcountry yeomen farmers by taxing land on the basis of acreage rather than value. Planter-legislators also spared themselves the cost of building fences around their fields by enacting laws that forced yeomen to fence in their livestock. Moreover, by the 1850s, wealthy legislators throughout the South began to encourage economic development by subsidizing canals and railroads and increasing allocations for public education.

Seen from one perspective, these measures were desperately needed. Even as the top 10 percent of the white population grew rich from the cotton, rice, tobacco, and sugar produced by their slaves, the economic well-being of ordinary southerners — white and black — did not improve significantly. In fact, the South's standard of living fell behind that of the North. Both in 1840 and in 1860, the per capita wealth of the South was only 80 percent of the national average, while that in the industrializing Northeast was 139 percent of the average.

Yet this comparison with the Northeast is a bit misleading. If the South had been a separate nation, its economy would have been the fourth most prosperous in the world, with a per capita income higher than that of France and Germany. It ranked second in the world in the construction of railroads, sixth in cotton textiles, and eighth in the smelting of pig iron. As a contributor to a Georgia newspaper argued in the 1850s, it was beside the point to protest "tariffs, and merchants, and manufacturers" because "the most highly prosperous people now on earth, are to be found in these very [slave] States."

The paradox of the southern economy is that he was both right and wrong. Many white southerners lived better than other peoples of the world did, but most African Americans — 30 percent of the population — did not. Perceptive southerners recognized that their farm-based economy failed to raise the living standards of the entire population. Pointing to South Carolina's fixation on an "exclusive and exhausting" system of agriculture, textile entrepreneur William Gregg asked, "Who can look forward to the future destiny of our State . . . without dark forebodings?" Other leaders acknowledged the South's predicament but blamed it on outsiders: "Purely agricultural people," intoned planter-politician James Henry Hammond, "have been in all ages the victims of rapacious tyrants grinding them down."

Attempts at Economic Diversification. Thinking like Hammond's discouraged purposeful private or government action to create a more diversified economy; so did the booming market in cotton. Wealthy southerners continued to invest in land and slaves, a strategy that brought substantial short-run profits but diverted capital resources and entrepreneurial energies from more-productive forms of economic activity. In particular, southerners failed to take advantage of the many opportunities created during the early nineteenth century by a series of technological innovations — water- and steam-powered factories, machine tools, steel plows, and macadamized roads, for example—that would have raised the region's productivity. Urban growth took place mostly in the commercial cities around the periphery of the South: New Orleans, St. Louis, and Baltimore. Factories—often staffed by slave labor—likewise appeared primarily in the Chesapeake, which had already diversified its economy and had a surplus of bound workers. Within the Cotton South, a few wealthy planters invested in railroads but only to open up new lands for commercial farming; when the Western & Atlantic Railroad reached the Georgia upcountry, the cotton crop quickly doubled. Cotton—and agriculture—remained "King."

Slavery worked in yet another way to deter industrialization. Fearing competition from slave labor, poor European immigrants refused to settle in the South, depriving the region of the laborers needed to drain swamps, dig canals, smelt iron, and work on railroads. Nor were there enough enslaved African Americans to undertake these tasks because slave owners often refused to rent their slaves to entrepreneurs. The work was dangerous, they said, and "a negro's life is too valuable to be risked at it." Other slave owners feared the work would make their slaves too independent. As one of them explained to Frederick Law Olmsted, rented-out workers "had too much liberty . . . and got a habit of roaming about and taking care of themselves."

Thus, despite the South's expansion in territory and exports, in 1860, it remained an economic colony of Great Britain and the North, which bought its staple crops and provided its manufactures, financial services, and shipping facilities. Most southerners—some 84 percent—still worked in agriculture, more than double the percentage in the northern states; and southern factories turned out only 10 percent of the nation's manufactured goods. Textile entrepreneur William Gregg lamented that the combination of cotton and slave labor had been to the South

> what the mines of Mexico were to Spain. It has produced us such an abundant supply of all the luxuries and elegances of life, with so little exertion on our part, that we have become enervated, unfitted for other and more laborious pursuits.

> ➤ How would you explain the large and expanding domestic trade in slaves between 1800 and 1860? What combination of factors produced this result?

> ➤ By 1860, what different groups made up the South's increasingly complex society? How did these groups interact in the political arena?

> ➤ Why in 1860 did the South remain committed to the institution of slavery and its expansion?

The African American World

By the 1820s, the cultural life of most slaves was a complex blend of African and American influences. It was shaped in part by the values and customs of their West African ancestors and in part by the language, laws, and religious beliefs of the dominant white society. Because blacks were denied access to the way of life in that society, they relied heavily on forms of cultural expression that reflected their African heritage and their condition as an enslaved people.

Evangelical Black Protestantism

The emergence of a black form of evangelical Christianity exemplified the synthesis of African and American cultures. Evangelical Protestantism came to the South in the late eighteenth century with the Second Great Awakening and the conversion by Baptist and Methodist preachers of thousands of white families and hundreds of enslaved blacks (see Chapter 8). Until that time, African-born blacks, often identifiable by their ritual scars, had maintained the religious practices of their homelands: Some practiced Islam, and the majority gave homage to African gods and spirits. As late as 1842, Charles C. Jones, a Presbyterian minister, noted that many of the blacks on his family's plantation in Georgia believed "in second-sight, in apparitions, charms, witchcraft . . . [and other] superstitions brought from Africa." Fearing "the consequences" for their own souls if they withheld "the means of salvation from them," Jones and other zealous white Protestant preachers and planters set out to save African American souls for Christ.

Other Protestant crusaders came from the ranks of pious black men and women. Converted in the Chesapeake and then swept off to the Cotton South by the domestic slave trade, they carried the evangelical message of emotional conversion, ritual baptism, and communal spirituality with them. Equally important, they adapted Protestant doctrines to black needs. Enslaved Christians pointed out that masters and slaves were all "children of God" and should be dealt with according to the Golden Rule—treat others as you would be treated by them. Moreover, black preachers generally ignored the doctrines of original sin and predestination as well as biblical passages that encouraged unthinking obedience to authority. A white minister in Liberty County, Georgia, reported that when he urged slaves to obey their masters, "one half of my audience deliberately rose up and walked off" (see Reading American Pictures, "How Did Slaves Live on Cotton Plantations?" p. 381).

Indeed, many African American converts saw themselves as "de people dat is born of God" and envisioned the deity as the Old Testament warrior who had liberated the Jews. Charles Davenport, a Mississippi slave, recalled black preachers' "exhort[ing] us dat us was the chillum o' Israel in de wilderness an' de Lawd done sont us to take dis lan' o' milk an' honey." And it was a vision of Christ

that impelled Nat Turner to lead a bloody rebellion against slavery in Virginia (see Chapter 11).

Although they now worshipped a European Christian god, slaves expressed their religiosity in distinctively African ways. The thousands of African Americans who joined the Methodist Church respected its ban on secular dancing but praised the Lord in the African-derived "ring shout." Minister Henry George Spaulding explained the "religious dance of the Negroes" this way:

Three or four, standing still, clapping their hands and beating time with their feet, commence singing in unison one of the peculiar shout melodies, while the others walk around in a ring, in single file, joining also in the song.

Plantation Burial, 1860

This painting by John Antrobus, who came to America from England in 1850, records the religious service following the death of an enslaved African American. A black preacher intones a prayer as the coffin is lowered into the ground. The burial comes at twilight, when the day's work is done, and friends and kin from neighboring plantations can attend. The Historic New Orleans Collection.

The songs themselves were usually collective creations, devised impromptu from bits of old hymns and tunes. Recalled an ex-slave:

> We'd all be at the "prayer house" de Lord's day, and de white preacher he'd splain de word and read whar Esekial done say — *Dry bones gwine ter lib ergin.* And, honey, de Lord would come a-shinin' thoo dem pages and revive dis ole nigger's heart, and I'd jump up dar and den and holler and shout and sing and pat, and dey would all cotch de words and I'd sing it to some ole shout song I'd heard 'em sing from Africa, and dey'd all take it up and keep at it, and keep a-addin' to it, and den it would be a spiritual.

By African-influenced means, black congregations devised a distinctive and joyous brand of Protestant worship to sustain them on the long journey to emancipation and the Promised Land. "O my Lord delivered Daniel," the slaves sang, "O why not deliver me too?"

Slave Society and Culture

Black Protestantism represented one facet of an increasingly homogeneous African American culture in the rural South. Even in South Carolina — a major point of entry for recently imported slaves — only 20 percent of the black residents in 1820 had been born in Africa. The rapid transfer of slaves from other regions into the Lower Mississippi Valley significantly reduced cultural differences. A prime example was the fate of the Gullah dialect (see Chapter 3). Long spoken by residents of the Carolina low country, Gullah did not take root on the cotton plantations of Alabama and Mississippi, where there were many more speakers of the black English spoken in the Chesapeake region. Black English, like Gullah, used double-negatives and other African grammatical forms but consisted primarily of English words rendered in an African manner (for example, with "th" spoken as "d" — "de preacher").

Although the black population was becoming more homogeneous, African cultural influences remained important. At least one-third of the slaves who entered the United States between 1776 and 1809 came from the Congo region of West-Central Africa, and they brought their culture with them. One traveler, Isaac Holmes, reported in 1821: "In Louisiana, and the state of Mississippi, the slaves . . . dance for several hours during Sunday afternoon. The general movement is in what they call the Congo dance." Similar descriptions of blacks who "danced the Congo and sang a purely African song to the accompaniment of . . . a drum" appeared as late as 1890.

Marriage and Kinship Relations. African Americans also continued to respect African incest taboos by shunning marriages between cousins. On the Good Hope Plantation on the Santee River in South Carolina, nearly half of the slave children born between 1800 and 1857 were related by blood to one another, yet only one marriage (out of forty-one) took place between cousins. This taboo was not learned from their white owners: Among the 440 South Carolina men and women who owned at least one hundred slaves in 1860, cousin marriages were frequent, in part because they kept wealth and political power within the extended family.

Unlike the marriages of whites, slave unions were not recognized by the law. Southern legislatures and courts prohibited legal marriages among slaves so that they could be sold without breaking a legal bond. Still, many young African Americans did have their marriage blessed by a Christian minister. Others marked their married state by following the African custom of jumping over a broomstick together in a public ceremony (see Reading American Pictures, "Jumping the Broomstick: Viewing an African Ceremony in South Carolina," p. 88). Once married, young couples in the Cotton South whose parents had remained behind in the Chesapeake often adopted elderly slaves in their new communities as their "aunts" and "uncles." The slave trade had destroyed their family but not their family values.

The creation of fictive kinship networks was part of a complex community-building process. Naming children was another. Recently imported slaves frequently gave their children African names. Males born on Friday, for example, were often called Cuffee — the name of that day in several West African languages. Many American-born parents chose names of British origin, but they usually named sons after fathers, uncles, or grandfathers, and daughters after grandmothers. Those transported to the Cotton South often named their children for relatives left behind. Like incest rules and marriage rituals, this intergenerational sharing of names solidified memories of a lost world and kinship ties in the present one.

By forming stable families and strong communities, African Americans gradually created a sense of order in the harsh and arbitrary world of slavery. Slaves in a few regions won substantial control over their lives. Blacks in the rice-growing lowlands of

How Did Slaves Live on Cotton Plantations?

What was it like to live as a slave on a large cotton plantation? Historians can consult a mass of evidence to answer this question: the testimonials of escaped slaves, the recollections of former slaves, masters diaries, travelers' accounts, and contemporary engravings and photographs. These two images tell a very small part of the story, and, like all historical sources, have to be carefully examined for bias and reliability.

ANALYZING THE EVIDENCE

➤ Who is harvesting the cotton in the photograph? Slaves of all ages, male and female, worked at picking cotton. Although the work was physically demanding, children had an advantage. Why? Notice the posture of the adult pickers. What were the physical effects of working like this all day?

➤ How would you describe the religious service pictured in the engraving *Family Worship in a Plantation in South Carolina*? How is the audience reacting to the minister's message? Is it significant that the minister is black? How do we know that he is literate?

➤ Whites are present in both images: an overseer in the photograph, and the master and mistress of the plantation and their children in the engraving. What is the effect of their presence on the African American workers and worshippers? What is the posture of the white onlookers? Is it significant? Why or why not?

Picking Cotton. National Archives.

Family Worship at a Plantation in South Carolina. *The Illustrated London News*/Picture Research Consultants & Archives.

➤ Would either of these images have been useful to abolitionists to support their demands for immediate emancipation? Would either image have furthered the cause of authors who extolled slavery? Imagine you are an advocate first of abolition and then of slavery. How would you fashion an argument using these pictures as evidence?

Antebellum Slave Quarters

During the colonial period, owners often housed their slaves in communal barracks by gender. In the nineteenth century, slaves usually lived in family units in separate cabins. The slave huts on this South Carolina plantation were sturdily built but had few windows. Inside, they were sparsely furnished. William Gladstone.

South Carolina successfully asserted the right to labor by the "task" rather than to work under constant supervision. Each day, task workers had to complete a precisely defined job — for example, turn over a quarter-acre of land, hoe half an acre, or pound seven mortars of rice. By working hard, many finished their tasks "by one or two o'clock in the afternoon," a Methodist preacher reported, and had "the rest of the day for themselves, which they spend in working their own private fields . . . planting rice, corn, potatoes, tobacco &c. for their own use and profit." Slaves on sugar and cotton plantations were less fortunate. The gang-labor system imposed a regimented work schedule, and many owners prohibited slaves from growing crops on their own. "It gives an excuse for trading," explained one slave owner, and that encouraged roaming.

Resistance. Planters worried constantly that enslaved African Americans — a majority of the population in the counties of the Cotton South — would rise in rebellion. They knew that in law, masters had virtually unlimited power over their slaves. Justice Thomas Ruffin of the North Carolina Supreme Court wrote in a decision in 1829: "The power of the master must be absolute to render the submission of the slave perfect." But absolute power required unremitting and brutal coercion, and only the most hardened or most sadistic master had the stomach for that, especially as slave prices rose.

Moreover, African American resistance seriously limited masters' power. Slaves slowed the pace of work by feigning illness and losing or breaking tools. Some blacks insisted that people be sold "in families." One Maryland slave, faced with transport to Mississippi and separation from his wife, "neither yields consent to accompany my people, or to be exchanged or sold," his owner reported. Because of the bonds of community among African Americans in the Chesapeake and Carolinas and the increasing black majorities in the Gulf states — masters ignored slaves' resistance at their peril. A slave (or his relatives) might retaliate by setting fire to the master's house and barns, poisoning his food, or destroying crops or equipment. Fear of resistance, as well as the increasingly critical scrutiny of abolitionists, prompted many masters to reduce their reliance on the lash. Instead, they tried to devise "a wholesome and well regulated system" of work discipline and to use positive incentives like food and special privileges to manage their laborers. Noted Frederick Law Olmsted: "Men of sense have discovered that it was better to offer them rewards than to whip them." Nonetheless, owners always had the option of resorting to

CLASS No. 1.

Comprises those prisoners who were found guilty and executed.

Prisoners Names.	Owners' Names.	Time of Commit.	How Disposed of.
Peter	James Poyas	June 18	
Ned	Gov. T. Bennett,	do.	Hanged on Tuesday
Rolla	do.	do	the 2d July, 1822,
Batteau	do.	do.	on Blake's lands,
Denmark Vesey	A free black man	22	near Charleston.
Jessy	Thos. Blackwood	23	
John	Elias Horry	July 5	Do on the Lines near
Gullah Jack	Paul Pritchard	do.	Ch.; Friday July 12.
Mingo	Wm. Harth	June 21	
Lot	Forrester	27	
Joe	P. L. Jore	July 6	
Julius	Thos. Forrest	8	
Tom	Mrs. Russell	10	
Smart	Robt. Anderson	do.	
John	John Robertson	11	
Robert	do.	do.	
Adam	do.	do.	
Polydore	Mrs. Faber	do.	Hanged on the Lines
Bacchus	Benj. Hammet	do.	near Charleston,
Dick	Wm. Sims	13	on Friday, 26th
Pharaoh	— Thompson	do.	July.
Jemmy	Mrs. Clement	18	
Mauidore	Mordecai Cohen	19	
Dean	— Mitchell	do.	
Jack	Mrs. Purcell	12	
Bellisle	Est. of Jos. Yates	18	
Naphur	do.	do.	
Adam	do.	do.	
Jacob	John S. Glen	16	
Charles	John Billings	18	
Jack	N. McNeill	22	
Cæsar	Miss Smith	do.	Do. Tues. July 30.
Jacob Stagg	Jacob Lankester	23	
Tom	Wm. M. Scott	24	
William	Mrs. Garner	Aug. 2	Do. Friday, Aug. 9.

"An Account of the Late Intended Insurrection, Charleston, South Carolina"

Charleston had a free black population of 1,500, which boasted an array of institutions, including a Brown Fellowship Society (for those of mixed racial ancestry) and an African Methodist Episcopal (AME) church. In 1822, Charleston authorities accused one of those free African Americans, Denmark Vesey, of organizing a rebellion to free the city's slaves, and historians have long accepted the validity of that charge. However, recent studies suggest that Vesey's only offense was antagonizing some whites by claiming his rights as a free man, and that the alleged insurrection was a figment of the imagination of fearful slave owners. In any event, South Carolina officials hanged Vesey and thirty-four alleged co-conspirators and tore down the AME church where they were said to have plotted the uprising. Rare Book, Manuscript & Special Collections, Duke University Library.

violence, and many masters continued to satisfy themselves sexually by raping their female slaves.

Slavery, then, remained an exploitative system grounded in fear and coercion. Over the decades, hundreds of individual slaves responded to this violence by attacking their masters and overseers. Blacks like Gabriel and Martin Prosser in Virginia (1800) plotted mass uprisings, but only a few—among them, Nat Turner (1831),—mounted revolts that

took revenge on their white captors. Most slaves recognized that uprisings would be futile. In most states they were outnumbered by whites, and everywhere they lacked the strong institutions—the communes of free peasants or serfs in Europe, for example—needed to organize a successful rebellion. Moreover, whites were well armed, unified, and determined to maintain their position of racial superiority (see Comparing American Voices, "Slaves and Masters," pp. 384–385).

Escape was equally problematic. Blacks in the Upper South could flee to the North, but only by leaving their family and kin. Slaves in the Lower South could seek freedom in Spanish Florida until 1819, when the United States annexed that territory. Even then, hundreds of blacks continued to flee to Florida, where they intermarried with the Seminole Indians. Elsewhere in the South, small groups of escaped slaves eked out a meager existence in deserted marshy areas or in mountain valleys.

Given these limited options, most slaves built the best possible lives for themselves on the plantations where they lived. In doing so, they developed a positive mode of resistance by demanding and, in many cases, winning a greater share of the product of their labor—much like unionized workers in the North were trying to do. Slaves insisted on getting paid for "overwork" and on the right to cultivate a garden and sell its produce. "De menfolks tend to de gardens round dey own house," recalled a Louisiana slave. "Dey raise some cotton and sell it to massa and git li'l money dat way." They then bought what they wished with the proceeds. An Alabama slave remembered buying "Sunday clothes with dat money, sech as hats and pants and shoes and dresses." By the 1850s, thousands of African Americans were reaping the rewards of this underground economy. But even as their material circumstances improved, few slaves accepted the legitimacy of their fate. Although well fed and never whipped, a former slave explained, "I was cruelly treated because I was kept in slavery."

The Free Black Population

Some African Americans managed to escape slavery through flight or manumission. The proportion of free blacks rose from 8 percent of the African American population in 1790 to about 13 percent between 1820 and 1840, and then fell to 11 percent by 1860. Nearly half of all free blacks in 1840 (some 170,000) and again in 1860 (250,000) lived in the North. Many of those African Americans were refugees from the South, either runaway

Slaves and Masters

Looked at closely, slavery was a multitude of individual relationships between African Americans and their white owners. But it was also a system of chattel property, forced labor, sexual abuse, and racial domination. As you read these selections, two documents excerpted from interviews with former slaves and one diary entry written by a cotton planter, think about how the system of slavery shaped the possibilities open to individuals.

MOLLIE DAWSON
Memories of a Slave Childhood

Mollie Dawson was born into slavery in Texas, where her owner had migrated from Tennessee. At the time Dawson told her story to the Writers' Project of the Work Projects Administration in the 1930s, she was eighty-five years old.

Dat makes me bo'n in january sometime, of 1852.... Mah maw was de slave of Nath Newman and dat made me his slave. Mah maw's name was Sarah Benjamin. Mah father's name was Carrol Benjamin, and he belonged ter different white folks....

De plantation dat he worked on was j'inin' our'n. I would go ovah ter see him once in a while when I was little, and de last time I goes ovah dar dey whips a man.... Dat was the only slave I ever seed gits a whippin', and I never did wants ter see dis white man anymo'....

Mah mother and father was slavery time married darkies. Dat didn't mean nuthin' dem days, but jest raisin' mo' darkies, and every slave darkie woman had ter do dat whether she wanted to or not. Dey would let her pick out a man, or a man pick him out a woman, and dey was married, and if de woman wouldn't have de man dat picks her, dey would take her ter a big stout high husky nigger somewhere and leave her a few days, jest lak dey do stock now'days, and she bettah begin raisin' chilluns, too....

Mah mother and father never did love each other lak dey ought to, so dey separated as soon as dey was free. Mah father married another woman by law. Mah mother married George Baldwin, and dey lives together fer about twelve years. Dey separated den, and she married Alfred Alliridge and dey lives together till she dies....

I was too young ter do much work durin' slavery time, but I picks lots of cotton, and all de pay we got fer it was a place ter stay, water ter drink, wood ter burn, food ter eat, and clothes ter wear, and we made de food and clothes ourselves. We eats corn pones three times a day, 'ceptin' Sunday and Christmas mornings; Maser Newman lets us have flour fer biscuits, den.

In de summah we wore cotton clothes. All of dem was made on de plantation. Some of de women would spin and some would weave and some would make clothes....

Maser Newman was a tall, slender man nearly six foot tall and was blue-eyed. He sho' was good ter all us slaves, but we all knew he means fer us ter work. He never whipped any of us slaves, but he hit one of de men wid a leather line 'bout two times once, 'cause dis slave kinda talked back ter him....

Maser Newman was a slow easy-goin' sort of a man who took everything as it comes, takin' bad and good luck jest alak.... Maser Newman was lots older dan his wife. She was a real young woman, and they 'peared ter think quite a bit of each other.... Maser and Missus Newman jest had two chilluns and both of dem was little girls.... Dey sho' was pretty little gals and dey was smart, too. Dey played wid de little slave chilluns all de time, and course dey was de boss, same as deir mother and father.

Maser Newman was a poor man, compared wid some of de other slave owners. He only had about seven slaves big enough ter work all de year round in de fields.... He didn't have no drivah; he would jest start dem all out ter work, and dey kept at it all day. But he generally worked around pretty close ter dem.

SOURCE: James Mellon, ed., *Bullwhip Days* (New York: Weidenfeld & Nicolson, 1988), 421–428.

LOUISA PICQUET
Sexual Exploitation under Slavery

Louisa Picquet was born into slavery in Georgia in 1827; around 1840, she became the property of a John Williams of New Orleans. On his death in 1848, she was freed and moved to Ohio with her four children. In 1860, she related the story of her life in an interview with Hiram Mattison, a white abolitionist minister, who published it the following year in Boston.

Q: How did you say you come to be sold?

A: Well, you see, Mr. Cook [my master] made great parties, and go off to watering-places, and get in debt, and had to break up, and then he took us to Mobile, and hired the most of us out, so the men he owe could not find us, and sell us for the debt. Then, after a while, the sheriff came from Georgia after Mr. Cook's debts, and found us all, and took us to auction, and sold us. My mother and brother was sold to Texas, and I was sold to New Orleans.

Q: How old were you, then?

A: Well, I don't know exactly, but the auctioneer said I wasn't quite fourteen. . . .

Q: Were there others there white like you?

A: Oh yes, plenty of them. . . . You see Mr. Cook had my hair cut off. My hair grew fast, and look so much better than Mr. Cook's daughter, and he fancy I had better hair than his daughter, and so he had it cut off to make a difference. . . . Then I was sold. . . . Mr. Williams allowed that he did not care what they bid, he was going to have me anyhow. Then he bid fifteen hundred. Mr. Horton said 'twas no use to bid anymore, and I was sold to Mr. Williams. I went right to New Orleans then.

Q: Who was Mr. Williams?

A: I didn't know then, only he lived in New Orleans. Him and his wife had parted, some way he had three children, boys. When I was going away I heard someone cryin' and prayin' the Lord to go with her only daughter, and protect me.

Q: Have you never seen her [Piquet's mother] since?

A: No, never since that time. I went to New Orleans, and she went to Texas. So I understood.

A: Mr. Williams told me what he bought me for, soon as we started for New Orleans. He said he was getting old, and when he saw me he thought he'd buy me, and end his days with me. He said if I behave myself he'd treat me well; but, if not, he'd whip me almost to death.

Q: How old was he?

A: He was over forty; I guess pretty near fifty. He was grayheaded. That's the reason he was always so jealous. He never let me go out anywhere. . . .

Q: Had you any children while in New Orleans?

A: Yes, I had four.

Q: Who was their father?

A: Mr. Williams. . . .

Q: Were your children mulattoes?

A: No, sir! They were all white. They look just like him. The neighbors all see that.

SOURCE: H. Mattison, Louisa Picquet, *The Octoroon: Or Inside Views of Southern Life* (New York: Published by the Author, 1861), 17–19.

BENNETT BARROW
Enforcing Labor Discipline

Bennett Barrow (1811–1854) inherited a substantial cotton plantation in Louisiana from his father. From 1837 to 1845, he kept a diary that consisted of brief remarks on the day's events, primarily on his plantation.

January 1838

14 Appearance of rain — pressed 7 B.[bales of cotton] last Sunday — pressing to day at Gibsons — will ship on Tuesday next 66 B . . . to Gin — On selling from 5 to 11½ cts. — The times are seriously hard all most impossible to raise one dollar . . . great Excitement in Congress, Northern States medling with slavery — first they com'ced by petition — now by openly speaking of the sin of Slavery in the southern states . . . must eventually cause a separation of the Union.

October 1838

12 Clear verry cold morning — hands picked worse yesterday than they have done this year. . . . Whiped near half the hands to day for picking badly & trashy. . . .

26 Clear pleasant weather — Cotton picks very trashy — Whiped 8 or 10 for weight today. . . .

May 1839

21 Clear verry warm — Finished hilling Cotton — Darcas & Fanny are the greatest shirks of any negroes I have — laid up twicet a month — Went to Town — man tried for whipping a negro to Death. trial will continue till to morrow — deserves death — Cleared!

July 1841

18 . . . Received a note from Ruffin stating that several of my negroes were implicated in an intended insurrection on the 1st of August next. . . . mine are O Fill O Ben Jack Dennis & Demps will go to Robert J. B. to have them examined . . .

27 Cloudy. Verry warm, Negros all Cleared. But will be tried by the Planters themselves &c.

SOURCE: Edwin Davis Adams, *Plantation Life in the Florida Parishes of Louisiana, 1836–1845 as Reflected in the Diary of Bennet H. Barrow* (New York: AMS Press, 1967 [c1943]), 105–106, 133, 135, 148, 236, 237.

ANALYZING THE EVIDENCE

➤ How strong is this evidence? Is there any reason to question its accuracy? Mollie Dawson was eighty-five when she was interviewed. How reliable do you think her memory was? Louisa Picquet's account was published by an abolitionist as an indictment of slavery. Is his account trustworthy? Is Bennett Barrow's diary a more reliable source than the other two? Explain your answer.

➤ Were you surprised by any of these accounts? If so, why? What did they tell you about day-to-day life under slavery that you did not know?

➤ Why do you suppose Picquet was freed in 1848?

A Master Bridge Builder

Horace King (1807–1885) was a self-made man of color, a rare achievement in the South in the nineteenth century. Born a slave of mixed European, African, and Native American (Catawba) ancestry, King built major bridges in Georgia, Alabama, and Mississippi during the early 1840s. After winning his freedom in 1846, he built and ran a toll bridge across the Chattahoochee River in Alabama. During the Civil War, King worked as a contractor for the Confederacy; during Reconstruction, he served two terms as a Republican member of the Alabama House of Representatives. Collection of the Columbus Museum, Columbus, Georgia; Museum purchase.

slaves or, more often, free blacks who feared reenslavement.

Even in the North, few free blacks enjoyed unfettered freedom. Most whites regarded all African Americans as their social inferiors and did all they could to confine them to low economic and political status. In rural areas, free blacks worked as farm laborers or tenant farmers; in towns and cities, they toiled as domestic servants, laundresses, or day laborers. Only a small number of free African Americans owned land. "You do not see one out of a hundred . . . that can make a comfortable living, own a cow, or a horse," a traveler in New Jersey noted. In addition, blacks were usually forbidden to vote, attend public schools, or sit next to whites in churches. Only a few states extended the vote to free blacks, and they could testify against whites in court only in Massachusetts. The federal government did not allow free African Americans to work for the postal service, claim pub-

lic lands, or hold a U.S. passport. Martin Delaney, a black activist, remarked in 1852: "We are slaves in the midst of freedom."

Of the few African Americans who were able to make full use of their talents, several achieved great distinction. Mathematician and surveyor Benjamin Banneker (1731–1806) published an almanac and helped lay out the new capital in the District of Columbia; Joshua Johnston (1765–1832) won praise for his portraiture; and merchant Paul Cuffee (1759–1817) acquired a small fortune from his business enterprises. More impressive and enduring were the community institutions created by the early generations of free African Americans. Throughout the North, they founded schools, mutual-benefit organizations, and fellowship groups, often called Free African Societies. Discriminated against by white Protestants, they formed their own congregations and a new religious denomination — the African Methodist Episcopal Church, headed by Bishop Richard Allen (see Chapter 8).

These institutions gave free African Americans a sense of cultural, if not political, autonomy. They also institutionalized sharp social divisions within the black community. "Respectable" blacks tried through their dress, conduct, and attitude to win the "esteem and patronage" of prominent whites, first Federalists and then Whigs and abolitionists, who were sympathetic to their cause. Those efforts separated them from impoverished blacks, who distrusted whites and those who "acted white."

The free black population in the slave states numbered approximately 94,000 in 1810 and 225,000 in 1860. Most of these men and women lived in coastal cities — Mobile, Memphis, New Orleans — and especially in the Upper South. In Maryland on the eve of the Civil War, half of the black population was free. But that freedom was fragile. Free blacks accused of crimes were often denied a jury trial, and those charged with vagrancy were sometimes forced back into slavery. To prove their free status, African Americans had to carry manumission documents, which did not necessarily protect them from being kidnapped and sold. However, because skilled as well as unskilled Europeans generally refused to migrate to the South, blacks became the backbone of the region's urban artisan workforce. African American carpenters, blacksmiths, barbers, butchers, and shopkeepers played prominent roles in the economies of Baltimore, Richmond, Charleston, and New Orleans.

A privileged group among African Americans, free blacks had divided loyalties. To advance the welfare of their families, they had to distance themselves from plantation slaves and assimilate white culture

An African American Clergyman

This flattering portrait is one of two paintings of African Americans by black artist Joshua Johnston (who also went by the name Johnson). Born into slavery in 1765, Johnston somehow became a free man and a successful artist. In an advertisement in the *Baltimore Intelligence* in 1798, he described himself as a "Portrait Painter . . . a self-taught genius deriving from nature and industry his knowledge of the Art." Merchant families in Maryland and Virginia held Johnston's work in high regard and commissioned most of his thirty or so extant works.

Bowdoin College Museum of Art, Brunswick, Maine. Museum purchase, George Otis Hamlin Fund.

and values. In fact, some privileged blacks adopted the perspective of the planter class. David Barland, one of twelve children born to a white Mississippi planter and his black slave Elizabeth, owned no fewer than eighteen slaves. In neighboring Louisiana, some free blacks supported secession because they "own slaves and are dearly attached to their native land."

But these men were exceptions. Most free African Americans acknowledged their unity with the great mass of impoverished slaves, which usually included some of their relatives. "We's different [from whites] in color, in talk and in 'ligion and beliefs," said one. White planters reinforced unity among blacks by justifying slavery as a "positive good" and, by the 1840s and 1850s, calling for the reenslavement of free African Americans. Knowing their own liberty was not secure so long as slavery existed, these blacks sought freedom for all those of African ancestry. As a delegate to the National Convention of Colored People in 1848 noted, "Our souls are yet dark under the pall of slavery." Free African Americans in the South—often the offspring of white planters—helped fugitive slaves, while northern blacks supported the antislavery movement. In the rigid caste system of American race relations, free blacks stood as symbols of hope to enslaved African Americans and as symbols of danger to most whites.

➤ Compare the religion and culture of enslaved African Americans with those of the other groups in southern society. What similarities do you find? How were they different?

➤ How do you explain the persistence in America of certain African practices (the ring shout and incest taboos, for example) and the gradual disappearance of others (among them ritual scarring)?

➤ Describe the place of free blacks in America. Where in the South in the mid-nineteenth century would free blacks most likely be found? What kind of work would they have been doing?

SUMMARY

In this chapter, we have seen how the theme of an expanding South ties together two important historical developments. First, there was the rapid expansion of the plantation system from its traditional home in the Upper South to the Mississippi Valley and beyond. Powered by cotton, this movement westward divided the planter elite into aristocratic paternalists and entrepreneurial capitalists, and involved the forced migration or sale of more than 1 million enslaved African Americans.

We also examined in detail the character of white and black societies in the Cotton South. We noted that after 1820, less than a third of white families owned slaves and that another third were yeoman farmers; propertyless tenant farmers and laborers made up the rest. Many of these whites joined evangelical Protestant churches, as did blacks, who infused them with African modes of expression. Indeed, church and family became the core institutions of African American society, providing strength and solace amid the tribulations of slavery.

Connections: Society and Culture

Following the Tobacco and Rice Revolutions around 1700 and the subsequent importation of tens of thousands of enslaved Africans, the South became a dual society. Those of English and African birth shared geographical space but little else. As we discovered in Chapter 3, they spoke different languages, worshipped different gods, and had different legal status. Coercion—forced work and forced sex—was a major factor in most interactions between the two peoples.

This dual society began to break down during the Revolutionary era (see Chapter 8). By 1780, most slaves had been born in America, and most spoke English; some had become Christians; and thousands would soon become free, the result of gradual emancipation in the North and individual manumissions in the Chesapeake region. Coercion remained a potent force in the slave system; but as masters and slaves negotiated work rules, the use of physical force became a measure of last resort for many planters. Thus, as we noted in the essay that opened Part Three (p. 269), it was not surprising that "southern planters increasingly defended slavery as a 'positive good'" and considered slaves to be a part of their extended family.

Of course, as we saw in this chapter, the behavior of most planters contradicted their words. They callously "sold south" hundreds of thousands of African Americans and treated the remaining black members of their "families" far differently than they did their white kin. Still, the social and cultural differences between the two peoples continued to diminish. By the 1840s, slaves spoke black English, practiced black Protestantism, and were on their way to becoming a black peasantry—a dependent agricultural people similar to the oppressed peasant peoples of Ireland and Central Europe. Indeed, as we shall see in Chapter 15, the abolition of slavery following the Civil War and the events of Reconstruction (1865–1877) would leave most African Americans poor sharecroppers, a peasantry in fact if not in name.

CHAPTER REVIEW QUESTIONS

➤ How did plantation crops and the slavery system change between 1800 and 1860? Why did these changes occur?

➤ Based on what you've learned so far in Part Three, compare and contrast society in the American South with that of the North. Is it fair to say that by 1860, America was, in fact, two distinct societies?

TIMELINE

1810s	Africans from Congo region influence black culture
	Natural increase produces surplus of slaves in Old South
	Domestic slave trade expands, disrupting black family life
1812	Louisiana becomes a state, and its sugar production increases
1817	Mississippi becomes a state; Alabama follows (1819)
1820s	Substantial growth in free black population in North and South
	Slave-owning aristocrats in Old South adopt paternalistic ideology
	Entrepreneurial planters in Cotton South turn to gang labor
	Southern Methodists and Baptists become socially conservative
	African Americans adopt Christian beliefs
1830s	Advocates of slavery argue it is a "positive good"
	Boom in cotton production
	Percentage of slave-owning families falls
	Yeomen farm families retreat to hill country
	Lawyers become influential in southern politics
1840s	Southern Whigs advocate economic diversification
	Gradual emancipation completed in North
1850s	Price of slaves and cotton rises, and production expands
	Southern states subsidize railroads, but industrialization remains limited

FOR FURTHER EXPLORATION

Charlene M. Boyer Lewis explores the lives of the planter class in *Ladies and Gentlemen on Display: Planter Society at the Virginia Springs, 1790–1860* (2001). Three other recent studies of slave owners are: William Kauffman Scarborough, *Masters of the Big House: Elite Slaveholders of the Mid-Nineteenth-Century South* (2003); Jeffrey Robert Young, *Domesticating Slavery: The Master Class in Georgia and South Carolina, 1670–1837* (1999); and James David Miller, *South by Southwest: Planter Emigration and Identity in the Slave South* (2002). For a look into the intellectual life of planters, see Michael O'Brien, *Conjectures of Order: Intellectual Life and the American South, 1810–1860* (2004). The story of Edward Ball's attempt to come to terms with his slaveholding ancestors appears in his *Slaves in the Family* (1998), winner of a National Book Award. For an audio interview recounting Ball's search for the slaves' descendants go to **www.albany.edu/talkinghistory/arch2000july-december .html**. Stephanie McCurry's *Masters of Small Worlds: Yeomen Households, Gender Relations, and the Political Culture of the Antebellum South Carolina Low Country* (1995) offers a brilliant analysis of yeomen families. For plantation discipline, see Sally E. Hadden, *Slave Patrols: Law and Violence in Virginia and the Carolinas* (2001), and John Hope Franklin and Loren Sweninger, *Runaway Slaves, Rebels on the Plantation* (1999).

Ira Berlin's *Generations of Captivity: A History of African American Slaves* (2003) offers a stimulating analysis of the changing character of slavery and African American society. See also the Web site to the PBS video on "Slavery and the Making of America" at **www.pbs.org/wnet/slavery/about/ index.html**. For primary documents that illustrate the ways in which African Americans acquired and transformed Protestant Christianity, log on to "Documenting the American South: The Church in the Southern Black Community" at **docsouth .unc.edu/church/index.html**. Marcus Wood, *Blind Memory: Visual Representations of Slavery in England and America, 1780–1865* (2000), offers many images of slave life, while Walter Johnson, *Soul by Soul: Life Inside the Antebellum Slave Market* (1999), closely examines the New Orleans slave mart. Two document-rich Web sites are "The African-American Mosaic" at **www.loc.gov/exhibits/african/intro.html** and "Slaves and the Courts, 1740–1860" at **lcweb2.loc.gov/ammem/aaohtml/**.

TEST YOUR KNOWLEDGE

To assess your command of the material in this chapter, see the Online Study Guide at **bedfordstmartins.com/henretta**.

For Web sites, images, and documents related to topics and places in this chapter, visit **bedfordstmartins.com/makehistory**.

13 The Crisis of the Union
1844–1860

THROUGHOUT THE NATION DURING THE 1850s, crusaders for temperance and abolition faced off against defenders of personal liberties and property rights. The struggle in South Carolina was especially intense. When temperance activists demanded a "Maine law" to prohibit the sale of intoxicants, Randolph Turner, a candidate for the South Carolina assembly, was outraged: "Legislation upon Liquor would cast a shade on my character which as a Caucassian and a white man, I am not willing to bear." Indeed, Turner vowed to shoulder his musket and, along with "hundreds of men in this district, . . . fight for individual rights, as well as State Rights."

In Washington, South Carolina congressman Preston Brooks battled for "Southern Rights." In an inflammatory speech in 1856, Senator Charles Sumner of Massachusetts denounced the South and, mixing invective with metaphor, declared that Senator Andrew P. Butler of South Carolina had taken "the harlot slavery" as his mistress. Outraged by Sumner's verbal attack on his uncle, Brooks accosted the Massachusetts legislator at his desk in the Senate chamber and beat him unconscious with a walking cane. As the impact of Brooks's attack reverberated throughout Washington and the nation, Axalla Hoole of South Carolina and other proslavery migrants in the Kansas Territory leveled their guns

◄ *War News from Mexico, 1848*

In this painting of a crowd gathered on the porch of the "American Hotel" in an unknown town, artist Richard Caton Woodville (1825–1855) captures the public's hunger for news of the Mexican War, the first military conflict with a foreign nation since the War of 1812. As a journalist in Baltimore, Woodville's hometown, noted, "People begin to collect every evening, about 5 o'clock at the telegraph and newspaper offices, waiting for extras and despatches, where they continue even to 12 or 1 o'clock at night, discussing the news that may be received." National Gallery of Art, Washington, D.C.

at an armed force of abolitionist settlers. Passion and violence had replaced political compromise as the hallmark of American public life.

The causes of the upsurge in political violence in the 1850s were complex. The immediate spark was the admission of Texas to the Union in 1845 and the acquisition of vast territories from Mexico in 1848. But at the root of the violence were the increasing differences between northern and southern states, and the resentment and alarm those differences raised in the South. White southerners feared the North's increasing wealth, political power, and moral righteousness, John C. Calhoun explained in 1850, especially its "long-continued agitation of the slavery question."

A massive surge of population in the West accentuated the importance of this sectional conflict. Emboldened by the nation's growing population and wealth, many Americans believed in **Manifest Destiny**—that it was their duty to extend republican institutions to the Pacific Ocean. But whose republican institutions: the aristocratic traditions and practices of the slaveholding South, or the more democratic customs and culture of the reform-minded North and Midwest? The answer to this question would determine the future of the nation. Beginning in 1844, Americans in the North, South, and West took up the challenge of answering it. In doing so, they would rip apart America's political and social institutions and, ultimately, the nation itself.

Manifest Destiny: South and North

The crisis over slavery in Missouri that began in 1819 (see Chapter 8) had frightened the nation's politicians. For the next two decades, the professional politicians who managed the Second Party System avoided policies that would spark another confrontation along regional lines. This strategy worked as long as the geographical boundaries of the United States remained unchanged. But during the 1840s, as the belief in Manifest Destiny led Americans toward the Pacific Ocean, the threat of confrontation loomed again.

The Independence of Texas

By the 1830s, settlers from the Ohio River Valley and the South had carried both yeoman farming and plantation slavery into Arkansas and Missouri. Between those states and the Rocky Mountains stretched the semiarid lands of the Great Plains. An army explorer, Major Stephen H. Long, labeled the area the **Great American Desert** and noted that it was "almost wholly unfit for cultivation." Settlers looking for land, then, turned south, to the Mexican province of Texas.

Although Texas was occupied primarily by Indian peoples and claimed by Spain, it had long been a zone of conflict between European nations. In the eighteenth century, Spanish authorities in Mexico dispatched a few military garrisons to the region, and Texas became a buffer zone against French settlements along the Mississippi River. After the Louisiana Purchase (1803), the Spanish saw the province as a shield against the expansion-minded American republic. Although some adventurers from the United States settled in Texas, the Adams-Onís Treaty of 1819 guaranteed Spanish sovereignty over the region.

Austin Family: Texas Pioneers and Speculators.

After winning independence from Spain in 1821, the Mexican government used lavish land grants to encourage both Mexicans and Americans to move to Texas. One early grantee was Moses Austin, an American land speculator who created a vast estate occupied by white tenants and smallholders. Adopting a paternalistic tone, Austin described the settlers as "one great family who are under my care." His son, Stephen F. Austin, acquired even more land from the Mexican government—some 180,000 acres—which he sold to incoming settlers. Most of these American residents did not assimilate Mexican culture. Equally important, in 1829, Austin and other grantees requested—and won—an exemption from a law ending slavery in Mexico. By 1835, about 27,000 white Americans and 3,000 African American slaves were raising cotton and cattle in eastern and central Texas. They far outnumbered the 3,000 Mexican residents, most of whom lived in the southwestern towns of Goliad and San Antonio (see Map 13.1).

As the Mexican government asserted greater political control over Texas in the 1830s, the American settlers split into two groups. Members of the "peace party," led by Stephen Austin and other longtime settlers, were content with Mexican rule but wanted greater political autonomy for the province; the "war party," headed mostly by recent migrants from Georgia, was demanding independence. Austin again won significant concessions from Mexican authorities. But in 1835, Mexico's president, General Antonio López de Santa Anna, began to strengthen national authority throughout Mexico, and he nullified those concessions. When Santa Anna appointed a military commandant for Texas, the war party provoked a rebellion that most

New York newspapers romanticized the heroism of the Texans and the deaths at the Alamo of folk heroes Davy Crockett and Jim Bowie. Drawing on anti-Catholic sentiment aroused by Irish immigrants in northern cities, American newspapers described the Mexicans as tyrannical butchers in the service of the pope. Hundreds of adventurers, lured by offers of land grants, flocked to Texas to join the rebel army. Led by General Sam Houston, the Texas rebels routed the Mexican army in the Battle of San Jacinto in April 1836, establishing de facto independence. The Mexican government refused to recognize the Texas Republic but abandoned efforts to reconquer it.

The Texans quickly voted by plebiscite for annexation by the United States, but President Martin Van Buren refused to bring the issue before Congress. As a Texas diplomat reported to his government, Van Buren and other American politicians feared that annexation would spark a war with Mexico and, beyond that, a "desperate death-struggle . . . between the North and the South; a struggle involving the probability of a dissolution of the Union."

"The Father of Texas"

Stephen F. Austin (1793–1836) grew up in Missouri, where he worked as the manager of a lead mine and a banker and served in the territory's legislature. In 1822, he established an American colony on the lower Colorado and Brazos rivers in the Mexican province of Texas, where he proudly posed for the original of this engraving. A skilled negotiator, Austin persuaded the Mexican government to allow the unrestricted migration of American planters — and their slaves — into Texas. Texas State Library and Archives Commission.

of the American settlers ultimately supported. On March 2, 1836, the American rebels proclaimed the independence of Texas and adopted a constitution that legalized slavery.

Rebellion and War. President Santa Anna vowed to put down the rebellion personally. On March 6, he led an army that wiped out the rebel garrison defending the Alamo in San Antonio and then took control of Goliad (Map 13.1). Santa Anna thought he had crushed the rebellion, but New Orleans and

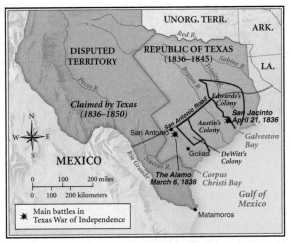

MAP 13.1   American Settlements and the Texas War of Independence

During the 1820s Mexican authorities granted huge tracts of land in Texas to Stephen F. Austin and other land speculators, who were expected to encourage Americans to migrate to Texas and grow cotton. By 1835, the nearly thirty thousand Americans in Texas far outnumbered Mexican settlers. To put down the American revolt, General Santa Anna led an army of six thousand men into Texas in early 1836. After overwhelming the Texans at the Alamo in March, Santa Anna set out to capture the Texas Provisional Government, which had fled to Galveston. But in April, his army was defeated and he was captured at the Battle of San Jacinto by a Texan force commanded by Sam Houston.

SIEGE OF THE ALAMO.

Assault on the Alamo

After a thirteen-day siege, on March 6, 1836, a Mexican army of 4,000 stormed the wall of the small fort—it was originally a Spanish mission—in San Antonio. "The first to climb were thrown down by bayonets ... or by pistol fire," reported a Mexican officer. After a half-hour of continuous and costly assaults, the attackers won control of the wall. This contemporary woodcut shows the fierceness of the battle, which took the lives of all 250 American defenders; 1,500 Mexicans were killed or wounded in the fighting. Archives Division, Texas State Library.

The Push to the Pacific

The annexation of Texas became a more pressing issue in the 1840s, as expansionists in the South and the North developed continental ambitions. The term Manifest Destiny, coined in 1845 by John L. O'Sullivan, the editor of the *Democratic Review*, captured those dreams. As O'Sullivan put it, "Our manifest destiny is to overspread the continent allotted by Providence for the free development of our yearly multiplying millions." Underlying the rhetoric of Manifest Destiny was a sense of American cultural and racial superiority: The "inferior" peoples who lived in the Far West—Native Americans and Mexicans—were to be brought under American dominion, taught republicanism, and converted to Protestantism (see Reading American Pictures, "Marching from the Atlantic to the Pacific: Visualizing Manifest Destiny," p. 396).

Oregon. Residents of the Ohio River Valley were already casting their eyes westward to the fertile lands of the Oregon Country. This region stretched along the Pacific Coast between the Russian-dominated lands of Alaska and the Mexican province of California, and was claimed by both Britain and the United States. Since 1818, a British-American convention had allowed fur traders and settlers from both nations to live in

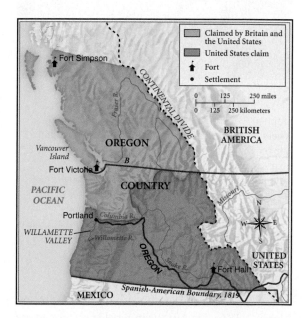

MAP 13.2 Territorial Conflict in Oregon, 1819–1846

As thousands of American settlers poured into the Oregon Country in the early 1840s, British authorities tried to keep them south of the Columbia River. However, the migrants—and fervent midwestern expansionists—asserted that Americans could settle anywhere in the territory, raising the prospect of armed conflict. In 1846, British and American diplomats resolved the dispute by dividing the region at the forty-ninth parallel.

the Oregon Country. The British-run Hudson's Bay Company developed a lucrative fur trade north of the Columbia River, while several hundred Americans settled to the south, mostly in the fertile lands of the Willamette Valley (see Chapter 16). Based on this settlement, the United States claimed ownership of the area between California and the Columbia River (Map 13.2).

In 1842, American interest in Oregon increased dramatically. The U.S. Navy published a glowing report of fine harbors in the Puget Sound, which was welcome news to New England merchants plying the China trade. In the same year, a party of one hundred farmers journeyed along the Oregon Trail, a route fur traders and explorers had blazed through the Great Plains and the Rocky Mountains (Map 13.3). Their reports from Oregon told of a mild climate and fertile soil.

"Oregon fever" suddenly raged. By May 1843, 1,000 men, women, and children—in more than one hundred wagons and with five thousand oxen and cattle—had gathered in Independence, Missouri, for the six-month trek to Oregon. The migrants were mostly yeomen farming families from the southern border states (Missouri, Kentucky, and Tennessee) who were looking for free land and a new life. They overcame flooding streams, dust storms, dying livestock, and a few armed encounters with Indians before they reached the Willamette Valley, a journey of 2,000 miles. Over the next two years, another 5,000 people reached Oregon, and the numbers continued to grow.

By 1860, about 350,000 Americans had braved the Oregon Trail. More than 34,000 of them died in the effort, mostly from disease and exposure; fewer than 500 deaths resulted from Indian attacks. The walking migrants wore three-foot-deep paths, and their wagons carved five-foot-deep ruts across sandstone formations in southern Wyoming— tracks that are visible today. Women found the trail especially difficult because it exaggerated the authority of their husbands, who directed the enterprise, and added the labor of driving wagons and animals to their usual chores. Hundreds of women endured pregnancy or gave birth during the long journey, and some did not survive the ordeal. "There was a woman died in this train yesterday," Jane Gould Tortillott noted in her diary. "She left six children, one of them only two day's old."

California. Some pioneers ended up in the Mexican province of California. They left the Oregon Trail along the Snake River, trudged down the California Trail, and settled in the interior along the Sacramento

MAP 13.3 Routes to the West, 1835–1860

By the 1840s, a variety of trails spanned the arid zone between the ninety-fifth meridian and the Pacific Coast. From the south, El Camino Real linked Mexico City to the California coast and to Santa Fe. From the east, the Mormon, Oregon, and Santa Fe trails carried tens of thousands of Americans from departure points on the Mississippi and Missouri rivers to new communities in Utah and along the Pacific Coast. By the 1860s, both the Pony Express and Butterfield Overland mail routes provided reliable communication between the eastern states and California.

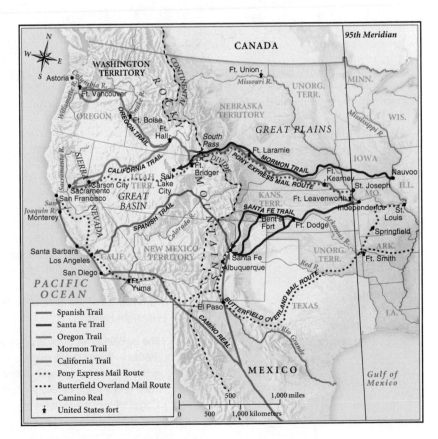

Visualizing Manifest Destiny

American Progress, John Gast. Library of Congress; Picture Research Consultants & Archives.

In 1845, John O'Sullivan, a newspaper and journal editor, coined the term *Manifest Destiny* to describe Americans' sudden — and urgent — longing to migrate westward and extend the boundaries of the nation to the Pacific Ocean. More than a quarter century later, John Gast's painting, *American Progress* (1872), gave visual form to that aspiration and was widely distributed in engravings and lithographs. What do the details of the painting tell us about the meaning of Manifest Destiny?

ANALYZING THE EVIDENCE

➤ The painting is an allegory: The artist uses symbols to depict America's expansion to the Pacific. The central symbol is the goddess Liberty; she floats westward, her forehead emblazoned with the "Star of Empire." Why do you think Gast chose Liberty to lead the republic to the West? What is the significance of the "School Book" in her right hand?

➤ The painting has three horizontal planes — foreground, middle ground, and background — and each tells a separate story. What stages of social evolution are pictured in each plane? What symbols of progress does Gast employ? How is technology depicted? What role does it play in the artistís depiction of progress?

➤ Gast also has divided the painting into two vertical planes. What do you think the transition from lightness to darkness symbolizes?

➤ In the background on the far right stands New York City, with the great Brooklyn Bridge (which was still being built in 1872) spanning the East River. Far off on the left, you can see the Pacific Ocean. Why did Gast include these elements in the painting?

River. The region was sparsely populated by native peoples or Mexicans. California had formed the remote northern corner of Spain's American empire, and Spanish authorities in Mexico established a significant foothold there only in the 1770s, when they built a chain of religious missions and forts (presidios) along the coast. New England merchants soon struck up trade with the Spanish settlers in California, buying sea otter pelts that the merchants then carried to China.

Commerce increased after Mexico won independence from Spain in 1821. To promote California's development, the Mexican government took over the Franciscan-run missions and liberated the twenty thousand Indians who had been induced to work on them. Some mission Indians rejoined their Native American tribes, but many intermarried with mestizos (Mexicans of mixed Spanish and Indian ancestry) and worked as laborers and cowboys on the large cattle ranches that the government in Mexico was promoting.

The rise of cattle ranching linked California to the American economy. New England merchants dispatched dozens of agents westward to buy leather and tallow for use in the booming Massachusetts boot and shoe industry. Many of those resident agents married into the families of the elite Mexican landowners and ranchers—the Californios—and adopted their dress, manners, outlook, and Catholic religion (see Chapter 16). A crucial exception was Thomas Oliver Larkin, the most successful merchant in the coastal town of Monterey. Larkin worked closely with Mexican ranchers, but he remained an American citizen and plotted for the peaceful annexation of California to the United States.

Like Larkin, the American migrants in the Sacramento River Valley did not want to assimilate into Mexican society. Many were squatters or held land grants of dubious legality. Some of them hoped to emulate the Americans in Texas by colonizing the country and then seeking annexation to the United States. However, these settlers numbered only about 700 in the early 1840s; by contrast, 7,000 Mexicans and 300 American traders lived along the coast.

The Fateful Election of 1844

The election of 1844 determined the American government's policy toward California, Oregon, and Texas. Since 1836, when Texas requested annexation, many southern leaders had advocated territorial expansion to extend slavery. Cautious party politicians and northern abolitionists resisted

A Californio Patriarch

The descendant of a Spanish family that had lived — and prospered — in Mexico since the Spanish conquest, Mariano Guadalupe Vallejo (1808–1890) served in Mexican California as a military officer. In the 1820s, he acquired title to 270,000 acres of land in the Sonoma Valley, north of San Francisco. Vallejo, the father of nine children, presents himself in this photograph as a proud patriarch, surrounded by two daughters and three granddaughters. During the American takeover in 1846, he was imprisoned for a short period and then, like many of the Californios, lost most of his vast land holdings to squatters and rival claimants. Bancroft Library, University of California, Berkeley.

their efforts. Now there were rumors that Britain wanted the Mexican government to cede California in payment for large debts owed to British investors. Southern leaders also believed that Britain was encouraging Texas to remain independent and had designs on Spanish Cuba, which some southerners wanted to annex. To thwart possible British schemes, southern expansionists demanded the immediate annexation of Texas.

At this crucial juncture, Oregon fever and Manifest Destiny opened up the possibility of annexing Texas by altering the political and diplomatic landscape in the North. In 1843, Americans in the Ohio River Valley and the Great Lakes states organized "Oregon conventions" that called on the federal government to end joint occupation of the region with Britain. In July, Democratic and Whig politicians met in a bipartisan national convention and demanded that the United States seize Oregon all the way to 54°40′ north latitude, the southern border of Russian Alaska.

With northern Democrats demanding expansion in Oregon, southern Democrats seized the opportunity to champion the annexation of Texas without threatening party unity. Moreover, they had the support of President John Tyler. Disowned by the Whigs because of his opposition to Henry Clay's nationalist economic program, Tyler hoped to win reelection in 1844 as a Democrat. To curry favor among expansionists, Tyler proposed to annex Texas and seize all of Oregon. In April 1844, Tyler and John C. Calhoun, an expansionist and the new secretary of state, sent the Senate a treaty to annex Texas. Two rival presidential candidates, Democrat Martin Van Buren and Whig Henry Clay, quickly declared their opposition. Knowing that annexation would raise the issue of the expansion of slavery and divide the nation, these cautious party politicians persuaded the Senate to defeat the treaty.

Expansion into Texas and Oregon became the central issue in the election of 1844. The Democrats passed over Tyler, whom they did not trust, and Van Buren, whom southerners despised for his opposition to the acquisition of Texas. They selected as their candidate Governor James K. Polk of Tennessee, a slave owner who favored annexation. Widely known as "Young Hickory," Polk was a protégé of Andrew Jackson and, like his mentor, was a man of iron will and boundless ambition for the nation. Accepting the claim of the Democratic Party platform that both areas already belonged to the United States, Polk campaigned for the "Re-occupation of Oregon and the Re-annexation of Texas—the whole of the territory of Oregon" to the Alaskan border. "Fifty-four forty or fight!" became the jingoistic cry of his expansionist campaign.

The Whigs nominated Henry Clay, who again championed his American System of internal improvements, high tariffs, and national banking. Clay initially dodged the issue of Texas but ultimately indicated support for annexation. His evasive position disappointed thousands of northern Whigs and Democrats, who opposed any expansion of slavery. Rather than vote for Clay, they cast their ballots for James G. Birney of the Liberty Party (see Chapter 11). Birney garnered less than 3 percent of the national vote but won enough support among Whigs in New York to cost Clay the state and the national election. By narrowly taking New York's thirty-six electoral votes, Polk won the presidency; without them, he would have lost by a margin of seven votes.

Following Polk's victory, Democrats in Congress called for the immediate annexation of Texas. When Whig opposition denied them the needed two-thirds majority in the Senate to ratify a treaty of annexation with the Republic of Texas, the Democrats approved the deal in February by a joint resolution of Congress, which required just a majority vote in each house. In a matter of months, a convention in Austin drafted a constitution and the people of Texas voted for statehood. On December 29, 1845, Texas joined the Union as the twenty-eighth state. Polk's strategy of linking Texas and Oregon had put him in the White House and Texas in the Union. Shortly, it would make the expansion of the South—and its system of slavery—the central topic of American politics.

➤ Both elected officials and private individuals shaped America's western policy. Which group was more important? Why?

➤ How did western expansion become linked with the sectional conflict between the North and the South? Why, after two decades of hesitation, did politicians support territorial expansion in the 1840s?

War, Expansion, and Slavery, 1846–1850

The acquisition of Texas whetted Polk's appetite. The president now saw an opportunity to assert American control over all Mexican territory between Texas and the Pacific Ocean. Moreover, he was prepared to go to war to get it. What he and the majority of the Democratic Party consciously ignored was the crisis over slavery they would unleash by pursuing this expansionist dream.

The War with Mexico, 1846–1848

Since gaining independence in 1821, Mexico had not prospered. Its stagnant economy yielded few surpluses and modest tax revenues, which were quickly devoured by interest payments on foreign debts and a bloated bureaucracy. The vast and distant northern provinces of California and New Mexico contributed little to the national economy and remained sparsely settled, with a Spanish-speaking population of only 75,000 in 1840. Still, Mexican officials vowed to preserve their nation's historical territories; and when the Texas constitutional convention voted to enter the American

Street Fighting in the Calle de Iturbide, 1846

The American conquest of Monterrey, which Spanish troops had been unable to capture during Mexico's war for independence (1820–1821), came after bloody house-to-house fighting. Protected by thick walls and shuttered windows, Mexican defenders poured a withering fire on the dark-uniformed American troops and buckskin-clad frontier fighters. A large Catholic cathedral looms in the background, its foundations obscured by the smoke from the Mexicans' cannons. West Point Museum, United States Military Academy, West Point, NY. From *The Old West: The Mexican War*, photographed by Paulus Lesser. © 1978 Time-Life Books.

Union on July 4, 1845, Mexico broke off diplomatic relations with the United States.

Polk's Expansionist Program. Taking advantage of this diplomatic rupture, President Polk set into motion his plans to acquire Mexico's far northern provinces. To intimidate the Mexican government, he ordered General Zachary Taylor and an American army of two thousand soldiers to occupy disputed lands between the Nueces River (the historical southern boundary of Texas) and the Rio Grande, which

the Republic of Texas had claimed as its border with Mexico (see Map 13.1, p. 393). Simultaneously, Polk launched a secret diplomatic initiative. He appointed John Slidell, a congressman from Louisiana, as minister to Mexico with instructions to win acceptance of the Rio Grande boundary and to buy the Mexican provinces of California and New Mexico, allotting up to $30 million for the purchase. When Slidell arrived in Mexico City in December 1845, Mexican officials refused to see him, reiterating their position that America's annexation of Texas was illegal. Purchasing

The Bear Flag Republic

When news of the war between the United States and Mexico reached California in June 1846, a group of American settlers captured the Mexican garrison at Sonoma and, raising a crude handmade flag, proclaimed California an independent republic. The star on the flag imitated the lone star of the Texas Republic, and the grizzly bear represented California. The Bear Flag Republic was short-lived; within a few months, American naval and ground forces had taken control of most of California. Society of California Pioneers.

New Mexico and California was now definitely out of the question.

Anticipating the failure of Slidell's mission, Polk had already embarked on an alternative plan. He hoped to foment a revolution in California that, like the rebellion in Texas, would lead to an independent republic and a request for annexation. In October 1845, Secretary of State James Buchanan told merchant Thomas Oliver Larkin, now the U.S. consul in the port of Monterey, to encourage influential Mexican residents to declare independence and support peaceful annexation. To add military muscle to the initiative, Polk ordered American naval commanders to seize San Francisco Bay and California's coastal towns in case of war with Mexico. The president also had the War Department dispatch Captain John C. Frémont and an "exploring" party of heavily armed soldiers into Mexican territory. By December 1845, Frémont had reached California's Sacramento River Valley.

Events now moved quickly toward war. Polk ordered General Taylor toward the Rio Grande to incite an armed response by Mexico. "We were sent to provoke a fight," recalled Ulysses S. Grant, then a young officer serving with Taylor, "but it was essential that Mexico should commence it." When the armies clashed near the Rio Grande in May 1846, Polk delivered the war message he had drafted long before. Taking liberties with the truth, the president declared that Mexico "has passed the boundary of the United States, has invaded our territory, and shed American blood upon the American soil." Ignoring Whig pleas for a negotiated settlement, the Democratic majority in Congress voted for war, a decision that was greeted with great popular acclaim. To avoid a simultaneous conflict with Britain, Polk retreated from "fifty-four forty or fight" and accepted a British proposal to divide the Oregon Country at the forty-ninth parallel.

American Military Successes. American forces in Texas quickly established their military superiority. Zachary Taylor's army crossed the Rio Grande, occupied Matamoros, and, after a fierce six-day battle in September 1846, took the interior Mexican town of Monterrey. Two months later, a U.S. naval squadron in the Gulf of Mexico seized Tampico, Mexico's second most important port. By the end of 1846, the United States controlled much of northeastern Mexico (Map 13.4).

Fighting had also broken out in California. In June 1846, naval commander John Sloat landed 250 marines in Monterey and declared that California "henceforward will be a portion of the United States." Almost simultaneously, American settlers in the Sacramento River Valley staged a revolt and, supported by Frémont's forces, captured the town of Sonoma and proclaimed an independent California—the "Bear Flag Republic." To cement these victories by American marines and settlers, Polk ordered army units to capture Santa Fe in New Mexico and then march to California. Despite stiff Mexican resistance, American forces secured control of California early in 1847.

Polk expected these American victories would end the war, but he had underestimated the Mexicans' national pride and the determination of President Santa Anna. Santa Anna went on the offensive and attacked Taylor's depleted units at Buena Vista in February 1847. Only superior artillery enabled Taylor to hold the American line in northeastern Mexico.

MAP 13.4 The Mexican War, 1846–1848

Departing from Fort Leavenworth in present-day Kansas, American forces commanded by Captain John C. Frémont and General Stephen Kearney defeated Mexican armies in California in 1846 and early 1847. Simultaneously, U.S. troops under General Zachary Taylor and Colonel Alfred A. Doniphan won victories over General Santa Anna's forces far to the south of the Rio Grande. In mid-1847, General Winfield Scott mounted a successful attack on Mexico City, ending the war.

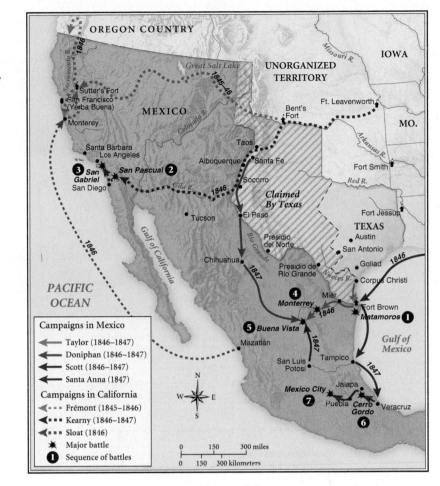

To bring Santa Anna to terms, Polk accepted General Winfield Scott's plan to strike deep into the heart of Mexico. In March 1847, Scott captured the port of Veracruz and began the 260-mile march to Mexico City. Leading Scott's 14,000 troops was a cadre of talented West Point officers who would become famous in the Civil War: Robert E. Lee, George Meade, and P. G. T. Beauregard. Scott's troops crushed Santa Anna's forces at Cerro Gordo and at Churubusco, just outside Mexico City, and seized the Mexican capital in September 1847. Those defeats cost Santa Anna his power, and a new Mexican government agreed to make peace with the United States.

A Divisive Victory

Initially, the war with Mexico sparked an explosion of patriotic support. Politicians and newspaper editors hailed the war as a noble struggle to extend American republican institutions. However, the conflict soon divided the nation. A few Whigs—among them Charles Francis Adams of Massachusetts (the son of President John Quincy Adams) and Joshua Giddings of Ohio—opposed the war from the beginning on moral grounds. Known as **conscience Whigs**, they warned of a southern conspiracy to add new slave states in the West. The expansion of slavery, they argued, would undermine the Jeffersonian ideal of a freeholder society and ensure permanent control of the federal government by slaveholding Democrats. These antislavery Whigs grew bolder after the elections of 1846 repudiated Polk's war policy and gave their party control of Congress.

The Wilmot Proviso. Polk's expansionist agenda split the Democrats into sectional factions. As early as 1839, Democratic senator Thomas Morris of Ohio had warned that "the power of slavery is aiming to govern the country, its Constitutions and laws." In August 1846, David Wilmot, a Democratic congressman from Pennsylvania, took up that refrain. To limit the spread of slavery, Wilmot proposed to prohibit slavery in any territories acquired from Mexico. His proposal rallied antislavery northerners. In the House of Representatives, northern Democratic allies of Martin Van Buren

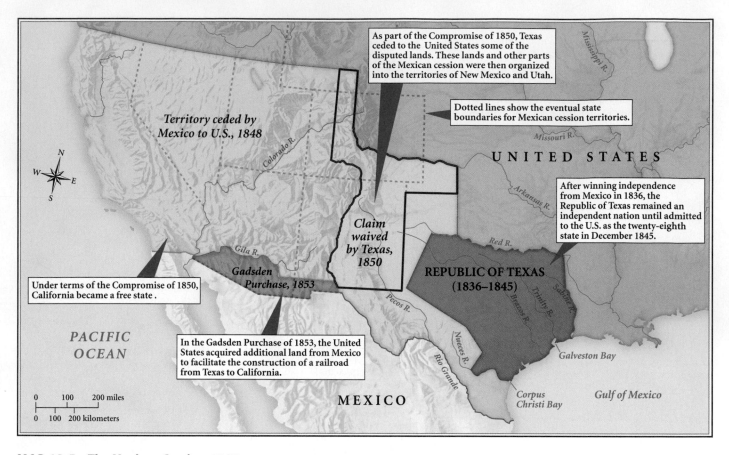

As part of the Compromise of 1850, Texas ceded to the United States some of the disputed lands. These lands and other parts of the Mexican cession were then organized into the territories of New Mexico and Utah.

Dotted lines show the eventual state boundaries for Mexican cession territories.

Territory ceded by Mexico to U.S., 1848

After winning independence from Mexico in 1836, the Republic of Texas remained an independent nation until admitted to the U.S. as the twenty-eighth state in December 1845.

UNITED STATES

Claim waived by Texas, 1850

REPUBLIC OF TEXAS (1836–1845)

Under terms of the Compromise of 1850, California became a free state.

Gadsden Purchase, 1853

In the Gadsden Purchase of 1853, the United States acquired additional land from Mexico to facilitate the construction of a railroad from Texas to California.

PACIFIC OCEAN

Galveston Bay

0   100   200 miles
0   100   200 kilometers

MEXICO

Corpus Christi Bay   *Gulf of Mexico*

MAP 13.5   The Mexican Cession, 1848

In the Treaty of Guadalupe Hidalgo (1848), Mexico ceded to the United States its vast northern territories—the present-day states of California, Nevada, Utah, Arizona, New Mexico, half of Colorado and Texas. These new territories, President Polk boasted to Congress, "constitute of themselves a country large enough for a great empire, and the acquisition is second in importance only to that of Louisiana in 1803."

joined forces with antislavery Whigs to pass the Wilmot Proviso. "The madmen of the North . . . ," declared the *Richmond Enquirer*, "have, we fear, cast the die and numbered the days of this glorious Union." Fearing just such an outcome, the Senate, dominated by southerners and proslavery northern Democrats, killed the proviso.

Fervent Democratic expansionists became even more aggressive. Polk, Secretary of State Buchanan, and Senators Stephen A. Douglas of Illinois and Jefferson Davis of Mississippi called for the United States to take Mexican territory south of the Rio Grande. However, to avoid a longer war and the assimilation of a huge number of Mexicans, John C. Calhoun and other southern leaders insisted that the United States should annex only California and New Mexico, Mexico's most sparsely populated provinces. "Ours is a government of the white man," Calhoun proclaimed, arguing that the United

States had never "incorporated into the Union any but the Caucasian race."

To reunify the Democratic Party before the next election, Polk and Buchanan abandoned their dreams to expand deep into Mexico and accepted Calhoun's policy. In February 1848, Polk signed the Treaty of Guadalupe Hidalgo, in which the United States agreed to pay Mexico $15 million in return for more than one-third of its territory: Texas, New Mexico, and California. The Senate ratified the treaty in March 1848 (Map 13.5).

Free Soil. The passions aroused by the war dominated the election of 1848. The Senate's rejection of the Wilmot Proviso prompted antislavery advocates to revive Thomas Morris's charge of a massive "Slave Power" conspiracy. To thwart any such plan, thousands of ordinary northerners joined a new movement, the **free-soil movement.** To Abijah

Beckwith of Herkimer County, New York, and other yeomen farmers, slavery was an institution of "aristocratic men" and a threat to the liberties of "the great mass of the people." "The curse of slavery," Beckwith told his grandson, "threatens the general and equal distribution of our lands into convenient family farms."

The free-soilers quickly organized as a political party. They abandoned the Liberty Party's emphasis on the sinfulness of slavery and the natural rights of African Americans. Instead, like Beckwith, they depicted slavery as a threat to republican liberties and white yeoman farming. The Wilmot Proviso's call for free soil was the first antislavery proposal to attract broad popular support. Hundreds of women in the Great Lakes states joined the female free-soil organizations formed by the American and Foreign Anti-Slavery Society. The Free-Soilers' shift in emphasis—from freeing slaves toward preserving the West for freehold farms—led abolitionist William Lloyd Garrison to denounce free-soil doctrine as racist "whitemanism."

Frederick Douglass: Political Abolitionist. But Frederick Douglass, the foremost black abolitionist, endorsed the Free-Soil movement. Born to a slave mother on a Maryland plantation in 1818, Douglass grew up as Frederick Bailey. He never knew the identity of his father, though it was undoubtedly his owner, Thomas Auld. Auld had Frederick raised by his brother in Baltimore, where he learned to read and mingled with the free blacks of the city. Later, when Frederick faced deportation to the Deep South for attempting to escape from plantation labor, Auld again intervened. In 1835, he returned Frederick to Baltimore, allowed him to hire himself out as caulker, and promised him freedom in eight years, at the age of twenty-five.

Frederick plunged enthusiastically into the life of Baltimore's free African American community. He courted a free black woman, Anna Murray; joined the East Baltimore Mental Improvement Society; and hatched a plan of escape. In 1838, he borrowed the identification papers of a free African American sailor and sailed to New York City. He took the last name Douglass, married Murray, and settled in New Bedford, Massachusetts. Inspired by Garrison, Douglass began to speak publicly on the issue of slavery and, in 1841, became a lecturer for Garrison's American Anti-Slavery Society. Soon, he became a celebrity. His partly African ancestry drew crowds to his lectures, as did his commanding presence, dramatic rhetoric, and forceful intellect.

In his speeches, Douglass denounced slavery in the South and racial discrimination in the North. Gradually, his views diverged from those of Garrison. To rid America of the sin of slavery, Garrison would expel the southern states from the Union. To Douglass, that policy was madness because it would perpetuate slavery. Rejecting Garrison's moral radicalism, he founded an antislavery newspaper, the *North Star*, and became a political abolitionist—dedicated to using political means and government power to overthrow slavery. In 1848, Douglass attended the Buffalo convention that established the Free-Soil Party and endorsed its political strategy as the best means of confronting the South.

The Election of 1848. The conflict over slavery took a toll on Polk and the Democratic Party. Opposed by Whigs and Free-Soilers and exhausted by his rigorous dawn-to-midnight work regime, Polk refused to run for a second term; he would die just three months after leaving office. In his place, the Democrats nominated Senator Lewis Cass of Michigan, an avid expansionist who had advocated buying Cuba, annexing Mexico's Yucatán Peninsula, and taking all of Oregon. To maintain party unity, Cass took a deliberately vague position on the question of slavery in the West. He promoted a new idea—squatter sovereignty—that would allow settlers in each territory to determine its status as free or slave.

Cass's political ingenuity failed to hold the Democracy together. Demanding unambiguous opposition to the expansion of slavery, some northern Democrats joined the newly formed Free-Soil Party, which nominated Martin Van Buren for president. Van Buren genuinely supported free soil, but he also wanted to punish southern Democrats for denying him the presidential nomination in 1844. To attract Whig votes, the Free-Soilers chose conscience Whig Charles Francis Adams as their candidate for vice president.

To keep their party intact, the Whigs nominated General Zachary Taylor for president. Taylor was a Louisiana slave owner, but he had not taken a position on the charged issue of slavery in the territories. Equally important, the general's military exploits had made him a popular hero. Known as "Old Rough and Ready," Taylor had a common

Frederick Douglass, c. 1848

This daguerreotype of Douglass was made when he was about thirty years old. Describing Douglass, an admirer wrote: "He was more than six feet in height, and his majestic form ... straight as an arrow, muscular, yet lithe and graceful, his flashing eye, and more than all, his voice, that rivaled Webster's in its richness and in the depth ... of Its cadences, made up such an ideal of an orator as the listeners never forgot." Chester County Historical Society.

touch that won him the affection of his troops. "Our Commander on the Rio Grande," wrote Walt Whitman, "emulates the Great Commander of our revolution"—George Washington.

In 1848, as in 1840, running a military hero worked for the Whigs. Taylor took 47 percent of the popular vote to Cass's 42 percent. However, he won a majority in the Electoral College (163 to 127) only because the Free-Soil ticket of Van Buren and Adams deprived the Democrats of enough votes in New York to cost Cass that state and the presidency. The bitter debate over the Wilmot Proviso had fractured the Democratic Party in the North and changed the dynamics of national politics.

1850: Crisis and Compromise

Even before Taylor took office, events in California triggered a new political crisis over slavery. In January 1848, workmen building a mill for John A. Sutter in the Sierra Nevada foothills in northern California discovered flakes of gold. Sutter was a Swiss immigrant who arrived in California in 1839, became a Mexican citizen, and established an estate in the Sacramento River Valley. He tried to keep the discovery a secret; but by May, American settlers from Monterey and San Francisco were pouring into the foothills. When President Polk confirmed the discovery in December, the gold rush was on. By January 1849, sixty-one crowded ships had left from northeastern ports to sail around Cape Horn to San Francisco; by May, twelve thousand wagons had crossed the Missouri River bound for the gold-fields (Map 13.6). In 1849 alone, more than eighty thousand "forty-niners" had arrived in California (see Chapter 16).

Statehood for California. The rapid influx of settlers revived the national debate over free soil. The forty-niners, who lived in crowded, chaotic towns and mining camps, demanded the formation of a territorial government to protect their lives and property. To avoid an extended debate over slavery, President Taylor advised the Californians to apply for statehood immediately; and in November 1849, they ratified a state constitution that prohibited slavery. Taylor had never believed that the defense of slavery in the South required its expansion into the territories. Now, urged on by William H. Seward, the former Whig governor of New York, Taylor tried to strengthen the Whig Party in the North by appealing to Free-Soilers and northern Democrats. As part of this political strategy, he urged Congress to admit California as a free state.

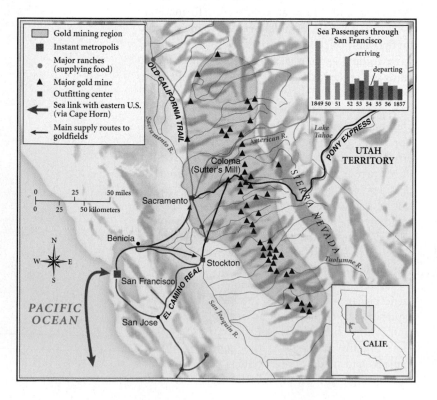

MAP 13.6   The California Gold Rush, 1849–1857

Traveling from all parts of the world—Europe, China, and Australia, as well as the eastern United States—hundreds of thousands of bonanza-seekers converged on the California goldfields. Miners traveling by sea landed at San Francisco, which quickly mushroomed into a substantial city; many other prospectors trekked overland to the goldfields on the Old California Trail. By the mid-1850s, the gold rush was over: Almost as many people were sailing from San Francisco each year as were arriving to seek their fortune.

A ROAD SCENE IN CALIFORNIA.

The Gold Rush Creates a Mix of Peoples

This well-composed drawing, sketched by German-born artist and California prospector Charles Nahl, captures the racial complexity of the gold rush. Displaced from their home by a horde of newcomers, a Native American family trudges away from the goldfields (left). Meanwhile, a contingent of Chinese miners marches toward the diggings (center), and a group of American men struggle to right their overturned wagon. University of California at Berkeley, Bancroft Library.

The swift triumph of antislavery forces in California alarmed southern politicians. Admitting California as a free state would prevent the expansion of slavery to the Pacific. More troubling, it would increase the number of free states in the Union to sixteen, giving the free states a one-state majority in the Senate. Fearing that the South would be placed at a permanent disadvantage in the national government, which they had long controlled, some southerners threatened secession. "[If] you seek to drive us from the territories of California and New Mexico," Representative Robert Toombs of Georgia warned northern congressmen, "*I am for disunion.*" However, the majority of southern politicians preferred a strategy of political resistance. They vowed to block California's admission unless the federal government guaranteed the future of slavery.

Constitutional Conflict. The resulting political impasse produced passionate debates in Congress and four distinct positions with respect to slavery in the territories. On the verge of death, John C. Calhoun took his usual extreme stance. Like Senator Albert Gallatin Brown of Mississippi, Calhoun had long resented the "social and sectional degradation" of the South by northern critics of slavery. To uphold southern honor, he now asserted the right of states to secede from the Union and proposed a constitutional amendment that would permanently balance the political power of the North and the South by creating a dual presidency. Calhoun also advanced the radical doctrine that Congress had no constitutional authority to regulate slavery in the territories. This argument ran counter to a half century of practice. In 1787, Congress had prohibited slavery in the Northwest Territory; and in the Missouri Compromise of 1820, it had extended that ban to most of the Louisiana Purchase.

Calhoun's assertion that the territories were open to slavery won support in the Deep South, but many southerners favored a second, more moderate, proposal to extend the Missouri Compromise line to the Pacific Ocean. This plan also won the support of Pennsylvanian James Buchanan, the former secretary of state, and other influential northern Democrats. Because an extension of the compromise line would guarantee slave owners access to at least some western territory, including a separate state in southern California, they championed it as a simple compromise that would resolve the crisis.

A third alternative for resolving the status of slavery in the territories was squatter sovereignty, the idea advanced by Lewis Cass in 1848 and now advocated by Democratic senator Stephen Douglas of Illinois. Douglas called his plan **popular sovereignty** to emphasize its roots in republican ideology, and it had considerable appeal. Politicians liked the fact that it would remove the explosive issue of slavery from national politics; and local settlers welcomed the power it would put in their hands. However, popular sovereignty was a vague and slippery concept. Could residents accept or ban slavery when a territory was first organized? Or must they delay that decision until a territory had enough people to frame a constitution and apply for statehood?

For their part, antislavery advocates were unwilling to accept any plan for California that might allow the expansion of slavery in the territories. Senator Salmon P. Chase of Ohio, elected by a Democratic–Free-Soil coalition, and Senator William H. Seward, a New York Whig, urged a fourth position—that federal authorities restrict slavery within its existing boundaries and then extinguish it completely. Condemning slavery as "morally unjust, politically unwise, and socially pernicious" and invoking "a higher law than the Constitution," Seward demanded bold action to protect freedom, "the common heritage of mankind."

A Complex Compromise. Standing on the brink of disaster, senior Whig and Democratic politicians desperately sought a compromise that would preserve the Union. With the help of Millard Fillmore, who became president in 1850, after Zachary Taylor died suddenly, Whig leaders Henry Clay and Daniel Webster and Democrat Stephen A. Douglas secured the passage of five separate laws known collectively as the Compromise of 1850. To mollify the South, the Compromise included a new Fugitive Slave Act that enlisted federal magistrates in the task of returning runaway slaves. To satisfy the North, the legislation admitted California as a free state, resolved a boundary dispute between New Mexico and Texas in favor of New Mexico, and abolished the slave trade (but not slavery) in the District of Columbia. Finally, the Compromise organized the rest of the lands acquired from Mexico into the territories of New Mexico and Utah and left the decision to allow or prohibit slavery in those vast areas to popular sovereignty (Map 13.7).

The Compromise averted a secession crisis in 1850, but only barely. In the middle of the political struggle, the governor of South Carolina declared that there was not "the slightest doubt" that his state would secede from the Union. He and other militant secessionists (known as "fire-eaters") in Georgia,

Mississippi, and Alabama organized special conventions to safeguard "Southern Rights" through secession. In Georgia, U.S. Congressman Alexander H. Stephens called on the delegates to make "the necessary preparations of men and money, arms and munitions, etc. to meet the emergency." However, most delegates to these conventions remained committed to the Union—though now only conditionally. Accepting the principle of secession, they agreed to leave the Union if Congress abolished slavery anywhere or refused to grant statehood to a territory with a proslavery constitution. Political wizardry had solved the immediate constitutional crisis, but the underlying issue of slavery remained unresolved.

➤ Why did President Polk go to war with Mexico? Why did the war become so divisive in Congress?

➤ What issues were resolved by the Compromise of 1850? Who benefited more from its terms, the North or the South? Why?

The End of the Second Party System, 1850–1858

The architects of the Compromise of 1850 expected it to last for at least a generation, as the Missouri Compromise had. Their hopes were quickly dashed. Demanding freedom for fugitive slaves and free soil in the West, antislavery northerners refused to accept the Compromise. For their part, proslavery southerners were plotting to extend slavery into the West, the Caribbean, and Central America. The resulting disputes destroyed the Second Party System and deepened the crisis of the Union.

Resistance to the Fugitive Slave Act

The Fugitive Slave Act proved the most controversial element of the Compromise. Under its terms, federal magistrates in the northern states determined the status of blacks who were alleged to be runaway slaves. The law denied a jury trial to the accused blacks and even their right to testify. Under its provisions, southern owners reenslaved about two hundred fugitives (as well as some free northern blacks).

The plight of runaways and the appearance of slave catchers in the North and Midwest aroused popular hostility. Free blacks and abolitionists openly resisted the new law, despite its provision of substantial fines and prison sentences for those who aided fugitive slaves or interfered with their capture. In October 1850, Boston abolitionists

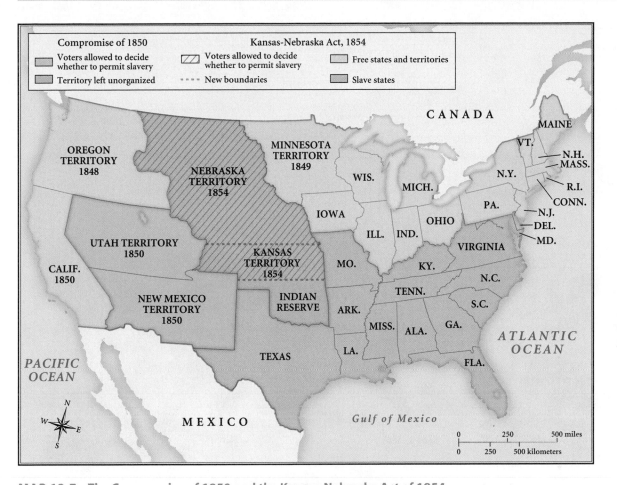

Compromise of 1850
- Voters allowed to decide whether to permit slavery
- Territory left unorganized

Kansas-Nebraska Act, 1854
- Voters allowed to decide whether to permit slavery
- New boundaries

- Free states and territories
- Slave states

MAP 13.7   The Compromise of 1850 and the Kansas-Nebraska Act of 1854

Vast territories were at stake in the contest over the expansion of slavery. The Compromise of 1850 resolved the status of lands in the Far West: California would be a free state, and the settlers of the Utah and New Mexico territories would vote for or against slavery (the doctrine of popular sovereignty). The decision in 1854 to void the Missouri Compromise (1820) and use popular sovereignty to decide the fate of slavery in the Kansas and Nebraska territories sparked a bitter local war and revealed a fatal flaw in the doctrine.

helped two slaves escape and drove a Georgia slave catcher out of town. The following year, rioters in Syracuse, New York, broke into a courthouse to free a fugitive slave. Abandoning his commitment to nonviolence, Frederick Douglass declared, "The only way to make a Fugitive Slave Law a dead letter is to make half a dozen or more dead kidnappers." As if in response, in September 1851, a deadly confrontation took place in the Quaker village of Christiana, Pennsylvania. About twenty African Americans exchanged gunfire with a party of slave catchers from Maryland, killing two of them. Federal authorities indicted thirty-six blacks and four whites for treason. But a Pennsylvania jury acquitted one defendant, and public opinion in the North forced the government to drop the charges against the rest.

Upping the ante was Harriet Beecher Stowe's abolitionist novel, *Uncle Tom's Cabin* (1852), which

magnified northern opposition to the Fugitive Slave Act. By translating the moral principles of abolitionism into heartrending personal situations, Stowe's melodramatic book evoked empathy and outrage throughout the North. Members of northern state legislatures were equally incensed that the act allowed the federal government to intervene in the internal affairs of their states. In response, they enacted **personal-liberty laws** that increased the legal rights of their residents, including accused fugitives. In 1857, the Wisconsin Supreme Court went even further. In *Ableman v. Booth,* it ruled that the Fugitive Slave Act was void in Wisconsin because it was contrary to state law and the constitutional rights of its citizens. Taking a states' rights stance—a position usually associated with the South—the Wisconsin court challenged the authority of federal courts to review its decision. When the case reached the U.S. Supreme Court in 1859,

Presidential Election of 1852

In this cartoon, Franklin Pierce races toward the White House on a fleet Democratic horse, while General Winfield Scott futilely beats his stubborn Whig mule, which is being pulled by members of the Know-Nothing Party ("Native Americans") and prodded by a group of African Americans. By identifying Scott and the Whigs as anti-foreigner and pro-black, the cartoonist hoped to garner votes for Pierce and the Democrats from New York's large population of Irish and German immigrants. Collection of Janice L. and David J. Frent.

Chief Justice Roger B. Taney led a unanimous Court in affirming the supremacy of federal courts over state courts—a position that has stood the test of time—and upheld the constitutionality of the Fugitive Slave Act. But by that time, popular opposition in the North had made it nearly impossible to catch fugitive blacks. As Frederick Douglass had hoped, the act had become a "dead letter."

The Political System in Decline

The conflict over slavery split both major political parties along sectional lines and stymied their leaders. The Whigs, weakened by the death of Henry Clay, chose General Winfield Scott, another hero of the war with Mexico, as their presidential candidate in 1852. However, many southern Whigs refused to support Scott because northern Whigs refused to support slavery. The Democrats were equally divided: Southerners wanted a candidate who would support Calhoun's constitutional argument that all territories should be open to slavery; but northern and midwestern Democrats advocated popular sovereignty, as did the three leading candidates—Lewis Cass of Michigan, Stephen Douglas of Illinois, and James Buchanan of Pennsylvania. Ultimately, the party settled on a compromise nominee, Franklin Pierce of New Hampshire, a congenial man reputed to be sympathetic to the South.

The Democrats' cautious strategy paid off, and they swept the election. Pleased by the admission of California as a free state, Martin Van Buren and many other Free-Soilers voted for Pierce, reuniting the Democratic Party. Conversely, disagreements over slavery fragmented the Whig Party into sectional wings; it would never again wage a national campaign.

As president, Pierce pursued an expansionist foreign policy. To assist northern merchants, he sent a mission to Japan to negotiate a commercial treaty. To mollify southern expansionists, he revived Polk's plan to annex extensive Mexican territories south of the Rio Grande. When Mexico rejected this initiative, Pierce settled for the purchase of a narrow slice of land that would enable his negotiator, James Gadsden, to build a transcontinental rail line from New Orleans to California (see Map 13.5, p. 402).

Pierce's most dramatic, and most controversial, foreign policy initiative came in the Caribbean and Central America. Southern expansionists had previously funded three clandestine military expeditions to Cuba, where they hoped to prod sugar-producing slave owners to declare independence from Spain and join the United States. Beginning in 1853, Pierce covertly supported new expeditions to Nicaragua and Cuba and, to further the venture in Cuba, threatened war with Spain over the seizure of an American ship. When northern Democrats in Congress refused to support this aggressive diplomacy, Pierce and Secretary of State William L. Marcy had to back down. Marcy then tried to buy the island from Spain. When that scheme also failed, Marcy arranged for American diplomats in Europe to inform Pierce, in the so-called Ostend Manifesto of 1854, that the United States would be justified "by every law, human and Divine" in seizing Cuba. Leaked to the press by antiexpansionists, the Ostend Manifesto revived fears of a "Slave Power" conspiracy; and determined northern resistance scuttled the planters' dreams of carving out an empire for slavery in the Caribbean.

The Kansas-Nebraska Act and the Rise of New Parties

In 1854, a new struggle over westward expansion deepened sectional divisions. Because the Missouri Compromise prohibited new slave states in the Louisiana Purchase north of 36°30′, southern senators had for two decades delayed the political organization of the area. Now residents of the Ohio River Valley and the Upper South were demanding

its settlement. Senator Stephen A. Douglas of Illinois became their spokesman, partly because he supported the construction of a transcontinental railroad linking Chicago to California. In 1854, Douglas introduced a bill to extinguish Native American rights on the central Great Plains and organize a large free territory to be called Nebraska.

Douglas's bill conflicted with the plans of southern politicians who wanted to extend slavery throughout the Louisiana Purchase and wanted a southern city—New Orleans, Memphis, or St. Louis—to serve as the eastern terminus of a transcontinental railroad. To win southern support for the organization of Nebraska, Douglas made two major concessions. First, he amended his bill so that it explicitly repealed the Missouri Compromise and organized the region on the basis of popular sovereignty. Second, Douglas agreed to the formation of two territories, Nebraska and Kansas. This provision would give southern planters the opportunity to settle Kansas and, through popular sovereignty, eventually make it a slave state (see Map 13.7, p. 407). Douglas knew that his bill would "raise a hell of a storm." To win the support of northern congressmen, he argued that Kansas was not suited to plantation agriculture and would become a free state. After weeks of bitter debate, the Senate enacted the Kansas-Nebraska Act. When sixty-six northern Democrats in the House of Representatives defied party policy to vote against the act, President Pierce used patronage and persuasion to get twenty-two members to change their votes, and the measure squeaked through.

The Republican and American Parties. The Kansas-Nebraska Act had disastrous consequences for the American political system. It completed the destruction of the Whig Party and nearly wrecked the Democratic Party. Denouncing the act as "part of a great scheme for extending and perpetuating supremacy of the slave power," northern Whigs and "anti-Nebraska" Democrats abandoned their respective parties. They joined with Free-Soilers and abolitionists in a new Republican Party. Although the new party was a coalition of "strange, discordant and even hostile elements," as one Republican put it, its founders shared a determination to ban slavery from the territories and a common economic philosophy. They condemned slavery because it degraded the dignity of manual labor and drove down the wages and working conditions of free white workers. Like Thomas Jefferson, they celebrated the moral virtues of a society based on "the middling classes who own the soil and work it with their own hands." Abraham Lincoln, an Illinois Whig who became a Republican, articulated the party's vision of social mobility. "There is no permanent class of hired laborers among us," he declared, which meant that every free man had a chance to become a property owner. In the face of increasing class divisions in the industrializing North and Midwest, Lincoln and his fellow Republicans asserted the values of republican liberty and individual enterprise.

The Republicans faced strong competition from the American, or Know-Nothing, Party. The party had its origins in the anti-immigrant and anti-Catholic organizations of the 1840s (see Chapter 9). In 1850, these secret nativist societies banded together as the Order of the Star-Spangled Banner; and the following year, they entered politics, forming the American Party. The secrecy-conscious members of the party often replied "I know nothing" to outsiders' questions, thus giving the party its nickname. But the party's program was far from secret: It wanted to unite all native-born Protestants against the "alien menace" of Irish and German Catholics, prohibit further immigration, and institute literacy tests for voting. In 1854, voters angered by the Kansas-Nebraska Act elected dozens of Know-Nothing candidates to the House of Representatives and gave the party control of the state governments of Massachusetts and Pennsylvania. The emergence of a major party led by nativists suddenly became a real possibility.

"Bleeding Kansas." The Kansas-Nebraska Act created yet another national political crisis. As soon as the act was passed, thousands of settlers rushed into the Kansas Territory, putting Douglas's theory of popular sovereignty to the test. On the side of slavery, Senator David R. Atchison of Missouri organized residents of his state to cross temporarily into Kansas and vote in crucial elections there. Opposing Atchison was the abolitionist New England Emigrant Aid Society, which dispatched hundreds of free-soilers to Kansas. In March 1855, the Pierce administration stepped into the fray by accepting the legitimacy of the territorial legislature sitting in Lecompton, Kansas, which had been elected primarily by border-crossing Missourians and had adopted proslavery legislation. However, the majority of Kansas residents favored free soil and refused allegiance to the Lecompton government.

In May 1856, both sides turned to violence and soon the territory was known as "Bleeding Kansas," a term coined by Horace Greeley of the *New York Tribune*. A proslavery gang, seven hundred strong, sacked the free-soil town of Lawrence; the gang wrecked two newspaper offices, looted stores, and burned down buildings. The attack enraged John Brown, a fifty-six-year-old abolitionist from New York and Ohio, whose free-state militia arrived too late to save the town. Brown was a complex man with a checkered financial past. Despite a long record of failed businesses, he had an intellectual and a moral intensity that won the trust of influential people. Taking vengeance for the sack of Lawrence, Brown and a few followers murdered and mutilated five proslavery settlers at Pottawatomie. We must "fight fire with fire" and "strike terror in the hearts of the proslavery people," Brown declared. The southerners' attack on Lawrence and the Pottawatomie killings started a guerrilla war in Kansas that took almost two hundred lives (see Comparing American Voices, "Civil Warfare in Kansas" pp. 412–413).

Armed Abolitionists in Kansas, 1859

The confrontation between North and South in Kansas took many forms. In the spring of 1859, Dr. John Doy (seated) slipped across the border into Missouri and tried to lead thirteen escaped slaves to freedom in Kansas, only to be captured and jailed in St. Joseph, Missouri. The serious-looking men standing behind Doy, well armed with guns and Bowie knives, attacked the jail and carried Doy back to Kansas. The photograph celebrated — and memorialized — their successful exploit. Kansas State Historical Society.

Buchanan's Failed Presidency

The violence in Kansas dominated the presidential election of 1856. The two-year-old Republican Party counted on anger over Bleeding Kansas to boost its fortunes. The party's platform denounced the Kansas-Nebraska Act and, alleging a Slave Power conspiracy, insisted that the federal government prohibit slavery in all the territories. Its platform also called for federal subsidies for transcontinental railroads, reviving an element of the Whig's economic program that was popular among midwestern Democrats. For president the Republicans nominated Colonel John C. Frémont, a free-soiler famous for his role in the conquest of Mexican California.

The Election of 1856. The American Party also entered the election with high hopes, but it quickly split along sectional lines over the conflict in Kansas. The southern faction of the party nominated former Whig president Millard Fillmore, while the northern contingent endorsed Frémont— thanks to clever maneuvering by Republican political operatives. During the campaign, Republicans won the votes of Know-Nothing workingmen in the North by demanding a ban on foreign immigrants and high tariffs on foreign manufactures. As

a Pennsylvania Republican put it, "Let our motto be, protection to everything American, against everything foreign." In New York, Republicans likewise shaped their policies "to cement into a harmonious mass . . . all of the Anti-Slavery, Anti-Popery and Anti-Whiskey" voters.

The Democrats reaffirmed their support for popular sovereignty and the Kansas-Nebraska Act, and nominated James Buchanan of Pennsylvania. A tall, dignified man, Buchanan was an experienced but unimaginative politician who was known for his support of the South. Drawing on that support and his party's organizational strength in the North, Buchanan won the three-way race with 1.8 million votes (45 percent) and 174 electoral votes. Frémont polled 1.3 million votes (33 percent) and 114 electoral votes Buchanan took only five free states; the Republican candidate took eleven. A small shift of the popular vote to Frémont in Illinois and Pennsylvania would have given him the presidency.

The dramatic restructuring of parties was now apparent (Map 13.8). With the splintering of the American Party, the Republicans had replaced the Whigs as the second major party. Moreover, because the Republicans had no support in the South, they would have to tread carefully; a Republican

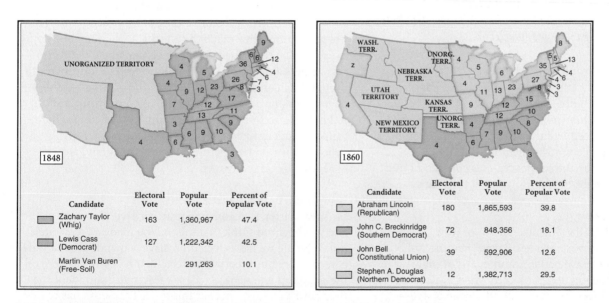

MAP 13.8 Political Realignment, 1848 and 1860
In the presidential election of 1848, both the Whig and the Democratic candidates won electoral votes in most parts of the nation. Subsequently, the political conflict over slavery and the Compromise of 1850 destroyed the Whig Party in the South. As the only nationwide party, the Democrats won easily over the Whigs in 1852 and, because of the split between Republicans and Know-Nothings, in 1856 as well. However, by 1860, a new regional party system had taken shape—and would persist for the next seventy years—with Democrats dominant in the South and Republicans dominant in the Northeast, Midwest, and Far West.

Civil Warfare in Kansas

The Kansas-Nebraska Act of 1854 and its doctrine of popular sovereignty set off a mad scramble. The New England Emigrant Aid Society provided support to antislavery northerners who wanted to settle in Kansas, while southern politicians mobilized supporters in Missouri and elsewhere to save the new territory for slavery. The no-holds-barred struggle for control of the territorial legislature led to fraud, intimidation, and, by 1856, the guerrilla warfare described in these letters.

Letters are valuable sources. Because they are written as private communications, they tend to depict the writers' values and passions frankly and realistically. What writers say in letters, they often mean. Still, letters—like all sources—have to be read carefully to probe the psychology and the motives of their authors.

AXALLA JOHN HOOLE
"Coming Here Will Do No Good at Last"

Early in 1856, Axalla John Hoole and his bride left South Carolina to build a new life in the Kansas Territory (K.T.). These letters from Hoole to his family show that things did not go well from the start and gradually got worse; after eighteen months, the Hooles returned to South Carolina. A Confederate militia captain during the Civil War, Axalla Hoole died in the Battle of Chickamauga in September 1863.

Kansas City, Missouri, Apl. 3d., 1856.

The Missourians . . . are very sanguine about Kansas being a slave state & I have heard some of them say it shall be. . . . But generally speaking, I have not met with the reception which I expected. Everyone seems bent on the Almighty Dollar, and as a general thing that seems to be their only thought. . . .

Well, dear brother, the supper bell has rung and I must close. Give my love to [the family] and all the Negroes. . . .

Lecompton, K.T., Sept. 12, 1856.

I have been unwell ever since the 9th of July. . . . I thought of going to work in a few days, when the Abolitionists broke out and I have had to stand guard of nights when I ought to have been in bed, took cold which . . . caused diarrhea, but . . . I feel quite well [now]. Betsie is well—

You perceive from the heading of this that I am now in Lecompton, almost all of the Proslavery party between this place and Lawrence are here. We brought our families here, as we thought that we would be better able to defend ourselves when altogether than if we scattered over the country. . . .

Lane [and a free-state army] came against us last Friday (a week ago to-day). As it happened we had about 400 men with two cannon—we marched out to meet him, though we were under the impression at the time that he had 1,000 men. We came in gunshot of each other, but the regular [U.S. Army] soldiers came and interferred, but not before our party had shot some dozen guns, by which it is reported that five of the Abolitionists had been killed or wounded. We had strict orders from our commanding officer (Gen'l Marshall) not to fire until they made the attack, but some of our boys would not be restrained. I was a rifleman and one of the skirmishers, but did all that I could to restrain our men though I itched all over to shoot myself. I drew a bead a dozen times on a big Yankee about 150 yards from me, but did not fire. . . . We were acting on the defensive, and did not think it prudent to commence the engagement. I firmly believe we would have whipped them, though we would have lost a good many men. . . .

Douglas, K.T., July the 5th., 1857.

I fear, Sister, that [our] coming here will do no good at last, as I begin to think that this will be made a Free State at last. 'Tis true we have elected Proslavery men to draft a state constitution, but I feel pretty certain, if it is put to a vote of the people, it will be rejected, as I feel pretty confident that they have a majority here at this time. The South has ceased all efforts, while the North is redoubling her exertions. We nominated a candidate for Congress last Friday—Ex-Gov. Ransom of Michigan. I must confess I have not much faith in him, tho he professes to hate the abolitionists bitterly, and I have heard him say that Negroes were a great deal better off with Masters. Still, I fear him, but it was the best we could do. If we had nominated a Southern man, he would have been sure to have been beaten and I doubt whether we can even elect a Northerner who favors our side. . . .

Give my love to Mother. . . . Tell all the Negroes howdie, and my best regards to enquiring friends.

SOURCE: William Stanley Hoole, ed., "A Southerner's Viewpoint of the Kansas Situation, 1856–1857," *Kansas Historical Quarterly* 3 (1934): 43–65, 149–171, passim.

JOHN LAWRIE
"A Few Goddamned White-livered Lawyers"

Unlike Axalla Hoole and his wife, Indiana farmer John Lawrie initially had no intention of settling in Kansas. However, after fighting there for ten months in 1856 and 1857, he seems to have warmed to the idea. When the Civil War broke out, Lawrie would join the Union army and serve for nearly four years.

Wolf Mound Farm, White Co., Indiana
Apl. 16th, 1857
Dear [brother] Art,

When I left home on the Fifteenth of last June I had no intention of making a home in Kansas. I intended in case I could find any organization ready to take the field against the Missourians, to use my utmost endeavors to change the attitude of the Free-State settlers from a defensive to an offensive warfare. When I reached Leavenworth, I was unable to find any organization of Free-State men, and could only tell one when I met him by his hanging head and subdued tone of voice. . . .

Hearing that people held up their heads and spoke what they thought in Lawrence, I started for that point and soon found myself at home as far as a hatred of tyranny and a thirst for vengeance for the insult [the sack of Lawrence] of the 21st of May was concerned. The people had concluded to try whether there was truth in the Border Ruffian assertion *The Damned Yankees won't fight!* There was quite a stir among the young men in the way of target firing and drilling in order to prepare themselves for any emergency that might arise requiring them *to contend with superior numbers*, the only thing that thus far had held them back. I found that arms were really scarce. I expected to find plenty of improved firearms, and it was with the greatest difficulty I succeeded in getting an old condemned musket.

I went up to Topeka [and] found the people discussing the propriety of defending the legislature against all who might attempt to disperse it. A few goddamned white-livered lawyers succeeded in getting through a resolution that it was the determination of the Free State men *not to molest or hinder the U.S. troops* [sent by authorities in Washington to preserve order]. On the fourth of July at an hour before noon the troops charged into town and dispersed the legislature and retired again unmolested.

I went back to the place where I worked near Lawrence, and did nothing but damn and curse lawyers and professional politicans until the sixth of August, when it was decided by some of the boys in town to go down to a block house erected by a company of Georgian robbers in the lower part of the territory and whip the robbers. . . .

We were all rather anxious to see how the boys would behave under fire, many of them never having as yet heard singing lead. The night was rather dark, and the enemy showed no light and made no noise. Our captain (who by the way was an old man of wars man) reconnoitered the ground and concluded to lead us right on to the place and take it by assault. . . . We went up as well as old veterans ever dared to go. . . . The sound of our steady *tramp! tramp!* was too much for the garrison and they incontinently fled. . . .

I shall remain here until the middle of June when I intend returning to Kansas.

SOURCE: V. E. Gibbens, ed., "Letters on the War in Kansas in 1856," *Kansas Historical Quarterly* 10 (1941): 370–373.

ANALYZING THE EVIDENCE

➤ What do these letters suggest about the character of the armed conflict in Kansas? Just how bloody was it?

➤ Why do you think Axalla Hoole and John Lawrie took up arms? Is it significant that both of them would go on to fight in the Civil War?

➤ Like most political or ideological doctrines, popular sovereignty only works well in certain circumstances. What were the conditions in Kansas between 1854 and 1860 that made it virtually unworkable? Can you see any parallels with the experiment of popular sovereignty in Iraq since 2004? Explain your answer.

triumph in the next presidential election might prompt the southern states to withdraw from the Union. A North Carolina newspaper threatened as much in 1856: "If the Republicans should succeed, the result will be a separation of the states. No human power can prevent it." The fate of the republic hinged on the ability of President Buchanan to defuse the passions of the past decade and devise a way of protecting free soil in the West and slavery in the South.

Dred Scott: Petitioner for Freedom. Events—and his own values and weaknesses—conspired against Buchanan. In 1856, the Supreme Court had considered the case of *Dred Scott v. Sandford*, which raised the controversial issue of Congress's constitutional authority to regulate slavery in the territories. Dred Scott was an enslaved African American who had lived for a time with his owner, an army surgeon, in the free state of Illinois and at Fort Snelling, then in the Wisconsin Territory, where the Northwest Ordinance (1787) prohibited slavery. Seeking freedom for himself and his family, Scott claimed in his suit that residence in a free state and a free territory had made him free. Hoping naively that a strong proslavery decision would settle the issue of slavery in the territories, Buchanan pressured several northern justices to vote in tandem with their southern colleagues. In the Court's decision, handed down in 1857, seven of the nine members of the Court agreed that Scott was still a slave; but the members of the majority were unable to agree on the legal issues, and each justice wrote a separate opinion.

Chief Justice Roger B. Taney of Maryland, a slave owner himself, composed the most influential opinion. He declared that Negroes, whether enslaved or free, could not be citizens of the United States, and that Scott therefore had no right to sue in federal court. That argument was controversial: Free blacks were citizens in many states, which presumably gave them access to the federal courts. But then Taney proceeded to make two even more controversial points. First, he endorsed John C. Calhoun's argument: Because the Fifth Amendment prohibited "takings" of property without due process of law, Taney ruled that Congress could not deny southern citizens the right to take their slave property into the territories and own it there. Consequently, the chief justice concluded, the provisions of the Northwest Ordinance and the Missouri Compromise that prohibited slavery had never been constitutional. Second, Taney declared that Congress could not give to territorial governments any powers that Congress itself did not possess. Because Congress had no authority to prohibit slavery in a territory, neither did a territorial government. Taney thereby endorsed Calhoun's interpretation of popular sovereignty: Only when settlers wrote a constitution and requested statehood could they prohibit slavery.

In a single stroke, Taney and the Democrat-dominated Supreme Court had declared the Republicans' antislavery platform to be unconstitutional. The Republicans could never accept the legitimacy of that decision. Led by Senator Seward of New York, they accused the Supreme Court and President Buchanan of participating in the Slave Power conspiracy.

Buchanan then added fuel to the raging constitutional fire. In early 1858, he recommended the admission of Kansas as a slave state under a constitution written by the proslavery Lecompton legislature, although the legitimacy of the constitution was widely questioned. Angered that Buchanan would not permit a popular referendum on the Lecompton constitution, Stephen Douglas, the most influential Democratic senator, broke with the president and persuaded Congress to deny statehood to Kansas. (Kansas would enter the Union as a free state in 1861.) By pursuing a proslavery agenda—first in the *Dred Scott* decision and then in Kansas—Buchanan had widened the split in his party and the nation.

➤ Why did the Compromise of 1850 fail?

➤ What did Stephen Douglas try to accomplish with the Kansas-Nebraska Act of 1854?

➤ Was that act any more successful than the Compromise of 1850? Explain your answer.

➤ What were the main constitutional arguments advanced during the debate over slavery in the territories? Which of those arguments influenced Chief Justice Taney's opinion in *Dred Scott*?

Abraham Lincoln and the Republican Triumph, 1858–1860

The crisis of the Union intensified as the Democratic Party fragmented along sectional lines and the Republicans gained support in the North and Midwest. Abraham Lincoln emerged as the pivotal figure in American politics, the only Republican leader whose policies and temperament might have saved the Union. But few southerners trusted Lincoln, and the prospect of his election to the presidency renewed the commitment of the southern secessionists who had been threatening to leave the Union since 1850.

Lincoln's Political Career

The middle-class world of storekeepers, lawyers, and entrepreneurs in the small towns of the Ohio River Valley shaped Lincoln's early career. He came from an impoverished yeoman farm family that had moved from Kentucky, where Lincoln was born in 1809, to Indiana and then to Illinois. In 1831, Lincoln rejected his father's life as a subsistence farmer and became a store clerk in New Salem. Socially ambitious, Lincoln sought entry into the middle class by mastering its literary and professional culture; he joined the New Salem Debating Society, read the works of Shakespeare, and studied law.

Admitted to the bar in 1837, Lincoln moved to Springfield, the new state capital. There he met Mary Todd, the cultured daughter of a Kentucky banker; they married in 1842. The couple was a picture in contrasts: Her tastes were aristocratic; his were humble. She was volatile; he was easygoing but suffered bouts of depression that tried her patience and tested his character.

Abraham Lincoln, 1859

Lincoln was not a handsome man, and he photographed poorly. In fact, his campaign photographs were often retouched to hide his prominent cheekbones and nose. More important, no photograph ever captured Lincoln's complex personality and wit or the intensity of his spirit and intellect. To grasp Lincoln, it is necessary to read his words. Chicago Historical Society.

Abraham Lincoln: Ambitious Politician. Lincoln's ambition was "a little engine that knew no rest," his closest associate remarked, and it prompted him to seek fame and fortune in politics. An admirer of Henry Clay, Lincoln joined the Whig Party and won election to four terms in the Illinois legislature, where he promoted education, state banking, and canals and railroads. He became a dexterous party politician, adept in the distribution of patronage and the passage of legislation.

In 1846, the rising lawyer-politician won election to a Congress that was bitterly divided over the Wilmot Proviso. Lincoln had long felt that human bondage was unjust but did not believe that the federal government had the constitutional authority to tamper with slavery in the South. With respect to the war with Mexico, he took the middle ground. He supported bills for military appropriations but, determined to exclude the institution of slavery from the territories, voted for Wilmot's proposal. He himself proposed that Congress enact legislation for the gradual (and compensated) emancipation of slaves in the District of Columbia. He argued that a series of measures—firm opposition to the

expansion of slavery, gradual emancipation, and the colonization of freed slaves in Africa—was the only practical way to address the issues of slavery and racial diversity. However, both abolitionists and proslavery activists rejected Lincoln's pragmatic policies, and he lost his bid for reelection. Dismayed at the rancor of ideological politics, he withdrew from the political arena and developed a lucrative legal practice representing railroads and manufacturers.

Lincoln returned to the political fray after passage of Stephen Douglas's Kansas-Nebraska Act. Shocked by the act's repeal of the Missouri Compromise, Lincoln warned the citizens of Illinois that the American "republican robe is soiled and trailed in the dust" and called on them to "repurify it and wash it white in the spirit, if not the blood of the Revolution." Rejecting Douglas's scheme to let residents decide the fate of slavery in the territories, Lincoln reaffirmed his position that slavery be allowed to continue in the states where it existed but that national authority should be used to exclude it from the territories. Confronting the moral issue of slavery, Lincoln declared that if the nation was going to uphold its republican ideals, it must eventually cut out slavery like a "cancer."

The Lincoln-Douglas Debates. Abandoning the Whig Party in favor of the Republicans, Lincoln quickly emerged as their leader in Illinois. Campaigning for the U.S. Senate against Douglas in 1858, Lincoln alerted his audiences to the dangers of the Slave Power. He warned that the proslavery Supreme Court might soon declare that the Constitution "does not permit a state to exclude slavery from its limits," just as it had decided in *Dred Scott* that "neither Congress nor the territorial legislature can do it." In that event, he continued, "we shall awake to the reality . . . that the Supreme Court has made Illinois a slave state." The prospect of slavery spreading into the North informed Lincoln's famous "House Divided" speech. Quoting from the Bible, "A house divided against itself cannot stand," he predicted a crisis: "I believe this government cannot endure permanently half slave and half free. . . . It will become all one thing, or all the other."

The contest in Illinois attracted national interest because of Douglas's prominence in the Democratic Party and Lincoln's reputation as a formidable speaker. During a series of seven debates, Douglas declared his support for white supremacy: "This government was made by our fathers, by white men for the benefit of white men and their posterity forever," he asserted, and he attacked Lincoln for supporting "negro equality." Put on the defensive by Douglas's racial rhetoric, Lincoln advocated economic opportunity for free blacks but not equal political rights. He asked how Douglas could accept the decision in *Dred Scott* (which protected slave owners' property in the territories) and yet advocate popular sovereignty (which asserted settlers' power to exclude slavery). Douglas responded with the so-called Freeport Doctrine, which suggested that a territory's residents could exclude slavery simply by not adopting a law to protect it. Although that doctrine pleased neither proslavery advocates nor abolitionists, the Democrats won a narrow victory over the Republicans in Illinois, and the state legislature reelected Douglas to the U.S. Senate.

The Union Under Siege

The debates with Douglas gave Lincoln a national reputation, and the election of 1858 established the Republican Party as a formidable political force.

Republicans won control of the House of Representatives and various state legislatures.

The Rise of Radicalism. Shaken by the Republican advance, southern Democrats divided into two groups: moderates and fire-eaters. The moderates, among them Senator Jefferson Davis of Mississippi, were known as Southern Rights Democrats; their goal was to win ironclad political commitments to protect slavery. The fire-eaters—men like Robert Barnwell Rhett of South Carolina and William Lowndes Yancey of Alabama—rejected that strategy; they repudiated the Union and actively promoted the secession of the southern states. Radical antislavery northerners played into their hands. Senator Seward of New York declared that freedom and slavery were locked in "an irrepressible conflict," and militant abolitionist John Brown demonstrated what that might mean. In October 1859, Brown led eighteen heavily armed black and white men in a raid on the federal arsenal at Harpers Ferry, Virginia. Brown hoped to secure hundreds of weapons, spark a slave rebellion, and establish a separate African American state in the South.

Republican leaders disavowed Brown's unsuccessful raid, but Democrats called his plot "a natural, logical, inevitable result of the doctrines and teachings of the Republican party." The state of Virginia charged Brown with treason, tried him in court, and sentenced him to be hanged. Virginians—and all white southerners—were horrified when reformer Henry David Thoreau called Brown "an angel of light" and other northerners leaped to Brown's defense. The slaveholding states looked to the future with fear. "The aim of the present black republican organization is the destruction of the social system of the Southern States, without regard to consequences," warned one newspaper. Once in power, another southern paper warned, the Republicans "would create insurrection and servile war in the South—they would put the torch to our dwellings and the knife to our throats." Brown had predicted as much. As he faced the gallows, Brown apocalyptically (and correctly) predicted "that the crimes of this guilty land will never be purged away but with blood."

Nor could the South count on the Democratic Party to protect its interests. At the party's convention in April 1860, northern Democrats rejected Jefferson Davis's proposal to protect slavery in the territories. In response, the delegates from eight southern states quit the meeting. At a second Democratic convention in Baltimore, northern and midwestern delegates

Harper's Ferry, Virginia

On Sunday evening, October 19, 1859, abolitionist John Brown and his band of nineteen men seized the federal armory and arsenal (the large buildings along the river) in the small industrial town of Harper's Ferry. The town lies at the junction of the Shenandoah (hidden behind the hill and house at right) and Potomac rivers in the Blue Mountains of northwestern Virginia. The Baltimore and Ohio Railroad crossed the Potomac on the bridge in the middle of the picture, and Hall's Rifle Works, where sixty gunsmiths produced firearms for the U.S. Army, occupied a nearby island in the Shenandoah. National Archives.

nominated Stephen Douglas for president; meeting separately, southern Democrats nominated the sitting Vice President, John C. Breckinridge of Kentucky.

The Election of 1860. With the Democrats divided, the Republicans sensed victory in the election of 1860. They courted white voters with a free-soil platform that opposed both slavery and racial equality: "Missouri for white men and white men for Missouri," declared that state's Republican platform. The national Republican convention chose Lincoln as its presidential candidate because his position on slavery was more moderate than that of the best-known Republicans, Senators Seward

of New York and Chase of Ohio, who were demanding abolition. Lincoln also conveyed a compelling egalitarian image that appealed to small-holding farmers and wage earners. And Lincoln's home territory—the rapidly growing Midwest—was crucial in the competition between Democrats and Republicans.

The Republican strategy worked. Although Lincoln received only 40 percent of the popular vote, he won a majority in the Electoral College by carrying every northern and western state except New Jersey. Douglas took 30 percent of the total vote, but won electoral votes only in Missouri and New Jersey. Breckinridge captured every state in the Deep South as well as Delaware, Maryland, and

Salomon de Rothschild

A French Banker Analyzes the Election of 1860 and the Threat of Secession

Salomon de Rothschild, the son of Baron James de Rothschild of Paris, traveled around the United States from 1859 to 1861. In a series of detailed letters to his cousin Nathaniel in London, Rothschild offered an astute (and often cynical) analysis of the sectional crisis. Although his comments are generally evenhanded, Rothschild feared social revolution and so favored the South; following secession, he supported diplomatic recognition of the Confederacy.

You know that the . . . United States was made up of two great parties, the Democrats and the Republicans. These two parties were subdivided into groups, only a few, but extremely violent ones. The abolitionists were the extremist Republicans; the "fire-eaters" or secessionists, the extremist Democrats. Fanaticism and the extremist parties always win out, and, exactly as I expressed my forebodings to you a very long time ago, abolitionism on one side and secession on the other dragged along the moderate neutrals despite themselves.

The point of departure was, as you know, the slavery question. Naturally, this institution, on which the wealth of the South was based, was defended to the limit by those who profited from it. Two reasons pushed the people of the North to seek to destroy slavery by any means. The first . . . was a simple humanitarian reason. In a free country like America, there must be no slaves, and complete equality must reign in all ranks of society. . . . But the real sentiment that guided them . . . was the spirit of leveling; everyone must be equal in abjection. They cannot tolerate someone in the South having 200 arms for his use while they have only their own two. This sentiment was the first seed of the social revolution which is at this very moment taking giant strides behind the political revolution.

You doubtless have read in the newspapers about the first effects of Lincoln's election; . . . several Southern states—Florida, Georgia, Alabama, and Mississippi, with South Carolina as their guide—have for all practical purposes seceded from the United States and are going to form a new confederation. . . . If this state of affairs should continue, the City of New York, whose interests are closely tied to those of the South, will secede from the State of New York, declare itself a free port, and form a new independent state. . . .

There may be two means of restoring the situation. The first (which seems impracticable to me) would be for Lincoln and [vice-President-elect] Hamlin, frightened by the political and financial crisis that their election has created, to submit their resignation. . . . The second expedient would be for those *slave* states which do not want to secede . . . to urge the two parties to make mutual concessions.

[However, Rothschild writes in another letter, compromise is unlikely because] the South is simply a producer and consumer; the West and the North, and especially the East, are almost entirely manufacturers, but they need strong protection. The South could supply itself with all necessary items in Europe, at prices from twenty-five to forty percent lower than what they have been paying up to now. It contends that these duties do it no good and that the money goes back into the pockets of the Northern manufacturers. Therefore it wants to escape from this tax. The suppression of, or even a strong reduction in, these duties would completely ruin the eastern states of New Jersey and Pennsylvania, which could not compete with the cheap prices attained by England and even by France. Thousands of men would find themselves unemployed and would therefore threaten the well-being and the very existence not only of their employers, but even of the merchants and the producers in those areas, leading to an imminent danger of social revolution, which the North must avoid at all costs. . . .

The future is as black as it can be. . . . For some months I have been predicting to you what is now happening. I was all alone in my opinion then, and the Americans, always optimistic in things that concern their country and themselves, laughed at my fears and my doubts. Now it is too late to change; half of America is ruined. . . .

SOURCE: Sigmund Diamond, ed., *A Casual View of America, 1859–1861: The Home Letters of Salomon de Rothschild* (Stanford, Calif.: Stanford University Press, 1961), 82–83, 118–119.

ANALYZING THE EVIDENCE

➤ Do you agree with Salomon de Rothschild's analysis of the motives of antislavery northern whites?

➤ Is Rothschild correct about the role of tariffs in the secession crisis? What happened to tariffs after the nullification crisis of the 1830s (see Chapter 10)?

➤ From what you have read in the text, is Rothschild's speculation that New York City will secede along with the South a realistic one? What argument does he make? Why was he wrong?

THE NATIONAL GAME. THREE "OUTS" AND ONE "RUN".
ABRAHAM WINNING THE BALL.

Lincoln on Home Base

As early as 1860, the language and imagery of sports had penetrated politics. Sporting a long raillike bat labeled "EQUAL RIGHTS AND FREE TERRITORY," Lincoln has scored a victory in the election. His three opponents—from left to right, Bell, Douglas, and Breckinridge—are "out." Indeed, they had been "skunk'd" and, as Douglas laments, their attempt to put a "short stop" to Lincoln's career had failed. Museum of American Political Life.

North Carolina; while John Bell, a former Tennessee Whig who was the nominee of the compromise-seeking Constitutional Union Party, carried the Upper South states where the Whigs had been strongest: Kentucky, Tennessee, and Virginia (see Voices from Abroad, "Salomon de Rothschild: A French Banker Analyzes the Election of 1860 and the Threat of Secession," p. 418.)

The Republicans had united voters in the Northeast, the Midwest, and California and Oregon behind free soil, and had gained national power. A revolution was in the making. Slavery had permeated the American federal republic for so long and so thoroughly that southerners had come to see it as part of the constitutional order—an order now under

siege. A Republican administration in Washington, warned John Townsend of South Carolina, might suppress "the inter-State slave trade" and thereby "*cripple this vital Southern institution* of slavery." To many southerners, it seemed time to think carefully about the meaning of Lincoln's words in 1858 that the Union must "become all one thing, or all the other."

➤ How did Lincoln's position on slavery differ from that of Stephen Douglas?

➤ Did the Republicans win the election of 1860, or did the Democrats lose it? Explain your answer.

SUMMARY

In this chapter, we have examined three important and related themes: the movement of Americans into Texas and Oregon in the 1830s and early 1840s, the causes and consequences of the war with Mexico in the late 1840s, and the gradual decline and destruction of the Second Party System during the 1850s. We saw that the coming of the Mexican War was a result of the political agendas of Presidents John Tyler and James Polk. Their determination to add territory, and slave states, to the Union pushed the United States into the war. As we have noted, the consequences of the war were immense because the acquisition of vast new territories raised the explosive and long-postponed question of the expansion of slavery.

To address this dangerous issue, Henry Clay and Daniel Webster devised the Compromise of 1850. As we have seen, their efforts were in vain. Antislavery northerners defied the Fugitive Slave Act, and expansionist-minded southerners sought to acquire new slave states in the Caribbean. Ideology—the pursuit of absolutes—replaced politics—the art of compromise—as the ruling principle of American political life.

The Second Party System rapidly disintegrated. The Whig Party crumbled and then vanished; two issue-oriented parties, the nativist American Party and the antislavery Republican Party, competed for its members. As the Republicans gained strength, the Democratic Party splintered into sectional factions over Bleeding Kansas and other slavery-related issues. The stage was set for Lincoln's victory in the climactic election of 1860.

Connections: Sectionalism

Sectionalism has been a constant factor in American history. In the seventeenth century, different groups of English settlers migrated to the Chesapeake and New England regions; and during the eighteenth century, their economies and societies developed along different lines. Then, as we pointed out in the essay that began Part Three, (p. 269), in the early nineteenth century,

the economic revolution and social reform sharpened sectional divisions: The North developed into an urban industrial society based on free labor, whereas the South remained a rural agricultural society dependent on slavery.

As we saw in Chapter 8, the first major conflict between North and South came in 1819 over the admission of Missouri to the Union as a slave state. A decade later, as we learned in Chapter 10, the Tariff of Abominations renewed the sectional struggle and sparked the nullification movement in South Carolina. Both the Missouri crisis of 1819–1821 and the tariff-nullification crisis of 1829–1832 ended with political compromises. And as we have just seen in this chapter, political leaders crafted the Compromise of 1850 to resolve yet another sectional conflict. However, as we will observe in the next chapter, the crisis sparked by the election of Abraham Lincoln, the presidential candidate of the northern- and midwestern-based Republican Party, could not be resolved through compromise. Nor did the Union's triumph in the Civil War end sectional strife. As Chapter 15 will demonstrate, Reconstruction created new sectional antagonisms and ended only with the Compromise of 1877—yet another political settlement of divisive social differences. Only in the mid-twentieth century, with the migration out of the South of millions of African Americans and the movement into the South of northern business corporations and millions of northern-born whites, would the sectional struggle begin to abate.

CHAPTER REVIEW QUESTIONS

➤ What were the links between the Mexican War of 1846–1848 and Abraham Lincoln's election as president in 1860?

➤ When and why did the Second Party System of Whigs and Democrats collapse?

➤ Some historians claim that the mistakes of a "Blundering Generation" of political leaders led, by 1860, to the imminent breakup of the Union. Do you agree with their assessment? Why or why not?

TIMELINE

1844	James Polk is elected president
1845	John Slidell's diplomatic mission to Mexico fails Texas admitted into the Union
1846	United States declares war on Mexico Treaty with Britain divides Oregon Country at forty-ninth parallel Wilmot Proviso is approved by House but not by Senate
1847	American troops under General Winfield Scott capture Mexico City
1848	Gold is discovered in California In Treaty of Guadalupe Hidalgo, Mexico cedes its provinces of California, New Mexico, and Texas to United States Free-Soil Party forms Zachary Taylor is elected president
1850	President Taylor dies, and Millard Fillmore assumes presidency Compromise of 1850 seeks to preserve the Union Northern abolitionists reject Fugitive Slave Act South seeks to expand slavery by acquiring Spanish Cuba
1851	American (Know-Nothing) Party forms
1852	Harriet Beecher Stowe publishes *Uncle Tom's Cabin* Franklin Pierce is elected president
1854	Ostend Manifesto promotes seizure of Cuba Kansas-Nebraska Act tests policy of popular sovereignty Republican Party forms
1856	Turmoil in Kansas undermines popular sovereignty James Buchanan is elected president
1857	Supreme Court's decision in *Dred Scott v. Sandford* allows slavery in U.S. territories
1858	President Buchanan backs Lecompton constitution Abraham Lincoln and Stephen Douglas debate in U.S. Senate race
1859	John Brown leads armed raid on federal arsenal at Harpers Ferry
1860	Abraham Lincoln is elected president in four-way contest

FOR FURTHER EXPLORATION

Patricia Nelson Limerick, *The Legacy of Conquest: The Unbroken Past of the American West* (1989), provides a sharply written interpretation of the struggle among individuals, groups, and nations for control of the West. "First-Person Narratives of California's Early Years, 1849–1900" is available through the Library of Congress (**lcweb2.loc.gov/ammem/cbhtml/cbhome.html**). *The West* (6 hours), a fine documentary by Ken Burns and Stephen Ives, has a useful Web site at **www.pbs.org/thewest**. For the early history of Texas, see **www.tsl.state.tx.us/treasures/**. The PBS documentary *U.S.-Mexican War: 1846–1848* (4 hours) and the companion Web site (**www.pbs.org/usmexicanwar**) view the war from both American and Mexican perspectives and draw on the expertise of historians from both countries.

David Potter, *The Impending Crisis, 1848–1861* (1976), presents a lucid account of the political history of the pre–Civil War years. For the role of slavery in sparking the Civil War, see episode 4 of the PBS documentary *Africans in America* and the related Web site (**www.pbs.org/wgbh/aia/home.html**). An audio discussion of the election of 1860 is available at **www.albany.edu/talkinghistory/arch2000july-december.html**. Two recent works—John Patrick Daly, *When Slavery Was Called Freedom: Evangelicalism, Proslavery, and the Causes of the Civil War* (2002), and Leonard L. Richards, *The Slave Power: The Free North and Southern Domination, 1780–1860* (2000)—offer a broad cultural analysis of the sectional conflict. For one state's struggle, see William A. Link, *Roots of Secession: Slavery and Politics in Antebellum Virginia* (2003). For proslavery ideology, consult Manisha Sinha, *The Counterrevolution of Slavery: Politics and Ideology in Antebellum South Carolina* (2000).

Eric Foner, *Free Soil, Free Labor, Free Men* (1970), provides an eloquent analysis of the ideology and politics of the Republican Party. Michael Holt's *The Political Crisis of the 1850s* (1978) shows how the collapse of the Second Party System allowed sectional rivalries to engulf the nation in war. For an evocative treatment of Lincoln, read Stephen Oates, *With Malice Toward None: A Life of Abraham Lincoln* (1977). The justices' opinions in the *Dred Scott* case are at **odur.let.rug.nl/~usa/D/1851-1875/dredscott/dredxx.htm**; for Lincoln's response, see **www.usconstitution.com/AbrahamLincolnonDredScottDecision.htm**. "*Uncle Tom's Cabin* and American Culture: A Multi-Media Archive" (**jefferson.village.virginia.edu/utc/**) is an extremely rich Web site that places the novel in its literary and cultural context.

TEST YOUR KNOWLEDGE

To assess your command of the material in this chapter, see the Online Study Guide at **bedfordstmartins.com/henretta**.

For Web sites, images, and documents related to topics and places in this chapter, visit **bedfordstmartins.com/makehistory**.

14

Two Societies at War
1861–1865

"**WHAT A SCENE IT WAS**," Union soldier Elisha Hunt Rhodes wrote in his diary as the Battle of Gettysburg ended. "Oh the dead and the dying on this bloody field." By July 1862, thousands of men had died in battle, and the slaughter would continue for two more years. "What is this all about?" asked Confederate lieutenant R. M. Collins at the end of another gruesome battle. "Why is it that 200,000 men of one blood and tongue . . . [are] seeking one another's lives? We could settle our differences by compromising and all be at home in ten days." But there was no compromise and no peace, a tragic outcome that President Lincoln found beyond human comprehension. "The Almighty has His own purposes," he reflected in 1862 and again in 1864. "God wills this contest, and wills that it shall not yet end."

To explain why Southerners seceded and then fought to the bitter end is not simple, but racial slavery is an important part of the answer. For southern political leaders, the Republican victory in 1860 presented a clear and immediate danger to the slave-owning republic that had existed since 1776. Lincoln was elected without a single electoral vote from the South, and Southerners knew that his Republican Party would prevent the extension of slavery into the territories.

◄ **Fields of Death**

Fought with mass armies and new weapons, the Civil War took a huge toll in human lives, as evidenced by this grisly photograph of a small section of the battlefield at Antietam, Maryland. At Shiloh, Tennessee, General Ulysses Grant surveyed a field "so covered with dead that it would have been possible to walk . . . in any direction, stepping on dead bodies, without a foot touching the ground." Library of Congress.

Moreover, they did not believe Lincoln when he promised not "directly or indirectly, to interfere with the institution of slavery in the States where it exists." "The mission of the Republican party," a southern newspaper declared, was "to meddle with everything—to meddle with the domestic institutions of other States, and to meddle with family arrangements in their own states—to overthrow Democracy, Catholicism and Slavery." Soon, a southern senator warned, "cohorts of Federal office-holders, Abolitionists, may be sent into [our] midst" to mobilize the African American population. The result would be bloody slave revolts and racial intermixture—by which was meant sexual relations between black men and white women, because white owners had already fathered untold numbers of children by their black women slaves. "Better, far better! endure all horrors of civil war," insisted a Confederate recruit from Virginia, "than to see the dusky sons of Ham leading the fair daughters of the South to the altar." To preserve black slavery and the supremacy of white men, radical southern leaders embarked on the dangerous journey of secession.

Lincoln and the North would not let them go in peace. Living in a world still ruled by kings and princes, northern leaders believed that the collapse of the American Union might destroy for all time the prospect of a republican government based on constitutional procedures, majority rule, and democratic elections. "We cannot escape history," the new president eloquently declared. "We shall nobly save, or meanly lose, the last best hope of earth." A young Union army recruit from Ohio put the issue simply: "If our institutions prove a failure . . . of what value will be house, family, or friends?"

And so came the Civil War. Called the War Between the States by Southerners and the War of the Rebellion by Northerners, the struggle continued until the great issues of the Union and slavery had finally been resolved. The cost was incredibly high: more lives lost than in all the nation's subsequent wars and a century-long legacy of bitterness between the triumphant North and the vanquished South.

Secession and Military Stalemate, 1861–1862

After Lincoln's election in November 1860, secessionist fervor swept through the Deep South and the future of the Union appeared dim. Still, the professional politicians in Washington—veteran party leaders who had run the country for a generation—did not give up. In the four months between Lincoln's election and his inauguration on March 4, 1861, they struggled to forge a new compromise that would preserve the Union.

The Secession Crisis

The movement toward secession was most rapid in South Carolina, the home of John C. Calhoun, nullification, and southern rights. Robert Barnwell Rhett and other fire-eaters had been calling for secession since the crisis of 1850; and with Lincoln's election, their goal was within reach. On December 20, a special state convention voted unanimously to dissolve "the union now subsisting between South Carolina and other States."

The Lower South Secedes. Moving quickly, fire-eaters elsewhere in the Lower South called similar conventions and mobilized vigilante groups and militia units to suppress local Unionists and prepare for war. In early January, in an atmosphere of public celebration, Mississippi enacted a secession ordinance. Within a month, Florida, Alabama, Georgia, Louisiana, and Texas had also left the Union (Map 14.1). In early February, the jubilant secessionists met in Montgomery, Alabama, to proclaim a new nation—the Confederate States of America. Adopting a provisional constitution, the delegates named Jefferson Davis of Mississippi, a former U.S. senator and secretary of war, as the Confederacy's president and Alexander Stephens, a congressman from Georgia, as vice president.

Secessionist fervor was less intense in the four states of the Middle South (Virginia, North Carolina, Tennessee, and Arkansas), where there were fewer slaves. Moreover, white opinion was sharply divided in the four border slave states (Maryland, Delaware, Kentucky, and Missouri), where yeomen farmers had greater political power. Yeomen had long resented the authority claimed by the slave-owning gentry, and some actively opposed it. In the 1850s, journalist Hinton Helper of North Carolina roused the "Non-slaveowners of the South! farmers, mechanics and workingmen," warning, "the slaveholders, the arrogant demagogues whom you have elected to offices of honor and profit, have hoodwinked you." Influenced partly by these sentiments, the legislatures of Virginia and Tennessee refused to join the secessionist movement in January 1861. Seeking a compromise, Upper South leaders proposed federal guarantees for slavery in the states where it existed.

Meanwhile, the Union government floundered. In his final message to Congress in December 1860, President Buchanan declared secession illegal but,

Agitating for Secession

Lincoln's election triggered a vigorous response from South Carolina's fire-eaters, who called a secession rally in Charleston. On December 1, 1860, hundreds of well-dressed planters and merchants met at the Mills Hotel to hear prominent secessionists demand withdrawal from the Union. Three weeks later, in a unanimous vote, a special state convention did just that. Library of Congress.

timid and indecisive, denied that the federal government had the authority to restore the Union by force. South Carolina viewed Buchanan's message as implicit recognition of its independence and demanded the surrender of Fort Sumter, a federal garrison in Charleston Harbor. To test the secessionists' resolve, Buchanan ordered that the fort be supplied by an unarmed merchant ship. When South Carolinians fired on the ship, Buchanan

showed his own lack of resolve by refusing to order the navy to escort it into the harbor.

The Crittenden Compromise. Instead, Buchanan urged Congress to find a compromise. The scheme proposed by Senator John J. Crittenden of Kentucky, an aging follower of Henry Clay, received the most support. Crittenden's plan had two parts. The first, which won congressional approval, called for a

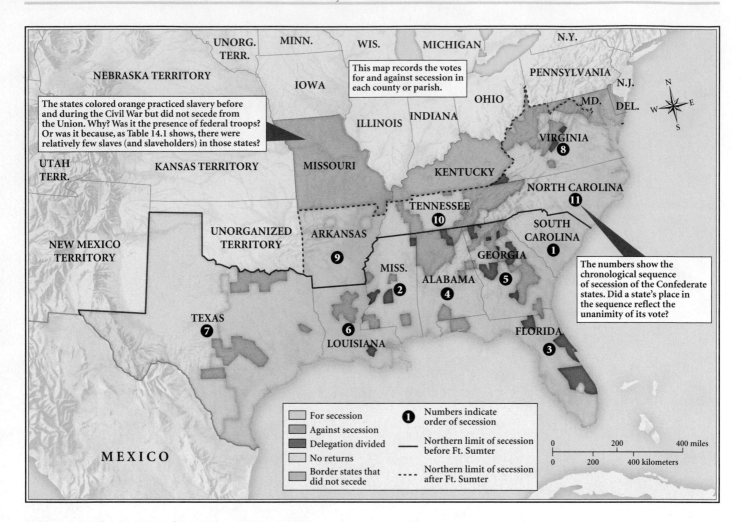

The states colored orange practiced slavery before and during the Civil War but did not secede from the Union. Why? Was it the presence of federal troops? Or was it because, as Table 14.1 shows, there were relatively few slaves (and slaveholders) in those states?

This map records the votes for and against secession in each county or parish.

The numbers show the chronological sequence of secession of the Confederate states. Did a state's place in the sequence reflect the unanimity of its vote?

	For secession		❶	Numbers indicate order of secession
	Against secession			
	Delegation divided			Northern limit of secession before Ft. Sumter
	No returns			
	Border states that did not secede			Northern limit of secession after Ft. Sumter

0   200   400 miles

0   200   400 kilometers

MAP 14.1   The Process of Secession, 1860–1861

The states of the Lower South had the highest concentration of slaves, and they led the secessionist movement. After the attack on Fort Sumter in April 1861, the states of the Upper South joined the Confederacy. Yeomen farmers in Tennessee and the backcountry of Alabama, Georgia, and Virginia opposed secession but, except in the future state of West Virginia, initially rallied to the Confederate cause. Consequently, the South entered the Civil War with its white population relatively united.

constitutional amendment to protect slavery from federal interference in any state where it already existed. Crittenden's second provision called for the westward extension of the Missouri Compromise line (36°30' north latitude) to the California border. Slavery would be barred north of the line and protected to the south, including any territories "hereafter acquired," thus holding out the prospect of future private military expeditions to acquire Cuba or Nicaragua.

On strict instructions from President-elect Lincoln, congressional Republicans rejected this part of Crittenden's plan. Lincoln was firmly committed to the doctrine of free soil and feared this compromise would encourage the South to

embark on new imperialist adventures in the Caribbean and Latin America. Crittenden's plan, Lincoln charged, would be "a perpetual covenant of war against every people, tribe, and State owning a foot of land between here and Tierra del Fuego [the southern tip of South America]." In 1787, 1820, and 1850, the political leaders of the North and South had found ways to resolve their differences over slavery. In 1861, there would be no compromise.

In his inaugural address in March 1861, Lincoln carefully articulated his position on slavery and the Union. He promised to safeguard slavery where it existed; however, there must be free soil in the territories. Most important, Lincoln stated that the

Union was "perpetual"; consequently, the secession of the Confederate states was illegal, and acts of violence in support of their action constituted insurrection. The new president clearly declared his intention to enforce federal law throughout the Union and—of particular relevance to Fort Sumter—to continue to "hold, occupy, and possess" federal property in the seceded states and "to collect duties and imposts" there. If force was necessary to preserve the Union, Lincoln—like Andrew Jackson during the nullification crisis—would use it. The choice was the South's: Return to the Union or face war.

The Upper South Chooses Sides

The South's decision came quickly. The garrison at Fort Sumter urgently needed food and medicine. Upholding his promise to defend federal property, Lincoln dispatched a relief expedition and assured the Confederate government of its peaceful mission. However, Jefferson Davis and his associates wanted a military confrontation to win the support of the states of the Middle and Border South; so Davis demanded the surrender of the fort. When Major Robert Anderson refused, the Confederate forces opened fire—ardent fire-eater Edmund Ruffin supposedly fired the first cannon on April 12. Isolated and under heavy bombardment, the Union forces capitulated on April 14. The next day, Lincoln called 75,000 state militiamen into federal service for ninety days to put down an insurrection "too powerful to be suppressed by the ordinary course of judicial proceedings." All talk of compromise was past.

The Bombardment of Fort Sumter, 1861

Currier & Ives, a New York publishing house, brought colorful art into thousands of middle-class homes by printing inexpensive lithographs of pastoral scenes and dramatic historical events. This fairly realistic depiction of the Confederate bombardment of Fort Sumter in Charleston Harbor in April 1861 was especially popular in the South. Library of Congress.

Northerners responded to Lincoln's call to arms with wild enthusiasm. Asked to provide thirteen regiments of volunteers, Republican governor William Dennison of Ohio sent twenty. Many northern Democrats declared their support for the Union cause, even as they prepared their party to function as the "loyal opposition," to oppose various initiatives of Lincoln's Republican administration. "Every man must be for the United States or against it," Stephen Douglas declared. "There can be no neutrals in this war, only patriots—or traitors."

The white residents of the Middle and Border South now had to choose between the Union and the Confederacy, and their decision was crucial. Those eight states accounted for two-thirds of the South's white population, more than three-fourths of its industrial production, and well over half of its food and fuel. They were home to many of the nation's best military leaders, including Colonel Robert E. Lee of Virginia, a career officer whom veteran General Winfield Scott recommended to Lincoln to lead the new Union army. And they were geographically strategic. Kentucky, with its 500-mile border on the Ohio River, was essential to the movement of troops and supplies. Maryland was vital to the Union's security because it bordered the nation's capital on the north.

The weight of history decided the outcome in Virginia, the original home of American slavery. Three days after the fall of Fort Sumter, a Virginia convention approved secession by a vote of 88 to 55, with the dissenters drawn mainly from the yeomen-dominated northwestern counties. Elsewhere, Virginia whites rallied to the Confederate cause. "The North was the aggressor," declared Richmond lawyer William Poague as he enlisted. "The South resisted her invaders." Refusing Scott's offer of the Union command, Robert E. Lee resigned from the U.S. Army. "Save in defense of my native state," Lee told Scott, "I never desire again to draw my sword." Arkansas, Tennessee, and North Carolina quickly joined Virginia in the Confederacy.

Lincoln moved aggressively to hold the states of the Border South, where relatively few families owned slaves (see Table 14.1). In May 1861, he ordered General George B. McClellan to take control of northwestern Virginia to secure the railway line between Washington and the Ohio River Valley. In October, voters in that yeoman region overwhelmingly approved the formation of a breakaway territory, West Virginia, which was admitted to the Union as a state in 1863. Unionists easily carried the day in Delaware but not in Maryland, where slavery was well entrenched. A pro-Confederate mob attacked Massachusetts troops marching between railroad stations in Baltimore, causing the war's first combat deaths: four soldiers and twelve civilians. When Maryland secessionists destroyed railroad bridges and telegraph lines, Lincoln ordered the military occupation of the state and the arrest of Confederate sympathizers, including legislators. He released them only in November 1861, after Unionists gained control of Maryland's government.

Lincoln was equally energetic and resourceful in the Southwest. To win Missouri (and control of the Missouri and upper Mississippi rivers), Lincoln mobilized the German American militia, which strongly opposed slavery; in July, it defeated a force of Confederate sympathizers commanded by the governor. Despite continuing raids by Confederate guerrilla bands, the Union retained control of Missouri (see Voices from Abroad, "Ernest Duvergier de Hauranne: German Immigrants and the Civil War Within Missouri," p. 429). In Kentucky, secessionist and Unionist sentiment was evenly balanced, so Lincoln moved cautiously. When Unionists took control of the state government in August, Lincoln ordered federal troops to halt Kentucky's thriving trade with the Confederacy. In September, Illinois volunteers under the command of a relatively unknown brigadier general named Ulysses S. Grant crossed the Ohio River into Kentucky and drove out an invading Confederate force. Lincoln had kept the four border states (Delaware, Maryland, Missouri, and Kentucky) and the northwestern portion of Virginia in the Union.

TABLE 14.1	**Slavery and Secession**		
Group	Percentage of Whites in Slave-owning Families	Percentage of Slaves in Population
Original Confederate states	38	47
Border states that later joined the Confederacy	24	32
Border states that remained in the Union	14	15

Ernest Duvergier
de Hauranne

German Immigrants and the Civil War Within Missouri

Tens of thousands of German immigrants settled in Missouri and other midwestern states in the two decades before the Civil War; and as this letter written by Ernest Duvergier de Hauranne indicates, most of them supported the Union cause. Duvergier de Hauranne (1843–1877), a Frenchman, traveled widely, and his letters home offer intelligent commentary on American politics and society during the Civil War.

St. Louis, September 12, 1864

Missouri is to all intents and purposes a rebel state, an occupied territory where the Federal forces are really nothing but a garrison under siege; even today it is not certain what would happen if the troops were withdrawn. Party quarrels here are poisoned by class hatreds. Not only are questions of peace and war, of national honor and humiliation, hotly debated, but so is the much more explosive question of slavery versus abolition. . . . It is a war over private interests between two irreconcilable classes. The old Anglo-French families, attached to Southern institutions, harbor a primitive, superstitious prejudice in favor of slavery. Conquered now, but full of repressed rage, they exhibit the implacable anger peculiar to the defenders of lost causes. They no longer have any hope of reviving slavery or their own past fortunes; . . . they seem to be lying low while hoping for an opportunity to take their revenge.

The more recent German population is strongly abolitionist. They have brought to the New World the instincts of European democracy, together with its radical attitudes and all-or-nothing doctrines. Ancient precedents and worn-out laws matter little to them. They have not studied history and have no respect for hallowed injustices; but they do have, to the highest degree, that sense of moral principle which is more or less lacking in American democracy. They aren't afraid of revolution: to destroy a barbarous institution they would, if necessary, take an axe to the foundations of society. Furthermore, their interests coincide with their principles. . . . Even if their democratic beliefs and innate sense of justice did not cause them to rise up against slavery, they would still detest it as an obstacle to their prosperity and as a source of unfair competition with their labor.

The immigrant arrives poor and lives by his work. A newcomer, having nothing to lose and caring little for the interests of established property owners, sees that the subjection of free labor to the ruinous competition of slave labor must be ended. At the same time, his pride rebels against the prejudice attached to work in a land of slavery; he wants to reestablish its value. . . .

There is no mistaking the hatred the two parties, not to say the two peoples, have for each other. . . . As passions were coming to a boil, the Federal government sent General [John C.] Frémont here as army commander and dictator. . . . An abolitionist and a self-made man, he put himself firmly at the head of the German party, determined to crush the friends of slavery. He formed an army of Germans who are completely devoted to their chief. . . . He left the abolitionist party in the West organized, disciplined, stronger and more resolute, but he also left the pro-Southern party more exasperated than ever, and society divided, without intermediaries, into two hostile camps. . . .

Everyone is an extremist; between the radical abolitionists and the friends of the South there is no moderate Unionist middle ground. Bands of guerrillas hold the countryside, where they raid as much as they please; politics serves as a fine pretext for looting. Their leaders are officers from the army of the South who receive their orders from the Confederate government. . . . These "bushwackers," who ordinarily rob indiscriminately, maintain their standing as political raiders by occasionally killing some poor, inoffensive person. Finally, people bent on personal vengeance take advantage of the state of civil war: sometimes one hears of villages divided against themselves so bitterly that massacres are carried on from door to door with incredible ferocity. . . . You can see what emotions are still boiling in this region that is supposed to be pacified.

SOURCE: Ernest Duvergier de Hauranne, *A Frenchman in Lincoln's America* (Chicago: Lakeside Press, 1974), 1: 305–309.

ANALYZING THE EVIDENCE

➤ According to Duvergier de Hauranne, why did German immigrants oppose slavery? How does his explanation help us understand the free-soil movement?

➤ Why, as late as 1864, did the federal government lack control over Missouri, a border state that remained in the Union? What clues does Duvergier de Hauranne provide?

➤ Ethnic rivalries loomed large in the civil warfare in Missouri. As you read the chapter, look for other ethnic conflicts that exploded during the war. Why did they do so?

Setting War Objectives and Devising Strategies

At his inauguration in February 1861, Jefferson Davis identified the Confederates' cause with that of the American revolutionaries: Like their grandfathers, white Southerners were fighting against tyranny and for the "sacred right of self-government." As Davis put it, the Confederacy sought "no conquest, no aggrandizement . . . ; all we ask is to be let alone." The South's decision to renounce expansion was ironic: It was the region's quest for western lands that had sparked the conflict. However, the decision simplified the Confederacy's military strategy; it needed only a stalemate to achieve the goal of independence. Ignoring the strong opposition to slavery among potential European allies, the Confederate constitution explicitly stated that "no . . . law denying or impairing the right of property in negro slaves shall be passed," and Vice President Alexander Stephens ruled out gradual emancipation. In Stephens's view, the Confederacy's "cornerstone rests upon the great truth that the Negro is not equal to the white man, that slavery—subordination to the superior race—is his natural or normal condition."

Lincoln outlined the Union's military goals in a speech to Congress on July 4, 1861. He portrayed secession as an attack on popular government, which was America's great contribution to world history; it tested "whether a constitutional republic . . . [can] maintain its territorial integrity against a domestic foe." Convinced that the Union had to crush the rebellion, Lincoln rejected General Winfield Scott's plan to use economic sanctions and a naval blockade to persuade the Confederates to return to the Union. Instead, the president insisted on an aggressive military strategy and a policy of unconditional surrender.

Union Thrusts Toward Richmond. The president hoped that a quick strike against the Confederate capital of Richmond, Virginia, would end the rebellion. So he dispatched General Irvin McDowell and an army of 30,000 men to attack General P. G. T. Beauregard's force of 20,000 troops at Manassas, a rail junction in Virginia 30 miles southwest of Washington. In July 1861, McDowell launched a strong assault near Manassas Creek (also called Bull Run), but panic swept his troops when the Confederate soldiers counterattacked. For the first time, Union soldiers heard the hair-raising rebel yell. "The peculiar corkscrew sensation that it sends down your backbone under these circumstances can never be told," one Union veteran wrote. "You

have to feel it." McDowell's troops—along with the many civilians who had come to observe the battle—retreated in disarray to Washington.

The rout of the Union army at Bull Run made it clear that the rebellion would not be easily crushed. Lincoln replaced McDowell with General McClellan and enlisted an additional million men who would serve for three years in the newly created Army of the Potomac. A cautious military engineer, McClellan spent the winter of 1861 training the recruits; then, early in 1862, he launched a major offensive. With great logistical skill, the Union general transported 100,000 troops by boat down the Potomac River and put them ashore on the peninsula between the York and James rivers (Map 14.2). Ignoring Lincoln's advice to "strike a blow" quickly, McClellan advanced slowly toward the South's capital, giving the Confederates time to mount a counterstroke. To relieve the pressure on Richmond, a Confederate army under Thomas J. "Stonewall" Jackson marched rapidly north up the Shenandoah Valley in western Virginia and threatened Washington. Lincoln recalled 30,000 troops from McClellan's army to protect the Union's capital, but Jackson, a brilliant general, tied down the larger Union forces. Then Jackson returned quickly to Richmond to bolster the main Confederate army commanded by General Robert E. Lee. Lee launched a ferocious attack that lasted for days (June 25–July 1), suffering 20,000 casualties to the Union's 10,000. When McClellan failed to exploit the Confederates' weakness, Lincoln ordered the withdrawal of the Army of the Potomac, and Richmond remained secure.

Lee Moves North: Antietam. Hoping for victories that would humiliate Lincoln's government, Lee went on the offensive. Joining with Jackson in northern Virginia, he routed Union troops in the Second Battle of Bull Run (August 1862) and then struck north through western Maryland. There, he nearly met with disaster. When Lee divided his force—sending Jackson to capture Harpers Ferry in West Virginia—a copy of his orders fell into McClellan's hands. The Union general again failed to exploit his advantage. He delayed his attack, thereby allowing Lee's depleted army to occupy a strong defensive position behind Antietam Creek, near Sharpsburg, Maryland. Outnumbered 87,000 to 50,000, Lee desperately fought off McClellan's attacks. Just as Union regiments were about to overwhelm Lee's right flank, Jackson's troops arrived and saved the Confederates from a major defeat. Appalled by the number of Union casualties, McClellan let Lee retreat to Virginia.

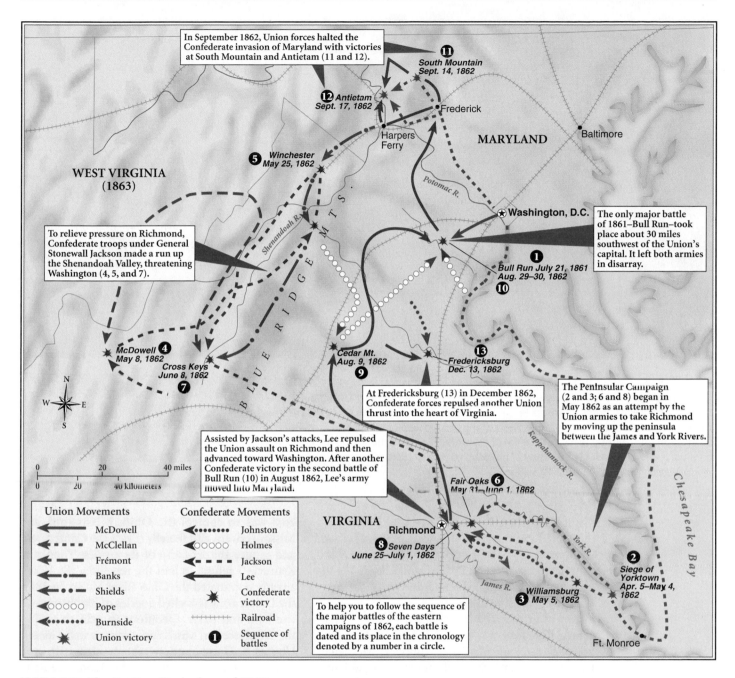

In September 1862, Union forces halted the Confederate invasion of Maryland with victories at South Mountain and Antietam (11 and 12).

To relieve pressure on Richmond, Confederate troops under General Stonewall Jackson made a run up the Shenandoah Valley, threatening Washington (4, 5, and 7).

The only major battle of 1861–Bull Run–took place about 30 miles southwest of the Union's capital. It left both armies in disarray.

At Fredericksburg (13) in December 1862, Confederate forces repulsed another Union thrust into the heart of Virginia.

The Peninsular Campaign (2 and 3; 6 and 8) began in May 1862 as an attempt by the Union armies to take Richmond by moving up the peninsula between the James and York Rivers.

Assisted by Jackson's attacks, Lee repulsed the Union assault on Richmond and then advanced toward Washington. After another Confederate victory in the second battle of Bull Run (10) in August 1862, Lee's army moved into Maryland.

To help you to follow the sequence of the major battles of the eastern campaigns of 1862, each battle is dated and its place in the chronology denoted by a number in a circle.

Union Movements

- McDowell
- McClellan
- Frémont
- Banks
- Shields
- Pope
- Burnside
- Union victory

Confederate Movements

- Johnston
- Holmes
- Jackson
- Lee
- Confederate victory
- Railroad
- Sequence of battles

MAP 14.2 The Eastern Campaigns of 1862

Many of the great battles of the Civil War took place in the 125 miles separating the Union capital, Washington, D.C., and the Confederate capital, Richmond, Virginia. During 1862, Confederate generals Robert J. "Stonewall" Jackson and Robert E. Lee won defensive victories that protected the Confederate capital (3, 6, 8, and 13) and launched offensive strikes against Union forces guarding Washington (1, 4, 5, 7, 9, and 10). They also suffered a defeat — at Antietam (12), in Maryland — that was almost fatal. As was often the case in the Civil War, the victors in these battles were either too bloodied or too timid to exploit their advantage.

The fighting at Antietam was savage. A Wisconsin officer described his men "loading and firing with demoniacal fury and shouting and laughing hysterically." At a critical point in the battle, a sunken road — nicknamed Bloody Lane — was filled with Confederate bodies two and three deep, and the attacking Union troops knelt on "this ghastly flooring" to shoot at the retreating Confederates. The battle at Antietam on September 17, 1862, remains the bloodiest single day in U.S. military

The Battle of Antietam: The Fight for Burnside's Bridge

Nearly eight thousand soldiers lost their lives at Antietam on September 17, 1862, many of them in the struggle for the Rohrback Bridge that crossed Antietam Creek. One of those who survived the battle, Captain James Hope of the Second Vermont Volunteers, recorded the event in this painting. In his description of the work, Hope gave the bridge the name of the Union general who sacrificed many of his troops trying to capture it. Antietam National Battlefield, National Park Service, Sharpsburg, Maryland.

history. Together, the Confederate and Union dead numbered 4,800 and the wounded 18,500, of whom 3,000 soon died. (By comparison, there were 6,000 American casualties on D-Day, which began the invasion of Nazi-occupied France in World War II.)

In public, Lincoln claimed Antietam as a Union victory; but privately he declared that McClellan should have fought Lee to the bitter end. A masterful organizer of men and supplies, McClellan lacked the stomach for an all-out attack. Dismissing McClellan as his chief commander, Lincoln began a long search for an effective replacement. His first choice was Ambrose E. Burnside, who proved to be more daring but less competent than his predecessor. In December, after heavy losses in futile attacks against well-entrenched Confederate forces at Fredericksburg, Virginia, Burnside resigned his command, and Lincoln replaced him with Joseph "Fighting Joe" Hooker. As 1862 ended, the Confederates were optimistic: The war in the East was stalemated.

The War in the West. In the West, Union commanders were more successful (Map 14.3). Their goal was to control the Ohio, Mississippi, and Missouri rivers, and thereby divide the Confederacy and reduce the mobility of its armies. Thanks to Kentucky's refusal to join the rebellion, the Union already dominated the Ohio River Valley. In 1862, the Union army launched a series of highly innovative land and water operations to gain control of the Tennessee and Mississippi rivers as well. General Ulysses S. Grant used riverboats clad with iron plates to take Fort Henry on the Tennessee River and Fort Donelson on the Cumberland River. Grant then moved south to seize critical railroad lines. On April 6, a Confederate army led by Albert Sidney Johnston and P. G. T. Beauregard caught Grant by surprise near a small log church named Shiloh. In the ensuing battle, Grant relentlessly committed troops until he forced a Confederate withdrawal. As the fighting ended on April 7, Grant looked out over a large field "so covered with dead that it would have been possible to walk over the clearing in any direction, stepping on dead bodies, without a foot touching the ground." The cost in lives was high, but Lincoln was pleased: "What I want . . . is generals who will fight battles and win victories."

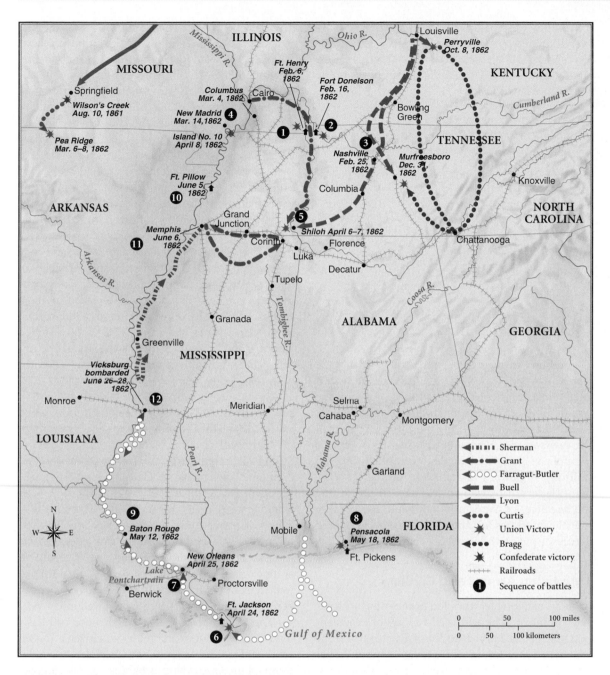

MAP 14.3 The Western Campaigns, 1861–1862

As the Civil War intensified in 1862, Union and Confederate military and naval forces fought to control the great valleys of the Ohio, Tennessee, and Mississippi rivers. From February through April 1862, Union armies moved south through western Tennessee (1–3 and 5). By the end of June, Union naval forces controlled the Mississippi River north of Memphis (4, 10, and 11) and from the Gulf of Mexico to Vicksburg (6, 7, 9, and 12). These military and naval victories gave the Union control of crucial transportation routes, kept Missouri in the Union, and carried the war to the borders of the states of the Deep South.

Less than three weeks later, Union naval forces commanded by David G. Farragut struck the Confederacy from the Gulf of Mexico. They captured New Orleans and took control of fifteen hundred plantations and fifty thousand slaves in the sur-rounding region. The Union now held the South's financial center and largest city, and were in a strong position to conduct future naval operations. Equally important, slaves on many plantations looted their owner's mansion and refused to work unless they were paid wages. Slavery there "is forever destroyed and worthless," declared one Northern reporter. Union victories in the West had significantly undermined Confederate strength in the Mississippi River Valley.

> ➤ Why was there no new compromise over slavery in 1861?
>
> ➤ Why did most of the border states remain in the Union?
>
> ➤ Why did the Confederacy—and the Union—decide to go to war in 1861? What were the military goals of each side?

Toward Total War

The military carnage in 1862 made it clear that the war would be long and costly. After Shiloh, Grant later remarked, he "gave up all idea of saving the Union except by complete conquest." The conflict became a **total war**, arraying the entire resources of the two societies against each other. Aided by the Republican Party and a talented cabinet, Lincoln skillfully organized an effective central government. Jefferson Davis had less success harnessing the resources of the South, a difficult task because the eleven states of the Confederacy remained deeply suspicious of centralized rule.

Mobilizing Armies and Civilians

Initially, patriotic fervor filled both armies with eager volunteers. The widowed mother of nineteen-year-old Elisha Hunt Rhodes of Pawtuxet, Rhode Island, sent her son to war, saying, "My son, other mothers must make sacrifices and why should not I?" The call for soldiers was especially successful in the South, which had a strong military tradition, an ample supply of trained officers, and a culture that stressed duty and honor. "Would you, My Darling, . . . be willing to leave your Children under such a [despotic Union] government?" James B. Griffin of Edgefield, South Carolina, asked his wife. "No—I know you would sacrifice every comfort on earth, rather than submit to it." However, enlistments fell off as potential recruits learned the realities of mass warfare: heavy losses to epidemic diseases in the camps and wholesale death on the battlefields. Both governments soon faced the necessity of conscription.

The Military Draft. The Confederacy was the first to act. In April 1862, following the bloody battle at Shiloh, the Confederate Congress imposed the first legally binding draft in American history. One law extended existing enlistments for the duration of the war; another required three years of military service from all men between the ages of eighteen and thirty-five. In September 1862, after the heavy casualties at Antietam, the age limit was raised to forty-five. The Confederate draft had two loopholes, both controversial. First, it exempted one white man—the planter, a son, or an overseer—for each twenty slaves, and so allowed some whites on large plantations to avoid military service. This provision, Mississippi senator James Phelan wrote to Jefferson Davis, "has aroused a sprit of rebellion in some places." Second, draftees could hire substitutes. Before this provision was repealed in 1864, the price for a substitute had risen to $300 in gold, about three times the annual wages of a skilled worker. Laborers and yeomen farmers angrily complained that it had become "a rich man's war and a poor man's fight."

Consequently, some Southerners refused to serve. Because the Confederate constitution vested sovereignty in the individual states, the government in Richmond could not compel military service. Strong governors like Joseph Brown of Georgia and Zebulon Vance of North Carolina simply ignored President Davis's first draft call in early 1862. Elsewhere, state judges issued writs of **habeas corpus**—a legal instrument used to protect people from arbitrary arrest—and ordered the Confederate army to release reluctant draftees. However, the Confederate Congress overrode the judges' authority to free conscripted men, enabling the government to keep substantial armies in the field well into 1864.

The Union government acted more ruthlessly toward potential foes and reluctant citizens. To prevent sabotage and resistance by Confederate sympathizers, Lincoln suspended habeas corpus and over the course of the war imprisoned about fifteen thousand people without trial. The president also extended martial law to civilians who discouraged enlistments or resisted the draft, putting them under the jurisdiction of military courts rather than local juries. These firm policies had the wanted effect. When the Militia Act of 1862 set local recruitment quotas, states and towns enticed volunteers with cash bounties and eventually signed up nearly a million men. In the North, as in the South, wealthy men could avoid military service by providing a substitute or paying a $300 commutation fee.

The Enrollment Act of 1863 initiated conscription in the North and was strongly opposed by recent responded by rushing in Union troops who had just fought at Gettysburg; the soldiers killed more than one hundred rioters and suppressed the insurrection.

Women and the War Effort. The Union government's campaign of total war won greater support among native-born middle-class citizens. In 1861, prominent New Yorkers established the U.S. Sanitary Commission to provide medical services and prevent the spread of epidemic diseases. Through its network of seven thousand local auxiliaries, the commission collected clothing, food, and medicine, and recruited battlefield nurses and doctors for the Union Army Medical Bureau. Despite the commission's efforts, dysentery, typhoid, and malaria spread through the camps, as did mumps and measles, childhood viruses to which many rural men had not developed immunity. Diseases and infections killed about 250,000 Union soldiers, roughly twice the number who died in combat. Still, better sanitation and high-quality food kept the mortality rate among Union troops significantly below that of soldiers in nineteenth-century European wars. Confederate soldiers were less fortunate. Thousands of women volunteered as nurses,

Draft Riots and Antiblack Violence in New York City

The Enrollment Act of 1863 enraged many workers in New York City, especially recent Irish and German immigrants who did not want to go to war. In July, they took out their anger on free blacks in a weeklong series of riots. This engraving depicts a mob burning the Colored Orphan Asylum on Fifth Avenue, home to two hundred African American children. All of the children escaped safely, but the fire spread to adjoining structures, forcing residents to flee with whatever possessions they could carry. Library of Congress.

Hospital Nursing

Working as nurses in battlefront hospitals, thousands of Union and Confederate women gained firsthand experience of the horrors of war. A sense of calm prevails in this behind-the-lines Union hospital in Nashville, Tennessee, as nurse Anne Belle tends to the needs of soldiers recovering from their wounds. Most Civil War nurses were volunteers; they spent time cooking and cleaning for their patients as well as tending their injuries. U.S. Army Military History Institute.

immigrants from Germany and Ireland, who protested that it was not their war. Northern Democrats, who became increasingly critical of Lincoln's policies as the war progressed, used the furor over conscription to bolster political support for their party. They accused Lincoln of drafting poor whites to win freedom for blacks, who would flood into the cities and take the whites' jobs. "Slavery is dead," declared a Democratic newspaper in Cincinnati, "the negro is not, there is the misfortune." In July 1863, the immigrants' hostility to the draft and to African Americans brought violence to the streets of New York City. For five days, Irish and German workers ran rampant, burning draft offices, sacking the homes of influential Republicans, and attacking the police. The rioters also lynched and mutilated a dozen African Americans, drove hundreds of black families from their homes, and burned down the Colored Orphan Asylum. Lincoln

but the Confederate health system was poorly organized. Scurvy was a special problem for southern soldiers, who lacked vitamin C in their diets, and they died from camp diseases at higher rates than did Union soldiers.

War-relief measures had a significant impact on women's lives. More than 200,000 northern women worked as volunteers in the Sanitary Commission and the Freedman's Aid Society, which collected supplies for liberated slaves, and some women took leading roles in wartime agencies. Dorothea Dix (see Chapter 11) served as superintendent of female nurses, the first woman to receive a major federal appointment. Dix successfully combated the prejudice against women's providing medical treatment to men and thereby opened a new occupation to women. Thousands of educated Union women joined the war effort as clerks in the expanding government bureaucracy, while in the South women staffed the efficient Confederate postal service. Indeed, in both sections of the country, millions of women assumed new economic responsibilities. They took over many farm tasks previously done by men and filled jobs not only in schools and offices but also in textile, clothing, and shoe factories. A number of women even took on military duties as spies, scouts, and (disguising themselves as men) soldiers. As nurse Clara Barton, who later founded the American Red Cross, recalled, "At the war's end, woman was at least fifty years in advance of the normal position which continued peace would have assigned her."

Mobilizing Resources

Wars are usually won by the side with greater resources and better economic organization. In this regard, the Union entered the war with a distinct advantage. With nearly two-thirds of the nation's population, two-thirds of the railroad mileage, and almost 90 percent of the industrial output, the North's economy was far superior to the South's (Figure 14.1). The North had an especially great advantage in the manufacture of cannon and rifles because many of its arms factories were equipped for mass production.

But the Confederate position was far from weak. Virginia, North Carolina, and Tennessee had substantial industrial capacity. Richmond, with its Tredegar Iron Works, was an important manufacturing center; and in 1861, the Confederacy moved the gun-making machinery from the U.S. armory at Harpers Ferry to Richmond. The production at the Richmond armory, the purchase of Enfield rifles from Britain, and the capture of 100,000 Union

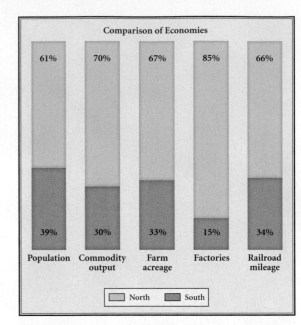

FIGURE 14.1   Economies, North and South, 1860

The military advantages of the North were even greater than this chart suggests because the population figures include slaves, whom the South feared to arm, and because its commodity output was primarily in farm goods rather than manufactures. Moreover, on average, southern factories were much smaller than those in the North. SOURCES: Stanley Engerman, "The Economic Impact of the Civil War," in *The Reinterpretation of American Economic History*, ed. Robert W. Fogel and Stanley L. Engerman (New York: Harper & Row, 1971); and U.S. census data.

guns enabled the Confederacy to provide every infantryman with a modern rifle-musket by 1863.

Moreover, with 9 million people, the Confederacy could mobilize enormous armies. Although more than one-third of that number were slaves, they contributed to the war effort by producing food for the army and cotton for export. Confederate leaders counted on **"King Cotton"** to provide the revenue to purchase clothes, boots, blankets, and weapons from abroad. They also counted on cotton as a diplomatic weapon that would persuade Britain and France, whose textile factories needed raw cotton, to grant the Confederacy diplomatic recognition. However, British manufacturers had stockpiled cotton; and when those stocks ran out, they found new sources in Egypt and India. Still, the South's hope was partially fulfilled. Although Britain never recognized the Confederacy as an independent nation, it granted the rebel government the status of a belligerent power—with the right under international law to borrow money and purchase weapons. The odds, then, did not necessarily favor the Union, despite its superior resources.

Richmond: Capital City and Industrial Center

The Confederacy chose Richmond as its capital because of the historic importance of Virginia as the home of Washington, Jefferson, Madison, and Monroe. However, Richmond was also a major industrial center. Exploiting the city's location at the falls of the James River, the city's entrepreneurs had developed a wide range of industries: flour mills, tobacco factories, railroad and port facilities, and, most important, a profitable and substantial iron industry. In 1861, the Tredegar Iron Works employed nearly one thousand workers and, as the only facility in the South that could manufacture large machinery and heavy weapons, made a major contribution to the Confederate war effort. Virginia State Library.

Forging New Economic Policies. To mobilize the resources of the North, the Republican-dominated Congress enacted a program of government-assisted national economic development that far surpassed Henry Clay's American System. First, the Republicans raised tariffs to win the political support of northeastern manufacturers and workers, who feared competition from cheaper foreign goods. Then Secretary of the Treasury Salmon P. Chase secured legislation that forced thousands of local banks to accept federal charters and regulations. This integrated national banking system was far more effective in raising capital and controlling inflation than the First and Second Banks of the United States had been. Finally, the Republican Congress implemented Clay's program for a nationally financed system of internal improvements. In 1862, it chartered the Union Pacific and Central

Pacific companies to build a transcontinental railroad line and assisted them with lavish subsidies. In addition, the Republicans provided northern and midwestern farmers with "free land." The Homestead Act of 1862 gave heads of families or individuals age twenty-one or older the title to 160 acres of public land after five years of residence. This economic program won the Republican Party the allegiance of many farmers, workers, and entrepreneurs, and bolstered the Union's ability to fight a long war.

New industries sprang up to meet the army's need for guns, clothes, and food. More than 1.5 million men served in the Union army, and they consumed more than half a billion pounds of pork and other packed meats. To supply this immense quantity, Chicago railroads built new lines to carry tens of thousands of hogs and cattle to the city's ever-larger stockyards and slaughtering houses. By 1862,

Chicago passed Cincinnati as the meatpacking capital of the nation, bringing prosperity to thousands of midwestern farmers and great wealth to Philip D. Armour and other entrepreneurs.

A similar concentration of capital took place in many industries. The war, an observer commented, gave a few men "the command of millions of money"; such massed financial power threatened not only the prewar society of small producers but also the future of democracy. Americans "are never again to see the republic in which we were born," lamented abolitionist and social reformer Wendell Phillips.

The Confederate government slowly developed a coherent economic policy. True to its states' rights philosophy, the Confederacy initially left most economic matters in the hands of the state governments. However, as the realities of total war became clear, the Davis administration took some extraordinary measures: It built and operated shipyards, armories, foundries, and textile mills; commandeered food and scarce raw materials like coal, iron, copper, and lead; requisitioned slaves to work on fortifications; and exercised direct control over foreign trade. Ordinary southern citizens increasingly resented and resisted these measures by the government in Richmond. To sustain the war effort, the Confederacy increasingly relied on white solidarity: Jefferson Davis warned that a Union victory would destroy slavery "and reduce the whites to the degraded position of the African race."

Raising Money in the North. For both sides, the cost of fighting a total war was enormous. The annual spending of the Union government shot up from $63 million in 1860 to more than $865 million in 1864 (Table 14.2). To meet that vast outlay, the Republicans established a powerful modern state that raised money in three ways. First, the government increased tariffs on consumer goods, placed high excise duties on alcohol and tobacco, and imposed direct taxes on business corporations, large inheritances, and incomes. These levies paid for about 20 percent of the cost of the war. The sale of treasury bonds financed another 65 percent. Led by Jay Cooke, a Philadelphia banker, the Treasury Department used newspaper advertisements and 2,500 subagents to persuade nearly a million northern families to buy war bonds. In addition, the National Banking Acts of 1863 and 1864 forced most banks to purchase treasury bonds.

The Union paid the remaining cost of the war by printing paper money. The Legal Tender Act of 1862 authorized the issue of $150 million in treasury notes—which soon became known as **greenbacks**—and required the public to accept them as legal tender. Like the Continental currency issued during the War of Independence, these treasury notes were not backed by specie; unlike the earlier currency, this paper money was printed in relatively limited amounts and so did not depreciate disastrously in value. By imposing broad-based taxes, borrowing from the middle classes, and creating a national monetary system, the Union government had created the financial foundations of a modern nation-state.

The South Resorts to Inflation. The financial demands on the South were just as great, but it lacked a powerful central government that could tax and borrow. The Confederate Congress fiercely opposed taxes on cotton exports and slaves, the most valuable property held by wealthy planters; and the urban middle class and yeoman farm families refused to bear the entire tax burden. Consequently, the Confederacy covered less than 5 percent of its expenditures through taxation. The government paid for another 35 percent by borrowing, although wealthy planters and foreign bankers became increasingly wary of investing in Confederate bonds that might never be redeemed.

TABLE 14.2	The Cost of War: Union Finances, 1860 and 1864	
	1860	**1864**
Income	$56.1 million	$264.6 million
Expenditures	$63.1 million	$865.3 million
General	32.0 million	35.1 million
Army and navy	27.9 million	776.5 million
Interest on debt	3.2 million	53.7 million
Public debt	$64.8 million	$1,815.8 million

In 1864, the Union government received almost five times as much revenue as it had in 1860, but it spent nearly fourteen times as much, mostly to pay soldiers and buy military supplies. In four years, the public debt had risen by a factor of twenty-eight, so that interest payments in 1864 nearly equaled the level of all federal government spending in 1860.

The War's Toll on Civilians

In the spring of 1862, fighting along the Mississippi River and the Union blockade in the Gulf of Mexico disrupted the commerce of New Orleans. By the time Union troops captured the city in May, the stock of food in the city was very low. In June, hungry citizens—men in top hats, fashionably dressed women, barefoot children, and white and black workers—stormed the stores and emptied them of their last supplies of food. This engraving, titled *Starving People of New Orleans*, appeared in *Harper's Weekly*, a prominent New York journal. Library of Congress.

This meant that the Confederacy had to finance about 60 percent of its expenses by printing paper money. The flood of currency created a spectacular inflation: By 1865, prices had risen to ninety-two times their 1861 level. As the vast supply of money (and a shortage of goods) caused food prices to soar, riots broke out in more than a dozen southern cities and towns. In Richmond, several hundred women broke into bakeries, crying, "Our children are starving while the rich roll in wealth." In Randolph County, Alabama, women confiscated grain from a government warehouse "to prevent starvation of themselves and their families." As inflation increased, Southerners refused to accept Confederate money, sometimes with serious consequences. When South Carolina storekeeper Jim Harris rejected the Confederate notes presented by a group of soldiers, they raided his storehouse and "robbed it of about five thousand dollars worth of goods." Army supply officers seized goods from storekeepers and merchants, and offered payment in worthless IOUs. Faced with a public that feared strong government and high taxation, the Confederacy could sustain the war effort only by seizing the property of its citizens.

➤ Which government—the Union or the Confederacy—imposed greater military and economic burdens on its citizens? How successful was that strategy?

➤ What were the main economic policies enacted by the Republican-controlled Congress?

The Turning Point: 1863

By 1863, the Lincoln administration had finally created an efficient war machine, a coherent financial system, and a set of strategic priorities. The perceptive young diplomat Henry Adams, the grandson of President John Quincy Adams and a future novelist and historian, noted the change from his post in London: "Little by little, one began to feel that, behind the chaos in Washington power was taking shape; that it was massed and guided as it had not been before." Slowly but surely, the tide of the struggle shifted toward the Union.

Emancipation

When the war began, antislavery Republicans demanded that their party make abolition—as well as restoration of the Union—a central goal. The fighting should continue, a Massachusetts abolitionist declared, "until the Slave power is completely subjugated, and *emancipation made certain.*" Because slave-grown crops sustained the Confederacy, antislavery activists argued for black emancipation on military grounds. As Frederick Douglass put it, "Arrest that hoe in the hands of the Negro, and you smite the rebellion in the very seat of its life." Initially, Lincoln subordinated demands for black freedom to the survival of the Union. "If I could save the Union without freeing any slave, I would do it," he told Horace Greeley in a letter published in the *New York Tribune* in August 1862, "and if I could save it by freeing all the slaves, I would do it." By implicitly asserting his constitutional authority to end slavery, Lincoln was beginning to define the conflict as both a struggle to preserve the Union and to destroy slavery, the cornerstone of southern society.

"Contrabands." As Lincoln moved cautiously toward emancipation, enslaved African Americans forced the issue by seizing freedom for themselves. Exploiting the disorder of wartime, tens of thousands of slaves fled their plantations and sought refuge behind Union lines. In May 1861, when three slaves reached the camp of General Benjamin Butler in Virginia, he labeled them "contraband of war" and refused to return them. The term stuck, and within a few months a thousand "contrabands" were camping with Butler's army. In August 1861, to provide these fugitives with legal status, Congress passed the Confiscation Act, authorizing the seizure of all property—including slaves—used to support the rebellion.

Radical Republicans—Treasury Secretary Salmon Chase, Senator Charles Sumner of Massachusetts, and Representative Thaddeus Stevens of Pennsylvania—now saw a way to use wartime legislation to destroy slavery. A longtime member of Congress, Stevens was a masterful politician and adept at fashioning legislation that could win majority support. In April 1862, Stevens and his Radical allies persuaded Congress to end slavery in the District of Columbia by providing compensation for owners. In June, Congress outlawed slavery in the federal territories (finally enacting the Wilmot Proviso of 1846); and in July, it passed a second Confiscation Act. This act simply overrode the property rights of Confederate slave owners by declaring "forever free" all fugitive slaves and all slaves captured by the Union army. Emancipation had become an instrument of war.

The Emancipation Proclamation. Lincoln built on the Radical Republicans' initiative. In July 1862, he prepared a general proclamation of emancipation; considering the Battle of Antietam "an indication of the Divine Will," he issued the proclamation five days later, on September 22, 1862. The statement relied for its legal authority on the president's responsibility as commander in chief to suppress the rebellion. It declared that slavery would be legally abolished in all states that remained out of the Union on January 1, 1863. The rebel states had a hundred days in which to preserve slavery by renouncing secession. None chose to do so.

The proclamation was politically astute. Lincoln wanted to avoid opposition from slave owners in the Union-controlled border states, such as Maryland and Missouri, so the proclamation left slavery intact in those states. It also left slavery intact in areas occupied by Union armies—western and central Tennessee, western Virginia, and southern Louisiana, including New Orleans. Consequently, the Emancipation Proclamation did not actually free a single slave, at least not immediately. Yet, as abolitionist Wendell Phillips perceived, Lincoln's proclamation had moved the institution of slavery to "the edge of Niagara," from where it would soon be swept over the brink. Indeed, advancing Union troops became the agents of its destruction. "I became free in 1863, in the summer, when the yankees come by and said I could go work for myself," Jackson Daniel of Maysville, Alabama, recalled. "I was farming after that [and also] . . . making shoes." As Lincoln now saw it, the conflict had become a war of "subjugation" in which "the old South is to be destroyed and replaced by new propositions and ideas" (see Comparing American Voices, "Blacks and Whites Describe the End of Slavery," pp. 442–443).

As an objective of the war, emancipation was controversial. In the Confederacy, Jefferson Davis labeled it the "most execrable measure recorded in the history of guilty man"; in the North, it produced a racist backlash among white voters. During the congressional election of 1862, the Democrats denounced emancipation as unconstitutional, warned of slave uprisings, and claimed that a "black flood" would take white jobs. Democrat Horatio Seymour won the governorship of New York by declaring that if abolition was a goal of the war, the South should not be conquered. Other Democrats swept to victory in Pennsylvania, Ohio, and Illinois, and the party gained thirty-four seats in Congress. But the Republicans still held a twenty-five-seat majority in the House and had gained five seats in the Senate. Lincoln refused to retreat. On New Year's Day 1863, he signed the Emancipation Proclamation. To reassure Northerners, Lincoln urged slaves to "abstain from all violence" and justified emancipation as an "act of justice." "If my name ever goes into history," he said, "it was for this act."

Vicksburg and Gettysburg

The fate of the proclamation would depend on the political success of the Republican Party and the military victories of the Union armies. The outlook was not encouraging on either front. Democrats had registered significant gains in the election of 1862, and popular support was growing for a negotiated peace. Two brilliant victories in Virginia by Lee, whose army defeated Hooker's forces at Fredericksburg (December 1862) and Chancellorsville (May 1863), caused further erosion of northern support for the war.

The Crucial Battles of July 1863. At this critical juncture, General Grant mounted a major offensive in the West designed to split the Confederacy in two. Grant drove south along the west bank of the Mississippi and then moved his troops across the river near Vicksburg, Mississippi, where he defeated two Confederate armies and laid siege to the city. After repelling Union assaults for six weeks, the exhausted and starving Vicksburg garrison surrendered on July 4, 1863. Five days later, Union forces took Port Hudson, Louisiana (near Baton Rouge), and established complete control of the Mississippi River. Grant had taken 31,000 prisoners; cut off Louisiana, Arkansas, and Texas from the rest of the Confederacy; and prompted thousands of slaves to desert their plantations or demand wages.

As Grant advanced along the Mississippi in May, Confederate leaders were arguing over the best strategic response. President Davis and other politicians wanted to reinforce Vicksburg and send another army to Tennessee to draw Grant out of Mississippi. But General Robert E. Lee, buoyed by his recent victories over Hooker, favored a new invasion of the North. That strategy, Lee suggested, would either draw Union armies to the east, thereby relieving the pressure on Vicksburg, or give the Confederacy a major victory that would undermine northern support for the war.

Lee won out. In June 1863, he maneuvered his army north through Maryland into Pennsylvania. The Union's Army of the Potomac moved along with him, positioning itself between Lee and Washington, D.C., the federal capital. On July 1, the two great armies met by accident at Gettysburg, Pennsylvania, in what became a decisive confrontation (Map 14.4). On the first day of battle, Lee drove the Union's advance guard to the south of town. General George G. Meade, who had just

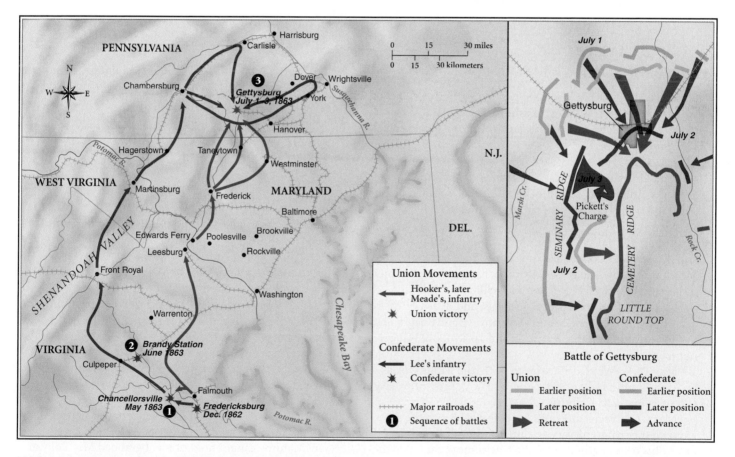

MAP 14.4 Lee Invades the North, 1863

After Lee's victories at Chancellorsville (1) in May and Brandy Station (2) in June, the Confederate forces moved northward, constantly shadowed by the Union army. On July 1, the two armies met accidentally near Gettysburg. In the ensuing battle (3), the Union army, commanded by General George Meade, emerged victorious, primarily because it was much larger than the Confederate force and held well-fortified positions along Cemetery Ridge, which gave its units a major tactical advantage.

Blacks and Whites Describe the End of Slavery

Ratification of the Thirteenth Amendment on December 6, 1865, legally ended chattel slavery—the ownership of people as property. In fact, slavery died a million deaths, each at a different time and under different circumstances. Some deaths happened years before 1865; others, long after. Because slavery was a personal as well as a property relationship, it ended in a psychological sense only when a slave claimed freedom. As you read these stories, consider the various ways in which slaves became free and the extent of their freedom.

These stories come from the journal of a slave-owning woman and from transcriptions of oral interviews of ex-slaves during the 1930s. Most of the interviewers, from the Federal Writers' Project, were white men and women. Most of the ex-slaves were in their eighties and nineties. Use this knowledge as you read these sources.

ELIZABETH MARY MEADE INGRAHAM

Elizabeth Mary Meade Ingraham was the mistress of Ashwood Plantation near Vicksburg, Mississippi. Her diary describes the impact on plantation life of General Grant's advance on Vicksburg in 1863.

May 4. [Union general] Osterhaus' Division, scum of St. Louis, camped in the big field. All the corn ruined in the field, and nearly all consumed in the granaries. . . .

May 8. The last thing Eddens [a slave] did was to save some meat for me. He slept in the spare room Sunday night, and Monday at noon he had quit our service. . . . Parker, Sol, Mordt, Jim Crow, Isaiah, and Wadloo, have quit us, but the rest are here, and very attentive and willing. . . .

May 13. Elsy still faithful, feeds us, and does what she can; Rita Jane too; Bowlegs very attentive. Emma beginning to tire of waiting on me, did not come up at noon; Nancy not true. . . .

May 18. [We] have reason to think the hands will all leave; only a question of time, they are not quite ready; Elsy still true; but Jack doubtful. . . .

May 27. Negro meetings are being held, and the few whites left begin to be very anxious. . . . Powers was burnt out by his own negroes. I fear the blacks more than I do the Yankees. Jack trying to persuade Elsy to leave. . . . She tells him to get her a home and a way of earning a living, and she is ready to go, but [I] told her, if he left here, to move up into the wash-house with her children. I would give her $12 a month and free her four children.

June 6–10. Martha with her three children and Emma, left at midnight Friday . . . and the rest are packing to-day. Hays resolved to go, and I dread lest he take his wife with him, for I can hardly get along as it is, and shall die if I have the cooking to do. . . . Those who have stayed are utterly demoralized; if they work for you, the job is only half done.

SARAH DEBRO

Sarah Debro grew up in slavery in Orange County, North Carolina.

I wuz to be a house maid [to Miss Polly]. The day she took me my mammy cried cauz she knew I never be 'lowed to live at de cabin wid her no more. . . . [Working in the big house] my dresses and apron was starched stiff. I had a clean apron every day. . . . I loved Mis' Polly an' loved stayin' at de big house. . . .

When de War was over, de Yankees was all roun' de place telling niggers what to do. Dey tole dem dey was free, dat dey didn' have to slave for de white folks no more.

One day my mammy come to de big house after me. I didn' want to go. I wanted to stay wid Mis' Polly. I 'gun to cry, an' Mammy caught hold of me. I grabbed Mis' Polly an' held so tight dat I tore her skirt bindin' loose, an' her skirt fell down 'bout her feets.

"Let her stay wid me," Mis' Polly said to Mammy. But Mammy shook her head. "You took her away from me an' didn' pay no mind to my cryin', so now I's takin' her back home. We's free now Mis' Polly. We ain' gwine be slaves no more to nobody." She dragged me away. I can see how Mis' Polly looked, now. She didn' say nothin', but she looked hard at Mammy, an' her face was white.

ALLEN WILLIAMS

Allen Williams lived as a slave on a small farm in Texas.

You ought to been behind a tree the day young Master George told me I was free. You would have laughed fit to kill. I was down on farm plowing, and Master George rid up on a hoss and say, "Morning, Allen." I say, "Morning, Master George." "Laying by the crap [crop]?" he say. "Yes, Sah," I told him. Then, he say, "Allen, you is free." I say, "What you mean, 'free'?" "The damn Yankees is freed you," he say.

I got off the plow, and he grabbed me by the arm, and pushed my sleeve up, and p'inted to my skin, and say, "Allen, my daddy give a thousand dollars in gold for that, didn't he?" "He sho' did," I told him. Then, he say, "Didn't my daddy give you to me? And didn't I put them clothes on you?" "Sho' 'nuf, you did," I say to him. Then, Master George say, "Yes, and the damn Yankees took you away from me. But them is my clothes." Then, he made like he was gonna take my clothes away from me, and we scuffled all round the field.

Then, Master George begin to laugh, and say, "Allen, I ain't gonna take your clothes. I's gonna put some better ones on you. You is free, but I want you to stay right on and tend to your mistress, like you been doing." I lived with them till after I was grown. I was in and out five or six years, 'fore married. When I couldn't get work, I went back to them and et Old Mistress' meat and bread.

ANNIE RO

Annie Ro worked as a household servant on a plantation in Alabama.

One day, aftah de am fightin' fo' mo' dan two yeahs, de marster gits a letter f'om Marster Billy. Dat letter says de niggar sho' am gwine to be free, de Wah am 'bout over, dat him will be home soon, an' dat John am killed. . . . De marster says nothin', jus' sit and stares. Den, suddenly, him jumps up an' stahts cussin' de War, de nigger, Abe Lincoln, an' ever'body . . . an' says, "Free de nigger, will dey? Ise free dem." . . . Den, him takes his gun off de rack an' stahts fo' de field whar de niggers am a-wukkin'. . . .

De good Lawd took a han' in dat mess, den. De marster ain' gone far in de field, when he draps [dead], all of a sudden.

DELICIA PATTERSON

Delicia Patterson was ninety-two when she was interviewed in St. Louis, Missouri.

I was born in Boonville, Missouri, January 2, 1845. My mother's name was Maria and my father's was Jack Wiley. Mother had five children but raised only two of us. I was owned by Charles Mitchell until I was fifteen years old. They were fairly nice to all of their slaves and they had several of us. . . . When I was fifteen years old, I was brought to the courthouse, put up on the auction block to be sold. . . . I was sold to a Southern Englishman named Thomas Steele for fifteen hundred dollars. . . . I lived in that family until after the Civil War was over. . . .

When freedom was declared Mr. Steele told me that I was as free as he was. He said I could leave them if I please or could stay, that they wanted me [to stay] . . . and his wife said, "Course she is our nigger. She is as much our nigger now as she was the day you bought her two years ago and paid fifteen hundred dollars for her."

That made me mad so I left right then, since she was so smart. . . . I hired myself out to a family named Miller at three dollars a week, and lived on the place. . . .

I don't know what the ex-slaves expected, but I do know they didn't get anything. After the War we just wandered from place to place, working for food and a place to stay.

SOURCES: W. Maury Darst, "The Vicksburg Diary of Mrs. Alfred Ingraham," *Journal of Mississippi History* 44 (May 1982): 148–179; James Mellon, ed., *The Slaves Remember: An Oral History* (New York: Avon Books, 1988), 347 (Williams), and 352 (Debro); and Norman Yetman, ed., *Memoirs from the Slave Narrative Collection* (New York: Dover, 2002), 72 (Ro) and 101–103 (Patterson).

ANALYZING THE EVIDENCE

➤ How does Elizabeth Mary Meade Ingraham react to the end of slavery? How does her reaction compare with those of the other slave owners described in the interviews? What are the owners' strategies and goals with regard to their workers?

➤ Do you think the interviewers' race or outlook affected the content of the interviews here? Is it important that some transcriptions are in Standard English and that others are in black dialect?

➤ What impact do you think the age of the ex-slaves had on their stories? How might the passage of decades have affected their memory of events? Is it significant that most of those interviewed were either children or teenagers when slavery ended?

➤ What specific event or set of factors prompted each of these former slaves to claim his or her freedom? Can you detect any patterns in the stories? What are they?

replaced Hooker as the Union commander, placed his troops in well-defended hilltop positions and called up reinforcements. By the morning of July 2, Meade had 90,000 troops to Lee's 75,000. Aware that he was outnumbered but bent on victory, Lee ordered assaults on both of Meade's flanks but failed to turn them. General Richard B. Ewell, assigned to attack the right side of the Union line, refused to risk his men in an all-out assault, and General Longstreet, on the Union left, failed to dislodge Meade's forces from a hill known as Little Round Top.

On July 3, Lee decided on a frontal assault against the center of the Union line. He recognized the danger of this tactic, but he had enormous confidence in his troops. After the heaviest artillery barrage of the war, Lee ordered General George E. Pickett and his 14,000 men to take Cemetery Ridge. Anticipating this attack, Meade had reinforced his line with artillery and his best troops. When Pickett's men charged across a mile of open terrain, they were met by deadly fire from artillery and rifle-muskets; thousands were killed, wounded, or captured. When the three-day battle ended, Lee had suffered 28,000 casualties, one-third of the Army of Northern Virginia, while 23,000 of Meade's soldiers lay killed or wounded. Shocked by the bloodletting, Meade allowed the remaining Confederate units to escape. Lincoln was furious: "As it is," the president brooded, "the war will be prolonged indefinitely."

Still, Gettysburg was a great Union victory and, together with the triumph at Vicksburg, was the major turning point in the conflict. Southern armies would never again invade the North, and the people in the South were growing increasingly weary of the war. The Confederate elections of 1863 went sharply against the politicians who supported Jefferson Davis. Many ordinary citizens, and even a few members of the Confederate Congress, began to criticize the war effort.

Vicksburg and Gettysburg also transformed the political situation in the North and in Europe. In the fall of 1863, Republicans swept state and local elections in Pennsylvania, Ohio, and New York. Equally important, American diplomats were finally able to prevent the Confederacy from acquiring advanced weapons. In 1862, British shipbuilders had supplied the Confederacy with an ironclad cruiser, the *Alabama*, which had sunk or captured more than one hundred Union merchant ships, and the delivery of two more ironclad cruisers was imminent. News of the Union victories in early July changed everything. Charles Francis Adams, the American minister, persuaded the British government to impound the ships. Britain did not want to risk Canada or its merchant marine by provoking the military might of the United States. Moreover, the country had become increasingly dependent for its food supply on imports of wheat from the American Midwest, and British workers and reformers were strongly opposed to slavery. "King Cotton" diplomacy had failed; "King Wheat" stood triumphant. "Rest not your hopes in foreign nations," President Jefferson Davis now advised his nation, "This war is ours; we must fight it ourselves."

➤ Antislavery Republican politicians and the thousands of "contrabands" played a role in President Lincoln's decision to declare and sign the Emancipation Proclamation. What role did each of them play?

➤ Why were the battles at Gettysburg and Vicksburg significant? How did they change the tide of war strategically? Diplomatically? Psychologically?

The Union Victorious, 1864–1865

The Union victories of 1863 meant that the South could not win its independence through a decisive military triumph. However, the Confederacy could still hope for a stalemate on the battlefield and a negotiated peace. Lincoln faced a daunting task as the bloody war entered its fourth year: He had to win an overwhelming victory, or he would lose the support of the northern voters.

Soldiers and Strategy

Two developments allowed the Union to prosecute the war with continued vigor: the enlistment of African American soldiers and the emergence of capable and determined generals.

The Impact of Black Troops. As early as 1861, free African Americans and fugitive slaves had volunteered for the Union army, and Frederick Douglass had embraced their cause: "Once let the black man get upon his person the brass letters, 'U.S.' . . . a musket on his shoulder and bullets in his pockets, and there is no power on earth which can deny that he has earned the right to citizenship in the United States." The prospect of citizenship for blacks frightened many northern whites, and most Union generals doubted that former slaves would make good soldiers. Consequently, the Lincoln administration initially refused to enlist African Americans. But by 1862, free and contraband blacks had formed regiments in New England, South Carolina, Louisiana, and Kansas, and were eager to join the fighting.

Black Soldiers in the Union Army

Determined to end racial slavery, tens of thousands of African Americans volunteered for service in the Union army in 1864 and 1865, boosting the northern war effort at a critical moment. These proud soldiers were members of the 107th Colored Infantry, stationed at Fort Corcoran near Washington, D.C. In January 1865, their regiment participated in the daring capture of Fort Fisher, which protected Wilmington, North Carolina, the last Confederate port open to blockade runners. Library of Congress.

The Emancipation Proclamation changed popular thinking and military policy with respect to black soldiers. The proclamation invited former slaves to serve in the Union army; northern whites, long suspicious of arming African Americans, now agreed that because blacks were to benefit from a Union victory, they should share in the fighting and dying. The valor exhibited by the first African American regiments to go into combat also influenced opinion in the North. In January 1863, Thomas Wentworth Higginson, the white abolitionist commander of the black First South Carolina Volunteers, wrote a glowing newspaper account of the regiment's military prowess: "No officer in this regiment now doubts that the key to the successful prosecution of the war lies in the unlimited employment of black troops." In July, a heroic and costly attack on Fort Wagner, South Carolina, by another black regiment, the Fifty-fourth Massachusetts Infantry, convinced many Union officers of the value of black soldiers. The War Department authorized black enlistment; and as white resistance to conscription increased, the Lincoln administration recruited as many African Americans as it could. Without black soldiers, the president suggested in the autumn of 1864, "we would be compelled to abandon the war in three weeks." By the spring of 1865, there were nearly 200,000 African American soldiers and sailors in the Union forces.

Military service did not end racial discrimination. Black soldiers served under white officers in segregated regiments and were used primarily to build fortifications, garrison forts, and guard supply lines. At first they were paid less than white soldiers ($10 a month versus $13) and won equal pay only by threatening to lay down their arms. Despite this treatment, African Americans volunteered for military service in disproportionate numbers and diligently served the Union cause. They were fighting for freedom and a new social order. "Hello, Massa," said one black soldier to his former master, who had been taken prisoner. "Bottom rail on top dis time." The worst fears of the secessionists had come true: Through the agency of the Union army, blacks had risen in a great rebellion against slavery.

Capable Generals Take Command. As African Americans joined the army's ranks, Lincoln finally found an efficient and ruthless commanding general. In March 1864, Lincoln placed General Ulysses S. Grant in charge of all the Union armies and created a unified structure of command. From then on, the president determined general strategy and Grant decided how to implement it. Lincoln directed Grant to advance simultaneously against all the major Confederate armies, a strategy Grant had long favored. Both the president and the general wanted a decisive victory before the election of 1864.

As the successful western campaign of 1863 showed, Grant knew how to fight a modern war, a war that relied on industrial technology and targeted an entire society. At Vicksburg, he had besieged the whole city and forced its surrender. Then, in November 1863, he had used railroad transport to charge to the rescue of a Union army near Chattanooga, Tennessee, and drive back an invading Confederate army. Moreover, Grant was willing to accept heavy casualties in assaults on strongly defended positions. The attempts of earlier Union commanders "to conserve life" through cautious tactics had prolonged the war, Grant argued. However, Grant's aggressiveness earned him a reputation as a butcher — of enemy armies and his own men.

In May 1864, Grant ordered major new offensives on two fronts. Personally taking charge of the

Grant Planning an Attack

On June 2, 1864, the day this photograph was taken, Grant moved his headquarters to Bethesda Church, moved its pews outside, under the shade of the surrounding trees, and planned the costly attack he would make at Cold Harbor, Virginia, the next day — a frontal assault that resulted in seven thousand Union casualties. While Grant (to the left) leaned over a pew, gesturing at a map, his officers smoked their pipes and read reports of the war in newspapers that had just arrived from New York City. Library of Congress.

115,000-man-strong Army of the Potomac, he set out to destroy Lee's force of 75,000 troops in Virginia. Simultaneously, he instructed General William Tecumseh Sherman, who shared his ruthless views on warfare, to invade Georgia and take Atlanta. As Sherman prepared for battle, he wrote that "all that has gone before is mere skirmish. The war now begins."

Grant advanced toward Richmond, hoping to force Lee to fight in open fields, where the Union's superior manpower and artillery would prevail. But remembering his tactical errors at Gettysburg, Lee remained in strong defensive positions and attacked only when he held an advantage. The Confederate general seized that opportunity twice: He won narrow victories in early May 1864 at the extraordinarily bloody battles of the Wilderness and Spotsylvania Court House. At Spotsylvania, the soldiers fought at point-blank range, often using their bayoneted rifles as spears. Despite heavy losses in these battles and at Cold Harbor, Grant drove on (Map 14.5). Although his attacks severely eroded Lee's forces, which suffered 31,000 casualties, Union losses were even higher: 55,000 men.

The fighting also took a heavy psychological toll. "Many a man has gone crazy since this campaign began from the terrible pressure on mind and body," observed a Union captain. As the morale and health of the soldiers on both sides weakened, many deserted. In June 1864, Grant laid siege to Petersburg, an important railroad center near Richmond. Protracted trench warfare—like that American troops would face in World War I—made the spade as important as the sword. Union and Confederate soldiers built complex networks of trenches, tunnels, and artillery emplacements for almost fifty miles around Richmond and Petersburg. Invoking the intense imagery of the Bible, an officer described the continuous artillery firing and sniping as "living night and day within the 'valley of the shadow of death.'" The stress was especially great for the outnumbered Confederate troops, who spent months in the muddy, sickening trenches without rotation to the rear.

As time passed, Lincoln and Grant felt pressures of their own. The enormous casualties and continued military stalemate threatened Lincoln with defeat in the November election. The outlook for the Republicans worsened in July 1864, when a raid near Washington by Jubal Early's cavalry forced Grant to divert his best troops from the Petersburg campaign. To punish farmers in the Shenandoah Valley, who had provided a base for Early and food for Lee's army, Grant ordered General Philip H. Sheridan to turn the region into "a barren waste." Sheridan's troops conducted a scorched-earth campaign, destroying grain supplies, barns, farming implements, and gristmills. These terrorist tactics went beyond the military norms of the day: Most

MAP 14.5 The Closing Virginia Campaign, 1864–1865

Beginning in May 1864, General Ulysses Grant launched an all-out campaign against Richmond. By threatening General Robert E. Lee's lines of supply from Richmond, Grant tried to lure him into open battle. Lee avoided a major test of strength. Instead, he retreated to defensive positions and inflicted heavy casualties on Union attackers at the Wilderness, Spotsylvania Court House, North Anna, and Cold Harbor (1–4). From June 1864 to April 1865, the two armies faced each other across defensive fortifications outside Richmond and Petersburg (5), a protracted siege finally broken by Grant's flanking maneuver at Five Forks (6). Lee's surrender followed shortly.

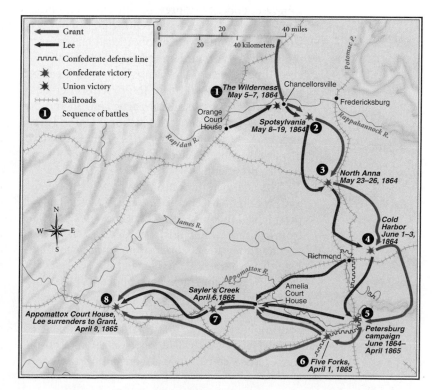

officers regarded civilians as noncombatants and feared that punishing them would erode military discipline. Grant's practice of carrying the war to Confederate civilians was changing the definition of conventional warfare.

The Election of 1864 and Sherman's March

As the siege at Petersburg dragged on, the president's hopes for reelection increasingly depended on General Sherman in Georgia. Sherman had gradually penetrated to within about thirty miles of Atlanta, a great railway hub at the heart of the Confederacy. Although his army outnumbered that of General Joseph E. Johnston—90,000 men to 60,000 men—Sherman avoided a direct attack and slowly pried the Confederates out of one defensive position after another. Finally, on June 27, at Kennesaw Mountain, Sherman engaged Johnston in a set battle, only to suffer 3,000 casualties, five times the losses he inflicted on Johnston's troops. By late July 1864, the Union general had laid siege to Atlanta on the north, but the next month brought little gain. Like Grant, Sherman seemed bogged down in a hopeless campaign.

The National Union Party Versus the Peace Democrats.
Meanwhile, the presidential campaign of 1864 was well under way. In June, a Republican convention attended by both Republicans and Unionist Democrats resisted the attempt of some Republicans to prevent Lincoln's renomination. The convention endorsed the president's war strategy, demanded the unconditional surrender of the Confederacy, and called for a constitutional amendment to abolish slavery. It likewise accepted Lincoln's political strategy. To attract border-state voters and create a national party, Lincoln and his allies took a new name, the National Union Party, and chose Andrew Johnson, a Tennessee slave owner and Unionist Democrat, as their candidate for vice president.

The Democratic convention met in late August and nominated General George B. McClellan for president. Lincoln had twice removed McClellan from military commands: first for an excess of caution and then for his opposition to emancipation. Like their candidate, the Democratic delegates rejected freedom for blacks and condemned Lincoln's uncompromising repression of domestic dissent. However, they split into two camps over the issue of continuing the war. A substantial contingent of "Peace Democrats" called for "a cessation of hostilities" and a constitutional convention to restore peace. Although personally a "War Democrat," McClellan promised if elected to recommend to Congress an immediate armistice and a peace convention. Rejoicing in "the first ray of real light I have seen since the war began," Confederate vice president Alexander Stephens declared that if Atlanta and Richmond held out, Lincoln could be defeated. Then, McClellan and the northern Democrats could be persuaded to accept an independent Confederacy.

The Fall of Atlanta and Lincoln's Victory.
Stephens's hopes collapsed on September 2, 1864, as Atlanta fell to Sherman's army. In a stunning move, the Union general pulled his troops from the trenches, swept around the city, and destroyed its rail links to the rest of the Confederacy. Fearing that Sherman would encircle and trap his army, Confederate general John B. Hood abandoned the city. "Atlanta is ours, and fairly won," Sherman telegraphed Lincoln, sparking hundred-gun salutes and wild Republican celebrations in northern cities. "The national resources . . . are unexhausted, and . . . unexhaustible," Lincoln warned Confederate leaders. "We are *gaining* strength, and may, if need be, maintain the contest indefinitely."

A deep pessimism settled over the Confederacy. Mary Chesnut, a plantation mistress, "felt as if all were dead within me, forever" and foresaw the end of the Confederacy: "We are going to be wiped off the earth," she wrote in her diary. Acknowledging the dramatically changed military situation, McClellan repudiated the Democratic peace platform, and dissident Republicans abandoned efforts to dump Lincoln. Instead, the National Union Party went on the offensive. Its newspapers charged that McClellan was still a peace candidate and that Peace Democrats were "copperheads" (poisonous snakes) who were hatching treasonous plots.

Sherman's success in Georgia gave Lincoln a clear-cut victory in November. The president received 55 percent of the popular vote and won 212 of 233 electoral votes. Republicans and National Unionists captured 145 of the 185 seats in the House of Representatives and increased their Senate majority to 42 of 52 seats. Many victories came from the votes of Union troops, who wanted the war to continue until the Confederacy met every Union demand, including emancipation.

Legal emancipation was already under way at the edges of the South. In 1864, Maryland and Missouri amended their constitutions to free their slaves, and the three occupied states—Tennessee, Arkansas, and Louisiana—followed suit. However, abolitionists were worried that the Emancipation

William Tecumseh Sherman

Sherman was a nervous man who smoked cigars and talked continuously. When he was seated, he crossed and uncrossed his legs incessantly, and a journalist described his fingers as constantly "twitching his red whiskers — his coat buttons — playing a tattoo on the table — or running through his hair." But Sherman was a decisive general who commanded the loyalty of his troops. This photograph was taken in 1865, after Sherman's devastating march through Georgia and the Carolinas. Library of Congress.

Proclamation, which was based on the president's wartime powers, would lose its force at the end of the war. Urged on by Lincoln and the black-organized National Equal Rights League, the Republican-dominated Congress took a major step to guarantee black freedom. On January 31, 1865, it approved the Thirteenth Amendment, which prohibited slavery throughout the United States, and sent it to the states for ratification. Slavery was nearly dead.

William Tecumseh Sherman: "Hard War" Warrior.
Thanks to William Tecumseh Sherman, the Confederacy was nearly dead as well. The Civil War had rescued Sherman from life as an undistinguished military officer and a failed businessman. An 1840 graduate of West Point, Sherman had missed out on the military action during the Mexican War and so rose slowly in the ranks. In 1860, he had just taken charge of the brand-new Louisiana Military

Seminary. Although he was born and raised in Ohio, Sherman had served in the South and mixed easily with the planter class. Moreover, he believed that slavery was necessary to maintain the stability of the southern social order.

But Sherman was a staunch nationalist and a firm supporter of the Union. Secession meant "anarchy," he told his southern friends in early 1861, and had to be crushed. "If war comes, as I fear it surely will, I must fight your people whom I best love." He resigned his position in Louisiana and took command of the Union forces in Kentucky, his first wartime command. There he was unsuccessful in recruiting troops—and so darkly pessimistic about Union prospects that Lincoln relieved him of his command.

Then Sherman got lucky. Assigned to serve under Ulysses S. Grant, Sherman took his commander as a model. After distinguishing himself during Grant's victories at Shiloh and Vicksburg, Sherman was given command of a Union army in Tennessee. There, finally, he achieved success both as a commanding general and as an architect of modern warfare. As he fought, Sherman developed the philosophy and tactics of "hard war." "When one nation is at war with another, all the people of one are enemies of the other," Sherman declared, as he turned his troops loose against pro-Confederacy civilians suspected of helping anti-Union guerrillas. After guerrillas fired on a boat with Unionist passengers near Randolph, Tennessee, Sherman sent a regiment to level the town, asserting, "We are justified in treating all inhabitants as combatants."

After he captured Atlanta, Sherman decided on a bold strategy based on hard-war tactics. Instead of following the retreating Confederate army northward into Tennessee, he proposed to move south and "cut a swath through to the sea." To persuade Lincoln and Grant to approve his unconventional plan to live off the land, Sherman pointed out that his march would devastate Georgia and score a major psychological victory. It would be "a demonstration to the world, foreign and domestic, that we have a power Davis cannot resist."

Sherman set out to fight a campaign that would destroy the South's economic resources and will to resist. "We are not only fighting hostile armies," Sherman wrote, "but a hostile people, and must make old and young, rich and poor, feel the hard hand of war." He left Atlanta in flames and, during his 300-mile march to the sea (Map 14.6), consumed or demolished everything in his path. A Union veteran wrote, "[We] destroyed all we could not eat, stole their niggers, burned their cotton & gins, spilled their sorghum, burned & twisted their R.Roads and raised Hell generally." The havoc so

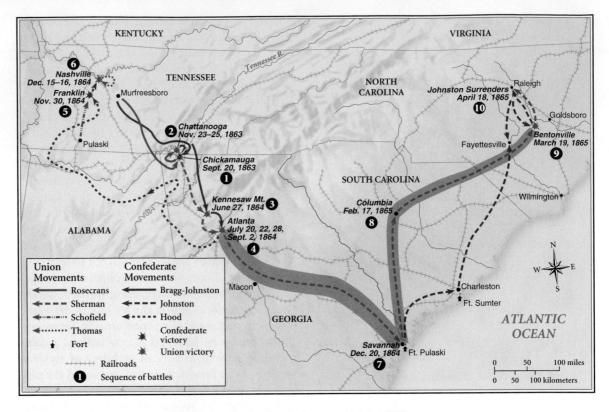

MAP 14.6   Sherman's March Through the Confederacy, 1864–1865

The Union victory in November 1863 at Chattanooga, Tennessee (2), was almost as critical as the victories in July at Gettysburg and Vicksburg, because it opened up a route of attack into the heart of the Confederacy. In mid-1864, General Sherman advanced on the railway hub of Atlanta (3 and 4). After finally taking the city in September 1864, Sherman relied on other Union armies to stem General Hood's invasion of Tennessee (5 and 6) while he began a devastating "March to the Sea." By December, he had reached Savannah (7); from there, he cut a swath through the Carolinas (8–10).

demoralized Confederate soldiers that many deserted their units and fled home to protect their farms and families. When Sherman reached Savannah in mid-December, the city's ten thousand defenders left without a fight.

Georgia's slaves treated Sherman as a savior. "They flock to me, old and young, they pray and shout and mix up my name with Moses . . . as well as 'Abram Linkom', the Great Messiah of 'Dis Jubilee.'" To provide for the hundreds of blacks now following his army, Sherman issued Special Field Order No. 15, which set aside 400,000 acres of prime rice-growing land for the exclusive use of freedmen. By June 1865, some 40,000 blacks were cultivating "Sherman lands," which many freedmen believed would be theirs forever, belated payment for generations of enslaved labor. "All the land belongs to the Yankees now and they gwine divide it out among de coloured people."

In February 1865, Sherman invaded South Carolina, both to link up with Grant at Petersburg and to punish the state where secession had begun. His troops ravaged the countryside as they cut a comparatively narrow swath across the state. After capturing South Carolina's capital, Columbia, they burned the business district, most churches, and the wealthiest residential neighborhoods. "This disappointment to me is extremely bitter," lamented Jefferson Davis. By March, Sherman had reached North Carolina and was on the verge of linking up with Grant and crushing Lee's army.

The Confederate Collapse. Grant's war of attrition had already exposed a weakness in the Confederacy: rising class resentment on the part of poor whites. Long angered by the "twenty-negro" exemption from military service given to slave owners and fearing that the Confederacy was doomed, ordinary southern farmers now repudiated the draft. "All they want is to git you . . . to fight for their infurnal negroes," grumbled an Alabama hill farmer. More and more soldiers fled their units. "I am now going to work instead of to the war," declared David Harris, a backcountry farmer. By 1865, at least 100,000 men had deserted from Confederate armies, and there were so few white recruits that southern leaders decided to take an extreme measure. Urged on by General Lee, the Confederate Congress voted to enlist black soldiers, and President Davis issued an executive order granting freedom to blacks who served in the Confederate army. But the war ended too soon to reveal whether any slaves would have fought for the Confederacy.

The symbolic end of the war took place in Virginia. In April 1865, Grant finally gained control of the crucial railroad junction at Petersburg and cut off Lee's supplies. Lee abandoned Richmond and retreated toward North Carolina, to join up with Confederate forces there. While Lincoln visited the ruins of the Confederate capital and was mobbed by joyful ex-slaves, Grant cut off Lee's escape route. On April 9, almost four years to the day after the attack

on Fort Sumter, Lee surrendered at Appomattox Court House. By late May, all the Confederate generals had stopped fighting, and the Confederate army and government simply dissolved (Map 14.7).

The hard and bitter war was finally over. Union armies had destroyed the Confederate government; and the South's factories, warehouses, and railroads were in ruins, as were many of its farms and some of its most important cities. Almost 260,000 Confederate soldiers had paid for secession with their lives. The cost to the North was equally great in money, resources, and lives. More than 360,000 Union soldiers had died, and hundreds of thousands had been maimed (see Reading American Pictures, "What Do Photographs Tell Us About the Civil War?" p. 452). Delivering his second inaugural address as the fighting continued, Abraham Lincoln confessed his inability to justify the hideous carnage of the war in human terms:

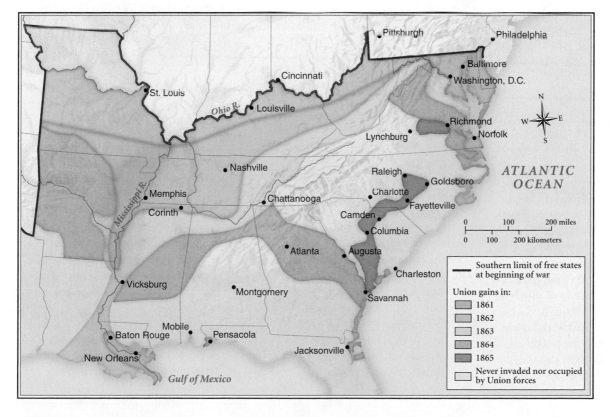

MAP 14.7 The Conquest of the South, 1861–1865
It took four years for the Union armies to defeat those of the Confederacy. Until the last year of the long conflict, most of the South remained in Confederate hands; even at the end of the war, Union armies had never entered many parts of the rebellious states. Most of the Union's territorial gains came on the vast western front, where its control of strategic lines of communication (the Mississippi River and major railroads) gave its forces a decisive advantage.

What Do Photographs Tell Us About the Civil War?

Captain George A. Custer and a Confederate Prisoner. Library of Congress.

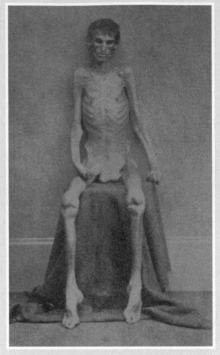

A Federal Prisoner. Library of Congress.

The Civil War was the first military conflict caught on film. As the full-page photograph at the beginning of Chapter 14 (p. 422) attests, the results were not pretty. Hundreds of Civil War photos show the bodies of dead men scattered across fields of battle—grim scenes, indeed. Hundreds of other images document the destruction of towns and cities, particularly in Virginia, the scene of much of the fighting (see the picture of Richmond on p. 453). But what did these photographs mean to the people of the era? And what insight can they give us into the nature of the conflict?

ANALYZING THE EVIDENCE

➤ Study the pictures on pages 422 and 453. Then look at the picture above of the emaciated body of a Massachusetts soldier who has just been freed from a Confederate military prison. Which image is more powerful intellectually? Emotionally? How do you think nineteenth-century Americans responded to the three photographs?

➤ The other image shows Captain (later General) George A. Custer (right) conversing quietly with a captured Confederate officer. These men had just tried to kill each other. Why are they now behaving with such civility? The rules of war? Respect between officers?

➤ Why did the photographer, the great Mathew Brady, take this picture of Custer? Brady chose his images carefully so that they conveyed meaning or a perspective on events. Is the black boy, the Southerner's slave property, the clue to the meaning of this picture? Do you think Brady is suggesting that the struggle is really about the values and ideology of white men?

➤ Look carefully at the picture of the destroyed buildings in Richmond on page 453. What does the presence of the two women in the right foreground add to the image and to its effect on the viewer?

➤ Go to **memory.loc.gov/ammem/ cwphtml/cwphome.html** for additional Civil War photographs available at the Library of Congress.

The Devastation of War

From June 1864 to April 1865, Union troops commanded by General Grant besieged Richmond and the neighboring city of Petersburg, Virginia. As this photograph from the studio of Mathew Brady shows, Union artillery destroyed large sections of the Confederate capital, especially its flour mills, tobacco factories, and ironworks. Library of Congress.

If God wills that it continue until all the wealth piled by the bondsman's two hundred and fifty years of unrequited toil shall be sunk, and until every drop of blood drawn with the lash shall be paid by another drawn with the sword, as was said three thousand years ago, so still it must be said "the judgments of the Lord are true and righteous altogether."

As a reunited nation turned to the tasks of peace, it found that they were to be equally hard and bitter.

➤ What was the effect of emancipation on the politics and military affairs of the North?

➤ What were the strengths and weaknesses of Grant's military strategy and tactics? How was Grant's way of warfare different from traditional military practice?

➤ Describe Sherman's hard-war strategy. How did he pursue this strategy? With what results?

SUMMARY

In this chapter, we have surveyed the dramatic events of the Civil War. Looking at the South, we watched the fire-eaters attack Fort Sumter, which prompted the secession of the states of the Middle South and greatly strengthened the Confederacy. The potential of that new nation grew as its generals repulsed Union attacks against Richmond and went on the offensive. However, as the war continued, the inherent economic and social weaknesses of the Confederacy came to the fore. Enslaved workers fled or refused to work; yeomen farmers refused to fight for an institution that benefited wealthy planters; and European nations refused to recognize a nation created to preserve racial slavery.

Examining the North, we witnessed the initial failure of its leaders to exploit the Union's significant advantages in industrial output, financial resources, and military manpower. The generals— McClellan and Meade—moved slowly to attack and refused to pursue their weakened foes. But over time, the inherent strengths of the Union became manifest. Congress created efficient systems of banking and war finance; Lincoln found efficient and ruthless generals; and the emancipation and recruitment of enslaved African Americans provided an abundant supply of soldiers determined to fight for their freedom.

Looking at both sides, we explored the impact of total war on civilians: the imposition of conscription and high taxes; the increased workload of farm women and the employment of urban women as nurses and postal workers; and the constant food shortages and soaring prices. Above all else, there was the omnipresent fact of death—a tragedy that touched nearly every family, North and South.

Connections: Government

Since the beginning of the American republic, political leaders have argued over the scope and powers of the national government. As we learned in Chapter 7, during the 1790s, Alexander Hamilton, reading the Constitution expansively, devised a policy of national mercantilism. In response, Thomas Jefferson and James Madison created the Republican Party, which reduced the scope of the national government when it came to power in 1800, and which encouraged state governments to promote economic development. In the 1820s, as we discussed in Chapter 10, Henry Clay and John Quincy Adams revived Hamilton's nationalistic program through their calls for an American System. It would consist of a national bank to oversee the financial system, national tariff protection for American manufacturers, and national subsidies for roads, canals, and other internal improvements. As we noted in the essay that opened Part Three (p. 269), Jacksonian Democrats condemned Clay's scheme and

in the 1830s and 1840s . . . led a political and constitutional revolution that cut government aid to financiers, merchants, and corporations.

As we saw in this chapter, during the Civil War, the Republican administration of Abraham Lincoln reversed the Jacksonian policies by enacting legislation that helped farmers, railroads, and corporations. Indeed, as we will see in Chapter 17, these Hamilton-Clay-Lincoln policies continued after the war. By enacting and upholding legislation favorable to banking enterprises and other businesses during the late nineteenth century, Congress and the federal judiciary actively promoted the development of a powerful industrial economy. Although the Jeffersonian-Jacksonian ideology of small government continued to command support in the South, it receded as a significant force in national life.

CHAPTER REVIEW QUESTIONS

➤ As the war began, politicians and ordinary citizens in both North and South were supremely confident of victory. Why did Southerners believe they would triumph? Why did the North ultimately win the Civil War?

➤ In 1860, the institution of slavery was firmly entrenched in the United States; by 1865, it was dead. How did this happen? How did Union policy toward slavery and enslaved people change over the course of the war? Why did it change?

TIMELINE

1860	Abraham Lincoln elected president (November 6)
	South Carolina votes to secede from the Union (December 20)
1861	President Lincoln inaugurated (March 4)
	Confederates fire on Fort Sumter (April 12)
	Virginia leads Upper South out of the Union (April 17)
	Union general Benjamin Butler declares runaway slaves "contraband of war" (May)
	Confederates rout Union forces at first Battle of Bull Run (July 21)
	First Confiscation Act authorizes seizure of all property, including slaves, used to support Confederacy's rebellion (August)
1862	Legal Tender Act authorizes issue of greenbacks (February)
	Battle of Shiloh advances Union cause in West (April 6–7)
	Confederacy introduces first draft (April)
	Congress passes Homestead Act, which provides free land to settlers (May)
	Congress gives federal subsidies to transcontinental railroads (July)
	Second Confiscation Act declares all fugitive and contraband slaves to be "forever free" (July)
	Union halts Confederate offensive at Antietam (September 17)
	Lincoln issues preliminary Emancipation Proclamation (September 22)
1863	Lincoln signs Emancipation Proclamation (January 1)
	Union wins battles at Gettysburg (July 1–3) and Vicksburg (July 4)
	Enrollment Act initiates draft in North (March), and leads to riots in New York City (July)
1864	President Lincoln gives Ulysses S. Grant command of all Union armies (March)
	Grant begins advance on Richmond (May)
	William Tecumseh Sherman takes Atlanta (September 2)
	President Lincoln is reelected (November 8)
	Sherman marches through Georgia (November and December)
1865	Congress approves Thirteenth Amendment, outlawing slavery (January 31)
	Robert E. Lee surrenders at Appomattox Court House (April 9)
	Lincoln assassinated by John Wilkes Booth (April 14)
	Thirteenth Amendment is ratified (December 6)

FOR FURTHER EXPLORATION

Charles P. Roland, *An American Iliad: The Story of the Civil War* (1991), is an excellent brief survey; James M. McPherson, *The Battle Cry of Freedom* (1988), offers a fine synthesis of the war. For the story of the complex mixture of policies, personalities, and accidents that precipitated the conflict, read Richard Current, *Lincoln and the First Shot* (1963). John Hope Franklin, *The Emancipation Proclamation* (1963), explains the background of Lincoln's edict and its impact.

Nancy Scott Anderson and Dwight Anderson, *The Generals: Ulysses S. Grant and Robert E. Lee* (1988), is a vivid popular account of the men's lives and exploits. For scholarly analyses of the war, consult Mark Grimsley, *The Hard Hand of War: Union Military Policy Toward Southern Civilians, 1861–1865* (1995), and Gary W. Gallagher, *The Confederate War* (1997). William W. Freehling in *The South vs. the South* (2001) explores the impact of anti-Confederate sentiment.

James M. McPherson, *For Cause and Comrades: Why Men Fought in the Civil War* (1997), allows ordinary soldiers to explain their commitment to the Union and Confederacy. For firsthand accounts of black soldiers, see Ira Berlin et al., eds., *Freedom's Soldiers: The Black Military Experience in the Civil War* (1998). Earl J. Hess, *The Union Soldier in Battle: Enduring the Ordeal of Combat* (1997), presents a vivid account of the smell, sound, and feel of combat, as does Michael Shaara's *Killer Angels* (1974), a masterful novel about the Battle of Gettysburg.

For an incisive portrait of southern society from the diary of a planter's wife, see *Mary Chesnut's Civil War*, edited by C. Vann Woodward (1981). Jane E. Schultz details the experiences of *Women at the Front: Hospital Workers in Civil War America* (2004); and Laura F. Edwards compellingly describes the war's impact on all southern women in *Scarlett Doesn't Live Here Anymore* (2000).

For Civil War photographs, log on to **memory.loc.gov/ ammem/ndlpcoop/nhihtml/cwnyhshome.html** and **memory .loc.gov/ammem/cwphtml/cwphome.html**. An award-winning Web site is "The Valley of the Shadow" (**jefferson.village .virginia.edu/vshadow2/**), which traces the parallel histories of a northern and a southern community using a multitude of hyperlinked sources; the companion book is Edward L. Ayers, *In the Presence of Mine Enemies: War in the Heart of America, 1859–1863* (2003). Another award-winning Web site that captures the drama of war and emancipation in the words of liberated slaves and defeated masters is "Freedmen and Southern Society Project" (**www.history.umd.edu/Freedmen/home.html**).

TEST YOUR KNOWLEDGE

To assess your command of the material in this chapter, see the Online Study Guide at **bedfordstmartins.com/henretta**.

For Web sites, images, and documents related to topics and places in this chapter, visit **bedfordstmartins.com/makehistory**.

15 Reconstruction

1865–1877

I N HIS SECOND INAUGURAL ADDRESS, President Lincoln spoke of the need to "bind up the nation's wounds." No one knew better than Lincoln how daunting a task that would be. Slavery was finished. That much was certain. But what system of labor should replace plantation slavery? What rights should the freedmen be accorded beyond emancipation? How far should the federal government go to settle these questions? And, most immediately pressing, on what terms should the rebellious states be restored to the Union?

The last speech Lincoln delivered, on April 11, 1865, demonstrated his grasp of these issues. Reconstruction, he said, had to be regarded as a practical, not a theoretical, problem. It could be solved only if Republicans remained united, even if that meant compromising on principled differences dividing them, and only if the defeated South gave its consent, even if that meant forgiveness of the South's transgressions. The speech revealed the middle ground, at once magnanimous and open-minded, on which Lincoln hoped to reunite a wounded nation.

What course Reconstruction might have taken had Lincoln lived is one of the unanswerable questions of American history. On April 14, 1865 — five days after Lee's surrender at Appomattox — Lincoln was shot in the head at Ford's Theatre in Washington by John Wilkes Booth, a

◄ **Chloe and Sam (1882)**

After the Civil War the country went through the wrenching peacemaking process known as Reconstruction. The struggle between the victorious North and the vanquished South was fought out on a political landscape, but Thomas Hovenden's heartwarming painting reminds us of the deeper meaning of Reconstruction: that Chloe and Sam, after lives spent in slavery, might end their days in the dignity of freedom. Thomas Colville Fine Art.

prominent Shakespearean actor and Confederate sympathizer who had been plotting to abduct Lincoln and rescue the South. After Lee's surrender, Booth became bent on revenge. Without regaining consciousness, Lincoln died on April 15, 1865.

With one stroke John Wilkes Booth sent Lincoln to martyrdom, hardened many Northerners against the South, and handed the presidency to a man utterly lacking in Lincoln's moral sense and political judgment, Vice President Andrew Johnson.

Presidential Reconstruction

The problem of Reconstruction—how to restore rebellious states to the Union—was not addressed by the Founding Fathers. The Constitution does not say which branch of government handles the readmission of rebellious states or, for that matter, even contemplates the possibility of secession. It was an open question whether, upon seceding, the Confederate states had legally left the Union. If so, their reentry surely required legislative action by Congress. If not, if even in defeat they retained their constitutional status, then the terms for restoring them to the Union might be treated as an administrative matter best left to the president. In a constitutional system based on the **separation of powers**, the absence of clarity on so fundamental a matter made for explosive politics. The ensuing battle between the White House and Capitol Hill over who was in charge became one of the fault lines in Reconstruction's stormy history.

Presidential Initiatives

Lincoln, as wartime president, had the elbow room to take the lead, offering in December 1863 a general amnesty to all but high-ranking Confederates willing to pledge loyalty to the Union. When 10 percent of a state's 1860 voters had taken this oath, the state would be restored to the Union, provided that it accepted the Thirteenth Amendment abolishing slavery (see Chapter 14). The Confederate states did not bite, however, and congressional Republicans proposed a harsher substitute for Lincoln's Ten Percent Plan. The Wade-Davis Bill, passed on July 2, 1864, laid down, as conditions on the rebellious states, an oath of allegiance to the Union by a majority of each state's adult white men; new governments formed only by those who had never borne arms against the North; and permanent disfranchisement of Confederate leaders. The Wade-Davis bill served notice that the con-gressional Republicans were not about to hand over Reconstruction policy to the president.

Lincoln executed a **pocket veto** of the Wade-Davis bill by not signing it before Congress adjourned. At the same time he initiated informal talks with congressional leaders aimed at a compromise. It was this stalemate that Lincoln was addressing when he appealed for Republican flexibility in the last speech of his life. Lincoln's successor, however, had no such inclinations. Andrew Johnson believed that Reconstruction was the president's prerogative, and by an accident of timing, he was free to act on his convictions. Under leisurely rules that went back to the early republic, the 39th Congress elected in November 1864 was not scheduled to convene until December 1865.

Andrew Johnson and Reconstruction. Johnson was a self-made man from the hills of eastern Tennessee. Born in 1808, he was apprenticed as a boy to a tailor and set up shop in Greeneville. Despite his lack of formal schooling—his wife was his teacher—Johnson prospered. His tailor shop became a political meeting place, and, natural leader that he was, he soon entered local politics with the backing of Greeneville's small farmers and laborers. In 1857, after a relentless climb up the political ranks, he became a U.S. Senator. A Jacksonian

Andrew Johnson

The president was not an easy man. This photograph of Andrew Johnson (1808–1875) conveys some of the prickly qualities that contributed so centrally to his failure to reach an agreement with Republicans on a moderate Reconstruction program. Library of Congress.

Democrat, Johnson despised equally the "bloated, corrupt aristocracy" of the Northeast and the Tennessee planter elite that dominated Memphis and its environs. It was the poor whites that Johnson championed, however, not the enslaved blacks nor, for that matter, emancipation.

Loyal to the Union, Johnson refused to leave the Senate when his state seceded. In this, he was utterly alone; no southern colleague stayed with him. When federal forces captured Nashville in 1862, Lincoln appointed Johnson Tennessee's military governor. Tennessee, one of the war's bloodiest battlefields, was bitterly divided along geographical lines: Unionist in the east and Rebel in the west. Johnson's assignment was to hold the state together, and he did so, with an iron hand. He was rewarded by being named Lincoln's running mate in 1864. Choosing this war Democrat seemed a smart move, designed to promote wartime unity and court the support of southern Unionists.

In May 1865, just a month after Lincoln's death, Johnson advanced his version of Reconstruction. He offered amnesty to all Southerners who took an oath of allegiance to the Constitution, except for high-ranking Confederate officials and wealthy planters, the elite whom Johnson blamed for secession. Johnson appointed provisional governors for the southern states, requiring as conditions for their restoration only that they revoke their ordinances of secession, repudiate their Confederate debts, and ratify the Thirteenth Amendment. Within months all the former Confederate states had met Johnson's terms and enjoyed functioning, elected governments.

At first Republicans responded favorably. The moderates among them were sympathetic to Johnson's argument that it was up to the states, not the federal government, to define the civil and political rights of the freedmen. Even the Radicals — the Republicans bent on a hard line toward the South — held their fire. They liked the stern treatment of Confederate leaders, and hoped that the new southern governments would show good faith by generous treatment of the freed slaves.

Nothing of the sort happened. The South lay in ruins (see Voices from Abroad, "David Macrae: The Devastated South," p. 460). But Southerners held fast to the old order. The newly seated legislatures moved to restore slavery in all but name. They enacted laws — known as **Black Codes** — designed to drive the former slaves back to the plantations. The new governments had been formed mostly by southern Unionists, but when it came to racial attitudes, little distinguished these loyalists from the Confederates. Despite his hard words against them, more-over, Johnson forgave ex-Confederate leaders easily, so long as he got the satisfaction of humbling them when they appealed for pardons. Soon the ex-Confederates, emboldened by Johnson's indulgence, were filtering back into the halls of power. Old comrades packed the delegations to the new Congress: nine members of the Confederate Congress, seven former officials of Confederate state governments, four generals and four colonels, and even the vice president of the Confederacy, Alexander Stephens. This was the last straw for the Republicans.

The Battle Joined. Under the Constitution, Congress is "the judge of the Elections, Returns and Qualifications of its own Members" (Article 1, Section 5). With this power the Republican majorities in both houses refused to admit the southern delegations when Congress convened in early December 1865, effectively blocking Johnson's Reconstruction program. In response the southern states backed away from the Black Codes, replacing them with regulatory ordinances silent on race yet, in practice, applying only to blacks, not to whites. On top of that, a wave of violence erupted across the South. In Tennessee a Nashville paper reported that white gangs "are riding about whipping, maiming and killing all negroes who do not obey the orders of their former masters, just as if slavery existed." Congressional Republicans concluded that the South had embarked on a concerted effort to circumvent the Thirteenth Amendment. They decided that the federal government had to intervene.

Back in March 1865, before adjourning, the 38th Congress had established the Freedmen's Bureau to aid ex-slaves during the transition from war to peace. Now in early 1866, under the leadership of the moderate Republican Senator Lyman Trumbull, Congress voted to extend the Freedmen's Bureau's life, gave it direct funding for the first time, and authorized its agents to investigate mistreatment of blacks.

More extraordinary was Trumbull's civil rights bill, declaring the ex-slaves to be citizens and granting them, along with every other citizen, equal rights of contract, access to the courts, and protection of person and property. Trumbull's bill nullified all state laws infringing on citizens' equal protection under the law, authorized U.S. attorneys to bring enforcement suits in the federal courts, and provided for fines and imprisonment for violators. Provoked by an unrepentant South, even the most moderate Republicans demanded that the federal government assume responsibility for the civil rights of the freedmen.

David Macrae

The Devastated South

In this excerpt from The Americans at Home *(1870), an account of his tour of the United States, the Scottish clergyman David Macrae describes the war-stricken South as he found it in 1867–1868, at a time when the crisis over Reconstruction was boiling over.*

I was struck with a remark made by a Southern gentleman in answer to the assertion that Jefferson Davis [the president of the Confederacy] had culpably continued the war for six months after all hope had been abandoned.

"Sir," he said, "Mr. Davis knew the temper of the South as well as any man in it. He knew if there was to be anything worth calling peace, the South must win; or, if she couldn't win, she wanted to be whipped—well whipped—thoroughly whipped."

The further south I went, the oftener these remarks came back upon me. Evidence was everywhere that the South had maintained the desperate conflict until she was utterly exhausted. . . . Almost every man I met at the South, especially in North Carolina, Georgia, and Virginia, seemed to have been in the army; and it was painful to find many who had returned were mutilated, maimed, or broken in health by exposure. When I remarked this to a young Confederate officer in North Carolina, and said I was glad to see that he had escaped unhurt, he said, "Wait till we get to the office, sir, and I will tell you more about that." When we got there, he pulled up one leg of his trousers, and showed me that he had an iron rod

there to strengthen his limb, and enable him to walk without limping, half of his foot being off. He showed me on the other leg a deep scar made by a fragment of a shell; and these were but two of seven wounds which had left their marks upon his body. When he heard me speak of relics, he said, "Try to find a North Carolina gentleman without a Yankee mark on him."

Nearly three years had passed when I traveled through the country, and yet we have seen what traces the war had left in such cities as Richmond, Petersburg, and Columbia. The same spectacle met me at Charleston. Churches and houses had been battered down by heavy shot and shell hurled into the city from Federal batteries at a distance of five miles. Even the valley of desolation made by a great fire in 1861, through the very heart of the city, remained unbuilt. There, after the lapse of seven years, stood the blackened ruins of streets and houses waiting for the coming of a better day. . . . Over the country districts the prostration was equally marked. Along the track of Sherman's army—especially, the devastation was fearful—farms laid waste, fences burned, bridges destroyed, houses left in ruins, plantations in many cases turned into wilderness again.

The people had shared in the general wreck, and looked poverty-stricken, careworn, and dejected. Ladies who before the war had lived in affluence, with black servants round them to attend to their every wish, were boarding together in half-furnished houses, cooking their own food and washing their own linen, some of them, I was told, so utterly destitute that they did not know when they finished one meal where they were to find the next. . . . Men who

had held commanding positions during the war had fallen out of sight and were filling humble situations—struggling, many of them, to earn a bare subsistence. . . . I remember dining with three cultured Southern gentlemen, one a general, the other, I think, a captain, and the third a lieutenant. They were all living together in a plain little wooden house, such as they would formerly have provided for their servants. Two of them were engaged in a railway office, the third was seeking a situation, frequently, in his vain search, passing the large blinded house where he had lived in luxurious ease before the war.

SOURCE: Allan Nevins, ed., *America through British Eyes* (Gloucester, MA: Peter Smith, 1968), 345–347.

ANALYZING THE EVIDENCE

➤ In general, we value accounts by foreigners for insights they provide into America that might not be visible to its own citizens. Do you find any such insights in the Reverend Macrae's account of the postwar South?

➤ The South proved remarkably resistant to northern efforts at reconstruction. Can we find explanations for that resistance in Macrae's account?

➤ The North quickly became disillusioned with radical Reconstruction (see p. 466). Is there anything in Macrae's sympathetic interviews with wounded southern gentlemen and destitute ladies that sheds light on the susceptibility of many Northerners to propaganda depicting a South in the grip of "a mass of black barbarism"?

Acting on Freedom

While Congress debated, emancipated slaves acted on their own ideas about freedom. News that their bondage was over left them exultant and hopeful (see Comparing American Voices, "Freedom," pp. 462–463). Freedom meant many things—the end of punishment by the lash; the ability to move around; the reuniting of families; and the opportunity to begin schools, to form churches and social clubs, and, not least, to engage in politics. Across the South blacks held mass meetings, paraded, and formed organizations. Topmost among their demands was the right to vote—"an essential and inseparable element of self-government." No less than their former masters, ex-slaves intended to be actors in the savage drama of Reconstruction.

Struggling for Economic Independence. Ownership of land, emancipated blacks believed, was the basis for true freedom. In the chaotic final months of the war, freedmen seized control of plantations where they could. In Georgia and South Carolina, General William T. Sherman reserved large coastal tracts for liberated slaves and settled them on 40-acre plots. Sherman just didn't want to be bothered with the refugees as his army drove across the Lower South, but the freedmen assumed that Sherman's order meant that the land would be theirs. When the war ended, resettlement became the responsibility of the Freedmen's Bureau, which was charged with distributing confiscated land to "loyal refugees and freedmen" and regulating labor contracts between freedmen and planters. Many black families stayed on their old plantations, awaiting redistribution of the land to them. When the South Carolina planter Thomas Pinckney returned home, his freed slaves told him: "We ain't going nowhere. We are going to work right here on the land where we were born and what belongs to us."

Johnson's amnesty plan, entitling pardoned Confederates to recover property seized during the war, blasted these hopes. In October 1865 Johnson ordered General Oliver O. Howard, head of the Freedmen's Bureau, to restore the plantations on the Sea Islands off the South Carolina coast to their white owners. When Howard reluctantly obeyed, the dispossessed blacks protested: "Why do you take away our lands? You take them from us who have always been true, always true to the Government! You give them to our all-time enemies! That is not right!"

In the Sea Islands and elsewhere, former slaves resisted efforts to evict them. Led by black veterans of the Union army, they fought pitched battles with plantation owners and bands of ex-Confederate soldiers. Landowners struck back hard. One black veteran wrote from Maryland: "The returned colard Solgers are in Many cases beten, and their guns taken from them, we darcent walk out of an evening. . . . They beat us badly and Sumtime Shoot us." Often aided by federal troops, the local whites generally prevailed in this land war.

Resisting Wage Labor. As planters prepared for a new growing season, a great battle took shape over the labor system that would replace slavery. Convinced that blacks needed supervision, planters wanted to retain the gang labor of the past, only now with wages replacing the food, clothing, and shelter their slaves had once received. The Freedmen's Bureau, although watchful against exploitative labor contracts, sided with the planters. The main thing, its reform founders believed, was not to encourage dependency under "the guise of guardianship." Rely on your "own efforts and exertions," an agent told a large crowd of freedmen in North Carolina, "make contracts with the planters" and "respect the rights of property."

This was advice given with little regard for the world in which those North Carolina freedmen lived. It was not only their unequal bargaining power they worried about or even that their ex-masters' real desire was to re-enslave them under the guise of "free" contracts. In their eyes the condition of wage labor was, by definition, debasing. The rural South was not like the North, where working for wages was by now the norm and qualified a man as independent. In the South, selling one's labor to another—and in particular, selling one's labor to work another's land—implied not freedom, but dependency. "I mean to own my own manhood," responded one South Carolina freedman to an offer of wage work. "I'm going to own my own land."

The wage issue cut to the very core of the former slaves' struggle for freedom. Nothing had been more horrifying than that as slaves their persons had been the property of others. When a master cast his eye on a slave woman, her husband had no recourse; nor, for that matter, was rape of a slave a crime. In a famous oration celebrating the anniversary of emancipation, the Reverend Henry M. Turner spoke bitterly of the time when his people had "no security for domestic happiness" and "our wives were sold and husbands bought, children were begotten and enslaved by their fathers." That was why formalizing marriage was so urgent a matter and why, when hard-pressed planters demanded that freedwomen go back into the fields, they resisted so resolutely. If the ex-slaves were to be free as white folk, then their wives could not, any

Freedom

In the annals of America, probably no human relationship was so conducive to mutual incomprehension as enslavement. Slavery meant one thing to the masters, something altogether different to the slaves. And when freedom came, there was no bridging this bottomless gulf. That, more than anything, explains the racial strife over land, over equal rights, and over political power that engulfed the Reconstruction South. The following documents offer vivid testimony to this bitter legacy of slavery.

EDWARD BARNELL HEYWARD

This letter is from the son of a (formerly) wealthy plantation owner, to his friend Jim, evidently a Northerner. Heyward has not quite gotten over the fact that he — and his northern friend — has survived the war, nor that he is now poor. And, in defeat, he feels deeply alienated from America; he is thinking of migrating to England. What is most telling about his letter, however, is his despair over the future of his ex-slaves. He is afraid, remarkably, that emancipation means "their best days are over."

E. B. Heyward
Gadsden P.O.
South Carolina
22 January 1866

My dear Jim

Your letter of date July 1865, has just reached me and you will be relieved by my answer, to find, that I am still alive, and extremely glad to hear from you. . . .

I have served in the Army, my brother died in the Army, and every family has lost members. No one can know how reduced we are, particularly the refined & educated. . . .

Our losses have been frightful, and we have now, scarcely a support. My Father had five plantations on the coast, and all the buildings were burnt, and the negroes, now left to themselves, are roaming in a starving condition . . . like lost sheep, with no one to care for them.

They find the Yankee only a speculator, and they have no confidence in anyone. They very naturally, poor things, think that freedom means doing nothing, and this they are determined to do. They look to the government, to take care of them, and it will be many years, before this once productive country will be able to support itself. The former kind and just treatment of the slaves, and their docile and generous temper, makes them now disposed to be

[quiet] and obedient: but the determination of your Northern people to give them a place in the councils of the Country and make them the equal of the white man, will at last, bear its fruit, and we may *then* expect them, to rise against the whites, and in the end, be exterminated themselves.

I am now interested in a school for the negroes, who are around me, and will endeavor to do my duty, to them, as ever before, but I am afraid their best days are past.

As soon as able, I shall quit the Country, and leave others to stand the storm, which I now see making up, at the North, which must soon burst upon *the whole* country, and break up everything which we have so long boasted of.

I feel now that I have *no country*, I *obey* like a subject, but I cannot love such a government. Perhaps the next letter, you get from me, will be from England.

I have, thank God! A house over my head & something to eat & am as ever always

your friend,
E. B. Heyward

JOURDON ANDERSON

This is a letter by Jourdan Anderson, a Tennessee slave who escaped with his family during the war and settled in Dayton, Ohio, to his former master. Folklorists have recorded the sly ways that slaves found, even in bondage, for "puttin' down" their masters. But only in freedom — and beyond reach in a northern state at that — could Anderson's sarcasm be expressed so openly, with the jest that his family might consider returning if they first received the wages due them, calculated to the dollar, for all those years in slavery. Anderson's letter, although probably written or edited by a white friend in Dayton, surely is faithful to what the ex-slave wanted to say.

Dayton, Ohio
August 7, 1865.

To My Old Master, Colonel P. H. Anderson, Big Spring, Tennessee.

Sir:

I got your letter, and was glad to find that you had not forgotten Jourdon. . . . I thought the Yankees would have hung you long before this, for harboring Rebs they found at your house. I suppose they never heard about your going to Colonel Martin's house to kill the union soldier that was left by his company in their stable. Although you shot at me twice before I left you, I did not want to hear of your being hurt, and am glad you are still living. It would do me good to go back to the dear old home again, and see Miss Mary and Miss Martha and Allen, Esther, Green, and Lee. Give my love to them all, and tell them I hope we will meet in the better world, if not in this. . . .

I want to know particularly what the good chance is you propose to give me. I am doing tolerably well here. I get twenty-five dollars a month, with victuals and clothing; have a comfortable home for Mandy,—the folks call her Mrs. Anderson,—and the children—Milly, Jane, and Grundy—go to school and are learning well. . . . We are kindly treated. Sometimes we overhear others saying, "Them colored people were slaves" down in Tennessee. The children feel hurt when they hear such remarks; but I tell them it was no disgrace in Tennessee to belong to Colonel Anderson. Many darkeys would have been proud, as I used to be, to call you master. . . .

Mandy says she would be afraid to go back without some proof that you were disposed to treat us justly and kindly; and we have concluded to test your sincerity by asking you to send us our wages for the time we served you. This will make us forget and forgive old scores, and rely on your justice and friendship in the future. I served you faithfully for thirty-two years, and Mandy twenty years. At twenty-five dollars a month for me and two dollars a week for Mandy, our earnings would amount to eleven thousand six hundred and eighty dollars. Add to this the interest for the time our wages have been kept back, and deduct what you paid for our clothing, and three doctor's visits to me, and pulling a tooth for Mandy, and the balance will show what we are in justice entitled to. . . .

In answering this letter, please state if there would be any safety for my Milly and Jane, who are now grown up, and both good-looking girls. . . . I would rather stay here and starve—and die, if it come to that—than have my girls brought to shame by the violence and wickedness of their young masters. You will also please state if there has been any schools opened for the colored children in your neighborhood. The great desire of my life now is to give my children an education, and have them form virtuous habits.

Say howdy to George Carter, and thank him for taking the pistol from you when you were shooting at me.

From your old servant,
Jourdon Anderson

SOURCE: Stanley I. Kutler, ed., *Looking for America: The People's History,* 2nd ed., 2 vols. (New York: W. W. Norton, 1979), 2: 4–6, 24–27.

ANALYZING THE EVIDENCE

➤ The South proved fiercely resistant to accepting the ex-slaves as citizens with equal rights. In what ways does Heyward's letter provide insight into that resistance and (despite Heyward's professed sympathy) help explain why so many blacks were beaten and killed when they tried to exercise their rights?

➤ In what ways does Anderson's letter suggest that, despite Heyward's dire prediction, the best days of the freed slaves were not "behind them" and that, on the contrary, they were hungry for the benefits of freedom?

➤ Once emancipated, ex-slaves were free to go wherever they wanted. Yet they mostly stayed put and, despite the bitterness of their enslavement, often became sharecroppers for their former masters, as, for example, on the Barrow plantation (see Map 15.2, p. 473). Does Anderson's letter suggest why they might have made that choice? Does it matter that his former master is also named Anderson?

Wage Labor of Former Slaves

This photograph, taken in South Carolina shortly after the Civil War, shows former slaves leaving the cotton fields. Ex-slaves were organized into work crews probably not that different from earlier slave gangs, although they now labored for wages and their plug-hatted boss bore little resemblance to the slave drivers of the past. New-York Historical Society.

more than white wives, labor for others. "I seen on some plantations," one freedman recounted, "where the white men would . . . tell colored men that their wives and children could not live on their places unless they work in the fields. The colored men [answered that] whenever they wanted their wives to work they would tell them themselves; and if he could not rule his own domestic affairs on that place he would leave it and go someplace else."

The reader will see the irony in this definition of freedom: It assumed the wife's subordinate role and designated her labor the husband's property. But if that was the price of freedom, freedwomen were prepared to pay it. Far better to take a chance with their own men than with their ex-masters.

Many former slaves voted with their feet, abandoning their old plantations and seeking better lives in the towns and cities of the South. Those who remained in the countryside refused to work the cotton fields under the hated **gang-labor system** or negotiated tenaciously over the terms of their labor contracts. Whatever system of labor finally might emerge, it was clear that the freedmen would never settle for anything resembling the old plantation system.

The efforts of former slaves to control their own lives challenged deeply entrenched white attitudes. "The destiny of the black race," asserted one Texan, could be summarized "in one sentence — subordination to the white race." Southern whites, a Freedmen's Bureau official observed, could not

"conceive of the negro having any rights at all." And when freedmen resisted, white retribution was swift and often terrible. In Pine Bluff, Arkansas, "after some kind of dispute with some freedmen," whites set fire to their cabins and hanged twenty-four of the inhabitants — men, women, and children. The toll of murdered and beaten blacks mounted into untold thousands. The governments established under Johnson's plan only put the stamp of legality on the pervasive efforts to enforce white supremacy. Blacks "would be *just as well* off with no law at all or no Government," concluded a Freedmen's Bureau agent, as with the justice they got under the restored white rule.

In this unequal struggle, blacks turned to Washington. "We stood by the government when it wanted help," a black Mississippian wrote President Johnson. "Now . . . will it stand by us?"

Congress versus President

Andrew Johnson was not the man to ask. In February 1866 he vetoed the Freedmen's Bureau bill. The bureau, Johnson charged, was an "immense patronage," showering benefits on blacks never granted to "our own people." Republicans could not muster enough votes to override his veto. A month later, again rebuffing his critics, Johnson vetoed Trumbull's civil rights bill, arguing that federal protection of black rights constituted "a stride toward centralization." His racism, hitherto muted, now blazed forth: "This is a country for white men, and by God, as long as I am president, it shall be government for white men."

Galvanized by Johnson's attack on their legislation, the Republicans went into action. In early April they got the necessary two-thirds majorities in both houses and enacted the Civil Rights Act. Republican resolve was reinforced by news of mounting violence in the South, culminating in three days of rioting in Memphis. Forty-six blacks were left dead, and hundreds of homes, churches, and schools were burned. In July an angry Congress renewed the Freedmen's Bureau over a second Johnson veto.

The Fourteenth Amendment. Anxious to consolidate their gains, Republicans moved to enshrine black civil rights in an amendment to the Constitution. The heart of the Fourteenth Amendment was Section 1, which declared that "all persons born or naturalized in the United States" were citizens. No state could abridge "the privileges or immunities of citizens of the United States," deprive "any person of life, liberty, or property, without due process of law," or deny anyone "the equal protection of the laws." These phrases were vague, intentionally so, but they established the constitutionality of the Civil Rights Act and, at the least, laid the groundwork for a federally enforced standard of equality before the law in the states.

For the moment, however, the Fourteenth Amendment was most important as a factor in partisan politics. With the 1866 congressional elections approaching, Johnson somehow figured he could turn the Fourteenth Amendment to his advantage. He urged the states not to ratify it. Months earlier, Johnson had begun maneuvering against the Republicans. He aimed at building a coalition of white Southerners, northern Democrats, and conservative Republicans under the banner of a new party, National Union. Any hope of launching it, however, was shattered by Johnson's intemperate behavior and by escalating violence in the South. A dissension-ridden National Union convention in July ended inconclusively, and Johnson's campaign against the Fourteenth Amendment became, effectively, a campaign for the Democratic Party.

"The First Vote"

This lithograph appeared in *Harper's Weekly* in November 1867. The voters represent elements of African American political leadership: an artisan with tools, a well-dressed member of the middle class, and a Union soldier. Corbis-Bettmann.

Republicans responded furiously, unveiling a practice that would become known as "waving the bloody shirt." The Democrats were traitors, charged Indiana governor Oliver Morton. Their party was "a common sewer and loathsome receptacle, into which is emptied every element of treason North and South." In late August Johnson embarked on a disastrous "swing around the circle"—a railroad tour from Washington to Chicago and St. Louis and back—that violated the custom against personal campaigning by presidents. Johnson made matters worse by engaging in shouting matches with hecklers and insulting the hostile crowds.

The 1866 congressional elections inflicted a humiliating defeat on Johnson. The Republicans won a three-to-one majority in Congress. They considered themselves "masters of the situation" and free to proceed "entirely regardless of [Johnson's] opinions or wishes." As a referendum on the Fourteenth Amendment, moreover, the election was a striking victory, demonstrating vast popular support for the civil rights of the former slaves. The Republican Party emerged with a new sense of unity—a unity coalescing not at the center, but on the left, around the unbending program of the Radical minority.

Radical Republicans. The Radicals represented the abolitionist strain within the Republican Party. Most of them hailed from New England or from the upper Midwest, which was heavily settled by New Englanders. In the Senate they were led by Charles Sumner of Massachusetts and in the House by Thaddeus Stevens of Pennsylvania. For them Reconstruction was never primarily about restoring the Union but about remaking southern society. "The foundations of their institutions . . . must be broken up and relaid," declared Stevens, "or all our blood and treasure will have been spent in vain."

Only a handful went as far as Stevens in demanding that the plantations be treated as "forfeited estates of the enemy" and broken up into small farms for the former slaves. About securing the freedmen's civil and political rights, however, there was agreement. In this endeavor Radicals had no qualms about expanding the powers of the national government. "The power of the great landed aristocracy in those regions, if unrestrained by power from without, would inevitably reassert itself," warned Congressman George W. Julian of Indiana. Radicals were aggressively partisan. They regarded the Republican Party as God's instrument for regenerating the South.

At first, in the months after Appomattox, few but the Radicals themselves imagined that so extreme a program had any chance of enactment. Black **suffrage** especially seemed beyond reach, since the northern states themselves (except in New England) denied blacks the vote. And yet, as fury mounted against the intransigent South, Republicans became ever more radicalized until, in the wake of the smashing congressional victory of 1866, they embraced the Radicals' vision of a reconstructed South.

➤ Why can the enactment of southern Black Codes in 1865 be considered a turning point in the course of Reconstruction?

➤ Why was working for wages resisted by ex-slaves struggling for freedom after emancipation?

➤ To what extent was President Johnson responsible for the radicalization of the Republican Party in 1866?

Radical Reconstruction

Afterward, thoughtful Southerners admitted that the South had brought radical Reconstruction on itself. "We had, in 1865, a white man's government in Alabama," remarked the man who had been Johnson's provisional governor, "but we lost it." The state's "great blunder" was not to "have at once taken the negro right under the protection of the laws." Remarkably, the South remained defiant even after the 1866 elections. Every state legislature but Tennessee's rejected the Fourteenth Amendment. It was as if they could not imagine that governments installed under the presidential imprimatur and fully functioning might be swept away. But that, in fact, is just what the Republicans intended to do.

Congress Takes Command

The Reconstruction Act of 1867, enacted in March by the Republican Congress, organized the South as a conquered land, dividing it into five military districts, each under the command of a Union general (Map 15.1). The price for reentering the Union was granting the vote to the freedmen and disfranchising those of the South's prewar leadership class who had participated in the rebellion. Each military commander was ordered to register all eligible adult males (black as well as white), supervise the election of state conventions, and make certain that

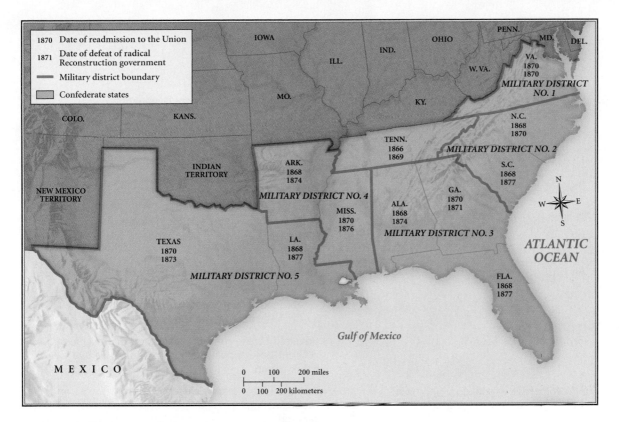

Map 15.1 Reconstruction

The federal government organized the Confederate states into five military districts during radical Reconstruction. For each state the first date indicates when that state was readmitted to the Union; the second date shows when Radical Republicans lost control of the state government. All the ex-Confederate states rejoined the Union from 1868 to 1870, but the periods of radical rule varied widely. Republicans lasted only a few months in Virginia; they held on until the end of Reconstruction in Louisiana, Florida, and South Carolina.

the new constitutions contained guarantees of black suffrage. Congress would readmit a state to the Union if its voters ratified the constitution, if that document proved acceptable to Congress, and if the new state legislature approved the Fourteenth Amendment (thus ensuring the needed ratification by three-fourths of the states). Johnson vetoed the Reconstruction Act, but Congress overrode the veto (Table 15.1).

Impeachment. The Tenure of Office Act, a companion to the Reconstruction Act, required Senate consent for the removal of any official whose appointment had required Senate confirmation. Congress chiefly wanted to protect Secretary of War Edwin M. Stanton, a Lincoln holdover and the only member of Johnson's cabinet who favored radical Reconstruction. In his position Stanton could do much to frustrate Johnson's anticipated efforts to undermine Reconstruction. The law also required the president to issue all orders to the

army through its commanding general, Ulysses S. Grant. In effect, Congress was attempting to reconstruct the presidency as well as the South.

Seemingly defeated, Johnson appointed generals recommended by Stanton and Grant to command the five military districts in the South. But he was just biding his time. In August 1867, after Congress had adjourned, he "suspended" Stanton and replaced him with Grant, believing that the general would be a good soldier and follow orders. Next Johnson replaced four of the commanding generals. Johnson, however, had misjudged Grant, who publicly objected to the president's machinations. When the Senate reconvened in the fall, it overruled Stanton's suspension. Grant, now an open enemy of Johnson's, resigned so that Stanton could resume his office.

On February 21, 1868, Johnson formally dismissed Stanton. The feisty secretary of war, however, barricaded the door of his office and refused to admit Johnson's appointee. Three days later, for the

Table 15.1	Primary Reconstruction Laws and Constitutional Amendments
Law (Date of Congressional Passage)	**Key Provisions**
Thirteenth Amendment (December 1865*)	Prohibited slavery
Civil Rights Act of 1866 (April 1866)	Defined citizenship rights of freedmen
	Authorized federal authorities to bring suit against those who violated those rights
Fourteenth Amendment (June 1866†)	Established national citizenship for persons born or naturalized in the United States
	Prohibited the states from depriving citizens of their civil rights or equal protection under the law
	Reduced state representation in House of Representatives by the percentage of adult male citizens denied the vote
Reconstruction Act of 1867 (March 1867)	Divided the South into five military districts, each under the command of a Union general
	Established requirements for readmission of ex-Confederate states to the Union
Tenure of Office Act (March 1867)	Required Senate consent for removal of any federal official whose appointment had required Senate confirmation
Fifteenth Amendment (February 1869‡)	Forbade states to deny citizens the right to vote on the grounds of race, color, or "previous condition of servitude"
Ku Klux Klan Act (April 1871)	Authorized the president to use federal prosecutions and military force to suppress conspiracies to deprive citizens of the right to vote and enjoy the equal protection of the law

*Ratified by three-fourths of all states in December 1865.
†Ratified by three-fourths of all states in July 1868.
‡Ratified by three-fourths of all states in March 1870.

first time in U.S. history, House Republicans introduced articles of **impeachment** against a sitting president, employing the power granted the House of Representatives by the Constitution to charge high federal officials with "Treason, Bribery, or other high Crimes and Misdemeanors." The House serves in effect as the prosecutor in such cases. Eleven counts of presidential misconduct were brought, nine of them violations of the Tenure of Office Act.

The case went to the Senate, which acts as the court in impeachment cases, with Chief Justice Salmon P. Chase presiding. After an eleven-week trial, thirty-five senators on May 15 voted for conviction, one vote short of the two-thirds majority required. Seven moderate Republicans broke ranks, voting for acquittal along with twelve Democrats. The dissenting Republicans felt that the Tenure of Office Act was of dubious validity (in fact, the Supreme Court subsequently declared it unconstitutional) and that removing a president for defying Congress was too extreme, too damaging to the constitutional system of checks and balances, even for the sake of punishing

Johnson. And they were wary of the alternative, the Radical Republican Benjamin F. Wade, the president pro tem of the Senate, who, since there was no vice president, stood next in line for the presidency.

Despite his acquittal, however, Johnson had been defanged. For the remainder of his term he was powerless to alter the course of Reconstruction.

The Election of 1868. The impeachment controversy made Grant, already the North's war hero, a Republican hero as well, and he easily won the party's presidential nomination in 1868. In the fall campaign he supported radical Reconstruction, but he also urged reconciliation between the sections. His Democratic opponent, Horatio Seymour, a former governor of New York, almost declined the nomination because he doubted that the Democrats could overcome the stain of disloyalty.

As Seymour feared, the Republicans "waved the bloody shirt," stirring up old wartime emotions against the Democrats to great effect. Grant did about as well in the North (55 percent) as had

Lincoln in 1864. Overall, he won by a margin of 52.7 percent and received 214 of 294 electoral votes. The Republicans also retained two-thirds majorities in both houses of Congress.

The Fifteenth Amendment. In the wake of their victory, the Republicans quickly produced the last major piece of Reconstruction legislation—the Fifteenth Amendment, which forbade either the federal government or the states from denying citizens the right to vote on the basis of race, color, or "previous condition of servitude." The amendment left room for **poll taxes** and property requirements or literacy tests that might be used to discourage blacks from voting, a necessary concession to northern and western states that already relied on such provisions to keep immigrants and the "unworthy" poor from the polls. A California senator warned that in his state, with its rabidly anti-Chinese sentiment (see Chapter 16), any restriction on that power would "kill our party as dead as a stone."

Despite grumbling by Radical Republicans, the amendment passed without modification in February 1869. Congress required the states still under federal control—Virginia, Mississippi, Texas, and Georgia—to ratify it as a condition for being readmitted to the Union. A year later the Fifteenth Amendment became part of the Constitution.

Woman Suffrage Denied

If the Fifteenth Amendment troubled some proponents of black suffrage, this was nothing compared to the outrage felt by women's rights advocates. They had fought the good fight for the abolition of slavery for so many years, only to be abandoned when the chance finally came to get the vote for women. All it would have taken was one more word in the Fifteenth Amendment, so that the protected categories for voting would have read "race, color, *sex,* or previous condition." Leading suffragists such as Susan B. Anthony and Elizabeth Cady Stanton did not want to hear from Radical Republicans that this was "the Negro's hour" and that women should wait for another day. How could suffrage be granted to former slaves, Stanton demanded, but not to them?

In a decisive debate in May 1869 at the Equal Rights Association, the champion of universal suffrage, the black abolitionist Frederick Douglass, pleaded for understanding. "When women, because they are women, are hunted down . . . dragged from their homes and hung upon lamp posts . . . when their children are not allowed to enter schools; then they will have an urgency to obtain the ballot equal to our own." Not even all his black sisters agreed. "If colored men get their rights, and not

colored women theirs," protested Sojourner Truth, "you see the colored men will be masters over the women, and it will be just as bad as it was before." As for white women in the audience, remarked Frances Harper in support of Douglass, they "all go for sex, letting race occupy a minor position," or worse. In her despair, Elizabeth Cady Stanton lashed out in ugly racist terms against "Patrick and Sambo and Hans and Ung Tung," aliens ignorant of the Declaration of Independence and yet entitled to vote while the most accomplished of American women remained voteless. Douglass's resolution in support of the Fifteenth Amendment failed, and the Equal Rights convention broke up in acrimony.

At this searing moment a rift opened in the ranks of the women's movement. The majority, led by Lucy Stone and Julia Ward Howe, reconciled themselves to disappointment and accepted the priority of black suffrage. Organized into the American Woman Suffrage Association, these moderates remained allied to the Republican Party, in hopes that once Reconstruction had been settled it would be time for the woman's vote. The Stanton-Anthony group, however, struck out in a new direction. The embittered Stanton declared that woman "must not put her trust in man." The new organization she headed, the New York–based National Woman Suffrage Association, accepted only women, focused exclusively on women's rights, and resolutely took up the battle for a federal woman suffrage amendment.

The fracturing of the women's movement obscured the common ground the two sides shared. Both appealed to constituencies beyond the narrow confines of abolitionism and evangelical reform. Both elevated suffrage into the preeminent women's issue. And both were energized for the battles that lay ahead. "If I were to give vent to all my pent-up wrath concerning the subordination of woman," Lydia Maria Child wrote the Republican warhorse Charles Sumner in 1872, "I might frighten *you.* . . . Suffice it, therefore, to say, either the theory of our government is *false,* or women have a right to vote." If radical Reconstruction seemed a barren time for women's rights, in fact it had planted the seeds of the modern feminist movement.

Republican Rule in the South

Between 1868 and 1871 all the southern states met the congressional stipulations and rejoined the Union. Protected by federal troops, state Republican organizations took hold across the South. The Reconstruction administrations they set up remained in power for periods ranging from a few months in Virginia to nine years in South Carolina, Louisiana, and Florida. Their core support came

Women's Rights, 1870s

This 1870s engraving reveals a distinguishing feature of the woman suffrage movement as it emerged after Reconstruction, which was that it became exclusively a movement of women (although there are a couple of men in the audience). Bettmann/Corbis.

from African Americans, who constituted a majority of registered voters in Alabama, Florida, South Carolina, and Mississippi.

Carpetbaggers and Scalawags. Ex-Confederates had a name for Southern whites who supported Reconstruction: **scalawags,** an ancient Scots-Irish term for runty, worthless animals. Whites who had come from the North they denounced as **carpetbaggers**—self-seeking interlopers who carried all their property in cheap suitcases called carpetbags. Such labels glossed over the actual diversity of these white Republicans.

Some carpetbaggers, while motivated by personal profit, also brought capital and skills. Others were Union army veterans taken with the South—its climate, people, and economic opportunities. And interspersed with the self-seekers were many idealists anxious to advance the cause of emancipation.

The scalawags were even more diverse. Some were former slave owners, ex-Whigs and even ex-Democrats, drawn to Republicanism as the best way to attract northern capital to southern railroads, mines, and factories. But most were yeomen farmers from the backcountry districts who wanted to rid the South of its slaveholding aristocracy. They had generally fought against, or at least refused to support, the Confederacy, believing that slavery had victimized whites as well as blacks. "Now is the time," a Georgia scalawag wrote, "for every man to come out and speak his principles publickly [sic] and vote for liberty as we have been in bondage long enough."

African American Leadership. The Democrats' scorn for black leaders as ignorant field hands was just as false as stereotypes about white Republicans. The first African American leaders in the South came from an elite of free blacks. They were joined by northern blacks who moved south heartened by the arrival of radical Reconstruction. Like their white allies, many were Union army veterans. Some had participated in the antislavery crusade; a number were employed by the Freedmen's Bureau or northern missionary societies. Others had escaped from slavery and were returning home. One of these was Blanche K. Bruce, who had been tutored on the Virginia plantation of his white father. During the war Bruce escaped and established a school for ex-slaves in Missouri. In 1869 he moved to Mississippi, became active in politics, and in 1874 became Mississippi's second black U.S. senator.

As the reconstructed Republican governments of 1867 began to function, this diverse group of ministers, artisans, shopkeepers, and former soldiers reached out to the freedmen. African American speakers, some financed by the Republican Party, fanned out into the old plantation districts and recruited ex-slaves for political roles. Still, few of the new leaders were field hands; most had been preachers or artisans. The literacy of one ex-slave, Thomas Allen, who was a Baptist minister and shoemaker, helped him win election to the Georgia legislature. "In my county," he recalled, "the colored people came to me for instructions, and I gave them the best instructions I could. I took the *New York Tribune* and other papers, and in that way I found out a great deal, and I told them whatever I thought was right."

Although never proportionate to their numbers in the population, black officeholders were prominent across the South. In South Carolina African Americans constituted a majority in the lower house of the legislature in 1868. Three were elected to Congress; another joined the state supreme court. Over the entire course of Reconstruction, twenty African Americans served in state administrations as governor, lieutenant governor, secretary of state, treasurer, or superintendent of education; more than six hundred served as state legislators; and sixteen were U.S. congressmen.

The Radical Program. The Republicans had ambitious plans for a reconstructed South. They wanted to end its dependence on cotton agriculture, build an entrepreneurial economy like the North's, and make a better life for all southerners. Although they fell short, they accomplished more than their critics gave them credit for.

The Republicans modernized state constitutions, eliminated property qualifications for the vote, and swept out the Black Codes restricting the lives of the freedmen. Women also benefited from the Republican defense of personal liberty. The new constitutions expanded the rights of married women, enabling them to hold property and earnings independent of their husbands—"a wonderful reform," a Georgia woman wrote, for "the cause of Women's Rights." Republican social programs called for the establishment of hospitals, more humane penitentiaries, and asylums for orphans and the mentally ill. Money poured into road-building projects and the region's shattered railroad network.

To pay for their ambitious programs the Republican governments copied taxes that Jacksonian reformers had earlier introduced in the North—in particular, property taxes on both real estate and personal wealth (see Chapter 10). The goal was to make planters pay their fair shares and to broaden the tax base. In many plantation counties, former slaves served as tax assessors and collectors, administering the taxation of their one-time owners.

Higher tax revenues never managed to overtake the huge obligations assumed by the Reconstruction governments. State debts mounted rapidly, and, as crushing interest on bonds fell due, public credit collapsed. On top of that, much spending was wasted or ended up in the pockets of public officials. Corruption was ingrained in American politics, rampant everywhere in this era, not least in the Grant administration itself. Still, in the free-spending atmosphere of the southern Republican regimes, corruption was especially luxuriant and damaging to the cause of radical Reconstruction.

Schools and Churches. Nothing, however, could dim the achievement in public education. Here the South had lagged woefully; only Tennessee had a system of public schooling before the Civil War. Republican state governments vowed to make up for lost time, viewing education as the foundation for a democratic order. African Americans of all ages rushed to the newly established schools, even when they had to pay tuition. An elderly man in Mississippi explained his hunger for education: "Ole missus used to read the good book [the Bible] to us . . . on Sunday evenin's, but she mostly read dem places where it says, 'Servants obey your masters.' . . . Now we is free, there's heaps of tings in that old book we is just suffering to learn."

Hiram R. Revels

In 1870 Hiram R. Revels (1822–1901) was elected to the U.S. Senate from Mississippi to fill Jefferson Davis's former seat. Revels was a free black from North Carolina who had migrated to the North and attended Knox College in Illinois. He recruited blacks for the Union army and, as an ordained Methodist minister, served as chaplain of a black regiment in Mississippi, where he settled after the war. Library of Congress.

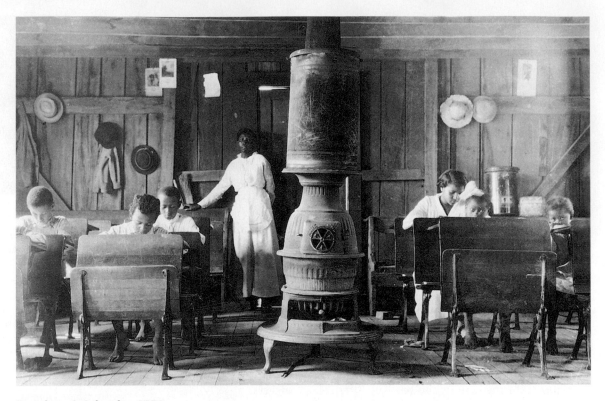

Freedmen's School, c. 1870

This rare photograph shows the interior of one of the three thousand freedmen's schools established across the South after the Civil War. Although many of these schools were staffed by white missionaries, a main objective of northern educators was to prepare blacks to take over the classrooms. The teacher shown here is surely one of the first. Library of Congress.

The building of schools was part of a larger effort by African Americans to fortify the institutions that had sustained their spirits in the slave days, most especially, Christianity. Now, in freedom, the African Americans left the white-dominated congregations, where they had been relegated to segregated balconies and denied any voice in church governance, and built churches of their own. These churches joined together to form African American versions of the Southern Methodist and Baptist denominations, including, most prominently, the National Baptist Convention and the African Methodist Episcopal Church. Everywhere the black churches served not only as places of worship but also as schools, social centers, and political meeting halls.

Black clerics were community leaders and often political leaders as well. As Charles H. Pearce, a Methodist minister in Florida, declared, "A man in this State cannot do his whole duty as a minister except he looks out for the political interests of his people." Calling forth the special destiny of the ex-slaves as the new "Children of Israel," black ministers provided a powerful religious underpinning for the Republican politics of their congregations.

The Quest for Land

In the meantime the freedmen were locked in a great economic struggle with their former owners. In 1869 the Republican government of South Carolina had established a land commission empowered to buy property and resell it on easy terms to the landless. In this way about 14,000 black families acquired farms. South Carolina's land distribution plan showed what was possible, but it was the exception and not the rule. Despite a lot of rhetoric, Republican regimes elsewhere did little to help the freedmen fulfill their dreams of becoming independent farmers. Federal efforts proved equally feeble. The Southern Homestead Act of 1866 offered 80-acre grants to settlers, limited for the first year to freedmen and southern Unionists. The advantage was mostly symbolic, however, since only marginal land was made available, off the beaten track in swampy, infertile parts of the Lower South. Few of the homesteaders succeeded.

There was no reversing President Johnson's order restoring confiscated lands to ex-Confederates. Property rights, it seemed, trumped everything else, even for most Radical Republicans. The Freedman's Bureau, which had earlier championed the land claims of the ex-slaves, now devoted itself to teaching them how to be good agricultural laborers.

Sharecropping. While they yearned for farms of their own, most freedmen started out landless, with no option but to work for their former owners — but not, they vowed, under the conditions of slavery — no gang work, no supervision by overseers, no fines or punishments, no regulation of their private lives. In certain parts of the agricultural South wage work became the norm — for example, on the great sugar plantations of Louisiana financed by northern capital. The problem was that cotton planters lacked the money to pay wages, at least not until the crop came in, and sometimes, in lieu of a straight wage, they offered a share of the crop. As a wage, this was a bad deal for the freedmen, but if they could be paid in shares for their work, why could they not pay in shares to rent the land they worked?

This form of land tenancy was already familiar in parts of the white South, and the freedmen now seized on it for the independence it offered them. Planters resisted, believing, as one wrote, that "wages are the only successful system of controlling hands." But, in a battle of wills that broke out all across the cotton South, the planters yielded to "the inveterate prejudices of the freedmen, who desire to be masters of their own time."

Thus there sprang up the distinctive laboring system of cotton agriculture called **sharecropping**, in which the freedmen worked as renters, exchanging their labor for the use of land, house, implements, seed, and fertilizer, and typically turning over one-half to two-thirds of their crops to the landlord (Map 15.2). The sharecropping system joined laborers and the owners of land and capital in a common sharing of risks and returns. But it

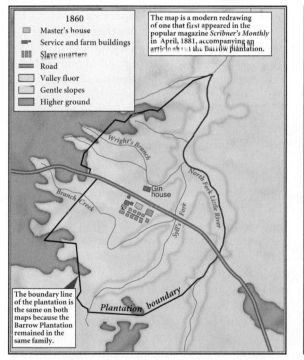
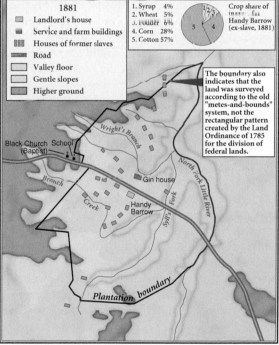

Map 15.2   The Barrow Plantation, 1860 and 1881

Comparing the 1860 map of this central Georgia plantation with the 1881 map reveals the impact of sharecropping on patterns of black residence. In 1860 the slave quarters were clustered near the planter's house. In contrast, by 1881 the sharecroppers scattered across the plantation's 2,000 acres, building cabins on the ridges between the low-lying streams. The name Barrow was common among the sharecropping families, which means almost certainly that they had been slaves on the Barrow plantation who, years after emancipation, still had not moved on. For all the croppers freedom surely meant not only their individual lots and cabins, but also the school and church shown on the map.

was a very unequal relationship, given the force of southern law and custom on the white landowner's side and the sharecroppers' dire economic circumstances. Starting out penniless, they had no way of making it through the first growing season without borrowing for food and supplies.

Country storekeepers stepped in. Bankrolled by their northern suppliers, they "furnished" the sharecropper and took as collateral a **lien** on the crop, effectively assuming ownership of the cropper's share and leaving him only the proceeds that remained after his debts had been paid. Once indebted at one store, sharecroppers were no longer free to shop around. They became an easy target for exorbitant prices, unfair interest rates, and crooked bookkeeping. As cotton prices declined during the 1870s, more and more sharecroppers failed to settle accounts and fell into permanent debt. And if the merchant was also the landowner, or conspired with the landowner, the debt became a pretext for forced labor, or **peonage,** although evidence now suggests that sharecroppers generally managed to pull up stakes and move on once things became hopeless. Sharecroppers always thought twice about moving, however, because part of their "capital" was being known and well reputed in their home communities. Freedmen who lacked that local standing generally found sharecropping hard going and ended up in the ranks of agricultural laborers.

In the face of so much adversity, black families struggled to better themselves. That it enabled family struggle was, in truth, the saving advantage of sharecropping because it mobilized husbands and wives in common enterprise while shielding both from personal subordination to whites. Wives were doubly blessed. Neither field hands for their ex-masters nor dependent housewives, they became partners laboring side by side with their husbands. The trouble with sharecropping, one planter grumbled, was that "it makes the laborer too independent; he becomes a partner, and has to be consulted." By the end of Reconstruction, about a quarter of sharecropping families had managed to save enough to rent with cash payments, and eventually black farmers owned about a third of the land they cultivated (see Reading American Pictures, "Why Sharecropping?," p. 475).

A Comparative Perspective. The battle between planters and freedmen over the land was by no means unique to the American South. Whenever slavery ended—in Haiti after the slave revolt of 1791, in the British Caribbean by abolition in 1833, in Cuba and Brazil by gradual emancipation during the 1880s—a fierce struggle ensued between planters bent on restoring a gang-labor system and ex-slaves bent on gaining economic autonomy. The outcome of this universal conflict depended on the ex-slaves' access to land. Where vacant land existed, as in British Guiana, or where plantations could be seized, as in Haiti, the ex-slaves became subsistence farmers, and insofar as the Caribbean plantation economy survived without the ex-slaves, it did so by the importation of indentured servants from India and China. Where land could not be had, as in British Barbados or Antigua, the ex-slaves returned to plantation labor as wage workers, although often in some combination with customary rights to housing and garden plots. The cotton South fit neither of these broad patterns. The freedmen did not get the land, but neither did the planters get field hands. What both got was sharecropping.

There are two ways of explaining this outcome. One is political. Outside the American South, emancipated slaves rarely got civil or political equality. Even in the British islands, where substantial self-government existed, high property qualifications effectively disfranchised the ex-slaves. In the United States, however, hard on the heels of emancipation came civil rights, manhood suffrage, and, for a brief era, a real measure of political power for the freedmen. Sharecropping took shape during Reconstruction, and there was no going back afterward.

That there was no going back suggests a second explanation for the triumph of sharecropping, namely, that it was a good fit for cotton agriculture. We can see this in the experience of other countries that became major producers in response to the global cotton famine set off by the Civil War. In all these places, in India, Egypt, Brazil and West Africa, some variant of the sharecropping system emerged. Most striking was the adoption everywhere of crop-lien laws, at the behest of the international merchants and bankers putting up the capital. Indian and Egyptian villagers got the advances they needed to shift from subsistence agriculture to cotton, but at the price of being placed, as in America, permanently under the thumb of the furnishing merchants. Implicit in advancing that money, of course, was the realization that cotton, unlike sugar cane, could be raised efficiently by small farmers (provided they had the lash of indebtedness always on their backs). American planters resisted sharecropping because they started at a different place: not traditional, subsistence economies that had to be converted to cotton but a proven plantation system over which they had been absolute masters.

Why Sharecropping?

Sharecroppers in Georgia. Brown Brothers.

The account of sharecropping on the neighboring pages describes the experience of hundreds of thousands of ex-slaves and plantation owners. How do we know that our generalizations are true? Or, more concretely, that a sharecropper reading our account would nod and say, "Yes, that's the way it was." One sliver of evidence is this photograph depicting a family of ex-slaves standing proudly by their new cabin and young cotton crop. In what ways does this contemporary photograph confirm or amplify our account of sharecropping?

ANALYZING THE EVIDENCE

➤ The cotton rows go right up to the house. Why would this family not have set aside land for a garden and for some livestock? And what does this suggest about the historians' claim that sharecropping doomed the South to a cash-crop monoculture?

➤ Note the gent in the background — most likely the landowner — with his handsome horse and carriage. The family is posing for the photograph, yet he pays no heed and breaks into the frame. And he seems to feel, although he has rented it out, that he still has the run of the place. What does this suggest about the limits of sharecropping as a means of achieving independence by the freedmen?

➤ In that struggle, of course, everything was relative. What elements in the photograph suggest that, compared to what they had known as slaves or, after emancipation, would have faced as day laborers, this family might have thought they had not fared so badly? (Students are urged to consult Map 15.2 on p. 473, bearing in mind of course that this family did not actually live on the Barrow plantation.)

For America's ex-slaves sharecropping was not the worst choice; it certainly beat laboring for their former owners. But for southern agriculture the costs were devastating. Sharecropping committed the South inflexibly to cotton because, as a market crop, it generated the cash required by landlords and furnishing merchants. Neither soil depletion nor low prices ever enabled sharecroppers to shift away from cotton. With farms leased year to year, neither tenant nor owner had much incentive to improve the property. And the crop-lien system lined merchants' pockets with unearned profits that might otherwise have gone into agricultural improvement. The result was a stagnant farm economy, blighting the South's future and condemning it to economic backwardness — a kind of retribution, in fact, for the fresh injustices visited on the people it had once enslaved.

➤ Do you think it was predictable in 1865 that five years later the ex-slaves would receive the constitutional right to vote? Or that, having gone that far, the nation would deny the vote to women?

➤ What do you regard as the principal achievements of radical Reconstruction in the South? Do you think the achievements outweigh the failures?

➤ Why did the ex-slaves' struggle for land end in the sharecropping system?

The Undoing of Reconstruction

Ex-Confederates were blind to the achievements of radical Reconstruction. Indeed, no amount of success could have persuaded them that it was anything but an abomination, undertaken without their consent and denying them their rightful place in southern society. Led by the planters, ex-Confederates staged a massive counterrevolution — one designed to "redeem" the South and restore them to political power under the banner of the Democratic Party. But the Redeemers could not have succeeded on their own. They needed the complicity of the North. The undoing of Reconstruction is as much about northern acquiescence as it is about southern resistance.

Counterrevolution

Insofar as they could win at the ballot box, southern Democrats took that route. They worked hard

to get ex-Confederates restored to the voting rolls, they appealed to southern patriotism, and they campaigned against black rule. But force was equally acceptable. Throughout the Deep South, especially where black voters were heavily concentrated, ex-Confederate planters and their supporters organized secretly and terrorized blacks and their white allies.

Nathan Bedford Forrest and the Politics of Terror. No one looms larger in this bloody story than Nathan Bedford Forrest, the Confederacy's most decorated cavalry general. Born in poverty in 1821, he scrambled up the booming cotton economy and became a big-time Memphis slaver trader and Mississippi plantation owner. A man of fiery temper, he championed secession. When the war broke out, Forrest immediately formed a Tennessee cavalry regiment, fought bravely (and was badly wounded) at the battle of Shiloh, and won fame as a daring cavalry raider. On April 12, 1864, his troopers perpetrated one of the war's worst atrocities, the slaughter of black troops at Fort Pillow, Tennessee, acting on rumors that they had harassed local whites. The Fort Pillow massacre foreshadowed the civil strife that would consume Tennessee during Reconstruction.

Nathan Bedford Forrest in Uniform, c. 1865

Before he became Grand Wizard of the Ku Klux Klan, Forrest had been a celebrated cavalry general in the Confederate army. This photograph shows him in uniform before he was mustered out. Library of Congress.

Although nominally in control since 1862, Union authorities never managed to subdue Tennessee's irreconcilable Confederate sympathizers. The Republican-elected governor in 1865, William G. Brownlow, was a tough man, a former Confederate prisoner not shy about calling his enemies to account. They struck back with a campaign of terror, targeting especially Brownlow's black supporters. It was amidst this general mayhem that the first den of the Ku Klux Klan emerged in Pulaski, Tennessee, in late 1865 or early 1866. As it proliferated across the state, the Klan turned to General Forrest, who had been trying, unsuccessfully, to rebuild his prewar fortunes. Late in 1866, at a clandestine meeting in Nashville, Forrest donned the robes of Grand Wizard. His activities are mostly cloaked in mystery, but there is no mystery about why Forrest gravitated to the Klan. For him, the Klan was politics by other means, the instrument by which disfranchised former Confederates like himself might strike a blow against the despised Republicans who ran Tennessee.

In many towns the Klan became virtually identical to the Democratic clubs. In fact, Klan members — including Forrest — dominated Tennessee's delegation to the Democratic national convention of 1868. The Klan unleashed a murderous campaign of terror against Republican sympathizers. Governor Brownlow responded resolutely, threatening to mobilize the state militia and root out the Klan. If Brownlow tried, answered Forrest, "There will be war, and a bloodier one than we have ever witnessed." In the end, it was the Republicans, not the Klan, who cracked. In March 1869 Brownlow retreated to the U.S. Senate. The Democrats were on their way back to power, and the Klan, having served its purpose, was officially disbanded in Tennessee.

Elsewhere, the Klan raged on, murdering Republican politicians, burning black schools and churches, and attacking party gatherings, with more or less the same results as in Tennessee. By 1870, the Democrats had seized power in Georgia and North Carolina and were making headway across the South.

The Federal Reaction. Congress responded by passing legislation, including the Ku Klux Klan Act of 1871, designed to enforce the rights of ex-slaves under the Fourteenth and Fifteenth Amendments. These so-called enforcement laws authorized federal prosecutions, military intervention, and martial

"Worse than Slavery," 1874

This cartoon by Thomas Nast registers the despair felt by advocates of racial equality at the failure of Reconstruction. The Klan ruffians and White Leaguers have prevailed, Nast is saying, and white terrorism has reduced the oppressed black family to conditions worse than slavery. Granger Collection.

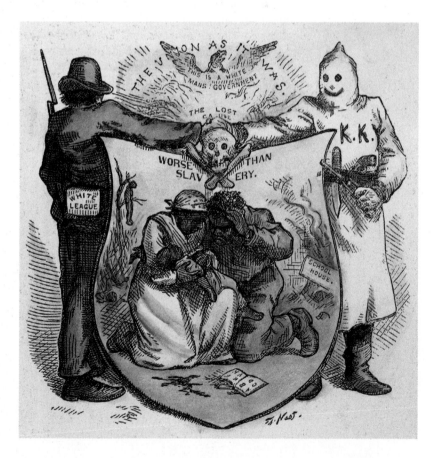

law to suppress terrorist activities that deprived citizens of their civil and political rights. In South Carolina, where the Klan became most deeply entrenched, federal troops occupied nine counties, made hundreds of arrests, and drove as many as two thousand Klansmen from the state.

The Grant administration's assault on the Klan raised the spirits of southern Republicans, but also revealed how dependent they were on the federal government. The potency of the Ku Klux Klan Act, a Mississippi Republican wrote, "derived alone from its source" in the federal government. "No such law could be enforced by state authority, the local power being too weak." If they were to prevail over antiblack terrorism, Republicans needed what one carpetbagger described as "steady, unswerving power from without."

But northern Republicans grew weary of Reconstruction and the endless bloodshed it seemed to produce. Prosecuting Klansmen was an uphill battle. U.S. attorneys usually faced all-white juries and unsympathetic federal judges, with scant resources for handling the cases. After 1872 prosecutions began to drop off; many Klansmen received hasty pardons. And then the constitutional underpinnings of the antiterrorist campaign came into question, culminating in the Supreme Court's decision in *United States v. Cruikshank* (1876) that the federal government had exceeded its authority under the Fourteenth Amendment. If the rights of the ex-slaves were being violated by individuals or private groups (like the KKK), that was a state responsibility and beyond the federal jurisdiction.

In a kind of self-fulfilling prophecy, the reluctance of the Grant administration to shore up Reconstruction guaranteed that it would fail. Republican governments that were denied federal help one by one fell victim to the massive resistance of their ex-Confederate enemies: Texas in 1873, Alabama and Arkansas in 1874, Mississippi in 1875.

The Mississippi campaign showed all too clearly what the Republicans were up against. As elections neared in 1875, paramilitary groups such as the Rifle Clubs and Red Shirts operated openly. Mississippi's Republican governor, Adelbert Ames, a Congressional Medal of Honor winner from Maine, appealed to President Grant for federal troops, but Grant refused. Brandishing their guns and stuffing the ballot boxes, the Redeemers swept the 1875 elections and took control of Mississippi. Facing impeachment, Governor Ames resigned his office and returned to the North.

By 1876 Republican governments, backed by token U.S. military units, remained in only three states—Louisiana, South Carolina, and Florida. Elsewhere, the former Confederates were back in power.

The Acquiescent North

The faltering of Reconstruction stemmed from more than discouragement about prosecuting the Klan, however. Sympathy for the freedman began to wane. The North was flooded with one-sided, often racist reports, such as James M. Pike's *The Prostrate State* (1873), describing South Carolina in the grip of "a mass of black barbarism." The impact of this propaganda could be seen in the fate of the Civil Rights bill, which Charles Sumner introduced in 1870 in an attempt to apply federal power against the discriminatory treatment of African Americans, guaranteeing them, among other things, equal access to public accommodation, schools, and jury service. By the time the bill passed in 1875, it had been stripped of its key provisions. The Supreme Court finished the demolition job when in 1883 it declared the remnant Civil Rights Act unconstitutional.

The political cynicism that overtook the Civil Rights Act signaled the Republican Party's reversion to the practical politics of earlier days. In many states a second generation took over the party—men like Roscoe Conkling of New York, who treated the Manhattan Customs House, with its regiment of political appointees, as an auxiliary of his organization. Conkling and similarly minded politicos had little enthusiasm for Reconstruction, except when it benefited the Republican Party. As the party lost headway in the South, Republicans lost interest in the battle for black rights. In Washington President Grant presided benignly over this transformation of his party, turning a blind eye on corruption even as its waters began to lap against the White House.

Not all Republicans embraced Grant's politics as usual. Yet even the high-minded, the heirs of antislavery Christian reform, turned against Reconstruction. The touchstone for them was "free labor," the idea of America as a land of self-reliant, industrious property owners. They had framed the Civil War as a battle between "free labor" and its antithesis, the plantation society of masters and slaves. And now, with the South defeated, the question became: Would the emancipated slaves embrace "free labor"? No, asserted Pike's *The Prostrate South* and similarly inflammatory reports. Instead of choosing self-reliance, the freedmen were running riot, demanding patronage, becoming dependents of the corrupt Reconstruction regimes they had voted into power. With this tragic misreading of the former slaves — and of their uphill struggle for land and self-rule — Republican allies drifted away and turned against radical Reconstruction.

More was at work, however, than disillusionment with the freedmen. In the aftermath of war, a broader loss of nerve gripped northern reformers. The meaning of "free labor" had not been uncontested. If middle-class Republicans juxtaposed it against black slavery, labor leaders juxtaposed it also against *wage* slavery, and suddenly, when peace arrived, there was a burst of trade-union activity, calls for sweeping labor reform, and a formidable new organization on the scene, the National Labor Union. Radical proposals came forth, most famously, Ira Steward's demand for the eight-hour day, which, by his cock-eyed theory, would close the gap between rich and poor "until the capitalist and laborer are one" — a true "free labor" society. The labor reform movement lacked staying power, however. The eight-hour drive failed, and so did campaigns for cooperative industry and currency reform. After an abortive effort at launching a labor party in 1872, the National Labor Union collapsed.

If the surge of labor agitation died, not so the fear it inspired among middle-class reformers. Intent on a "harmony of interests," they got instead a strong whiff of class conflict. These advocates of "free labor," once zealous for black freedom and equal rights, clambered to the safer ground of civil-service reform. Henceforth it was the evils of corrupt politics that would claim their attention. They repudiated the wartime expansion of federal power and refashioned themselves as **liberals** — believers in free trade, market competition, and limited government. And, with unabashed elitism, they denounced universal suffrage, which "can only mean in plain English the government of ignorance and vice." American reform had arrived at a dispiriting watershed. The grand impulse that had driven the antislavery struggle, insofar as it survived the trauma of Reconstruction, now took the form of pallid efforts at purifying American politics, with Grant as the first target.

The Liberal Republicans and the Election of 1872. As Grant's administration lapsed into cronyism, a revolt took shape inside the Republican Party, led by an influential collection of intellectuals, journalists, and reform-minded businessmen. Unable to deny Grant renomination, the dissidents broke away and formed a new party under the name Liberal Republican. Their candidate was

Horace Greeley, longtime editor and publisher of the *New York Tribune* and veteran of American reform in all its variety, including antislavery. The Democrats, still in disarray, also nominated Greeley, notwithstanding his editorial diatribes against them. A poor campaigner, Greeley was assailed so bitterly that, as he said, "I hardly knew whether I was running for the Presidency or the penitentiary."

Grant won overwhelmingly, capturing 56 percent of the popular vote and every electoral vote. Yet the Liberal Republicans had managed to shift the terms of political debate in the country. The agenda they had established — civil service reform, limited government, reconciliation with the South — was adopted by the Democrats as they shed their disloyal reputation and reclaimed their place as a legitimate national party.

Scandal and Depression. Charges of Republican corruption, mounting ever since Grant's reelection, came to a head in 1875. The scandal involved the Whiskey Ring, a network of liquor distillers and treasury agents who defrauded the government of millions of dollars of excise taxes on whiskey. The ringleader was a Grant appointee, and Grant's own private secretary, Orville Babcock, had a hand in the thievery. The others went to prison, but Grant stood by Babcock, possibly perjuring himself to save his secretary from jail. The stench of scandal, however, had engulfed the White House.

On top of this, a financial panic struck in 1873, triggered by the bankruptcy of the Northern Pacific Railroad and its main investor, Jay Cooke. Both Cooke's privileged role as financier of the Civil War and the generous federal subsidies to the Northern Pacific caused many economically pressed Americans to blame Republican financial mismanagement and thievery. Grant's administration responded ineffectually, rebuffing the pleas of debtors for relief by increasing the money supply (see Chapter 19).

Among the casualties of the bad economy was the Freedman's Savings and Trust Company, which held the small deposits of thousands of ex-slaves. When the bank failed in 1874, Congress refused to compensate the depositors, and many lost their life savings. In denying their pathetic pleas, Congress was signaling also that Reconstruction had lost its moral claim on the country. National politics had moved on; concerns about the economy and political fraud, not the plight of the ex-slaves, absorbed the northern voter as another presidential election approached in 1876.

The Political Crisis of 1877

Abandoning Grant, the Republicans nominated Rutherford B. Hayes, governor of Ohio, a colorless figure but untainted by corruption or by strong convictions — in a word, a safe man. His Democratic opponent was Samuel J. Tilden, governor of New York, a wealthy lawyer with ties to Wall Street and a reform reputation for his role in cleaning up New York City politics. The Democrat Tilden, of course, favored **home rule** for the South, but so, more discreetly, did the Republican Hayes. Reconstruction actually did not figure prominently in the campaign and was mostly subsumed under

broader Democratic charges of "corrupt centralism" and "incapacity, waste, and fraud." By now Republicans had essentially written off the South. Not a lot was said about the states still ruled by Reconstruction governments — Florida, South Carolina, and Louisiana.

Once the returns started coming in on election night, however, those three states began to loom very large indeed. Tilden led in the popular vote and, victorious in key northern states, he seemed headed for the White House until sleepless politicians at Republican headquarters realized that if they kept Florida, South Carolina, and Louisiana, Hayes would win by a single electoral vote. Republicans still controlled the state election machinery and, citing Democratic fraud and intimidation, they certified Republican victories. The audacious announcement came forth from Republican headquarters: Hayes had carried Florida, South Carolina, and Louisiana and won the election. Newly elected Democratic officials also sent in electoral votes for Tilden, and, when Congress met in early 1877, it faced two sets of electoral votes from those states.

The Constitution does not provide for this contingency. All it says is that the president of the Senate (in 1877, a Republican) opens the electoral certificates before the House (Democratic) and the Senate (Republican) and that "the Votes shall then be counted" (Article 2, Section 1). Suspense gripped the country. There was talk of inside deals, of a new election, even of a violent coup. Just in case, the commander of the army, General William T. Sherman, deployed four artillery companies in Washington. Finally, Congress appointed an electoral commission to settle the question. The commission included seven Republicans, seven Democrats, and, as the deciding member, David Davis, a Supreme Court justice not known to have fixed party loyalties. Davis, however, disqualified himself by accepting an Illinois seat in the Senate. He was replaced by Republican justice Joseph P. Bradley, and by 8 to 7 the commission awarded the disputed votes to Hayes.

Outraged Democrats had one more trick up their sleeves. They controlled the House, and they stalled a final count of the electoral votes so as to prevent Hayes's inauguration on March 4. But a week before, secret Washington talks had begun between southern Democrats and Ohio Republicans representing Hayes. Everything turned on South Carolina and Louisiana, where rival governments were encamped at the state capitols, with federal soldiers holding the Democrats at bay. Exactly what deal was struck or how involved Hayes himself was will probably never be known, but on March 1 the House Democrats suddenly ended their delaying tactics, the ceremonial counting of votes went forward, and Hayes was inaugurated on schedule. He soon ordered the Union troops back to their barracks, the Republican governors in South Carolina and Louisiana fled the unprotected statehouses, and Democratic claimants took control. Reconstruction had ended.

In 1877 political leaders on all sides seemed ready to say that what Lincoln had called "the work" was complete. But for the former slaves, the work had only begun. Reconstruction turned out to have been a magnificent aberration, a leap beyond what most white Americans actually felt was due their black fellow citizens. Still, something real

had been achieved — three rights-defining amendments to the Constitution, some elbow room to advance economically, and, not least, a stubborn confidence among blacks that, by their own efforts, they could lift themselves up. Things would get worse, in fact, before they got better, but the work of Reconstruction was imperishable and could never be erased.

> ➤ Why did the Redeemers resort to terror in their campaign to regain political control of the South?

> ➤ What changes in the North explain why the Republicans abandoned the battle for Reconstruction?

> ➤ Explain how the contested presidential election of 1876–1877 brought an end to Reconstruction.

SUMMARY

By any measure — in lives, treasure, or national amity — the Civil War was the most shattering event in American history. In this chapter we describe how the nation picked up the pieces. Reconstruction confronted two great tasks: first, restoring the rebellious states to the union, and second, incorporating the emancipated slaves into the national citizenry. Separable perhaps in theory, the two tasks were inseparably part of a single grand struggle.

Reconstruction went through three phases. In what has been called the presidential phase, Lincoln's successor Andrew Johnson unilaterally offered the South easy terms for reentering the Union. This might have succeeded had Southerners responded with restraint, but instead they adopted oppressive Black Codes and welcomed ex-Confederates back into power. Infuriated by southern arrogance, congressional Republicans closed ranks behind the Radicals, embraced the freedmen's demand for full equality, placed the South under military rule in 1867, and inaugurated radical Reconstruction.

In this second phase, the new Republican state governments tried to transform the South's decrepit economic and social structures, while on the plantations ex-slaves battled for economic independence. No amount of accomplishment, however, could reconcile the ex-Confederates to Republican rule, and they staged a violent counterrevolution in the name of white supremacy and "redemption."

Distracted by Republican scandals and economic problems, the Grant administration had little stomach for a protracted guerrilla war in the

South. Left on their own, the Reconstruction governments fell one by one to Redeemer intimidation and violence. In this third phase, as Reconstruction wound down, the concluding event was the contested election of 1876, which the Republicans resolved by trading their last remaining southern strongholds, South Carolina and Louisiana, for retention of the White House. On that unsavory note, Reconstruction ended.

Connections: Sectionalism

In many ways, Reconstruction marked the final stage in a titanic sectional struggle whose origins went back to the early nineteenth century. As we noted in the essay opening Part Three (p. 269):

> The North developed into an urbanizing and industrializing society based on free labor, whereas the South remained a rural, agricultural society dependent on slavery.

In Chapter 13 we described how the sectional crisis arising from these differences broke apart the Union in 1861. The Civil War (Chapter 14) tested the war-making capacities of the rival systems. At first the advantage lay with the military prowess of the agrarian South, but in the end the superior resources of the industrial North prevailed. Even in defeat, however, the South could not be forced into a national mold. That was the ultimate lesson of Reconstruction. In the aftermath, the South persisted on its own path, as we will see in Chapter 17, which discusses the emergence of its distinctive low-wage labor system, and Chapter 19, which describes the development of its one-party, whites-only politics. The gradual, if partial, dissolution of southern uniqueness in the twentieth century is a theme of later chapters of this book.

CHAPTER REVIEW QUESTIONS

➤ Why did the debate over restoring the South to the Union devolve into an institutional struggle between the presidency and the Congress?

➤ Do you believe that the failure of Reconstruction was primarily a failure of leadership? Or, to put it more concretely, that the outcome might have been different had Lincoln lived? Or chosen a different vice president?

➤ Was there any way of reconciling the Republican desire for equality for the ex-slaves with the ex-Confederate desire for self-rule in the South?

TIMELINE

1863	Lincoln announces his Ten Percent Plan
1864	Wade-Davis Bill passed by Congress
	Lincoln "pocket" vetoes Wade-Davis Bill
1865	Freedmen's Bureau established
	Lincoln assassinated; Andrew Johnson succeeds as president
	Johnson implements his restoration plan
1866	Civil Rights Act passes over Johnson's veto
	Johnson makes disastrous "swing around the circle"; defeated in congressional elections
1867	Reconstruction Act
	Tenure of Office Act
1868	Impeachment crisis
	Fourteenth Amendment ratified
	Ulysses S. Grant elected president
1870	Ku Klux Klan at peak of power
	Fifteenth Amendment ratified
1872	Grant's reelection
1873	Panic of 1873 ushers in depression of 1873–1877
1875	Whiskey Ring scandal undermines Grant administration
1877	Compromise of 1877; Rutherford B. Hayes becomes president
	Reconstruction ends

FOR FURTHER EXPLORATION

The best current book on Reconstruction is Eric Foner's major synthesis, *Reconstruction: America's Unfinished Revolution, 1863–1877* (1988), available also in a shorter version. *Black Reconstruction in America* (1935), by the African American activist and scholar W. E. B. Du Bois, deserves attention as the first book on Reconstruction that stressed the role of blacks in their own emancipation. For the presidential phase of Reconstruction, see Dan T. Carter, *When the War Was Over: The Failure of Self-Reconstruction in the South, 1865–1867* (1985). On the freedmen, Leon F. Litwack, *Been in the Storm So Long: The Aftermath of Slavery* (1979), provides a stirring account. More recent emancipation studies emphasize slavery as a labor system: Julie Saville, *The Work of Reconstruction: From Slave to Wage Laborer in South Carolina, 1860–1870* (1994), and Amy Dru Stanley, *From Bondage to Contract* (1999), which expands the discussion to show what the onset of wage labor meant for freedwomen. In *Gendered Strife & Confusion: The Political Culture of Reconstruction* (1997), Laura F. Edwards explores via a local study the impact of "peripheral" people — the ordinary folk of both races — on Reconstruction politics. Eric Foner, *Nothing But Freedom: Emancipation and Its Legacy* (1983), helpfully places emancipation in a comparative context. William S. McFeely, *Grant: A Biography* (1981), deftly explains the politics of Reconstruction. The emergence of the sharecropping system is explored in Gavin Wright, *Old South, New South* (1986), and Edward Royce, *The Origins of Southern Sharecropping* (1993). On the Compromise of 1877, see C. Vann Woodward's classic *Reunion and Reaction* (1956). A helpful Web site on Reconstruction, with documents and illustrations, can be found at **www. pbs.org/wgbh/amex/reconstruction/ index.html**, which derives from the PBS documentary in the *American Experience* series.

TEST YOUR KNOWLEDGE

To assess your command of the material in this chapter, see the Online Study Guide at **bedfordstmartins.com/henretta**.

For Web sites, images, and documents related to topics and places in this chapter, visit **bedfordstmartins.com/makehistory**.

The Declaration of Independence

In Congress, July 4, 1776,
The Unanimous Declaration of the
Thirteen United States of America

When in the Course of human events, it becomes necessary for one people to dissolve the political bands which have connected them with another, and to assume among the Powers of the earth, the separate and equal station to which the Laws of Nature and of Nature's God entitle them, a decent respect to the opinions of mankind requires that they should declare the causes which impel them to the separation.

We hold these truths to be self-evident, that all men are created equal, that they are endowed by their Creator with certain unalienable rights, that among these are Life, Liberty, and the pursuit of Happiness. That to secure these rights, Governments are instituted among Men, deriving their just powers from the consent of the governed. That whenever any Form of Government becomes destructive of these ends, it is the Right of the People to alter or to abolish it, and to institute new Government, laying its foundation on such principles and organizing its powers in such form, as to them shall seem most likely to effect their Safety and Happiness. Prudence, indeed, will dictate that Governments long established should not be changed for light and transient causes; and accordingly all experience hath shown, that mankind are more disposed to suffer, while evils are sufferable, than to right themselves by abolishing the forms to which they are accustomed. But when a long train of abuses and usurpations, pursuing invariably the same Object evinces a design to reduce them under absolute Despotism, it is their right, it is their duty, to throw off such Government, and to provide new Guards for their future security. — Such has been the patient sufferance of these Colonies; and such is now the necessity which constrains them to alter their former Systems of Government. The history of the present King of Great Britain is a history of repeated injuries and usurpations, all having in direct object the establishment of an absolute Tyranny over these States. To prove this, let Facts be submitted to a candid world.

He has refused his Assent to Laws, the most wholesome and necessary for the public good.

He has forbidden his Governors to pass Laws of immediate and pressing importance, unless suspended in their operation till his Assent should be obtained; and, when so suspended, he has utterly neglected to attend to them.

He has refused to pass other Laws for the accommodation of large districts of people, unless those people would relinquish the right of Representation in the Legislature, a right inestimable to them and formidable to tyrants only.

He has called together legislative bodies at places unusual, uncomfortable, and distant from the depository of their public Records, for the sole purpose of fatiguing them into compliance with his measures.

He has dissolved Representative Houses repeatedly, for opposing with manly firmness his invasions on the rights of the people.

He has refused for a long time, after such dissolutions, to cause others to be elected; whereby the Legislative powers, incapable of Annihilation, have returned to the People at large for their exercise; the State remaining in the mean time exposed to all the dangers of invasion from without and convulsions within.

He has endeavoured to prevent the population of these States; for that purpose obstructing the Laws of Naturalization of Foreigners; refusing to pass others to encourage their migrations hither, and raising the conditions of new Appropriations of Lands.

He has obstructed the Administration of Justice, by refusing his Assent to Laws for establishing Judiciary powers.

He has made Judges dependent on his Will alone, for the tenure of their offices, and the amount and payment of their salaries.

He has erected a multitude of New Offices, and sent hither swarms of Officers to harass our People, and eat out their substance.

He has kept among us, in times of peace, Standing Armies without the Consent of our legislature.

He has combined with others to subject us to a jurisdiction foreign to our constitution, and unacknowledged by our laws; giving his Assent to their Acts of pretended Legislation:

For quartering large bodies of armed troops among us:

For protecting them, by a mock Trial, from Punishment for any Murders which they should commit on the Inhabitants of these States:

For cutting off our Trade with all parts of the world:

For imposing taxes on us without our Consent:

For depriving us, in many cases, of the benefits of Trial by jury:

For transporting us beyond Seas to be tried for pretended offences:

For abolishing the free System of English Laws in a neighbouring Province, establishing therein an Arbitrary government, and enlarging its Boundaries so as to render it at once an example and fit instrument for introducing the same absolute rule into these Colonies:

For taking away our Charters, abolishing our most valuable Laws, and altering fundamentally the Forms of our Governments:

For suspending our own Legislatures, and declaring themselves invested with Power to legislate for us in all cases whatsoever.

He has abdicated Government here, by declaring us out of his Protection and waging War against us.

He has plundered our seas, ravaged our Coasts, burnt our towns, and destroyed the lives of our people.

He is at this time transporting large armies of foreign mercenaries to compleat the works of death, desolation, and tyranny, already begun with circumstances of Cruelty & perfidy scarcely paralleled in the most barbarous ages, and totally unworthy the Head of a civilized nation.

He has constrained our fellow Citizens taken Captive on the high Seas to bear Arms against their Country, to become the executioners of their friends and Brethren, or to fall themselves by their Hands.

He has excited domestic insurrections amongst us, and has endeavoured to bring on the inhabitants of our frontiers, the merciless Indian Savages, whose known rule of warfare, is an undistinguished destruction of all ages, sexes, and conditions.

In every stage of these Oppressions We have Petitioned for Redress in the most humble terms: Our repeated Petitions have been answered only by repeated injury. A Prince, whose character is thus marked by every act which may define a Tyrant, is unfit to be the ruler of a free people.

Nor have We been wanting in attention to our British brethren. We have warned them from time to time of attempts by their legislature to extend an unwarrantable jurisdiction over us. We have reminded them of the circumstances of our emigration and settlement here. We have appealed to their native justice and magnanimity, and we have conjured them by the ties of our common kindred to disavow these usurpations, which would inevitably interrupt our connections and correspondence. They too have been deaf to the voice of justice and of consanguinity. We must, therefore, acquiesce in the necessity, which denounces our Separation, and hold them, as we hold the rest of mankind, Enemies in War, in Peace Friends.

We, therefore, the Representatives of the United States of America, in General Congress, Assembled, appealing to the Supreme Judge of the world for the rectitude of our intentions, do, in the Name, and by Authority of the good People of these Colonies, solemnly publish and declare, That these United Colonies are, and of Right ought to be FREE AND INDEPENDENT STATES; that they are Absolved from all Allegiance to the British Crown, and that all political connection between them and the State of Great Britain, is and ought to be totally dissolved; and that as Free and Independent States, they have full Power to levy War, conclude Peace, contract Alliances, establish Commerce, and to do all other Acts and Things which Independent States may of right do. And for the support of this Declaration, with a firm reliance on the Protection of Divine Providence, we mutually pledge to each other our Lives, our Fortunes, and our sacred Honor.

John Hancock

Button Gwinnett	George Wythe	James Wilson	Josiah Bartlett
Lyman Hall	Richard Henry Lee	Geo. Ross	Wm. Whipple
Geo. Walton	Th. Jefferson	Caesar Rodney	Matthew Thornton
Wm. Hooper	Benja. Harrison	Geo. Read	Saml. Adams
Joseph Hewes	Thos. Nelson, Jr.	Thos. M'Kean	John Adams
John Penn	Francis Lightfoot Lee	Wm. Floyd	Robt. Treat Paine
Edward Rutledge	Carter Braxton	Phil. Livingston	Elbridge Gerry
Thos. Heyward, Junr.	Robt. Morris	Frans. Lewis	Step. Hopkins
Thomas Lynch, Junr.	Benjamin Rush	Lewis Morris	William Ellery
Arthur Middleton	Benja. Franklin	Richd. Stockton	Roger Sherman
Samuel Chase	John Morton	John Witherspoon	Sam'el Huntington
Wm. Paca	Geo. Clymer	Fras. Hopkinson	Wm. Williams
Thos. Stone	Jas. Smith	John Hart	Oliver Wolcott
Charles Carroll of Carrollton	Geo. Taylor	Abra. Clark	

The Articles of Confederation and Perpetual Union

Agreed to in Congress, November 15, 1777;
Ratified March 1781

BETWEEN THE STATES OF NEW HAMPSHIRE, MASSACHUSETTS BAY, RHODE ISLAND AND PROVIDENCE PLANTATIONS, CONNECTICUT, NEW YORK, NEW JERSEY, PENNSYLVANIA, DELAWARE, MARYLAND, VIRGINIA, NORTH CAROLINA, SOUTH CAROLINA, GEORGIA.*

Article 1

The stile of this confederacy shall be "The United States of America."

Article 2

Each State retains its sovereignty, freedom and independence, and every power, jurisdiction, and right, which is not by this confederation expressly delegated to the United States, in Congress assembled.

Article 3

The said states hereby severally enter into a firm league of friendship with each other for their common defence, the security of their liberties and their mutual and general welfare; binding themselves to assist each other against all force offered to, or attacks made upon them, or any of them, on account of religion, sovereignty, trade, or any other pretence whatever.

Article 4

The better to secure and perpetuate mutual friendship and intercourse among the people of the different states in this union, the free inhabitants of each of these states, paupers, vagabonds, and fugitives from justice excepted, shall be entitled to all privileges and immunities of free citizens in the several states; and the people of each State shall have free ingress and regress to and from any other State, and shall enjoy therein all the privileges of trade and commerce, subject to the same duties, impositions, and restrictions, as the inhabitants thereof respectively; provided, that such restrictions shall not extend so far as to prevent the removal of property, imported into any State, to any other State of which the owner is an inhabitant; provided also, that no imposition, duties, or restriction, shall be laid by any State on the property of the United States, or either of them.

If any person guilty of, or charged with treason, felony, or other high misdemeanor in any State, shall flee from justice and be found in any of the United States, he shall, upon demand of the governor or executive power of the State from which he fled, be delivered up and removed to the State having jurisdiction of his offence.

Full faith and credit shall be given in each of these states to the records, acts, and judicial proceedings of the courts and magistrates of every other State.

Article 5

For the more convenient management of the general interests of the United States, delegates shall be annually appointed, in such manner as the legislature of each State shall direct, to meet in Congress, on the 1st Monday in November in every year, with a power reserved to each State to recall its delegates, or any of them, at any time within the year, and to send others in their stead for the remainder of the year.

No State shall be represented in Congress by less than two, nor by more than seven members; and no person shall be capable of being a delegate for more than three years in any term of six years; nor shall any person, being a delegate, be capable of holding any office under the United States, for which he, or any other for his benefit, receives any salary, fees, or emolument of any kind.

Each State shall maintain its own delegates in a meeting of the states, and while they act as members of the committee of the states.

In determining questions in the United States, in Congress assembled, each State shall have one vote.

Freedom of speech and debate in Congress shall not be impeached or questioned in any court or place out of Congress: and the members of Congress shall be protected in their

*This copy of the final draft of the Articles of Confederation is taken from the *Journals*, 9:907-25, November 15, 1777.

persons from arrests and imprisonments, during the time of their going to and from, and attendance on Congress, except for treason, felony, or breach of the peace.

Article 6

No State, without the consent of the United States, in Congress assembled, shall send any embassy to, or receive any embassy from, or enter into any conference, agreement, alliance, or treaty with any king, prince, or state; nor shall any person, holding any office of profit or trust under the United States, or any of them, accept of any present, emolument, office or title, of any kind whatever, from any king, prince, or foreign state; nor shall the United States, in Congress assembled, or any of them, grant any title of nobility.

No two or more states shall enter into any treaty, confederation, or alliance, whatever, between them, without the consent of the United States, in Congress assembled, specifying accurately the purposes for which the same is to be entered into, and how long it shall continue.

No state shall lay any imposts or duties which may interfere with any stipulations in treaties entered into by the United States, in Congress assembled, with any king, prince, or state, in pursuance of any treaties already proposed by Congress to the courts of France and Spain.

No vessels of war shall be kept up in time of peace by any State, except such number only as shall be deemed necessary by the United States, in Congress assembled, for the defence of such State or its trade; nor shall any body of forces be kept up by any State, in time of peace, except such number only as, in the judgment of the United States, in Congress assembled, shall be deemed requisite to garrison the forts necessary for the defence of such State; but every State shall always keep up a well regulated and disciplined militia, sufficiently armed and accoutred, and shall provide, and constantly have ready for use, in public stores, a due number of field pieces and tents, and a proper quantity of arms, ammunition and camp equipage.

No State shall engage in any war without the consent of the United States, in Congress assembled, unless such State be actually invaded by enemies, or shall have received certain advice of a resolution being formed by some nation of Indians to invade such State, and the danger is so imminent as not to admit of a delay till the United States, in Congress assembled, can be consulted; nor shall any State grant commissions to any ships or vessels of war, nor letters of marque or reprisal, except it be after a declaration of war by the United States, in Congress assembled, and then only against the kingdom or state, and the subjects thereof, against which war has been so declared, and under such regulations as shall be established by the United States, in Congress assembled, unless such State be infested by pirates, in which case vessels of war may be fitted out for that occasion, and kept so long as the danger shall continue, or until the United States, in Congress assembled, shall determine otherwise.

Article 7

When land forces are raised by any State for the common defence, all officers of or under the rank of colonel, shall be appointed by the legislature of each State respectively, by whom such forces shall be raised, or in such manner as such State shall direct; and all vacancies shall be filled up by the State which first made the appointment.

Article 8

All charges of war and all other expences, that shall be incurred for the common defence or general welfare, and allowed by the United States, in Congress assembled, shall be defrayed out of a common treasury, which shall be supplied by the several states, in proportion to the value of all land within each State, granted to or surveyed for any person, as such land and the buildings and improvements thereon shall be estimated according to such mode as the United States, in Congress assembled, shall, from time to time, direct and appoint.

The taxes for paying that proportion shall be laid and levied by the authority and direction of the legislatures of the several states, within the time agreed upon by the United States, in Congress assembled.

Article 9

The United States, in Congress assembled, shall have the sole and exclusive right and power of determining on peace and war, except in the cases mentioned in the 6th article; of sending and receiving ambassadors; entering into treaties and alliances, provided that no treaty of commerce shall be made, whereby the legislative power of the respective states shall be restrained from imposing such imposts and duties on foreigners as their own people are subjected to, or from prohibiting the exportation or importation of any species of goods or commodities whatsoever; of establishing rules for deciding, in all cases, what captures on land or water shall be legal, and in what manner prizes, taken by land or naval forces in the service of the United States, shall be divided or appropriated; of granting letters of marque and reprisal in times of peace; appointing courts for the trial of piracies and felonies committed on the high seas, and establishing courts for receiving and determining, finally, appeals in all cases of captures; provided, that no member of Congress shall be appointed a judge of any of the said courts.

The United States, in Congress assembled, shall also be the last resort on appeal in all disputes and differences now subsisting, or that hereafter may arise between two or more states concerning boundary, jurisdiction or any other cause whatever; which authority shall always be exercised in the manner following: whenever the legislative or executive authority, or lawful agent of any State, in controversy with another, shall present a petition to Congress, stating the matter in question, and praying for a hearing, notice thereof shall be given, by order of Congress, to the legislative or executive authority of the other State in controversy, and a day assigned for the appearance of the parties by their lawful agents, who shall then be directed to appoint, by joint consent, commissioners or judges to constitute a court for hearing and determining the matter in question; but, if they cannot agree, Congress shall name three persons out of each of the United States, and from the list of such persons each party shall alternately strike out one, the petitioners beginning, until the number shall be reduced to thirteen; and from that number not less than seven, nor more than nine names, as Congress shall direct, shall, in the presence of Congress, be drawn out by lot; and the persons whose names shall be so drawn, or any five of them, shall be commissioners or judges to hear and finally determine the controversy, so always as a major part of the judges who shall hear the cause shall agree in the determination; and if either party shall neglect to attend at the day appointed, without shewing reasons which Congress shall judge sufficient, or, being present, shall refuse to strike, the Congress shall proceed to nominate three persons out of each State, and the secretary of Congress shall strike in behalf of such party absent or refusing; and the judgment and sentence of the court to be appointed, in the manner before prescribed, shall be final and conclusive; and if any of the parties shall refuse to submit to the authority of such court, or to appear or defend their claim or cause, the court shall nevertheless proceed to pronounce sentence or judgment, which shall, in like manner, be final and decisive, the judgment or sentence and other proceedings begin, in either case, transmitted to Congress, and lodged among the acts of Congress for the security of the parties concerned: provided, that every commissioner, before he sits in judgment, shall take an oath, to be administered by one of the judges of the supreme or superior court of the State where the cause shall be tried, "well and truly to hear and determine the matter in question, according to the best of his judgment, without favour, affection, or hope of reward:" provided, also, that no State shall be deprived of territory for the benefit of the United States.

All controversies concerning the private right of soil, claimed under different grants of two or more states, whose jurisdictions, as they may respect such lands and the states which passed such grants, are adjusted, the said grants, or either of them, being at the same time claimed to have originated antecedent to such settlement of jurisdiction, shall, on the petition of either party to the Congress of the United States, be finally determined, as near as may be, in the same manner as is before prescribed for deciding disputes respecting territorial jurisdiction between different states.

The United States, in Congress assembled, shall also have the sole and exclusive right and power of regulating the alloy and value of coin struck by their own authority, or by that of the respective states; fixing the standard of weights and measures throughout the United States; regulating the trade and managing all affairs with the Indians not members of any of the states; provided that the legislative right of any State within its own limits be not infringed or violated; establishing and regulating post offices from one State to another throughout all the United States, and exacting such postage on the papers passing through the same as may be requisite to defray the expences of the said office; appointing all officers of the land forces in the service of the United States, excepting regimental officers; appointing all the officers of the naval forces, and commissioning all officers whatever in the service of the United States; making rules for the government and regulation of the said land and naval forces, and directing their operations.

The United States, in Congress assembled, shall have authority to appoint a committee to sit in the recess of Congress, to be denominated "a Committee of the States," and to consist of one delegate from each State, and to appoint such other committees and civil officers as may be necessary for managing the general affairs of the United States, under their direction; to appoint one of their number to preside; provided that no person be allowed to serve in the office of president more than one year in any term of three years; to ascertain the necessary sums of money to be raised for the service of the United States, and to appropriate and apply the same for defraying the public expences; to borrow money or emit bills on the credit of the United States, transmitting, every half year, to the respective states, an account of the sums of money so borrowed or emitted; to build and equip a navy; to agree upon the number of land forces, and to make requisitions from each State for its quota, in proportion to the number of white inhabitants in such State; which requisitions shall be binding; and thereupon, the legislature of each State shall appoint the regimental officers, raise the men, and cloathe, arm, and equip them in a soldier-like manner, at the expence of the United States; and the officers and men so cloathed, armed, and equipped, shall march to the place appointed and within the time agreed on by the United States, in Congress assembled; but if the United States, in Congress assembled, shall, on consideration of circumstances, judge proper that any State should not raise men, or should raise a smaller number than its quota, and that any other State should raise a greater number of men than the quota thereof, such extra number shall be raised, officered, cloathed, armed, and equipped in the same manner as the quota of such State, unless the legislature of such State shall judge that such extra number cannot be safely spared out of the same, in which case they shall raise, officer, cloathe, arm, and equip as many of such extra number as they judge can be safely spared. And the officers and men so cloathed, armed, and equipped, shall march to the place appointed and within the time agreed on by the United States, in Congress assembled.

The United States, in Congress assembled, shall never engage in a war, nor grant letters of marque and reprisal in time of peace, nor enter into any treaties or alliances, nor coin money, nor regulate the value thereof, nor ascertain the sums and expences necessary for the defence and welfare of the United States, or any of them: nor emit bills, nor borrow money on the credit of the United States, nor appropriate money, nor agree upon the number of vessels of war to be built or purchased, or the number of land or sea forces to be raised, nor appoint a commander in chief of the army or navy, unless nine states assent to the same; nor shall a question on any other point, except for adjourning from day to day, be determined, unless by the votes of a majority of the United States, in Congress assembled.

The Congress of the United States shall have power to adjourn to any time within the year, and to any place within the United States, so that no period of adjournment be for a longer duration than the space of six months, and shall publish the journal of their proceedings monthly, except such parts thereof, relating to treaties, alliances or military operations, as, in their judgment, require secrecy; and the yeas and nays of the delegates of each State on any question shall be entered on the journal, when it is desired by any delegate; and the delegates of a State, or any of them, at his, or their request, shall be furnished with a transcript of the said journal, except such parts as are above excepted, to lay before the legislatures of the several states.

Article 10

The committee of the states, or any nine of them, shall be authorized to execute, in the recess of Congress, such of the powers of Congress as the United States, in Congress assembled, by the consent of nine states, shall, from time to time, think expedient to vest them with; provided, that no power be delegated to the said committee, for the exercise of which, by the articles of confederation, the voice of nine states, in the Congress of the United States assembled, is requisite.

Article 11

Canada acceding to this confederation, and joining in the measures of the United States, shall be admitted into and entitled to all the advantages of this union; but no other colony shall be admitted into the same, unless such admission be agreed to by nine states.

The Constitution of the United States of America

Agreed to by Philadelphia Convention,
September 17, 1787
Implemented March 4, 1789

We the People of the United States, in Order to form a more perfect Union, establish Justice, insure domestic Tranquility, provide for the common defence, promote the general Welfare, and secure the Blessings of Liberty to ourselves and our Posterity, do ordain and establish this Constitution for the United States of America.

Article I

Section 1. All legislative Powers herein granted shall be vested in a Congress of the United States, which shall consist of a Senate and a House of Representatives.

Section 2. The House of Representatives shall be composed of Members chosen every second Year by the People of the several States, and the Electors in each State shall have the Qualifications requisite for Electors of the most numerous Branch of the State Legislature.

No Person shall be a Representative who shall not have attained to the Age of twenty-five Years, and been seven Years a Citizen of the United States, and who shall not, when elected, be an Inhabitant of that State in which he shall be chosen.

Representatives and direct Taxes shall be apportioned among the several States which may be included within this Union, according to their respective Numbers, *which shall be determined by adding to the whole Number of free Persons, including those bound to Service for a Term of Years, and excluding Indians not taxed, three fifths of all other Persons.** The actual Enumeration shall be made within three Years after the first Meeting of the Congress of the United States, and within every subsequent Term of ten Years, in such Manner as they shall by Law direct. The Number of Representatives shall not exceed one for every thirty Thousand, but each State shall have at Least one Representative; and *until such enumeration shall be made, the State of New Hampshire shall be entitled to chuse three, Massachusetts eight, Rhode Island and Providence Plantations one, Connecticut five, New York six, New Jersey four, Pennsylvania eight, Delaware one, Maryland six, Virginia ten, North Carolina five, South Carolina five, and Georgia three.*

When vacancies happen in the Representation from any State, the Executive Authority thereof shall issue Writs of Election to fill such Vacancies.

The House of Representatives shall chuse their Speaker and other Officers; and shall have the sole Power of Impeachment.

Section 3. The Senate of the United States shall be composed of two Senators from each State, *chosen by the Legislature thereof,*† for six Years; and each Senator shall have one Vote.

Immediately after they shall be assembled in Consequence of the first Election, they shall be divided as equally as may be into three Classes. The Seats of the Senators of the first Class shall be vacated at the Expiration of the second Year, of the second Class at the Expiration of the fourth Year, and of the third Class at the Expiration of the sixth Year, so that one-third may be chosen every second Year; and if Vacancies happen by Resignation, or otherwise, during the Recess of the Legislature of any State, the Executive thereof may make temporary Appointments until the next Meeting of the Legislature, which shall then fill such Vacancies.‡

No person shall be a Senator who shall not have attained to the Age of thirty Years, and been nine Years a Citizen of the United States, and who shall not, when elected, be an Inhabitant of that State for which he shall be chosen.

The Vice President of the United States shall be President of the Senate, but shall have no Vote, unless they be equally divided.

The Senate shall chuse their other Officers, and also a President pro tempore, in the absence of the Vice President, or when he shall exercise the Office of President of the United States.

The Senate shall have the sole Power to try all Impeachments. When sitting for that Purpose, they shall be on Oath or Affirmation. When the President of the United States is tried, the Chief Justice shall preside: And no Person shall be convicted without the Concurrence of two-thirds of the Members present.

Note: The Constitution became effective March 4, 1789. Provisions in italics are no longer relevant or have been changed by constitutional amendment.
*Changed by Section 2 of the Fourteenth Amendment.

---

†Changed by Section 1 of the Seventeenth Amendment.
‡Changed by Section 2 of the Seventeenth Amendment.

Judgment in Cases of Impeachment shall not extend further than to removal from Office, and disqualification to hold and enjoy any Office of honor, Trust or Profit under the United States: but the Party convicted shall nevertheless be liable and subject to Indictment, Trial, Judgment and Punishment, according to Law.

Section 4. The Times, Places and Manner of holding Elections for Senators and Representatives, shall be prescribed in each State by the Legislature thereof; but the Congress may at any time by Law make or alter such Regulations, except as to the Places of Chusing Senators.

The Congress shall assemble at least once in every Year, and such Meeting *shall be on the first Monday in December, unless they shall by Law appoint a different Day.**

Section 5. Each House shall be the Judge of the Elections, Returns and Qualifications of its own Members, and a Majority of each shall constitute a Quorum to do Business; but a smaller number may adjourn from day to day, and may be authorized to compel the Attendance of absent Members, in such Manner, and under such Penalties, as each House may provide.

Each House may determine the Rules of its Proceedings, punish its Members for disorderly Behavior, and, with the Concurrence of two-thirds, expel a Member.

Each House shall keep a Journal of its Proceedings, and from time to time publish the same, excepting such Parts as may in their Judgment require Secrecy; and the Yeas and Nays of the Members of either House on any question shall, at the Desire of one-fifth of those Present, be entered on the Journal.

Neither House, during the Session of Congress, shall, without the Consent of the other, adjourn for more than three days, nor to any other Place than that in which the two Houses shall be sitting.

Section 6. The Senators and Representatives shall receive a Compensation for their Services, to be ascertained by Law, and paid out of the Treasury of the United States. They shall in all Cases, except Treason, Felony and Breach of the Peace, be privileged from Arrest during their Attendance at the Session of their respective Houses, and in going to and returning from the same; and for any Speech or Debate in either House, they shall not be questioned in any other Place.

No Senator or Representative shall, during the Time for which he was elected, be appointed to any civil Office under the Authority of the United States, which shall have been created, or the Emoluments whereof shall have been increased, during such time; and no Person holding any Office under the United States, shall be a Member of either House during his Continuance in Office.

*Changed by Section 2 of the Twentieth Amendment.

Section 7. All Bills for raising Revenue shall originate in the House of Representatives; but the Senate may propose or concur with Amendments as on other Bills.

Every Bill which shall have passed the House of Representatives and the Senate, shall, before it becomes a Law, be presented to the President of the United States; If he approve he shall sign it, but if not he shall return it, with his Objections to that House in which it shall have originated, who shall enter the Objections at large on their Journal, and proceed to reconsider it. If after such Reconsideration two-thirds of that House shall agree to pass the Bill, it shall be sent, together with the Objections, to the other House, by which it shall likewise be reconsidered, and if approved by two-thirds of that House, it shall become a Law. But in all such Cases the Votes of both Houses shall be determined by Yeas and Nays, and the Names of the Persons voting for and against the Bill shall be entered on the Journal of each House respectively. If any Bill shall not be returned by the President within ten Days (Sundays excepted) after it shall have been presented to him, the Same shall be a Law, in like Manner as if he had signed it, unless the Congress by their Adjournment prevent its Return, in which Case it shall not be a Law.

Every Order, Resolution, or Vote to which the Concurrence of the Senate and the House of Representatives may be necessary (except on a question of Adjournment) shall be presented to the President of the United States; and before the Same shall take Effect, shall be approved by him, or being disapproved by him, shall be repassed by two-thirds of the Senate and House of Representatives, according to the Rules and Limitations prescribed in the Case of a Bill.

Section 8. The Congress shall have Power To lay and collect Taxes, Duties, Imposts and Excises, to pay the Debts and provide for the common Defence and general Welfare of the United States; but all Duties, Imposts and Excises shall be uniform throughout the United States;

To borrow money on the credit of the United States;

To regulate Commerce with foreign Nations, and among the several States, and with the Indian Tribes;

To establish an uniform Rule of Naturalization, and uniform Laws on the subject of Bankruptcies throughout the United States;

To coin Money, regulate the Value thereof, and of foreign Coin, and fix the Standard of Weights and Measures;

To provide for the Punishment of counterfeiting the Securities and current Coin of the United States;

To establish Post Offices and post Roads;

To promote the Progress of Science and useful Arts, by securing for limited Times to Authors and Inventors the exclusive Right to their respective Writings and Discoveries;

To constitute Tribunals inferior to the supreme Court;

To define and punish Piracies and Felonies committed on the high Seas, and Offenses against the Law of Nations;

To declare War, grant Letters of Marque and Reprisal, and make Rules concerning Captures on Land and Water;

To raise and support Armies, but no Appropriation of Money to that Use shall be for a longer Term than two Years;

To provide and maintain a Navy;

To make Rules for the Government and Regulation of the land and naval Forces;

To provide for calling forth the Militia to execute the Laws of the Union, suppress Insurrections and repel Invasions;

To provide for organizing, arming, and disciplining the Militia, and for governing such Part of them as may be employed in the Service of the United States, reserving to the States respectively, the Appointment of the Officers, and the Authority of training the Militia according to the discipline prescribed by Congress;

To exercise exclusive Legislation in all Cases whatsoever, over such District (not exceeding ten Miles square) as may, by Cession of particular States, and the acceptance of Congress, become the Seat of Government of the United States, and to exercise like Authority over all Places purchased by the Consent of the Legislature of the State in which the Same shall be, for the Erection of Forts, Magazines, Arsenals, dock-Yards, and other needful Buildings; — And

To make all Laws which shall be necessary and proper for carrying into Execution the foregoing Powers, and all other Powers vested by this Constitution in the Government of the United States, or in any Department or Officer thereof.

Section 9. The Migration or Importation of such Persons as any of the States now existing shall think proper to admit, shall not be prohibited by the Congress prior to the Year one thousand eight hundred and eight but a tax or duty may be imposed on such Importation, not exceeding ten dollars for each Person.

The privilege of the Writ of Habeas Corpus shall not be suspended, unless when in Cases of Rebellion or Invasion the public Safety may require it.

No Bill of Attainder or ex post facto Law shall be passed.

*No capitation, or other direct, Tax shall be laid, unless in Proportion to the Census or Enumeration herein before directed to be taken.**

No Tax or Duty shall be laid on Articles exported from any State.

No Preference shall be given by any Regulation of Commerce or Revenue to the Ports of one State over those of another: nor shall Vessels bound to, or from, one State, be obliged to enter, clear, or pay Duties in another.

No Money shall be drawn from the Treasury, but in Consequence of Appropriations made by law; and a regular Statement and Account of the Receipts and Expenditures of all public Money shall be published from time to time.

No Title of Nobility shall be granted by the United States: And no Person holding any Office of Profit or Trust under them, shall, without the Consent of the Congress, accept of any present, Emolument, Office, or Title, of any kind whatever, from any King, Prince, or foreign State.

---

*Changed by the Sixteenth Amendment.

Section 10. No State shall enter into any Treaty, Alliance, or Confederation; grant Letters of Marque and Reprisal; coin Money; emit Bills of Credit; make any Thing but gold and silver Coin a Tender in Payment of Debts; pass any Bill of Attainder, ex post facto Law, or Law impairing the Obligation of Contracts, or grant any Title of Nobility.

No State shall, without the Consent of the Congress, lay any Imposts or Duties on Imports or Exports, except what may be absolutely necessary for executing its inspection Laws: and the net Produce of all Duties and Imposts, laid by any State on Imports or Exports, shall be for the Use of the Treasury of the United States; and all such Laws shall be subject to the Revision and Control of the Congress.

No State shall, without the Consent of the Congress, lay any duty of Tonnage, keep Troops, or Ships of War in time of Peace, enter into any Agreement or Compact with another State, or with a foreign Power, or engage in War, unless actually invaded, or in such imminent Danger as will not admit of delay.

Article II

Section 1. The executive Power shall be vested in a President of the United States of America. He shall hold his Office during the Term of four Years, and, together with the Vice President, chosen for the same Term, be elected, as follows:

Each State shall appoint, in such Manner as the Legislature thereof may direct, a Number of Electors, equal to the whole Number of Senators and Representatives to which the State may be entitled in the Congress; but no Senator or Representative, or Person holding an Office of Trust or Profit under the United States, shall be appointed an Elector.

The Electors shall meet in their respective States, and vote by Ballot for two Persons, of whom one at least shall not be an Inhabitant of the same State with themselves. And they shall make a List of all the Persons voted for, and of the Number of Votes for each; which List they shall sign and certify, and transmit sealed to the Seat of the Government of the United States, directed to the President of the Senate. The President of the Senate shall, in the Presence of the Senate and House of Representatives, open all the Certificates, and the Votes shall then be counted. The Person having the greatest Number of Votes shall be the President, if such Number be a Majority of the whole Number of Electors appointed; and if there be more than one who have such Majority, and have an equal Number of Votes, then the House of Representatives shall immediately chuse by Ballot one of them for President; and if no Person have a Majority, then from the five highest on the List the said House shall in like Manner chuse the President. But in chusing the President, the Votes shall be taken by States, the Representation from each State having one Vote; a quorum for this Purpose shall consist of a Member or Members from two thirds of the States, and a Majority of all the States shall be necessary to a Choice. In every Case, after the Choice of the President, the Person having the greatest Number of Votes of the

Electors shall be the Vice President. But if there should remain two or more who have equal Votes, the Senate shall chuse from them by Ballot the Vice President.[*]

The Congress may determine the Time of chusing the Electors, and the Day on which they shall give their Votes; which Day shall be the same throughout the United States.

No Person except a natural born Citizen, or a Citizen of the United States, at the time of the Adoption of this Constitution, shall be eligible to the Office of President; neither shall any Person be eligible to that Office who shall not have attained to the Age of thirty five Years, and been fourteen Years a Resident within the United States.

In Case of the Removal of the President from Office, or of his Death, Resignation, or Inability to discharge the Powers and Duties of the said Office, the same shall devolve on the Vice President, *and the Congress may by Law provide for the Case of Removal, Death, Resignation, or Inability, both of the President and Vice President, declaring what Officer shall then act as President, and such Officer shall act accordingly, until the Disability be removed, or a President shall be elected.*[†]

The President shall, at stated Times, receive for his Services a Compensation, which shall neither be increased nor diminished during the Period for which he shall have been elected, and he shall not receive within that Period any other Emolument from the United States, or any of them.

Before he enter on the Execution of his Office, he shall take the following Oath or Affirmation: — "I do solemnly swear (or affirm) that I will faithfully execute the Office of President of the United States, and will to the best of my Ability, preserve, protect and defend the Constitution of the United States."

Section 2. The President shall be Commander in Chief of the Army and Navy of the United States, and of the Militia of the several States, when called into the actual Service of the United States; he may require the Opinion, in writing, of the principal Officer in each of the executive Departments, upon any Subject relating to the Duties of their respective Offices, and he shall have Power to Grant Reprieves and Pardons for Offences against the United States, except in Cases of Impeachment.

He shall have Power, by and with the Advice and Consent of the Senate, to make Treaties, provided two thirds of the Senators present concur; and he shall nominate, and by and with the Advice and Consent of the Senate, shall appoint Ambassadors, other public Ministers and Consuls, Judges of the supreme Court, and all other Officers of the United States, whose Appointments are not herein otherwise provided for, and which shall be established by Law: but the Congress may by Law vest the Appointment of such inferior Officers, as they think proper, in the President alone, in the Courts of Law, or in the Heads of Departments.

The President shall have Power to fill up all Vacancies that may happen during the Recess of the Senate, by granting Commissions which shall expire at the End of their next Session.

Section 3. He shall from time to time give to the Congress Information of the State of the Union, and recommend to their Consideration such Measures as he shall judge necessary and expedient; he may, on extraordinary Occasions, convene both Houses, or either of them, and in Case of Disagreement between them, with Respect to the Time of Adjournment, he may adjourn them to such Time as he shall think proper; he shall receive Ambassadors and other public Ministers; he shall take Care that the Laws be faithfully executed, and shall Commission all the Officers of the United States.

Section 4. The President, Vice President and all civil Officers of the United States, shall be removed from Office on Impeachment for, and Conviction of, Treason, Bribery, or other high Crimes and Misdemeanors.

Article III

Section 1. The judicial Power of the United States, shall be vested in one supreme Court, and in such inferior Courts as the Congress may from time to time ordain and establish. The Judges, both of the supreme and inferior Courts, shall hold their Offices during good Behaviour, and shall, at stated Times, receive for their Services a Compensation, which shall not be diminished during their Continuance in Office.

Section 2. The judicial Power shall extend to all Cases, in Law and Equity, arising under this Constitution, the Laws of the United States, and Treaties made, or which shall be made, under their Authority; — to all Cases affecting Ambassadors, other public Ministers and Consuls; — to all Cases of admiralty and maritime Jurisdiction; — to Controversies to which the United States shall be a Party; — to Controversies between two or more States; — *between a State and Citizens of another State*;[‡] — between Citizens of different States; — between Citizens of the same State claiming Lands under Grants of different States, and between a State, or the Citizens thereof, and foreign States, Citizens or Subjects.

In all Cases affecting Ambassadors, other public Ministers and Consuls, and those in which a State shall be Party, the supreme Court shall have original Jurisdiction. In all the other Cases before mentioned, the supreme Court shall have appellate Jurisdiction, both as to Law and Fact, with such Exceptions, and under such Regulations as the Congress shall make.

---

[*]Superseded by the Twelfth Amendment.
[†]Modified by the Twenty-fifth Amendment.

[‡]Restricted by the Eleventh Amendment.

The trial of all Crimes, except in Cases of Impeachment, shall be by Jury; and such Trial shall be held in the State where said Crimes shall have been committed; but when not committed within any State, the Trial shall be at such Place or Places as the Congress may by Law have directed.

Section 3. Treason against the United States, shall consist only in levying War against them, or in adhering to their Enemies, giving them Aid and Comfort. No Person shall be convicted of Treason unless on the Testimony of two Witnesses to the same overt Act, or on Confession in open Court.

The Congress shall have Power to declare the Punishment of Treason, but no Attainder of Treason shall work Corruption of Blood, or Forfeiture except during the Life of the Person attainted.

Article IV

Section 1. Full Faith and Credit shall be given in each State to the public Acts, Records, and judicial Proceedings of every other State. And the Congress may by general Laws prescribe the Manner in which such Acts, Records, and Proceedings shall be proved, and the Effect thereof.

Section 2. The Citizens of each State shall be entitled to all Privileges and Immunities of Citizens in the several States.

A Person charged in any State with Treason, Felony, or other Crime, who shall flee from Justice, and be found in another State, shall on demand of the executive Authority of the State from which he fled, be delivered up, to be removed to the State having Jurisdiction of the Crime.

No Person held to Service or Labour in one State, under the Laws thereof, escaping into another, shall, in Consequence of any Law or Regulation therein, be discharged from such Service or Labour, but shall be delivered up on Claim of the Party to whom such Service or Labour may be due.*

Section 3. New States may be admitted by the Congress into this Union; but no new State shall be formed or erected within the Jurisdiction of any other State; nor any State be formed by the Junction of two or more States, or parts of States, without the Consent of the Legislatures of the States concerned as well as of the Congress.

The Congress shall have Power to dispose of and make all needful Rules and Regulations respecting the Territory or other Property belonging to the United States; and nothing in this Constitution shall be so construed as to Prejudice any Claims of the United States, or of any particular State.

Section 4. The United States shall guarantee to every State in this Union a Republican Form of Government, and shall protect each of them against Invasion; and on Application of the Legislature, or of the Executive (when the Legislature cannot be convened) against domestic Violence.

Article V

The Congress, whenever two-thirds of both Houses shall deem it necessary, shall propose Amendments to this Constitution, or, on the Application of the Legislatures of two-thirds of the several States, shall call a Convention for proposing Amendments, which, in either Case, shall be valid to all Intents and Purposes, as Part of this Constitution, when ratified by the Legislatures of three-fourths of the several States, or by Conventions in three-fourths thereof, as the one or the other Mode of Ratification may be proposed by the Congress; Provided that no Amendment which may be made prior to the Year One thousand eight hundred and eight shall in any Manner affect the first and fourth Clauses in the Ninth Section of the first Article; and that no State, without its Consent, shall be deprived of its equal Suffrage in the Senate.

Article VI

All Debts contracted and Engagements entered into, before the Adoption of this Constitution, shall be as valid against the United States under this Constitution, as under the Confederation.

This Constitution, and the Laws of the United States which shall be made in Pursuance thereof; and all Treaties made, or which shall be made, under the Authority of the United States, shall be the supreme Law of the Land; and the Judges in every State shall be bound thereby, any Thing in the Constitution or Laws of any State to the Contrary notwithstanding.

The Senators and Representatives before mentioned, and the Members of the several State Legislatures, and all executive and judicial Officers, both of the United States and of the several States, shall be bound by Oath or Affirmation, to support this Constitution; but no religious Test shall ever be required as a Qualification to any Office or public Trust under the United States.

Article VII

The Ratification of the Conventions of nine States shall be sufficient for the Establishment of this Constitution between the States so ratifying the Same.

Done in Convention by the Unanimous Consent of the States present the Seventeenth Day of September in the Year of our Lord one thousand seven hundred and Eighty seven and of the Independence of the United States of America the Twelfth. In Witness whereof We have hereunto subscribed our Names.

---

*Superseded by the Thirteenth Amendment.

Go. Washington
President and deputy from Virginia

New Hampshire
John Langdon
Nicholas Gilman

Massachusetts
Nathaniel Gorham
Rufus King

Connecticut
Wm. Saml. Johnson
Roger Sherman

New York
Alexander Hamilton

New Jersey
Wil. Livingston
David Brearley
Wm. Paterson
Jona. Dayton

Pennsylvania
B. Franklin
Thomas Mifflin
Robt. Morris
Geo. Clymer
Thos. FitzSimons
Jared Ingersoll
James Wilson
Gouv. Morris

Delaware
Geo. Read
Gunning Bedford jun
John Dickinson
Richard Bassett
Jaco. Broom

Maryland
James McHenry
Dan. of St. Thos. Jenifer
Danl. Carroll

Virginia
John Blair
James Madison, Jr.

North Carolina
Wm. Blount
Richd. Dobbs Spaight
Hu Williamson

South Carolina
J. Rutledge
Charles Cotesworth Pinckney
Pierce Butler

Georgia
William Few
Abr. Baldwin

Amendments to the Constitution with Annotations (Including the Six Unratified Amendments)

In their effort to gain Antifederalists' support for the Constitution, Federalists frequently pointed to the inclusion of Article 5, which provides an orderly method of amending the Constitution. In contrast, the Articles of Confederation, which were universally recognized as seriously flawed, offered no means of amendment. For their part, Antifederalists argued that the amendment process was so "intricate" that one might as easily roll "sixes an hundred times in succession" as change the Constitution.

The system for amendment laid out in the Constitution requires that two-thirds of both houses of Congress agree to a proposed amendment, which must then be ratified by three-quarters of the legislatures of the states. Alternatively, an amendment may be proposed by a convention called by the legislatures of two-thirds of the states. Since 1789, members of Congress have proposed thousands of amendments. Besides the seventeen amendments added since 1791, only the six "unratified" ones included here were approved by two-thirds of both houses but not ratified by the states.

Among the many amendments that never made it out of Congress have been proposals to declare dueling, divorce, and interracial marriage unconstitutional as well as proposals to establish a national university, to acknowledge the sovereignty of Jesus Christ, and to prohibit any person from possessing wealth in excess of $10 million.*

Among the issues facing Americans today that might lead to constitutional amendment are efforts to balance the federal budget, to limit the number of terms elected officials may serve, to limit access to or prohibit abortion, to establish English as the official language of the United States, and to prohibit flag burning. None of these proposed amendments has yet garnered enough support in Congress to be sent to the states for ratification.

Although the first ten amendments to the Constitution are commonly known as the Bill of Rights, only Amendments 1 through 8 provide guarantees of individual rights. Amendments 9 and 10 deal with the structure of power within the constitutional system. The Bill of Rights was promised to appease Antifederalists who refused to ratify the Constitution without guarantees of individual liberties and limitations to federal power. After studying more than two hundred amendments recommended by the ratifying conventions of the states, Federalist James Madison presented a list of seventeen to Congress, which used Madison's list as the foundation for the twelve amendments that were sent to the states for ratification. Ten of the twelve were adopted in 1791. The first on the list of twelve, known as the Reapportionment Amendment, was never adopted (p. D-16). The second proposed amendment was adopted in 1992 as Amendment 27 (p. D-24).

Amendment I [1791]†

Congress shall make no law respecting an establishment of religion, or prohibiting the free exercise thereof; or abridging the freedom of speech, or of the press; or the right of the people peaceably to assemble, and to petition the Government for a redress of grievances.

. . .

The First Amendment is a potent symbol for many Americans. Most are well aware of their rights to free speech, freedom of the press, and freedom of religion and their rights to assemble and to petition, even if they cannot cite the exact words of this amendment.

The First Amendment guarantee of freedom of religion has two clauses: the "free exercise clause," which allows individuals to practice or not practice any religion, and the "establishment clause," which prevents the federal government from discriminating against or favoring any particular religion. This clause was designed to create what Thomas Jefferson referred to as "a wall of separation between church and state." In the 1960s the Supreme Court ruled that the First Amendment prohibits prayer and Bible reading in public schools.

Although the rights to free speech and freedom of the press are established in the First Amendment, it was not until the twentieth century that the Supreme Court began to explore the full meaning of these guarantees. In 1919 the Court ruled in Schenck v. United States that the government could suppress free expression only where it could cite a "clear and present danger." In a decision that continues to raise controversies, the Court ruled in 1990, in Texas v. Johnson, that flag burning is a form of symbolic speech protected by the First Amendment.

---

*Richard B. Bernstein, *Amending America* (New York: Times Books, 1993), 177–81.

†The dates in brackets indicate when the amendment was ratified.

Amendment II [1791]

A well regulated Militia, being necessary to the security of a free State, the right of the people to keep and bear Arms shall not be infringed.

. . .

Fear of a standing army under the control of a hostile government made the Second Amendment an important part of the Bill of Rights. Advocates of gun ownership claim that the amendment prevents the government from regulating firearms. Proponents of gun control argue that the amendment is designed only to protect the right of the states to maintain militia units.

In 1939 the Supreme Court ruled in United States v. Miller *that the Second Amendment did not protect the right of an individual to own a sawed-off shotgun, which it argued was not ordinary militia equipment. Since then, the Supreme Court has refused to hear Second Amendment cases, whereas lower courts have upheld firearm regulations. Several justices currently on the bench seem to favor a broader interpretation of the Second Amendment, which would affect gun-control legislation. The controversy over the impact of the Second Amendment on gun owners and gun-control legislation will certainly continue.*

Amendment III [1791]

No Soldier shall, in time of peace, be quartered in any house, without the consent of the Owner, nor in time of war, but in a manner to be prescribed by law.

. . .

The Third Amendment was extremely important to the framers of the Constitution, but today it is nearly forgotten. American colonists were especially outraged that they were forced to quarter British troops in the years before and during the American Revolution. The philosophy of the Third Amendment has been viewed by some justices and scholars as the foundation of the modern constitutional right to privacy.

Amendment IV [1791]

The right of the people to be secure in their persons, houses, papers, and effects, against unreasonable searches and seizures, shall not be violated, and no Warrants shall issue, but upon probable cause, supported by Oath or affirmation, and particularly describing the place to be searched, and the persons or things to be seized.

. . .

In the years before the Revolution, the houses, barns, stores, and warehouses of American colonists were ransacked by British authorities under "writs of assistance" or general warrants. The British, thus empowered, searched for seditious material or smuggled goods that could then be used as evidence against colonists who were charged with a crime only after the items were found.

The first part of the Fourth Amendment protects citizens from "unreasonable" searches and seizures. The Supreme Court has interpreted this protection as well as the words search *and* seizure *in different ways at different times. At one time, the Court did not recognize electronic eavesdropping as a form of search and seizure, although it does today. At times, an "unreasonable" search has been almost any search carried out without a warrant, but in the two decades before 1969 the Court sometimes sanctioned warrantless searches that it considered reasonable based on "the total atmosphere of the case."*

The second part of the Fourth Amendment defines the procedure for issuing a search warrant and states the requirement of "probable cause," which is generally viewed as evidence indicating that a suspect has committed an offense.

In Weeks v. U.S. *(1994) and* Mapp v. Ohio *(1962), the Court excluded evidence seized in violation of constitutional standards. The justification is that excluding such evidence deters violations of the amendment, but doing so may allow a guilty person to escape punishment.*

Amendment V [1791]

No person shall be held to answer for a capital or otherwise infamous crime, unless on a presentment or indictment of a Grand Jury, except in cases arising in the land or naval forces, or in the Militia, when in actual service in time of War or public danger; nor shall any person be subject for the same offence to be twice put in jeopardy of life or limb; nor shall be compelled in any criminal case to be a witness against himself, nor be deprived of life, liberty, or property, without due process of law; nor shall private property be taken for public use, without just compensation.

. . .

The Fifth Amendment protects people against government authority in the prosecution of criminal offenses. It prohibits the state, first, from charging a person with a serious crime without a grand-jury hearing to decide whether there is sufficient evidence to support the charge and, second, from charging a person with the same crime twice. The best-known aspect of the Fifth Amendment is that it prevents a person from being "compelled . . . to be a witness against himself." The last clause, the "takings clause," limits the power of the government to seize property.

Although invoking the Fifth Amendment is popularly viewed as a confession of guilt, a person may be innocent yet still fear prosecution. For example, during the cold war era of the late 1940s and 1950s, many people who had participated in legal activities that were associated with the Communist Party claimed the Fifth Amendment privilege rather than testify before the House Un-American Activities Committee because the mood of the times cast those activities in a negative light. Because "taking the Fifth" was viewed as an admission of guilt, those people often lost their jobs or became unemployable. Nonetheless, the right to protect oneself against self-incrimination plays an important role in guarding against the collective power of the state.

Amendment VI [1791]

In all criminal prosecutions, the accused shall enjoy the right to a speedy and public trial, by an impartial jury of the State and district wherein the crime shall have been committed, which district shall have been previously ascertained by law, and to be informed of the nature and cause of the accusation; to be confronted with the witnesses against him; to have compulsory process for obtaining witnesses in his favor, and to have the Assistance of Counsel for his defence.

• • •

The original Constitution put few limits on the government's power to investigate, prosecute, and punish crime. This process was of great concern to many Antifederalists, and of the twenty-eight rights specified in the first eight amendments, fifteen have to do with it. Seven rights are specified in the Sixth Amendment. These include the right to a speedy trial, a public trial, a jury trial, a notice of accusation, confrontation of opposing witnesses, testimony by favorable witnesses, and the assistance of counsel.

Amendment VII [1791]

In suits at common law, where the value in controversy shall exceed twenty dollars, the right of trial by jury shall be preserved, and no fact tried by a jury, shall be otherwise reexamined in any Court of the United States, than according to the Rules of the common law.

• • •

This amendment guarantees people the same right to a trial by jury as was guaranteed by English common law in 1791. Under common law, in civil trials (those involving money damages) the role of the judge was to settle questions of law and that of the jury was to settle questions of fact. The amendment does not specify the size of the jury or its role in a trial, however. The Supreme Court has generally held that those issues be determined by English common law of 1791, which stated that a jury consists of twelve people, that a trial must be conducted before a judge who instructs the jury on the law and advises it on facts, and that a verdict must be unanimous.

Amendment VIII [1791]

Excessive bail shall not be required, nor excessive fines imposed, nor cruel and unusual punishments inflicted.

• • •

The language used to guarantee the three rights in this amendment was inspired by the English Bill of Rights of 1689. The Supreme Court has not had a lot to say about "excessive fines." In recent years it has agreed that despite the provision against "excessive bail," persons who are believed to be dangerous to others can be held without bail even before they have been convicted.

Although opponents of the death penalty have not succeeded in using the Eighth Amendment to achieve the end of capital punishment, the clause regarding "cruel and unusual punishments" has been used to prohibit capital punishment in certain cases, such as minors and the mentally retarded.

Amendment IX [1791]

The enumeration in the Constitution, of certain rights, shall not be construed to deny or disparage others retained by the people.

• • •

Some Federalists feared that inclusion of the Bill of Rights in the Constitution would allow later generations of interpreters to claim that the people had surrendered all rights not specifically enumerated there. To guard against this, James Madison added language that became the Ninth Amendment. Interest in this heretofore largely ignored amendment revived in 1965 when it was used in a concurring opinion in Griswold v. Connecticut *(1965). While Justice William O. Douglas called on the Third Amendment to support the right to privacy in deciding that case, Justice Arthur Goldberg, in the concurring opinion, argued that the right to privacy regarding contraception was an unenumerated right that was protected by the Ninth Amendment.*

In 1980 the Court ruled that the right of the press to attend a public trial was protected by the Ninth Amendment. Although some scholars argue that modern judges cannot identify the unenumerated rights that the framers were trying to protect, others argue that the Ninth Amendment should be read as providing a constitutional "presumption of liberty" that allows people to act in any way that does not violate the rights of others.

Amendment X [1791]

The powers not delegated to the United States by the Constitution, nor prohibited by it to the States, are reserved to the States respectively, or to the people.

• • •

The Antifederalists were especially eager to see a "reserved powers clause" explicitly guaranteeing the states control over their internal affairs. Not surprisingly, the Tenth Amendment has been a frequent battleground in the struggle over states' rights and federal supremacy. Prior to the Civil War, the Jeffersonian Republican Party and Jacksonian Democrats invoked the Tenth

Amendment to prohibit the federal government from making decisions about whether people in individual states could own slaves. The Tenth Amendment was virtually suspended during Reconstruction following the Civil War. In 1883, however, the Supreme Court declared the Civil Rights Act of 1875 unconstitutional on the grounds that it violated the Tenth Amendment. Business interests also called on the amendment to block efforts at federal regulation.

The Court was inconsistent over the next several decades as it attempted to resolve the tension between the restrictions of the Tenth Amendment and the powers the Constitution granted to Congress to regulate interstate commerce and levy taxes. The Court upheld the Pure Food and Drug Act (1906), the Meat Inspection Acts (1906 and 1907), and the White Slave Traffic Act (1910), all of which affected the states, but it struck down an act prohibiting interstate shipment of goods produced through child labor. Between 1934 and 1935 a number of New Deal programs created by Franklin D. Roosevelt were declared unconstitutional on the grounds that they violated the Tenth Amendment. As Roosevelt appointees changed the composition of the Court, the Tenth Amendment was declared to have no substantive meaning. Generally, the amendment is held to protect the rights of states to regulate internal matters such as local government, education, commerce, labor, and business as well as matters involving families such as marriage, divorce, and inheritance within the state.

Unratified Amendment

Reapportionment Amendment (proposed by Congress September 25, 1789, along with the Bill of Rights)

After the first enumeration required by the first article of the Constitution, there shall be one Representative for every thirty thousand, until the number shall amount to one hundred, after which the proportion shall be so regulated by Congress, that there shall be not less than one hundred Representatives, nor less than one Representative for every forty thousand persons, until the number of Representatives shall amount to two hundred; after which the proportion shall be so regulated by Congress, that there shall not be less than two hundred Representatives, nor more than one Representative for every fifty thousand persons.

• • •

If the Reapportionment Amendment had passed and remained in effect, the House of Representatives today would have more than 7,000 members rather than 435 to reflect the current U.S. population.

Amendment XI [1798]

The Judicial power of the United States shall not be construed to extend to any suit in law or equity, commenced or prosecuted against one of the United States by Citizens of another State, or by Citizens or subjects of any foreign state.

• • •

In 1793 the Supreme Court ruled in favor of Alexander Chisholm, executor of the estate of a deceased South Carolina merchant. Chisholm was suing the state of Georgia because the merchant had never been paid for provisions he had supplied during the Revolution. Many regarded this Court decision as an error that violated the intent of the Constitution.

Antifederalists and many other Americans feared a powerful federal court system because they worried that it would become like the British courts of this period, which were accountable only to the monarch. Furthermore, Chisholm v. Georgia prompted a series of suits against state governments by creditors and suppliers who had made loans during the war.

In addition, state legislators and Congress feared that the shaky economies of the new states, as well as the country as a whole, would be destroyed, especially if Loyalists who had fled to other countries sought reimbursement for land and property that had been seized. The day after the Supreme Court announced its decision, a resolution proposing the Eleventh Amendment, which overturned the decision in Chisholm v. Georgia, *was introduced in the U.S. Senate.*

Amendment XII [1804]

The Electors shall meet in their respective States and vote by ballot for President and Vice-President, one of whom, at least, shall not be an inhabitant of the same State with themselves; they shall name in their ballots the person voted for as President, and in distinct ballots the person voted for as Vice-President, and they shall make distinct lists of all persons voted for as President, and of all persons voted for as Vice-President, and of the number of votes for each, which lists they shall sign and certify, and transmit sealed to the seat of government of the United States, directed to the President of the Senate;—the President of the Senate shall, in the presence of the Senate and House of Representatives, open all the certificates and the votes shall then be counted;—The person having the greatest number of votes for President, shall be the President, if such number be a majority of the whole number of Electors appointed; and if no person have such majority, then from the persons having the highest numbers not exceeding three on the list of those voted for as President, the House of Representatives shall choose immediately, by ballot, the President. But in choosing the President, the votes shall be taken by States, the representation from each State having one vote; a quorum for this purpose shall consist of a member or members from two-thirds of the States, and a majority of all the States shall be necessary to a choice. And if the House of Representatives shall not choose a President whenever the right of choice shall devolve upon them, before *the fourth day of March* next following, then the Vice-President shall act as

President, as in the case of the death or other constitutional disability of the President.* — The person having the greatest number of votes as Vice-President, shall be the Vice-President, if such number be a majority of the whole number of Electors appointed; and if no person have a majority, then from the two highest numbers on the list, the Senate shall choose the Vice-President; a quorum for the purpose shall consist of two-thirds of the whole number of Senators, and a majority of the whole number shall be necessary to a choice. But no person constitutionally ineligible to the office of President shall be eligible to that of Vice-President of the United States.

• • •

The framers of the Constitution disliked political parties and assumed that none would ever form. Under the original system, electors chosen by the states would each vote for two candidates. The candidate who won the most votes would become president, and the person who won the second-highest number of votes would become vice president. Rivalries between Federalists and Republicans led to the formation of political parties, however, even before George Washington had left office. In 1796 Federalist John Adams was chosen as president, and his great rival, Thomas Jefferson (whose party was called the Republican Party), became his vice president. In 1800 all the electors cast their two votes as one of two party blocs. Jefferson and his fellow Republican nominee, Aaron Burr, were tied with seventy-three votes each. The contest went to the House of Representatives, which finally elected Jefferson after thirty-six ballots. The Twelfth Amendment prevents these problems by requiring electors to vote separately for the president and vice president.

Unratified Amendment

Titles of Nobility Amendment
(proposed by Congress May 1, 1810)

If any citizen of the United States shall accept, claim, receive or retain any title of nobility or honor or shall, without the consent of Congress, accept and retain any present, pension, office or emolument of any kind whatever, from any emperor, king, prince or foreign power, such person shall cease to be a citizen of the United States, and shall be incapable of holding any office of trust or profit under them, or either of them.

• • •

This amendment would have extended Article I, Section 9, Clause 8 of the Constitution, which prevents the awarding of titles by the United States and the acceptance of such awards from foreign powers without congressional consent. Historians speculate that general nervousness about the power of the Emperor Napoleon, who was at that time extending France's empire throughout Europe, may have prompted the proposal. Though it

fell one vote short of ratification, Congress and the American people thought the proposal had been ratified, and it was included in many nineteenth-century editions of the Constitution.

The Civil War and Reconstruction Amendments (Thirteenth, Fourteenth, and Fifteenth Amendments)

In the four months between the election of Abraham Lincoln and his inauguration, more than two hundred proposed constitutional amendments were presented to Congress as part of a desperate attempt to hold the rapidly dissolving Union together. Most of these were efforts to appease the southern states by protecting the right to own slaves or by disfranchising African Americans through constitutional amendment. None were able to win the votes required from Congress to send them to the states. Ultimately, the Corwin Amendment seemed to be the only hope for preserving the Union by amending the Constitution.

The northern victors in the Civil War tried to restructure the Constitution just as the war had restructured the nation. Yet they were often divided in their goals. Some wanted to end slavery; others hoped for social and economic equality regardless of race; others hoped that extending the power of the ballot box to former slaves would help create a new political order. The debates over the Thirteenth, Fourteenth, and Fifteenth Amendments were bitter. Few of those who fought for these changes were satisfied with the amendments themselves; fewer still were satisfied with their interpretation. Although the amendments put an end to the legal status of slavery, it was nearly a hundred years after the amendments' passage before most of the descendants of former slaves could begin to experience the economic, social, and political equality the amendments were intended to provide.

Unratified Amendment

Corwin Amendment
(proposed by Congress March 2, 1861)

No amendment shall be made to the Constitution which will authorize or give to Congress the power to abolish or interfere, within any State, with the domestic institutions thereof, including that of persons held to labor or service by the laws of said State.

• • •

Following the election of Abraham Lincoln, Congress scrambled to try to prevent the secession of the slaveholding states. House member Thomas Corwin of Ohio proposed the "unamendable" amendment in the hope that by protecting slavery where it existed, Congress would keep the southern states in the Union. Lincoln indicated his support for the proposed amendment in his first inaugural address. Only Ohio and Maryland ratified the Corwin Amendment before the war caused it to be forgotten.

*Superseded by Section 3 of the Twentieth Amendment.

Amendment XIII [1865]

Section 1. Neither slavery nor involuntary servitude, except as a punishment for crime whereof the party shall have been duly convicted, shall exist within the United States, or any place subject to their jurisdiction.

Section 2. Congress shall have power to enforce this article by appropriate legislation.

• • •

Because the Emancipation Proclamation of 1863 abolished slavery only in the parts of the Confederacy still in rebellion, Republicans proposed a Thirteenth Amendment that would extend abolition to the entire South. In February 1865, when the proposal was approved by the House, the gallery of the House was newly opened to black Americans who had a chance at last to see their government at work. Passage of the proposal was greeted by wild cheers from the gallery as well as tears on the House floor, where congressional representatives openly embraced one another.

The problem of ratification remained, however. The Union position was that the Confederate states were part of the country of thirty-six states. Therefore, twenty-seven states were needed to ratify the amendment. When Kentucky and Delaware rejected it, backers realized that without approval from at least four former Confederate states, the amendment would fail. Lincoln's successor, President Andrew Johnson, made ratification of the Thirteenth Amendment a condition for southern states to rejoin the Union. Under those terms, all the former Confederate states except Mississippi accepted the Thirteenth Amendment, and by the end of 1865 the amendment had become part of the Constitution and slavery had been prohibited in the United States.

Amendment XIV [1868]

Section 1. All persons born or naturalized in the United States, and subject to the jurisdiction thereof, are citizens of the United States and of the State wherein they reside. No State shall make or enforce any law which shall abridge the privileges or immunities of citizens of the United States; nor shall any State deprive any person of life, liberty, or property, without due process of law; nor deny to any person within its jurisdiction the equal protection of the laws.

Section 2. Representatives shall be apportioned among the several States according to their respective numbers, counting the whole number of persons in each State, excluding Indians not taxed. But when the right to vote at any election for the choice of electors for President and Vice-President of the United States, Representatives in Congress, the Executive and Judicial officers of a State, or the members of the Legislature

thereof, is denied to any of the male inhabitants of such State, being twenty-one years of age and citizens of the United States, or in any way abridged, except for participation in rebellion, or other crime, the basis of representation therein shall be reduced in the proportion which the number of such male citizens shall bear to the whole number of male citizens twenty-one years of age in such State.

Section 3. No person shall be a Senator or Representative in Congress, or Elector of President and Vice-President, or hold any office, civil or military, under the United States, or under any State, who, having previously taken an oath, as a member of Congress, or as an officer of the United States, or as a member of any State legislature, or as an executive or judicial officer of any State, to support the Constitution of the United States, shall have engaged in insurrection or rebellion against the same, or given aid or comfort to the enemies thereof. Congress may, by a vote of two-thirds of each house, remove such disability.

Section 4. The validity of the public debt of the United States, authorized by law, including debts incurred for payment of pensions and bounties for services in suppressing insurrection or rebellion, shall not be questioned. But neither the United States nor any State shall assume or pay any debt or obligation incurred in aid of insurrection or rebellion against the United States, or any claim for the loss or emancipation of any slave; but all such debts, obligations, and claims shall be held illegal and void.

Section 5. The Congress shall have power to enforce, by appropriate legislation, the provisions of this article.

• • •

Less than a year after Lincoln's assassination, Andrew Johnson was ready to bring the former Confederate states back into the Union and Confederate leaders back into Congress. Anxious Republicans drafted the Fourteenth Amendment to prevent that from happening. Moreover, most Southern states had enacted "Black Codes" that restricted the legal, political, and civil rights of former slaves. The most important provisions of this complex amendment made all native-born or naturalized persons American citizens and prohibited states from abridging the "privileges or immunities" of citizens; depriving them of "life, liberty, or property, without due process of law"; and denying them "equal protection of the laws." In essence, it made all former slaves citizens and protected the rights of all citizens against violation by their own state governments.

As occurred in the case of the Thirteenth Amendment, former Confederate states were forced to ratify the amendment as a condition of representation in the House and the Senate. The intentions of the Fourteenth Amendment, and how those intentions should be enforced, have been the most debated point of constitutional history. The terms due process *and* equal protection *have been especially troublesome. Was the amendment designed to outlaw racial segregation? Or was the goal simply to prevent the leaders of the rebellious South from gaining political power?*

The framers of the Fourteenth Amendment hoped Section 2 would produce black voters who would increase the power of the Republican Party. The federal government, however, never used its power to punish states for denying blacks their right to vote. Although the Fourteenth Amendment had an immediate impact in giving black Americans citizenship, it did nothing to protect blacks from the vengeance of whites once Reconstruction ended. In the late nineteenth and early twentieth centuries, Section 1 of the Fourteenth Amendment was often used to protect business interests and strike down laws protecting workers on the grounds that the rights of "persons," that is, corporations, were protected by "due process." More recently, the Fourteenth Amendment has been used to justify school desegregation and affirmative action programs, as well as to dismantle such programs.

Amendment XV [1870]

Section 1. The right of citizens of the United States to vote shall not be denied or abridged by the United States or by any State on account of race, color, or previous condition of servitude —

Section 2. The Congress shall have power to enforce this article by appropriate legislation.

• • •

The Fifteenth Amendment was the last major piece of Reconstruction legislation. Although earlier Reconstruction acts had already required black suffrage in the South, the Fifteenth Amendment extended black voting rights to the entire nation. Some Republicans felt morally obligated to do away with the double standard between the North and South because many northern states had stubbornly refused to enfranchise blacks. Others believed that the freedman's ballot required the extra protection of a constitutional amendment to shield it from white counterattack in the South. But partisan advantage also played an important role in the amendment's passage because Republicans hoped that by giving the ballot to blacks, they could lessen their party's political vulnerability.

Many women's rights advocates had fought for the amendment. They had felt betrayed by the inclusion of the word male *in Section 2 of the Fourteenth Amendment and were further angered when the proposed Fifteenth Amendment failed to prohibit denial of the right to vote on the grounds of sex as well as "race, color, or previous condition of servitude." In this amendment, for the first time, the federal government exerted its power to regulate the franchise, or vote. It was also the first time the Constitution placed limits on the power of the states to regulate access to the franchise. Although ratified in 1870, the amendment was not enforced until the twentieth century.*

The Progressive Amendments (Sixteenth– Nineteenth Amendments)

No amendments were added to the Constitution between the Civil War and the Progressive Era. America was changing, however, in fundamental ways. The rapid industrialization of the United States after the Civil War led to many social and economic problems. Hundreds of amendments were proposed, but none received enough support in Congress to be sent to the states. Some scholars believe that regional differences and rivalries were so strong during this period that it was almost impossible to gain a consensus on a constitutional amendment. During the Progressive Era, however, the Constitution was amended four times in seven years.

Amendment XVI [1913]

The Congress shall have power to lay and collect taxes on incomes, from whatever source derived, without apportionment among the several States, and without regard to any census or enumeration.

• • •

Until passage of the Sixteenth Amendment, most of the money used to run the federal government came from customs duties and taxes on specific items, such as liquor. During the Civil War the federal government taxed incomes as an emergency measure. Pressure to enact an income tax came from those who were concerned about the growing gap between rich and poor in the United States. The Populist Party began campaigning for a graduated income tax in 1892, and support continued to grow. By 1909 thirty-three proposed income tax amendments had been presented in Congress, but lobbying by corporate and other special interests had defeated them all. In June 1909 the growing pressure for an income tax, which had been endorsed by presidents Roosevelt and Taft, finally pushed an amendment through the Senate. The required thirty-six states had ratified the amendment by February 1913.

Amendment XVII [1913]

Section 1. The Senate of the United States shall be composed of two Senators from each State, elected by the people thereof, for six years; and each Senator shall have one vote. The electors in each State shall have the qualifications requisite for electors of [voters for] the most numerous branch of the State legislatures.

Section 2. When vacancies happen in the representation of any State in the Senate, the executive authority of such State shall issue writs of election to fill such vacancies: Provided, that the Legislature of any State may empower the executive thereof to make temporary appointments until the people fill the vacancies by election as the Legislature may direct.

Section 3. This amendment shall not be so construed as to affect the election or term of any Senator chosen before it becomes valid as part of the Constitution.

. . .

The framers of the Constitution saw the members of the House as the representatives of the people and the members of the Senate as the representatives of the states. Originally, senators were to be chosen by the state legislators. According to reform advocates, however, the growth of private industry and transportation conglomerates during the late nineteenth century had created a network of corruption in which wealth and power were exchanged for influence and votes in the Senate. Senator Nelson Aldrich, who represented Rhode Island in this period, for example, was known as "the senator from Standard Oil" because of his open support of special business interests.

Efforts to amend the Constitution to allow direct election of senators had begun in 1826, but because any proposal had to be approved by the Senate, reform seemed impossible. Progressives tried to gain influence in the Senate by instituting party caucuses and primary elections, which gave citizens the chance to express their choice of a senator who could then be officially elected by the state legislature. By 1910 fourteen of the country's thirty senators received popular votes through a state primary before the state legislature made its selection. Despairing of getting a proposal through the Senate, supporters of a direct-election amendment had begun in 1893 to seek a convention of representatives from two-thirds of the states to propose an amendment that could then be ratified. By 1905 thirty-one of forty-five states had endorsed such an amendment. Finally, in 1911, despite extraordinary opposition, a proposed amendment passed the Senate; by 1913 it had been ratified.

Amendment XVIII [1919; repealed 1933 by Amendment XXI]

Section 1. After one year from the ratification of this article the manufacture, sale, or transportation of intoxicating liquors within, the importation thereof into, or the exportation thereof from the United States and all territory subject to the jurisdiction thereof, for beverage purposes, is hereby prohibited.

Section 2. The Congress and the several States shall have concurrent power to enforce this article by appropriate legislation.

Section 3. This article shall be inoperative unless it shall have been ratified as an amendment to the Constitution by the legislatures of the several States, as provided by the Constitution, within seven years from the date of the submission thereof to the States by the Congress.

. . .

The Prohibition Party, formed in 1869, began calling for a constitutional amendment to outlaw alcoholic beverages in 1872. A prohibition amendment was first proposed in the Senate in 1876

and was revived eighteen times before 1913. Between 1913 and 1919 another thirty-nine attempts were made to prohibit liquor in the United States through a constitutional amendment. Prohibition became a key element of the Progressive agenda as reformers linked alcohol and drunkenness to numerous social problems, including the corruption of immigrant voters. Whereas opponents of such an amendment argued that it was undemocratic, supporters claimed that their efforts had widespread public support. The admission of twelve "dry" western states to the Union in the early twentieth century and the spirit of sacrifice during World War I laid the groundwork for passage and ratification of the Eighteenth Amendment in 1919. Opponents added a time limit to the amendment in the hope that they could thereby block ratification, but this effort failed. (See also Amendment XXI.)

Amendment XIX [1920]

Section 1. The right of citizens of the United States to vote shall not be denied or abridged by the United States or by any State on account of sex.

Section 2. Congress shall have the power to enforce this article by appropriate legislation.

. . .

Advocates of women's rights tried and failed to link woman suffrage to the Fourteenth and Fifteenth Amendments. Nonetheless, the effort for woman suffrage continued. Between 1878 and 1912 at least one and sometimes as many as four proposed amendments were introduced in Congress each year to grant women the right to vote. Although over time women won very limited voting rights in some states, at both the state and federal levels opposition to an amendment for woman suffrage remained very strong. President Woodrow Wilson and other officials felt that the federal government should not interfere with the power of the states in this matter. And many people were concerned that giving women the vote would result in their abandoning traditional gender roles. In 1919, following a protracted and often bitter campaign of protest in which women went on hunger strikes and chained themselves to fences, an amendment was introduced with the backing of President Wilson. It narrowly passed the Senate (after efforts to limit the suffrage to white women failed) and was adopted in 1920 after Tennessee became the thirty-sixth state to ratify it.

Unratified Amendment

Child Labor Amendment (proposed by Congress June 2, 1924)

Section 1. The Congress shall have power to limit, regulate, and prohibit the labor of persons under eighteen years of age.

Section 2. The power of the several States is unimpaired by this article except that the operation of State laws shall be suspended to the extent necessary to give effect to legislation enacted by Congress.

. . .

Throughout the late nineteenth and early twentieth centuries, alarm over the condition of child workers grew. Opponents of child labor argued that children worked in dangerous and unhealthy conditions, that they took jobs from adult workers, that they depressed wages in certain industries, and that states that allowed child labor had an economic advantage over those that did not. Defenders of child labor claimed that children provided needed income in many families, that working at a young age helped to develop character, and that the effort to prohibit the practice constituted an invasion of family privacy.

In 1916 Congress passed a law that made it illegal to sell through interstate commerce goods made by children. The Supreme Court, however, ruled that the law violated the limits on the power of Congress to regulate interstate commerce. Congress then tried to penalize industries that used child labor by taxing such goods. This measure was also thrown out by the courts. In response, reformers set out to amend the Constitution. The proposed amendment was ratified by twenty-eight states, but by 1925 thirteen states had rejected it. Passage of the Fair Labor Standards Act in 1938, which was upheld by the Supreme Court in 1941, made the amendment irrelevant.

Amendment XX [1933]

Section 1. The terms of the President and Vice-President shall end at noon on the 20th day of January, and the terms of Senators and Representatives at noon on the 3rd day of January, of the years in which such terms would have ended if this article had not been ratified; and the terms of their successors shall then begin.

Section 2. The Congress shall assemble at least once in every year, and such meeting shall begin at noon on the 3rd day of January, unless they shall by law appoint a different day.

Section 3. If, at the time fixed for the beginning of the term of the President, the President-elect shall have died, the Vice-President-elect shall become President. If a President shall not have been chosen before the time fixed for the beginning of his term, or if the President-elect shall have failed to qualify, then the Vice-President-elect shall act as President until a President shall have qualified; and the Congress may by law provide for the case wherein neither a President-elect nor a Vice-President-elect shall have qualified, declaring who shall then act as President, or the manner in which one who is to act shall be selected, and such person shall act accordingly until a President or Vice-President shall have qualified.

Section 4. The Congress may by law provide for the case of the death of any of the persons from whom the House of Representatives may choose a President whenever the right of choice shall have devolved upon them, and for the case of the death of any of the persons from whom the Senate may choose a Vice-President whenever the right of choice shall have devolved upon them.

Section 5. Sections 1 and 2 shall take effect on the 15th day of October following the ratification of this article.

Section 6. This article shall be inoperative unless it shall have been ratified as an amendment to the Constitution by the Legislatures of three-fourths of the several States within seven years from the date of its submission.

. . .

Until 1933, presidents took office on March 4. Because elections are held in early November and electoral votes are counted in mid-December, this meant that more than three months passed between the time a new president was elected and when he took office. Moving the inauguration to January shortened the transition period and allowed Congress to begin its term closer to the time of the president's inauguration. Although this seems like a minor change, an amendment was required because the Constitution specifies terms of office. This amendment also deals with questions of succession in the event that a president- or vice-president-elect dies before assuming office. Section 3 also clarifies a method for resolving a deadlock in the electoral college.

Amendment XXI [1933]

Section 1. The eighteenth article of amendment to the Constitution of the United States is hereby repealed.

Section 2. The transportation or importation into any State, Territory, or Possession of the United States for delivery or use therein of intoxicating liquors, in violation of the laws thereof, is hereby prohibited.

Section 3. This article shall be inoperative unless it shall have been ratified as an amendment to the Constitution by conventions in the several States, as provided in the Constitution, within seven years from the date of the submission thereof to the States by the Congress.

. . .

Widespread violation of the Volstead Act, the law enacted to enforce prohibition, made the United States a nation of lawbreakers. Prohibition caused more problems than it solved by encouraging crime, bribery, and corruption. Further, a coalition of liquor and beer manufacturers, personal liberty advocates, and constitutional scholars joined forces to challenge the amendment. By 1929 thirty proposed repeal amendments had been introduced in Congress, and the Democratic Party made repeal part of its platform in the 1932 presidential campaign. The Twenty-first Amendment was proposed in February 1933 and ratified less than a year later. The failure of the effort to enforce prohibition through a constitutional amendment has often been cited by opponents of subsequent efforts to shape public virtue and private morality.

Amendment XXII [1951]

Section 1. No person shall be elected to the office of the President more than twice, and no person who has held the office of President, or acted as President, for more than two years of a term to which some other person was elected President shall be elected to the office of President more than once. But this article shall not apply to any person holding the office of President when this Article was proposed by the Congress, and shall not prevent any person who may be holding the office of President, or acting as President, during the term within which this Article becomes operative from holding the office of President or acting as President during the remainder of such term.

Section 2. This article shall be inoperative unless it shall have been ratified as an amendment to the Constitution by the legislatures of three-fourths of the several States within seven years from the date of its submission to the States by the Congress.

• • •

George Washington's refusal to seek a third term of office set a precedent that stood until 1912, when former president Theodore Roosevelt sought, without success, another term as an independent candidate. Democrat Franklin Roosevelt was the only president to seek and win a fourth term, though he did so amid great controversy. Roosevelt died in April 1945, a few months after the beginning of his fourth term. In 1946 Republicans won control of the House and the Senate, and early in 1947 a proposal for an amendment to limit future presidents to two four-year terms was offered to the states for ratification. Democratic critics of the Twenty-second Amendment charged that it was a partisan posthumous jab at Roosevelt.

Since the Twenty-second Amendment was adopted, two of the three presidents who might have been able to seek a third term, had it not existed, were Republicans Dwight Eisenhower and Ronald Reagan. Since 1826, Congress has entertained 160 proposed amendments to limit the president to one six-year term. Such amendments have been backed by fifteen presidents, including Gerald Ford and Jimmy Carter.

Amendment XXIII [1961]

Section 1. The District constituting the seat of Government of the United States shall appoint in such manner as

the Congress may direct: A number of electors of President and Vice-President equal to the whole number of Senators and Representatives in Congress to which the District would be entitled if it were a State, but in no event more than the least populous State; they shall be in addition to those appointed by the States, but they shall be considered for the purposes of the election of President and Vice-President, to be electors appointed by a State; and they shall meet in the District and perform such duties as provided by the twelfth article of amendment.

Section 2. The Congress shall have the power to enforce this article by appropriate legislation.

• • •

When Washington, D.C., was established as a federal district, no one expected that a significant number of people would make it their permanent and primary residence. A proposal to allow citizens of the district to vote in presidential elections was approved by Congress in June 1960 and was ratified on March 29, 1961.

Amendment XXIV [1964]

Section 1. The right of citizens of the United States to vote in any primary or other election for President or Vice-President, for electors for President or Vice-President, or for Senator or Representative in Congress, shall not be denied or abridged by the United States or any State by reason of failure to pay any poll tax or other tax.

Section 2. The Congress shall have the power to enforce this article by appropriate legislation.

• • •

In the colonial and Revolutionary eras, financial independence was seen as necessary to political independence, and the poll tax was used as a requirement for voting. By the twentieth century, however, the poll tax was used mostly to bar poor people, especially southern blacks, from voting. Although conservatives complained that the amendment interfered with states' rights, liberals thought that the amendment did not go far enough because it barred the poll tax only in national elections and not in state or local elections. The amendment was ratified in 1964, however, and two years later the Supreme Court ruled that poll taxes in state and local elections also violated the equal protection clause of the Fourteenth Amendment.

Amendment XXV [1967]

Section 1. In case of the removal of the President from office or of his death or resignation, the Vice-President shall become President.

Section 2. Whenever there is a vacancy in the office of the Vice-President, the President shall nominate a Vice-President who shall take office upon confirmation by a majority vote of both Houses of Congress.

Section 3. Whenever the President transmits to the President pro tempore of the Senate and the Speaker of the House of Representatives his written declaration that he is unable to discharge the powers and duties of his office, and until he transmits to them a written declaration to the contrary, such powers and duties shall be discharged by the Vice-President as Acting President.

Section 4. Whenever the Vice-President and a majority of either the principal officers of the executive departments or of such other body as Congress may by law provide, transmit to the President pro tempore of the Senate and the Speaker of the House of Representatives their written declaration that the President is unable to discharge the powers and duties of his office, the Vice-President shall immediately assume the powers and duties of the office as Acting President.

Thereafter, when the President transmits to the President pro tempore of the Senate and the Speaker of the House of Representatives his written declaration that no inability exists, he shall resume the powers and duties of his office unless the Vice-President and a majority of either the principal officers of the executive department[s] or of such other body as Congress may by law provide, transmit within four days to the President pro tempore of the Senate and the Speaker of the House of Representatives their written declaration that the President is unable to discharge the powers and duties of his office. Thereupon Congress shall decide the issue, assembling within forty-eight hours for that purpose if not in session. If the Congress, within twenty-one days after receipt of the latter written declaration, or, if Congress is not in session, within twenty-one days after Congress is required to assemble, determines by two-thirds vote of both Houses that the President is unable to discharge the powers and duties of his office, the Vice-President shall continue to discharge the same as Acting President; otherwise, the President shall resume the powers and duties of his office.

• • •

The framers of the Constitution established the office of vice president because someone was needed to preside over the Senate. The first president to die in office was William Henry Harrison, in 1841. Vice President John Tyler had himself sworn in as president, setting a precedent that was followed when seven later presidents died in office. The assassination of President James A. Garfield in 1881 posed a new problem, however. After he was shot, the president was incapacitated for two months before he died; he was unable to lead the country, and his vice president, Chester A. Arthur, was unable to assume leadership. Efforts to

resolve questions of succession in the event of a presidential disability thus began with the death of Garfield.

In 1963 the assassination of President John F. Kennedy galvanized Congress to action. Vice President Lyndon Johnson was a chain-smoker with a history of heart trouble. According to the 1947 Presidential Succession Act, the two men who stood in line to succeed him were the seventy-two-year-old Speaker of the House and the eighty-six-year-old president of the Senate. There were serious concerns that any of these men might become incapacitated while serving as chief executive. The first time the Twenty-fifth Amendment was used, however, was not in the case of presidential death or illness, but during the Watergate crisis. When Vice President Spiro T. Agnew was forced to resign following allegations of bribery and tax violations, President Richard M. Nixon appointed House Minority Leader Gerald R. Ford vice president. Ford became president following Nixon's resignation eight months later and named Nelson A. Rockefeller as his vice president. Thus, for more than two years, the two highest offices in the country were held by people who had not been elected to them.

Amendment XXVI [1971]

Section 1. The right of citizens of the United States, who are eighteen years of age or older, to vote shall not be denied or abridged by the United States or by any State on account of age.

Section 2. The Congress shall have power to enforce this article by appropriate legislation.

• • •

Efforts to lower the voting age from twenty-one to eighteen began during World War II. Recognizing that those who were old enough to fight a war should have some say in the government policies that involved them in the war, Presidents Eisenhower, Johnson, and Nixon endorsed the idea. In 1970 the combined pressure of the antiwar movement and the demographic pressure of the baby-boom generation led to a Voting Rights Act lowering the voting age in federal, state, and local elections.

In Oregon v. Mitchell (1970), the state of Oregon challenged the right of Congress to determine the age at which people could vote in state or local elections. The Supreme Court agreed with Oregon. Because the Voting Rights Act was ruled unconstitutional, the Constitution had to be amended to allow passage of a law that would lower the voting age. The amendment was ratified in a little more than three months, making it the most rapidly ratified amendment in U.S. history.

Unratified Amendment

Equal Rights Amendment (proposed by Congress March 22, 1972; seven-year deadline for ratification extended to June 30, 1982)

Section 1. Equality of rights under the law shall not be denied or abridged by the United States or by any State on account of sex.

Section 2. The Congress shall have the power to enforce, by appropriate legislation, the provisions of this article.

Section 3. This amendment shall take effect two years after the date of ratification.

• • •

In 1923, soon after women had won the right to vote, Alice Paul, a leading activist in the woman suffrage movement, proposed an amendment requiring equal treatment of men and women. Opponents of the proposal argued that such an amendment would invalidate laws that protected women and would make women subject to the military draft. After the 1964 Civil Rights Act was adopted, protective workplace legislation was partially removed.

The renewal of the women's movement, as a by-product of the civil rights and antiwar movements, led to a revival of the Equal Rights Amendment (ERA) in Congress. Disagreements over language held up congressional passage of the proposed amendment, but on March 22, 1972, the Senate approved the ERA by a vote of 84 to 8, and it was sent to the states. Six states ratified the amendment within two days, and by the middle of 1973 the amendment seemed well on its way to adoption, with thirty of the needed thirty-eight states having ratified it. In the mid-1970s, however, a powerful "Stop ERA" campaign developed. The campaign portrayed the ERA as a threat to "family values" and traditional relationships between men and women. Although thirty-five states ratified the ERA, five of those state legislatures voted to rescind ratification, and the amendment was never adopted.

Unratified Amendment

D.C. Statehood Amendment
(proposed by Congress August 22, 1978)

Section 1. For purposes of representation in the Congress, election of the President and Vice President, and article V of this Constitution, the District constituting the seat of government of the United States shall be treated as though it were a State.

Section 2. The exercise of the rights and powers conferred under this article shall be by the people of the District constituting the seat of government, and as shall be provided by Congress.

Section 3. The twenty-third article of amendment to the Constitution of the United States is hereby repealed.

Section 4. This article shall be inoperative, unless it shall have been ratified as an amendment to the Constitution by the legislatures of three-fourths of the several states within seven years from the date of its submission.

• • •

The 1961 ratification of the Twenty-third Amendment, giving residents of the District of Columbia the right to vote for a president and vice president, inspired an effort to give residents of the district full voting rights. In 1966 President Lyndon Johnson appointed a mayor and city council; in 1971 D.C. residents were allowed to name a nonvoting delegate to the House; and in 1981 residents were allowed to elect the mayor and city council. Congress retained the right to overrule laws that might affect commuters, the height of District buildings, and selection of judges and prosecutors. The district's nonvoting delegate to Congress, Walter Fauntroy, lobbied fiercely for a congressional amendment granting statehood to the district. In 1978 a proposed amendment was approved and sent to the states. A number of states quickly ratified the amendment, but, like the ERA, the D.C. Statehood Amendment ran into trouble. Opponents argued that Section 2 created a separate category of "nominal" statehood. They argued that the federal district should be eliminated and that the territory should be reabsorbed into the state of Maryland. Most scholars believe that the fears of Republicans that the predominantly black population of the city would consistently elect Democratic senators constituted a major factor leading to the defeat of the amendment.

Amendment XXVII [1992]

No law varying the compensation for the services of the Senators and Representatives, shall take effect, until an election of Representatives shall have intervened.

• • •

Whereas the Twenty-sixth Amendment was the most rapidly ratified amendment in U.S. history, the Twenty-seventh Amendment had the longest journey to ratification. First proposed by James Madison in 1789 as part of the package that included the Bill of Rights, this amendment had been ratified by only six states by 1791. In 1873, however, it was ratified by Ohio to protest a massive retroactive salary increase by the federal government. Unlike later proposed amendments, this one came with no time limit on ratification. In the early 1980s Gregory D. Watson, a University of Texas economics major, discovered the "lost" amendment and began a single-handed campaign to get state legislators to introduce it for ratification. In 1983 it was accepted by Maine. In 1984 it passed the Colorado legislature. Ratifications trickled in slowly until May 1992, when Michigan and New Jersey became the thirty-eighth and thirty-ninth states, respectively, to ratify. This amendment prevents members of Congress from raising their own salaries without giving voters a chance to vote them out of office before they can benefit from the raises.

The American Nation

Admission of States into the Union

State	Date of Admission	State	Date of Admission	State	Date of Admission
1. Delaware	December 7, 1787	18. Louisiana	April 30, 1812	35. West Virginia	June 20, 1863
2. Pennsylvania	December 12, 1787	19. Indiana	December 11, 1816	36. Nevada	October 31, 1864
3. New Jersey	December 18, 1787	20. Mississippi	December 10, 1817	37. Nebraska	March 1, 1867
4. Georgia	January 2, 1788	21. Illinois	December 3, 1818	38. Colorado	August 1, 1876
5. Connecticut	January 9, 1788	22. Alabama	December 14, 1819	39. North Dakota	November 2, 1889
6. Massachusetts	February 6, 1788	23. Maine	March 15, 1820	40. South Dakota	November 2, 1889
7. Maryland	April 28, 1788	24. Missouri	August 10, 1821	41. Montana	November 8, 1889
8. South Carolina	May 23, 1788	25. Arkansas	June 15, 1836	42. Washington	November 11, 1889
9. New Hampshire	June 21, 1788	26. Michigan	January 26, 1837	43. Idaho	July 3, 1890
10. Virginia	June 25, 1788	27. Florida	March 3, 1845	44. Wyoming	July 10, 1890
11. New York	July 26, 1788	28. Texas	December 29, 1845	45. Utah	January 4, 1896
12. North Carolina	November 21, 1789	29. Iowa	December 28, 1846	46. Oklahoma	November 16, 1907
13. Rhode Island	May 29, 1790	30. Wisconsin	May 29, 1848	47. New Mexico	January 6, 1912
14. Vermont	March 4, 1791	31. California	September 9, 1850	48. Arizona	February 14, 1912
15. Kentucky	June 1, 1792	32. Minnesota	May 11, 1858	49. Alaska	January 3, 1959
16. Tennessee	June 1, 1796	33. Oregon	February 14, 1859	50. Hawaii	August 21, 1959
17. Ohio	March 1, 1803	34. Kansas	January 29, 1861		

Territorial Expansion

Territory	Date Acquired	Square Miles	How Acquired
Original states and territories	1783	888,685	Treaty of Paris
Louisiana Purchase	1803	827,192	Purchased from France
Florida	1819	72,003	Adams-Onís Treaty
Texas	1845	390,143	Annexation of independent country
Oregon	1846	285,580	Oregon Boundary Treaty
Mexican cession	1848	529,017	Treaty of Guadalupe Hidalgo
Gadsden Purchase	1853	29,640	Purchased from Mexico
Midway Islands	1867	2	Annexation of uninhabited islands
Alaska	1867	589,757	Purchased from Russia
Hawaii	1898	6,450	Annexation of independent country
Wake Island	1898	3	Annexation of uninhabited island
Puerto Rico	1899	3,435	Treaty of Paris
Guam	1899	212	Treaty of Paris
The Philippines	1899–1946	115,600	Treaty of Paris; granted independence
American Samoa	1900	76	Treaty with Germany and Great Britain
Panama Canal Zone	1904–1978	553	Hay–Bunau-Varilla Treaty
U.S. Virgin Islands	1917	133	Purchased from Denmark
Trust Territory of the Pacific Islands*	1947	717	United Nations Trusteeship

*A number of these islands have been granted independence: Federated States of Micronesia, 1990; Marshall Islands, 1991; Palau, 1994.

Presidential Elections

Year	Candidates	Parties	Percentage of Popular Vote	Electoral Vote	Percentage of Voter Participation
1789	**George Washington**	No party designations	*	69	
	John Adams[†]			34	
	Other candidates			35	
1792	**George Washington**	No party designations		132	
	John Adams			77	
	George Clinton			50	
	Other candidates			5	
1796	**John Adams**	Federalist		71	
	Thomas Jefferson	Democratic-Republican		68	
	Thomas Pinckney	Federalist		59	
	Aaron Burr	Democratic-Republican		30	
	Other candidates			48	
1800	**Thomas Jefferson**	Democratic-Republican		73	
	Aaron Burr	Democratic-Republican		73	
	John Adams	Federalist		65	
	Charles C. Pinckney	Federalist		64	
	John Jay	Federalist		1	
1804	**Thomas Jefferson**	Democratic-Republican		162	
	Charles C. Pinckney	Federalist		14	
1808	**James Madison**	Democratic-Republican		122	
	Charles C. Pinckney	Federalist		47	
	George Clinton	Democratic-Republican		6	
1812	**James Madison**	Democratic-Republican		128	
	De Witt Clinton	Federalist		89	
1816	**James Monroe**	Democratic-Republican		183	
	Rufus King	Federalist		34	
1820	**James Monroe**	Democratic-Republican		231	
	John Quincy Adams	Independent Republican		1	
1824	**John Quincy Adams**	Democratic-Republican	30.5	84	26.9
	Andrew Jackson	Democratic-Republican	43.1	99	
	Henry Clay	Democratic-Republican	13.2	37	
	William H. Crawford	Democratic-Republican	13.1	41	
1828	**Andrew Jackson**	Democratic	56.0	178	57.6
	John Quincy Adams	National Republican	44.0	83	
1832	**Andrew Jackson**	Democratic	54.5	219	55.4
	Henry Clay	National Republican	37.5	49	
	William Wirt	Anti-Masonic	8.0	7	
	John Floyd	Democratic	‡	11	
1836	**Martin Van Buren**	Democratic	50.9	170	57.8
	William H. Harrison	Whig		73	
	Hugh L. White	Whig		26	
	Daniel Webster	Whig	49.1	14	
	W. P. Mangum	Whig		11	
1840	**William H. Harrison**	Whig	53.1	234	80.2
	Martin Van Buren	Democratic	46.9	60	
1844	**James K. Polk**	Democratic	49.6	170	78.9
	Henry Clay	Whig	48.1	105	
	James G. Birney	Liberty	2.3		

Year	Candidates	Parties	Percentage of Popular Vote	Electoral Vote	Percentage of Voter Participation
1848	**Zachary Taylor**	Whig	47.4	163	72.7
	Lewis Cass	Democratic	42.5	127	
	Martin Van Buren	Free Soil	10.1		
1852	**Franklin Pierce**	Democratic	50.9	254	69.6
	Winfield Scott	Whig	44.1	42	
	John P. Hale	Free Soil	5.0		
1856	**James Buchanan**	Democratic	45.3	174	78.9
	John C. Frémont	Republican	33.1	114	
	Millard Fillmore	American	21.6	8	
1860	**Abraham Lincoln**	Republican	39.8	180	81.2
	Stephen A. Douglas	Democratic	29.5	12	
	John C. Breckinridge	Democratic	18.1	72	
	John Bell	Constitutional Union	12.6	39	
1864	**Abraham Lincoln**	Republican	55.0	212	73.8
	George B. McClellan	Democratic	45.0	21	
1868	**Ulysses S. Grant**	Republican	52.7	214	78.1
	Horatio Seymour	Democratic	47.3	80	
1872	**Ulysses S. Grant**	Republican	55.6	286	71.3
	Horace Greeley	Democratic	43.9		
1876	**Rutherford B. Hayes**	Republican	48.0	185	81.8
	Samuel J. Tilden	Democratic	51.0	184	
1880	**James A. Garfield**	Republican	48.5	214	79.4
	Winfield S. Hancock	Democratic	48.1	155	
	James B. Weaver	Greenback-Labor	3.4		
1884	**Grover Cleveland**	Democratic	48.5	219	77.5
	James G. Blaine	Republican	48.2	182	
1888	**Benjamin Harrison**	Republican	47.9	233	79.3
	Grover Cleveland	Democratic	48.6	168	
1892	**Grover Cleveland**	Democratic	46.1	277	74.7
	Benjamin Harrison	Republican	43.0	145	
	James B. Weaver	People's	8.5	22	
1896	**William McKinley**	Republican	51.1	271	79.3
	William J. Bryan	Democratic	47.7	176	
1900	**William McKinley**	Republican	51.7	292	73.2
	William J. Bryan	Democratic; Populist	45.5	155	
1904	**Theodore Roosevelt**	Republican	57.4	336	65.2
	Alton B. Parker	Democratic	37.6	140	
	Eugene V. Debs	Socialist	3.0		
1908	**William H. Taft**	Republican	51.6	321	65.4
	William J. Bryan	Democratic	43.1	162	
	Eugene V. Debs	Socialist	2.8		
1912	**Woodrow Wilson**	Democratic	41.9	435	58.8
	Theodore Roosevelt	Progressive	27.4	88	
	William H. Taft	Republican	23.2	8	
	Eugene V. Debs	Socialist	6.0		
1916	**Woodrow Wilson**	Democratic	49.4	277	61.6
	Charles E. Hughes	Republican	46.2	254	
	A. L. Benson	Socialist	3.2		

Year	Candidates	Parties	Percentage of Popular Vote	Electoral Vote	Percentage of Voter Participation
1920	**Warren G. Harding**	Republican	60.4	404	49.2
	James M. Cox	Democratic	34.2	127	
	Eugene V. Debs	Socialist	3.4		
1924	**Calvin Coolidge**	Republican	54.0	382	48.9
	John W. Davis	Democratic	28.8	136	
	Robert M. La Follette	Progressive	16.6	13	
1928	**Herbert C. Hoover**	Republican	58.2	444	56.9
	Alfred E. Smith	Democratic	40.9	87	
1932	**Franklin D. Roosevelt**	Democratic	57.4	472	56.9
	Herbert C. Hoover	Republican	39.7	59	
1936	**Franklin D. Roosevelt**	Democratic	60.8	523	61.0
	Alfred M. Landon	Republican	36.5	8	
1940	**Franklin D. Roosevelt**	Democratic	54.8	449	62.5
	Wendell L. Willkie	Republican	44.8	82	
1944	**Franklin D. Roosevelt**	Democratic	53.5	432	55.9
	Thomas E. Dewey	Republican	46.0	99	
1948	**Harry S Truman**	Democratic	49.6	303	53.0
	Thomas E. Dewey	Republican	45.1	189	
1952	**Dwight D. Eisenhower**	Republican	55.1	442	63.3
	Adlai E. Stevenson	Democratic	44.4	89	
1956	**Dwight D. Eisenhower**	Republican	57.6	457	60.6
	Adlai E. Stevenson	Democratic	42.1	73	
1960	**John F. Kennedy**	Democratic	49.7	303	64.0
	Richard M. Nixon	Republican	49.5	219	
1964	**Lyndon B. Johnson**	Democratic	61.1	486	61.7
	Barry M. Goldwater	Republican	38.5	52	
1968	**Richard M. Nixon**	Republican	43.4	301	60.6
	Hubert H. Humphrey	Democratic	42.7	191	
	George C. Wallace	American Independent	13.5	46	
1972	**Richard M. Nixon**	Republican	60.7	520	55.5
	George S. McGovern	Democratic	37.5	17	
1976	**Jimmy Carter**	Democratic	50.1	297	54.3
	Gerald R. Ford	Republican	48.0	240	
1980	**Ronald W. Reagan**	Republican	50.7	489	53.0
	Jimmy Carter	Democratic	41.0	49	
	John B. Anderson	Independent	6.6	0	
1984	**Ronald W. Reagan**	Republican	58.4	525	52.9
	Walter F. Mondale	Democratic	41.6	13	
1988	**George H. W. Bush**	Republican	53.4	426	50.3
	Michael Dukakis	Democratic	45.6	111**	
1992	**Bill Clinton**	Democratic	43.7	370	55.1
	George H. W. Bush	Republican	38.0	168	
	H. Ross Perot	Independent	19.0	0	
1996	**Bill Clinton**	Democratic	49	379	49.0
	Robert J. Dole	Republican	41	159	
	H. Ross Perot	Reform	8	0	
2000	**George W. Bush**	Republican	47.8	271	51.3
	Albert Gore	Democratic	48.4	267	
	Ralph Nader	Green	0.4	0	
2004	**George W. Bush**	Republican	50.7	286	60.3
	John Kerry	Democratic	48.3	252	
	Ralph Nader	Independent	.38	0	

*Prior to 1824, most presidential electors were chosen by state legislators rather than by popular vote.

†Before the Twelfth Amendment was passed in 1804, the Electoral College voted for two presidential candidates; the runner-up became vice president.

‡Percentages below 2.5 have been omitted. Hence the percentage of popular vote might not total 100 percent.

**One Dukakis elector cast a vote for Lloyd Bentsen.

Supreme Court Justices

Name	Terms of Service	Appointed by	Name	Terms of Service	Appointed by
John Jay,* N.Y.	1789–1795	Washington	Samuel Blatchford, N.Y.	1882–1893	Arthur
James Wilson, Pa.	1789–1798	Washington	Lucius Q. C. Lamar, Miss.	1888–1893	Cleveland
John Rutledge, S.C.	1790–1791	Washington	**Melville W. Fuller,** Ill.	1888–1910	Cleveland
William Cushing, Mass.	1790–1810	Washington	David J. Brewer, Kan.	1890–1910	B. Harrison
John Blair, Va.	1790–1796	Washington	Henry B. Brown, Mich.	1891–1906	B. Harrison
James Iredell, N.C.	1790–1799	Washington	George Shiras Jr., Pa.	1892–1903	B. Harrison
Thomas Johnson, Md.	1792–1793	Washington	Howell E. Jackson, Tenn.	1893–1895	B. Harrison
William Paterson, N.J.	1793–1806	Washington	Edward D. White, La.	1894–1910	Cleveland
John Rutledge, S.C.	1795	Washington	Rufus W. Peckham, N.Y.	1896–1909	Cleveland
Samuel Chase, Md.	1796–1811	Washington	Joseph McKenna, Cal.	1898–1925	McKinley
Oliver Ellsworth, Conn.	1796–1800	Washington	Oliver W. Holmes, Mass.	1902–1932	T. Roosevelt
Bushrod Washington, Va.	1799–1829	J. Adams	William R. Day, Ohio	1903–1922	T. Roosevelt
Alfred Moore, N.C.	1800–1804	J. Adams	William H. Moody, Mass.	1906–1910	T. Roosevelt
John Marshall, Va.	1801–1835	J. Adams	Horace H. Lurton, Tenn.	1910–1914	Taft
William Johnson, S.C.	1804–1834	Jefferson	Charles E. Hughes, N.Y.	1910–1916	Taft
Brockholst Livingston, N.Y.	1807–1823	Jefferson	**Edward D. White**, La.	1910–1921	Taft
Thomas Todd, Ky.	1807–1826	Jefferson	Willis Van Devanter, Wy.	1911–1937	Taft
Gabriel Duvall, Md.	1811–1835	Madison	Joseph R. Lamar, Ga.	1911–1916	Taft
Joseph Story, Mass.	1812–1845	Madison	Mahlon Pitney, N.J.	1912–1922	Taft
Smith Thompson, N.Y.	1823–1843	Monroe	James C. McReynolds, Tenn.	1914–1941	Wilson
Robert Trimble, Ky.	1826–1020	J. Q. Adams	Louis D. Brandeis, Mass.	1916–1939	Wilson
John McLean, Ohio	1830–1861	Jackson	John H. Clarke, Ohio	1916–1922	Wilson
Henry Baldwin, Pa.	1830–1844	Jackson	**William H. Taft**, Conn.	1921–1930	Harding
James M. Wayne, Ga.	1835–1867	Jackson	George Sutherland, Utah	1922–1938	Harding
Roger B. Taney, Md.	1836–1864	Jackson	Pierce Butler, Minn.	1923–1939	Harding
Philip P. Barbour, Va.	1836–1841	Jackson	Edward T. Sanford, Tenn.	1923–1930	Harding
John Cartron, Tenn.	1837–1865	Van Buren	Harlan F. Stone, N.Y.	1925–1941	Coolidge
John McKinley, Ala.	1838–1852	Van Buren	**Charles E. Hughes**, N.Y.	1930–1941	Hoover
Peter V. Daniel, Va.	1842–1860	Van Buren	Owen J. Roberts, Pa.	1930–1945	Hoover
Samuel Nelson, N.Y.	1845–1872	Tyler	Benjamin N. Cardozo, N.Y.	1932–1938	Hoover
Levi Woodbury, N.H.	1845–1851	Polk	Hugo L. Black, Ala.	1937–1971	F. Roosevelt
Robert C. Grier, Pa.	1846–1870	Polk	Stanley F. Reed, Ky.	1938–1957	F. Roosevelt
Benjamin R. Curtis, Mass.	1851–1857	Fillmore	Felix Frankfurter, Mass.	1939–1962	F. Roosevelt
John A. Campbell, Ala.	1853–1861	Pierce	William O. Douglas, Conn.	1939–1975	F. Roosevelt
Nathan Clifford, Me.	1858–1881	Buchanan	Frank Murphy, Mich.	1940–1949	F. Roosevelt
Noah H. Swayne, Ohio	1862–1881	Lincoln	**Harlan F. Stone**, N.Y.	1941–1946	F. Roosevelt
Samuel F. Miller, Iowa	1862–1890	Lincoln	James R. Byrnes, S.C.	1941–1942	F. Roosevelt
David Davis, Ill.	1862–1877	Lincoln	Robert H. Jackson, N.Y.	1941–1954	F. Roosevelt
Stephen J. Field, Cal.	1863–1897	Lincoln	Wiley B. Rutledge, Iowa	1943–1949	F. Roosevelt
Salmon P. Chase, Ohio	1864–1873	Lincoln	Harold H. Burton, Ohio	1945–1958	Truman
William Strong, Pa.	1870–1880	Grant	**Frederick M. Vinson**, Ky.	1946–1953	Truman
Joseph P. Bradley, N.J.	1870–1892	Grant	Tom C. Clark, Texas	1949–1967	Truman
Ward Hunt, N.Y.	1873–1882	Grant	Sherman Minton, Ind.	1949–1956	Truman
Morrison R. Waite, Ohio	1874–1888	Grant	**Earl Warren**, Cal.	1953–1969	Eisenhower
John M. Harlan, Ky.	1877–1911	Hayes	John Marshall Harlan, N.Y.	1955–1971	Eisenhower
William B. Woods, Ga.	1881–1887	Hayes	William J. Brennan Jr., N.J.	1956–1990	Eisenhower
Stanley Matthews, Ohio	1881–1889	Garfield	Charles E. Whittaker, Mo.	1957–1962	Eisenhower
Horace Gray, Mass.	1882–1902	Arthur	Potter Stewart, Ohio	1958–1981	Eisenhower

Name	Terms of Service	Appointed by	Name	Terms of Service	Appointed by
Bryon R. White, Colo.	1962–1993	Kennedy	Antonin Scalia, Va.	1986–	Reagan
Arthur J. Goldberg, Ill.	1962–1965	Kennedy	Anthony M. Kennedy, Cal.	1988–	Reagan
Abe Fortas, Tenn.	1965–1969	Johnson	David H. Souter, N.H.	1990–	Bush, G. H. W.
Thurgood Marshall, Md.	1967–1991	Johnson	Clarence Thomas, Ga.	1991–	Bush, G. H. W.
Warren E. Burger, Minn.	1969–1986	Nixon	Ruth Bader Ginsburg, N.Y.	1993–	Clinton
Harry A. Blackmun, Minn.	1970–1994	Nixon	Stephen G. Breyer, Mass.	1994–	Clinton
Lewis F. Powell Jr., Va.	1971–1987	Nixon	**John G. Roberts, Jr.**, Md.	2005–	Bush, G. W.
William H. Rehnquist, Ill.	1971–1986	Nixon	Samuel A. Alito Jr., N.J.	2006–	Bush, G. W.
John Paul Stevens, Ill.	1975–	Ford			
Sandra Day O'Connor, Ariz.	1981–2006	Reagan			
William H. Rehnquist, Va.	1986–2005	Reagan			

*Chief Justices are printed in bold type.

The American People: a Demographic Survey

A Demographic Profile of the American People

Year	Life Expectancy from Birth		Average Age at First Marriage		Number of Children Under 5 (per 1,000 Women Aged 22–24)	Percentage of Persons in Paid Employment		Percentage of Paid Workers Who Are Women
	White	Black	Men	Women		Men	Women	
1820					1,295		6.2	7.3
1830					1,145		6.4	7.4
1840					1,085		8.4	9.6
1850					923		10.1	10.8
1860					929		9.7	10.2
1870					839		13.7	14.8
1880					822		14.7	15.2
1890			26.1	22.0	716	84.3	18.2	17.0
1900	47.6	33.0	25.9	21.9	688	85.7	20.0	18.1
1910	50.3	35.6	25.1	21.6	643	85.1	24.8	20.0
1920	54.9	45.3	24.6	21.2	604	84.6	22.7	20.4
1930	61.4	48.1	24.3	21.3	511	82.1	23.6	21.9
1940	64.2	53.1	24.3	21.5	429	79.1	25.8	24.6
1950	69.1	60.8	22.8	20.3	589	81.6	29.9	27.8
1960	70.6	63.6	22.8	20.3	737	80.4	35.7	32.3
1970	71.7	65.3	22.5	20.6	530	79.7	41.4	38.0
1980	74.4	68.1	24.7	22.0	440	77.4	51.5	42.6
1990	76.1	69.1	26.1	23.9	377	76.4	57.4	45.2
2000	77.6	71.7	26.7	25.1	365	74.8	58.9	46.3
2004	78.2	73.4	27.4	25.8		73.3	59.2	46.5

SOURCE: U.S. Bureau of the Census, *Historical Statistics of the United States, Colonial Times to 1970 (1975); Statistical Abstract of the United States, 2001; Statistical Abstract of the United States, 2006.*

American Population

Year	Population	Percentage Increase	Year	Population	Percentage Increase
1610	350	—	1820	9,638,453	33.1
1620	2,300	557.1	1830	12,866,020	33.5
1630	4,600	100.0	1840	17,069,453	32.7
1640	26,600	478.3	1850	23,191,876	35.9
1650	50,400	90.8	1860	31,443,321	35.6
1660	75,100	49.0	1870	39,818,449	26.6
1670	111,900	49.0	1880	50,155,783	26.0
1680	151,500	35.4	1890	62,947,714	25.5
1690	210,400	38.9	1900	75,994,575	20.7
1700	250,900	19.2	1910	91,972,266	21.0
1710	331,700	32.2	1920	105,710,620	14.9
1720	466,200	40.5	1930	122,775,046	16.1
1730	629,400	35.0	1940	131,669,275	7.2
1740	905,600	43.9	1950	150,697,361	14.5
1750	1,170,800	29.3	1960	179,323,175	19.0
1760	1,593,600	36.1	1970	203,235,298	13.3
1770	2,148,100	34.8	1980	226,545,805	11.5
1780	2,780,400	29.4	1990	248,709,873	9.8
1790	3,929,214	41.3	2000	281,421,906	13.2
1800	5,308,483	35.1	2005	296,410,404	5.0
1810	7,239,881	36.4			

Note: These figures largely ignore the Native American population. Census takers never made any effort to count the Native American population that lived outside their reserved political areas and compiled only casual and incomplete enumerations of those living within their jurisdictions until 1890. In that year the federal government attempted a full count of the Indian population: The Census found 125,719 Indians in 1890, compared with only 12,543 in 1870 and 33,985 in 1880.

SOURCES: U.S. Bureau of the Census, *Historical Statistics of the United States, Colonial Times to 1970* (1975); *Statistical Abstract of the United States, 2001*; U.S. Bureau of the Census, Population Finder, http://factfinder.census.gov.

White/Nonwhite Population

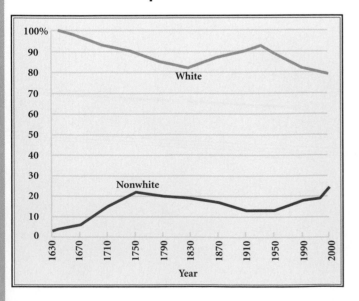

Urban/Rural Population

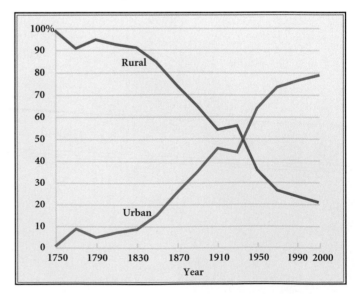

The Ten Largest Cities by Population, 1700–2000

		City	Population			City	Population
1700	1.	Boston	6,700	1930	1.	New York	6,930,446
	2.	New York	4,937*		2.	Chicago	3,376,438
	3.	Philadelphia	4,400†		3.	Philadelphia	1,950,961
1790	1.	Philadelphia	42,520		4.	Detroit	1,568,662
	2.	New York	33,131		5.	Los Angeles	1,238,048
	3.	Boston	18,038		6.	Cleveland	900,429
	4.	Charleston, S.C.	16,359		7.	St. Louis	821,960
	5.	Baltimore	13,503		8.	Baltimore	804,874
	6.	Salem, Mass.	7,921		9.	Boston	781,188
	7.	Newport, R.I.	6,716		10.	Pittsburgh	669,817
	8.	Providence, R.I.	6,380	1950	1.	New York	7,891,957
	9.	Marblehead, Mass.	5,661		2.	Chicago	3,620,962
	10.	Portsmouth, N.H.	4,720		3.	Philadelphia	2,071,605
1830	1.	New York	197,112		4.	Los Angeles	1,970,358
	2.	Philadelphia	161,410		5.	Detroit	1,849,568
	3.	Baltimore	80,620		6.	Baltimore	949,708
	4.	Boston	61,392		7.	Cleveland	914,808
	5.	Charleston, S.C.	30,289		8.	St. Louis	856,796
	6.	New Orleans	29,737		9.	Washington, D.C.	802,178
	7.	Cincinnati	24,831		10.	Boston	801,444
	8.	Albany, N.Y.	24,209	1970	1.	New York	7,895,563
	9.	Brooklyn, N.Y.	20,535		2.	Chicago	3,369,357
	10.	Washington, D.C.	18,826		3.	Los Angeles	2,811,801
1850	1.	New York	515,547		4.	Philadelphia	1,949,996
	2.	Philadelphia	340,045		5.	Detroit	1,514,063
	3.	Baltimore	169,054		6.	Houston	1,233,535
	4.	Boston	136,881		7.	Baltimore	905,787
	5.	New Orleans	116,375		8.	Dallas	844,401
	6.	Cincinnati	115,435		9.	Washington, D.C.	756,668
	7.	Brooklyn, N.Y.	96,838		10.	Cleveland	750,879
	8.	St. Louis	77,860	1990	1.	New York	7,322,564
	9.	Albany, N.Y.	50,763		2.	Los Angeles	3,485,398
	10.	Pittsburgh	46,601		3.	Chicago	2,783,726
1870	1.	New York	942,292		4.	Houston	1,630,553
	2.	Philadelphia	674,022		5.	Philadelphia	1,585,577
	3.	Brooklyn, N.Y.	419,921‡		6.	San Diego	1,110,549
	4.	St. Louis	310,864		7.	Detroit	1,027,974
	5.	Chicago	298,977		8.	Dallas	1,006,877
	6.	Baltimore	267,354		9.	Phoenix	983,403
	7.	Boston	250,526		10.	San Antonio	935,933
	8.	Cincinnati	216,239	2000	1.	New York	8,008,278
	9.	New Orleans	191,418		2.	Los Angeles	3,694,820
	10.	San Francisco	149,473		3.	Chicago	2,896,016
1910	1.	New York	4,766,883		4.	Houston	1,953,631
	2.	Chicago	2,185,283		5.	Philadelphia	1,517,550
	3.	Philadelphia	1,549,008		6.	Phoenix	1,321,045
	4.	St. Louis	687,029		7.	San Diego	1,223,400
	5.	Boston	670,585		8.	Dallas	1,188,580
	6.	Cleveland	560,663		9.	San Antonio	1,144,646
	7.	Baltimore	558,485		10.	Detroit	951,270
	8.	Pittsburgh	533,905				
	9.	Detroit	465,766				
	10.	Buffalo	423,715				

*Figure from a census taken in 1698.
†Philadelphia figures include suburbs.
‡Annexed to New York in 1898.
SOURCE: U.S. Census data.

Immigration by Decade

Year	Number	Percentage of Total Population	Year	Number	Percentage of Total Population
1821–1830	151,824	1.6	1921–1930	4,107,209	3.9
1831–1840	599,125	4.6	1931–1940	528,431	0.4
1841–1850	1,713,251	10.0	1941–1950	1,035,039	0.7
1851–1860	2,598,214	11.2	1951–1960	2,515,479	1.6
1861–1870	2,314,824	7.4	1961–1970	3,321,677	1.8
1871–1880	2,812,191	7.1	1971–1980	4,493,000	2.2
1881–1890	5,246,613	10.5	1981–1990	7,338,000	3.0
1891–1900	3,687,546	5.8	1991–2000	9,095,083	3.7
1901–1910	8,795,386	11.6	**Total**	**32,433,918**	
1911–1920	5,735,811	6.2			
Total	**33,654,785**		1821–2000		
			GRAND TOTAL	**66,088,703**	

SOURCES: U.S. Bureau of the Census, *Historical Statistics of the United States, Colonial Times to 1970* (1975), part 1, 105–106; *Statistical Abstract of the United States, 2001.*

Regional Origins

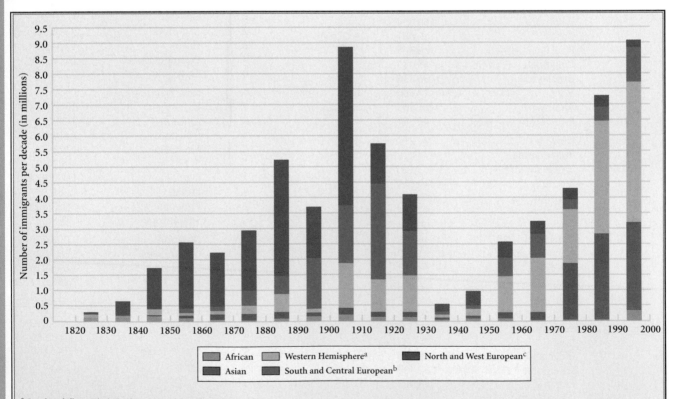

a Canada and all countries in South America and Central America.
b Italy, Spain, Portugal, Greece, Germany (Austria included, 1938–1945), Poland, Czechoslovakia (since 1920), Yugoslavia (since1920), Hungary (since 1861), Austria (since 1861, except 1938–1945), former USSR (excludes Asian USSR between 1931 and 1963), Latvia, Estonia, Lithuania, Finland, Romania, Bulgaria, Turkey (in Europe), and other European countries not classified elsewhere.
c Great Britain, Ireland, Norway, Sweden, Denmark, Iceland, Netherlands, Belgium, Luxembourg, Switzerland, France.
SOURCES: Stephan Thernstrom, ed., *Harvard Encyclopedia of American Ethnic Groups* (1980), 480; U.S. Bureau of the Census, *Statistical Abstract of the United States, 1991;* U.S. Immigration and Naturalization Service, *Statistical Yearbook, 2000.*

The Labor Force (Thousands of Workers)

Year	Agriculture	Mining	Manufacturing	Construction	Trade	Other	Total
1810	1,950	11	75	—	—	294	2,330
1840	3,570	32	500	290	350	918	5,660
1850	4,520	102	1,200	410	530	1,488	8,250
1860	5,880	176	1,530	520	890	2,114	11,110
1870	6,790	180	2,470	780	1,310	1,400	12,930
1880	8,920	280	3,290	900	1,930	2,070	17,390
1890	9,960	440	4,390	1,510	2,960	4,060	23,320
1900	11,680	637	5,895	1,665	3,970	5,223	29,070
1910	11,770	1,068	8,332	1,949	5,320	9,041	37,480
1920	10,790	1,180	11,190	1,233	5,845	11,372	41,610
1930	10,560	1,009	9,884	1,988	8,122	17,267	48,830
1940	9,575	925	11,309	1,876	9,328	23,277	56,290
1950	7,870	901	15,648	3,029	12,152	25,870	65,470
1960	5,970	709	17,145	3,640	14,051	32,545	74,060
1970	3,463	516	20,746	4,818	15,008	34,127	78,678
1980	3,364	979	21,942	6,215	20,191	46,612	99,303
1990	3,223	724	21,346	7,764	24,622	60,849	118,793
2000	2,464	475	19,644	9,931	15,763	88,260	136,891

SOURCES: U.S. Bureau of the Census, *Historical Statistics of the United States, Colonial Times to 1970* (1975), 139; *Statistical Abstract of the United States, 1998*, table 675; *Statistical Abstract of the United States, 2006.*

Changing Labor Patterns

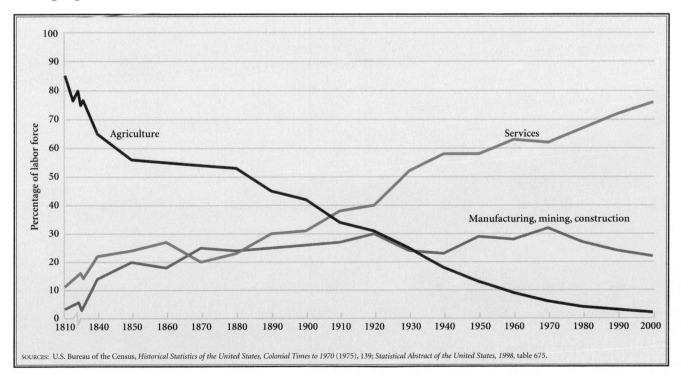

SOURCES: U.S. Bureau of the Census, *Historical Statistics of the United States, Colonial Times to 1970* (1975), 139; *Statistical Abstract of the United States, 1998*, table 675.

Birth Rate, 1820–2000

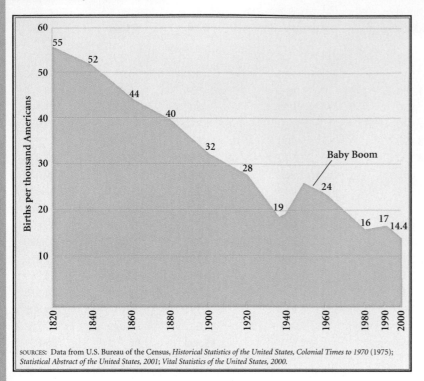

SOURCES: Data from U.S. Bureau of the Census, *Historical Statistics of the United States, Colonial Times to 1970* (1975); *Statistical Abstract of the United States, 2001; Vital Statistics of the United States, 2000.*

Death Rate, 1900–2000

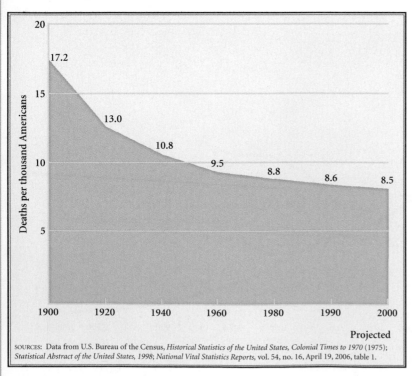

SOURCES: Data from U.S. Bureau of the Census, *Historical Statistics of the United States, Colonial Times to 1970* (1975); *Statistical Abstract of the United States, 1998; National Vital Statistics Reports,* vol. 54, no. 16, April 19, 2006, table 1.

Life Expectancy (at birth), 1900–2000

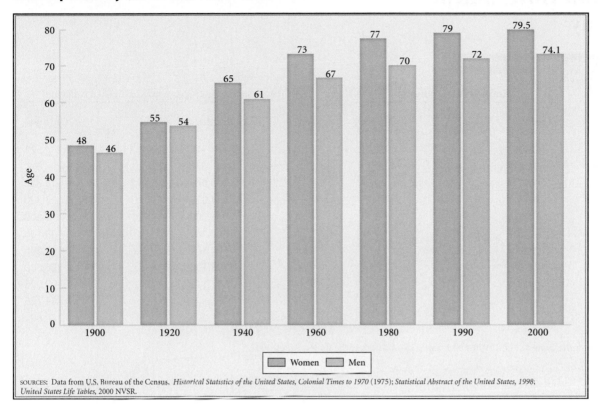

SOURCES: Data from U.S. Bureau of the Census, *Historical Statistics of the United States, Colonial Times to 1970* (1975); *Statistical Abstract of the United States, 1998*; *United States Life Tables*, 2000 NVSR.

The Aging of the U.S. Population, 1850–2000

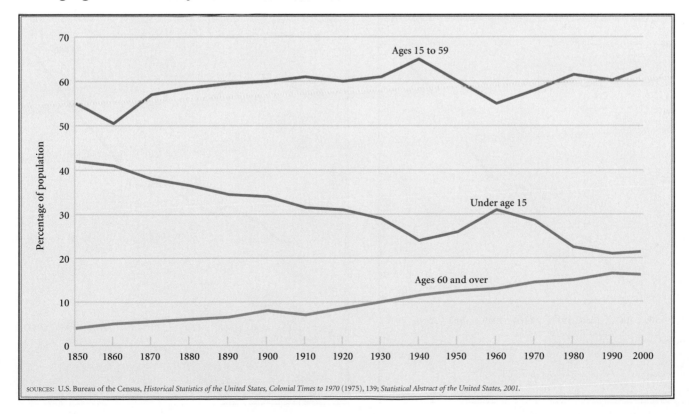

SOURCES: U.S. Bureau of the Census, *Historical Statistics of the United States, Colonial Times to 1970* (1975), 139; *Statistical Abstract of the United States, 2001.*

The American Government and Economy

The Growth of the Federal Government

Year	Employees (millions)		Receipts and Outlays ($ millions)	
	Civilian	Military	Receipts	Outlays
1900	0.23	0.12	567	521
1910	0.38	0.13	676	694
1920	0.65	0.34	6,649	6,358
1930	0.61	0.25	4,058	3,320
1940	1.04	0.45	6,900	9,600
1950	1.96	1.46	40,900	43,100
1960	2.38	2.47	92,500	92,200
1970	3.00	3.06	193,700	196,600
1980	2.99	2.05	517,112	590,920
1990	3.13	2.07	1,031,321	1,252,705
2000	2.88	1.38	2,025,200	1,788,800

SOURCES: *Statistical Profile of the United States, 1900–1980; Statistical Abstract of the United States, 2001.*

Gross Domestic Product, 1840–2000

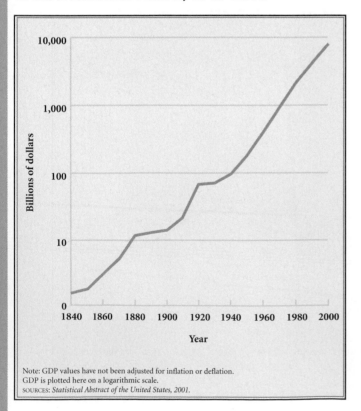

Note: GDP values have not been adjusted for inflation or deflation.
GDP is plotted here on a logarithmic scale.
SOURCES: *Statistical Abstract of the United States, 2001.*

GDP per Capita, 1840–2000

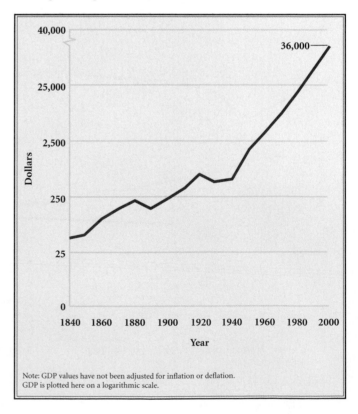

Note: GDP values have not been adjusted for inflation or deflation.
GDP is plotted here on a logarithmic scale.

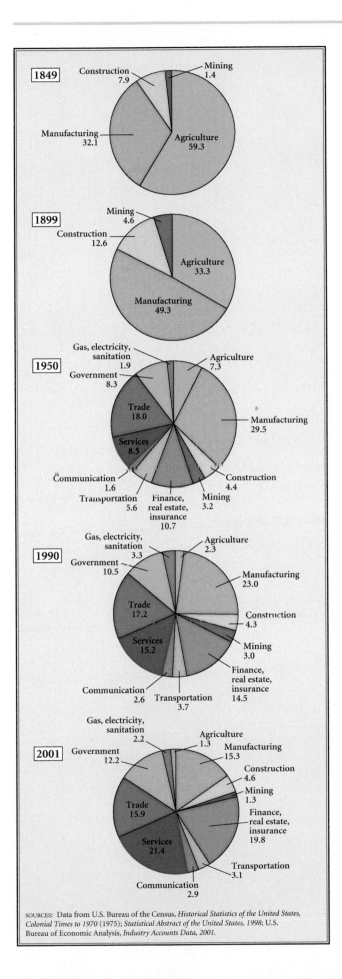

◄ Main Sectors of the U.S. Economy: 1849, 1899, 1950, 1990, and 2001

SOURCES: Data from U.S. Bureau of the Census, *Historical Statistics of the United States, Colonial Times to 1970* (1975); *Statistical Abstract of the United States, 1998*; U.S. Bureau of Economic Analysis, *Industry Accounts Data, 2001.*

Consumer Price Index

$100 in the year		
$100 in the year	1790 is equivalent to	$2,204 in 2005
	1800	1,605
	1810	1,640
	1820	1,720
	1830	2,185
	1840	2,330
	1850	2,580
Civil War Inflation	1860	2,425
	1870	1,540
	1880	1,970
$100 in the year	1890 is equivalent to	2,210 in 2005
	1900	2,400
World War I Inflation	1910	2,120
	1920	975
	1930	1,170
Post World War II	1940	1,400
Inflation	1950	810
	1960	660
	1970	500
	1980	240
$100 in the year	1990 is equivalent to	150 in 2005
	2000	115

This index provides a very rough guide to the purchasing power of $100 in various periods of American history. For example, in the early 1830s, day laborers earned about $1 a day or about $300 a year. This sum is the equivalent of about $6,555 a year in 2005 (3 × $2,185 = $6,555) or sixty percent of the gross income of a worker earing the federal government-designated minimum wage of $5.15 per hour.
SOURCE: Lawrece H. Officer and Samuel H. Williamson, "Purchasing Power of Money…1774–2005," MeasuringWorth.com, August 2006. www.measuringworth.com/calculculators/ppowerus/

American Renaissance   A burst of American literature during the 1840s, highlighted by the novels of Herman Melville and Nathaniel Hawthorne; the essays of Ralph Waldo Emerson, Henry David Thoreau, and Margaret Fuller; and the poetry of Walt Whitman. (p. 252)

American System   A political program conceived in the early 1820s to expand economic development through a federally funded system of internal improvements (roads and canals), tariffs, and a national bank. Such policies marked a shift toward government involvement in the economy, reflecting the growing strength of commercial interests. (p. 304)

artisan republicanism   An ideology that celebrated small-scale producers, men and women who owned their own shops (or farms) and defined the ideal republican society as one constituted by, and dedicated to the welfare of, independent workers and citizens. (p. 280)

Benevolent Empire   A broad-ranging campaign of moral and institutional reforms inspired by evangelical Christian ideals and endorsed by upper-middle-class men and women in the 1820s. Ministers who promoted benevolent reform insisted that people who had experienced saving grace should provide moral guidance and charity to the less fortunate. (p. 290)

bills of exchange   Credit slips that British manufacturers, West Indian planters, and American merchants used in the eighteenth century in place of currency to settle transactions. (p. 90)

Black Codes   Laws passed by southern states after the Civil War denying ex-slaves the civil rights enjoyed by whites and intended to force blacks back to the plantations. (p. 459)

blacklist   Procedure used by employers throughout the nineteenth century to label and identify workers affiliated with unions. In the 1950s, blacklists were utilized to exclude alleged Communists from jobs in government service, the motion picture business, and many industries and unions. (p. 322)

business cycle   The periodic rise and fall of business activity that is characteristic of market-driven, capitalist economies. To increase profits, producers increase production and lower wages, which means workers cannot buy all the goods they produce. The surplus prompts a cutback in output and an economic recession. In the United States, major periods of expansion (1802–1818, 1824–1836, 1846–1856, 1865–1873, 1896–1914, and 1922–1928) were followed by either relatively short financial panics (1819–1822 and 1857–1860) or extended economic depressions (1837–1843, 1873–1896, and 1929–1939). (p. 239)

capitalism   A system of economic production based on the private ownership of property and the contractual exchange for profit of goods, labor, and money (capital). Although some elements of capitalism existed in the United States before 1820, a full-scale capitalist economy—and society—emerged only with the Market Revolution (1820–1850) and reached its pinnacle during the final decades of the century. *See* Market Revolution. (p. 237)

carpetbaggers   A derisive name given by Southerners to Northerners who moved to the South during Reconstruction. Former Confederates despised these Northerners as transient exploiters. Carpetbaggers actually were a varied group, including Union veterans who had served in the South, reformers eager to help the ex-slaves, and others looking for business opportunities. (p. 470)

caste system   A form of social organization that divides a society along relatively rigid lines of status based primarily on birth. (p. 28)

chattel slavery   A system of bondage in which a slave has the legal status of property and so can be bought and sold like property. (p. 52)

civic humanism   The belief that individuals owe a service to their community and its government. During the Renaissance, political theorists argued that selfless service was of critical importance in a republic, a form of government in which authority lies in the hands of some or all of the citizenry. (p. 20)

civil religion   A term used by historians to refer to a religious-like reverence for various political institutions and ideologies. An example is the belief in "republicanism" after the American Revolution. (p. 200)

clan   A group of related families that share a real or legendary common ancestor. Most Native peoples north of the Rio Grande organized their societies around clan groups, which combined to form a distinct people based on language and culture. (p. 9)

classical liberalism   The political ideology, dominant in England and the United States during the nineteenth century, that celebrated individual liberty, private property, a competitive market economy, free trade, and limited government. In the late-twentieth-century United States, many economic conservatives embrace the principles of classical liberalism (and oppose the principles of social welfare liberalism). (p. 318)

closed-shop agreement   Labor agreement in which an employer agrees to hire only union members. Many employers viewed these agreements as illegal and worked to overturn them in the courts. Closed-shops became popular in the United States in the early part of the twentieth century. In 1947, under the Taft-Hartley Act, the closed-shop was declared illegal, but they continue to exist in practice. (p. 322)

Columbian Exchange   The transfer in the sixteenth century of agricultural products and diseases from the Western Hemisphere to other continents, and from those other continents to the Western Hemisphere. (p. 25)

common law   Centuries-old body of English law based on custom and judicial interpretation, not legislation, and evolving case by case on the basis of precedent. The common law was transmitted to America along with English settlement and became the foundation of American law at the state and local levels. In the United States, even more than in Britain, the common law gave the courts supremacy over the legislatures in many areas of law. (p. 52)

companionate marriage A marriage based on equality and mutual respect—both republican values. Although husbands in these marriages retained significant legal power, they increasingly came to see their wives as loving partners rather than as inferiors or dependents. (p. 245)

conscience Whigs Whig politicians who opposed the Mexican War (1846–1848) on moral grounds. They maintained that the purpose of the war was to expand and perpetuate slavery. They feared that the addition of more slave states would ensure the South's control of the national government and undermine a society of yeomen farmers and "free labor" in the North. (p. 401)

craft worker An artisan or other worker who has a specific craft or skill. For example, a mason, a cabinetmaker, a printer, or a weaver. (p. 279)

deist, deism The Enlightenment-influenced belief that the Christian God created the universe and then left it to run according to natural laws. (p. 117)

division of labor A system of manufacture that assigns specific—and repetitive—tasks to each worker. The system was first implemented between 1800 and 1830 in the shoe industry and soon became general practice throughout the manufacturing sector of the U.S. economy. Although it improved productivity, it eroded workers' control and sense of achievement. (p. 272)

dower, dower right A legal right originating in Europe and carried to the American colonies that provided a widow with the use of one-third of the family's land and goods during her lifetime. (p. 16)

enclosure acts Laws passed in sixteenth-century England that allowed landowners to fence in the open fields that surrounded many villages and use them for grazing sheep. This enclosure of the fields left peasants in those villages without land to cultivate, forcing them to work as wage laborers or as wool spinners and weavers. (p. 33)

encomiendas Land grants in America given by the Spanish kings to privileged landholders (*encomenderos*) in the sixteenth century. *Encomiendas* also gave the landholders legal control over Native peoples who lived on or near their estates. (p. 25)

established church A church given privileged legal status by the government. Historically, established churches in Europe and America were supported by public taxes, and were often the only legally permitted religious institutions. (p. 258)

factory A structure first built by manufacturers in the early nineteenth century to concentrate all aspects of production—and the machinery needed to increase output—in one location. (p. 273)

Federalists Supporters of the Constitution of 1787, which created a strong central government, were called Federalists; those who feared that a strong central government would corrupt the nation's newly won liberty were called Antifederalists. (p. 195)

franchise The right to vote. The franchise was gradually widened in the United States to include groups such as blacks and women, who had no vote in federal elections when the Constitution was ratified. In 1971, the Twenty-Sixth Amendment lowered the voting age from twenty-one to eighteen. (p. 302)

free market A system of economic exchange in which prices are determined by supply and demand and no producer or consumer dominates the market. The term also refers to markets that are not subject to government regulation. (p. 194)

free-soil movement A political movement of the 1840s that opposed the expansion of slavery. Motivating its members—mostly white yeomen farmers—was their belief that slavery benefited "aristocratic men." They wanted farm families to settle the western territories and install democratic republican values and institutions there. The short-lived Free-Soil Party (1848–1854) stood for "free soil, free labor, free men," which subsequently became the program of the Republican Party. (p. 402)

freehold, freeholder Property owned in its entirety, without feudal dues or landlord obligations. Freeholders have the legal right to improve, transfer, or sell their property. (p. 53)

gang-labor system A system of work discipline used on southern cotton plantations in the mid-nineteenth century. White overseers or black drivers constantly supervised gangs of enslaved laborers to enforce work norms and achieve greater productivity. (p. 373)

gentility A refined style of living and elaborate manners that came to be highly prized among well-to-do English families after 1600. (p. 90)

gentry A class of Englishmen and -women who were substantial landholders but lacked the social privileges and titles of nobility. During the Price Revolution of the sixteenth century, the relative wealth and status of the gentry rose while those of the aristocracy fell. (p. 33)

Great American Desert The name given to the drought-stricken Great Plains by Euro-Americans in the early nineteenth century. Believing the region was unfit for cultivation or agriculture, Congress designated the Great Plains as permanent Indian country in 1834. (p. 392)

greenbacks Paper money issued by the U.S. Treasury during the Civil War to finance the war effort. Greenbacks had the status of legal tender in all public and private transactions. Because they were issued in large amounts and were not backed by gold or silver, the value of a greenback dollar fell during the war to 40 cents (but much less than the notes issued during the Revolutionary War, which became virtually worthless) and recovered only as the Union government won the war and proceeded to reduce its war-related debt. (p. 438)

guild An organization of skilled workers in medieval and early modern Europe that regulated the entry into and the practice of a trade. Guilds did not develop in colonial America because artisans generally were in short supply. (p. 20)

habeas corpus Latin for "bring forth the body," a legal writ forcing government authorities to justify their arrest and detention of an individual. Rooted in English common law, habeas corpus was given the status of a formal privilege in the U.S. Constitution (Article 1, Section 9), which also allows its suspension in cases of invasion or insurrection. During the Civil War, Lincoln suspended habeas corpus to stop protests against the draft and other anti-Union activities. The USA PATRIOT Act (2001) likewise suspends this privilege in cases of suspected terrorism, but the constitutional legitimacy of this and other provisions of the act have yet to be decided by the courts. (p. 434)

heresy A religious doctrine that is inconsistent with the teachings of a church. Some of the Crusades between 1096 and 1291 targeted groups of Christians whose beliefs the Roman Catholic Church judged to be heretical. (p. 16)

home rule A rallying cry used by southern Democrats painting Reconstruction governments as illegitimate—imposed on the

South—and themselves as the only party capable of restoring the South to "home rule." By 1876, northern Republicans were inclined to accept this claim. (p. 480)

homespun Cloth spun and woven by American women and traditionally worn by poorer colonists. During the boycotts of British goods in the 1760s, wearing homespun clothes took on a political meaning, and even those who could easily afford finer clothing began wearing clothes made of homespun fabrics. Their work making homespun fabrics allowed women to contribute directly to the Patriot movement. (p. 148)

ideology A systematic philosophy or political theory that purports to explain the character of the social world or to prescribe a set of values or beliefs. (p. 20)

impeachment First step in the constitutional process for removing the president from office, in which charges of wrongdoing (articles of impeachment) are passed by the House of Representatives. A trial is then conducted by the Senate to determine whether the impeached president is guilty of the charges. (p. 468)

indenture, indentured servants A seventeenth-century labor contract that required service for a period of time in return for passage to North America. Indentures were typically for a term of four or five years, provided room and board in exchange for labor, and granted free status at the end of the contract period. (p. 34)

indulgence A certificate granted by the Catholic Church that claimed to pardon a sinner from punishment in the afterlife. In his *Ninety-five Theses,* written in 1517, Martin Luther condemned the sale of indulgences, a common practice among Catholic clergy. (p. 29)

joint-stock corporation A financial organization devised by English merchants around 1550 that subsequently facilitated the colonization of North America. In these companies, a number of investors pooled their capital and, in return, received shares of stock in the enterprise in proportion to their share of the total investment. (p. 56)

"King Cotton" A term used to describe the importance of raw cotton in the nineteenth-century economy. More specifically, the Confederate belief during the Civil War that their cotton was so important to the British and French economies that those governments would recognize the South as an independent nation and supply it with loans and arms. (p. 436)

labor theory of value The belief that human labor produces value. Adherents argued that the price of a product should be determined not by the market (supply and demand) but by the amount of work required to make it, and that most of the price should be paid to the person who produced it. The idea was popularized by the National Trades' Union and other labor leaders in the mid-nineteenth century. (p. 280)

laissez-faire The doctrine, based on economic theory, that government should not interfere in business or the economy. Laissez-faire ideas guided American government policy in the late nineteenth century and conservative politics in the twentieth. Business interests that supported laissez-faire in the late nineteenth century accepted government interference when it took the form of tariffs or subsidies that worked to their benefit. Broader uses of the term refer to the simple philosophy of abstaining from all government interference. (p. 318)

land bank An institution, established by a colonial legislature, that printed paper money and lent it to farmers, taking a lien on their land to ensure repayment. (p. 99)

liberal, liberalism The ideology of individual rights and private property outlined by John Locke (circa 1690) and embodied in many American constitutions, bills of rights, and institutions of government. *See also* classical liberalism. (p. 479)

lien (crop lien) A legal device enabling a creditor to take possession of the property of a borrower, including the right to have it sold in payment of the debt. Furnishing merchants took such liens on cotton crops as collateral for supplies advanced to sharecroppers during the growing season. This system trapped farmers in a cycle of debt and made them vulnerable to exploitation by the furnishing merchant. (p. 474)

machine tools Cutting, boring, and drilling machines used to produce standardized metal parts that were assembled into products like sewing machines. The development of machine tools by American inventors in the early nineteenth century facilitated the rapid spread of the Industrial Revolution. (p. 278)

Manifest Destiny A term coined by John L. O'Sullivan in 1845 to describe the idea that Euro-Americans were fated by God to settle the North American continent from the Atlantic to the Pacific Ocean. Adding geographical and secular dimensions to the Second Great Awakening, Manifest Destiny implied that the spread of American republican institutions and Protestant churches across the continent was part of God's plan for the world. In the late nineteenth century, the focus of the policy expanded to include overseas expansion. (p. 392)

manorial system A quasi-feudal system of landholding in the Hudson River valley in which wealthy landlords leased out thousands of acres to tenant farmers in exchange for rent, a quarter of the value of all improvements (houses and barns, for example), and a number of days of personal service. (p. 70)

manumission From the Latin *manumittere,* "to release from the hand," the legal act of relinquishing property rights in slaves. In 1782, the Virginia assembly passed an act allowing manumission; and within a decade, planters had freed ten thousand slaves. Worried that a large free black population would threaten the institution of slavery, the assembly repealed the law in 1792. (p. 252)

Market Revolution The dramatic increase between 1820 and 1850 in the exchange of goods and services in market transactions. The Market Revolution resulted from the combined impact of the increased output of farms and factories, the entrepreneurial activities of traders and merchants, and the development of a transportation network of roads, canals, and railroads. (p. 272)

mass production A system of factory production that often combines sophisticated machinery, a disciplined labor force, and assembly lines to turn out vast quantities of identical goods at low cost. In the nineteenth century, the textile and meatpacking industries pioneered mass production, which eventually became the standard mode for making consumer goods from cigarettes to automobiles, to telephones, radios, televisions, and computers. (p. 286)

matrilineal Describes a system of family organization in which social identity and property descend through the female line. Children are usually raised in their mother's household, and her brother (their uncle) plays an important role in their lives. (p. 14)

mechanic   A term used in the nineteenth century to refer to a skilled craftsman and inventor who built and improved machinery and machine tools for industry. Mechanics developed a professional identity and established institutes to spread their skills and knowledge. (p. 274)

mercantilism   A set of parliamentary policies, first enacted in 1650 and constantly updated, that regulated colonial commerce and manufacturing for the enrichment of Britain. The policies ensured that the American colonies produced agricultural goods and raw materials for export to Britain, where they were sold to other European nations or made into finished goods. (p. 32)

mestizo   A person of mixed blood; specifically, the child of a European and a Native American. (p. 28)

middle class   In Europe, the class of traders and townspeople who were not part of either the aristocracy or the peasantry. The term was introduced in America in the early nineteenth century to describe both an economic group (of prosperous farmers, artisans, and traders) and a cultural outlook (of self-discipline, hard work, and social mobility). (p. 243)

Middle Passage   The brutal sea voyage from Africa to the Americas in the eighteenth and nineteenth centuries that cost nearly a million African slaves their lives. (p. 82)

Minutemen   Colonial militiamen who stood ready to mobilize on short notice during the imperial crisis of the 1770s. These volunteers formed the core of the citizens' army that met British troops at Lexington and Concord in April 1775. (p. 160)

national debt   The financial obligations of the U.S. government for money borrowed from its citizens and foreign investors. Alexander Hamilton wanted wealthy Americans to invest in the national debt so that they would support the new national government. In recent decades, that same thinking has led the United States to encourage individuals and institutions in crucial foreign nations—Saudi Arabia and Japan, for example—to invest billions of dollars in the American national debt. (p. 206)

nullification   Idea stating that a state convention could declare federal laws unconstitutional if they were seen to overstep Congressional powers. South Carolina politicians advanced this idea in 1828 as a response to Congress's so-called "Tariff of Abominations." After a heated confrontation, Congress passed a more moderate tariff in 1833. The question of federal power versus states' rights, however, was far from settled. The implied threat of nullification was secession and the South later acted upon this threat when they felt the federal government compromised their perceived right to slavery. (p. 309)

outwork   A system of manufacturing, also known as *putting out*, used extensively in the English woolen industry in the sixteenth and seventeenth centuries. Merchants bought wool and then hired landless peasants who lived in small cottages to spin and weave it into cloth, which the merchants would sell in English and foreign markets. (p. 32)

pagan   A person whose spiritual beliefs center on the natural world. Pagans do not worship a supernatural God; instead, they pay homage to spirits and spiritual forces that dwell in the natural world. (p. 16)

party caucus   An informal meeting of politicians held by political parties to make majority decisions and enforce party discipline. Traditionally members of Congress meet in party caucuses to select Congressional leaders. In the early history of America, small groups of party leaders chose candidates for office in party caucuses. Since the 1830s the major political parties have switched to using a national convention to nominate their candidates. (p. 303)

patronage   The power of elected officials to grant government jobs. Beginning in the early nineteenth century, politicians systematically used—and abused—patronage to create and maintain strong party loyalties. After 1870, political reformers gradually introduced merit-based civil service systems in the federal and state governments. (p. 303)

peasant   The traditional term for a farmworker in Europe. Some peasants owned land, while others leased or rented small plots from landlords. In some regions, peasants lived in compact communities with strong collective institutions. (p. 14)

peonage (debt peonage)   As cotton prices declined during the 1870s, many sharecroppers fell into permanent debt. Merchants often conspired with landowners to make the debt a pretext for forced labor, or peonage. (p. 474)

personal-liberty laws   Laws enacted in many northern states to protect free blacks and fugitive slaves from southern slave catchers. Early laws required a formal hearing before a local court. When these kinds of provisions were declared unconstitutional by the Supreme Court in *Prigg v. Pennsylvania* (1842), new laws prohibited state officials from helping slave catchers. (p. 407)

pocket veto   Presidential way to kill a piece of legislation without issuing a formal veto. When congressional Republicans passed the Wade-Davis Bill in 1864, a harsher alternative to President Lincoln's restoration plan, Lincoln used this method to kill it by simply not signing the bill and letting it expire after Congress adjourned. (p. 458)

political machines   Nineteenth-century term for highly organized groups operating within and intending to control political parties. Machines were regarded as antidemocratic by political reformers and were the target especially of Progressive era leaders such as Robert La Follette. The direct primary was the factored antimachine instrument because it made the selection of party candidates the product of a popular ballot rather than conventions that were susceptible to machine control. (p. 303)

poll taxes   A tax paid for the privilege of voting, used in the South beginning during Reconstruction to disfranchise freedmen. Nationally, the northern states used poll taxes to keep immigrants and others deemed unworthy from the polls. (p. 469)

polygamy   The practice of marriage by a man to multiple wives. Polygamy was customary among many African peoples and was practiced by many Mormons in the United States, particularly between 1840 and 1890 (p. 39).

popular sovereignty   The republican principle that ultimate power resides in the hands of the electorate. Popular sovereignty dictates that voters directly or indirectly (through their elected representatives) ratify the constitutions of their state and national governments and amendments to those fundamental laws. During the 1850s, the U.S. Congress applied the principle to western lands by enacting legislation that gave residents there the authority to determine the status of slavery in their own territories. (p. 166)

praying town   A Native American settlement in seventeenth-century New England supervised by a Puritan minister. Puritans used these settlements to encourage Indians to adopt English culture and Protestant Christianity. (p. 62)

predestination   The idea that God chooses certain people for salvation even before they are born. Sixteenth-century theologian John Calvin was the main proponent of this doctrine, which became a fundamental tenet of Puritan theology. (p. 29)

Price Revolution   The impact of the high rate of inflation in Europe in the mid-1500s. American gold and silver, brought to Europe by Spain, doubled the money supply at a time when the population also was increasing. The increase in prices caused profound social changes — reducing the political power of the aristocracy and leaving many peasant families on the brink of poverty — setting the stage for substantial migration to America. (p. 32)

primogeniture   The practice of passing family land, by will or by custom, to the eldest son. Republican-minded Americans of the Revolutionary era felt this practice was unfair, but they did not prohibit it. However, most state legislatures eventually passed laws providing that if a father dies without a will, all his children must receive an equal portion of his estate. (p. 16)

probate inventory   An accounting of a person's property at the time of death, as recorded by court-appointed officials. Probate inventories are of great value to historians: These detailed lists of personal property, household items, and financial assets and debts tell us a good deal about people's lives. (p. 93)

proprietors   Groups of settlers who received land grants from the General Courts of Massachusetts Bay and Connecticut, mostly between 1630 and 1720. The proprietors distributed the land among themselves, usually based on social status and family need. This system encouraged widespread ownership of land in New England. (p. 61)

protective tariff   A tax on imports levied to protect domestic products from foreign competition. A hot political issue throughout much of American history, protective tariffs became particularly controversial in the 1830s and again between 1880 and 1914, when Republicans (for protectionism) and Democrats (for free trade) centered their political campaigns on the issue. (p. 207)

pueblos   Multistory and multiroom stone or mud-brick buildings built as residences by native peoples in the southwestern United States. (p. 11)

Radical Whigs   Eighteenth-century faction in Parliament that protested corruption in government, the growing cost of the British empire, and the rise of a wealthy class of government-related financiers. (p. 95)

reconquista   The campaign by Spanish Catholics to drive North African Moors (Muslim Arabs) from the European mainland. After a centuries-long effort to recover their lands, the Spaniards defeated the Moors at Granada in 1492 and secured control of all of Spain. (p. 23)

republic   A state without a monarch that is ruled by a representative system of government. In designing governments for the newly independent American states, Patriot leaders chose a republican form. They considered it an antidote to the poisonous corruption they had seen in the British monarchy. (p. 20)

republicanism   A political ideology that repudiates rule by kings and princes and celebrates a representative system of government and a virtuous, public-spirited citizenry. Historically, most republics have limited active political participation to those with a significant amount of property. After 1800, the United States became a democratic republic, with widespread participation by white adult men of all social classes and, after 1920, by adult women. (p. 183)

republican motherhood   The idea that the primary political role of American women was to instill a sense of patriotic duty and republican virtue in their children and mold them into exemplary republican citizens. (p. 248)

revenue tariff   A tax on imports levied to raise money for the government. *See* protective tariff. (p. 207)

revival, revivalism   An outburst of religious enthusiasm, often prompted by the preaching of a charismatic Baptist or Methodist minister. The Great Awakening of the 1740s was significant, but it was the revival that swept across the United States between the 1790s and 1850s that imparted a deep religiosity to the culture. Subsequent revivals in the 1880s and 1890s and in the late twentieth century helped maintain a strong evangelical Protestant culture in America. (p. 118)

rotten boroughs   Tiny electoral districts for Parliament whose voters were controlled by wealthy aristocrats or merchants. In the 1760s, Radical Whig John Wilkes called for the elimination of rotten boroughs to make Parliament more representative of the property-owning classes. (p. 140)

salutary neglect   A term often used to describe British colonial policy during the reigns of George I (r. 1714–1727) and George II (r. 1727–1760). By relaxing their supervision of internal colonial affairs, royal bureaucrats contributed significantly to the rise of self-government in North America. (p. 94)

scalawags   Southern whites who joined the Republicans during Reconstruction and were ridiculed by ex-Confederates as worthless traitors. They included ex-Whigs and yeomen farmers who had not supported the Confederacy and who believed that an alliance with the Republicans was the best way to attract northern capital and rebuild the South. (p. 470)

secret ballot   Before 1890, most Americans voted in "public." That is, voters either announced their vote to a clerk or handed in a ballot that had been printed by — and so was recognizable as the work of — a political party. Voting in "private" or in "secret" was first used on a wide scale in Australia. When the practice was adopted in the United States, it was known as the Australian ballot. (p. 376)

self-made man   A nineteenth-century ideal that celebrated men who rose to wealth or social prominence from humble origins through self-discipline, hard work, and temperate habits. (p. 289)

sentimentalism   A European cultural movement that emphasized emotions and a physical appreciation of God, nature, and people. Sentimentalism came to the United States in the early nineteenth century and was a factor in the shift to marriages based on love rather than on financial considerations. (p. 244)

separate spheres   Term used by historians to describe the nineteenth-century view that men and women have different gender-defined characteristics and, consequently, that the sexes inhabit — and should inhabit — different social worlds. Men should dominate the public sphere of politics and economics, while women should manage the private spheres of home and family. In mid-nineteenth-century America, this cultural understanding was both sharply defined and hotly contested. (p. 356)

separation of powers The constitutional arrangement that gives the three governmental branches — executive, legislative, and judicial — independent standing, thereby diffusing the federal government's overall power and reducing the chances that it might turn tyrannical and threaten the liberties of the people. (p. 458)

sharecropping The labor system by which freedmen agreed to exchange a portion of their harvested crops with the landowner for use of the land, a house, and tools. A compromise between freedmen and white landowners, this system developed in the cash-strapped South because the freedmen wanted to work their own land but lacked the money to buy it, while white landowners needed agricultural laborers but did not have money to pay wages. (p. 473)

socialism A theory of social and economic organization based on the common ownership of goods. Utopian socialists of the early nineteenth century envisioned small planned communities; later socialists campaigned for state ownership of railroads and large industries. (p. 338)

Sons of Liberty Colonists — primarily middling merchants and artisans — who banded together to protest the Stamp Act and other imperial reforms of the 1760s. The group originated in Boston in 1765 but soon spread to all the colonies. (p. 145)

spoils system The widespread award of public jobs to political supporters following an electoral victory. Underlying this practice was the view that in a democracy rotation in office was preferable to a permanent class of officeholders. In 1829 Andrew Jackson began this practice on the national level, and it became a central, and corrupting, feature of American political life. (p. 303)

states' rights An interpretation of the Constitution that exalts the sovereignty of the states and circumscribes the authority of the national government. Expressed first by Antifederalists in the debate over the Constitution, and then in the Virginia and Kentucky resolutions of 1798, the ideology of states' rights became especially important in the South. It informed white southerners' resistance to the high tariffs of the 1820s and 1830s, to legislation to limit the spread of slavery, and to attempts by the national government in the mid-twentieth century to end Jim Crow practices. (p. 211)

suffrage The right to vote. The classical republican ideology current before 1810 limited suffrage to those who held property and thus had "a stake in society." However, between 1810 and 1860, state constitutions extended the vote to virtually all adult white men and some free black men. Over the course of American history, suffrage has expanded as barriers of race, gender, and age have fallen. (p. 244)

temperance, temperance movement A long-term series of activities by reform organizations to encourage individuals and governments to limit the consumption of alcoholic beverages. Leading temperance groups include the American Temperance Society of the 1830s, the Washingtonian Association of the 1840s, the Women's Christian Temperance Union of the late nineteenth century, and Alcoholics Anonymous, which was founded in the 1930s. (p. 293)

total war A form of warfare, new to the nineteenth and twentieth centuries, that mobilized all of a society's resources — economic, political, and cultural — in support of the military effort. Governments now mobilized massive armies of conscripted civilians rather than small forces of professional soldiers. Moreover, they attacked civilians and industries that supported the war efforts of their enemies. Witness Sherman's march through Georgia in the Civil War, and the massive American bombing of Dresden, Hamburg, and Tokyo during World War II and of North Vietnam during the Vietnam War. (p. 434)

town meeting A system of local government in New England in which all male heads of households met regularly to elect selectmen, levy local taxes, and regulate markets, roads, and schools. (p. 61)

trade slaves West Africans who were sold by one African kingdom to another and who were not considered members of the society that had enslaved them. For centuries, Arab merchants carried trade slaves to the Mediterranean region; around 1440, Portuguese ship captains joined in this trade and began buying slaves from African princes and warlords. (p. 23)

transcendentalism A nineteenth-century intellectual movement that posited the importance of an ideal world of mystical knowledge and harmony beyond the world of the senses. As articulated by Ralph Waldo Emerson and Henry David Thoreau, transcendentalism called for the critical examination of society and emphasized individuality, self-reliance, and nonconformity. (p. 332)

vice-admiralty court A tribunal presided over by a judge, with no jury. The Sugar Act of 1764 required that offenders be tried in a vice-admiralty court rather than in a common-law tribunal, where a jury decides guilt or innocence. This provision of the act provoked protests from merchant-smugglers accustomed to acquittal by sympathetic local juries. (p. 142)

virtual representation The claim made by British politicians that the interests of the American colonists were adequately represented in Parliament by merchants who traded with the colonies and by absentee landlords (mostly sugar planters) who owned estates in the West Indies. (p. 143)

war of attrition A military strategy of small-scale attacks used, usually by the weaker side, to sap the resources and morale of the stronger side. Examples include the attacks carried out by Patriot militias in the South during the War of Independence, and the guerrilla tactics of the Vietcong and North Vietnamese during the Vietnam War. (p. 179)

Whigs In the United States, a political party that began in 1834 with the opponents of Andrew Jackson, who they thought was treating the presidency like a monarchy. They took their name from a British political party with a reputation for supporting liberal principles and reform. The British Whigs rose in power during the Glorious Revolution of 1688 and favored "mixed government" in which the House of Commons would have a voice in shaping policies, especially the power of taxation, as opposed to a monarchy. The Whig party in the United States dissolved in the 1850s over the question of whether or not to extend slavery to the territories. (p. 318)

yeoman In England between 1500 and 1800, a farmer who owned enough land to support his family in reasonable comfort. In America, Thomas Jefferson envisioned a nation of yeomen, of politically and financially independent farmers. (p. 14)

Chapter 1

Comparing American Voices: Friar Bernardino de Sahagun, "Aztec Elders Describe the Spanish Conquest." Excerpt from *The Florentine Codex: General History of the Things of New Spain*, translated by Arthur J.O. Anderson and Charles E. Dibble. Copyright © 1975 by the University of Utah Press and the School of American Research. Reprinted courtesy of the University of Utah Press.

Chapter 2

Table 2.3. "Environment, Disease and Death in Virginia, 1618–1624." Adapted from table 3 in *The Chesapeake in the Seventeenth Century* by Thad W. Tate and David L. Ammerman, eds. Published by W.W. Norton (1979). © University of North Carolina Press. Reprinted by permission.

Chapter 4

Voices from Abroad: Gottlieb Mittelberger, "The Perils of Migration." Excerpt from "The Crossing to Pennsylvania" in *Journey to Pennsylvania* by Gottlieb Mittelberger, edited and translated by Oscar Handlin and John Clive, pp. 11–21: The Belknap Press of Harvard University Press. Copyright © 1960 by the President and Fellows of Harvard College. Reprinted by permission of the publisher.

Table 4.1: "Estimated European Migration to the British Mainland Colonies, 1700–1780."

Adapted (and altered from) *The Journal of Interdisciplinary History*, XXII (1992), 628, with the permission of the editors of *The Journal of Interdisciplinary History* and The MIT Press, Cambridge, Massachusetts. © 1992 by the Massachusetts Institute of Technology and The Journal of Interdisciplinary History, Inc.

Chapter 6

Fig. 6.1: "Middling Men Enter the Halls of Government, 1765–1790." Adapted from "Government by the People: The American Revolution and the Democratization of the Legislature" by Jackson T. Main. From *William and Mary Quarterly*, 3rd series, vol. 23 (1996). Reprinted by permission of the Omohundro Institute of Early American History and Culture.

Chapter 7

Voices from Abroad: William Cobbett, "Peter Porcupine Attacks Pro-French Americans." Excerpted from *Peter Porcupine in America: Pamphlets on Republicanism and Revolution* edited by David A. Wilson. Copyright © 1994 by Cornell University. Used by permission of the publisher, Cornell University Press.

Chapter 8

Comparing American Voices: Caroline Howard Gilman. "Female Submission in Marriage." Abridged version from *Major Problems in the History of American Families and Children* by Ayna Jabour, editor. Copyright © 2005 by Ayna Jabour. Reprinted with permission of Houghton Mifflin. All rights reserved.

Comparing American Voices: Martha Hunter Hitchcock. "Isolation, Unmentionable Sorrows and Suffering." Abridged versions from *Major Problems in the History of American Families and Children*. Copyright © 2005 by Ayna Jabour. Reprinted with permission of Houghton Mifflin. All rights reserved.

Comparing American Voices: Elizabeth Scott Neblett. "My Seasons of Gloom and Despondency." Abridged versions from *Major Problems in the History of American Families and Children* by Ayna Jabour, editor. Reprinted with the permission of Houghton Mifflin. All rights reserved.

Table 8.1. "African Slaves Imported into the United States, by Ethnicity, 1776–1809." Adapted from table A-6, "From Slaves, Convicts and Servants to Free Passengers" as published in the *Journal of American History* 85 (June 1998). Reprinted by permission.

Chapter 9

Voices from Abroad: German Immigrants in the Midwest. Excerpts from *News from the Land of Freedom: German Immigrants Write Home* by Walter D. Kamphoefner, Wolfgang Helbid, and Ulrike Sommer, ed. Translated by Susan Carter Vogel. Copyright © 1991 by Cornell University Press. Reprinted with permission of the publisher, Verlag C H Beck Press.

Table 9.1. "Leading Branches of Manufacture, 1860." Adapted from data (p.26) published in *Economic Growth of the U.S. 1790–1860* by Douglas C. North. © Douglas C. North. Reprinted by permission of Pearson Education, Inc. Upper Saddle River, NJ.

Chapter 10

Voices from Abroad: Alexis de Toqueville. "Parties in the United States." From *Democracy in America* by Alexis de Toqueville. Translated by Henry Reeve. Copyright © 1945 and renewed 1973 by Alfred A. Knopf, a division of Random House, Inc. Used by permission of Alfred A. Knopf, a division of Random House, Inc.

Chapter 11

Voices from Abroad: Noel Rae. "The Mystical World of the Shakers" from *Witnessing America* by Noel Rae. Copyright © by Noel Rae and The Stonesong Press, LLC. Used with permission Stonesong Press, LLC.

Comparing American Voices: David Brion Davis. American Temperance Magazine "You Shall Not Sell." From *Antebellum American Culture: An Interpretive Anthology* by David Brion Davis. Copyright © 1997 by David Brion Davis. Reprinted by permission of The Pennsylvania State University and the author.

Fig. 11.2. "The Surge in Immigration, 1842–1855." Adapted from *Division and the Stresses of Renunion 1845–1876* by David M. Potter. © David M. Potter. Reprinted by permission.

Understanding History through Maps

Working with maps deepens your understanding of the basic issues of geography and how they relate to historical studies. Understanding these five themes — location, place, region, movement, and interaction — will enrich your readings of maps and the historical situation they depict.

Location "When?" and "where?" are the first questions asked by historians and cartographers. Every event happens somewhere and at some point in time, and maps are the best devices to show a particular location at a particular time.

Place Human activity creates places. Locations exist on their own without the presence of people, but they become places when people use the spots in some way. As human enterprise thickens and generation after generation use a place, it accumulates artifacts, develops layers of remains, and generates a variety of associations held in a society's history and memory.

Region A region highlights common elements, tying certain places together as a group distinguishable from other places. Perceiving regional ties helps the reader of historical maps because they suggest the forces binding individual interests together and encouraging people to act in common.

Movement All historical change involves movement. People move in their daily activities, in seasonal patterns, and in migration to new places of residence. To understand a map fully, the reader must always envision it as one part of a sequence, not unlike a "still" excerpted from a motion picture.

Interaction The interaction between people and the environment goes both ways. On the one hand, people change their environment to suit their needs. Human ingenuity has found ways to put almost all places to some use. On the other hand, climate and topography present constraints on how people use the land and force people to change their behavior and culture as they adapt to their natural surroundings.